INTERMEDIATE MICROECONOMICS AND ITS APPLICATION
Fourth Edition

INTERMEDIATE MICROECONOMICS AND ITS APPLICATION
Fourth Edition

Walter Nicholson
Amherst College

The Dryden Press
Chicago New York San Francisco
Philadelphia Montreal Toronto
London Sydney Tokyo

Acquisitions Editor: Elizabeth Widdicombe
Developmental Editor: Deborah Acker
Project Editor: Holly Crawford
Production Manager: Mary Jarvis
Director of Editing, Design, and Production: Jane Perkins

Text and Cover Designer: Jeanne Calabrese
Copy Editor: Michele Heinz
Compositor: Waldman Graphics
Text Type: 10/12 Sabon

Library of Congress Cataloging-in-Publication Data

Nicholson, Walter.
    Intermediate microeconomics and its application.

    Includes bibliographies and indexes.
    1. Microeconomics.   I. Title.
HB172.N48   1987   338.5   86-19713
ISBN 0-03-007799-0

Printed in the United States of America
 89-016-987654

Address orders:
111 Fifth Avenue
New York, NY 10003

Address editorial correspondence:
One Salt Creek Lane
Hinsdale, IL 60521

The Dryden Press
Holt, Rinehart and Winston
Saunders College Publishing

Cover Source: Copyright Barbara Kasten, courtesy of John Weber Gallery, New York

To Dorothy Ives

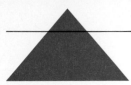

THE DRYDEN PRESS SERIES IN ECONOMICS

Preface

This fourth edition of *Intermediate Microeconomics and Its Application,* like its predecessors, has two principal goals: (1) to provide a clear, concise, and accurate introduction to the subject of microeconomics; and (2) to make that introduction interesting to students so that they will want to learn more. Many changes have been made in the book over its various editions in the pursuit of these goals. This edition, however, continues to offer a concise, nontechnical presentation of the basic theories of microeconomics together with a wide variety of applications. Concepts are developed intuitively and graphically, and many include simple numerical examples. The text always stresses the relationships of these theories to the real world by supplying each concept with an empirical application taken from actual data.

New to This Edition

The most visible change in *Intermediate Microeconomics* is the adoption of a two-color format, which greatly improves the book's visual appeal and increases the clarity and usefulness of its graphs. As a result of this change, I have had to drop my joking reference in earlier editions to the absence of two colors.

Even more important than the change to two colors are several substantive changes in the content of the book that I believe will improve its already strong appeal to instructors and students alike. Most importantly, the principal focus of this revision has been on developing a book that is consistently easy to read, easy to use, and easy to learn from. To achieve these goals, many parts of the book have been completely rewritten, some of the more complex topics from the prior editions have been dropped, entirely new and timely topics have been added, and many new learning aids appear for the first time.

Major new topic areas include:

- A new chapter on the modern theory of the firm, including issues in implicit labor contracts, the principal-agent problem, and the market for corporate control (Chapter 10).
- A new chapter on public goods and public choice theory (Chapter 19).
- A thoroughly revised and updated treatment of general equilibrium and welfare economics (Chapter 17).
- Expanded background material in elementary algebra, game theory, and the mathematics of compound interest (Chapter 2, Appendix to Chapter 13, and Appendix to Chapter 16, respectively).

New learning aids include:

- Marginal glossary definitions of key terms that are cross-referenced with the complete glossary and with the index.
- Additional simplified problems together with solutions to all odd-numbered problems.
- Thought-provoking questions about the empirical applications, now titled "Applying Economics," which are set off more effectively in colored boxes in this edition.
- Thoroughly revised and expanded chapter summaries.
- Completely redrawn graphs with improved labeling.
- Many new numerical examples that illustrate basic analytical concepts.

In making these additions I have tried to retain the book's primary focus on the careful development and application of economic analysis. The learning aids are intended to assist in that process, not substitute for it.

New Ancillaries. In addition to these changes within the text, this new edition also has a companion workbook and study guide—*Problems and Exercises for Intermediate Microeconomics*—prepared by my friend and colleague, Frank Westhoff of Amherst College. This guide offers students a wide variety of learning exercises, including chapter summaries, multiple-choice questions, and many additional problems. A version of *Problems and Exercises for Intermediate Microeconomics* including much of the content of the study guide (together with some additional features as well) is available on a computer disk for IBM PC (and most compatibles) called *Computer Problems and Exercises for Intermediate Microeconomics*. We have used many of the components of the study guide in our own teaching for several years and have found it to be quite helpful for students, and hope that others will have a similar experience.

To the Instructor

Although this edition generally follows the organization of prior ones, some specific changes should be noted. Despite the addition of two new chapters (on the theory of the firm and public choice) there are only 19 chapters in the present edition. This reduction in number of chapters has been achieved primarily by combining related material that previously appeared in two or more separate chapters. Such combinations occur in Chapter 6, "Applications of Utility Analysis"; Chapter 11, "Pricing in Perfectly Competitive Markets," which now covers both the short run and the long run in a single chapter; Chapter 14, "The Demand for Factors of Production," which now includes both the perfectly and imperfectly competitive cases; and Chapter 17, "General Equilibrium and Economic Efficiency." Much of this reorganization was done at the request of users of the book for a more compact, streamlined treatment. I believe the new organization meets this goal without compromising the coverage of essential material.

I also hope instructors will find helpful the many new problems and the discussion questions that appear with the applications in this edition. Most of the problems added here are quite straightforward. Their general goal is to help students to become more comfortable with numerical and graphic material. Some of the more difficult problems from prior editions have now been eliminated and those difficult ones that remain are denoted by an asterisk in the text. Solutions to odd-numbered problems appear in an appendix at the back of this edition. Solutions to all of the problems together with some discussion suggestions focusing on the economic applications appear in the *Instructor's Manual and Test Bank*, available to all adopters. The *Instructor's Manual and Test Bank* includes over 300 multiple choice test questions as well as sample examinations.

As always, I would be most happy to hear from users of this book. Most of what I know about the strengths and weaknesses of prior editions comes from such feedback. Such interaction can't help but improve the final product.

To the Student

The primary goal of this edition is to make *Intermediate Microeconomics and Its Application* even more helpful to students. I hope that the new two-color format combined with numerous student aids such as the marginal glossary, simple numerical illustrations, problems and solutions, and the concise chapter summaries will make the book both easier to learn from and helpful in reviewing for the inevitable tests and exams. Perhaps more important than these visible features are changes in the text and graphs that were made to add to the clarity of the overall presentation. In writing I have tried to provide both complete and intuitive explanations of the ideas being discussed, and I have (I hope) kept the graphs as simple and uncluttered as possible.

Students will be the ultimate judge of how well I have succeeded in making this book a good one to learn from. I would be happy to hear from you about the places where I have fallen short. Words of praise would, of course, also be acceptable.

Acknowledgments

So many of the ideas used in this new edition came from colleagues and friends that it is hard to be sure which are my own and which are theirs. It is also difficult to remember everyone who has given me helpful advice on the book since much of the most important advice I received was delivered in informal ways and in unlikely places (Fenway Park, for example). Still, I have some obvious debts that clearly deserve acknowledgment. Detailed reviews for this new edition were provided by Ted Amato, University of North Carolina, Charlotte; Taeho Bark, Georgetown University; David Emmons, Wayne State; Simon Hakim, Temple University; Dean Hiebert, Illinois State University; Gillian Hunter, Syracuse University; Ali Khan, University of Illinois; David Mills, University of Virginia; and Paul D. Thistle, University of Alabama. The contribution of these reviewers is apparent throughout the book and I am most thankful for their insights. Additional guidance came from the ten economists who helped me address some remaining issues by participating in an in-depth survey: Jere R. Behrman, University of Pennsylvania; Steven Craig, University of Houston; Bill Even, Miami University; D. Allen Dalton, Boise State University; Wayne Gray, Clark University; Alice M. Hughes, Clark University; Janet E. Kohler, University of Houston, University Park; Sharon Berstein Megdal, University of Arizona; Scott S. Monroe, Oakland University; and Arthur Woolf, University of Vermont. A special thanks is owed to Gillian Hunter of Syracuse University, who reviewed all of the problems in the book and offered many helpful suggestions on them. Other users of the book who offered good advice on many topics were: Lee Friedman, University of California, Berkeley; Bernard Saffron, Swarthmore College; and Gordon Winston, Williams College. My colleagues at Amherst, Frank Westhoff and Beth Yarbrough, also clarified my thinking about the proper way to proceed in several places, and I think the book benefited greatly from their suggestions.

David Macoy of the Amherst College class of 1987 provided assistance to me at several spots in the book, especially in the development of some problems. His work and the fine work of earlier students (Adrian Dillon, Jeff Rodman, Katie Merrell, and Mark Bruni) clearly made this a better book. Readers who object to what passes for humor in the problems should take the matter up with these students, however.

The effort of the entire staff at The Dryden Press played an important role in shaping this edition. Liz Widdicombe offered numerous stylistic and substantive suggestions that provided overall direction to the project. Her attention to details (such as the labeling of graphs) was remarkable and I greatly appreciate her help. Debby Acker also provided a great deal of overall guidance and kept the project moving ahead. The copyediting work of Michele Heinz and the supervision of the art by Jeanne Calabrese provided two other important components to the success of the final product. Everything in the production stage of the book was coordinated by Holly Crawford. How she managed to keep all the components straight is beyond me. All in all then, this edition is as much the product of the Dryden staff as it is mine, and I think the book was greatly improved by this joint effort.

Happi Cramer typed the entire manuscript for this book, all on a rather tight schedule. Her work was exceptional for both its high quality and for the speed in which it was accomplished. I consider myself very lucky that Happi could take on this project on short notice when the press of other events prevented Dorothy Ives from working on this edition. After three editions of this book, three editions of *Microeconomic Theory,* and numerous instructor's manuals, Dorothy clearly deserved a break and I'm pleased that the transition went so smoothly. My dedication of this edition to Dorothy Ives is just one small indication of the many debts I owe her and of the love everyone in our department has for her. I only hope we can talk her out of this foolish talk of retirement.

As always, my children—Kate, David, Tory, and Paul—want to be mentioned. They are a bit older now than when first mentioned in my prefaces (aren't we all!). They have even started to argue with me about some of the statements made in this book. But getting their names in print has become a habit I can't seem to break.

Walter Nicholson
Amherst, Massachusetts
September 1986

ABOUT THE AUTHOR

Walter Nicholson is professor of economics at Amherst College. He received a B.A. degree in mathematics from Williams College and a Ph.D. in economics from Massachusetts Institute of Technology. Professor Nicholson's primary research interests are in the econometric analysis of labor markets. He has published many articles on topics related to unemployment, job search, welfare policy, and the domestic impact of international trade. He is also the author of *Microeconomic Theory: Basic Principles and Extensions,* third edition (The Dryden Press, 1985). Professor Nicholson lives in Amherst, Massachusetts. He and his wife, Susan, have four children—Kate, David, Tory, and Paul—all of whom like to see their names in print.

CONTENTS

PART 4   PRICING OF GOODS   271

INTRODUCTION

Part 1 gives some background for the study of economics. Chapter 1 investigates various definitions of ''economics'' and talks about how economic tools help us understand how real-world economies work. The chapter also reviews briefly some basic principles of supply and demand, which should look familiar from your introductory economics course. This review is especially important because supply and demand serve as a starting point for much of the deeper theory covered later in this book. Chapter 1 ends with a short outline of the text that shows how several important themes are repeated throughout.

Since mathematical tools are now widely used in economics, Chapter 2 covers the math that is frequently used in later chapters. Most of these basic principles are usually covered in high school algebra. Most important are the relationships between algebraic functions and how these functions are represented in graphs. Because we will be using graphs heavily throughout the book (and because they are widely used in the field of economics as a whole), be sure you understand the material presented. ▲

CHAPTER 1

Why Economic Models are Useful

In 1789 the British political philosopher Edmund Burke noted: "The Age of Chivalry is gone: that of sophisters, economists, and calculators has succeeded."[1] What was true in eighteenth-century England is even truer today—chivalry is long gone, and the age of economists (and certainly calculators if not sophisters) is upon us. Not a day goes by when the economy is not front-page news. Oil prices, layoffs in the automobile industry, skyrocketing real estate values, and new and complex environmental concerns, such as acid rain, increasingly affect our lives. Just because economic issues have become such a part of our lives, however, does not mean they are well understood. There is probably no field in which uninformed opinions can be so misleading as in economics. The purpose of this particular book and of the study of economics as a whole is to make some sense of the subject. After studying the analysis presented in this book, you should be better able to tell good economic arguments from bad ones and to develop more informed judgments about the many economic issues important today. This book introduces how economists think, how economic decisions are made, and how the economic decisions of one group affect those of another. A step-by-step, commonsense study of these relationships is what economics is all about.

This first chapter introduces the philosophy behind the study of economics. It first defines the subject, and then looks at simple theoretical models for making sense out of the economy. The chapter ends with an overview of the remainder of the book.

---

[1]Edmund Burke, in *Reflections on the French Revolution*, F. G. Selby, ed. (London: The Macmillan Co., 1902), p. 84.

Defining Economics

There are several definitions of economics in use today. The most widely quoted definition describes economics as the "study of the allocation of scarce resources among alternative end uses." This definition introduces two important aspects of society that concern economists: *scarce resources* and *alternative end uses*.

Resources are scarce—there are simply not enough resources available to satisfy all human wants and desires. The amount of land, labor, and capital that is available and the technology that exists for using them limit what society can produce. Second, these scarce resources are devoted to alternative end uses. For example, a society may choose to have television sets or automobiles or clean air or beautiful cities. In fact, a society is likely to choose some combination of all of those "end uses" of its resources. Economists are particularly interested in studying the alternative end uses a society has for its resources and how it chooses among them. "Applying Economics: Scarcity among Ants and Termites" shows how the economic tools used to study scarcity have a wide variety of uses.

A second definition, building on these ideas, describes economics as the "study of the ways in which choices are made." Not only does society as a whole, through governmental decisions, choose how its resources are used, but, more importantly, the people in that society also make a wide variety of decisions on their own. They choose what to buy with their incomes, how to spend their leisure time, for whom to vote, how many (if any) children to have, and so on. Beyond these personal decisions, people also make choices in their jobs. A manager of a firm, for example, must decide the techniques to use and the resources to obtain (both labor and raw materials) to make the firm's product. **Microeconomics** focuses on these kinds of choices. Understanding the factors that influence people's choices and how these choices affect each other can help you understand how society uses or allocates its resources.

Microeconomics
The study of the economic choices individuals and firms make.

A final definition of economics not completely seriously describes it as "what economists do." This definition shows how difficult it is to describe all the questions that interest economists. Economists ask "large" questions, such as whether capitalism or socialism is better or the proper role of government in a free market economy. They also study "small" questions, such as why farmers choose to plant hybrid seeds to grow corn or what rates an electric utility company should charge its customers. Even though these questions are very different, all economic studies use the same theories and the same methods to focus these theories on a particular issue. This book is about those theories and methods.

Why Economists Use Theoretical Models

The most striking feature of any developed economy is its overall complexity. Thousands of firms produce millions of different products and services. Millions of people work in all kinds of jobs and buy a bewildering variety of

Scarcity among Ants and Termites

Scarcity is as important in the nonhuman biological world as it is in the human world. Just as human societies choose how to use their resources, animal societies must make "choices" about how to use *their* resources. Of course, even the most social and intelligent animals' choices do not reflect the complexity, sophistication, and free will that characterize human choices. Biological societies usually evolve slowly through time in response to various environmental pressures. These pressures are in many ways similar to the forces that shape the evolution of human societies. It is no accident that Charles Darwin, in his theories of evolution, drew from the writings of nineteenth-century economists on scarcity.

The impact of scarcity is most visible in the behavior of social insects, such as ants and termites. These insects face scarcity in the availability of their food supply and in the amount of work each individual insect is able to do. In order to insure their survival (which is based on the survival of their queens) an elaborate system of castes has evolved. Different members of the species perform different specialized tasks to promote the overall welfare of the hive. For example, worker insects may forage for food or nurse the young, and soldier insects defend the hive.

A number of biological researchers have applied economic logic to these activities and have concluded that social insects operate very efficiently.[2] In particular, the degree of specialization in various species of termites and ants is based on the number of problems the hive may face (providing these problems occur with some regularity). Social insects in tropical climates tend to have a greater number of castes than do those in temperate climates because tropical problems (such as floods and droughts) happen less regularly there. The number of insects in each caste in a given hive is also based on regularly recurring problems. There are more insects in those castes that must deal with the most frequently recurring problem. In this way the threat from the environment is minimized.

Later chapters show how the economic logic to the problem of scarcity predicts exactly these results—specialization and the allocation of resources among those members of society with specialized skills is a principal reaction to resource scarcity. Since humans are but one part of a much larger biological world, it is not surprising that economics is relevant to other parts of that world.

To Think About

1. How can insects such as ants choose the best policies for dealing with their environment? An ant's brain is smaller than a pinhead; can its behavior be compared to human behavior? If ants really behave in efficient ways, who makes their plans?
2. Are there other animals that choose efficient strategies to cope with scarcity? What kinds of choices (if any) are open to these animals? How would you explain the choices they make?

products, ranging from bread to movies to house trailers. These actions must somehow work together. Wheat, for example, must be harvested at the right time; the farmer must ship it to a miller, who grinds it and ships it to a baker, who bakes it into bread. Enough bread must be sent to the grocery store for people to buy. To describe every action of an economy in such complete detail would be impossible—lengthy books on every product and job could be written! Instead, economists develop simple **models** to capture the "essentials" of how the economy works. Just as a road map does not need to show every

Models
In economics, theories that capture the essentials of how the economy works.

---

[2]See E. O. Wilson, "The Ergonomics of Caste in the Social Insects," *American Economic Review*, December 1978, pp. 25–35.

house to be useful, economic models are useful in understanding the real world even though they do not record every feature of the economy. This book covers the most widely used of these economic models.

The use of models is widespread both in the sciences (including economics) and in everyday life. In physics, for example, scientists use abstractions of the "perfect" vacuum or the "ideal" gas to study real-world physical happenings in simplified settings. Chemistry uses the atom or the molecule as a very simplified model of the structure of matter. In more everyday life, architects use scale models to plan buildings. Television repairers use wiring diagrams in their work, and dressmakers use patterns and plans.

In much the same way economists use models to understand the infinitely complex real world. These models show how people make decisions, how firms make decisions, and how these two types of decisions relate to each other in the market.

Developing a Basic Economic Model: The Theory of Value

To develop an economic model we will look at how economists explain the way prices are determined. Although this discussion ends with the standard model of supply and demand that you should have studied in introductory economics, some of the predecessors of that model are first covered to show how economic models are developed and how they are improved upon over time.

Definition of Value

Theory of value
Study of the factors that determine relative prices.

The study of price determination traditionally is known as the **theory of value.** The meaning of *value* has changed over time. Today value is considered to be the same as price.[3] Earlier, however, the market price of a good (the price it would get if sold on the market) and its value were separate ideas. Value then was defined as importance, essentiality, and sometimes even godliness. When price and value did not have the same meaning, early economists could focus on their differences.

"Just" Price: Price versus Value

Saint Thomas Aquinas (1225–1274) believed value was divinely determined. Prices, being set by people, could differ from value. A person who set a price in excess of a good's value might be accused of charging an unjust price. For

---

[3]Part 6 of this text (especially Chapter 18) discusses how value and price are not always considered the same today.

example, Saint Thomas believed the just rate of interest to be zero. Any lender who demanded interest for the use of money was charging an unjust price and could be—and often was—prosecuted by church officials.

Controversies over the just price for goods dominated the economic discussions of the Middle Ages. The notion of a just price became less important as economists moved away from the concept of natural law toward the scientific method. Rather than looking for a divine pattern, economists began to study economic actions in their own right. The scientific method of proposing and testing alternative theories became the most important means of investigation, both in economics and in most other areas of knowledge, in the eighteenth century.

Value in Exchange: The Labor Theory of Value

The early scientific economists, such as Adam Smith (1723–1790) and David Ricardo (1772–1823), still saw value and price as different. Smith defined the *value* of a good as value in use and *price* as value in exchange (exchange in the market). The difference between these two definitions is illustrated in the **water-diamond paradox.** Water has great value in use, since it is necessary to all life, but little value in exchange, as it has a low price. Diamonds, on the other hand, have less value in use but great value in exchange. Like water, some very useful items have low prices whereas certain nonessential items, like diamonds, have high prices.

This paradox was never satisfactorily resolved by either Smith or Ricardo. Philosophers continued to argue over the concept of value in use while economists turned to explaining value in exchange or relative prices. One obvious possible explanation is that the prices of goods are the same as the costs to produce them. Since the biggest cost of production was for labor in the times of Smith and Ricardo, it was only a short step for economists to embrace a *labor theory of value*. For example, to paraphrase Adam Smith, if it takes twice as long to catch a deer as to catch a beaver, then one deer should be worth two beavers. The labor theory of value would explain the water-diamond paradox: diamonds are more costly than water because they require substantially more labor to produce.

How can this explanation of exchange value be applied to other productive resources, such as payment for rent and for capital equipment, that have no labor cost? Ricardo argued that the cost of capital equipment could also be regarded as a labor cost, in that the labor was invested when the machines were made. Using this argument any capital cost could be traced back to its labor cost. Ricardo also argued that rent was a result and not a cause of a good's price (as discussed in detail in Chapter 14). These arguments result in a pure **labor theory of value.** The price of a good is determined by the labor cost used in making it.

Anyone with a passing knowledge of the law of supply and demand will find Ricardo's explanation strange. What about the effect of demand on price? When prices rapidly rose or fell, Ricardo did see them as reacting to a change

Water-diamond paradox
If water is so much more important to life than diamonds, how can diamonds be more expensive than water?

Labor theory of value
Relative prices of goods are determined only by the relative amounts of labor used to make them.

in demand. However, he believed these price changes were abnormal and that they affected price only temporarily. Ricardo did not see demand as important in determining market value; he felt long-run prices were determined solely by labor costs.

Karl Marx (1818–1883) used Ricardo's ideas as the cornerstone for his theory of political economy. If labor is the source of all value, Marx reasoned, the workers should receive all the proceeds from the goods they produce. According to this theory, capitalists and landowners siphon off the proceeds that belong to the workers. Marx's theories challenged future economists to come up with another theory of value to serve as the cornerstone for a more general theory of price determination.

Value in Use Reconsidered: The Marginalist Revolution

Between 1850 and 1880 economists realized that to construct an adequate alternative to Ricardo's theory of value, they first had to come to grips with the paradox of value in use. Several economists saw that it is not the total usefulness of a good that determines its exchange value but the usefulness of the *last unit consumed*. For example, although water is very useful, since it is relatively plentiful one *more* gallon has very little use. These economists defined value in use as marginal, or incremental, usefulness—the usefulness of an *additional unit of a good*.

This concept of the demand for an additional unit of a good, when combined with Ricardo's theory, which also stressed incremental, or "marginal," costs, gives a comprehensive picture of price determination. The knowledge that both marginal usefulness (demand) and marginal costs (supply) influence the price of a good revolutionized economic theory.

Marshallian Supply and Demand

The clearest statement of these ideas was presented by the English economist Alfred Marshall (1842–1924) in his *Principles of Economics,* published in 1890. Marshall showed how demand and supply *simultaneously* determine price—neither demand nor supply alone determines price, just as only one blade of a scissors does not cut alone. Marshall's analysis is illustrated by the familiar cross shown in Figure 1.1.

In this graph the amount of a good purchased per period (say, each week) is shown on the horizontal axis, and the price of the good appears on the vertical axis. The curve labeled Demand shows the amount of the good demanded at each price. This curve slopes down as you move to the right. This negative slope shows the marginalist principle: as the amount of the good increases, the price falls because people are willing to pay less and less for the last unit purchased. The curve labeled Supply shows that the cost of making the good rises as more units are produced. This curve goes up as you move to the right. This positive slope shows the increasing cost of making one more

Figure 1.1
The Marshall Supply-
Demand Cross

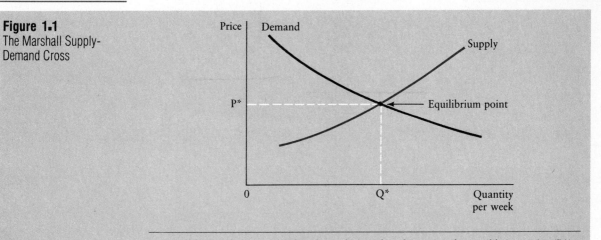

Marshall believed that demand and supply together determine the equilibrium price (P*) and quantity (Q*) of a good. Just as only one blade of a scissors does not do the cutting, neither demand nor supply alone determines price, and neither cost nor usefulness to buyers alone determines exchange value.

unit of the good as the total amount of the good increases. In other words, the upward slope of the supply curve reflects *increasing* marginal costs, just as the downward slope of the demand curve reflects *decreasing* marginal usefulness. The two curves intersect at P*, Q*. Here P* is an **equilibrium price**—both buyers and sellers are content with the amount of goods being traded and the price at which they are traded.

Equilibrium price
The price at which both buyers and sellers are in agreement about the amount of the good being sold.

If the good is sold at a price above P*, people will want to buy *less* than the amount being made. There would be too much of this good being supplied. On the other hand, if the good is sold at a price below P*, people will want to buy more of the good than is being made—demand will exceed supply. Only at the equilibrium price of P* do the demand of buyers and the supply from the sellers agree.

If either the demand or supply curve should shift, however, the equilibrium price would also change. In Figure 1.2, people's demand for the good increases. In this case the demand curve moves outward (from curve D to curve D'). At each price people now want to buy more of the good. The equilibrium price increases (from P* to P**). This higher price both tells firms to supply more goods and restrains the people's demand for the good. At the new equilibrium price of P** supply and demand again balance—at this price the amount of goods demanded is exactly the same as the amount supplied.

Marshall's model of supply and demand resolved the water-diamond paradox. The price of a good actually reflects both the marginal usefulness of the good to a buyer (demand) and the marginal costs to make the good (supply). Now there is no paradox. Water is low in price because it has both a low marginal value and a low marginal cost of production. On the other hand, diamonds are high in price because they have both a high marginal value

Figure 1.2
An Increase in Demand
Alters Equilibrium Price
and Quantity

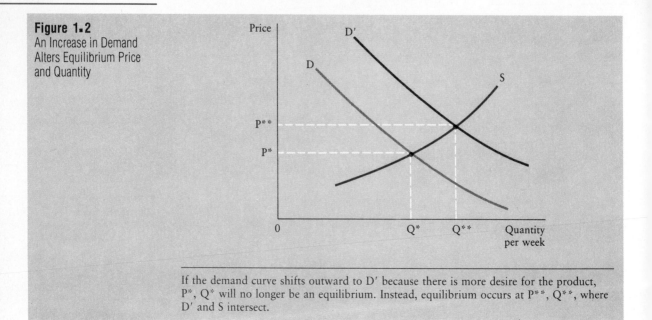

If the demand curve shifts outward to D' because there is more desire for the product,
P*, Q* will no longer be an equilibrium. Instead, equilibrium occurs at P**, Q**, where
D' and S intersect.

(since they are relatively scarce) and a high marginal cost of production. The
price of diamonds is higher than water as a result of the forces of both supply
and demand.

Since Marshall introduced his model of supply and demand in the late
nineteenth century, it has been the basis for all later economic theory. The
model and the concepts of marginal value and cost that underlie it can be used
to explain a wide variety of real-world situations. "Applying Economics: Water
Demand and the 1977 Drought in California" adapts these ideas to one such
situation. In general, Marshall's model underlies most of the analysis in this
book.

Models of Many Markets: The Production Possibility Frontier

Probably the most important recent use of Marshall's model of supply and
demand is to show how different markets work together in an economy. The
basic model pictured in Figures 1.1 and 1.2 is a **partial equilibrium model** of
a single market. It does not show how results in one market affect those in
another. For example, Figure 1.2 shows how an increase in demand for a good
causes its price to rise, but not how that price increase might affect other
markets.

If we were examining the market for imported French wine, say, we know
that an increase in demand would result in a rise in price. But it also seems
likely that this price rise would have effects on the market for California wine

**Partial equilibrium
model**
An economic model of
a single market.

Water Demand and the 1977 Drought in California

Water is necessary to all life, and how it is used is dominated by this fact. Water supply planners, for example, may assume that each user (a residential household, an industrial firm, a vegetable farmer, and so on) needs a certain amount, and water is assumed to have equal value for all users. But, as the marginalists' solution to the water-diamond paradox shows, water is not of equal value to all users. The overall usefulness of water (that is, that it is a necessity), however, is not as important as its marginal value—the value of one more gallon to a user. This distinction is especially clear during periods of water shortage, such as the drought in the Pacific Coast states in 1976 and 1977.

The year 1977 was the driest in California since rainfall records began to be kept in the mid-1800s.[4] Following a very dry 1976, this absence of rainfall meant water use needed to be cut back. Households were asked to take extraordinary measures ("shower with a friend," "flush once a day") to save water. Agricultural water users in the Central Valley were allowed to use only between 25 and 50 percent of their normal water requirements. Using the assumption that water is a necessity, the cutbacks were made across the board to all users so that the shortage was shared "equally." This cutback policy did not consider the marginal valuation of water for different types of farmers. Before the drought, water allocations were based largely on historical accident; the differences in marginal value were therefore extreme. By some estimates, water was worth only about $1 per acre foot (326,000 gallons) to farmers growing

rice—that is, a cutback of an acre foot of water use would reduce the rice crop output by only $1. On the other hand, water valuations for farmers with high-priced vegetables (tomatoes, cucumbers, and so forth) ran as high as $800 to $1,000 per acre foot. The cutback in water to these farmers was much costlier *at the margin* than to rice farmers, but this fact was ignored since water was considered equally necessary to both crops.

The farmers themselves knew differences in water valuation. Many farmers who valued water highly tried to buy water from farmers with a lower valuation. Most of these purchases were prevented by water laws and at first by the high costs of moving large quantities of water. As the drought wore on, water transfers were increasingly made. The rains of the winter of 1977 and 1978 finally eliminated the need to think about such matters—until the next drought.

To Think About
1. Why would water even have a market price? Isn't it usually provided free of charge from rain? Does a person who collects rain water (say, in a pond) have any right to sell it to someone else?
1. Rights to water in California are mainly determined by history—whoever claimed the flow of water from a river first has the right to that water. Does this legal principle make sense? How else might rights to water from a river be determined? Should the owner of water rights be able to sell this water? What would happen if these sales were prohibited?

(where demand would increase as people shifted from French to California products). Indeed, the effects could be far more widespread than this, including repercussions in the market for fine cheeses (to consume with wine), for wine glasses and cork screws, and possibly even affecting the wages of California grape harvesters. And, to complicate the story, some of these effects may have repercussions on the original market with which we started our discussion

---

[4]This discussion draws on the background papers of the water transfers workshop held at the Graduate School of Public Policy, University of California, Berkeley, May 20, 1977.

General equilibrium
model
An economic model of
several related markets.

Production possibility
frontier
A graph showing all
possible combinations
of goods that can be
produced with a fixed
amount of resources.

Opportunity cost
How much of one good
will not be able to be
produced if more of
some other good is
produced?

(the market for French wine). Suppose, for example, that California grape
harvesters just happen to like French wine. Then a rise in their wages might
cause them to buy more of this product and that would disturb the initial
equilibrium. To show all the effects of a change in one market on other
markets, we need a **general equilibrium model**, which includes workings of
all markets together. Later sections of this book look closely at some of these
multimarket models.

Here these models are introduced using another graph you should remember from introductory economics—the **production possibility frontier**. This
graph shows the various amounts of two goods that an economy can produce
during some period (again, say one week). Because the production possibility
frontier shows two goods, rather than the single good in Marshall's model, it
is used as a basic building block for general equilibrium models.

Figure 1.3 shows the production possibility frontier for two goods, food
and clothing. The graph looks at the supply of these goods by showing the
combinations that can be produced with this economy's resources. For example, ten pounds of food and three units of clothing could be made, or four
pounds of food and twelve units of clothing. Many other combinations of
food and clothing could also be produced. The production possibility frontier
shows all of them. Combinations of food and clothing outside the frontier
cannot be made because there are not enough resources available. The production possibility frontier reminds us of the basic economic fact that resources are scarce—there are not enough resources available to produce all
we might want of every good.

This scarcity means that we must choose how much of each good to produce. Figure 1.3 makes clear that each choice has its costs. For example, if
this economy produces ten pounds of food and three units of clothing at point
A, producing one more unit of clothing would "cost" one-half pound of food—
to increase the output of clothing by one unit means the production of food
would have to decrease by one-half pound. Economists would say that the
opportunity cost of one unit of clothing at point A is one-half pound of food.
On the other hand, if the economy initially makes four pounds of food and
twelve units of clothing at point B, it would cost two pounds of food to make
one more unit of clothing. The opportunity cost of one more unit of clothing
at point B has increased to two pounds of food. Because more units of clothing
are produced at point B than at point A, both Ricardo's and Marshall's ideas
of increasing incremental costs suggest that the opportunity cost of an additional unit of clothing will be higher at point B than at point A. This effect is
just what Figure 1.3 shows.

The production possibility frontier in Figure 1.3 gives us two general equilibrium results that are not clear in Marshall's supply and demand model of
a single market. The first result is that producing more of one good means
producing less of another good because resources are scarce. Economists often
(perhaps too often!) use the expression "there is no such thing as a free lunch"
to explain that everything has opportunity costs. The second result shown by
the production possibility frontier is that these opportunity costs depend on
how much of each good is produced. The frontier is like a supply curve for

Figure 1.3
Production Possibility
Frontier

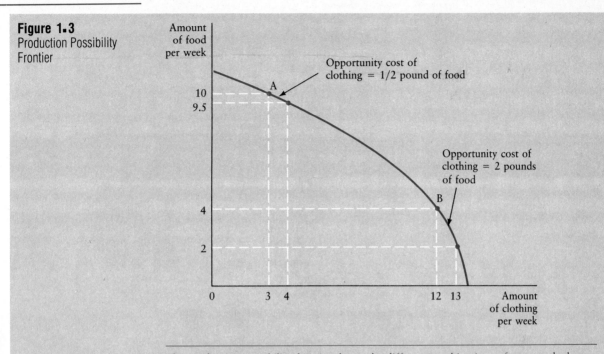

The production possibility frontier shows the different combinations of two goods that can be produced from a certain amount of scarce resources. It also shows the opportunity cost of producing more of one good as how much of the other good then cannot be produced. The opportunity cost at two different levels of production of a good can be seen by comparing points A and B.

two goods—it shows the opportunity cost of producing more of one good as the decrease in the amount of a second good. The production possibility frontier is therefore a particularly useful tool to study several markets at the same time.

How Economists Verify Theoretical Models

Direct approach
To verify economic models, the direct approach examines the validity of the assumptions on which the model is based.

Of course, not all models are as useful as Marshall's model of supply and demand. For example, Ptolemy's theory of planetary motion put earth as the center of the universe; it could not be believed when it could not explain the movement of the planets around the sun. An important purpose of scientific investigation is to sort out such "bad" models from "good" ones. Two methods are used to test economic models. The **direct approach** looks at the assumptions upon which a model is based; the **indirect approach,** on the other hand, uses a simple version of a model to see if it can correctly predict real-world events. Each approach is used in this book to try to illustrate the validity of the models that are presented. The differences between these two approaches are discussed on the following page.

The Direct Approach

The direct approach to testing the assumptions of an economic model might begin with intuition. Do the model's assumptions seem "reasonable"? Unfortunately, this question is fraught with problems, since what appears reasonable to one person may seem preposterous to someone else (try arguing with a non-economics student about whether people behave rationally, for example).

Assumptions can also be tested with empirical evidence. For example, economists usually assume that firms are in business to "maximize profits" or make as much money as possible—in fact, much of our discussion in this book is based on that assumption. Using the direct approach to test this assumption with real-world data, you might send questionnaires to managers asking them how they make decisions and whether they really do try to maximize profits. This approach has been used many times; but the results are difficult to interpret and do not shed much light on the profit maximization assumption. Even this kind of gathering of information may not be too helpful to decide if the model's basic assumptions are correct.

Indirect approach
To verify economic models, the indirect approach asks if the model can accurately predict real-world events.

The Indirect Approach

Many economists, such as Milton Friedman, do not believe that a theory can be tested through its assumptions.[5] They argue that all theories are based on unrealistic assumptions; the very nature of theorizing demands that we make these unrealistic assumptions. These economists believe that we must see if the theory is capable of explaining and predicting real-world events in order to see if it is valid. The real test of an economic theory is whether it can be used with events from the economy itself.

Friedman gives a good example of this idea by asking what theory explains the shots an expert pool player will make. He argues that the laws of velocity, momentum, and angles from classical physics make a suitable theoretical model, because the pool player certainly shoots *as if* he or she followed these laws. If we asked the players whether they understood these physical principles, they would undoubtedly answer that they did not. That does not matter, Friedman argues, because the physical laws give very accurate predictions of the shots made and are therefore useful as theoretical models.

Going back to the question of whether firms try to maximize profits, the indirect approach would try to predict the firms' behavior by assuming that they do act *as if* they were maximizing profits. If we find that they do, then we can believe the profit-maximization hypothesis. Even if these firms said on

---

[5]Milton Friedman, *Essays in Positive Economics* (Chicago: University of Chicago Press, 1953), Chapter 1. Another view stressing the importance of realistic assumptions can be found in H. A. Simon, "Rational Decision Making in Business Organizations," *American Economic Review,* September 1979, pp. 493–513.

questionnaires that they do not try to maximize profits, the theory will still be valid, much as the pool player's disclaiming knowledge of the laws of physics does not make these laws untrue. The ultimate test in both cases is the theory's ability to predict real-world events.

Using Empirical Examples

This book is about economic theories. Because our real objective is to learn about the real world, we must be able to prove those theories. This book uses both the direct and indirect methods to test them. Occasionally, we will follow the direct approach by pointing out that a model is based on "reasonable" assumptions. More often, however, we will look at examples from the real world in which behavior can be predicted using economic theory. These real-world examples are included not only because they are interesting applications of economics in their own right, but also because they are used as empirical support for the theories presented here. They are especially important to understanding economic model building. "Applying Economics: Economic Models and the Limits to Growth Debate" looks at some predictions based on rather poor economic models and shows why we might want to reject those models.

Positive versus Normative Economics

Positive economic analysis
Theories that explain how resources actually are used in an economy.

Normative analysis
Theories that make judgments about how the economy's resources should be used.

So far we have been talking about **positive economic analysis,** which uses the real world as an object to be studied to explain economic events. Positive economics tries to determine how resources actually are used in an economy. A somewhat different use of economic theory is **normative analysis.** In this type of economic theory, economists have a great deal to say about how an economy's resources *should* be used. For example, an economist engaged in positive analysis might look at health care prices in terms of the behavior of doctors, patients, hospitals, insurance companies, and so forth. The economist might also measure the costs and benefits of devoting more resources to health care. But if the economist says that more resources should be allocated to health care, he or she has moved into normative analysis. By suggesting what policies should be undertaken, the economist is making judgments that go beyond how prices and quantities of health care are determined.

Some economists believe that only positive analysis is proper. They argue that economics should be as scientific as the physical sciences, and should only describe and possibly predict real-world events. Moralistic positions and special interests are improper for an economist. According to this view, the choice of a particular health care policy should be left to the political process, not to the economist.

This book takes a positive economic approach by explaining actual economic behavior. At the same time we consider several normative questions. For example, our discussion of monopoly shows how monopolistic firms may misallocate resources. Our analysis of incomplete property rights shows how they can cause goods to be misallocated as well. Each of these conclusions

Economic Models and the Limits to Growth Debate

In the early 1970s many books and reports predicted dire consequences for the future of humanity. *World Dynamics* by Jay W. Forrester and *The Limits to Growth* by Donnella H. Meadows *et al.* (based largely on the Forrester book) were very influential.[6] Using complex computer models, these books suggested strongly that by the mid-1980s and on into the twenty-first century the world would experience major economic disruptions, with per capita availability of food and other necessities falling at a disturbingly rapid rate. These authors raised the fears first suggested in the writings of T. R. Malthus in the late eighteenth century that world population growth would exceed increases in production of food and other necessities of life. We need to ask if the evidence supports this model before we can trust its predictions.

Of course, the twenty-first century has not yet arrived, so actual evidence that would test the model's predictions is not available. Since the models were first published, their assumptions have been looked at closely, however. Not only do these assumptions seem faulty, but there is increasing evidence that the predictions as well may be wrong.[7]

Economists criticized these books because they did not consider how people might change their behavior in response to changing market prices. For example, the models assumed that a certain amount of natural resources was needed for each unit of goods produced by the economy. The models assumed that increasing production would put equally increasing strains on the world's resources. This assumption ignores how the price of resources works to make producers use these resources more efficiently. One of the most dramatic re-

cent examples is the case of energy, particularly oil. During the 1970s the real price of oil to users increased more than sixfold, mostly because the Organization of Petroleum Exporting Countries (the infamous OPEC cartel) was formed to control oil production early in the decade. This huge increase led to large increases in the price of all types of energy. The world economy responded to these energy price increases by cutting back on the use of energy in many ways, such as developing more efficient, smaller cars and more efficient industrial machines. In the United States, for example, real energy prices rose about 60 percent between 1973 and 1980, but energy use per dollar of real gross national product declined by nearly 20 percent. The models used in the *Limits* book did not, however, allow for such possibilities.

The limits to growth debate is not settled, and the world economy may still face serious problems into the 1990s and beyond. The criticisms of the *Limits* books clearly show that more accurate models need to be used to predict these problems.

To Think About

1. What does it mean to be "running out" of some resource? Hasn't the world been running out of resources since Adam and Eve? Does the market price of a resource tell whether or not it is scarce, or should other factors be considered too?

2. Should the authors of the *Limits* books have assumed that there is a fixed relationship between economic growth and resource use? What factors might influence the amount of natural resources needed for economic growth? Can you think of situations where growth would require relatively few resources?

---

[6]J. W. Forrester, *World Dynamics* (Cambridge, Mass.: Wright Allen Press, 1971), and Donnella H. Meadows *et al.*, *The Limits to Growth* (New York: Universe Books, 1972).

[7]W. D. Nordhaus, "World Dynamics: Measurement without Data," *Economic Journal,* December 1973, pp. 1156–1183.

may suggest a change in policy (such as regulation of monopoly or full legal specification of property rights), but by pointing out the problems we are not necessarily recommending specific corrections. Our goal is to show the consequences of undertaking any policy.

An Overview of the Book

This book is divided into six parts. Each part explains a broad area of economic analysis in several closely related chapters.

Part 1 introduces the topics that follow later. Chapter 1 discusses some of the methodological issues arising in economic analysis. This chapter also reviews the basic model of supply and demand developed by economists to explain how prices are determined, which is the framework for most of the analysis in this book. Chapter 2 reviews basic concepts of algebra, especially algebraic functions and graphs. These concepts are widely used in economics and are essential to this book.

Parts 2 and 3 examine the two important participants in the economic process. Part 2 develops in detail the economic theory of *individual behavior*. It explains how economists treat individuals' preferences and how these preferences affect decisions, which leads to the concept of demand. Part 3 is concerned with *firms' behavior*. Part 3 focuses primarily on firms' costs and on how firms' decisions affect costs; this leads to the idea of supply.

Parts 4 and 5 show how the preferences of individuals (demand) and the costs of firms (supply) create markets and determine prices. The allocation of goods and resources takes place in these markets. Part 4 discusses markets for goods and looks at how these markets are organized. Part 5 then looks at markets for productive resources. Both parts build on the analysis of individuals' and firms' decisions in Parts 2 and 3.

Part 6 raises general questions about the desirability of market operations. Economic efficiency and social welfare are discussed, and "ideal" situations are described (as well as not so ideal situations!). Advantages and disadvantages of government dealing with these situations are intensively investigated.

Three Important Recurring Themes

Although many economic models are discussed in this book, they are all based on a few simple ideas. Three specific themes are repeated throughout the book.

The Benefits of Free Exchange

If Smith has something Jones wants, and Jones has something Smith wants, it is possible that they both will be better off by exchanging these goods. Much of this book, especially the sections about competitive markets, applies this commonsense idea.

The Limit of Exchange

In many situations, the free exchange of goods may not produce socially desirable results. For example, people on their own probably would not choose to provide adequate mosquito control. Each person would probably say "let the other guy do it," hoping to benefit from the other guy's insecticides. If everyone believed this, then mosquitos would never be controlled. Because free exchange cannot guarantee that enough resources will go to mosquito control, there may be a need for government action.

The Value of the "Maximization Hypothesis"

In order to understand economic behavior, we usually assume that the actors (individuals, firms, labor unions, and others) are working toward some goal. The actor will choose the action that best achieves (that is, maximizes) the goal. As we saw earlier, the most familiar example of this hypothesis is the assumption that firms act to maximize profits. Using this one basic assumption, several implications about a firm's behavior can be made and tested in the real world. In this book, similar assumptions are made about most economic actors, which then shed light on how choices are made and how scarce resources are allocated.

These three themes are basic to most of microeconomics. You will encounter them in many different forms in this book since they apply to a wide range of questions. In many respects these three simple ideas summarize the way in which economists look at the world.

Summary

This chapter provides you with the background to begin your study of microeconomics. Much of this material should be familiar to you from your introductory economics course, but that should come as no surprise. In many respects the study of economics repeatedly investigates the same questions with an increasingly sophisticated set of tools. This course gives you some more of these tools. In establishing the basis for that investigation, this chapter reminds you of several important ideas:

- Economics is the study of allocating scarce resources among possible uses. Because resources are scarce, choices have to be made on how they will be used. Economists develop theoretical models to explain these choices.
- The most commonly used model of the allocation of resources is the model of supply and demand developed by Alfred Marshall in the latter part of the nineteenth century. That model shows how prices are determined with an equilibrium between the amount people want to buy and the amount firms are willing to produce. If supply and demand curves shift, new prices are established to restore equilibrium to the market.

- Marshall's model of supply and demand is a "partial equilibrium" model because it looks at only one market. Models of many markets are complicated by the number of relationships among them.

- The production possibility frontier provides a simple illustration of the supply conditions in two markets. The curve clearly shows the limits imposed on any economy because resources are scarce. Producing more of one good means that less of something else must be produced. This reduction in output elsewhere is called the opportunity cost. The size of the opportunity cost depends on how much of various goods are being produced.

- Proving the validity of economic models is difficult and sometimes controversial. Occasionally the validity of a model can be determined by whether it is based on reasonable assumptions. More often, however, models are judged by how well they explain actual economic events.

CHAPTER 2

Mathematical Tools Used in Economics

Mathematics began to be widely used in economics near the end of the nineteenth century. Marshall's *Principles of Economics,* published in 1890, included a lengthy mathematical appendix that developed his arguments more systematically than the book itself. Today, mathematics is indispensable for economists. They use it not to hide behind symbols or to make their arguments hard to understand, but to show their results precisely. Just as the physical sciences use mathematics, economists use it to move logically from the basic assumptions of a theory to predicting the results of those assumptions. Without mathematics, this process would be both more cumbersome and less accurate.

The models we discuss in this book are based on mathematical arguments. Sometimes these arguments are presented step by step, and in other cases they are discussed in a less rigorous, more literary way. Although the mathematics we use here is no more complex than high school algebra, some of the theories themselves are based on more advanced mathematics. That level of mathematics may be presented in footnotes, but more often you will be told to go to advanced works.

This chapter reviews some of the basic concepts of algebra. We then discuss a few issues that arise in applying those concepts to the study of economics. We use the tools introduced here throughout the rest of the book.

Functions of One Variable

The basic elements of algebra are called **variables.** These are usually called X and Y and may be given any numerical value. In this equation:

$$Y = f(X) \qquad [2.1]$$

Variables
The basic elements of algebra, usually called X, Y, and so on, that may be given any numerical value in an equation.

Independent variable
In an algebraic equation, a variable that is unaffected by the action of another variable and may be assigned any value.

Dependent variable
In algebra, a variable whose value is determined by another variable.

you would say, "Y is a function of X," meaning that the value of Y depends on the value given to X. For example, if we make X calories eaten per day and Y body weight, then Equation 2.1 shows the relationship between the amount of food intake and an individual's weight. The form of Equation 2.1 also shows causality. X is an **independent variable** and may be given any value. On the other hand, the value Y receives is completely determined by X; Y is a **dependent variable.** The functional notation in Equation 2.1 shows that "X causes Y."

The exact functional relationship between X and Y may take on a wide variety of forms. There are two common forms.

1. Y is a *linear function* of X. In this case

$$Y = a + bX \qquad [2.2]$$

where a and b are constants that may be given any numerical value. For example, if a = 2 and b = 2, Equation 2.2 would be written as

$$Y = 2 + 2X. \qquad [2.3]$$

We could give Equation 2.3 an economic interpretation. For example, if we make Y the labor costs of a firm and X the number of labor hours hired, then the form of Equation 2.3 could record the relationship between costs and workers hired. In this case there is a fixed cost of $2 (when X = 0, Y = $2), and the wage rate is $2 per hour. The cost of X labor hours would be 2X.

2. Y is a *quadratic function* of X. In this case

$$Y = a + bX + cX^2 \qquad [2.4]$$

where a, b, and c are constants that may be given any numerical value. One specific example of a quadratic function would make a = −5, b = 6, and c = −1; Equation 2.4 would then be written as

$$Y = -5 + 6X - X^2. \qquad [2.5]$$

We could also give an economic interpretation to Equation 2.5. Suppose we make Y the output of corn on an acre of land and X the amount of fertilizer applied to that land. In this case, the ability of fertilizer to raise corn output declines as more fertilizer is added. This decline can be easily seen using the quadratic curve in the graph of this equation in Figure 2.5.

Sometimes it may be useful to look at the relationship between X and Y for several different values of X. Table 2.1 lists the values for Y for the integral values of X between −3 and +6 for both the linear and quadratic functions. Of course, many more values of X (including fractional values) could have

Table 2.1
Values of X and Y for
Linear and Quadratic
Functions

	Linear Function		Quadratic Function
X	$Y = f(X)$ $= 2 + 2X$	X	$Y = f(X)$ $= -5 + 6X - X^2$
-3	-4	-3	-32
-2	-2	-2	-21
-1	0	-1	-12
0	2	0	-5
1	4	1	0
2	6	2	3
3	8	3	4
4	10	4	3
5	12	5	0
6	14	6	-5

been included in this table, and you should be able to compute the value for Y for any preassigned value of X.

Graphing Functions of One Variable

When we write down the functional relationship between X and Y, we are summarizing all there is to know about that relationship. In principle, this book, or any book that uses mathematics, could be written using only these equations. Graphs of some of these functions, however, are very helpful. Graphs not only make it easier for us to understand certain arguments, they also can take the place of a lot of the mathematical notation that must be developed. For these reasons, this book relies heavily on graphs of its topics, using some of the following basic techniques.

A graph is simply one way to show the relationship between two variables. Usually the values of the dependent variable (Y) are shown on the vertical axis, and the values of the independent variable (X) are shown on the horizontal axis.[1] Figure 2.1 uses this form to graph Equation 2.3. Although we use heavy dots to show only the points of this function that are listed in Table 2.1, the graph applies to the function of every possible value of X. The graph of Equation 2.3 is a straight line, which is why this is called a **linear function**. In Figure 2.1, X and Y can take on both positive and negative values. The variables used in economics generally take on only positive values, and therefore we only have to use the upper righthand (positive) quadrant of the axes.

Linear function
An equation that is represented by a straight line graph.

---

[1] In economics this convention is not always followed. Sometimes a dependent variable is shown on the horizontal axis as, for example, in the case of demand and supply curves. In that case the independent variable (price) is shown on the vertical axis and the dependent variable (quantity) on the horizontal axis.

Figure 2.1
Graph of the Linear
Function Y = 2 + 2X

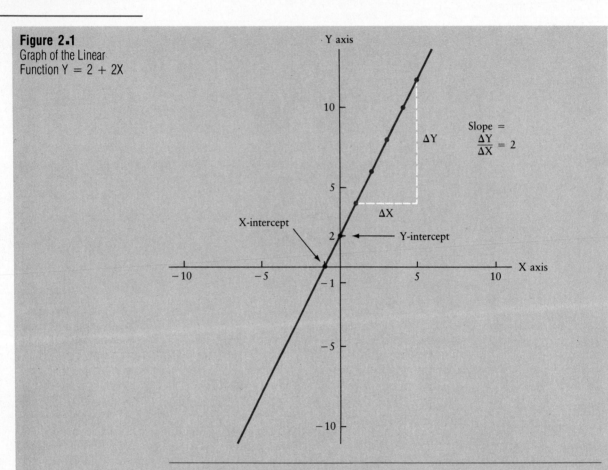

The Y-intercept is 2, when X = 0, Y = 2. The slope of the line is 2: an increase in X by 1 will increase Y by 2.

Linear Functions: Intercepts and Slopes

Slope
The direction of a line on a graph. Shows the change in Y that results from a change in X.

Intercept
The value of Y when X equals zero.

Two important features of the graph in Figure 2.1 are its **slope** and its **intercept** on the Y axis. The Y-intercept is the value of Y when X is equal to 0. For example, as we can see in Figure 2.1, when X = 0, Y = 2; this means that 2 is the Y-intercept.[2] In the general linear form of Equation 2.2,

$$Y = a + bX,$$

---

[2]One can also speak of the X-intercept of a function, which is defined to be that value of X for which Y = 0. For Equation 2.3 it is easy to see that Y = 0 when X = −1, which is then the X-intercept. The X-intercept for the general linear function in Equation 2.2 is given by X = −a/b, as may be seen by substituting that value into the equation.

the Y-intercept will be $Y = a$, since this is the value of Y when $X = 0$.

We define the slope of any straight line to be the ratio of the change in Y to the change in X for a movement along the line. The slope can be defined mathematically as

$$\text{Slope} = \frac{\text{Change in Y}}{\text{Change in X}} = \frac{\Delta Y}{\Delta X},$$

where the Δ ("delta") notation simply means "change in." For the particular function shown in Figure 2.1, the slope is equal to 2. We can clearly see from the dashed lines, representing ΔY and ΔX, that a given change in X is met by a change of twice that amount in Y. Table 2.1 shows the same change—for example, as X increases from 0 to 1, Y increases from 2 to 4. Consequently

$$\text{Slope} = \frac{\Delta Y}{\Delta X} = \frac{4 - 2}{1 - 0} = 2.$$

It should be obvious that this is true for all the other points in Table 2.1. Everywhere along the straight line, the slope is the same. Generally, for any linear function, the slope is given by b in Equation 2.2.[3] The slope of a straight line may be positive (as it is in Figure 2.1) or it may be negative, in which case the line would run from upper left to lower right.

A straight line may also have a slope of 0, which is horizontal. In this case the value of Y is constant; changes in X will not affect Y. The function would be $Y = a + 0X$, or $Y = a$. This equation is represented by a horizontal line (parallel to the X axis) through point a on the Y axis.

The slope of a function depends on the units in which X and Y are measured. For example, we might see a relationship in which the number of oranges (Y) purchased in a week is equal to $2 + 2X$, where X is an individual's income measured in hundreds of dollars per week. Consequently, $\Delta Y/\Delta X = 2$: that is, a $100 increase in income one week causes 2 more oranges to be purchased. If income (X) is measured in single dollars, the relationship is $Y = 2 + .02X$ and $\Delta Y/\Delta X = .02$. In this case, although the interpretation of this slope is the same (a $100 increase in income still increases orange purchases by 2), the numerical value of the slope is very different. In later chapters we look at some methods that might solve this "units" problem.

Changes in Slope

Quite often in this text we are interested in changing the parameters (that is, a and b) of a linear function. We can do this in two ways; we can change the

---

[3]In calculus, mathematicians call the slope of a function "the derivative" and denote this concept by dY/dX where the d means the change in Y brought about by a very small change in X. For the general linear Equation 2.2, $dY/dX = b$.

Figure 2.2
Changes in the Slope of a
Linear Function

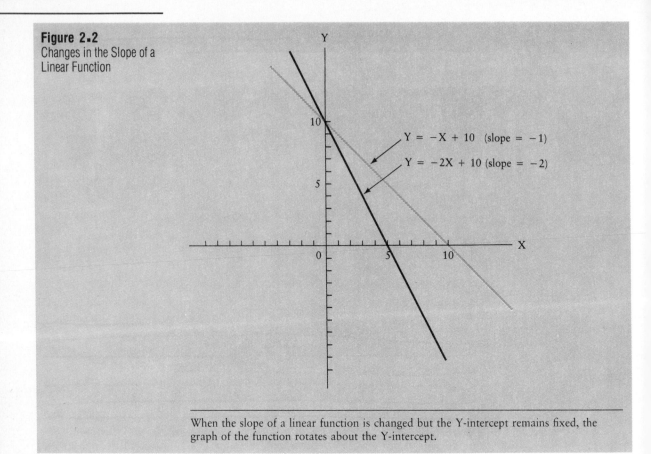

When the slope of a linear function is changed but the Y-intercept remains fixed, the graph of the function rotates about the Y-intercept.

Y-intercept, or we can change the slope. Figure 2.2 shows the graph of the function

$$Y = -X + 10. \qquad [2.6]$$

This linear function has a slope of -1 and a Y-intercept of $Y = 10$. Figure 2.2 also shows the function

$$Y = -2X + 10. \qquad [2.7]$$

We have doubled the slope of Equation 2.6 from -1 to -2 and kept the Y-intercept at $Y = 10$. This causes the graph of the function to become steeper and to rotate about the Y-intercept. In general, a change in the slope of a function will cause this kind of rotation without changing the value of its Y-intercept.

Figure 2.3
Changes in the Y-Intercept
of a Linear Function

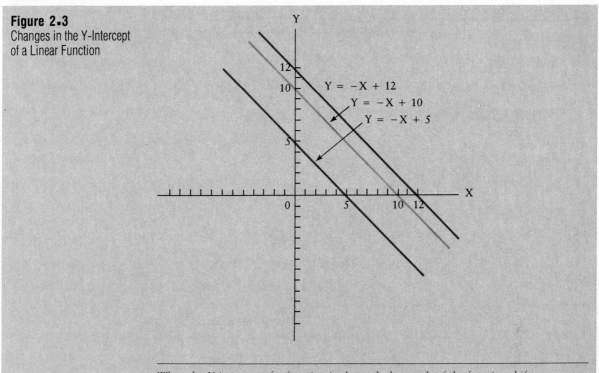

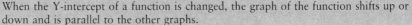

When the Y-intercept of a function is changed, the graph of the function shifts up or down and is parallel to the other graphs.

Changes in Intercept

Figure 2.3 also shows a graph of the function $Y = -X + 10$. It shows the effect of changes in the constant term, that is, the Y-intercept only, while the slope stays at -1. Figure 2.3 shows the graphs of

$$Y = -X + 12 \qquad\qquad [2.8]$$

and

$$Y = -X + 5. \qquad\qquad [2.9]$$

All three lines are parallel; they have the same slope. Changing the Y-intercept only makes the line shift up and down; its slope does not change. Of course, changes in the Y-intercepts also cause the X-intercepts to change, and you can see these new intercepts.

You should also be able to see that the graphs of any two linear functions are different only in their slopes and Y-intercepts. In this book we usually

Property Tax Assessment

Property taxes are the most important source of local revenues in the United States. In most communities they pay for schools, local police forces, the fire department, and so forth. Conceptually, figuring what a property owner owes in taxes is a simple matter—the town assessors multiply the tax rate by the market value of the property. A major problem with this procedure is that precise current market values for most properties are not known since properties only rarely change hands. Less recent sales prices of properties can be very misleading measures of current values, especially in time of rapid inflation. To come up with more accurate market values, localities increasingly have turned toward sophisticated computer methods to assess properties. These methods provide a good illustration of the use of linear functions in economics.

Consider the case of houses. Local property assessors begin by collecting information on all houses that were recently sold. With these data they can estimate a relationship between sales price (Y) and some relevant characteristic of the house, say its square footage (X). Such a relationship might be stated as

$$Y = \$10{,}000 + \$50X. \qquad [2.10]$$

This equation means that a house with zero square footage (X = 0) should sell for $10,000 (because of the value of its land) and each square foot of living space adds $50 to the value of the house. Using this relationship the assessor does not need current sales prices to assess a property's market value. Using the square footage of a house, the assessor can "predict" its current value by using Equation 2.10. This procedure is shown in Figure 2.4. According to the figure, a house with 2,000 square feet of living space would have a market value of $110,000, and one with 3,000 square feet is worth $160,000.

Of course, the procedures used in actual property assessment are considerably more complicated than this. For example, assessors must take into account far more features of houses than square footage. One way to do that is to use current sales information to value other factors, such as a nice view. Suppose current sales suggest that a view is worth $30,000 in the current housing market. Assuming Equation 2.10 reflects the values of houses without views, the values for houses with views can be computed by

Figure 2.4
Relationship between Floor Area of a House and Its Market Value

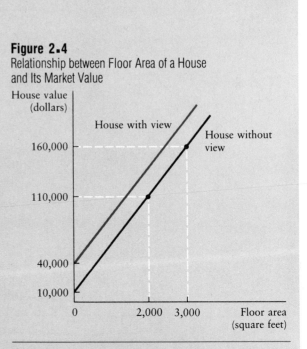

Using data on recent house sales, real estate appraisers can calculate a relationship between floor area (X—measured in square feet) and market value (Y). This relationship can then be used to predict sales prices of homes of any specified floor area. The entire relationship shifts upward by $30,000 if a house has a nice view.

$$\begin{aligned} Y &= \$30{,}000 + \$10{,}000 + \$50X \\ &= \$40{,}000 + \$50X. \end{aligned} \qquad [2.11]$$

That is, having a view shifts the relationship between living space and value up by a constant $30,000. This relationship is also shown in Figure 2.4. You can now use this figure to predict what 2,000 and 3,000 square foot houses with views are worth.

To Think About
1. Suppose spectacular views are more valuable in large houses than in small ones because large houses have more space for picture windows. How would this effect be represented with algebra and in a graph for property tax assessment?
2. Do you think that using these mathematical methods for assessment ends people's disputes over their tax bills? How would you argue with an assessor who tried to use the equations in this example to calculate your taxes?

Figure 2.5
Graph of a Quadratic
Function

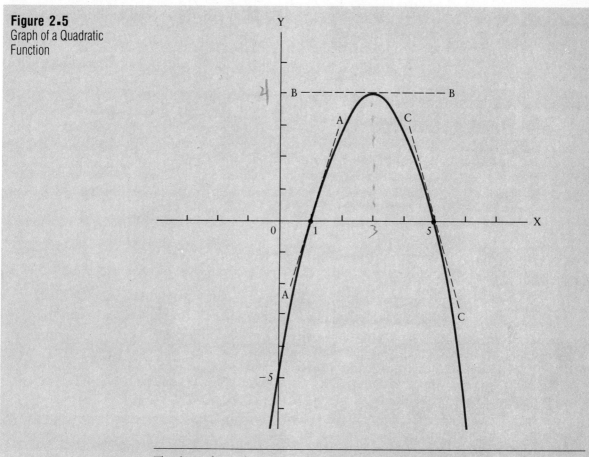

The slope of a nonlinear curve at any point is the slope of a line tangent to the curve at that point. For example, at the point X = 3, Y = 4, the slope of the diagrammed function is 0. This is the slope of the line BB.

discuss changes in slopes and changes in Y-intercepts separately. Although the economic context will vary, the mathematics form of these changes will be of the general type shown in Figures 2.2 and 2.3. These graphs are quite helpful to show the effects of changes in economic circumstances. "Applying Economics: Property Tax Assessment" uses these linear concepts with a real-world problem.

Nonlinear Functions

Nonlinear functions of one variable are also simple to graph. Figure 2.5 shows the graph of the **quadratic function** in Equation 2.5:

$$Y = -5 + 6X - X^2.$$

Quadratic function
An equation that includes terms in X^2.

Heavy dots again show the points listed in Table 2.1, although fractional values of X as well as integral values apply. The Y-intercept is the constant term (-5) in Equation 2.5.[4] In general, the slope of a nonlinear function is not the same everywhere, unlike linear functions.

We define the slope of a nonlinear function at some particular point as the slope of the straight line that is tangent to the function at that point. For example, the slope of the function in Figure 2.5 at the point X = 1, Y = 0 is given by the slope of the line AA. The slope at the point X = 3, Y = 4 is given by the slope of the line BB; at the point X = 5, Y = 0, the slope is given by the line CC. When the function reaches its highest point (at X = 3, Y = 4) the slope of the function is 0. To the left of this highest point the graph has a positive slope, and to the right of it the slope is negative. We can define the slopes of much more complex curves in the same way by looking at the slope of the straight line tangent to the curves.[5]

Whenever a function reaches its maximum value, the slope of the function generally will be 0 at that point. To use a mountain as an illustration, the slope of the ground at the mountaintop must be 0. Otherwise you would not be on the top, since walking in the appropriate direction will put you higher. Only if the slope is 0 will you not be able to go higher. Since throughout this book we are interested in maximum (that is highest) points, this mountain example is very helpful to keep in mind.

The fact that the slope of a function (or its graph) must be 0 at a maximum point is very important in economics. The marginalist ideas in Chapter 1 grew directly out of this mathematical law. "Applying Economics: The U.S. Income Tax Structure" relates these marginal ideas to another important situation.

Functions of Two or More Variables

Economists are usually concerned with functions of more than just one variable, since there is almost always more than a single cause of an economic outcome. To see the effects of many causes, economists must work with functions of several variables. A two-variable function might be written as

$$Y = f(X,Z). \tag{2.12}$$

---

[4] The X-intercepts (the values of X for which Y = 0) are called the "roots" of the quadratic function. They may be found by using the quadratic formula, which states that if $Y = a + bX + cX^2$, the roots are given by

$$X = \frac{-b \pm \sqrt{b^2 - 4ac}}{2c}.$$

You should be able to show that this formula provides the roots X = 1 and X = 5 for the example shown in the text.

[5] In elementary calculus it is shown that the slope of Y = f(X) at some point is given by the value of the derivative of this function at that point. For Equation 2.5, $dY/dX = -2X + 6$. At X = 1 the slope is +4, at X = 3 it is 0, and at X = 5 the slope is -4. The function reaches its maximum value when the derivative (and the slope) is equal to 0.

Table 2.4
Values of X, Z, and Y That
Satisfy the Relationship
$Y = X \cdot Z$

X	Z	Y
1	1	1
1	2	2
1	3	3
1	4	4
2	1	2
2	2	4
2	3	6
2	4	8
3	1	3
3	2	6
3	3	9
3	4	12
4	1	4
4	2	8
4	3	12
4	4	16

This equation shows that Y's values depend on the values of two independent variables, X and Z. For example, an individual's weight (Y) depends not only on calories eaten (X), but also on how much the individual exercises (Z). We could also have Y depend on the values of more than two variables, but this simple two-variable function can be used to explain how multiple variable functions in general work.

To show a function of two variables, suppose the relationship between Y, X, and Z is given by

$$Y = X \cdot Z. \qquad [2.13]$$

The form of this particular function is widely used in economics. Later chapters use a closely related form to show the utility (Y) that an individual receives from using two goods (X and Z), and also to show the production relationship between an output (Y) and two inputs (say, labor, X, and capital, Z). Here, however, we are interested mainly in the function's mathematical properties.

Some values for the function in Equation 2.13 are recorded in Table 2.4. Two things are especially important about these values. First, even if one of the variables is held constant (say at X = 2), changes in the other independent variable (Z) will cause the value of the dependent variable (Y) to change. The value of Y increases from 4 to 6 as Z rises from 2 to 3, even though X is held constant. Second, several different combinations of X and Z will result in the same value of Y. For example, Y = 4 if X = 2, Z = 2 or if X = 1, Z = 4 (or indeed, for an infinite number of other X, Z combinations if fractions are used). Using this equality of values of Y for a number of X, Z combinations, functions of two variables can be graphed rather simply.

The U.S. Income Tax Structure

The mathematical concept of slope and the economic idea of marginalism are clearly related. We can see this relationship in the determination of income taxes.

Many governments use income taxes as their principal source of revenue, and most of the rate schedules for those taxes are "progressive": that is, the proportion of income paid in taxes is greater for people with high incomes than for people with low incomes. Marginal tax rates (that is, the rate of tax on the last dollar earned) increase with increasing income levels. Table 2.2 shows a typical rate schedule for married taxpayers in the United States for 1980. The lowest marginal tax rate (other than 0) is 14 percent for households with taxable incomes between $3,400 and $5,500. For each extra dollar earned by a person in this category, taxes rise by 14 cents. Households with taxable income of $3,400 pay

nothing in taxes, whereas households with $5,500 in taxable income pay $294 (14 percent of the extra $2,100). At the other extreme, households with taxable income over $215,400 face a marginal tax rate of 70 percent. Seventy cents of every extra dollar earned is paid in taxes (maximum tax rates are a lot lower than this now).

The U.S. tax schedule in Table 2.2 is distinctly nonlinear, as we can see by graphing the relationship between taxable income (X) and tax liability (Y). The tax schedule is used to compute tax liabilities for various income levels up to $60,000. These figures are computed in Table 2.3 and shown graphically in Figure 2.6.

The progressive nature of the U.S. tax system is clearly illustrated in the figure. As income rises the taxation curve (OT) assumes a steeper upward slope. That increasing slope reflects the increasing marginal tax rates, since the slope shows how taxes (Y) change for a small change in income (X). The relationship is quite general: the marginal influence of one variable on another at some point can always be shown as the slope of the graph of the relationship between the variables at that point. The mathematical notion of slope and the economic concept of marginal changes are identical.

Average rates of taxation can also be seen in Figure 2.6, although they are a bit more difficult to show. We

Table 2.2
U.S. Income Tax Rates for Married Couples Filing Jointly, 1980

Taxable Income Bracket	Tax at Lower End of Bracket	Marginal Tax Rate	Average Tax Rate at Lower End of Bracket
$0–$3,400	$ 0	0%	0%
$3,400–$5,500	0	14	0
$5,500–$7,600	294	16	5
$7,600–$11,900	630	18	8
$11,900–$16,000	1,404	21	12
$16,000–$20,200	2,265	24	14
$20,200–$24,600	3,273	28	16
$24,600–$29,900	4,505	32	18
$29,900–$35,200	6,201	37	21
$35,200–$45,800	8,162	43	23
$45,800–$60,000	12,720	49	28
$60,000–$85,600	19,678	54	33
$85,600–$109,400	33,502	59	39
$109,400–$162,400	47,544	64	43
$162,400–$215,400	81,464	68	50
Over $215,400	117,504	70	55

Source: From 1040 U.S. Individual Income Tax Return 1981, Department of the Treasury, Internal Revenue Service.

Table 2.3
Income Tax Liabilities and Marginal and Average Tax Rates for Selected Income Levels

(1) Income	(2) Tax Liability	(3) Marginal Tax Rate	(4) Average Tax Rate (Col. 2 ÷ Col. 1)
$ 5,000	$ 224	14%	4%
10,000	1,062	18	11
15,000	2,055	21	14
20,000	3,225	24	16
30,000	6,238	37	21
40,000	10,226	43	26
50,000	14,778	49	30
60,000	19,678	54	33

Source: Calculated from Table 2.2.

Figure 2.6
Graphic Representation of the Relationship between Taxable
Income and Tax Liability

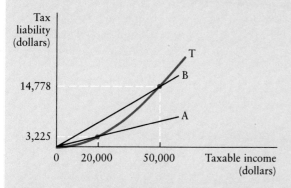

The line 0T shows the relationship between taxable
income and tax liability. The curve's increasing slope
illustrates increasing marginal tax rates. Average tax rates
are given by the slope of lines drawn through the origin
to the appropriate point on the curve. The slope of 0B,
for example, is the average tax rate for someone with a
taxable income of $50,000 (30 percent).

need to know the ratio of tax liabilities to taxable income for various levels of income. It can be calculated
by drawing a ray through the origin to the appropriate
point on the taxation curve (0T). The slope of the ray
shows the desired average tax rate.[6] For example, the
average tax rate for a household income of $20,000 is
shown by the slope of the ray 0A (which is .16, or 16
percent). The rate for a household income of $50,000
is given by the slope of 0B (30 percent). Increasing average tax rates are shown by the increase in the slope of
the rays as income increases. It is also clear from the
figure that, for any income level, the marginal tax rate
(the slope of the 0T curve) exceeds the average tax rate
(the slope of the ray through the origin).

Although we are looking at income taxes, the concepts are quite general. The ratio of the dependent variable (Y) to the independent variable (X) at one point
on a graph can always be found by calculating the slope
of a ray through the origin to that point. This idea is
used frequently in this book, particularly to show the
relationship between average and marginal magnitudes.

To Think About
1. The U.S. income tax schedule has a top marginal rate
of 70 percent—no matter how high a person's income
is, an extra dollar of income never increases the tax
liability by more than 70 cents. How would this feature
of the tax schedule be shown in Figure 2.6? Would average tax rates continue to rise once the 70 percent marginal rate is reached? Would the average rate ever reach
70 percent?
2. Develop a graph for a tax schedule under which the
first $10,000 of income is tax-free and then all addi-
tional income is subject to a 50 percent marginal tax
rate. How would such a system compare to the present
one? Who would gain under this alternative system?
Who would lose?

Graphing Functions of Two Variables

We would need to use three dimensions to graph a function of two variables
completely: one axis for X, one for Z, and one for Y. Drawing three-dimensional graphs in a two-dimensional book is very difficult. Not only must an
artist be good enough to be able to show depth in only two dimensions, but

---

[6]Remember the slope was defined as $\Delta Y/\Delta X$. Here, for a taxable income of $20,000, say, $\Delta Y =$
taxes on $20,000 − 0 = $3225 − 0; $\Delta X = $20,000 − 0 = $20,000. Therefore the slope is
$\Delta Y/\Delta X = $3225/$20,000 = 0.16$.

Figure 2.7
Contour Lines for
$Y = X \cdot Z$

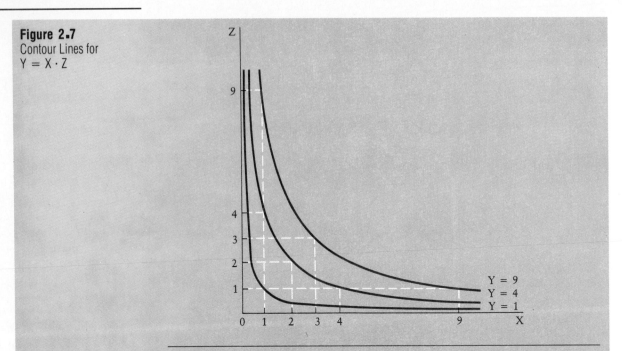

Contour lines for the function $Y = X \cdot Z$ are rectangular hyperbolas. They can be represented by making Y equal to various supplied values (here $Y = 1$, $Y = 4$, and $Y = 9$), and then graphing the relationship between the independent variables X and Z.

the reader must have enough imagination to read the graph as a three-dimensional model. Since economists are not necessarily good artists (and some would argue because economists lack imagination), they graph these functions another way that is much like the techniques mapmakers use.

Mapmakers are also confined to working with two-dimensional drawings. They use **contour lines** to show the third dimension. These are lines of equal altitude that outline the physical features of the territory being mapped. For example, a contour line labeled "1000 feet" on a map shows all those points of land that are 1000 feet above sea level. By using a number of contour lines, mapmakers can show the heights and steepness of mountains and the depths of valleys and ocean trenches. In this way they add the third dimension to a two-dimensional map.

Economists also use contour lines—that is, lines of equal "altitude." Equation 2.13 can be graphed in two dimensions (one each for the values of X and Z), with contour lines to show the values of Y, the third dimension. This equation is graphed in Figure 2.7, with three contour lines: one each for $Y = 1$, $Y = 4$, and $Y = 9$.

Each of the contour lines in Figure 2.7 is a rectangular hyperbola. The contour line labeled "Y = 4" is a graph of

$$Y = 4 = X \cdot Z, \qquad\qquad [2.14]$$

Contour lines
Lines in two dimensions that show the sets of values of the independent variables that yield the same value for the dependent variable.

Oil Pipelines

The amount of crude oil that can be put through a pipeline depends on the diameter of the pipe and the force with which the oil is pumped. Although there are a number of other engineering issues involved, a simple mathematical model of pipeline throughput closely resembles the algebraic example discussed in the previous section. Specifically, if we make Y the amount of oil pumped (measured in thousands of barrels per day), X the pumping force applied (in thousands of horsepower), and Z the pipe diameter (in inches), the approximate relationship is[7]

$$Y = 4\sqrt{X \cdot Z}. \qquad [2.16]$$

This equation makes clear that there are many ways to obtain a throughput of, say, 50,000 barrels per day. A 12-inch pipeline requires about 13,000 horsepower to pump this amount. A 16-inch pipeline needs only 10,000 horsepower to pump the same amount. These combinations are shown in Figure 2.8, which shows a portion of the Y = 50 contour line for Equation 2.16. This contour line is a graph of the equation

$$Y^2 = 2500 = 16X \cdot Z$$
$$156.25 = X \cdot Z. \qquad [2.17]$$

Other contour lines for higher and lower levels of oil pipeline throughout can be calculated in the same manner.

The importance of this kind of information to pipeline planners should be obvious. Knowing that they can achieve pipeline throughput a number of different ways, they can figure out how to do so in the least costly way, including the prices of pipe and pumps, for example. In Chapter 7 we examine the general issue of input choices and how they are affected by input prices in considerable detail.

To Think About
1. Suppose a pipeline firm wished to move 50,000 barrels of crude oil per day as cheaply as possible. What

Figure 2.8
Alternative Combinations of Pumping Force and Pipeline Diameter That Allow a Throughput of 50,000 Barrels per Day

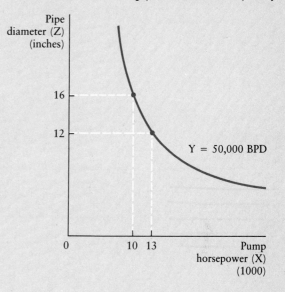

Using the relationship between output (Y), pumping force (X), and pipeline diameter (Z), we can draw a contour line for Y = 50 (thousand barrels per day). This curve shows that there are a number of ways to achieve this same level of throughput.

would this firm need to know in order to decide what size pipeline to build? Can you illustrate this choice in Figure 2.8?
2. Suppose pipeline throughput depends not only on pipe diameter and horsepower, but also on the nature of the terrain (whether the pipeline goes uphill or downhill). How might this be reflected in Equation 2.17? How would it alter Figure 2.8?

---

[7]This relationship is adapted from L. Cookenboo, *Crude Oil Pipelines and Competition in the Petroleum Industry* (Cambridge, Mass.: Harvard University Press, 1955).

and the line labeled "Y = 9" is a graph of

$$Y = 9 = X \cdot Z. \qquad [2.15]$$

Some of the values for these lines are shown in Table 2.4. It would be easy to compute other points on the curves. Other contour lines for the function could also be drawn by making Y equal to the desired level and graphing the resulting relationship between X and Z. Since we can give any value we want, there is an infinite number of contour lines we could draw. In this way we could show the original function in Equation 2.13 as accurately as we want without even resorting to three dimensions. One practical application of this type of graph is discussed in Applying Economics: Oil Pipelines.

Simultaneous Equations

Simultaneous equations
A set of equations with more than one variable that must be solved together for a particular solution.

Another mathematical concept that is often used in economics is **simultaneous equations.** When two variables (say X and Y) are related by two different equations it is sometimes, though not always, possible to solve these equations together for a single set of values for X and Y that satisfies both of the equations. For example, it is easy to see that two equations

$$\begin{aligned} X + Y &= 3 \\ X - Y &= 1 \end{aligned} \qquad [2.18]$$

have a unique solution of

$$\begin{aligned} X &= 2 \\ Y &= 1. \end{aligned} \qquad [2.19]$$

These equations operate "simultaneously" to determine the solutions for X and Y. One of the equations alone cannot determine each variable—the solution depends on both of the equations. It makes no sense in these equations to ask how a change in, say, X would affect the solution for Y. There is only one solution for X and Y using these equations. So long as both equations must hold, the values of neither X nor Y can change. Of course, if the equations themselves are changed, then their solution will also change. For example, the equation system

$$\begin{aligned} X + Y &= 5 \\ X - Y &= 1 \end{aligned} \qquad [2.20]$$

is solved as

$$\begin{aligned} X &= 3 \\ Y &= 2. \end{aligned} \qquad [2.21]$$

Figure 2.9
Solving Simultaneous
Equations

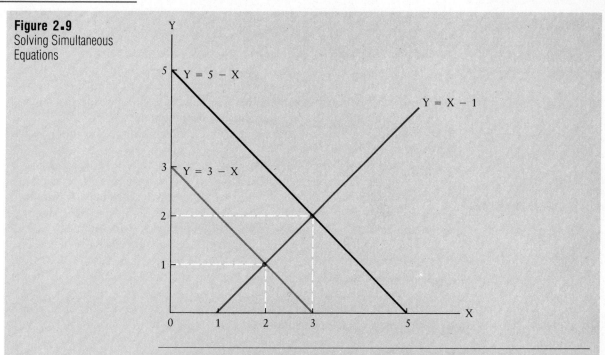

The linear equations X + Y = 3 (Y = 3 − X) and X − Y = 1 (Y = X − 1) can be
solved simultaneously to find X = 2, Y = 1. This solution is shown by the point of
intersection of the graphs of the two equations. If the first equation is changed (to X +
Y = 5, or Y = 5 − X), the solution will also change (to X = 3, Y = 2).

Changing just one of the parameters in Equation 2.18 gives us an entirely
different solution set.

These results are illustrated in Figure 2.9. The two equations in Equation
2.18 are straight lines that intersect at point 2, 1. This point is the solution
to the two equations since it is the only one that lies on both lines. Changing
the constant in the first equation of this system gives us a different intersection
for Equation 2.20. In that case the lines intersect at point 3,2, and that is the
new solution. Even though only one of the lines shifted, both X and Y take
on new values.

The similarity between the algebraic graph in Figure 2.9 and the supply
and demand graphs in Figures 1.1 and 1.2 is striking. The point of intersection
of two curves is called a "solution" in algebra and an "equilibrium" in economics, but in both cases we are finding the point that satisfies both relationships. The shift of the demand curve in Figure 1.2 clearly resembles the
simultaneous equation set in Figure 2.9. In both cases the shift in one of the
curves results in new solutions for both of the variables. Marshall's analogy
of the blades of the supply and demand "scissors" determining market price
and quantity can be seen in the algebraic notion of simultaneous systems and
their solutions.

Special Features of Mathematics in Economics

A few peculiarities arise when the mathematical tools described in this chapter are applied to economic problems. First, as we mentioned before, practically all the variables used in economic analysis can take on only positive values. Economists talk about prices, quantities of output, and quantities of factors of production. In most situations these variables are either positive or zero; a negative price or quantity would have no meaning. Most graphs in this book show only the positive quadrant and its axes, where both of the variables are always non-negative.

A second peculiarity is the economist's tendency to "reverse" the axes in a graph by putting the dependent variable on the horizontal axis. The supply and demand graphs in Figures 1.1 and 1.2 show this arrangement. Economists usually assume that price is the independent variable in a supply and demand situation and that individuals and firms react to this price by choosing the quantities they will demand and the quantities they will produce, respectively. As we show later in Part 3, economists use the vertical axis to record the independent variable (price) in these relations and the horizontal axis to record the dependent variable (quantity).

Of course, the nature of an equation is not affected by which variables are put on which axes. The equation

$$Y = 2 + 2X \qquad\qquad [2.22]$$

is identical to the equation

$$X = \tfrac{1}{2}Y - 1 \qquad\qquad [2.23]$$

in that the same set of points satisfies both equations. Nevertheless, the equations are written differently (for example, the slope of Equation 2.23 is the reciprocal of the slope of Equation 2.22), and we should keep in mind this departure from standard conventions.

Finally, economists frequently use more than two or three variables in their work and identify them with **subscripts.** Instead of using more letters in addition to the familiar X, Y, and Z, economists identify variables as

Subscripts
The use of small numbers at the bottom of variables to identify them as separate variables.

$$X_1, X_2, X_3, \ldots, X_n,$$

where each X_i is a separate variable. In this way many variables can be used with a very compact notation.

Subscripts are particularly useful in writing long and complex sums. For example, instead of writing

$$Y = X_1 + X_2 + X_3 + X_4 + X_5 + X_6, \qquad\qquad [2.24]$$

we can write

$$Y = \sum_{i=1}^{6} X_i \qquad\qquad [2.25]$$

where the symbol Σ means to add together all the Xs for which the subscript i is equal to the integers from 1 to 6. This symbol is used at a few points in this book; it is nothing more than a compact way of showing addition.

Summary

This chapter reviews material that should be familiar to you from math classes in high school. What we have done here is to go over some basic algebra and show how some simple functions can be graphed. Some of the results presented here that will be used throughout the rest of this book are:

- Linear equations have graphs that are straight lines. These lines are described by their slopes and by their intercepts with the Y axis. Changes in the slope cause the graph of a linear equation to rotate about its Y-intercept. Changes in the Y-intercept cause the graph to shift in a parallel way.
- Non-linear equations have graphs which have many curved shapes. The most common such shapes are parabolas and hyperbolas.
- Economists often use functions of two or more variables because economic outcomes have many causes. These functions can sometimes be graphed in two dimensions by using contour lines.
- Simultaneous equations determine solutions for two (or more) variables that satisfy all of the equations. An important use of such equations is to show how supply and demand curves determine equilibrium prices. For that reason, such equations are widely encountered in economics.

Problems

2.1 Consider the equation

$$Y = 15 + 3X.$$

a. If $X = 0$ what is the value of Y?
b. If $Y = 0$ what is the value of X?
c. Calculate Y for $X = 3$ and for $X = 4$. What do you conclude about the relationship between changes in Y and changes in X?
d. Graph the equation.
e. Graph the equation for

$$Y = 20 + 3X$$

and answer parts a through c for this equation.

f. Graph the equation

$$Y = 15 + 5X$$

and answer parts a through c for that equation.

g. Briefly describe why your answers to parts a through c differ for these three examples.

2.2 Consider the equation

$$Y = X^2 - 6X + 8.$$

a. If $X = 0$ what is the value of Y?
b. For what values of X does $Y = 0$?
c. If $X = 3$ what does Y equal? Can Y ever be less than this amount?
d. Graph the equation.
e. Using calculus it can be shown that the slope of the equation at any point is given by

$$Slope = 2X - 6.$$

Show that this slope is negative for $X < 3$ and positive for $X > 3$.

f. Explain intuitively why the Y takes on its minimum value at $X = 3$ and the slope of the equation is zero there.

2.3 The demand for potatoes is given by

$$Q_D = 40 - 2P + .001I$$

where Q_D = Quantity of potatoes in millions of pounds
       P = Price of potatoes in cents per pound
       I = Average income in dollars.

a. If $I = 10,000$, graph the demand curve for potatoes. How many potatoes are demanded at a price of 0? How many are demanded at a price of 10 cents per pound? At what price does $Q_D = 0$?

b. Suppose now $I = 20,000$. How would your answers to part a change? Graph your results.

c. Suppose the government imposes an excise tax of 10 cents per pound on potatoes. Now

$$P = P_P + 10$$

where P is the price paid by potato consumers and P_P is the price received by producers. If producers charge 10 cents per pound, if $I = \$10,000$, how many potatoes will be demanded? If producers charge 0, how many will be demanded? At what producer price will potato demand go to zero? Graph the new demand curve and compare them to your results from part a.

2.4 The supply curve for flounder is given by

$$Q_S = -100 + 5P \text{ (for } Q_S > 0)$$

where Q_S is the quantity of flounder supplied in tons and P is the wholesale price of flounder received by producers in cents per pound.

a. Graph the flounder supply curve. At what price will producers actually start supplying flounder to the market?
b. Suppose the government imposes a 25 percent tax on flounder production. Hence

$$P_M = 1.25P$$

where P_M is the market price of flounder. What will be the market supply curve for flounder (with Q_S as a function of P_M)? At what market price will any flounder be produced? Graph your results and compare them to your graph for part a.

2.5 This problem involves solving demand and supply equations together to determine price and quantity.

a. Consider a demand curve of the form

$$Q_D = -2P + 20$$

where Q_D is the quantity demanded of a good and P is the price of the good. Graph this demand curve. Also draw a graph of the supply curve

$$Q_S = 2P - 4$$

where Q_S is the quantity supplied. Be sure to put P on the vertical axis and Q on the horizontal axis. Assume that all the Q's and P's are nonnegative for parts a, b, and c. At what values of P and Q do these curves intersect—that is, where does $Q_D = Q_S$?
b. Now suppose at each price that individuals demand four more units of output—that the demand curve shifts to

$$Q_D' = -2P + 24.$$

Graph this new demand curve. At what values of P and Q does the new demand curve intersect the old supply curve—that is, where does $Q_D' = Q_S$?

c. Now, finally, suppose the supply curve shifts to

$$Q'_S = 2P - 8.$$

Graph this new supply curve. At what values of P and Q does $Q'_D = Q'_S$? You may wish to refer back to this simple problem when we discuss shifting supply and demand curves in later sections of this book.

2.6 a. Graph the demand curve

$$Q_D = -4P + 32.$$

At what value of P does $Q_D = 0$? At $P = 0$ what is Q_D?

b. Now graph the demand curve

$$Q'_D = -2P + 16.$$

Again, at what value of P does $Q'_D = 0$; what is Q'_D when $P = 0$? Call this value Q^*.

c. Referring back to the demand curve Q_D, what are demanders willing to pay for Q^*? Call this price P^*. What is the product $P^* \times Q^*$? Can you give an economic interpretation to this figure?

d. Now consider all possible products of $P \times Q$ where both P and Q lie on the demand curve Q_D. Show that $P^* \times Q^*$ is the largest value of these products.

   We consider an example similar to this one in Chapter 8 when we discuss the concept of marginal revenue.

2.7 Taxes in Oz are calculated according to the formula

$$T = .01I^2$$

where T represents thousands of dollars of tax liability and I represents income measured in thousands of dollars. Using this formula answer the following questions:

a. How much in taxes is paid by individuals with incomes of $10,000, $30,000, and $50,000? What are the average tax rates for these income levels? At what income level does tax liability equal total income?

b. Graph the tax schedule for Oz. Use your graph to estimate marginal tax rates for the income levels specified in part a. Also show the average tax rates for these income levels on your graph.

2.8 Consider the function

$$Y = \sqrt{X \cdot Z}$$

where $X > 0$, $Z > 0$. Draw the contour lines (in the positive quadrant) for this function for $Y = 4$, $Y = 5$, and $Y = 10$. What do we call the shape of these contour lines? Where does the line $20X + 10Z = 200$ intersect the contour line $Y = \sqrt{50}$? (Hint: as in Chapter 2, it may be easier to graph the contour lines for Y^2 here.)

*2.9 Using the function $Y = \sqrt{X \cdot Z}$ from the previous problem, find that combination of X and Z for which Y is as large as possible and which also satisfies the following linear equations. Graph your results using contour lines for Y. (Hint: for this problem the slope of Y contour lines is given by $-Z/X$.)

a. $2X + Z = 20$.
b. $X + Z = 20$.
c. $X + 2Z = 40$.
d. $X + 5Z = 100$.
e. $2X + Z = 40$.
f. $X + Z = 40$.

---

*Denotes a problem that is rather difficult. Answers to all odd-numbered problems appear at the end of the book.

PART 2

CHOICE AND DEMAND

Part 2 covers how economists look at people's demand for the goods they buy. Our main goal in this part is to develop Marshall's demand curve for a product and to show why this demand curve is likely to be downward sloping. You will see how economists treat the way people make choices and also how the choices of many individuals can be summarized by a market demand curve. The way people make choices has many applications that are discussed here and elsewhere in this book.

Economists explain consumer demand as the interaction of two forces: (1) consumers have preferences or desires for goods, but (2) they have limited incomes to purchase these commodities. How the consumer resolves these conflicting forces determines which commodities he or she will purchase. For example, the first force may tell the consumer to buy a car (since a car provides desirable services), but the second warns not to (since there are many other uses for the income). Only when the right balance in expenditures is reached will the individual consumer obtain as much satisfaction as the available income allows. Part 2 shows how this balance is reached and how changes in preferences, income, or prices affect the consumer's choices.

Chapter 3 describes how economists treat the consumer's decision problem. We first define the concept of utility, which represents a consumer's preferences. Since not everyone likes the same thing, economists work with models that can deal with these differences. The first half of Chapter 3 develops the idea of a person's tastes. These tastes are the first force that influences demand decisions. The second half of the chapter discusses how

people decide to spend their incomes on different goods to get the greatest satisfaction possible—that is, to "maximize" their utility. Because this is the first example of the maximization hypothesis you encounter in this book, it is covered in detail.

Chapter 4 investigates how people change their choices when their income changes or as prices change. This is the first example in the book of "comparative statics" analysis. In this analysis we compare two situations to see how the choices in these situations differ. Most economic analysis is comparative. The results of such comparisons can be very interesting. For example, they can show how people react to changes in the price of a commodity. The analysis can then be used to draw an individual demand curve for the commodity since we now know how the person reacts to price changes.

Chapter 5 shows how these individual demand curves can be "added up" to make market demand curves. These curves are basic to the price determination process. By constructing market demand curves from the decisions that individual consumers make, we are in a good position to see how changing influences on people may affect the market curve. Chapter 5 also discusses how market demand is measured in the real world.

The final chapter in Part 2, Chapter 6, applies the theory of individual choice developed in Chapters 3 through 5 to three other economic topics. First, the model of utility maximization is used to study trading between individuals. Since the mutually beneficial nature of trade gives rise to organized markets, trading between individuals can be used as the foundation for supply and demand analysis. Second, the utility maximization model is used to analyze price indices, such as the gross national product (GNP) price deflator and the Consumer Price Index (CPI). Since these indices are widely used in economics, showing how they are arrived at is an especially important application of microeconomic theory. The third major topic in Chapter 6 is how people act in uncertain or risky situations.

In this application of the utility maximization model we show why people dislike risk and are usually willing to "pay" something to avoid it. "Risk aversion" is especially important to some economic decisions, such as buying insurance and investing in risky assets, that cannot be understood without considering the uncertainties involved in them. ▲

CHAPTER 3

Utility Maximization: How People Make Economic Choices

An economic system is nothing more than a collection of people and a set of institutions (such as firms or government agencies) that these people operate. Economists therefore place the study of people's behavior at the center of their models. People's desires are assumed to have a strong effect in determining what goods are demanded and ultimately produced by the economy; people, to a large extent, decide what levels of productive services (labor and capital) they will supply; and, through their political activities, people influence the government's goals, including its economic goals.

These roles cannot be separated from one another. Any decision a person makes as a consumer, say to buy a new car, will affect his or her decisions as a provider of resources (to save less or to work harder to pay for the car) and also his or her decisions as a voter (he or she may now favor government spending for new or better highways on which to drive the new car). Economic texts used to refer to "economic man" (*homo economicus*) and considered the individual's role as a consumer only. Even though most authors recognized the individual's other roles, they were never explicitly discussed. Modern microeconomics does consider the mixture of the individual's roles and has developed tools to help understand the interrelationships among them.

This book looks at the economic theory that has been developed to explain the actions of individuals in various activities. Part 2 concentrates on people as consumers of goods; Part 5 investigates people's roles as suppliers of labor and capital; and Part 6 examines the insights that economic analysis can provide us about people's actions in the political process.

Definition of Utility

Economists have developed a useful model to simplify their analysis of the individual's decision problem. This model formalizes the concepts of prefer-

Theory of choice
The interaction of preferences and income that causes people to make the choices they do.

Utility
The pleasure, satisfaction, or need fulfillment that people get from their economic activity.

Ceteris paribus assumption
In economic analysis, holding all other factors constant so that only the factor being studied is allowed to change.

ences and income, and it lets us describe how these two forces determine the choices that are made. This conceptual apparatus more than anything else underlies the economists' thinking about people's decisions—it is the fundamental economic **theory of choice**.

People's preferences can be formalized with the concept of **utility**, which is defined as the satisfaction that a person receives from his or her activities. This concept is very broad and in the next few sections we define it more precisely. We use the simple case of a single consumer who receives utility from just two commodities. We will eventually analyze how that person chooses to allocate income between these two goods, but first we need to develop a better understanding of utility itself.

Ceteris Paribus Assumption

To identify all the factors affecting a person's feelings of satisfaction would be a lifelong task for an imaginative psychologist; to measure these factors precisely would probably be impossible. Economists focus on basic, quantifiable economic factors and look at how people choose among them. Economists clearly recognize that nonmeasurable factors (aesthetics, love, security, envy, and so forth) affect behavior, but they develop models in which these kinds of factors are held constant and are not specifically analyzed.

Much economic analysis is based on this *ceteris paribus* (other things being equal) **assumption**. We can simplify the analysis of a person's consumption decisions by assuming that satisfaction is affected only by the choices being considered and that other effects on satisfaction remain constant. In this way we can isolate the economic factors that affect consumption behavior. This narrow focus is not intended to imply that other things that affect utility are "unimportant"—we are conceptually holding these other factors constant so that we may study consumption choices in a simplified setting.

Utility from Consuming Two Goods

This chapter concentrates on an individual's problem of choosing the quantities of two goods (X and Y) to consume.[1] We assume that the person receives utility from these goods and that we can show this utility in functional notation (see Chapter 2) by

$$\text{Utility} = U (X, Y; \text{other things}).$$

[3.1]

$$U = \sqrt{XY}$$

---

[1]See Walter Nicholson, *Microeconomic Theory: Basic Principles and Extensions*, 3d ed. (Hinsdale, Ill.: Dryden Press, 1985) and Paul A. Samuelson, *Foundations of Economic Analysis* (Cambridge, Mass.: Harvard University Press, 1947), to investigate the analysis of the consumption of many goods. In most ways the many-good case is identical to the two-good case.

This notation indicates that the utility an individual receives from consuming X and Y over some period of time depends on the quantities of X and Y consumed and on "other things." These other things might include easily quantifiable items such as the amounts of other kinds of goods consumed, the number of hours worked, or the amount of time spent sleeping. They might also include such unquantifiable items as love, security, and feelings of self-worth. These other things appear after the semicolon in Equation 3.1 because we assume that they are held constant while we examine the individual's choice between X and Y. If one of the other things should change, the utility from some particular amounts of X and Y might be very different than it was before.

For example, several times in this chapter we consider the case of a person choosing how many hamburgers (Y) and soft drinks (X) to consume during one week. Although our example uses seemingly trivial commodities, the analysis is quite general and will apply to any two goods. In analyzing the hamburger–soft drink choices, we assume that all other factors affecting utility are held constant. The weather, the person's preferences, the quantity of food eaten for breakfast, and everything else is assumed not to change during the analysis. If the weather, for instance, were to become warmer we might expect soft drinks to become relatively more desirable, and we wish to eliminate such effects from our analysis, at least for the moment. We usually write the utility function in Equation 3.1 as

$$\text{Utility} = U(X, Y) \qquad [3.2]$$

with the understanding that many other things are being held constant. All economic analyses impose some form of *ceteris paribus* assumption so that the relationship between a selected few variables can be studied. You should try to identify the "important" things that are being held constant in this book as we explore the notion of utility in many things.

Measurability of Utility

The first economists to deal with the concept of utility thought that it might be measurable. Some early psychological experiments on people's responses to electrical stimuli gave rise to the mistaken belief that all individual reactions were not only quantifiable but also of the same general type. If utility were measurable, many economic questions could be easily answered. Not only could we understand and predict individual consumer behavior, for example, but we could, if we wished, also produce a "fair" distribution of goods (and utility) among people.

The obstacles to measuring utility have proved to be insurmountable, with two major problems. The first concerns what to use for a unit of measurement. We have no very good psychological idea of what a *util* (that is, a unit of utility) might be. There is also no way of determining how one person's utils compare to another's. When asked, "How happy are you?" for example, people respond in very different ways. The second problem arises in imposing the *ceteris paribus* assumption. In simple psychological experiments it may be possible to hold everything except the stimulus under question constant (that is, to provide an adequate experimental "control"). In economics, however, the myriad factors that affect a person's economic choices are impossible to list and quantify. To hold some of them constant in order to measure an economically relevant concept of utility is out of the question.

Consequently, we must expect much less than measurability from a utility theory. All that can be assumed is that people rank bundles of commodities in some consistent way. To say that the utility of a **consumption bundle** of goods, A, is greater than that of another bundle, B, only means that A is preferred to B. We cannot say how much A is preferred to B, since a hard-and-fast measure of utility is beyond our grasp. For example, we may be able to assert that a person prefers a roast beef dinner to a fried chicken dinner, but we cannot say that he or she is "5 percent happier" with the roast beef or that the chicken provides "7 fewer utils." There are many things we can say about individual choices despite this problem, however. Most observable economic behavior can be explained without having to measure utility. The next section looks at how preferences can be described in a simple way.

Consumption bundles
The combinations of goods or services that an individual chooses.

Assumptions about Utility

What do we mean by saying that people's preferences are "consistent"? Can these preferences (utility) be shown graphically? This section's principal goal is eventually to demonstrate the trade-offs that people make in their consumption choices.

Consistency of Preferences

Although we cannot expect to be able to measure utility, we might expect people to express their preferences in a reasonably consistent manner. Between two consumption bundles, A and B, we would expect a person to be able to state either "I prefer A to B," or "I prefer B to A," or "A and B are equally attractive to me." We do not expect the individual to be paralyzed by indecision, but rather to be able to state clearly how he or she feels about any potential consumption possibilities. This rules out such situations as the mythical jackass, who, finding himself midway between a pile of hay and a bag of oats, starved to death because he was unable to decide which way to go.

In addition to expecting people to be able to state preferences clearly and completely, we might also expect people's preferences not to be self-contradictory. We do not expect a person to make statements about his or her preferences that conflict with each other. In other words, we assume that preferences are **transitive**. If a person says, "I prefer A to B," and "I prefer B to C," then he or she can be expected to say, "I prefer A to C." A person who then states the contrary (that is, "I prefer C to A") would appear to be

Transitive
The property that if A is preferred to B, and B is preferred to C, then A must be preferred to C.

Figure 3.1
More of a Good Is
Preferred to Less

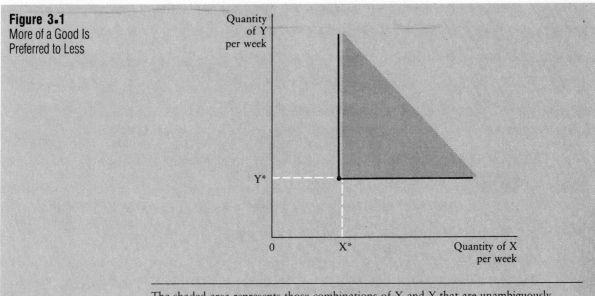

The shaded area represents those combinations of X and Y that are unambiguously preferred to the combination X*, Y*. In a sense this is why goods are called "goods"; other things being the same, individuals prefer having more of any good rather than less.

hopelessly inconsistent. We wish to rule out such inconsistency from our analysis. In "Applying Economics: Transitivity in Football, Choice of Marriage Partners, and Pizza" we discuss some of the ways in which economists have tried to investigate whether people's choices really are transitive.

More is Better and the Definition of a "Good"

A third assumption we make about individual preferences is that a person prefers more of a good to less. In Figure 3.1 all points in the shaded area are preferred to the amounts X* of good X and Y* of good Y. Movement from point X*, Y* to any point in the shaded area is an unambiguous improvement, since the individual in this area can obtain more of one good without taking less of another. This idea of preferences is implicit in a definition of "goods" as items that yield positive benefits to people. It would be relatively simple to develop a theory of "bads" (garbage, termites, or, for the author, lima beans) where less is preferred to more.

Trades and Substitution

How people feel about getting more of some good when they must give up an amount of some other good is another important aspect of preferences.

Transitivity in Football, Choice of Marriage Partners, and Pizza

Whether or not people obey the assumption of transitivity and thereby make consistent decisions has been a subject of some controversy among economists and psychologists. Many examples have been proposed that purport to show the assumption is widely violated in the real world. One popular example is scoring at sporting events. By invoking (incorrectly) the assumption of transitivity it is often possible to draw absurd conclusions about how games might turn out. Consider the following question: Can Amherst College (a major football power of the Connecticut Valley) beat the University of Oklahoma? Using the assumption of transitivity the answer is a definite yes. In the 1975 season, for example, Amherst beat Bowdoin, Bowdoin beat Bates, Bates beat C. W. Post, and (to make a very long story short) C. W. Post beat a team that beat a team that beat a team that beat Pitt. Since Pitt beat Kansas and (in that year) Kansas beat Oklahoma, the result is proved.[2] An Amherst-Oklahoma match-up would be no contest since the law of transitivity assures that Amherst would win in a walk-away.

The absurdity of the above conclusion stems from the fact that football games do not necessarily obey the assumption of transitivity. Rather, the outcomes of games depend mostly on relatively random happenings between the players; drawing conclusions from comparative scores is a very inexact business.

Of greater interest to economists is whether individuals' choices obey or violate the transitivity assumption. A number of experiments have been undertaken to try to answer that question. Here we describe two of them.

In a 1958 study, J. M. Davis asked a group of undergraduate male students to express their marital preferences from among a set of written descriptions of nine women.[3] These descriptions included (relatively sexist) adjectives such as: woman 1—plain, average charm, wealthy; woman 2—pretty, average charm, wealthy; woman 3—pretty, very charming, average income; and so forth. The students were then asked to make choices between pairs of women. Such choices were judged intransitive if a subject reported, for example, that he preferred woman 1 to woman 3, that he preferred woman 3 to woman 7, and that he preferred woman 7 to woman 1. In all, Davis examined nearly 4,000 such triples, looking for intransitivities and finding relatively few. Only about 1 out of 8 of the triples examined showed

Whether a trade would increase utility is not clear. We need some additional terminology to be able to look into this situation. Studying the effects of trades is very common in economics. Giving up units of one commodity to get back some other commodity is what gives rise to trade and organized markets.

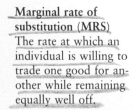

Marginal Rate of Substitution (MRS)

Marginal rate of substitution (MRS) The rate at which an individual is willing to trade one good for another while remaining equally well off.

To study a person's giving up some amount of one good to get some amount of another good, we introduce the concept of the **marginal rate of substitution (MRS).** The marginal rate of substitution is used by economists to record how much of one good (say Y) a person is willing to give up in order to get *one*

---

[2]This example was developed by Frank Westhoff, an economist and die-hard football fan.

[3]J. M. Davis, "Transitivity of Preferences," *Behavioral Science,* Fall, 1958, pp. 26–33.

intransitivity, and most of those failed to be repeated in a second test on the same subjects. Fewer than 1 percent of all the triples examined were intransitive on both replications of the test. Davis concluded that the vast majority of preferences were transitive, and those intransitivities that were observed could probably be explained as random choices among women judged to be equally desirable by the subjects.

A similar approach to the study of consistency of preferences was taken by A. A. Weinstein in a 1968 experiment that examined how individuals ranked consumption items.[4] Overall, 10 items were used (ranging from $3 in cash to three Beatles records or a 15-inch pizza) and, following the Davis study, the author looked at individuals' ranking of three items to see how many intransitivities occurred. For example, an inconsistency would occur if someone reported preferring the cash to the Beatles records and the records to the pizza, but that he or she preferred pizza to cash. Among adults, Weinstein found few (less than 7 percent) such intransitivities. Again, those that did occur might be attributed to relatively random rankings among goods viewed as equally attractive to the subjects being examined. The

author did find, however, that younger people (notably children ages 9 through 12) exhibited considerably more intransitivities (about 20 percent of choices made). This led him to conclude that consistency may to some extent be an acquired skill.

Overall, then, it appears that individuals (as opposed to football teams) make relatively consistent choices. Certainly a theory that assumes consistency (as we will) cannot be too far wrong for explaining the behavior of the average person.

To Think About

1. Do people have to learn to behave "rationally?" Don't young children, even babies, seem to know exactly what they want? If that is so, how do you explain the fact that children seem to make a fairly large number of inconsistent choices? How do you explain the fact that adults exhibit any such inconsistencies?

2. Are sporting matches between individuals (say, tennis or boxing) transitive? Do the people who usually lose to you at some game also lose to the people who can beat you? How do you explain any of the intransitivities that occur in such activities?

more unit of some other good (say X). For example, suppose we let Y represent hamburgers and X represent soft drinks. In this case, if we say that the MRS is 2, we mean that the person in question is willing to give up two hamburgers to get one additional soft drink in return. If we said that the MRS is ⅔, we would mean that the person is willing to give up two-thirds of a hamburger only if one additional soft drink will be received in return. To be consistent throughout our discussion, we denote the marginal rate of substitution by MRS (of X for Y) to make clear that the person we are studying is increasing X consumption by one unit and reducing Y consumption: X is being *substituted for* Y by replacing it in the bundle of goods that the person purchases. We are asking how many units of Y is this person willing to trade away to get one more X.

It seems reasonable to assume that a person's MRS depends in some way

[4]A. A. Weinstein, "Transitivity of Preferences," *Journal of Political Economy*, March/April 1968, pp. 307–311.

on how much X and Y he or she is currently consuming. Surely the rate at which you would be willing to give up hamburgers to get soft drinks would depend (among other things) on how many hamburgers you had just eaten. If someone has eaten many hamburgers and few soft drinks, it seems plausible that he or she will be willing to trade quite a few hamburgers for an additional soft drink. For example, if an individual has six hamburgers and two soft drinks, we might expect that he or she would willingly trade a few hamburgers (say two) to get one more soft drink. In this case, with X = 2, Y = 6, the individual's MRS would be 2.

On the other hand, if this person starts with a large supply of soft drinks (say six) and few hamburgers (say two) we might assume that the MRS would be low. He or she might be willing to give up only one-half of a hamburger to get one additional soft drink now. In this case the MRS (at the point X = 6, Y = 2) would be ½, which indicates the individual's diminished desire for additional soft drinks when he or she has many of them already. As the person substitutes soft drinks for hamburgers, he or she becomes less willing to give up hamburgers to get even more soft drinks.

An assumption that this will be the case reflects the simple notion that people prefer some balance in their consumption choices. We now develop a graphic analysis of this notion.

Indifference Curves

Indifference curve
All the combinations of goods or services that provide the same level of utility.

We can illustrate the principle of a diminishing marginal rate of substitution using an **indifference curve** with our hamburger–soft drink example. These two goods are used for purposes of explanation only—the same development could be presented for any other two goods.

Figure 3.2 records the quantity of soft drinks consumed by an individual in one period (again, say, one week) on the horizontal axis and the quantity of hamburgers consumed on the vertical axis. The curve U_1 in Figure 3.2 includes all those combinations of hamburgers and soft drinks with which the individual is equally happy. For example, the curve shows that the individual would be just as happy with six hamburgers and two soft drinks as with four hamburgers and three soft drinks or with three hamburgers and four soft drinks. In other words, this person is "indifferent" about which of the consumption bundles on the curve U_1 he or she actually receives, since they all provide the same level of enjoyment. Stated more formally, the points on U_1 all provide the same level of utility to the individual, and therefore he or she does not have any particular reason for preferring any point on U_1 to any other point. For this reason the curve U_1 is called an *indifference curve*.

The indifference curve U_1 is similar to a contour line on a map (discussed in Chapter 2) in that it shows those combinations of hamburgers and soft drinks that provide an identical "altitude" (that is, amount) of utility. Points to the northeast of U_1 promise a higher level of satisfaction and are preferred to points on U_1. Point E (five soft drinks and four hamburgers) is preferred to point C because it provides more of both goods. Combinations of hamburgers and soft drinks that lie below U_1, on the other hand, are less desirable

Figure 3.2
Indifference Curve · *all the combinations of goods & services that provide the same level of utility*

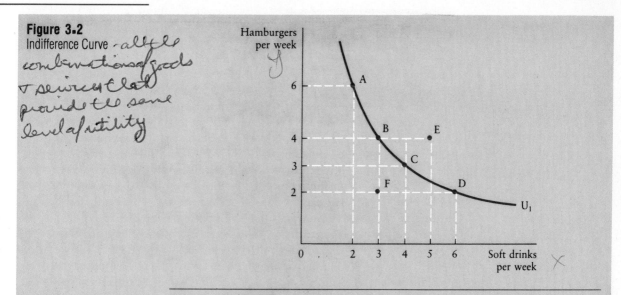

The curve U_1 shows the combinations of hamburgers and soft drinks that provide the same level of utility to an individual. The slope of the curve shows the trades an individual will freely make. For example, in moving from point A to point B, the individual will give two hamburgers to get one additional soft drink. In other words, MRS is approximately 2 in this range. Points below U_1 (such as F) provide less utility than points on U_1. Points above U_1 (such as E) provide more utility than U_1.

to the individual since they offer less satisfaction. Point F offers less of both goods than does point C. The fact that the indifference curve U_1 has a negative slope (that is, the curve runs from the upper left portion of the figure to the lower right portion) indicates that if an individual is forced to give up some hamburgers, he or she must receive additional soft drinks to remain equally well off. This type of movement along U_1 represents those trades that a person might freely make, which we wish to look at here.

Indifference Curves and the Marginal Rate of Substitution

What happens when an individual moves from point A (six hamburgers and two soft drinks) to point B (four hamburgers and three soft drinks)? The individual remains equally well off since the two commodity bundles lie on the same indifference curve. The individual will voluntarily give up two of the hamburgers that were being consumed at point A in exchange for one additional soft drink. The slope of the curve U_1 between A and B is therefore approximately $-2/1 = -2$. That is, Y (hamburgers) declines two units in response to a one-unit increase in X (soft drinks). Another way of recording this fact is to say that the MRS (of soft drinks for hamburgers) between points A and B is 2: the individual is willing to give up two hamburgers in order to get one more soft drink. The slope of the indifference curve U_1 and the MRS record the same thing—how this individual is willing to trade one good for another.

Diminishing Marginal Rate of Substitution

The MRS varies along the curve U_1. For points such as A the individual has quite a few hamburgers and is relatively willing to trade them for soft drinks. On the other hand, for consumption bundles such as those represented by point D, the individual has an abundance of soft drinks and is reluctant to give up any more hamburgers to get more soft drinks. This increasing reluctance to trade away hamburgers follows the notion that the consumption of any one good (here soft drinks) can be pushed too far. This characteristic can be seen by considering the trades that take place in moving from points A to B, from points B to C, and from points C to D. In the first trade two hamburgers are given up to get one more soft drink—the MRS is 2 (as we have already shown). The second trade involves giving up one hamburger to get one additional soft drink. In this trade, the MRS has declined to 1, reflecting the individual's increased reluctance to give up hamburgers to get more soft drinks. Finally, for the third trade (from points C to D), the individual is willing to give up a hamburger only if two soft drinks are received in return. In this final trade, the MRS is ½ (the individual is willing to give up one-half of a hamburger to get one more soft drink), which is a further decline from the MRS of the previous trades.

The convex shape of the indifference curve U_1 reflects the diminishing marginal rate of substitution. As we consider consumption bundles that contain increasing quantities of soft drinks and decreasing quantities of hamburgers, the indifference curve becomes flatter. The slope of the curve approaches zero. This slope reflects another basic assumption that economists make about people's preferences: people become increasingly reluctant to trade away an increasingly scarce good, and prefer some balance in their consumption.[5]

---

[5]If we assume utility is measurable we can provide an alternative analysis of a diminishing MRS. To do so we introduce the concept of the marginal utility of a good X (denoted by MU_X). Marginal utility is defined as the extra utility obtained by consuming one more unit of good X. The concept is meaningful only if utility can be measured and is not as useful as the MRS. If the individual is asked to give up some Y (ΔY) to get some additional X(ΔX) the change in utility is given by

$$\text{Change in utility} = MU_Y \cdot \Delta Y + MU_X \cdot \Delta X. \qquad \text{[i]}$$

It is equal to the utility gained from the additional X less the utility lost from the reduction in Y. Since, along an indifference curve, utility does not change, we can use Equation (i) to derive

$$-\frac{\Delta Y}{\Delta X} = \frac{MU_X}{MU_Y}. \qquad \text{[ii]}$$

Along an indifference curve, the negative of its slope is given by MU_X/MU_Y. That slope is, by definition, the MRS. Hence we have

$$MRS = MU_X/MU_Y. \qquad \text{[iii]}$$

For example, if an extra hamburger yields two utils ($MU_Y = 2$) and an extra soft drink yields one util ($MU_X = 1$), MRS = ½ since the individual will be willing to trade away one-half of a hamburger to get an additional soft drink. If it is assumed that MU_X falls and MU_Y increases as X is substituted for Y, Equation (iii) shows that MRS will fall.

Figure 3.3
Balance in Consumption
Is Desirable

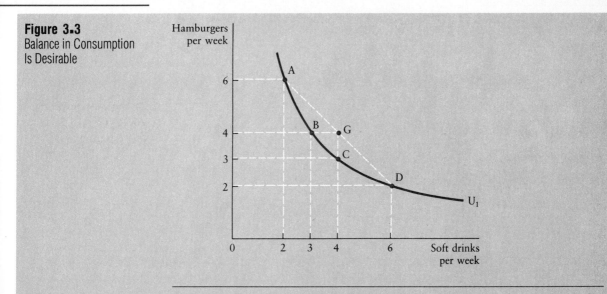

The consumption bundle G (four hamburgers, four soft drinks) is preferred to either of
the extreme bundles A and D. This is a result of the assumption of a diminishing MRS.
Because individuals become progressively less willing to give up hamburgers as they move
in a southeasterly direction along U_1, the curve U_1 will have a convex shape.
Consequently all points on a straight line joining two points such as A and D will lie
above U_1. Points such as G will be preferred to any of those on U_1.

Balance in Consumption and the Assumption of a Diminishing MRS

Our conclusion of a diminishing MRS is based on the idea that people prefer
balanced consumption bundles to unbalanced ones. This assumption is illustrated precisely in Figure 3.3, where the indifference curve U_1 from Figure 3.2
is redrawn. Our discussion here concerns the two extreme consumption bundles A and D. In consuming bundle A the individual receives six hamburgers
and two soft drinks; the same satisfaction could be received by consuming
bundle D (two hamburgers and six soft drinks). Now consider a bundle of
commodities (say G) "between" these extremes. With G (four hamburgers and
four soft drinks) the individual obtains a higher level of satisfaction (point G
is northeast of the indifference curve U_1) than with either of the extreme
bundles A or D.

The reason for this increased satisfaction should be geometrically obvious.
All of the points on the straight line joining A and D lie above U_1. Point G is
one of these points (as the figure shows, there are many others). So long as
the indifference curve obeys the assumption of a diminishing MRS, it will be
convex; any bundle that represents an "average" between two equally attractive extremes will be preferred to those extremes. The assumption of a diminishing MRS is consistent with the notion that people prefer some variety in
consumption.

Figure 3.4
Indifference Curve Map
for Hamburgers and
Soft Drinks

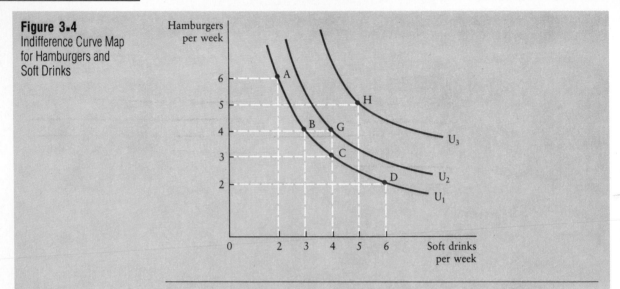

The positive quadrant is full of indifference curves that each reflect a different level of
utility. Three such curves are illustrated. Combinations of goods on U_3 are preferred to
those on U_2, which in turn are preferred to those on U_1. This is simply a reflection of the
assumption that more of a good is preferred to less, as may be seen by comparing points
C, G, and H.

Indifference Curve Maps

Although Figures 3.2 and 3.3 each show only one indifference curve, the
positive quadrant contains many such curves, each one corresponding to a
different level of utility. Since every combination of hamburgers and soft drinks
must yield some level of utility, every point must have one (and only one)
indifference curve passing through it. These curves are, as we said earlier,
similar to the contour lines that appear on topographical maps in that they
each represent a different "altitude" of utility. In Figure 3.4 three of these
curves have been drawn and are labeled U_1, U_2, and U_3. These are only three
of the infinite number of curves that characterize an individual's entire indifference curve map. Just as a map may have many contour lines (say one for
each inch of altitude), so too the gradations in utility could be very fine, as
shown by very closely spaced indifference curves. For graphic convenience,
our analysis generally deals with only a few indifference curves that are relatively widely spaced.

The labeling of the indifference curves in Figure 3.4 has no special meaning
except to indicate that utility increases as we move from combinations of
goods on U_1 to those on U_2 and then to those on U_3. As we have repeatedly
pointed out, there is no precise way to measure the level of utility associated
with (say) U_2. Similarly, we have no way of measuring the amount of extra

utility an individual receives from consuming bundles on U_3 instead of U_2. All we can assume is that utility increases as the individual moves to higher indifference curves.

The indifference curve map shown in Figure 3.4 summarizes a person's preferences about all possible combinations of the two goods shown. The basic assumptions we have made about these preferences assure that the indifference curve map will exhibit the general shape shown in the figure. First, the assumption that more is preferred to less implies that utility increases as we move from U_1 to U_2 to U_3. This increase can be seen by comparing the utility provided by commodity bundles C, G, and H. Second, the notion of a diminishing MRS implies that the indifference curves will have the convex shape shown in the figure. Balanced bundles will be preferred to unbalanced ones.

Utility-Maximization Hypothesis: An Initial Survey

Economists assume that when a person is faced with a choice from among a number of possible options, he or she will choose the one that yields the highest utility. As Adam Smith remarked more than two centuries ago, "We are not ready to suspect any person of being defective in selfishness."[6] In other words, economists assume that people know their own minds and make choices consistent with their preferences. This section surveys how such choices might be made.

The most interesting feature of the utility-maximization problem is that people are constrained in what they can buy by the size of their incomes. Of those combinations of goods that an individual can afford, he or she will choose the one that is most preferred. This most preferred bundle of goods may not provide complete bliss; it may even leave this person in misery. It will, however, reflect the best use of limited income. All other bundles of goods that can be bought with that limited income would leave him or her even worse off. It is the limitation of income that makes the individual's problem of choice an economic one of allocating a scarce resource (the limited income) among alternative end uses. Our "Applying Economics: Irrational Behavior" example illustrates how general this notion of making the best of one's situation is.

The Basic Result

This section considers the simple problem of how an individual chooses to allocate income in purchasing two goods (hamburgers and soft drinks) to obtain the highest level of utility possible. This analysis of choice is perhaps the most basic in all of microeconomics. The result can easily be stated at the

---

[6]Adam Smith, *The Theory of Moral Sentiments* (New Rochelle, N.Y.: Arlington House, 1969), p. 446. First published 1759.

APPLYING ECONOMICS

Irrational Behavior

The assumption that people seek to maximize their utility is essentially an assumption that individuals act in a "rational" way to achieve certain ends. To many noneconomists such an assumption seems preposterous. Instead, they argue that people are "irrational" in that they make unsystematic decisions dominated as much by whim and ignorance as by any sort of rational thought process. Here we examine a few examples of allegedly irrational behavior in order to show how economists explain these examples.

Much purportedly irrational behavior represents differences in tastes between the observer and the person being observed. Some critics may assert it is "irrational" for people to eat at McDonald's or to watch soap operas, but such statements really amount to assertions that the speakers' preferences are "superior" to those being observed; economists wish to make no such value judgment. Similarly, much of what is described as "irrational" behavior (such as living in dilapidated housing or consuming poor diets) is actually a reflection of the constraint imposed by low income. As for the case of differing preferences, to regard such behavior as irrational is to misuse the term. Here instead we are interested in the type of behavior that suggests that people make decisions that are not in their own best interest.

Self-Imposed Constraints

One type of behavior that might be termed irrational occurs when individuals impose additional constraints on their own actions. People participate in compulsory savings plans (such as Christmas Clubs) that pay very low rates of interest; they pay to join stop-smoking clinics to break the cigarette habit; and they hide the key to the freezer to make sure they stay on a diet. These types of behavior seem irrational because people are voluntarily subjecting themselves to unnecessary constraints. Recent examinations of the notion of "self control" have shown why such behavior is indeed rational.[7] Introducing constraints for a specific purpose allows individuals to attain long-term goals (saving for a specific goal, stopping smoking, or losing weight) while maintaining considerable discretion in day-to-day decision making. Self-imposed constraints are therefore just one way in which individuals rationally pursue certain goals.

Criminal Behavior

To most people criminal behavior is regarded as "deviant." Economists would not deny that many criminals exhibit antisocial characteristics or that some crimes are particularly bizarre. However, economists differ from many other social scientists in viewing much criminal behavior (particularly property crimes such as burglary, robbery, and auto theft) as fundamentally rational. Rather than viewing criminals as psychotic, economists treat them as utility maximizers who are responding to the incentives they face. For example, in one study of how various factors affect crime rates, Isaac Ehrlich found that each 1 percent increase in the likelihood that some-

$MRS: \dfrac{P_x}{P_y}$

outset. In order to maximize utility given a fixed amount of income to spend on two goods, an individual will spend the entire income and will choose a bundle of goods for which the marginal rate of substitution between two goods is equal to the ratio of those goods' market prices.

The reasoning behind the first part of this proposition is straightforward. Because we assume that "more is better," an individual will spend the entire amount budgeted for the two items. The only alternative here to spending on

[7]See, for example, R. H. Thaler and H. M. Shefrin, "An Economic Theory of Self-Control," *Journal of Political Economy*, April 1981, pp. 392–406.

one committing a property crime will be caught was associated with a reduction in such crimes of 0.8 percent. Ehrlich also found that each 1 percent increase in the severity of the penalty imposed on a convicted felon reduced the rate of property crime by nearly 1 percent.[8] Similar results were found for specific categories of property crimes such as burglary or auto theft. Ehrlich's most controversial finding was that criminal sanctions had relatively large negative effects on crimes against other persons such as rape and aggravated assault. Even for the types of crimes that seem least subject to rational economic calculation, there was some evidence that the incentives faced by criminals had an impact on observed crime rates.

Psychiatric Patients

That institutionalized psychiatric patients behave "irrationally" seems almost self-evident—if such patients behaved rationally they would probably not be institutionalized. There can be no doubt that many such patients do behave in ways that are not socially acceptable. But there is also considerable evidence that these patients often make the kinds of rational responses to economic incentives that are not very different from those made by "normal" society. Economists have, for example, studied a number of "token economies"—therapeutic communities for psychiatric patients in which patients earn tokens for performing various tasks and spend those tokens to purchase a variety of consumption items. Behavior in such communities in response to changes in the redemption value of tokens has been found to be remarkably similar to the way in which demanders in general respond to changing prices. Similarly, patients seem to respond to changes in the token compensation rate for specific jobs in much the same way that workers in the economy at large respond to wage changes.[9] The usual utility-maximizing model may serve equally well to explain the economic behavior of individuals judged to be irrational in other types of behavior.

These are just a few examples of the ways in which economists approach rational decision making by utility-maximizing individuals. Of course, there will always be examples of peculiar behavior not explicable by any model of rational choice. But as a starting place, the utility-maximization model can go a long way in providing insights about how choices are made in the vast majority of situations.

To Think About

1. How might you explain the following types of "irrational" behavior as being completely in accord with the notion of utility maximization: (a) never shopping for bargains; (b) refusing to use a seat belt; (c) living in an "unsafe" neighborhood; (d) smoking; (e) drinking "too much" alcohol?

2. What types of "irrational" behavior do you engage in (if in doubt, ask your parents or roommate)? How do you explain your behavior in such situations? Does it represent utility maximization on your part or not?

the two goods is throwing the money away, which is obviously less desirable than buying something.

The reasoning behind the second part of the proposition can be seen with our hamburger–soft drink example. Suppose that an individual is currently consuming some combination of hamburgers and soft drinks for which the MRS is equal to 1; he or she is willing to trade away one hamburger in order

---

[8]Isaac Ehrlich, "Participation in Illegitimate Activities: A Theoretical and Empirical Investigation," *Journal of Political Economy*, May/June 1973, p. 550.

[9]This evidence is reviewed in J. H. Kugel, "Token Economies and Experimental Economics," *Journal of Political Economy*, July/August 1972, pp. 779–785.

to get an additional soft drink. Assume, on the other hand, that the price of hamburgers is $.20 and that of soft drinks is $.10. The ratio of their prices is $.10/$.20 = ½. The individual is able to obtain an extra soft drink in the market by giving up only one-half of a hamburger. In this situation the individual's MRS is not equal to the ratio of the goods' market prices, and there is another bundle of goods that provides more utility.

Suppose this person consumes one less hamburger. This frees $.20 in purchasing power, since one hamburger costs $.20. He or she can now buy one more soft drink (at a price of $.10) and is now as well off as before since the MRS was assumed to be 1. However, there is still $.10 (= $.20 − $.10) unspent that can be spent on either soft drinks or hamburgers (or some combination of the two), thereby making the individual better off than in the initial situation.

Any time that the individual selects a bundle of goods for which the MRS differs from the price ratio a similar beneficial change in spending patterns can be made. This reallocation will continue until the MRS is brought into line with the price ratio. We now turn to presenting a more formal proof of this.

Graphic Analysis of Utility Maximization

To develop a graphic demonstration of the process of utility maximization we will begin by showing how to illustrate an individual's **budget constraint.** This constraint shows which bundles of commodities are affordable. From among these we assume that the bundle that provides the most utility will be chosen. To demonstrate that choice we use an indifference curve map, as introduced in the first part of this chapter.

Budget constraint
The limit that income places on the combinations of goods and services that an individual can afford.

The Budget Constraint

Figure 3.5 shows the combinations of goods X and Y that an individual with a fixed amount of money to spend can afford. If all available income is spent on good X, the number of units that can be purchased is recorded as X_{max} in the figure. If all available income is spent on Y, Y_{max} is the amount that can be bought. The line joining X_{max} to Y_{max} represents the various mixed bundles of goods X and Y that can be purchased using all the available funds. Points in the shaded area below the budget line are also affordable, but these leave some portion of funds unspent, so these points would usually not be chosen.

The downward slope of the budget line shows that the individual can afford more X only if Y purchases are cut back. The precise slope of this relationship depends on the unit prices of the two goods. If Y is expensive and X is cheap, the line will be relatively flat since choosing to consume one less Y will permit purchasing many units of X (an individual who decides not to purchase a new designer suit can instead choose to purchase many pairs of socks). Alternately, if Y is relatively cheap per unit and X is expensive, the budget line will be steep. Reducing Y consumption does not permit very much more of good X

Figure 3.5
Individual's Budget
Constraint for Two Goods

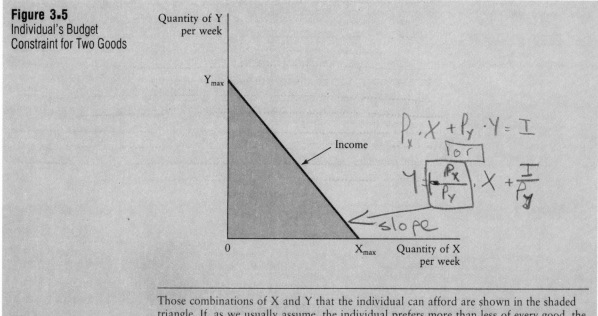

Those combinations of X and Y that the individual can afford are shown in the shaded triangle. If, as we usually assume, the individual prefers more than less of every good, the outer boundary of this triangle is the relevant constraint where all of the available funds are spent either on X or Y. The slope of this straight boundary is given by $-P_X/P_Y$.

to be bought. All of these relationships can be made clearer by using a bit of algebra.

Suppose that the individual has I dollars to spend on either good X or good Y. Suppose also that P_X represents the price of good X and P_Y the price of good Y. The total amount spent on X is given by the price of X times the amount purchased. Similarly, $P_Y \cdot Y$ represents total spending on good Y. Since the available income must be spend on either X or Y we have

$$\text{Amount spent on X} + \text{Amount spend on Y} = \text{I}$$

or

$$P_X \cdot X + P_Y \cdot Y = \text{I}. \qquad [3.3]$$

Equation 3.3 is an algebraic statement of the budget line shown in Figure 3.5. To make the relationship clearer we can solve Equation 3.3 for Y so that the budget line has the standard form for a linear equation (Y = a + bX) discussed in Chapter 2. This solution of Equation 3.3 gives

$$Y = -\frac{P_X}{P_Y} \cdot X + \frac{I}{P_Y}. \qquad [3.4]$$

Although Equations 3.3 and 3.4 say exactly the same thing, the relationship between Equation 3.4 and Figure 3.5 should be somewhat clearer. It is obvious from Equation 3.4 that if the individual chooses to spend all available funds on Y (that is, if X = 0), he or she can buy I/P_Y units. That point is the Y-intercept in the figure, which we previously called Y_{max}. Similarly, a slight manipulation of the budget equation shows that if Y = 0, all income will be devoted to X purchases, and the X-intercept will be I/P_X. Again, this point is labeled X_{max} in the figure. Finally, the slope of the budget constraint is given by the ratio of the goods' prices, $-P_X/P_Y$. This shows the ratio at which Y can be given up to get more X in the market. As we noted before, if P_X is low and P_Y is high, the slope will be small and the budget line will be flat. On the other hand, a high P_X and a low P_Y will make the budget line steep.

To reinforce these ideas let's return to our hamburger–soft drink example. Remember that the price of hamburgers was assumed to be $.20 (that is, P_Y = $.20) and the price of soft drinks was assumed to be $.10 ($P_X$ = $.10). Suppose also that total funds are $1. When the entire dollar is devoted to hamburger purchases, five hamburgers (= I/P_Y = $1/$.20) can be purchased. At the other extreme, if the dollar is spent on soft drinks, a total of ten drinks (= I/P_X = $1/$.10) can be bought. As before, the ratio of the goods' prices ($.10/$.20 = ½) records the fact that one hamburger is worth two soft drinks in the market.

Utility Maximization

The individual can afford all bundles of X and Y that fall within the shaded triangle in Figure 3.5. From among these, this person will choose the one that offers the greatest utility. The budget constraint can be used together with the individual's indifference curve map to show this utility-maximization process. Figure 3.6 illustrates the procedure. The individual would be irrational to choose a point such as A—he or she can get to a higher utility level just by spending some of the unspent portion of his or her income. Similarly, by reallocating expenditures the individual can do better than point B. This is the case in which the MRS and the price ratio differ, and the individual can move to a higher indifference curve by choosing to consume less Y and more X. Point D is out of the question because income is not large enough to permit purchase of D. It is clear that the position of maximum utility will be at point C where the combination X^*, Y^* is chosen. This is the only point on indifference curve U_2 that can be bought with I dollars, and no higher utility level can be bought. C is a point of tangency between the budget constraint and the indifference curve. Therefore all funds are spent and:

$$\text{Max Utility} = \begin{array}{|c} \text{Slope of} \\ \text{budget constraint} \end{array} = \begin{array}{c|} \text{Slope of} \\ \text{indifference curve} \end{array} \text{ or} \qquad [3.5]$$

or (neglecting the fact that both slopes are negative)

Figure 3.6
Graphic Demonstration of
Utility Maximization

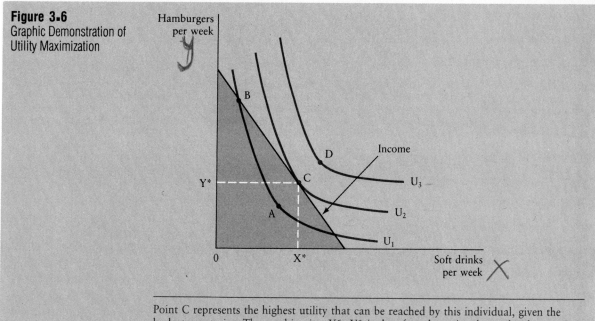

Point C represents the highest utility that can be reached by this individual, given the budget constraint. The combination X*, Y* is therefore the rational way for this person to use the available purchasing power. Only for this combination of goods will two conditions hold: all available funds will be spent; and the individual's psychic rate of trade-off (MRS) will be equal to the rate at which the goods can be traded in the market (P_X/P_Y).

$$\frac{P_X}{P_Y} = MRS. \qquad\qquad [3.6]$$

The result is proved—for a utility maximum the MRS should equal the ratio of the prices of the goods. The diagram shows that if this condition is not fulfilled, this person could be made better off by reallocating expenditures.[10]

---

[10]If we use the results of note 5 on the assumption that utility is measurable, Equation 3.6 can be given an alternative interpretation. Since

$$P_X/P_Y = MRS = MU_X/MU_Y \qquad\qquad [i]$$

for a utility maximum, we have

$$\frac{MU_X}{P_X} = \frac{MU_Y}{P_Y}. \qquad\qquad [ii]$$

The ratio of the extra utility from consuming one more unit of a good to its price should be the same for each good. Each good should provide the same extra utility per dollar spent. If that were not true, total utility could be raised by reallocating funds from a good that provided a relatively low level of marginal utility per dollar to one that provided a high level. Goods that do not offer this common marginal benefit/marginal cost ratio to a person will not be bought at all.

You may wish to try several other combinations of X and Y that the individual can afford in order to show that they provide a lower utility level than does combination C. In "Applying Economics: Rationing" we examine a case in which people may not have such complete freedom in how they spend their incomes. We will show why this results in a lower level of utility than when they do have this freedom.

Figure 3.6 can be given a concrete interpretation by again using the hamburger–soft drink example. Point A might represent a choice of two hamburgers and three soft drinks. The choice does not maximize utility since some part of the individual's dollar will not be spent. With the $.30 [(= $1 − (2 × $.20) − (3 × $.10)] that is left over, it would be possible for this consumer to buy more of either good and thereby increase utility. Point B (four hamburgers, two soft drinks) is also inefficient, even though the entire dollar is spent. At this point relatively too much of the dollar has been spent on hamburger purchases. The consumer could enjoy a higher level of utility by reducing hamburger purchases and increasing soft drink purchases in the market. He or she would do so until reaching a point such as C (three hamburgers, four soft drinks) at which the entire dollar is spent *and* the psychic rate of trade-off (the MRS) between soft drinks and hamburgers is exactly equal to that rate that is provided by the market in terms of the goods' prices (P_X/P_Y = ½). Combinations such as D (four hamburgers, five soft drinks), although preferred to point C, are not affordable because their total costs exceed $1.

Importance of Diminishing Marginal Rate of Substitution

If the individual is to maximize utility subject to a budget constraint, he or she must choose consumption bundles that exhaust income and whose MRS is equal to P_X/P_Y. Points of maximum satisfaction are characterized by a tangency between an individual's indifference curve map and the budget constraint. Not every such point of tangency must provide maximum satisfaction, however, as Figure 3.7 illustrates. Here a point of tangency (C) is inferior to a point of nontangency (B). The true maximum is, as it must be, at another point of tangency (A). The failure of the tangency condition to produce an unambiguous maximum can be attributed to the peculiar shape of the indifference curves in Figure 3.7. If the indifference curves are shaped as are those in Figure 3.6, no such problem can arise. But it was shown previously that "normally" shaped indifference curves are a result of the assumption of a diminishing MRS. Therefore, if the MRS is assumed to be diminishing, the condition of tangency assures a true maximum. Without this assumption, we would have to be very careful in applying the tangency rule. Since this book always assumes a diminishing MRS, we do not need to be particularly concerned with the type of problems illustrated in Figure 3.7.

Figure 3.7
Example of an Indifference
Curve Map for Which the
Tangency Condition Does
Not Insure a Maximum

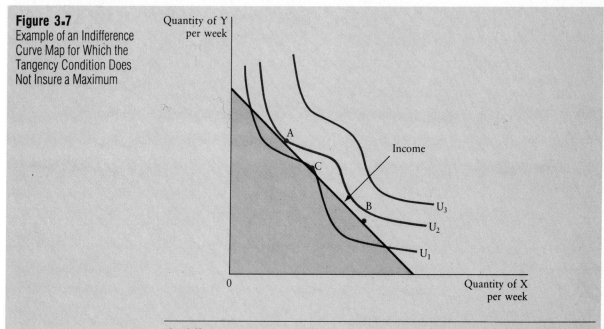

If indifference curves do not obey the assumption of a diminishing MRS, not all points of tangency (points for which MRS = P_X/P_Y) may truly be points of maximum utility. In this example, tangency point C is inferior to many other points that can also be purchased with the available funds.

A Numerical Example of Utility Maximization

We can give a numerical example of utility maximization if we assume for the moment that utility is measurable. Again suppose that an individual is choosing between hamburgers (Y) and soft drinks (X) and that the prices of these goods are $P_Y = \$.20$, $P_X = \$.10$. Assume also that the individual now has $2 to spend (since the numbers work out more easily in this case than when there is only $1 to spend). Finally, suppose that the utility from consuming X and Y is given by

$$ \text{Utility} = U(X,Y) = \sqrt{XY}. \qquad [3.7]$$

We are assuming not only that utility can be measured but also that its value is given by the square root (denoted by $\sqrt{\ }$) of the product of X times Y. This particular utility function is suitable for our purposes because its indifference curves (contour lines) have the familiar convex shape (see the numerical example of contour lines in Chapter 2).

Table 3.1
Alternative Combinations of Hamburgers and Soft Drinks That Can Be Bought with $2 and the Utility of Each Combination (P_Y = $.20, P_X = $.10)

Hamburgers Y	Soft Drinks X	$U(X,Y) = \sqrt{XY}$
0	20	$\sqrt{0} = 0$
1	18	$\sqrt{18} = 4.2$
2	16	$\sqrt{32} = 5.7$
3	14	$\sqrt{42} = 6.5$
4	12	$\sqrt{48} = 6.9$
5	10	$\sqrt{50} = 7.1$
6	8	$\sqrt{48} = 6.9$
7	6	$\sqrt{42} = 6.5$
8	4	$\sqrt{32} = 5.7$
9	2	$\sqrt{18} = 4.2$
10	0	$\sqrt{0} = 0$

Table 3.1 lists several possible ways in which the individual might spend $2 and calculates the utility associated with each choice. For example, if the individual buys six hamburgers and eight soft drinks (totally exhausting the $2), utility will be 6.9 (= $\sqrt{48}$). The other entries in the table should be interpreted accordingly. We consider only those combinations of X and Y that cost exactly $2. The individual cannot spend more than that and would be irrational to spend less since, in this problem, unspent income just disappears. From the table we can see that the combination Y = 5, X = 10 provides the maximum utility (7.1 = $\sqrt{50}$) of those combinations listed. Figure 3.8 shows that this is indeed a true maximum. With the budget constraint

$$\$.10X + \$.20Y = \$2,$$

the individual can just reach the indifference curve U = $\sqrt{50}$ at the single point Y = 5, X = 10. Any other choices that cost $2 or less yield a lower utility. At the point Y = 5, X = 10 the budget constraint is just tangent to the indifference curve;[11] the MRS is equal to the ratio of the goods' prices.

This example is presented for teaching purposes only. We are not able to measure an individual's utility function; even if we could, it is highly unlikely it would depend only on hamburgers and soft drinks and take the simple form we have used. There are, however, economic maximization problems in which the goal being sought is (at least in principle) measurable. Examples of these appear in Part 3 when we discuss production functions and cost curves.

---

[11]This indifference curve is a graph of $\sqrt{XY} = \sqrt{50}$ or, more simply, XY = 50. Hence it is similar to the contour lines graphed in Chapter 2.

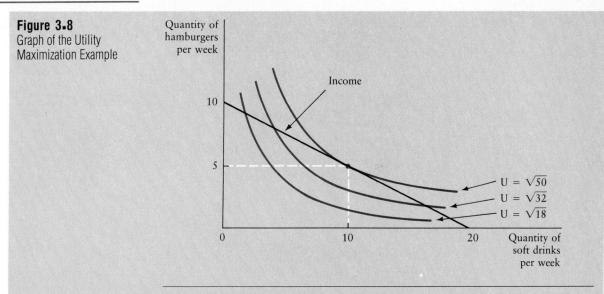

Figure 3.8
Graph of the Utility Maximization Example

If P_X = \$.10, P_Y = \$.20, and I = \$2, then the utility-maximizing choice for X and Y is X^* = 10, Y^* = 5. At this point, the budget constraint is just tangent to the indifference curve U = $\sqrt{XY}$ = $\sqrt{50}$ (or X · Y = 50), and this is the highest utility level obtainable.

Generalizations

Although the previous example (and most of the analysis in this chapter so far) studied only the individual's problem in choosing between two specific goods, the approach is quite general. In any situation in which people must make choices that are constrained by their economic circumstances a very similar analysis could be used.[12] Because economics is in many respects the study of how choices are made when scarcity is present, this model of choice lies behind many of the approaches taken by economists to study real-world questions. Before turning to another example that shows how the model is used, one common graphic procedure might be mentioned. Often we wish to study a person's decisions about only one particular good and are not concerned about any other specific goods. In this case we could record the good that is the object of attention on the horizontal (X) axis and treat all other goods as one single commodity shown on the vertical (Y) axis. That is, good Y is treated as a "composite good" that includes everything except the good

---

[12]The analysis can be easily applied to choices among any number of goods. To examine such cases requires the use of mathematics since graphical techniques cannot be easily adapted to many dimensions. A relatively simple treatment of these mathematical derivations can be found in Walter Nicholson, *Microeconomic Theory: Basic Principles and Extensions,* 3d ed. (Hinsdale, Ill: Dryden Press, 1985), pp. 74–76. For a more complex discussion, see Paul A. Samuelson, *Foundations of Economic Analysis* (Cambridge, Mass.: Harvard University Press, 1947), Chapter 5.

APPLYING ECONOMICS

Rationing

Because economic goods do not exist in quantities sufficient to satisfy all human wants, such goods must always in some way be allocated among individuals. The
most common method of allocation is through the price
system. The study of that process is the central focus of
this book. At times, however, goods may be allocated
by nonmarket means.

Government rationing is one of the most common
of these methods. Either because a society may not wish
to allocate goods by price for ideological or humanitar-
ian reasons (as with rice allotments in China) or because
temporary shortages arise that, it is believed, should be
shared by all (as was the case in many countries during
World War II), governments may choose to ration existing stocks of goods equally (or nearly equally) among
everyone.

Such a situation is illustrated in Figure 3.9. Given
market prices and income, the individual wishes to consume the combination X^*, Y^*. If rationing limits the
quantity of X available to any individual to an amount
X_R (which must still be purchased at the prevailing price),
that preferred point will be unattainable. Rather, the
effective budget constraint then becomes the line segment BI, and some other utility-maximizing point must
be chosen. From the figure it is clear that point B provides the maximum utility given this additional constraint. Rationing of X has reduced the individual's utility
from U_2 to U_1 by forcing the purchase of less X (and
more Y) than is desired.[13]

Two aspects of the solution pictured in Figure 3.9
might be highlighted. First, rationing has an effect on
the individual's choices only if $X_R < X^*$. If $X_R > X^*$,
the individual is permitted to purchase more of good X
than would be freely chosen, and rationing is, for this

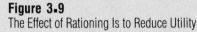

Figure 3.9
The Effect of Rationing Is to Reduce Utility

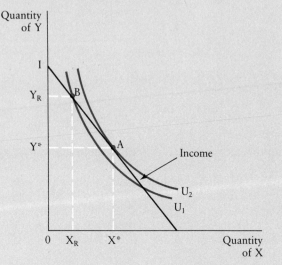

Rationing that allows an individual to purchase only X_R
reduces utility (if $X_R < X^*$) from U_2 to U_1. Rationing is
more likely to affect the choices of high-income
consumers than of low-income consumers.

person, ineffective. Since, as we show in the next chapter, it is likely that X^* will be greater the higher is an
individual's income, the probability that rationing will
effectively limit choices is greater for high-income persons than for low-income persons.

Table 3.2 illustrates this presumption for the case of
food rationing in Germany, Poland, and the United

---

[13]For example, rationing of consumer goods in the United States during World War II caused the
personal saving rate to triple (from around 7 to 8 percent of disposable income to nearly 25
percent). Constrained consumption choices meant that individuals made use of the only other
beneficial use for their incomes—additional savings. In fact, these savings were later used to
finance the postwar boom in durable goods purchases.

Table 3.2

Ration Allotment of Food during World War II as a Percent of Peacetime Consumption by Income Class

Food	Germany			Poland			United Kingdom		
	Low Income	Medium Income	High Income	Low Income	Medium Income	High Income	Low Income	Medium Income	High Income
Bread	99.0%	103.0%	103.0%	48.6%	42.4%	44.7%	Not rationed		
Meat	71.8	45.9	32.9	34.9	22.7	15.5	91.3%	55.3%	43.8%
Milk	150.0	109.1	96.8	71.4	45.5	31.3	500.0	168.2	94.6
Fats	75.0	47.6	36.6	NA	NA	NA	93.0	67.9	61.0

Source: Wartime Rationing and Consumption: League of Nations Intelligence Service (1941, 11a, 2) pp. 58–59.

Kingdom during World War II. The table shows the wartime food allotment as a percentage of peacetime consumption for food items: bread, meat, milk, and fats. For all items, high-income consumers appear to have been more constrained than low-income consumers. In Germany, for example, meat allotments were nearly 72 percent of peacetime consumption for low-income families, but only about 33 percent of peacetime consumption for high-income families. Rationing also had a much greater effect on those goods whose purchase might be expected to rise rapidly with family income (meat and fats) than on those whose purchase was relatively little affected by greater income (bread and milk).

A second feature of this problem concerns the stability of the rationed solution. Since the unrationed optimal choice (A) provides more utility than does the rationed choice (B), there is an incentive for the individual to find some way of moving from B to A. The appearance of black markets in rationed commodities attests to the strength of this incentive. Our observations also suggest that high-income individuals would be more likely to make black market purchases because they would have more to gain by doing so.

To Think About

1. Are the "black markets" that almost always arise in situations of rationing undesirable? Why should anyone object to people trading away their rations if they choose to? Should the government discourage black markets in some kinds of goods and encourage them in other kinds of goods?

2. Suppose the government required people to buy more of some good than they would freely choose to purchase. Use a diagram similar to Figure 3.9 to show that this would also result in a lower utility than in the absence of such a requirement. Can you think of any examples for which such an analysis would be appropriate (that is, what kinds of things does the government require you to buy that you would not freely choose)?

being explicitly examined. In this way, the standard two-dimensional analysis of choice is more general than might first appear to be the case.[14] In "Applying Economics: Taxation and Lump-Sum Principle," we use this technique to illustrate an important result about taxes and their effects on the way people behave.

---

[14]To make this convention rigorously correct requires that we assume that the relative prices of all the goods that constitute "everything else" are not changing during the analysis.

APPLYING ECONOMICS

Taxation and Lump-Sum Principle

The utility-maximization model can also be used to demonstrate that taxes on general purchasing power are more efficient than taxes on a single item. Here the term "more efficient" is taken to mean that if the two taxes yield equal governmental revenues, the general purchasing power tax can be shown to reduce utility less (and, therefore, have a smaller "burden") than does the tax on a single commodity. Hence consumers should favor such taxes. The proof is shown in Figure 3.10. Initially, the individual has I to spend and chooses to consume X* and Y* since that point obeys the budget constraint

$$I = P_X X^* + P_Y Y^* \qquad [3.9]$$

and the tangency condition for a maximum. A tax on good (X) of t dollars per unit would raise its price to $P_X + t$, and the budget constraint would become:

$$I = (P_X + t)X + P_Y Y. \qquad [3.10]$$

With that budget constraint (shown as line I′ in Figure 3.10) this person would be forced to accept a lower utility level (U_1) and would choose to consume the combination X_1, Y_1. Suppose now that the government decided to institute a general income (purchasing power) tax that raised the same revenue as this sales tax. This would shift the individual's budget constraint to I″. The fact that I″ passes through X_1, Y_1 shows that both taxes have reduced the individual's purchasing power by the same amount.[15]

However, with budget constraint I″, this person will choose to consume X_2, Y_2 (rather than X_1, Y_1) as shown in Figure 3.10. Even though the individual pays the same tax bill in both instances, the combination chosen under the purchasing power tax yields a higher utility (U_2) than does the single commodity tax. An intuitive explanation of this result is based on the recognition that a single commodity tax affects people's well-being in two ways: it reduces general purchasing power and it directs consumption away from the taxed commodity. A purchasing power tax incorporates only the first effect, and individuals are better off under it.

This analysis provides a formal rationale for the belief that lump-sum taxes (those that reduce purchasing power on an across-the-board basis) are superior to excise or sales taxes on individual items. One must be careful not to apply that argument uncritically, however. Lump-sum taxes are more efficient only to the extent that they do not incorporate distorting price effects. The most commonly proposed real-world approximation to a lump-sum tax is a general tax on income. That tax may not be free of price effects. As we show in detail in Chapter 15, an income tax affects an individual's hourly wage and may therefore affect his or her decisions about how many hours to work. Whether or not an income tax is the best available approximation of the lump-sum principle remains an open question.

---

[15]Some algebra may clarify this. Total taxes collected under sales tax are given by $T = tX_1$. An income tax of T dollars would leave aftertax income of

$$I'' = I - T = I - tX_1.$$

But remember

$$I = (P_X + t)X_1 + P_Y Y_1,$$

so

$$I'' = P_X X_1 + P_Y Y_1,$$

which shows that I″ passes through X_1, Y_1.

Figure 3.10
The Efficiency of Lump-Sum Taxes

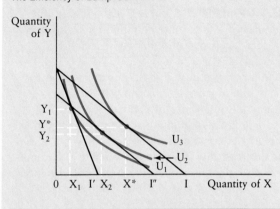

A per-unit tax on good X causes the utility-maximizing point to shift to X_1, Y_1 and utility to fall from U_3 to U_1. A lump-sum tax that collects the same revenue would shift the budget constraint to I'' and would only reduce utility to U_2. The lump-sum tax may therefore be preferred on efficiency grounds.

The argument presented here for positive taxes applies to negative taxes (that is, income subsidies) as well. A general income subsidy can be shown to be a more efficient way of raising utility than would be the provision of some goods at below market prices. That conclusion (which is subject to the caveats raised previously about the lump-sum properties of income taxes) has important policy implications for antipoverty programs. In recent years the most rapidly growing programs to aid the poor have been those that provide certain goods at subsidized prices. Food stamps, subsidized housing programs, and Medicaid are the most notable examples. Our analysis suggests that antipoverty funds might be more effectively allocated (in terms of raising the utility of poor people) by a greater reliance on direct income grants. A number of current welfare reform plans suggest moving in that direction.

To Think About
1. What kinds of taxes seem to come closest to the lump-sum principle? That is, which actual taxes seem to have the least distorting effect on the economic choices people make? Should we make more use of such taxes? Or are there good reasons to have some taxes (for example, taxes on cigarettes) that do distort people's choices?
2. If direct income grants are more effective in raising people's utility than subsidies on particular goods, why does the government operate so many subsidy programs (in food, housing, medical care, legal services, and education, to name just a few)? Couldn't these all be "cashed out" to provide a great deal more utility to the low income people for whom they are intended? Or, are there good reasons to retain subsidies on specific goods?

Summary

This chapter covers a lot of ground. In it we have seen how economists explain the kinds of choices people make and the ways in which those choices are constrained by economic circumstances. The chapter has been rather tough going in places. The theory of choice is one of the most difficult parts of any study of microeconomics, and it is unfortunate that it usually comes at the very start of the course. But that placement clearly shows why the topic is so important—practically every model of economic behavior we will study starts with the building blocks introduced in this chapter. Developing a good understanding of the material will be very useful to you later in this book.

Our principal conclusions in this chapter are:

- Economists use the term "utility" to refer to the satisfaction that people derive from their economic activities. Usually only a few of the things that affect utility are examined in any particular analysis. All other factors are assumed to be held constant so that a person's choices can be studied in a simplified setting.
- Utility can be represented by an indifference curve map. Each indifference curve shows those bundles of goods that the individual considers to be equally attractive. Higher levels of utility are represented by higher indifference curve "contour" lines.
- The slope of indifference curves shows how individuals are willing to trade one good for another while remaining equally well off. The negative of this slope is called the "marginal rate of substitution" (MRS), since it shows the degree to which an individual is willing to substitute one good for another in his or her consumption choices.
- People are limited in what they can buy. Economists refer to such limits as "budget constraints." When a person is choosing between two goods, his or her budget constraint is usually a straight line. The negative of the slope of this line represents the price ratio of the two goods—it shows what one of the goods is worth in terms of the other in the marketplace.
- If individuals are to obtain the maximum possible utility from their limited incomes, they should spend all the available funds and they should choose a bundle of goods for which the MRS is equal to the price ratio of the two goods. Such a utility maximum is shown graphically by a tangency between the individual's budget constraint and the highest indifference curve that his or her income can afford.

Problems

3.1 Suppose a person has $8 to spend only on apples and oranges. Suppose apples cost $.40 each and oranges cost $.10 each.

   a. If this person buys *only* apples, how many can be bought?
   b. If the person buys *only* oranges, how many can be bought?
   c. If the person were to buy 10 apples, how many oranges could be bought with the funds left over?
   d. If the person consumes one less apple (that is, nine) how many more oranges could be bought? Is this rate of trade-off the same no matter how many apples are relinquished?
   e. Write down the algebraic equation for this person's budget constraint and graph it showing the points mentioned in parts a through d (using graph paper would improve the accuracy of your work).

3.2 Suppose the person faced with the budget constraint described in problem 3.1 has preferences for applies (A) and oranges (O) given by

$$\text{Utility} = \sqrt{A \cdot O}.$$

     a.   If A = 5 and O = 80 what will utility be?

     b.   If A = 10 what value for O will provide the same utility as in part a?

     c.   If A = 20 what value for O will provide the same utility as in parts a and b?

     d.   Graph the indifference curve implied by parts a through c.

     e.   Given the budget constraint from problem 3.1, which of the points identified in parts a through c can be bought by this person?

     f.   Show through some examples that every other way of allocating income provides less utility than does the point identified in part e. Graph this utility-maximizing situation.

3.3   Show that it is impossible for a person's indifference curves to intersect. To do this, draw two intersecting indifference curves and make use of the "more is better" assumption introduced at the start of Chapter 3.

3.4   People do not typically buy some of every good available on supermarket shelves. Rather, they limit their purchases to relatively few items that they know they like. For example, some people (such as the author) never buy lima beans or calf's liver, although others obviously do. Show the utility-maximizing situation for such people and explain precisely why no lima beans are bought. Use this analysis to explain what people mean when they say some good "isn't worth its price."

3.5   Oliver D. Dancefloor gets his utility by going to discos or rock concerts. His utility function is $U = \sqrt{D \cdot C}$, where D = the number of discos and C = the number of concerts he attends in a month. Draw the contour lines (in the positive quadrant) for this function for utility levels of 4, 5, and 10 (that is, for U = 4, U = 5, and U = 10). What do we call the shape of these contour lines? (Hint: here it may be easier to graph U^2 rather than U.)

     If concert tickets are \$4, the cover charge at the disco is \$2, and Oliver's monthly entertainment budget is \$64, his budget constraint is 2D + 4C = 64. Where does this line intersect the indifference curve for $U = \sqrt{128}$? Does this seem to be the highest utility possible given the budget constraint?

3.6   Ms. Caffeine enjoys coffee (C) and tea (T) according to the function $U(C,T) = 3C + 4T$. What does her utility function say about her MRS of coffee for tea? What do her indifference curves look like? If coffee and tea cost \$3 each and Ms. Caffeine has \$12 to spend on these products, how much coffee and tea should she buy to maximize her utility? Draw the graph of her indifference curve map and her budget constraint, and show that the utility-maximizing point occurs only on the T axis where no coffee is bought. Would she buy any coffee if she had more money to spend? How would her consumption change if the price of coffee fell to \$2?

3.7   Mr. A derives utility from martinis in proportion to the number he drinks, $U(M) = M$. Mr. A is very particular about his martinis, however: he only enjoys them made in the exact proportion of two parts gin (G) to one part vermouth (V). Graph Mr. A's indifference curve in terms of G and V for various levels of martini consumption. (Hint: Does Mr. A have an MRS of G for V?) Show that regardless of the prices of the two ingredients, Mr. A will never alter the way he mixes martinis. Graph this result.

3.8   Assume consumers are choosing between housing services (H) measured in square feet and consumption of all other goods (C) measured in dollars.

   a.   Show the equilibrium position in a diagram.
   b.   Now suppose the government agrees to subsidize consumers by paying 50 percent of their housing cost. How will their budget line change? Show the new equilibrium.
   c.   Show in a diagram the minimum amount of income supplement the government would have to give individuals instead of housing subsidy to make them as well off as they were in part b.

*3.9   Suppose low-income people have preferences for nonfood consumption (NF) and for food consumption (F). In the absence of any income transfer programs a person's budget constraint is given by

$$NF + P_F F = I$$

where P_F is the price of food relative to nonfood items and NF and I are measured in terms of nonfood prices (that is, dollars).

   a.   Graph the initial utility-maximizing situation for this low-income person.
   b.   Suppose now that a food stamp program is introduced that requires low-income people to pay C (measured in terms of nonfood prices) in order to receive food stamps sufficient to buy F* units of food (presumably $P_F F^* > C$). Show this person's budget constraint if he or she participates in the food stamp program.
   c.   Show graphically the factors that will determine whether the person chooses to participate in the program.
   d.   Show graphically what it will cost the government to finance benefits for the typical food stamp recipient. Show also that this person could reach a higher utility level if this amount were simply given with no strings attached.

*3.10 Suppose individuals derive utility from two goods, housing (H) and all other consumption (C). Show that if the government requires individuals to buy more housing than they would freely choose (say, by setting minimum housing "standards") such a policy may reduce utility. Which group would you expect to suffer the greatest losses of utility from such a policy? (Hint: Use Figure 3.9.)

---

*Denotes a problem that is rather difficult.

CHAPTER 4

How Changes in Income and Prices Affect Choices

This chapter studies how people change their choices when conditions change. In particular we will study how changes in incomes, changes in the price of one good, and changes in the price of some other good affect the amount that people choose to consume. We will compare the new choices with those that were made before conditions changed. This kind of investigation is sometimes called **comparative statics** analysis because it compares two utility-maximizing choices. One result of this approach will be to construct the individual's demand curve for some good.

You need to be careful about two aspects of this kind of approach. First, the *ceteris paribus* assumption is important here. We are changing only one thing at a time that affects choices; everything else is being held constant. In particular, we are assuming that people's preferences do not change. In graphic terms, we will be keeping the individual's indifference curve map unchanged and studying the effects of shifting the budget constraint to alternative positions.

Second, you should understand that the general notion of "changing conditions" is only a beginning for our investigation. Ideally, we would like to explain why conditions change. Instead of supposing that, say, the price of potatoes has risen, we will eventually be more interested in finding out *why* the price of potatoes has risen. This chapter is only the first step in answering this larger question, which we will not discuss in detail until Part 4.

Comparative statics The investigation of new choices people make when conditions change, as compared to the choices they made under the former conditions.

Demand Functions

Chapter 3 shows that the quantities of X and Y that an individual chooses depend on the person's preferences (that is, on the shape of the indifference curve map) and on the budget constraint. That is, if we knew a person's preferences and all of the economic forces that affect the choices, we could predict how much of each good would be chosen. We can summarize this conclusion using the demand function for some particular good, say X:

$$\text{Quantity of X demanded} = X = D_X(P_X, P_Y, I; \text{preferences}). \qquad [4.1]$$

This equation contains the three elements that determine what the individual can buy—the prices of X and Y and the person's income (I)—as well as a reminder that choices are also affected by preferences for the goods.

These preferences appear to the right of the semicolon in Equation 4.1 because for most of our analysis we assume that preferences do not change. People's basic likes and dislikes are assumed to be developed through a lifetime of experience. They are unlikely to change as we examine their reactions to relatively short-term changes in their economic circumstances caused by changes in commodity prices or incomes.

The quantity demanded of good Y depends on these same general influences, and can be summarized by

$$\text{Quantity of Y demanded} = Y = D_Y(P_X, P_Y, I; \text{preferences}). \qquad [4.2]$$

Preferences again appear to the right of the semicolon in Equation 4.2 because we assume that the person's taste for good Y will not change during our analysis. Here we are interested only in examining how choices change when economic conditions change.

Homogeneity

One important rule that follows directly from Chapter 3 is that if the prices of X and Y and income (I) were all to double (or to change by any identical percentage), the same quantities of X and Y would be demanded. The budget constraint

$$P_X X + P_Y Y = I \qquad [4.3]$$

is identical to the budget constraint

$$2P_X X + 2P_Y Y = 2I. \qquad [4.4]$$

Graphically, Equations 4.3 and 4.4 are exactly the same lines. Consequently, both budget constraints are tangent to the individual's indifference curve map at precisely the same point. The quantities of X and Y the individual chooses when faced with the constraint in Equation 4.3 are exactly the same as when the individual is faced by the constraint in Equation 4.4.

The quantities an individual demands depend not on prices or on income alone but on the relative prices of X and Y and on the "real" value of income. Proportional changes in the prices of X and Y and in income change only the

Figure 4.1
Effect of Increasing
Income on Quantities
of X and Y Chosen

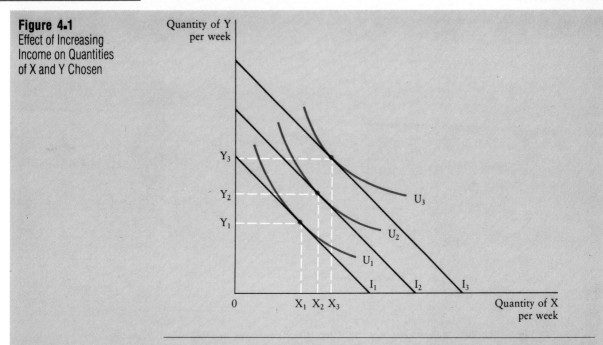

As income increases from I_1 to I_2 to I_3, the optimal (utility-maximizing) choices of X and Y are shown by the successively higher points of tangency. The budget constraint shifts in a parallel way because its slope (given by the ratio of the goods' prices) does not change.

Homogeneous demand
Demand does not change when prices and income increase in the same proportion.

units we count in (such as dollars instead of cents). They do not affect the quantities demanded. Individual demands are said to be **homogeneous** for identical changes in all prices and income.[1] People are not hurt by general inflation of prices if their incomes increase in the same proportion. They will be on exactly the same indifference curve both before and after the inflation. Only if inflation increases some incomes faster or slower than prices change does it have an effect on budget constraints, on the quantities of goods demanded, and on people's well-being.

Changes in Income

As a person's total income rises, assuming prices don't change, we might expect the quantity purchased of each good to also increase. This situation is illustrated in Figure 4.1. As income increases from I_1 to I_2 to I_3, the quantity of X demanded increases from X_1 to X_2 to X_3, and the quantity of Y increases

---

[1]Technically, a function f(X,Y) is said to be homogeneous of degree zero in X and Y if f(tX,tY) = f(X,Y) for any t > 0. Doubling X and Y for a function homogeneous of degree zero leaves the value of f unchanged. This is precisely the case for demand functions.

Figure 4.2
Engel Curves Derived
from the Individual's
Indifference Curves

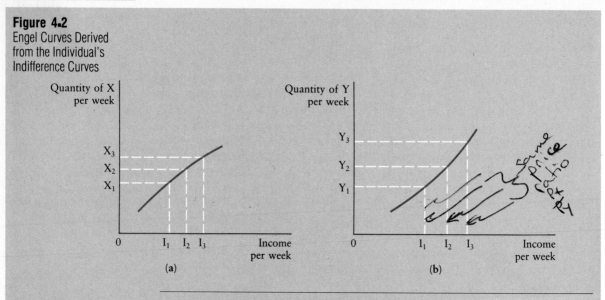

Engel curves show the relationship between total expenditures and the quantity purchased of a particular good. In Graphs (a) and (b), both goods are normal—the quantity purchased increases as income increases. Graph (a) shows a "necessary" normal good in that purchases of it rise less rapidly than income. On the other hand, the good in Graph (b) is a "luxury" because purchases of it rise rapidly as income increases. These Engel curves were constructed directly from Figure 4.1.

from Y_1 to Y_2 to Y_3. Budget lines I_1, I_2, and I_3 are all parallel because we are changing only income, not the relative prices of X and Y. Remember the slope of the budget constraint is given by the ratio of the two goods' prices, and these prices are not changing in this analysis.

Engel Curves

Engel curves
Curves that record the
relationship between the
quantity demanded of a
good and total income.

By using the information from Figure 4.1 we can construct two **Engel curves**, which are shown in Figure 4.2.[2] These curves record the relationship between the quantity of X purchased and total income. These curves are not necessarily straight lines. The demand for some "luxury" goods (such as Y) may increase more rapidly than income, but the demand for "necessities" (such as X) may grow less rapidly than income. The precise shape of the curve depends on the person's preferences for X and Y and how consumption of these items would

---

[2]The curves are named for the Prussian economist Ernst Engel (1821–1896), who was one of the first to study systematically the relationship between the quantity of a good demanded and income.

Figure 4.3
Indifference Curve Map
Showing Inferiority

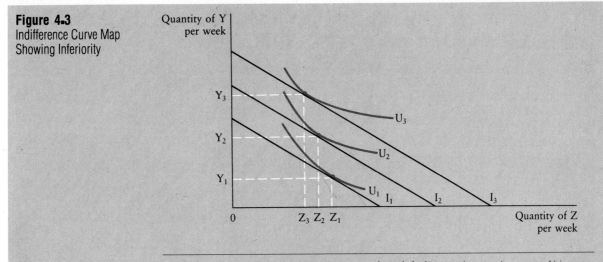

Good Z is inferior because the quantity purchased declines as income increases. Y is a normal good (as it must be if there are only two goods available), and purchases of it increase as total expenditures increase.

change as the person has more income to spend. The indifference curve map shows these preferences.

In Figures 4.1 and 4.2 both X and Y increase as income increases. Goods that follow this tendency are called **normal goods**. Most goods seem to be normal goods—as their incomes increase people tend to buy more of practically everything. The study of Engel curves is discussed further in "Applying Economics: Engel's Law."

Normal good
A good that is bought in greater quantities as income increases.

Inferior Goods

Inferior good
A good that is bought in smaller quantities as income increases.

The demand for certain goods decreases as income increases. Some examples of these goods are "rotgut" whiskey, potatoes, and secondhand clothing. This kind of good is an **inferior good.** How the demand for an inferior good changes is shown in Figure 4.3. The good Z is inferior because as income increases the individual chooses less of it. Although the curves in Figure 4.3 continue to obey the assumption of a diminishing MRS, they exhibit inferiority. Good Z is inferior only because of the way it relates to the other goods available (good Y here), not because of its own qualities. Purchases of rotgut whiskey decline as income increases, for example, because there are more expensive goods (such as French wine) that an individual becomes able to afford. Contrary to the Engel curves in Figure 4.2, the Engel curves for an inferior good are negatively sloped because the quantity demanded declines as income increases.

An interesting example of seemingly inferior goods is discussed in "Applying Economics: Are Children Inferior?"

APPLYING ECONOMICS

Engel's Law

The relationship between income and the consumption of certain goods has been studied by economists since the eighteenth century. Data on spending are usually collected from a sample of families. These data are then classified by income levels (or by social class) to see if there are any important regularities.

Probably the most famous sample data are those used by Engel himself in his original studies. An abbreviated set of these data is shown in Table 4.1. They show the spending patterns of 153 Belgian families in 1853. Engel drew one major conclusion from these data: the proportion of income spent on food declines as income rises. In other words, food is a necessity in the sense that consumption of it rises less rapidly than does income.

This hypothesis has come to be known as Engel's law. It has been verified in hundreds of studies. It holds true not only within a particular geographic area: cross-country comparisons also show that, on average, people in less-developed countries spend more of their incomes on food than people in richer industrial countries.

Over time the percentage of income spent on food also tends to decline as incomes rise. For example, in nineteenth-century America people spent nearly 50 percent of their incomes on food. Today, as we show below, that figure has fallen to about 20 percent.

Engel was cautious about making conclusions from the other data in Table 4.1. Even today no other laws of consumption are believed as true as Engel's law of food consumption. For example, according to the data in Table 4.1 shelter expenses seem to be a constant fraction of income. That conclusion has been hotly debated for many years, particularly as to how property taxes affect various income groups. The data also seem to indicate that spending on services increases more rapidly than income, but "services" does not always mean "luxury" goods (such as in the case of medical care).

Table 4.1
Percent of Total Expenditures on Various Items by Belgian Families in 1853

| Expenditure Item | Annual Income | | |
	$225–$300	$450–$600	$750–$1,000
Food	62.0%	55.0%	50.0%
Clothing	16.0	18.0	18.0
Lodging, light, and fuel	17.0	17.0	17.0
Services (education, legal, health)	4.0	7.5	11.5
Comfort and recreation	1.0	2.5	3.5
Total	100.0	100.0	100.0

Source: Reproduced in A. Marshall, *Principles of Economics*, 8th ed. (London: Macmillan & Co., Ltd., 1920), p. 97. Some items have been aggregated.

Changes in a Good's Price

Substitution effect
The part of the change in quantity demanded of a good whose price has changed that is caused by substitution of the good that is now relatively cheaper for the other that is now relatively more costly. A movement along an indifference curve.

How a price change affects the quantity demanded of a good is somewhat more complex than the effect of a change in income on the quantity demanded. Changing the price geometrically involves not only changing the intercept of the budget constraint but also changing its slope. Moving to the new utility-maximizing choice means moving to another indifference curve and also changing the MRS.

When a price changes, it has two different effects on people's choices. With the **substitution effect,** even if the individual stays on the same indifference curve, consumption has to be changed to equate MRS to the new price ratio of the two goods. With the **income effect,** because the price change also changes "real" purchasing power, people will move to a new indifference curve that is consistent with their new purchasing power. We now look at these two effects of price changes in several different situations.

Table 4.2
Percentage of Total Consumption by Income Class
for All U.S. Families, 1972

| | Annual Income | | |
Consumption Item	$3,000–$4,000	$7,000–$8,000	$12,000–$15,000
Food	24.5%	21.3%	19.7%
Clothing	7.1	7.6	8.1
Housing (including Furniture, Light, and Fuel)	34.7	30.7	29.9
Medical and Educational Services	7.8	7.3	6.8
Personal Care, Comfort, and Recreation	9.3	10.8	11.7
Transportation and Other	16.6	22.3	23.8
Total	100.0	100.0	100.0

Source: U.S. Dept. of Labor, Bureau of Labor Statistics Consumer Expenditure Survey Series, Report 455 (Washington, D.C., 1973), Table 1a.

Recent Data
Table 4.2 updates Engel's data using the United States in 1972. Although there have been vast changes since 1853 in the types of goods that people consume (which means the categories in Tables 4.1 and 4.2 are not directly comparable), some of Engel's conclusions remain valid. Most importantly, Engel's law continues to hold for the 1972 data. Higher-income people still spend less of their income on food than people with lower incomes do. There is again some evidence that housing expenditures are a relatively constant proportion of income, especially for incomes above the very lowest level. That finding is not as consistent as in Engel's original data, however.

To Think About
1. Since Engel's law of food consumption seems to be so universal, some economists have suggested that people be defined as "poor" if they spend, say, more than 35 percent of their income on food. Would this definition be better or worse than one which bases a definition of poverty on income? Which definition would provide a fairer way of comparing the situations of different families?
2. Suppose it is true, as the figures in this application suggest, that spending on housing is, more or less, a constant fraction of people's incomes. How does this fact square with the commonsense idea that housing is a necessity? Is it possible in this situation to define people as "poor" if they "have to" spend a very high fraction of their income on shelter?

Income effect
The part of the change in quantity demanded of a good whose price has changed that is caused by the change in real income that results from the price change.

Substitution and Income Effects from a Fall in Price

How does the quantity consumed of good X change in response to a fall in its price? This situation is illustrated in Figure 4.4. Initially the individual maximizes utility by choosing the combination X*, Y*. Suppose that the price of X falls. The budget constraint now shifts outward to the new budget constraint. Remember that the budget constraint meets the Y axis at the point where all available income is spent on good Y. But, since neither the person's income nor the price of good Y has changed here, this Y-intercept is the same for both constraints. The new X-intercept is to the right of the old one, because the lower price of X means that more of it can now be bought. The flatter

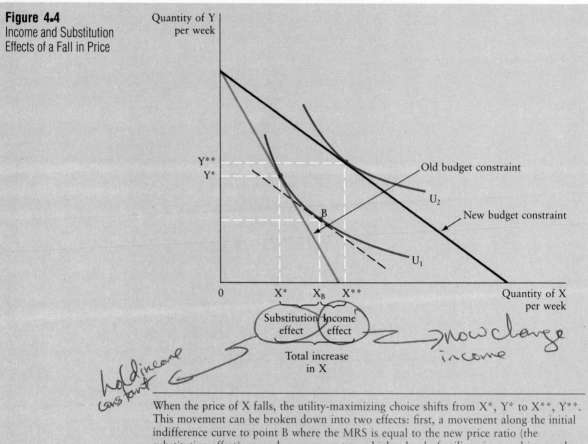

Figure 4.4
Income and Substitution
Effects of a Fall in Price

Quantity of Y
per week

Y**
Y*

B

Old budget constraint

U_2

New budget constraint

U_1

0   X*   X$_B$ X**   Quantity of X
                                                       per week

Substitution Income
effect   effect

Total increase
in X

hold income constant

now change income

When the price of X falls, the utility-maximizing choice shifts from X*, Y* to X**, Y**.
This movement can be broken down into two effects: first, a movement along the initial
indifference curve to point B where the MRS is equal to the new price ratio (the
substitution effect); second, a movement to a higher level of utility, since real income has
increased (the increase effect). Both the substitution and income effects cause more X to
be bought when its price declines. The Y-intercept is the same for both budget
constraints, because both P_Y and I are held constant.

slope of the budget constraint shows us that the relative price of X to Y (that
is, P_X/P_Y) has fallen.

With this change in the budget constraint, the new position of maximum
utility is at X**, Y**. There the new budget line is tangent to the indifference
curve U_2. The movement to this new set of choices is caused by two effects.
First, the change in the slope of the budget constraint would have motivated
the individual to move to point B even if the person had stayed on the original
indifference curve U_1. The dashed line in Figure 4.4 has the same slope as the
new budget constraint but it is tangent to U_1 because we are holding "real"
income (that is, utility) constant. A relatively lower price for X causes the

Are Children Inferior?

One decision that seems to involve an inferior good is the decision to have children. Table 4.3 lists U.S. birth rates and average annual earnings (adjusted to 1980 dollars) from 1890 to 1980. During that period, except for a temporary increase in the years after World War II, birth rates fell rather sharply. At the same time average real income nearly quadrupled. As Americans have become richer they seem to choose to demand fewer children. This pattern is also found in most other countries throughout the world. Does this pattern mean that children are "inferior" goods? Somehow the notion that people's preferences for children are similar to their preferences for rotgut whiskey or used clothing is a bit hard to believe. People seem to enjoy parenthood too much and spend too much money on their children for us to accept such a conclusion.

Economists are reluctant to accept at face value data that seems to show inferiority. They look for other explanations for the data. Most commonly, economists argue in this case that many other factors besides the decline in the birth rate go along with rising income levels. Interpreting the relationship of income and birth rates is more difficult than it at first appears. The figures in Table 4.3 do not hold other things constant and therefore do not truly reflect inferiority. Two of the explanations that follow this route deal with the quality versus quantity distinction and the cost of children.

Table 4.3
U.S. Birth Rates and Earnings since 1890

Year	Birth Rate per 1,000 Population	Average Annual Earnings in 1980 Dollars
1890	33.7	$ 4,210
1900	32.3	4,515
1910	30.1	4,905
1920	27.7	5,370
1930	21.3	6,275
1940	19.4	7,104
1950	24.1	9,580
1960	23.7	12,694
1970	18.4	15,239
1980	15.3	15,475

Source: Computed from various series in *U.S. Historical Statistics from Colonial Times to 1970* and *U.S. Statistical Abstract, 1980.*

Quality versus Quantity

Economist Gary Becker was one of the first to point out that a couple's decision to have children really has two dimensions: a decision about how many to have (quantity) and a series of decisions about how much money to spend on their upbringing (quality).[3] As people earn more money it seems likely that they will be more in-

(continued)

individual to move from X*, Y* to B if he or she is not better off as a result of the lower price. This movement is a graphic demonstration of the substitution effect. Even though the individual is no better off, the change in price still causes a change in consumption choices.

Second, the further move from B to the final consumption choice X**, Y** is identical to the kind of movement we described in Figure 4.1 for changes

---

[3]Gary S. Becker, "An Economic Analysis of Fertility," in *Demographic and Economic Change in Developed Countries,* National Bureau Conference Series 11 (Princeton, N.J.: Princeton University Press, 1960).

terested in the quality dimension of their children (by buying braces, violin lessons, college educations, and so forth). They may choose to have fewer children but to spend much more in total on the quality of their upbringing. Hence, the data on number of children may be entirely consistent with the notion that children are "normal" goods, just as the fact that individuals purchase more expensive cars as their incomes rise must be taken into account in determining how car purchases respond to changes in income.

The Price of Children
Another view of the data on birth rates considers how the cost of having children changes with increasing levels of affluence. This view argues that costs rise rapidly primarily because of the opportunity cost of the wages that are no longer earned by parents who stay home to provide child care. In the United States during the past hundred years, for example, it is argued that rising wages for women have sharply increased the opportunity cost of childbearing, and that is why birth rates have fallen.

Once this cost is taken into account, many authors find that the direction of the relationship between income and birth rate is reversed—that is, children do seem to be a "normal" good once other things (most importantly the "price" of children) are held constant.[4]

To Think About
1. Many less developed countries have attempted to control the size of their populations by adopting stringent birth control programs. How would the analysis provided in this application explain the rapid population growth rates of many less developed countries and what would it suggest about the likely success of such birth control programs? Would economic growth be a successful way to limit population growth?
2. How do high income tax rates affect couples' decisions to have children? Might such taxes have different effects depending on which family member we examine? Should tax rates be varied to take family responsibilities into account?

in income. Because the price of X has fallen, but nominal income (I) has stayed the same, the individual has a greater "real" income and can afford a higher utility level (U_2). If X is a normal good the individual will now demand more of it. This is the income effect of changing only the price of X. Both the substitution effect and the income effect cause the individual to choose more X when the price of X declines.

People do not actually move from X^*, Y^* to point B and then to X^{**}, Y^{**} when the price of a good changes. We never observe the point B; only the two actual choices of X^*, Y^* and X^{**}, Y^{**} are made. The analysis of income and substitution effects in this way is still valuable because it shows that a price change affects the quantity demanded of a good in two conceptually different ways.

We can use the hamburger–soft drink example to show these effects at work. Suppose that the price of soft drinks falls to $.05 from the earlier price of $.10. This price change will increase the individual's purchasing power.

---

[4] A great deal of this evidence is reviewed in T. W. Schultz, ed., "New Economic Approaches to Fertility," *Journal of Political Economy*, March/April 1973.

Whereas earlier 10 soft drinks could be bought with a dollar, now a dollar can buy 20 of them. The price decrease shifts the budget constraint and increases utility. The individual now will choose some different combination of hamburgers and soft drinks than before—if only because the previous choice of three hamburgers and four soft drinks (under the old budget constraint) now leaves $.20 in income unspent.

In making the new choices the individual is influenced by two different effects. First, even if we hold constant the individual's utility by compensating for the positive effect the price change has on utility, the individual will still act so that the MRS is brought into line with the new price ratio (now one hamburger to four soft drinks). This compensated response is the substitution effect. Even with a constant real income the individual will still choose more soft drinks and fewer hamburgers.

In actuality, real income has also increased; in order to assess the total effect of the price change on the demand for soft drinks, we must also investigate the effect of the change in purchasing power. Because the individual's real income has increased, this (assuming soft drinks are normal goods) would be another reason to expect soft drink purchases to increase.

Substitution and Income Effects from an Increase in Price

We can use a similar analysis to see what happens if the price of good X increases. The budget line in Figure 4.5 shifts inward because of an increase in the price of X. The Y-intercept for the budget constraint again does not change since neither income nor P_Y has changed. The slope of the budget constraint is now steeper, however, because X costs more than it did before.

The movement from the initial point of utility maximization (X^*, Y^*) to the new point X^{**}, Y^{**} is again caused by two forces. First, even if the individual stayed on the initial indifference curve (U_2), he or she would substitute Y for X and move along U_2 to point B. At this point the dashed line (with the same slope as the new budget constraint) is just tangent to the indifference curve U_2. The movement from X^*, Y^* to B along U_2 is the substitution effect. However, because purchasing power is reduced by the increase of the price of X (the amount of income remains constant, but now X costs more), the person must move to a lower level of utility, which is the income effect of the higher price. In Figure 4.5 both the income and substitution effects work in the same direction and cause the quantity demanded of X to fall in response to an increase in its price.

Summary of Substitution and Income Effects

How does the quantity demanded of X change graphically in response to changes in the price of $X(P_X)$? Because of the substitution effect, the quantity demanded of X always moves in a direction opposite to the direction of the

Figure 4.5
Income and Substitution
Effects of an Increase
in Price

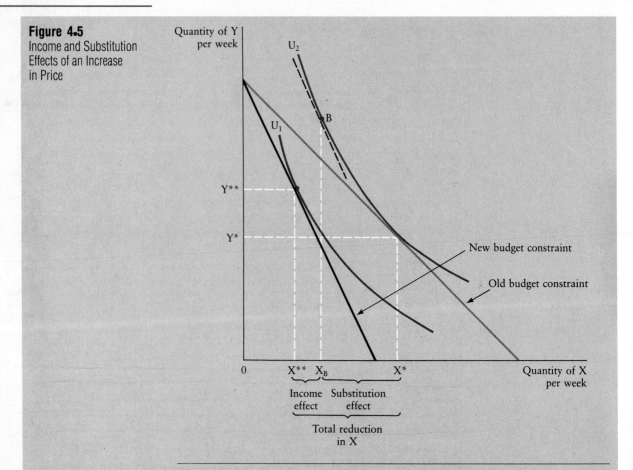

When the price of good X increases, the budget constraint shifts inward. The movement from the initial utility-maximizing point (X*, Y*) to the new point (X**, Y**) can be analyzed as two separate effects. The substitution effect causes a movement to point B on the initial indifference curve (U₂). The price increase would also create a loss of purchasing power. This income effect causes a consequent movement to a lower indifference curve. The income and substitution effects together cause the quantity demanded of X to fall as a result of the increase in its price. Again, the Y-intercept of the budget constraint is not affected by the change in the price of X.

price change. A decrease in P_X lowers the price ratio (P_X/P_Y). To reestablish the tangency condition for utility maximization, the MRS must also fall. In order to reduce the MRS, the person will choose more X and less Y by moving in a southeasterly direction along the indifference curve. Consequently the quantity of X increases as a result of the substitution effect. This result is a direct consequence of the assumption (introduced in Chapter 3) of a diminishing MRS.

Similarly, an increase in the price of X raises the price ratio (P_X/P_Y). The individual moves to a point on the indifference curve with a higher MRS. This

APPLYING ECONOMICS

The Substitution Effect with a Gasoline Tax and Tax Rebate

Substitution effects are sometimes called "compensated price effects" to show that real income (that is, utility) is being held constant. The importance of holding real income constant can be shown using a policy that was proposed (but never implemented) to reduce U.S. gasoline use after the 1973 Arab oil embargo. The proposal called for a large excise tax on gasoline of at least $.25 per gallon to discourage its use. Economic policymakers were afraid that this tax would dangerously reduce consumer purchasing power and add to recessionary pressures. They also proposed that the revenues collected under the tax be fully returned to consumers as a tax rebate.[5] The total proposal was a way to make a "compensated" price change in order to reduce gasoline sales.

The proposal is illustrated in Figure 4.6. Gasoline purchases (X) are shown on the horizontal axis and purchases of all other goods (Y) are shown on the vertical axis. With the initial budget constraint, the consumer chooses combination X^*, Y^*. The new gasoline tax alone would shift the budget constraint to the line labeled "excise tax" and the individual would now choose combination X', Y'. Gasoline purchases would decrease from X^* to X' and utility would be reduced from U_2 to U_1.

When the effects of the proposed tax rebate are also considered, the budget constraint would shift outward to the "excise tax and rebate" line. The consumer would now choose X'', Y''. With the rebate gasoline consumption would increase slightly over what it would have been under the pure excise tax ($X'' > X'$). Still, the combination of the tax and the rebate would cause a

Figure 4.6
The Gasoline Excise Tax and Tax Rebate Proposal

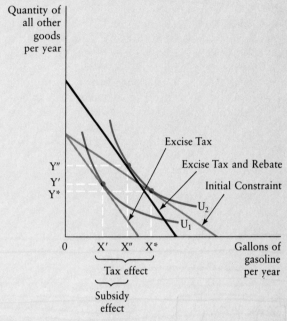

An excise tax on gasoline that shifts the budget constraint inward would reduce gasoline purchases from X^* to X' and utility from U_2 to U_1. Adding a tax rebate shifts the excise tax budget constraint outward to restore utility nearly to the U_2 level. Gasoline purchases are reduced under the policy combination (from X^* to X'') because of a "compensated" price effect.

(continued)

means choosing more Y and less X; the quantity demanded of X decreases. The assumption of a diminishing MRS means that the substitution effect will always cause the quantity demanded of X to change in the direction opposite to the direction of the change in its price.

---

[5]It was not proposed that each rebate would be equal to the exact amount paid by the individual in gasoline taxes. That would cause no actual price effect and (presumably) no change in consumption. Rather, the proposed tax rebate was planned only to compensate the "average" taxpayer.

reduction in the purchase of gasoline from its original level, with little loss in utility.[6]

What would the expected change in gasoline sales be as a result of this policy combination? Historical data suggest that the $.25 increase in gasoline price would reduce the average family's purchases by about 250 gallons per year from 1,250 gallons per year to about 1,000 gallons in 1973. The average tax collected would amount to $250 (= $0.25 × 1,000). This means that the tax would reduce the family's income by $250, and also would result in a $250 rebate check.

Historical data also suggest that this $250 gain in annual income would cause a 20-gallon increase in annual gasoline purchases per family, since gasoline is a normal good. The overall effect of the excise tax and tax rebate would be to reduce annual gasoline sales by a total of 230 gallons per family (about 23 percent) of its previous level).

Even though this proposal was never enacted (it was rather unpopular politically), it is one of the clearest examples of how important it is to consider both the substitution and income effects of a price change. We can see how it might be possible to compensate for the income effect of a tax meant to reduce consumption of a particular good.

To Think About

1. Under what conditions would this combined tax-rebate plan have had no effect on the amount of gasoline bought by the typical consumer? Why might such a result occur? Would you expect such a result to be more likely to represent only a short-term response, or would it be likely to hold over the longer term, too?

2. Suppose that the government had not rebated the gasoline tax revenues, but instead had spent the proceeds on government programs. Would it make a difference (in terms of the ultimate effect on gasoline purchases) what the government spent these proceeds on?

Substitution effects are only part of the story. To determine the total effect of a change in P_X on the quantity demanded of X, we must also consider income effects. Now the analysis may become somewhat more complex. A change in the price of good X affects an individual's real income, and we must analyze how this income change affects quantity demanded. When X is a normal good (that is, the quantity demanded of X increases as income increases), income effects reinforce substitution effects: again, price and quantity move in opposite directions. For example, a decrease in P_X causes real income to rise, and the person will choose to consume more X (since X is a normal good). The substitution effect is reinforced by the income effect. Similarly, when P_X increases, real income falls and the quantity of X demanded falls; this also reinforces the substitution effect. For normal goods, then, income and substitution effects reinforce each other, and both cause the price of X

---

[6]Although Figure 4.6 draws the rebate budget constraint precisely tangent to the original indifference curve (U_2), that construction is not strictly correct. Even if the excise tax revenues were fully rebated, the typical individual would not be able to reach his or her original indifference curve (see Problem 4.10. Here is another example of the lump-sum principle of taxation discussed in Applying Economics: Taxation and Lump-Sum Principle in Chapter 3. Because the gasoline excise tax distorts people's consumption choices, its effect on utility can be compensated for only by rebating more than the tax revenues collected. Conversely, as we show in Chapter 6, a subsidy to offset a price increase (as in cost-of-living adjustments) may overcompensate people if the possible substitution effects to rising prices are ignored.

Figure 4.7
Income and Substitution
Effects for an Inferior Good

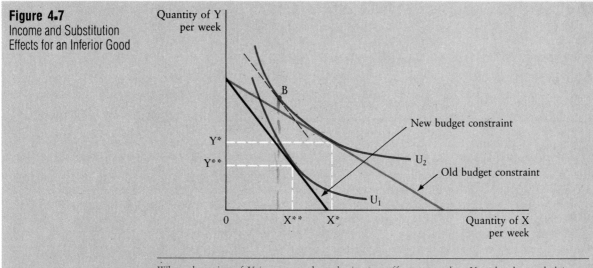

When the price of X increases, the substitution effect causes less X to be demanded (as shown by a movement to point B on the indifference curve U_2). However, because good X is inferior, the lower real income brought about by its price increase causes the quantity demanded of X to increase from B to X**. In this particular example, the substitution effect outweighs the income effect and X** < X*.

and the quantity demanded of X to move in opposite directions. That was the case in both Figures 4.4 and 4.5. As we can see in these figures, both the substitution and the income effects cause the quantity demanded of X to move in a direction opposite to the assumed direction of change in P_X.

Applying Economics: The Substitution Effect with a Gasoline Tax and Tax Rebate focuses on the substitution effect of a real-world price change. Applying Economics: Rising Gasoline Prices and Increasing Substitution Effects looks at the long-term effect of such a price change.

Substitution and Income Effects for an Inferior Good

We cannot predict exactly the effect of a price change on consumption of an inferior good. The income and substitution effects of this good's price change have opposite effects on the quantity demanded. Because inferior goods are relatively rare, we will only briefly look at this case.

Figure 4.7 shows the income and substitution effects from an increase in P_X when X is an inferior good. As the price of X rises, the substitution effect causes the individual to choose less X. This substitution effect is represented by a movement from the initial point X*, Y* to point B. This movement is exactly the same as in Figure 4.5 for a normal good. Because P_X has increased, however, the individual now has a lower real income and must move to a lower indifference curve, U_1. The individual will choose X**, Y**. At X** more X is chosen than at point B. This happens because good X is an inferior

Rising Gasoline Prices and Increasing Substitution Effects

The substitution effect of a price change may change with the length of time during which an individual adapts to the new price. If only a short period is involved, people may find it difficult to change their behavior very much for several reasons. It takes time for the price change to affect people; their reaction to it may require a change in well-established routines; and they may need to proceed slowly in deciding which of a wide variety of substitute products to buy. These reasons may have a different effect in the long run when people have the time and opportunity to make complete adjustments to new prices.

People's reactions to the rapidly rising gasoline prices during the 1970s are an excellent example of these long-term effects. The adjustment people can make to a price change depends a great deal on how long the change is in place. Over the short term, gasoline purchases are relatively difficult to alter. People own particular types of cars they must drive to work and for other necessary reasons. Everyone will complain about the higher gasoline prices, but in the short run there is little they can do about it. However, if prices stay high for a long period, a number of adjustments can be made. People may change their commuting patterns by joining car pools, they may take fewer spur-of-the-moment trips to the store or to visit friends, and, eventually, they may buy more fuel-efficient automobiles. Even though people would take a while to adapt to higher gasoline prices, the changes resulting from the higher prices could be substantial.

Some of these changes are presented in Table 4.4, which shows estimated responses in the United States to a 50 percent increase in the price of gasoline. This is approximately the level of increase both in 1973–1974 and in 1979–1980. It is estimated that this increase causes a decrease in gasoline consumption of about 15 percent over the short term. Roughly half of that adjustment is caused by a reduction in the number of miles driven. The other half comes from an increase in the number of miles per gallon experienced by the total fleet of cars in the United States. Since this stock of cars does not change much in the short run, the mileage improvement must result from better automobile maintenance and

Table 4.4
Estimated Reaction of U.S. Consumers to a 50 Percent Rise in the Retail Price of Gasoline

Time Period	Reduction in Miles Driven	Increase in Miles per Gallon	Total Change in Consumption
Short term	−7%	+8%	−15%
Long term	−4	+24	−28

Source: Calculated from figures given in Carol A. Dahl, "Consumer Adjustment to a Gasoline Tax," *Review of Economics and Statistics,* August 1979, pp. 427–431.

lower highway speeds. In the long run, older, low-mileage cars may be traded in for more fuel-efficient models, and the mileage effect becomes substantial.

Table 4.4 indicates that a 50 percent increase in gasoline price would cause a 24 percent increase in miles per gallon (say, from an average of 14 miles per gallon to over 17 miles per gallon) in the long term, and that effect provides the bulk of the overall long-term response to the price change. The lesson in the gasoline price increase is that it may take time for people to react and adjust to price changes. That is especially true when major changes in behavior (such as buying a new car) must be made before long-term adjustments are completed and their effect calculated.

To Think About
1. During the 1970s, the federal government implemented "fuel economy standards" that U.S. auto makers were required to meet by 1985. Can you think of any reasons why the government should require people to buy more fuel-efficient cars than they would choose to buy on their own? Should the standards be different depending on whether gasoline prices are high or low?
2. Higher energy prices during the 1970s caused people to economize on many other kinds of energy use in addition to automobiles. What were some of these other types of energy consumption? Do you think these markets adjusted more or less quickly to rising energy prices than did the auto market?

good: as real income falls, the quantity demanded of X increases rather than declines as it would for a normal good. In Figure 4.7, however, X** is less than X*; less X is ultimately demanded in response to the rise in its price. In our example here the substitution effect is strong enough to outweigh the "perverse" income effect of an inferior good's price change. The next section shows how these results can vary, using a famous example.

Giffen's Paradox

If the income effect of a price change is strong enough, the change in P_X and the resulting change in the quantity demanded of X actually could move in the same direction. Legend has it that the English economist Robert Giffen observed this paradox in nineteenth-century Ireland—when the price of potatoes rose, people reportedly consumed more of them. This peculiar result can be explained by looking at the size of the income effect of a change in the price of potatoes. Potatoes were not only inferior goods but also used up a large portion of the Irish people's income. An increase in the price of potatoes therefore reduced real income substantially. The Irish were forced to cut back on other luxury food consumption in order to buy more potatoes. Even though this rendering of events is historically implausible, the possibility of an increase in the quantity demanded in response to the price increase of a good has come to be known as **Giffen's Paradox.**[7]

Giffen's Paradox A situation in which the increase in a good's price leads people to consume more of the good.

The paradox is illustrated graphically in Figure 4.8, which shows potato consumption on the X axis and all other goods on the Y axis. The graph shows that in response to the increase in the price of potatoes, more are demanded. Even though the substitution effect reduces consumption, the "perverse" income effect is strong enough to make the total effect of the price increase positive. Real income falls and, since potatoes are inferior goods, the demand for them increases.

This paradox is probably quite rare in the real world—not only must the good be inferior, but the positive income effect must be strong enough to outweigh the negative substitution effect. A strong income effect will not usually exist unless the good makes up a large part of the individual's expenditures (as with potatoes in nineteenth-century Ireland). We can therefore conclude that price and quantity demanded of a good will usually move in opposite directions, even when the good is inferior. That is, Giffen's Paradox will not occur except in unusual circumstances.

---

[7]A major problem with this explanation is that it disregards Marshall's observation that both supply and demand factors must be taken into account when analyzing price changes. If potato prices increased because of the potato blight in Ireland, then supply should have become smaller, so how could *more* potatoes possibly have been consumed? Also, since many Irish people were potato farmers, the potato price increase should have increased real income for them. For a detailed discussion of these and other fascinating bits of potato lore, see G. P. Dwyer and C. M. Lindsey, "Robert Giffen and the Irish Potato," *American Economic Review,* March 1984, pp. 188–192.

Figure 4.8
Giffen's Paradox

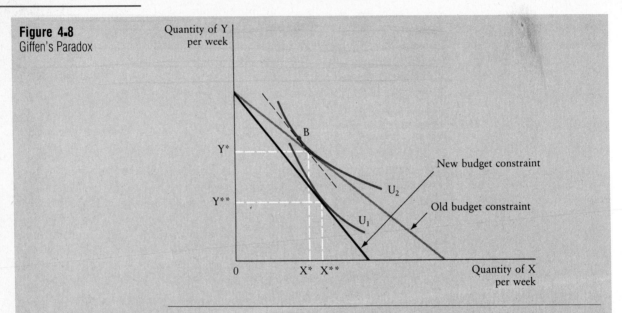

An increase in the price of X increases the quantity demanded of X. The substitution effect (the movement from X*, Y* to point B) is outweighed by the strong positive income effect from the inferiority of good X (compare this to Figure 4.7). Not every inferior good would exhibit Giffen's Paradox.

Changes in the Price of Another Good

Figures 4.4, 4.5, and 4.7 show that a change in the price of X will have an effect on the quantity demanded of the other good (Y). In Figure 4.4, for example, a decrease in the price of X causes not only the quantity demanded of X to increase, but the quantity demanded of Y to increase as well. We can explain this result by looking at the substitution and income effects on the demand for Y associated with the decrease in the price of X.

First, as we see in Figure 4.4, the substitution effect caused less Y to be demanded. In moving along the indifference curve U_1 from X*, Y* to point B, X is substituted for Y because the lower ratio of P_X/P_Y required an adjustment in the MRS. In this figure the income effect of the decline in the price of good X is strong enough to reverse this result. Since Y is a normal good, and since real income has increased, more Y is demanded: the individual

Figure 4.9
Effect on the Demand for a
Good of a Decrease in
Price of a Second Good

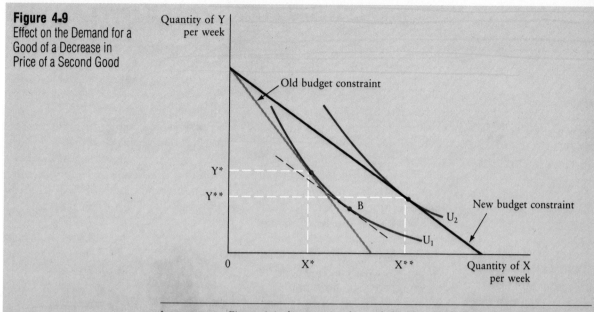

In contrast to Figure 4.4, the quantity demanded of Y now declines (from Y* to Y**) in response to a decrease in the price of X. The relatively flat indifference curves cause the substitution effect to be very large. Moving from X*, Y* to point B means giving up a substantial quantity of Y for additional X. This effect more than outweighs the positive income effect (from B to X**, Y**), and the quantity demanded of Y declines. Purchases of Y may either rise or fall when the price of X falls.

moves from point B to X**, Y**. Here Y** exceeds Y*, and the total effect of the price change is to increase the demand for Y.

A slightly different set of indifference curves (that is, different preferences) could have shown different results. Figure 4.9 shows a relatively flat set of indifference curves where the substitution effect of a decline in the price of X is very large. In moving from X*, Y* to point B, a large amount of X is substituted for Y. The income effect on Y is not strong enough to reverse this large substitution effect. In this case the quantity of Y finally chosen (Y**) is smaller than the original amount. The effect a price change of one good has on the quantity demanded of some other good is ambiguous—it all depends on what the indifference curve map looks like. We have to carefully examine income and substitution effects that (at least in the case of only two goods) work in opposite directions.

Using our hamburger–soft drink example, we have already discussed the substitution and income effects that a change in the price of soft drinks (from $.10 to $.05) will have on the number of soft drinks bought. What happens to the number of hamburgers chosen? The substitution effect predicts that fewer hamburgers will be purchased. Since hamburgers are now relatively more expensive than they were before soft drink prices fell, the initial level of utility can be achieved at lower cost by drinking more soft drinks and eating fewer hamburgers.

The total effect of the soft drink price decrease on hamburger purchases depends also on the income effect of the price change, however. As a result of the decrease in the price of soft drinks, the person has a higher real income and may buy more soft drinks and more hamburgers. The total effect of the price change on hamburger purchases is therefore ambiguous. This substitution effect works to decrease hamburger purchases, whereas the income effect works to increase such purchases.

Substitutes and Complements

Economists use the terms substitutes and complements to describe the way people may see the relationship between two goods. Complements are goods that go together in the sense that people will increase their use of both goods simultaneously. Examples of complements might be coffee and cream, fish and chips, peanut butter and jelly, or brandy and cigars. Substitutes, on the other hand, are goods that replace one another. Tea and coffee, hamburgers and hot dogs, or wheat and corn are some goods that are substitutes for each other.

Whether two goods are substitutes or complements of each other is primarily a question of the shape of people's indifference curves. The market behavior of individuals in their purchases of goods helps define these relationships. Two goods are **complements** if an increase in the price of one causes a decrease in quantity consumed of the other. For example, an increase in the price of coffee might cause not only the quantity demanded of coffee to decline, but also the demand for cream to decrease because of the complementary relationship between cream and coffee. Similarly, coffee and tea are **substitutes** because an increase in the price of coffee might cause the quantity demanded of tea to increase, as tea replaces coffee in use.

How the demand for one good relates to the price increase of another good is a result of both income and substitution effects. It is only the combined "gross" result of these two effects that we can observe. Including both income and substitution effects of price increases in our definitions of substitutes and complements can sometimes lead to problems, however. For example, it is theoretically possible for X to be a complement for Y and at the same time for Y to be a substitute for X. This perplexing state of affairs has led some economists to favor a definition of substitutes and complements that looks

Complements
Two goods such that when the price of one increases, the quantity demanded of the other falls. $P_x \uparrow Q_y \downarrow$

Substitutes
Two goods such that if the price of one increases, the quantity demanded of the other rises. $P_x \uparrow Q_y \uparrow$

only at the direction of substitution effects. We do not make that distinction in this book.[8]

Construction of Individual Demand Curves

We have now completed our discussion of how the individual's demand for good X is affected by various changes in economic circumstances. We started by writing the demand function for good X as

$$\text{Quantity of X demanded} = X = D_X (P_X, P_Y, I; \text{preferences}) \quad [4.1]$$

And then we examined how changes in each of the economic factors P_X, P_Y, and I might affect an individual's decision to purchase good X. The principal purpose of this examination has been to permit us to derive individual demand curves and to analyze those factors that might cause a demand curve to shift its position. This section shows how a demand curve can be constructed. The next section analyzes why this curve might shift.

Individual demand curve
A graphic representation of the relationship between the price of a good and the quantity of it demanded by a person.

An **individual demand curve** shows the *ceteris paribus* relationship between the quantity demanded of a good (say X) and its price (P_X). Not only are preferences held constant under the *ceteris paribus* assumption (as they have been throughout our discussion in this chapter), but the other economic factors in the demand function (that is, the price of good Y and income) are also held constant. In demand curves we are limiting our study to only the relationship between the quantity of a good chosen and its price.

Figure 4.10 shows how we can construct the demand curve for good X. In Graph (a) the individual's indifference curve map is drawn using three different budget constraints in which the price of X decreases. These decreasing prices are P_X', P_X'', and P_X'''. The other economic factors that affect the position of the budget constraint (the price of good Y and income) do not change. In graphic terms, all three constraints have the same Y-intercept. The lower prices of X rotate this constraint outward. Given the three separate budget constraints, the individual's utility-maximizing choices of X are given by X', X'', and X'''. These three choices show that the quantity demanded of X increases as the price of X falls.

Shape of the Demand Curve

The information in Graph (a) in Figure 4.10 can be used to construct the demand curve shown in Graph (b). The price of X is shown on the vertical

---

[8]For a slightly more extended treatment of this subject, see Walter Nicholson, *Microeconomic Theory: Basic Principles and Extensions,* 3d ed. (Hinsdale, Ill.: Dryden Press, 1985), pp. 142–145. For a complete treatment, see J. R. Hicks, *Value and Capital* (London: Cambridge University Press, 1939), Chapter 3 and the mathematical appendix.

Figure 4.10
Construction of an
Individual's Demand Curve

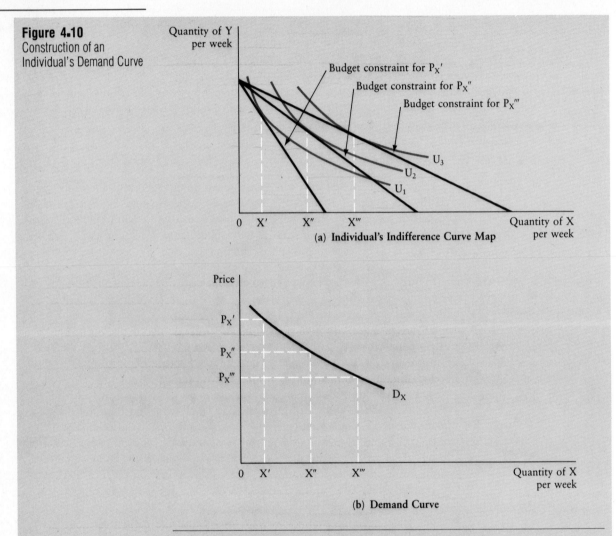

In Graph (a) the individual's utility-maximizing choices of X and Y are shown for three successively lower prices of X. In Graph (b) this relationship between P_X and X is used to construct the demand curve for X. The demand curve is drawn on the assumption that the price of Y and money income remain constant as the price of X varies.

axis, and the quantity chosen continues to be shown on the horizontal axis. The demand curve (D_X) is downward sloping, showing that when the price of X falls, the quantity demanded of X increases.

The precise shape and slope of the demand curve is determined by the income and substitution effects when the price of X changes. An individual's demand curve may be either rather flat or quite steeply sloped, depending on the nature of his or her indifference curve map. If X has many close substitutes, the indifference curves will be nearly straight lines (such as those shown in Figure 4.9), and the substitution effect from a price change will be very large. The quantity of X chosen may change substantially in response to the change in its price; consequently the demand curve will be relatively flat. For example, consider a person's demand for one particular brand of cereal (say, the famous Brand X). Since any one brand has many close substitutes, the demand curve for Brand X will be relatively flat. A rise in the price of Brand X will cause people to shift easily to other kinds of cereal, and the quantity demanded of Brand X will be reduced significantly.

On the other hand, the individual's demand curve for some goods may be steeply sloped. That is, price changes will not affect consumption very much. This might be the case if the good has no close substitutes. For example, consider a person's demand for water. Because water satisfies many unique needs, it is unlikely that it would have any substitutes when the price of water rose, and the substitution effect would be very small. However, since water does not use up a large portion of a person's total income, the income effect of the increase in the price of water would also not be large. The quantity demanded of water probably would not respond greatly to changes in its price; that is, the demand curve would be nearly vertical.

As a third possibility, consider the case of food. Because food as a whole has no substitutes (although individual food items obviously do), an increase in the price of food will not induce important substitution effects. In this sense, food is similar to our water example. However, food is a major item in a person's total expenditures, and an increase in its price will have a significant effect on purchasing power. It is possible, therefore, that the quantity demanded of food may be reduced substantially in response to a change in its price because of this income effect. The demand curve for food might be flatter (that is, demand reacts more to price) than we might expect if we thought of food only as a "necessity" with few, if any, substitutes.[9]

The individual's demand curve summarizes the *ceteris paribus* relationship between the price of X and the quantity demanded of X. The income and substitution effects of changes in that price cause the person to move along his or her demand curve. If one of the factors (the price of Y, income, or preferences) that we have so far been holding constant were to change, the entire curve would shift. The demand curve remains fixed only while the *ceteris paribus* assumption is in effect.

---

[9]For this reason sometimes it is convenient to talk about demand curves that reflect only substitution effects. These compensated demand curves are constructed on the assumption that any effect of a price change on the individual's purchasing power is automatically compensated for. Hence, real income rather than nominal income is being held constant. We will not cover these compensated demand curves in this book, but they are fairly widely used in economics. For a detailed treatment, see Walter Nicholson, *Microeconomic Theory: Basic Principles and Extensions,* 3d ed. (Hinsdale, Ill.: Dryden Press, 1985), pp. 133–135.

Figure 4.11
Shifts in an Individual's
Demand Curve

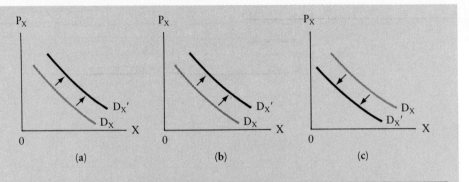

In Graph (a) the demand curve shifts outward because the individual's income has increased. More X is now demanded at each price. In Graph (b) the demand curve shifts outward because the price of Y has increased, and X and Y are substitutes for the individual. In Graph (c) the demand curve shifts inward because of the increase in the price of Y—X and Y are complements.

Shifts in an Individual's Demand Curve

When one of the factors held constant in a demand curve changes, the entire demand curve shifts to a new position. Figure 4.11 shows the kinds of shifts that might take place. In Graph (a) the effect on good X of an increase in income is shown. Assuming that good X is a normal good, an increase in income causes more X to be demanded at each price. This is the kind of effect we described early in this chapter (Figure 4.1). When income increases, people buy more X even though its price has not changed, and the demand curve shifts outward. Graphs (b) and (c) in Figure 4.11 record two possible effects that an increase in the price of Y might have on the demand curve for good X. In Graph (b), X and Y are assumed to be substitutes—for example, coffee (X) and tea (Y). An increase in the price of tea causes the individual to substitute coffee for tea. More coffee (that is, good X) is demanded at each price than was previously the case. Consequently, the demand curve shifts outward.

On the other hand, suppose X and Y are complements—for example, coffee (X) and cream (Y). An increase in the price of cream causes the demand curve for coffee to shift inward. Because coffee and cream "go together," less coffee (that is, good X) will now be demanded at each price. This shift in the demand curve is shown in Graph (c).

Changes in preferences might also cause the demand curve to shift. For example, a sudden warm spell would undoubtedly shift the entire demand curve for soft drinks outward. More drinks would be demanded at each price because now the individual's desire for them has increased. Similarly, the fashion for longer hairstyles for men in the 1960s shifted many men's demand curves for haircuts toward the origin. At each price a man would buy fewer haircuts per year than he would have in the past. "Applying Economics: Religious Practices and Fish Consumption" shows another situation that caused the position of an entire demand curve to shift.

APPLYING ECONOMICS

Religious Practices and Fish Consumption

The Roman Catholic Church has required its members to abstain from eating meat during certain periods of the year. Because fish is considered a substitute for meat, this abstinence increases the demand for fish during those periods. We can use the results of a statistical study of the demand for fish by F. W. Bell to show the effects of these shifts in demand.[10] Table 4.5 reports the estimated shifts in the demand curves in the New England states for four species of fish.

The effects of abstinence from eating meat during Lent and the end of the "meatless Friday" practice in December 1966 are shown here. For both cases the shifts in demand curves have been measured in a horizontal direction: that is, the figures report the total change in quantity of fish consumed, holding price constant.

As Table 4.5 shows, the increase in demand for fish during Lent is substantial. During this period people substitute fish for meat, thereby shifting their demand curves for various species of fish to the right. This type of seasonal influence on demand is quite common. For example, demand for ice cream and air conditioning increases during the summer months, demand for turkeys increases at Thanksgiving, and demand for wedding cakes increases in June. Since these shifts are reasonably predictable, firms can take them into account in planning their production and their inventory holdings.

In December 1966, Roman Catholic bishops in America ended mandatory meatless Fridays. As Table 4.5 shows, the demand for some kinds of fish decreased as people changed their purchases back to meat. Unexpected reductions in demand for other goods in recent years have been related to health concerns (cranberries, swordfish, and artificially sweetened beverages have all been subject to "cancer scares"), political motivations (boycotting table grapes or certain textile manufactur-

Table 4.5
Effects of Religious Practices on Fish Consumption in the New England States (in Thousands of Pounds per Month)

Species	Increase in Demand during Lent	Reduction in Demand after December 1966
Yellowtail flounder	+17.8	−4.4
Large haddock	+25.3	−7.1
Small haddock (scrod)	+13.3	−0.6
Cod	+29.0	−4.5

Source: F. W. Bell. "The Pope and the Price of Fish," *American Economic Review,* December 1968, pp. 1346–1350.

ers), or development of superior substitutes (slide rules and mechanical calculators being replaced by electronic calculators). Some of these shifts were relatively permanent (rather than seasonal) and may have imposed hardships on some producers. In the case of fish, that hardship is ironic since one reason for the original meatless Friday decree more than one thousand years ago was to aid the fishing industry in Naples.

To Think About

1. In this chapter we have identified three factors that shift a demand curve: changes in income, changes in the price of some other good, and changes in preferences. Which of these explanations best fits the case described in this example? Might it be possible to use two of the explanations?

2. Why do fish prices change so sharply in response to such a readily predictable event as Lent? Can't a speculator make a lot of money by buying fish when they are cheap prior to Lent and selling them when they are in high demand?

---

[10]F. W. Bell, "The Pope and the Price of Fish," *American Economic Review,* December 1968, pp. 1346–1350. The original Bell study reported shifts in the vertical (price) direction. We have recalculated them here to show quantity changes.

Increase or decrease in quantity demanded
The increase or decrease in quantity demanded caused by a change in the good's price. Graphically represented by the movement along a demand curve.

Increase or decrease in demand
The change in demand for a good caused by changes in the price of another good, income, or preferences. Graphically represented by a shift of the entire demand curve.

It is important that we keep the distinction between the shift in a demand curve and movement along a stationary demand curve clearly in mind. Changes in the price of X lead to movements along the demand curve for good X. Changes in other economic factors (such as a change in income or a change in another good's price) cause the entire demand curve for X to shift. If we wished to see how a change in the price of steak would affect a person's steak purchases, we would use a single demand curve and study movements along it. On the other hand, if we wanted to know how a change in income would affect the quantity of steak purchased, we would have to study the shift in the position of the entire demand curve.

The movement downward along a stationary demand curve is an **increase in quantity demanded**. A shift outward in the entire curve is an **increase in demand**. A rise in the price of a good causes a **decrease in quantity demanded** (a move along the demand curve), whereas a change in some other factor may cause a **decrease in demand** (a shift of the entire curve to the left). It is important to be precise in using those terms; they are not interchangeable.

Summary

This chapter uses the model of individual choice to examine how people react to changes in income or prices. We come to four major conclusions about the factors that affect the demand for a good:

- When income increases, the demand for a good will increase unless that good is inferior.
- A change in the price of a good has substitution and income effects that together cause changes in consumption choices. Except in the unlikely case of Giffen's Paradox, a reduction in a good's price will cause more of it to be demanded. An increase in price will cause less of the good to be demanded.
- A change in the price of one good will usually affect the demand for other goods. If two goods are complements, an increase in the price of one will reduce the demand for the other. If the goods are substitutes an increase in the price of one will increase the demand for the other.
- The demand for a good is also affected by preferences. Preferences are usually held constant under the *ceteris paribus* assumption in theoretical analysis.

Probably the most important tool developed in this chapter is the individual's demand curve, which shows the relationship between the quantity demanded of a product and its price (when all other influences are held constant). Demand curves are usually drawn downward sloping. They shift if one of the factors held constant (income, other prices, preferences) changes. In Chapter 5 we show how individual demand curves can be combined to come up with the market demand curve, which helps to determine market prices.

Problems

4.1 Ms. Boring maximizes her utility by spending her entire income on goods A, B, and C (whose prices stay constant in this problem). Ms. Boring makes $300 per week and purchases 10 units of good A, 10 units of good B, and 10 units of good C. When Ms. Boring's income rises to $400 per week, she buys 9 units of good A, 17 units of good B, and 14 units of good C. Finally, Ms. Boring gets another pay increase to $500 per week and purchases 8 units of good A, 26 units of good B, and 16 units of good C.

    a. Using the above information, construct the Engel curve for goods A, B, and C.

    b. Explain the nature of each good: is it normal or inferior? A "luxury" or "necessity?"

4.2 Elizabeth M. Suburbs makes $200 a week at her summer job and spends her entire weekly income on new sweaters and designer jeans since these are the only two items that provide utility to her. Furthermore, Elizabeth insists that for every sweater she buys, she must also buy a pair of jeans (without the jeans, the new sweater is worthless). Therefore, she buys the same number of sweaters and jeans in any given week.

    a. If jeans cost $20 and sweaters cost $20, how many will Elizabeth buy of each?

    b. Suppose that the price of jeans rises to $30 a pair. How many sweaters and jeans will she buy?

    c. Show your results by graphing the budget constraints from parts a and b. Also draw Elizabeth's indifference curves. Why do these "curves" look different than those you have seen before? (Hint: Elizabeth insists on buying in a fixed proportion of one sweater to one pair of jeans. Buying one more sweater without purchasing jeans does *not* increase her utility.)

    d. To what effect (income or substitution) do you attribute the change in utility levels between parts a and b?

4.3 Mr. Wright, a clothing salesman, is forced to spend at least a large minimum amount of his income on clothing. Show that his utility level is lower than if he could freely allocate his income.

4.4 Pete Moss buys 100 units of fertilizer and 80 units of grass seed along with quantities of other goods. The price of fertilizer rises by $.40 per unit and the price of grass seed drops by $.50 per unit; other prices and Pete's income remain unchanged. Will Pete buy more, less, or the same amount of fertilizer? Explain.

4.5 Show that if there are only two goods (X and Y) to choose from, both cannot be inferior goods.

4.6 Show that if there are only two goods (X and Y) to choose from, whether they are substitutes or complements will depend on whether the substitution or income effect is larger. Illustrate each case with a carefully drawn graph.

4.7 If a person consumes only two goods, X and Y, and good X exhibits Giffen's Paradox, how does an increase in the price of X affect the quantity of Y purchased? What happens to total spending on X and Y?

*4.8 David N. gets $3 per month as an allowance to spend any way he pleases. Since he only likes peanut butter and jelly sandwiches, he spends the entire amount on peanut butter (at $.05 per ounce) and jelly (at $.10 per ounce). Bread is provided free of charge by a concerned neighbor. David is a particular eater and makes his sandwiches with exactly 1 oz. of jelly and 2 oz. of peanut butter. He is set in his ways and will never change these proportions.

a. How much peanut butter and jelly will David buy with his $3 allowance in a week?

b. Suppose the price of jelly were to rise to $.15 per ounce. How much of each commodity would be bought?

c. By how much should David's allowance be increased to compensate for the rise in the price of jelly in part b?

d. Graph your results of parts a to c.

e. In what sense does this problem only involve a single commodity, peanut butter and jelly sandwiches? Graph the demand curve for this single commodity.

f. Discuss the results of this problem in terms of the income and substitution effects involved in the demand for jelly.

*4.9 Each year Sam Mellow grows 200 units of wheat and 100 units of sunflower seeds for his own consumption and for sale to the outside world. Wheat and sunflower seeds are the only two items that provide utility to Sam. They are also his only source of income. Sam cannot save his proceeds from year to year. Hint: To start this problem show that Sam's budget constraint always passes through the point

Wheat = 200, Sunflower seeds = 100.

a. If the price of wheat is $2 per unit and sunflower seeds sell for $10 per unit, Sam chooses to sell 20 units of the sunflower seeds he produces while retaining 80 units for his own use. Show Sam's utility-maximizing situation and indicate both his initial production levels and the amount of additional wheat he will buy with the proceeds from his sunflower seed sales.

b. Suppose sunflower seed prices fall to $6 per unit while wheat prices remain unchanged. Will Sam be made better or worse off by this price decline? Or is the situation ambiguous? Explain carefully us-

---

*Denotes a problem that is rather difficult.

ing a graphic analysis. Show that if Sam is to be made better off by the price decline he must become a seller of wheat and a buyer of sunflower seeds.

c. Explain using the terms "income effect" and "substitution effect" why the analysis in part b differs from the usual case in which a price decline always increases an individual's utility level.

4.10 Suppose the government imposes an excise tax on gasoline and rebates the complete proceeds to the taxpayers as discussed in "Applying Economics: The Substitution Effect with a Gasoline Tax and Tax Rebate."

a. Show that the size of the average tax rebate will generally not be large enough to permit the average consumer to return to his or her pretax utility level.

b. Show that if gasoline and other goods must be used in fixed proportion (that is, that there are no substitutes for gasoline) the tax rebate is just sufficient to return to the original equilibrium.

c. What can you conclude about the relationship between substitution effects and the inefficiency of various taxation schemes?

CHAPTER 5

Market Demand

Chapter 4 demonstrates how an individual's demand curve for a good can be constructed using an indifference curve map. This demand curve generally will be downward sloping, and the curve will shift when factors such as income and other prices change. Chapter 5 now deals with "adding up" individual demand curves to create the market demand curve. Market demand curves reflect the actions of many people and show how these actions are affected by market price.

We also will define a few ways of measuring market demand curves. We introduce the concept of elasticity, and show how we can use it to record the changes in the quantity demanded of a good in response to changes in income and prices. The final section of the chapter reviews some empirical evidence relating to real-world demand curves, and we show how this evidence can be used to predict changes in people's consumption patterns.

Market Demand Curves

Market demand
The total quantity of a good or service demanded by all potential buyers.

The **market demand** for a good is the total quantity of the good demanded by all potential buyers. The **market demand curve** shows the relationship between this demand and the market price of the good, when all other factors are held constant. The market demand curve's shape and position are determined by the shape of individuals' demand curves for the product in question. Market demand is nothing more than the combined effect of many people's economic choices.

Figure 5.1
Constructing a Market
Demand Curve from
Individual Demand Curves

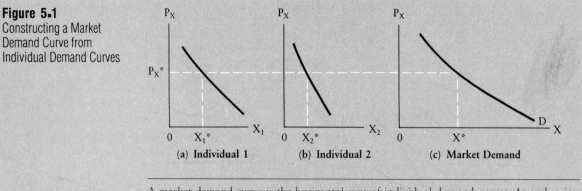

(a) Individual 1   (b) Individual 2   (c) Market Demand

A market demand curve is the horizontal sum of individual demand curves. At each price the quantity demanded in the market is the sum of the amounts each person demands. For example, at P_X^* the demand in the market is $X_1^* + X_2^* = X^*$.

Market demand curve
The relationship between the total quantity demanded of a good or service and its price holding all other factors constant.

Construction of the Market Demand Curve

Figure 5.1 shows the construction of the market demand curve for good X when there are only two buyers. For each price, the point on the market demand curve is found by summing the quantities demanded by each individual. For example, at a price of P_X^*, Individual 1 demands X_1^*, and Individual 2 demands X_2^*. The total quantity demanded at the market at P_X^* is therefore the sum of these two amounts: $X^* = X_1^* + X_2^*$. Consequently the point X^*, P_X^* is one point on the market demand curve D. The other points on the curve are plotted in the same way. The market curve is simply the "sum" of each individual's demand curve. At every possible price, we ask how much is demanded by each person, and then we sum up these amounts to arrive at the quantity demanded by the whole market.

Shifts in the Market Demand Curve

The demand curve summarizes the *ceteris paribus* relationship between the quantity demanded of X and its price. If the other factors do not change, the position of the curve will remain fixed and will reflect how people as a group respond to price changes. Why would the market demand curve shift? To answer that question, we must first find out how individual demand curves shift and then compare the combination of these new demand curves with the old market demand. In some cases the direction of the market demand curve shift is reasonably predictable. For example, using our two buyers, if both of their incomes increase and both regard X as a normal good, then each person's demand curve would shift outward, and the market demand curve would also

Figure 5.2
Increases in Each
Individual's Income Cause
the Market Demand Curve
to Shift Outward

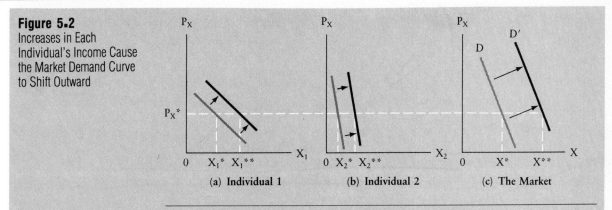

(a) Individual 1   (b) Individual 2   (c) The Market

An increase in income for each individual causes the individual demand curve for X to shift out (assuming X is a normal good). For example, at P_X^*, Individual 1 now demands X_1^{**} instead of X_1^*. The market demand curve shifts out to D'. X^* was demanded at P_X^* before the income increase. Now X^{**} ($= X_1^{**} + X_2^{**}$) is demanded.

shift outward. At each price more would be demanded in the market because each person's income had increased. This situation is illustrated in Figure 5.2.

In other cases the shifts may be more ambiguous. For example, suppose that the first person's income increases but the second person's income decreases. The location of the market demand curve now depends on the relative shifts in the individual demand curves that these income changes cause.

Figure 5.3 shows the market demand curve shifting to a different position because of different income changes for our two buyers. Individual 2's demand curve shifts inward more than Individual 1's shifts outward. The net result of these shifts is to shift the market demand curve inward to D'. If the income changes were different again, the market demand curve shift would also be different.

What holds true for our simple two-person example also applies to much larger groups of demanders—perhaps even the entire economy. In this case, the market demand summarizes the behavior of all possible consumers. If personal income in the United States as a whole were to rise, the effect on the market demand curve for pizza would depend greatly on whether the income gains went to people who love pizza or to people who never touch it. If the gains went to pizza lovers, the U.S. market demand for pizza would shift outward significantly. It would be little changed if the income gains went to pizza haters.

A change in the price of some other good (Y) will also affect the market demand for X. If the price of Y rises, for example, the market demand for X will shift outward if X and Y are regarded as substitutes by the buyers. On the other hand, an increase in the price of Y will cause the market demand curve for X to shift inward if most people regard the two goods as complements.

Figure 5.3
Effect of Income Changes
on Market Demand
Depends on How These
Changes Are Distributed

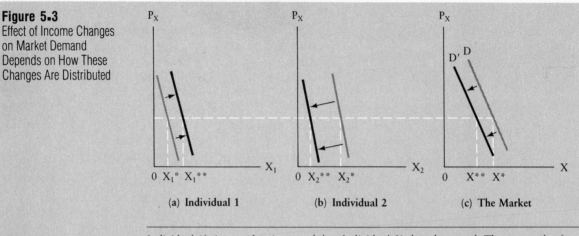

(a) **Individual 1**   (b) **Individual 2**   (c) **The Market**

Individual 1's income has increased, but Individual 2's has decreased. The net result of
these changes is to shift the market demand curve inward to D'.

A Word on Notation and Terms

Often in this book we will be looking only at one market. In order to simplify
the notation, we use the letter Q for the quantity of a good demanded (per
week) in this market, and we use P for its price. When we draw a demand
curve in the Q · P plane, we will assume that all other factors affecting demand
are held constant. That is, income, the price of other goods, and preferences
are assumed not to change. (If one of these factors should change, the demand
curve would probably shift.) As was the case for individual demand curves,
the term "change in quantity demanded" is used for a movement along a given
market demand curve, and the term "change in demand" is used for a shift
in the entire curve.

Elasticity

Economists frequently need to show how changes in one variable, say A, affect
some other variable, say B. For example, how much does the change in the
price of a good affect the quantity demanded, or how does a change in income
affect total expenditures? One problem in determining these kinds of effects
is that economic goods are measured in different units. For example, steak is
typically sold per pound, whereas oranges are sold per dozen. A $.10 per
pound rise in the price of steak might cause consumption of it to fall by two
pounds per week, and a $.10 per dozen rise in the price of oranges might
cause orange purchases to fall by one-half dozen per week. When two goods
are measured in different units, we cannot make a straight comparison between them to determine which item is more price responsive (that is, which
item's quantity demanded changes more because of a change in price).

Elasticity
The measure of the percentage change in one variable brought about by a 1 percent change in some other variable.

To be able to make these comparisons, economists use the concept of **elasticity**. In general, the elasticity of variable B with respect to changes in variable A is defined as the percentage change in B brought about by a 1 percent change in A. Elasticity is "unit-free"—it compares one percentage to another, and the units disappear. In our oranges and steak example, a 1 percent change in the price of steak might lead to a 2 percent change in the quantity bought, whereas a 1 percent change in the price of oranges might lead to only a 1 percent change in the quantity bought. Steak purchases in this example are more responsive to price than orange purchases. The fact that steak and oranges are measured in different units is no longer a problem because we can use percentage changes, which do not depend on how the good is measured.

Price Elasticity of Demand

Price elasticity of demand
The percentage change in the quantity demanded of a good in response to a 1 percent change in its price.

Although there are many different applications of elasticity in this book, probably the most important is **price elasticity of demand**. Changes in P (the price of a good) will lead to changes in Q (the quantity purchased), and the price elasticity of demand measures this relationship. Specifically, the price elasticity of demand ($e_{Q,P}$) is defined as the percentage change in quantity in response to a 1 percent change in price. In mathematical terms:

$$\text{Price elasticity of demand} = e_{Q,P} = \frac{\text{Percent change in Q}}{\text{Percent change in P}}. \quad \boxed{\frac{\%\Delta Q}{\%\Delta P}}$$

This elasticity records how Q changes in percentage terms in response to a percentage change in P. Since P and Q move in opposite directions (except in the rare case of Giffen's Paradox) $e_{Q,P}$ will be negative.[1] For example, a value of $e_{Q,P}$ of -1 means that a 1 percent rise in price leads to a 1 percent decline in quantity, whereas a value of $e_{Q,P}$ of -2 shows that a 1 percent rise in price causes quantity to decline by 2 percent.

Values of the Price Elasticity of Demand

A distinction is often made among values of $e_{Q,P}$ that are less than, equal to, or greater than -1. Table 5.1 lists the terms used for each value. For an elastic curve ($e_{Q,P}$ is less than -1), the price increase causes a more than proportional quantity decrease. For a unit elastic curve ($e_{Q,P}$ is equal to -1), the price increase and the quantity decrease are proportionally identical. For an inelastic curve ($e_{Q,P}$ is greater than -1), price increases proportionally more than quan-

[1]Sometimes the elasticity of demand is defined as the absolute value of the definition in Equation 5.1. Using this definition, elasticity is never negative; curves are classified as elastic, unit elastic, or inelastic depending on whether e_{QP} is greater than, equal to, or less than 1. You need to recognize this distinction since there is no consistent use in economic literature.

Table 5.1
Terminology of the Three
Values of $e_{Q,P}$

Value of $e_{Q,P}$ at a Point on Demand Curve	Terminology of Curve at this Point
$e_{Q,P} < -1$ so $-2, -3, -4$	Elastic
$e_{Q,P} = -1$	Unit elastic
$e_{Q,P} > -1$ so $0, 1, 2$	Inelastic

tity decreases. If a curve is elastic, price affects quantity "a lot"; if a curve is inelastic, price does not have much of an effect on quantity demanded.

We often classify goods by their price elasticities of demand. For example, the quantity of medical services demanded is undoubtedly very inelastic. The market demand curve here may be almost vertical, showing that the quantity demanded is not responsive to price changes. On the other hand, price changes will have a greater effect on the quantity demanded of a particular kind of candy bar (the demand is elastic). Here the market demand curve would be relatively flat. If market price were to change even slightly, the quantity demanded would change significantly because people would buy other candy bars.

The price elasticity of demand is a convenient way to compare the responsiveness of the quantity demanded of a good to changes in its price. The discussion of income and substitution effects in Chapter 4 gives us some theoretical basis for judging what the size of the price elasticity for particular goods might be. Goods with many close substitutes (brands of breakfast cereal, small cars, brands of electronic calculators, and so on) are subject to large substitution effects from a price change. For these kinds of goods we can presume that demand will be relatively elastic ($e_{Q,P} < -1$). On the other hand, goods with few close substitutes (water, insulin, and salt, for example) have small substitution effects when their price changes. Demand for such goods will probably be inelastic with respect to price changes ($e_{Q,P} > -1$—that is, $e_{Q,P}$ is between 0 and -1). Of course, as we mentioned previously, price changes also create income effects on the quantity demanded of a good, which we must consider to completely assess the likely size of overall price elasticities. Still, the existence (or nonexistence) of substitutes is probably the principal determinant of price elasticity.

Price Elasticity and Total Expenditures

The price elasticity of demand can be used to evaluate how total expenditures on a good change in response to a price change. Total expenditures on a good are the product of the good's price (P) times the quantity purchased (Q). If demand is elastic a price decline will cause total expenditures to increase, since

Table 5.2
Relationship between Price Changes and Changes in Total Expenditure

If Demand Is	In Response to an Increase in Price PQ Will	In Response to a Decrease in Price PQ Will
Elastic	Fall	Rise
Unit elastic	Not change	Not change
Inelastic	Rise	Fall

the percentage decline in price is more than counterbalanced by the resulting large increase in quantity demanded. For example, suppose people are currently buying 1 million automobiles at $2,000 each. Total expenditures on automobiles amount to $2 billion. Suppose also that the elasticity of demand for automobiles is −2. Now, if the price declines to $1,800 (a 10 percent drop) the quantity purchased would rise to 1.2 million cars (a 20 percent increase). Total expenditures are now $2.16 billion. Because demand is elastic, the price decline causes total expenditures to increase. This example can be easily reversed to show that if demand is elastic a price rise will cause total expenditures to fall.

If demand is unit elastic ($e_{Q,P} = -1$), total expenditures stay the same when prices change. A movement of P in one direction causes an exactly opposite proportional movement in Q, and the total price-times-quantity stays fixed.

Finally, when demand is inelastic, a price reduction will cause total expenditures to fall. There is not enough additional demand generated by the price fall to keep total expenditures from falling. A price rise in an inelastic situation, on the other hand, does not cause a very large reduction in quantity, and total revenues will increase. For example, suppose people buy 100 million bushels of wheat per year at a price of $3 per bushel. Total expenditures on wheat are $300 million. Suppose also that the price elasticity of demand for wheat is −0.5 (demand is inelastic). If the price of wheat rises to $3.60 per bushel (a 20 percent increase) quantity demanded will fall by 10 percent (to 90 million bushels). The net result of these actions is to increase total expenditures on wheat to $324 million. Because the quantity of wheat demanded is not very responsive to changes in price, total revenues are increased by a price rise. This same example could also be reversed to show that, in the inelastic case, total revenues are reduced by a fall in price.

These relationships between price elasticity and total expenditures are summarized in Table 5.2. You should think through the logic of each entry in the table to obtain a working knowledge of the elasticity concept. These relationships are used again in later chapters.

"Applying Economics: The Paradox of Agriculture" shows the effect of price inelasticity in agriculture. Elastic demand of another "good," betting on horses, is illustrated in "Applying Economics: The States' Take at the Track."

The Paradox of Agriculture

Demand for most agricultural products is relatively inelastic; even sharp changes in price do not have much effect on the quantity of food that people demand. This inelasticity of demand implies that even small changes in agricultural output can have a major impact on market prices, since these prices will have to change substantially in order to restore market equilibrium. This result gives rise to what is sometimes called the "paradox of agriculture." During periods of drought, crops are reduced and farm prices (and farmers' incomes) rise substantially. What is bad weather for the crops ends up being good for farmers. Similarly, good weather results in bumper crops and much lower agricultural prices, which may ultimately be a disaster for farmers' incomes. Because of the nature of the demand for agricultural products, the notions of "good" and "bad" weather are redefined from farmers' points of view.

Table 5.3 shows this paradox clearly with data on farm output and prices for a few recent periods. These data show that when agricultural output expanded rather rapidly (in 1951–1954, 1966–1967, and 1975–1977), prices tended to fall more than proportionally. When output fell (in 1972–1974), prices rose significantly. Real farm income followed the trends in farm prices, falling when prices fell and rising when prices rose.

The data in the table do not identify all of the factors that affected farm prices during these periods. For example, the explosion in agricultural prices during 1972–1974 was probably caused more by an unusually large sale of grain to the Soviet Union (primarily because the Soviets experienced a very poor harvest) than by the rather slight fall of U.S. output. Still, the data clearly show the importance of the relatively inelastic nature of agricultural demand in predicting the impact of external events on farm prices and incomes.

To Think About
1. This example suggests that farmers as a whole benefit from poor weather because they receive higher prices for their crops. How does that notion square with the more common-sense idea that farmers are impoverished by droughts? How are the income gains from poor weather distributed among farmers?
2. Would farmers be better off if the prices of their crops did not fluctuate so much? Would farmers take in more revenue if, say, the price of a bushel of wheat was fixed at $3 rather than constantly fluctuating between $2.50 and $3.50?

Table 5.3
The Paradox of Agriculture during Four Recent Periods

| | Percentage Change in | | |
Period	Farm Output	Farm Prices	Real Farm Income
1951–1954	+5.3%	−19.0%	−24.9%
1966–1967	+5.3	−5.7	−14.6
1972–1974	−3.6	+53.6	+39.6
1975–1977	+4.4	−4.5	−35.5

Source: Calculated from *Economic Report of the President, 1981,* Tables B-92, 94, and 95.

Is the Price Elasticity of Demand Constant?

So far in this section we have treated the price elasticity of demand as if it had the same value at every point on a demand curve. In the first Applying Economics example, when we report that the demand for agricultural products is inelastic, we assume that demand would be inelastic no matter what the market price is. In the racetrack wagering Applying Economics example we assert that demand for betting was elastic, implying that it is elastic at all possible prices. Although this rather loose use of the terms elastic and inelastic is quite common, it is important to point out that it is not strictly correct.

APPLYING ECONOMICS ▲

The States' Take at the Track

A good example of elastic demand is the case of wagering at the track. Betting on horses is big business in the United States, and many states obtain substantial revenues by taxing parimutuel wagering. New York and other states also operate off-track betting (OTB) parlors, where betting is also taxed. Since these taxes raise the "price" that bettors must pay for gambling, states pay close attention to how increases in the taxes affect the total amount bet. According to some estimates the demand for parimutuels wagering is very elastic with respect to the states' take: too high a tax rate will divert many would-be bettors to illegal bookmakers who do not collect such taxes.[2] Choosing how much tax to take out is an important practical problem for state regulators.

In one study of wagering in southern California, for example, W. D. Morgan and J. D. Vasche found that the state take-out rate of 15.75 percent in 1978 was not optimal from the state government's point of view.[3] They argued that a lower rate (of about 12 percent) would have generated enough additional attendance and wagering at thoroughbred racing to raise state revenues. As for any elastic demand curve, a reduction in price would have increased total revenues. Similar suggestions have been made for the New York OTB operation. In particular, several observers have suggested that a special 5 percent surcharge placed on OTB bets in 1974 actually resulted in a loss in total state revenues from OTB since average bets per parlor fell dramatically. It appears that the main beneficiaries of this surcharge were the illegal bookmakers (who provide the major substitute to OTB) rather than the state treasury.

To Think About
1. Do people really recognize that states tax their betting at the track? Isn't racetrack betting by its very nature an irrational, emotional activity not really subject to very careful economic calculations? Is this just one more example of carrying economic analysis too far?
2. The relatively elastic demand for betting at the track reported here implies that there must be close substitutes for such activities. What are these substitutes? How will the demand for them respond to the state's tax policies? Are these effects desirable? How would this case compare to other state taxes on specific commodities (for example, cigarettes and liquor) for which there are no close substitutes?

Nothing in economic theory requires that the elasticity of demand be the same everywhere along a demand curve. We would be more correct to say that *at current prices* the demand for agricultural products is inelastic, or that *at current prices* parimutuel wagering has an elastic demand. We need to leave open the possibility that elasticities could differ at other, different price levels.

This distinction may not be very important when only relatively small price changes are considered. When large changes in price are being considered, the possibility that the elasticity may change must be taken into account. This distinction is also true for all of the other elasticity concepts developed in this book. Even though we usually treat the elasticities as being unchanged throughout the ranges of the demand and supply curves we are examining for convenience in teaching, you still must remember that the elasticities can change.

---

[2] D. B. Suits estimates the elasticity of demand for betting to be −1.59: that is, each 10 percent increase in the take-out rate causes wagering to fall by 15.9 percent. See D. B. Suits, "The Elasticity of Demand for Gambling," *Quarterly Journal of Economics,* Summer 1979, p. 160.

[3] W. D. Morgan and J. D. Vasche, "Horseracing Demand, Parimutuel Taxation and State Revenue Potential," *National Tax Journal,* June 1979, pp. 185–194.

Figure 5.4
Elasticity of Demand Varies
along a Straight-Line
Demand Curve

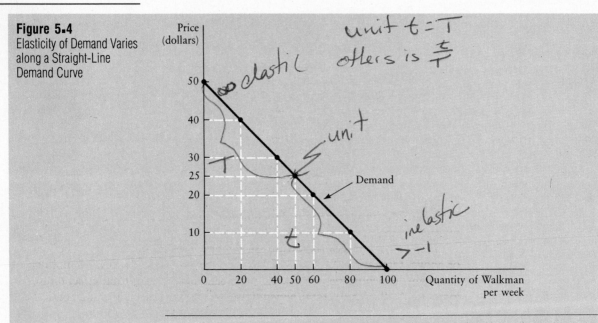

A straight-line demand curve is elastic in its upper portion, inelastic in its lower portion. This relationship is illustrated by considering how total expenditures change for different points on the demand curve.

Linear Demand Curves and Price Elasticity

Probably the most important illustration of this warning about elasticities occurs in the case of a linear (straight-line) demand curve. As one moves along such a curve the price elasticity of demand is always changing in value. At high price levels, demand is elastic: that is, a fall in price increases quantity purchased more than proportionally. At low prices, on the other hand, demand is inelastic—a further decline in price has relatively little proportional effect on quantity.

This result can be most easily proved graphically. Figure 5.4 illustrates a straight-line (linear) demand curve for, say, Walkman cassette tape players. In looking at the changing elasticity of demand along this curve, we will assume it has the specific algebraic form

$$Q = 100 - 2P \qquad [5.2]$$

(where Q is the quantity of players demanded per week and P is their price). The demonstration would be the same for any other linear equation we might choose. Table 5.4 shows a few price-quantity combinations that lie on the demand curve, and these points are also reflected in Figure 5.4. Notice, in particular, that the quantity demanded is zero for prices of $50 or greater.

Table 5.4

Price, Quantity, and Total
Expenditures on Walkmans
for the Demand Function
$Q = 100 - 2P$

Price (P)	Quantity (Q)	Total Expenditures (P · Q)
$50	0	$ 0
40	20	800
30	40	1,200
25	50	1,250
20	60	1,200
10	80	800
0	100	0

Table 5.4 also records total expenditures on Walkmans (P · Q) represented by each of the points on the demand curve. These expenditures are also represented by the areas of the various rectangles in Figure 5.4. For prices of $50 or above, total expenditures are $0. No matter how high the price, if nothing is bought, expenditures are $0. As price falls below $50, total expenditures increase. At P = $40, total expenditures are $800 ($40 · 20), and for P = $30 the figure rises to $1,200 ($30 · 40).

For relatively high prices, the demand curve in Figure 5.4 is elastic—a fall in price causes enough additional sales to increase total expenditures. This increase in total expenditures begins to slow as price drops still further. In fact, total expenditures reach a maximum at a price of $25. When P = $25, Q = 50 and total expenditures on tape players are $1,250. For prices below $25, reductions in price cause total expenditures to fall. At P = $20, expenditures are $1,200 ($20 · 60), whereas at P = $10, they are only $800 ($10 · 80). At these lower prices the increase in quantity demanded brought about by a further fall in price is simply not large enough to compensate for the price decline itself, and total expenditures fall.

This relationship is quite general. At relatively high prices on a linear demand curve, demand is elastic ($e_{Q,P} < -1$). Demand is unit elastic ($e_{Q,P} = -1$) at a price halfway between $0 and the price at which demand drops to nothing (given by P = $50 in the prior example). Below that price demand is inelastic. Further reductions in price actually reduce total revenues.

Because of this property of linear demand curves, it is particularly important when using them to note clearly the point at which price elasticity is to be measured.[4] If the price being examined has not changed very much over the period being analyzed, the distinction may be relatively unimportant. But, if

---

[4]In some empirical work, demand curves are assumed to be linear in the logarithms of Q and P, that is, it is assumed that

$$\log Q = a + b \log P$$

where a and b are constants. In this case it is easy to show that the price elasticity of demand is given by b (which will be negative) and is the same at every point on the demand curve.

the analysis is being conducted over a period of substantial price change, the possibility that elasticity may have changed should be considered.[5]

Income Elasticity of Demand

Income elasticity of demand
The percentage change in the quantity demanded of a good in response to a 1 percent change in income.

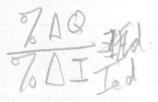

Another type of elasticity is the **income elasticity of demand** ($e_{Q,I}$). This concept records the relationship between income changes and change in quantity demanded.

$$\text{Income elasticity of demand} = e_{Q,I} = \frac{\text{Percent change in Q}}{\text{Percent change in I}}. \quad [5.3]$$

For a normal good, $e_{Q,I}$ is positive since increases in income lead to increases in purchases of the good. For the unlikely case of an inferior good, on the other hand, $e_{Q,I}$ would be negative, implying that income increases lead to decreases in quantity purchased.

Among normal goods, there is considerable interest about whether $e_{Q,I}$ is greater than or less than 1. Goods for which $e_{Q,I} > 1$ might be called luxury goods, in that purchases of these goods increase more rapidly than income. For example, if the income elasticity of demand for automobiles is 2, then a 10 percent increase in income will lead to a 20 percent increase in automobile purchases. On the other hand, a good such as food probably has an income elasticity of less than 1. If the income elasticity of demand for food were 0.5, for example, then a 10 percent rise in income would result in only a 5 percent increase in food purchases.[6] Considerable research has been done to determine the actual values of income elasticities for various items, and we discuss the results of some of these studies in the final section of this chapter.

Cross-Price Elasticity of Demand

Cross-price elasticity of demand
The percentage change in the quantity demanded of a good in response to a 1 percent change in the price of another good.

In Chapter 4 we showed that a change in the price of one good will affect the quantity demanded of most other goods. To measure such effects, economists use the **cross-price elasticity of demand**. This concept records the percentage change in quantity demanded (Q) that results from a 1 percentage point change in the price of some other good (call this other price P'). That is,

---

[5]A commonly used formula for the elasticity of demand at some point (P^*, Q^*) on a linear demand curve (given by $Q = a + bP$) can be derived directly from the definition. If

$$e_{Q,P} = \frac{\text{Percent change in Q}}{\text{Percent change in P}} = \frac{\Delta Q/Q}{\Delta P/P} = \frac{\Delta Q}{\Delta P} \cdot \frac{P}{Q}$$

and, at P^*, Q^*

$$e_{Q,P} = \frac{\Delta Q}{\Delta P} \cdot \frac{P^*}{Q^*} = b \cdot \frac{P^*}{Q^*}.$$

This formula also shows that the greater is the ratio P/Q, the greater will be the value of the point elasticity.

[6]It seems obvious that not every good can have an income elasticity greater than 1. People cannot, in total, increase their expenditures to more than their incomes. In general, it can be shown that goods for which $e_{Q,I} > 1$ must be roughly balanced by those for which $e_{Q,I} < 1$.

$$CPed = \frac{\%\Delta Q}{\%\Delta P_i}$$

$$\begin{array}{c} \text{Cross-price elasticity} \\ \text{of demand} \end{array} = e_{Q,P'} = \frac{\text{Percent change in Q}}{\text{Percent change in P}'} \qquad [5.4]$$

If these two goods are substitutes, the cross-price elasticity of demand will be positive since the price of one good and the quantity demanded of the other good will move in the same direction. For example, the cross-price elasticity for changes in the price of tea on coffee demand might be 0.5. Each 1 percentage point increase in the price of tea results in a 0.5 percentage point rise in the demand for coffee since coffee and tea are substitutes in peoples' consumption choices. A fall in the price of tea would cause the demand for coffee to fall also since people would choose to drink tea rather than coffee.

If two goods are complements, the cross-price elasticity will be negative showing that the price of one good and the quantity of the other good move in opposite directions. The cross-price elasticity of doughnut prices on coffee demand might be, say, -1.0. This would imply that a 1 percent increase in the price of doughnuts would cause the demand for coffee to fall by 1 percent. When doughnuts are more expensive, it becomes less attractive to drink coffee since many people like to have a doughnut with their morning coffee. A fall in the price of doughnuts would raise coffee demand since, in that case, people will choose to consume more of both complementary products.

As for the other elasticities we have examined, considerable empirical research has been conducted to try to measure actual cross-price elasticities of demand. Although we will not explicitly discuss these estimates in this chapter, they are discussed in several other places in this book. For example, our illustration of the effect of gasoline price changes on the demand for smaller cars in Chapter 4 implicitly involved this concept—since automobiles and gasoline are complementary goods, a rise in the price of gasoline causes people to consume "less" (that is, smaller) cars. Later (in Chapter 13), we will see that the concept of cross-price elasticity is sometimes quite important in antitrust cases since the number of competitors that a firm has can be defined by the number of products that are close substitutes (that is, have large, positive cross-price elasticities) for the product that the firm makes. More generally, cross-price elasticities describe the ways in which various markets are related and throughout this book we will be interested in showing such connections.

Empirical Studies of Demand

Economists have for many years studied the demand for all sorts of goods. Some of the earliest studies generalized from the expenditure patterns of a small sample of families.[7] Probably the most widely quoted result of those early studies was Engel's law (see Chapter 4). This "law" states that the percentage of income families spend on food declines as family income rises.

---

[7]For an interesting survey of some of the early empirical work in demand analysis see George J. Stigler, "The Early History of Empirical Studies of Consumer Behavior," *Journal of Political Economy,* April 1954, pp. 95–113.

Figure 5.5
Fitting a Demand Curve to
Empirical Observations

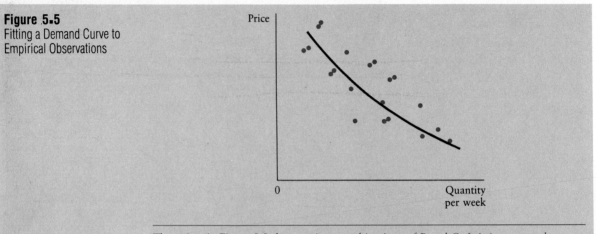

The points in Figure 5.5 show various combinations of P and Q. It is important that these points be observed while holding constant the other factors that affect the demand for Q. Otherwise they will not lie on a single demand curve.

The conclusion is that the income elasticity of the demand for food, although positive, is well below 1.

Estimating Demand Curves

More recent studies have examined a wide variety of goods to estimate both income and price elasticities. Although it is not possible for us to discuss here the statistical techniques used in such studies, we can show how these economists proceeded.

The first important problem faced in any empirical investigation is how to implement the *ceteris paribus* assumption. In studying the relationship between the price of a good and the quantity demanded, for example, our theory requires that we hold income, other prices, and preferences constant. Otherwise, if income and other prices are not held constant, observed combinations of P and Q will lie on many different demand curves rather than on the single curve we are trying to measure. Ideally we would find several people to study who are identical in every respect except that each faces a different price for the good in question. We could then plot the price and quantity chosen on a graph such as that shown in Figure 5.5. If we were sure that our individuals were, in fact, identical, the points in Figure 5.5 would indeed reflect the *ceteris paribus* influence of price on quantity.

Of course, it is impossible for us to impose the *ceteris paribus* assumption in this way in practice. Finding a group of people identical in every respect but one is impossible. It may be possible in the experimental sciences (such as biology) to isolate a single factor, but economists usually rely on the real world for their data. Consequently, they use statistical techniques to impose the *ceteris paribus* assumption. The most widely used technique is "multiple regression analysis."[8] While we will not examine this technique here, this technique was used to estimate all of the elasticities we will discuss below.

Once the problem of the *ceteris paribus* assumption has been resolved, how do we decide which curve to use to fit the data points? Since a large number of possible curves could represent the points in Figure 5.5, we must develop some criteria for choosing which of them is the "best." Again, this is a statistical problem that we cannot investigate in detail here. Usually the decision depends on which curve comes closest to the observed points and which curve seems most intuitively plausible.

Some Elasticity Estimates

Table 5.5 lists a few income and price elasticities of demand that economists have estimated. Although these estimates come from many sources, they do have certain similarities. The income elasticities for necessities (food and medical services) are considerably below those for luxuries (automobiles), as we might expect from the way purchases of these types of goods respond to income changes. A second observation is that most of the price elasticities are fairly low (although, as we expected, they are all negative). Price changes do not induce substantial proportional changes in quantities demanded.

A few of the elasticities in Table 5.5 are worth looking at more closely. For example, the table suggests that the demand for electricity is price elastic. One result of sharply increasing energy prices in the 1970s was a significant decrease in the demand for electric power. This decrease in demand caused a number of utility companies to cancel large power plant projects as they discovered that historical patterns significantly overstated the actual growth in electricity demand. Major bankruptcies resulted from some of these cancellations. For example, the default on Washington Water Power System bonds (which were used to pay for nuclear power plants) was the largest in history.

For housing, the finding that income elasticity of demand equals or exceeds 1 has interesting implications for the fairness of property taxation. If spending on housing increases more rapidly than income, a proportional tax on housing values will actually be relatively progressive since higher income people will pay proportionally more in taxes than low income people. The "common sense notion" that property taxes are regressive because housing is a necessity is erroneous using these data.

Finally, the price elasticity for giving to charity refers to how people respond to the favorable tax treatment of charitable contributions under the federal

---

[8]Multiple regression analysis, instead of looking only at the simple relationship $Q = a + bP$, attempts to estimate a relationship of the form $Q = a + bP + cI + dP' +$ other terms. Once this relationship is estimated, all the terms other than P can be held constant while the partial relationship between Q and P is examined. This is precisely what is required by the *ceteris paribus* assumption.

Table 5.5
Representative Income
and Price Elasticities

Item	Income Elasticity	Price Elasticity
Food	0.28	−0.21
Medical services	0.22	−0.20
Automobiles	3.00	−1.20
Housing		
Rental	1.00	−0.18
Owner occupied	1.20	−1.20
Gasoline	1.06	−0.54
Electricity	0.61	−1.14
Giving to charity	0.70	−1.29
Beer	0.93	−1.13
Marijuana	0	−1.50

Source: Food—H. Wold and L. Jureen, *Demand Analysis* (New York: John Wiley & Sons, Inc., 1953), p. 203. Medical services—income elasticity from R. Andersen and L. Benham, "Factors Affecting the Relationship between Family Income and Medical Care Consumption"; price elasticity from G. Rosenthal, "Price Elasticity of Demand for Short-Term General Hospital Services"; both in *Empirical Studies in Health Economics,* Herbert Klarman, ed. (Baltimore: Johns Hopkins Press, 1970). Automobiles—Gregory C. Chow, *Demand for Automobiles in the United States* (Amsterdam: North-Holland Publishing Co., 1957). Housing—income elasticities from F. deLeeuw, "The Demand for Housing," *Review of Economics and Statistics,* February 1971; price elasticities from H. S. Houthakker and L. D. Taylor, *Consumer Demand in the United States* (Cambridge, Mass.: Harvard University Press, 1970), pp. 166–167. Gasoline—Data Resources, Inc., "A Study of the Quarterly Demand for Gasoline." A study prepared for the Council on Environmental Quality, December 1973. Electricity—R. F. Halvorsen, "Residential Demand for Electricity," unpublished Ph.D. dissertation, Harvard University, December 1972. Giving to charity—M. Feldstein and A. Taylor, "The Income Tax and Charitable Contributions," *Econometrica,* November 1976, pp. 1201–1222. Beer—T. F. Hogarty and K. G. Elsinger, "The Demand for Beer," *Review of Economics and Statistics,* May 1972, pp. 195–198. Marijuana—T. C. Misket and F. Vakil, "Some Estimates of Price and Expenditure Elasticities among UCLA Students," *Review of Economics and Statistics,* November 1972, pp. 474–475.

income tax law. Under current law, these contributions may be deducted from taxable income, which reduces the net cost of making them. For example, a person whose income is taxed at 30 percent essentially pays only 70 percent of his or her gifts to charity; the government pays the remainder in terms of reduced tax revenues. People in higher tax brackets find the net price of giving even lower, and have greater incentives to give. Because the elasticity estimate in Table 5.5 is below −1 (that is, demand is elastic), the special tax treatment of contributions can be shown to generate a greater total amount in contributions than is lost in forgone tax revenues. The special tax treatment for charitable contributions is more effective in helping charitable purposes than if the government made all contributions directly. The data also suggest that dropping the charitable deduction (as many tax reform proposals have suggested) might have a large effect on charitable giving.

"Applying Economics: National Health Insurance" and "Applying Economics: Federal Tax Benefits for Homeowners" show in somewhat more detail how estimates of particular demand elasticities can be used by governments to study the effects of policies.

National Health Insurance

Most developed countries have some form of a national health insurance plan. A number of possible plans have been proposed for the United States in recent years. These plans vary greatly in cost, with a price tag of more than $200 billion per year for some of them. A principal determinant of a plan's cost is the precise mix of services that it covers. Very basic plans cover only hospital stays and physicians' costs for major illnesses, whereas more extensive plans may cover a wide variety of additional services such as family counseling or dental care. An important question in choosing among such plans is how their adoption will affect the demand for specific medical services. Because insurance lowers the out-of-pocket cost to patients (who don't have to pay for services as they use them), there is certain to be some increase in demand. The empirical question is how large that increase might be.

The estimated price elasticity of demand for medical services given in Table 5.5 is −.20. This figure might be a starting point in predicting the effect of insurance on demand for medical services. This value indicates that, as might be expected, the demand for medical services is quite inelastic. There probably still will be some expansion in demand as effective prices fall through insurance coverage. Of course, the data in Table 5.5 apply to all medical services. What really would happen may differ significantly among different medical specialties. For example, in a study of patients' responses to actual out-of-pocket costs for medical services, J. P. Newhouse and C. E. Phelps found very low (between 0 and −.10) price elasticities of demand for the lengths of stays in hospitals and for office visits to physicians.[9]

These services might show relatively little increase in demand if they were included in national health insurance plans.

On the other hand, several authors have found much larger price elasticities for services such as dental care, ophthalmological care, and psychiatric counseling. These services may have a somewhat greater discretionary element to their consumption. For these items a substantial increase in demand as a result of insurance coverage might be expected. Suggestions for ways of limiting this increase in demand have ranged from outright exclusion of such services from national health insurance plans to cost sharing by patients using the services. Information on price elasticities will continue to play a major role in shaping legislation in this area.

To Think About

1. Does the relatively high price elasticity of demand for some medical services imply that these services are not really "necessary?" Should health care planners use such elasticity estimates as a guide for the kinds of services people really need, or are there important drawbacks to basing such a judgment on people's responses to prices? How would you judge what medical services are really necessary for a person's well-being?

2. Isn't the use of demand concepts in the health care field inappropriate since a great deal of medical demand is determined by physicians, not by the patient? Is there any reason for physicians to take the price of a service into account when deciding what to prescribe? Does the model of a utility-maximizing consumer have any validity in this case?

Summary

In this chapter we have developed the market demand curve by adding up the demands of many consumers. This curve shows the relationship between the market price of a good and the amount that people choose to purchase of

---

[9]J. P. Newhouse and C. E. Phelps, "Price and Income Elasticities for Medical Care Services," in M. Perlman, ed., *The Economics of Health and Medical Care* (New York: John Wiley & Sons, 1974), pp. 139–161.

that good assuming all the other factors that affect demand do not change. When factors such as individuals' incomes, the prices of other goods, or preferences do change, the market demand curve will shift to a new position.

The market demand curve is a basic building block for the theory of price determination. We will be using the concept frequently throughout the remainder of this book. You should therefore keep in mind the following points about this concept:

- The market demand curve represents the summation of the demands of a given number of potential consumers of a particular good. The curve shows the *ceteris paribus* relationship between the market price of the good and the amount demanded by all consumers.
- Factors that shift individual demand curves also shift the market demand curve to a new position. Such factors include changes in incomes, changes in the prices of other goods, and changes in people's preferences.
- The price elasticity of demand provides a convenient way of measuring the extent to which market demand responds to price changes. Specifically, the price elasticity of demand shows the percent change in quantity demanded in response to a 1 percent change in market price. Demand is said to be "elastic" if a 1 percent change in price leads to a greater than 1 percent change in quantity demanded. Demand is "inelastic" if a 1 percent change in price leads to a smaller than 1 percent change in quantity.
- There is a close relationship between the price elasticity of demand and total expenditures on a good. If demand is elastic, a rise in price will reduce total expenditures. If demand is inelastic, a rise in price will increase total expenditures.
- Other elasticities of demand are defined in a way similar to that used for the price elasticity. For example, the income elasticity of demand measures the percent change in quantity demanded in response to a 1 percent change in income.
- Economists have estimated elasticities of demand for many different goods based on real world data. A major problem in making such estimates is to devise ways of holding all other factors that affect demand constant so that the points being used lie on a single demand curve.

Problems

5.1 Suppose the demand curve for flyswatters is given by

$$Q = 500 - 50P$$

where Q is the number of flyswatters demanded per week and P is the price in dollars.

Federal Tax Benefits for Homeowners

Elasticity estimates can be used to suggest how current federal tax benefits to people living in their own homes affect the demand for owner-occupied housing. Federal tax policy makes it more advantageous to own rather than rent housing because owners can deduct mortgage interest payments and property taxes from taxable income, whereas a renter (who ultimately pays these same costs to the landlord) cannot. Homeowners benefit directly since deductible interest payments and property taxes make up a substantial fraction of the total costs of housing. Most authors estimate that these two costs in fact make up about 70 percent of costs. Consequently it is argued that homeowners are permitted by law to deduct about 70 percent of housing costs from their income before they pay taxes, whereas renters are not able to do so.

The value of this tax benefit depends on the income tax rate that a particular family pays. For a home-owning family whose income is taxed at 30 percent, the government essentially pays 21 percent of the true housing costs (= 70 percent deduction times 30 percent tax rate). The effective price of owner-occupied housing is 21 percent lower than it would be in the absence of preferential tax treatment.

This subsidy may or may not be desirable from the viewpoint of national policy, but its effect on the demand for housing is clear: people will respond to the lower effective price by demanding more owner-occu-

pied housing. In fact, we can use the price elasticity for housing reported in Table 5.5, which is −1.20, to estimate that the 21 percent reduction in price will lead to approximately a 25 percent (= 21 percent times 1.20) increase in the quantity of owner-occupied housing demanded. For families facing a higher tax rate, the subsidy (and the impetus to own their homes) is even greater.

The effect of the government subsidy is to provide a considerable impetus to home ownership. At times, various tax reform programs (such as those proposed at the start of President Reagan's second term) have contained provisions to limit such subsidies. But, as might be expected, the tax benefits are quite popular and it can be political suicide to suggest limiting them.

To Think About
1. Why does the federal government provide a tax break for homeowners? Can you think of any general social goals that are fostered by such a break? Or does the special treatment of homeownership simply reflect the political strength of the middle class in the United States?
2. Housing prices tend to rise along with prices generally. Should these "capital gains" be taxed as income to the homeowner? Is an owner any better off if the price of his or her home doubles? Would your answer depend on how prices of other houses are also changing or on whether prices of other goods are rising also?

a. How many flyswatters are demanded at a price of $2? How about a price of $3? $4? Suppose flyswatters were free; how many would be bought?

b. Graph the flyswatter demand curve—remember to put P on the vertical axis and Q on the horizontal axis. To do so, you may wish to solve for P as a function of Q.

c. Suppose during July the flyswatter demand curve shifts to

$$Q = 1,000 - 50P.$$

Answer parts a and b for this new demand curve.

5.2 The market demand for potatoes is given by:

$$Q = 1,000 + 0.3I - 300P + 200P'$$

where:

$$Q = \text{Annual demand in pounds}$$

$$I = \text{Average income in dollars per year}$$

$$P = \text{Price of potatoes in cents per pound}$$

$$P' = \text{Price of rice in cents per pound.}$$

a. Suppose $I = \$10,000$ and $P' = \$.25$; what would be the market demand for potatoes? At what price would $Q = 0$? Graph this demand curve.

b. Suppose I rose to $\$20,000$ with P' staying at $\$.25$. Now what would the demand for potatoes be? At what price would $Q = 0$? Graph this demand curve. Explain why more potatoes are demanded at every price in this case than in part a.

c. If I returns to $\$10,000$ but P' falls to $\$.10$, what would the demand for potatoes be? At what price would $Q = 0$? Graph this demand curve. Explain why fewer potatoes are demanded at every price in this case than in part a.

5.3 Tom, Dick, and Harry constitute the entire market for scrod. Tom's demand curve is given by:

$$Q_1 = 100 - 2P$$

for $P \leq 50$. For $P > 50$, $Q_1 = 0$. Dick's demand curve is given by:

$$Q_2 = 160 - 4P$$

for $P \leq 40$. For $P > 40$, $Q_2 = 0$. Harry's demand curve is given by:

$$Q_3 = 150 - 5P$$

for $P \leq 30$. For $P > 30$, $Q_3 = 0$. Using this information, answer the following.

a. How much scrod is demanded by each person at $P = 50$? At $P = 35$? At $P = 25$? At $P = 10$? And at $P = 0$?

b. What is the total market demand for scrod at each of the prices specified in part a?

c. Graph each individual's demand curve.

d. Use the individual demand curves and the results of part b to construct the total market demand for scrod.

5.4 Suppose the quantity of good X demanded by individual 1 is given

$$X_1 = 10 - 2P_X + 0.01I_1 + 0.4P_Y.$$

and the quantity of X demanded by individual 2 is

$$X_2 = 5 - P_X + 0.02I_2 + 0.2P_Y.$$

a. What is the market demand function for total X $(= X_1 + X_2)$ as a function of P_X, I_1, I_2, and P_Y?
b. Graph the two individual demand curves (with X on the horizontal axis, P_X on the vertical axis) for the case $I_1 = 1,000$, $I_2 = 1,000$, and $P_Y = 10$.
c. Using these individual demand curves, construct the market demand curve for total X. What is the algebraic equation for this curve?
d. Now suppose I_1 increases to 1,100 and I_2 decreases to 900. How would the market demand curve shift? How would the individual demand curves shift? Graph these new curves.
e. Finally, suppose P_Y rises to 15. Graph the new individual and market demand curves that would result.

5.5 Assume that $e_{X,P_X} = -2$, $e_{X,P_Y} = .5$, and $e_{X,I} = .8$.

a. If originally $P_X = \$10$, $P_Y = \$10$, average $I = \$20,000$, and total consumption of good X is 1,000 units, how much of good X will be consumed when P_X rises to $10.10?
b. If P_Y rises to $10.10 instead and P_X stays at $10, how will consumption of good X be affected?
c. Now assume that P_X and P_Y stay constant at $10 but average I rises by $200. How will consumption of good X be affected?

5.6 The market demand for cashmere socks is given by:

$$Q_c = 1,000 + .5I - 400P_c + 200P_w$$

where

$$Q_c = \text{Annual demand in number of pairs}$$

$$I = \text{Average income in dollars per year}$$

$$P_c = \text{Price of one pair of cashmere socks}$$

$$P_w = \text{Price of one pair of wool socks.}$$

Given that $I = \$20,000$, $P_c = \$10$, and $P_w = \$5$, determine e_{Q_c,P_c}, e_{Q_c,P_w}, and $e_{Q_c,I}$ at this point.

5.7 Suppose ham and cheese are pure complements—they are always used in the ratio of one slice of ham to one slice of cheese to make a sandwich. Suppose also that ham and cheese sandwiches are the only goods that consumers can buy and that bread is free.

a. Show that if the price of a slice of ham equals the price of a slice of cheese, the price elasticity of demand for ham is $-\frac{1}{2}$.
b. Show that if the price of a slice of ham equals the price of a slice of

cheese, the cross-price elasticity of a change in the price of cheese on ham consumption is also $-\frac{1}{2}$.

   c. How would your answers to parts a and b change if a slice of ham cost twice as much as a slice of cheese?

5.8 A *luxury* is defined as a good for which the income elasticity of demand is greater than 1. Show that for a two-good economy, both goods cannot be luxuries. Hint: What happens if both goods are luxuries and income is increased by 10 percent?

5.9 If $e_{X,P_X} = -.6$ and $e_{X,P_Y} = -.8$ in a two-good economy, what is $e_{X,I}$? Hint: A 10 percent increase in income can be seen as a 10 percent drop in all prices.

5.10 For the linear demand curve shown in Figure A show that the price elasticity of demand at any given point (say, point E) is given by minus the ratio of distance X to distance Y in the figure. Hint: Use footnote 5 of this chapter.

Figure A

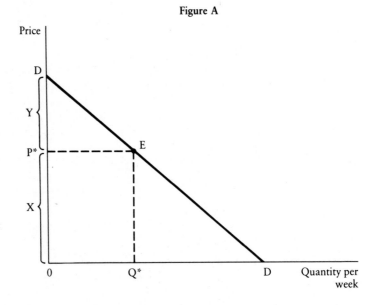

CHAPTER 6

Further Applications of the Theory of Choice

Chapters 4 and 5 use the utility-maximization model of people's consumption choices to develop the market demand curve. Although this is probably the model's most important application, it is by no means the only one. Because the notion of utility maximization is a very general theory of how choices are made, it can be (and is) applied to a wide variety of economic issues. This chapter looks at a few of these additional applications.

We begin with a discussion of the "gains from trade." We use the utility-maximization model to show how voluntary trading between two people can make both of them better off. Although our demonstration is quite simple, this action is the basis of many economic activities, including the law of contracts between individuals and, on a much larger scale, the benefits of international trade between nations. Some of these applications are examined here and later in this book (in Part 6).

Our second application of the utility-maximizing model concerns the properties of "index numbers." This concept is frequently encountered in economics—measuring "real" (inflation-adjusted) gross national product (GNP) and defining the Consumer Price Index (CPI) are the two most important examples. This chapter shows how the consumer choice model can be used to investigate the accuracy of how these measurements are arrived at, using the case of the CPI.

The final application of utility theory in this chapter concerns individual behavior in uncertain or risky situations. When people buy lottery tickets, invest in common stocks, or purchase used cars, they are engaging in activities with uncertain outcomes. Many different things might happen and whatever does occur will affect the individual's level of well-being. We focus on why economists generally believe people dislike risky situations and are usually

Table 6.1
A Trade in Which Both
Parties Gain

	Initial Quantity		Results of Trade		Final Quantity	
	X	Y	X	Y	X	Y
Person 1	5	10	+1	−1	6	9
Person 2	10	5	−1	+1	9	6

willing to pay something (such as an insurance premium) to avoid risk. A few instances of risk aversion are described, along with some more general issues about the value of information to people faced with uncertainty.

Gains from Voluntary Trade

One of the most elementary, yet far-reaching results that can be shown using utility analysis is that two people can be made better off by voluntary trading with each other. Two-person trades may not have a "winner" and a "loser," but can be mutually beneficial. For example, everyone participates in voluntary trade by giving up some amount of money to buy something (say, a candy bar) that he or she values more highly than the cash. The seller also benefits from this transaction—the seller values the cash more highly than the candy bar. Although we begin by studying mutually beneficial transactions in a very simple setting, the results of our examination are quite general and reappear in various forms throughout this book.

A Simple Exchange Situation

We can begin by assuming that only two goods, hamburgers (which we will call Y) and soft drinks (which we will call X) are available. Assume also that there are fixed amounts of X = 15 and Y = 15, and that persons 1 and 2 have unequal amounts of X and Y. Person 1 starts out with X = 5 and Y = 10, and person 2 starts out with X = 10 and Y = 5. These initial quantities appear in the first columns of Table 6.1.

To look at voluntary trades away from this initial position, we need to know these people's preferences to determine what trades would make each of them better off. Figure 6.1 presents indifference curve maps for our two traders, including the initial allocations of X and Y. At X = 5, Y = 10, person 1 has a marginal rate of substitution (MRS) of 2—because she has an abundance of hamburgers, she is willing to give up two of them to get one more soft drink. For person 2, on the other hand, the MRS is ½—because she has quite a lot of softdrinks already, she is rather unwilling to give up hamburgers to get even more of them.

Figure 6.1
Both Individuals Gain
from a Trade

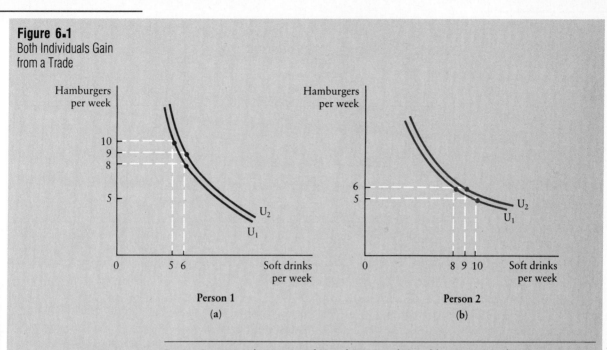

Person 1 | (a)

Person 2 | (b)

Person 1 starts with 10 units of Y and 5 units of X and has an MRS of 2. Person 2 starts with 10 units of X and 5 units of Y and has an MRS of ½. If person 1 trades one X to person 2 for one Y, each person will be on a higher indifference curve than in their initial situation. In other examples the actual distribution of the trading gains depends on the terms of trade that are established.

Suppose now that these two people reach an agreement under which person 1 trades one Y to person 2 for one X. Results of this trade are recorded in Table 6.1 and shown graphically in Figure 6.1. The striking fact of the trade is that it makes both people better off. Person 1 now has X = 6 and Y = 9. Since she would have been as well off as in her initial situation if the trade resulted in X = 6, Y = 8 (because her MRS is assumed to be 2), the posttrade allocation is clearly better—she still gets the same amount of X and more Y. Person 2 now has X = 9, Y = 6, which improves her utility. She would have been willing to accept X = 8, Y = 6 (with her assumed MRS of ½), but the proposed trade leaves her with one more X over what would have been acceptable. The proposed voluntary trade would make both people better off.

A similar demonstration could be made any time two people have combinations of goods that result in their having different marginal rates of substitution (if MRSs were the same, there would be no gains to trade). If they agree to trade goods in some ratio that lies between these two MRSs, both will be made better off.

Table 6.2
Distribution of Gains
from Trade Depends
on Terms of Trade

Case 1: 1 X trades for 2 Y—only person 2 gains

	Initial Quantity		Quantity Traded		Final Quantity	
	X	Y	X	Y	X	Y
Person 1	5	10	+1	−2	6	8
Person 2	10	5	−1	+2	9	7

Case 2: 2 X trades for 1 Y—only person 1 gains

	Initial Quantity		Quantity Traded		Final Quantity	
	X	Y	X	Y	X	Y
Person 1	5	10	+2	−1	7	9
Person 2	10	5	−2	+1	8	6

Distribution of the Gains from Trade

Although both individuals may gain from a voluntary trading situation, the gains may sometimes be unevenly divided. We would not expect people to agree to a trade that actually resulted in lower utility (people might be forced into such trades, however—a gun is an effective form of coercion for a mugger!). But, even in voluntary trades, one person may get the bulk of the gains. Two such situations are illustrated in Table 6.2. In Case 1, our two people have decided to exchange Y for X in the ratio of two Y for one X. This trade leaves person 1 (with X = 6, Y = 8) precisely as well off as before the trade. As shown in Figure 6.1, both the initial combination of goods and this new posttrade combination lie on the same indifference curve, U_1. Although person 1 doesn't lose from the trade, she doesn't gain anything either.

In this new trade, person 2 is the big winner. She now has X = 9, Y = 7, which, as Figure 6.1 shows, is not only preferred to her initial position, but also makes her better off than in our first trading example.

Case 2 of Table 6.2 shows a trade in which person 1 gets the better deal. Now the two individuals have agreed to trade at a ratio of one Y for two X. After this trade person 2 is still on her initial indifference curve. Person 1 with X = 7, Y = 9 is now better off than in any of the previous cases. With these "terms-of-trade," person 1 is the primary gainer from trading.

Generalizations

The elements in this simple demonstration of the gains from voluntary trade reappear at many other places in this book. The key feature is that people are willing to make trade-offs in their consumption choices and that some trades may improve their well-being. Whether a person will find such a favorable trading opportunity depends on how the external terms of trade (whether given by market prices or by the kinds of deals other people are willing to make) compare to the person's internal willingness to trade (as represented by the MRS). If these rates differ, a utility-improving trade may be made. The extent of gains usually depends on the divergence between these external and internal terms of trade. If the divergence is relatively small, the gains will be small; if it is large, significant gains from trade are possible. This basic principle can be applied to the trivial—when should you repair your own car or have someone else do it? It also applies to the profound, as "Applying Economics: The Gains from International Trade" shows. The possibility of gains from voluntary trade is at the base of organized markets and, indeed, provides the fundamental subject matter for the study of economic behavior.

Index Numbers

Index number
An average of many different trends into one number.

Economists frequently need to average many different trends into a single number. In measuring "the" rate of inflation, for example, some method must be found for averaging the different price trends of a wide variety of commodities. Calculating changes in the real quantity of production (that is, changes in real gross national product) means finding some way to add up changes in the quantities produced of a number of different goods. Although these kinds of constructions are often thought of as tedious exercises in "number-crunching," the development of **index numbers** raises a number of interesting conceptual issues. As a second major application of the model of utility maximization, we examine a few of these issues. Some of the problems discussed here that arise in constructing the Consumer Price Index as a measure of inflation are representative of the issues involved in all index number construction.

The Consumer Price Index

Consumer Price Index (CPI)
The current value of the market basket of goods and services purchased by a typical household compared to a base year value of the same market basket.

One of the principal measures of inflation in the United States is provided by the **Consumer Price Index** (CPI), which is published monthly by the U.S. Department of Labor. To construct the CPI the Bureau of Labor Statistics first defines a typical market basket of commodities purchased by consumers in some base year (1967 is the year presently used). Then data are collected every month about how much this market basket of commodities currenty costs the consumer. The ratio of the current cost to the bundle's original cost (in 1967) is then published as the current value of the price index, and the rate of change in this index between two periods is reported to be the rate of inflation.

This construction can be clarified with a simple two good example. Suppose that in 1967 the typical market basket contained X^{67} of good X and Y^{67} of

APPLYING ECONOMICS

The Gains from International Trade

The analysis of the gains from trading between two individuals also applies to a situation such as the California drought of 1977, discussed in Chapter 1 in "Applying Economics: Water Demand and the 1977 Drought in California." In that example farmers who had plenty of water were willing, even anxious, to sell to other farmers, who were equally anxious to part with cash to get it. The analysis applies to far more complex trading situations as well. Consider, for example, the case of trading among nations. In this situation there may be gains to all parties from voluntary trade. A principle source of much of those gains derives from production efficiency considerations discussed in Chapter 17.

Most countries restrict international trade using tariffs, quotas, and various nonquantitative restrictions. During the late 1970s, for example, tariff rates averaged about 11 percent in the major industrialized countries. Rates were considerably higher than 11 percent on some items and lower or nonexistent on others, but overall, countries had adopted fairly significant barriers to trade. Table 6.3 shows a series of estimates of how much trade would be created (and welfare improved) by elimination of such barriers, based on the Tokyo round of tariff negotiations in the late 1970s. For example, the complete elimination of tariffs would have resulted in a nearly $17 billion (in 1974 dollars) expansion in the annual level of trade among countries, and it is estimated that real income in those countries would have increased by about $2 billion. The estimated welfare gains reported in the table are probably substantial underestimates of the true gains. They take no account of the side benefits of freer trade (a more efficient economy, greater technical advancement, better relations among nations, and so forth), nor of the fact that the gains are expected to occur each year into the future. Some authors have estimated that the overall true gains from tariff reductions may be about one hundred times those listed in the table, or actually $200 billion if tariffs were completely eliminated.

The effects of tariff reduction formulas proposed, respectively, by the United States, Japan, and the European Economic Community (EEC) are also reported in Table 6.3. Although the welfare gains under these proposals are not so large as those for complete tariff elimination, they are nevertheless quite substantial. The

Table 6.3
Estimated Trade and Welfare Gains for Industrial Countries from the Tokyo Round of Tariff Reductions

Plan	Average Reduction	Additional Trade per Year ($ Billions)	Basic Welfare Gain per Year ($ Billions)
Complete elimination	100%	$16.9	$2.0
United States	65	11.0	1.7
Japanese	46	8.0	1.6
European Economic Community	33	5.7	1.4

Source: W. R. Cline, N. Kawanaabe, T. O. M. Kronsjo, and T. Williams, *Trade Negotiations in the Tokyo Round* (Washington, D.C.: Brookings, 1978).

different reduction formulas probably relate to the different countries' domestic political situations, since free trade can be very controversial if some workers' jobs are threatened by eliminating tariffs. Differences in the formulas also relate to how specific goods would be treated under each proposal, and how the countries feel about expanding trade in those items. For example, the United States has generally advocated freer trade in agricultural products, whereas the EEC and Japan have tried to protect their own farmers. The United States has tended to restrict trade in steel whereas Japan (and to a much lesser extent the EEC) has sought to expand such trade. Analysis developed later in this book may help to explain such preferences.

To Think About

1. Does "everyone" gain from trade between nations? Who might lose in such trading? Are these people "voluntary" participants in the trading?

2. Some authors claim that less developed countries do not gain very much from trade since prices for internationally traded goods are determined by markets in the industrialized countries. How does this notion relate to our simple example of who gains from voluntary trade?

good Y. The prices of these goods are given by P_X^{67} and P_Y^{67}. The cost of this bundle in the 1967 base year would be written as

$$\text{Cost of bundle in 1967} = B^{67} = P_X^{67} \cdot X^{67} + P_Y^{67} \cdot Y^{67}. \qquad [6.1]$$

To compute the cost of the same bundle of goods in 1987, we must first collect information on the goods' prices in that year (P_X^{87}, P_Y^{87}) and then compute

$$\text{Cost of bundle in 1987} = B^{87} = P_X^{87} \cdot X^{67} + P_Y^{87} \cdot Y^{67}. \qquad [6.2]$$

The CPI would then be defined as the ratio of the cost of these two figures:

$$\text{CPI (for 1987)} = \frac{B^{87}}{B^{67}}. \qquad [6.3]$$

The rate of inflation can be computed from this index. For example, if a market basket of items that cost \$100 in 1967 cost \$350 in 1987, the value of the CPI would be 3.5, and we would say there had been a 350 percent increase in prices over this 20-year period.[1] It might be said that people would need three-and-one-half times their 1967 income to enjoy the same standard of living in 1987 that they had in 1967. Cost-of-living adjustments in social security benefits and in many job agreements are calculated in precisely this way.

The CPI and True Inflation

The problem with the above calculation of inflation should be obvious from the material presented in the previous three chapters. This calculation assumes that people who are faced with 1987 prices will continue to demand the same basket of commodities that they consumed in 1967. The analysis makes no allowance for substitutions among commodities in response to changing prices. The calculation may overstate the decline in purchasing power that inflation has caused, since it takes no account of how people will seek to get the most utility for their dollars.

In Figure 6.2, for example, a typical individual initially is consuming X^{67}, Y^{67}. Presumably this choice provides maximum utility (U_1), given the budget constraint (I). Suppose that by 1987 relative prices have changed in such a way that P_X/P_Y has fallen—that is, assume that good X becomes less expen-

---

[1]Frequently, index numbers are multiplied by 100 to avoid computation to several decimal places. Instead of reporting the CPI as 3.50, a value of 350 would be reported. Each figure shows a 350 percent gain in the index over the base period.

Figure 6.2
Substitution Bias of the
Consumer Price Index

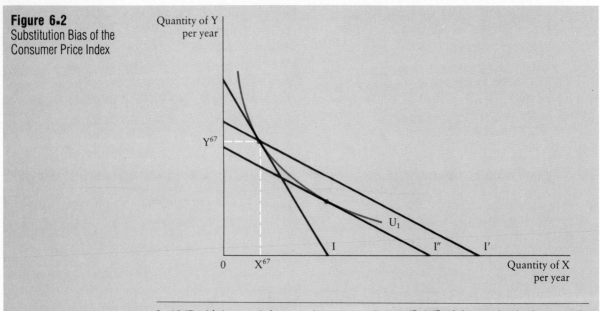

In 1967 with income I the typical consumer chose X^{67}, Y^{67}. If this market basket is used to construct a price index when different relative prices prevail, the basket's cost will be given by I'. This cost exceeds what is actually required to permit the consumer to reach the original level of utility, I".

sive. Using these new prices, the CPI calculates what X^{67}, Y^{67} would cost. This cost would be reflected by the budget constraint I', which is flatter than I (to reflect the changed prices) and passes through X^{67}, Y^{67}. As the figure makes clear, the erosion in purchasing power that has occurred is overstated. With I' our typical individual could now reach a higher utility level than could be attained in 1967.

A true measure of inflation would be provided by evaluating the income level I", which reflects the new prices but just permits the individual to remain on U_1. By failing to take account of these substitutions in consumption that people might make in response to changed prices (they would consume more X and less Y in moving along U_1), the CPI has exaggerated the true decline in purchasing power. In "Applying Economics: Substitution Biases and Revising Consumer Price Index" we show how large this error might be.

This problem of determining inflation is not an easy one to solve. Without knowing an individual's actual preferences, there is no precise way to know how much real purchasing power has been eroded through price changes. An individual's actual spending patterns may not provide sufficient information. For example, using the 1987 market basket to calculate the CPI leads to the same sort of problems that are illustrated in Figure 6.2. Economists have experimented with a variety of more sophisticated indices of price change, but

APPLYING ECONOMICS

Substitution Biases and Revising Consumer Price Index

Several economists have tried to estimate the extent to which a fixed market basket-type price index overstates the true rate of price increase by failing to consider the types of substitutions individuals make in response to changing relative prices. Table 6.4 reports the results of one such study by S. D. Braithwait. In this study the author compared the actual performance of the U.S. Consumer Price Index over the period 1958–73 to the performance of an estimated true cost of living index that takes account of substitution in consumption. As the table shows, the actual CPI rose 47.5 percent during the 15 year interval being examined (from 100 to 147.5) whereas the true index rose only 46.0 percent. Hence over the entire period the CPI tended to overstate inflation by about 1.5 percent by failing to consider substitution among items in the market basket. The resulting bias worked out to about one-tenth of a percent per year.

For major consumption categories within the CPI, rather different patterns emerged. In the case of food and clothing, little substitution tended to occur among specific items within each category in response to changing relative prices (and, indeed, relative prices within the categories changed only slightly) so the bias was quite small—less than one percent over the entire period. In the recreation and entertainment category, on the other hand, relative prices changed more significantly and substitution was more prevalent. Hence the bias was larger, amounting to nearly one half a percentage point per year. By failing to account for individuals' shifting demands among such items as televisions, spectator events, and use of hotels and motels, the CPI tended to exaggerate the general inflation rate for the goods in this category.

One question that the data in Table 6.4 shed some light on is how often CPI weights should be revised. Since gathering new data with which to develop weights is quite costly (the 1967 revisions cost about $100 million), there is a natural desire to delay in doing so. From the table, it appears that the 15 year period between revisions did not, at least during the years 1958–72, seriously bias the index. There is some evidence that delays of longer periods would, however, result in much larger biases. Of course, the judgment that 15 years is about the right length of time for a CPI revision depends

Table 6.4

Estimated Substitution Bias in the Consumer Price Index, 1958–73

Category	Actual CPI (1958 = 100)	True Cost of Living Index (1958 = 100)	Bias (Column 1– Column 2)
Food	156.1	155.4	0.7
Clothing	149.3	148.5	0.8
Shelter	136.8	135.8	1.0
Transportation	134.0	132.5	1.5
Personal Services	172.6	168.1	4.5
Recreation and Entertainment	146.9	139.9	7.0
Total Consumption	147.5	146.0	1.5

Source: S. D. Braithwait, "The Substitution Bias of the Laspeyres Price Index: An Analysis Using Estimated Cost of Living Indices," *American Economic Review*, March 1980, p. 70.

on whether the 1958–73 period was a normal period and whether more recent experience suggests more frequent revisions. Changes in energy prices in the late 1970s, for example, may have changed relative prices to a much greater extent than experienced previously and a more frequent revision may have been required. Similarly, during a period where many new goods are coming on the market (such as the number of home computer-related products in the early 1980s) more frequent revisions may also be called for.

To Think About

1. This example shows that the bias of the CPI during the period 1958–73 was fairly small. How do you think this result would hold up for the period after 1973? Explain why rapidly rising energy prices may have made substitution effects larger in this latter period? Can you think of some examples of such substitutions?

2. How should new or improved goods be handled in constructing the CPI? What would be the consequences of disregarding quality improvements in some goods when computing the CPI? What would be the consequences of completely excluding newly invented goods?

none of these has proven to be completely satisfactory.[2] Some care must always be taken in interpreting the CPI (and other index number) statistics.

Other Problems with the CPI

Two additional problems with this type of price index construction are related to the need to choose a base year "market basket." The first problem concerns what specific commodities should be included in the basket. Both everyday observations and more sophisticated studies (as shown in our earlier discussion of Engel's Law) suggest that people's consumption choices may vary greatly depending on their circumstances. It has been proposed that a separate index be constructed for poor people to reflect the kinds of goods they can afford, and that people living in colder climates also need a separate index to reflect costs of goods such as heating and ear muffs. The choice of a market basket has important implications for the performance of the index and for the calculation of cost-of-living adjustments. Seemingly "objective" questions about how to measure inflation have become highly politicized in recent years.

The development of new or improved goods presents a second problem in the construction of the CPI. Some products that are currently sold (such as videocassette recorders, pocket calculators, and oversized tennis rackets) were not even available in 1967. Modern color televisions are much more reliable and longlasting than those from the 1960s. Deciding how these new or improved products should be included in the CPI market basket (if at all) brings up many issues that have not been completely resolved.

Index Number Problems

The difficulties in constructing the CPI are fairly typical of a broad class of problems in developing any index numbers that average together various economic magnitudes. Whenever trends in two or more different commodities must be averaged to form a single index, some sort of weighting scheme is always necessary. In the case of the CPI, the 1967 market basket is used to average together the prices for goods X and Y in various years. Calculating real inflation-adjusted gross national product figures reverses this process with a set of base year prices to value the physical quantities of commodities produced in successive years. "Applying Economics: International Comparisons of Real Income" contains some examples of this sort of calculation. In the case of international currency values, the amount of trade between the United States and other nations is used to compute an average overall monetary exchange rate for the dollar.

---

[2]For a detailed treatment of index numbers and their associated problems, see R. G. D. Allen, *Index Numbers in Theory and Practice* (London: Macmillan, 1975).

APPLYING ECONOMICS

International Comparisons of Real Income

A problem similar to the substitution bias in the CPI arises in comparing real income (or GNP) between two countries. Ideally data are available on the quantities of various goods produced in each country, but the problem is choosing the set of prices to use in adding up these quantities into a real income measure. Two solutions might be adopted. First, we could use the prices that actually prevail in each country: for example, to compare U.S. and Colombian real GNP, we could use U.S. prices to compute U.S. GNP and Colombian prices to compute Colombian GNP. To do this we would need some method to convert Colombian pesos into U.S. dollars (or vice versa) so that our comparison will be meaningful. Determining the exchange rate for this calculation can be a difficult and controversial exercise.

A second solution is to use only one nation's prices to evaluate GNP in both countries. For example, both U.S. and Colombian GNP could be computed using U.S. prices for the quantities of goods. This approach, although it solves the exchange rate problem (since now dollars are compared to dollars), raises another problem of its own. We can assume that Colombian consumers buy relatively little of goods that are especially expensive in Colombia (household appliances, for example) and that U.S. consumers have similarly economized on items that are expensive in the United States (coffee, for example). If different goods are expensive in each country (as with household appliances and coffee), this method may produce biases since some high U.S. prices (for coffee, say) will be applied to goods which Colombians consume in large amounts, whereas low U.S. prices will be applied to goods on which Colombians economize (appliances). Real Colombian income will be overstated.

Table 6.5 shows 1973 data on various countries' per capita GNPs (actually per capita gross domestic products—GDPs) as a percentage of the per capita GDP in the United States. Table 6.5 compares GDPs in two ways: in terms of each country's own prices and in terms of only U.S. prices. As you can see, which prices are used can make a big difference in the comparison. In the case of India, the lowest income country compared, per capita GDP is less than 4 percent of that in the United States when India's GDP is evaluated using India's own prices, but nearly 8 percent of the U.S. GDP when India's GDP is evaluated using U.S. prices. Colombia is another

Table 6.5

International Comparisons of Gross Domestic Product per Capita as a Percentage of the U.S. Level of GDP

	Own Domestic Prices	U.S. Prices
India	3.8%	7.9%
South Korea	8.2	15.3
Colombia	11.9	26.1
Hungary	36.0	51.7
Japan	54.5	66.0
United Kingdom	54.7	66.4
West Germany	65.0	79.8
United States	100.0	100.0

Source: I. B. Kravis et al., *International Comparisons of Real Product and Purchasing Power* (Baltimore: Johns Hopkins University Press, 1978), p. 219.

country whose relative position to the U.S. level is more than doubled by using U.S. rather than local prices (from 11.9 percent to 26.1 percent). As the table seems to indicate, large differences may occur primarily for low income countries, whereas they are less dramatic for high income countries, such as Japan or Germany. Higher income countries' expenditure patterns are probably more like those in the United States than low income countries' are, so the effect of using different prices should be less noticeable. Nevertheless, the problem of which country's prices to use in comparing international GNPs has no completely satisfactory solution.

To Think About

1. Comparisons of real gross national product among countries usually include only those goods which are traded in organized markets. Non-market transactions (such as trading among farmers or the revenue from illegal activities) are not included in the calculations. How do you think these exclusions affect comparisons among nations? Would the poor nations look relatively poorer or relatively richer if such transactions were included in GNP?

2. Would problems similar to those which arise in comparing GNP among countries arise in comparing the real incomes of people living in different parts of the United States? Can you think of reasons why such comparisons might be easier to make than are comparisons among countries?

For these calculations and others, the precise weights that are used have a major impact on the final averages obtained. That choice (as in the case of the CPI) will always be arbitrary to some extent. For economists to study the properties of these calculations requires an economic model of the concept being measured to establish standards of accuracy. The study of index numbers is another major area in economics in which issues of measurement are closely linked to the underlying theory.

Uncertainty

The problem of uncertainty is our final application of utility theory here. So far in this book we have assumed that people's choices are not uncertain; that once they decide how to spend their income, they get what they want. In many real-world situations, that is not the way things always work. When you buy a lottery ticket, invest in shares of common stock, or play poker, what you get back is subject to chance. Many of the choices that people must make involve incomplete information (such as who knows which used car is a lemon and which isn't), and these choices are made somewhat "in the dark." Two questions are raised by the economic problems of uncertainty: why do people generally dislike risky situations, and what can they do to avoid or reduce risks?

Probability and Expected Value

Central to both questions are some simple mathematical ideas. The study of individual behavior under uncertainty and the mathematical study of probability and statistics have a common historical origin in games of chance. Gamblers who try to devise ways of winning at blackjack and casinos trying to keep the game profitable for them are a modern example of this endlessly popular pastime. Two statistical concepts that originated in the study of games of chance that are quite useful in the remainder of this chapter are probability and expected value.

Probability
The relative frequency with which an event will occur.

The **probability** of an event happening is, roughly speaking, the relative frequency with which it will occur. For example, to say that the probability of a head coming up on the flip of a fair coin is ½ means that if a coin is flipped a large number of times, we can expect a head to come up in approximately one-half of the flips. The probability of rolling a 2 on a single die is ⅙. In approximately one out of every six rolls, a 2 should come up. Of course, before a coin is flipped or a die is rolled, we have no idea what will come up, so each flip or roll still has an uncertain outcome as reflected by these probabilities.

Expected value
For a gamble with a number of uncertain outcomes, the outcome that will occur on average.

The **expected value** of a game with a number of uncertain outcomes (or prizes) is the size of the prize that the player will win on average. Suppose Jones and Smith agree to flip a coin once. If a head comes up, Jones will pay Smith \$1; if a tail comes up Smith will pay Jones \$1. From Smith's point of view there are two prizes (or outcomes) (X_1 and X_2) in this game: If the coin

APPLYING ECONOMICS

Blackjack Systems

The game of blackjack (or twenty-one) is an interesting illustration of the expected value notion and its relevance to people's behavior in uncertain situations. This game is a very simple one. Each player is dealt two cards (with the dealer coming last). The dealer asks each player if he or she wishes another card. The player getting a hand that totals closest to 21, without going over 21, is the winner. If receipt of a card puts a player over 21, that player automatically loses. Played in this way, blackjack offers a number of advantages to the dealer. Most important, the dealer, who plays last, is in a somewhat more favorable position since other players can go over 21 (and therefore lose) before the dealer plays. Under the usual rules, the dealer has the additional advantage of winning ties. These two advantages give the dealer a margin of winning in the game of about 6 percent on average. Players can expect to win 47 percent of all hands played, whereas the dealer will win 53 percent of the time.

Because the rules of blackjack make it relatively unfair to the players, casinos have gradually liberalized them to entice more players. At Las Vegas casinos, for example, dealers must play under fixed rules that allow no discretion depending on the individual game situation, and dealers must return bets to the players in the case of ties rather than winning them. These rules change the fairness of the game quite a bit. By some estimates, Las Vegas casinos enjoy an advantage in blackjack of as little as 0.1 percent, if that. Indeed, in recent years a number of systems have been developed by some players that they claim result in a net advantage for the player.[3]

These systems involve card counting, systematic varying of bets, and numerous other strategies for special situations that arise in the game. Computer simulations of literally billions of potential blackjack hands have shown that careful adherence to a correct strategy can result in an advantage to the player of as much as 1 or 2 percent.

It should come as no surprise that players' use of these blackjack systems is not particularly welcome by the casinos. The casinos made several rule changes (such as using multiple card decks to make card counting more difficult) to reduce system players' advantages. They also started to refuse admission to known system players. Recent books on blackjack systems have long sections on how to avoid detection.

All of this turmoil shows us the importance of small changes in expected values for a game such as blackjack that involves many repetitions. The systems pay relatively little attention to the variability of outcomes on a single hand. Instead they focus on improving the average outcome after many hours at the card table.

To Think About
1. If blackjack systems increase people's expected winnings, why doesn't everyone use them? Who would you expect to be most likely to learn how to use the systems? Who would be least likely?
2. Casinos make money by gearing their games of chance to have a positive expected value for them. With many players they are therefore assured of making a profit. Explain how the house wins, on average, in slot machines; craps; roulette; and stud poker.

is a head, $X_1 = +\$1$; if a tail comes up, $X_2 = -\$1$ (the minus sign indicates that Smith must pay). From Jones' point of view the game is exactly the same, except that the signs of the outcomes are reversed. The expected value of the game is then:

$$\tfrac{1}{2}X_1 + \tfrac{1}{2}X_2 = \tfrac{1}{2}(\$1) + \tfrac{1}{2}(-\$1) = 0. \qquad [6.4]$$

[3]For an amusing although slightly outdated introduction, see E. O. Thorpe, *Beat the Dealer*, new ed. (New York: Vintage Press, 1966).

The expected value of this game is zero. If the game were played a large number of times, it is not likely that either player would come out very far ahead.

Now suppose the prizes of the game were changed slightly so that, from Smith's point of view, $X_1 = \$10$, and $X_2 = -\$1$. Smith will win \$10 if a head comes up, but will lose only \$1 if a tail comes up. The expected value of this game is \$4.50:

$$
\begin{aligned}
\tfrac{1}{2}X_1 + \tfrac{1}{2}X_2 &= \tfrac{1}{2}(\$10) + \tfrac{1}{2}(-\$1) \\
&= \$5 - \$.50 = \$4.50.
\end{aligned}
\tag{6.5}
$$

If this game is played many times, Smith will certainly end up the big winner. In fact, Smith might be willing to pay Jones something for the privilege of playing the game. Smith might even be willing to pay as much as \$4.50, the expected value, for a chance to play. Games such as the one in Equation 6.4 with an expected value of zero and games such as the one in Equation 6.5 that cost their expected values for the right to play (here \$4.50) are called actuarially **fair games**. If fair games are played many times, the monetary losses or gains are expected to be rather small. "Applying Economics: Blackjack Systems" shows the importance of the expected value concept in the game of blackjack.

Fair games
Games with an expected value of zero.

Risk Aversion

Why would people refuse to bet in fair games? Economists have found that when people are faced with a risky but fair game or situation, they will usually choose not to participate.[4] A major reason for this **risk aversion** was first identified by the Swiss mathematician Daniel Bernoulli in the eighteenth century.[5] In his early study of behavior under uncertainty, Bernoulli theorized that it is not the strictly monetary payoff of a game that matters to people. Rather, it is the utility (what Bernoulli called the "moral value") associated with the game's prizes that is important for people's decisions. If the game's money prizes do not completely reflect utility, people may find that games that are fair in dollar terms are in fact unfair in terms of utility. Specifically, Bernoulli (and most later economists) assumed that the utility associated with the payoffs in a risky situation increases less rapidly than the dollar value of

Risk aversion
The tendency of people to refuse to accept fair games.

---

[4]The games we discuss here are assumed to yield no utility in their play other than the prizes. The observation that many people gamble at "unfair" odds (for instance, in the game of roulette there are 38 possible outcomes, but the house pays only 36 to 1 for a winning number) is not necessarily a refutation of risk aversion. These people can reasonably be assumed to derive some utility from the circumstances associated with the play of the game (perhaps playing the game makes them feel like James Bond). We can differentiate the consumption aspect of gambling from the pure risk aspect.

[5]Bernoulli's original article is well worth reading in Daniel Bernoulli, "Exposition of a New Theory on the Measurement of Risk," *Econometrica*, January 1954, pp. 23–36.

Figure 6.3
Relationship between
Income and Utility

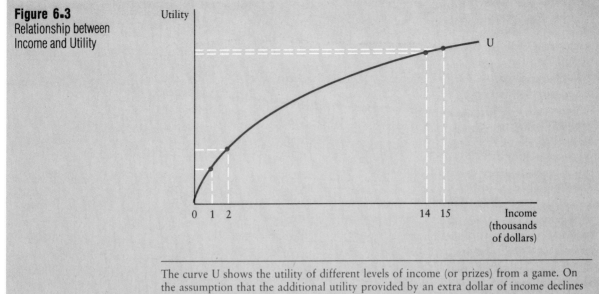

The curve U shows the utility of different levels of income (or prizes) from a game. On the assumption that the additional utility provided by an extra dollar of income declines as income increases, the curve will have the concave shape shown in the figure. This can be seen by comparing the utility gain associated with going from $1,000 to $2,000 to the gain associated with going from $14,000 to $15,000.

these payoffs. That is, the extra (or marginal) utility that winning an extra dollar in prize money provides is assumed to decline as more dollars are won.

This assumption is illustrated in Figure 6.3, which shows the utility associated with possible prizes (or incomes) from $0 to $15,000. The concave shape of the curve reflects the assumed diminishing marginal utility of these prizes. Although additional income always raises utility, the increase in utility resulting from an increase in income from $1,000 to $2,000 is much greater than the increase in utility that results from an increase in income from $14,000 to $15,000. It is this assumed diminishing marginal utility of income (which is in some ways similar to the assumption of a diminishing MRS introduced in Chapter 3) that gives rise to risk aversion. For example, a fair game that promises a gain of $1,000 when you win and a loss of $1,000 when you lose is not "fair" in utility terms. The $1,000 loss brings more pain than the $1,000 gain brings pleasure. Consequently, most people will refuse to play the game. People are more averse to playing fair games with big prizes than to playing fair games with small prizes for the same reason.

Figure 6.4 illustrates risk aversion. The figure repeats the utility of income curve from Figure 6.3 and assumes that there are three options open to this person. He or she may: (1) retain the current level of income ($10,000) without taking any risk; (2) take a fair bet with a 50–50 chance of winning or losing $2,000; or (3) take a fair bet with a 50–50 chance of winning or losing $5,000. To examine the person's preferences among these options, we must compute the expected utility available from each.

Figure 6.4
Risk Aversion

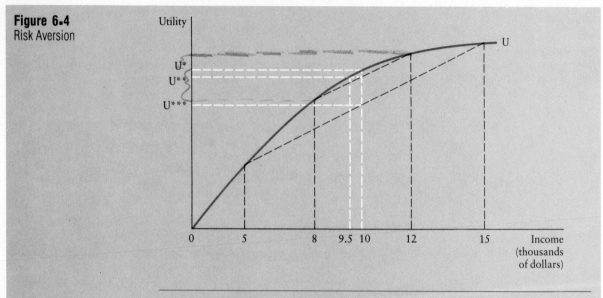

An individual characterized by the utility of income curve U will obtain a higher utility (U*) from a risk-free income of $10,000 than from a 50–50 chance of winning or losing $2,000 (U**). He or she will be willing to pay up to $500 to avoid having to take this bet. An uninsured fair bet of $5,000 provides even less utility (U***) than the $2,000 bet.

The utility received by staying at the current $10,000 income is given by U*. The U curve shows directly how the individual feels about this current income. The utility level obtained from the $2,000 bet is simply the average of the utility of $12,000 (which the individual will end up with by winning the game) and the utility of $8,000 (which he or she will end up with when the game is lost). This average utility is given by U**.[6] Because it falls short of U*, we can assume that the person will refuse to make the $2,000 bet. Finally, the utility of the $5,000 bet is the average of the utility from $15,000 and the utility from $5,000. This is given by U***, and falls below U**. In other words, the person dislikes the risky $5,000 bet even more than the $2,000 bet.

Diminished marginal utility of income, as Figure 6.4 implies, means that people will be averse to risk. Among options with the same expected dollar values ($10,000 in all of our examples), people will prefer risk-free incomes to risky options. In fact, an individual would be willing to give up some amount of certain income to avoid taking a risk. In Figure 6.4, for example, a risk-free income of $9,500 provides the same utility as does the $2,000 bet.

---

[6]Through simple geometry this average utility can be found by drawing the chord joining U($12,000) and U($8,000) and finding the midpoint of that chord. Since the vertical line at $10,000 is midway between $12,000 and $8,000, it will also bisect the chord.

Risk Aversion

People are averse to risk in a variety of ways. Three of the ways they react to risk are in diversification, insurance, and employment choices.

Diversification

"Don't put all your eggs in one basket" is advice based on risk aversion. Suppose there is a 50–50 chance of a shopping basket falling on the way home from the market and all the eggs in it breaking. Why is it better to make two trips (taking half the eggs in each trip) than to make one trip? Using either strategy, *on average* half the eggs will be broken. But the two-trip strategy is far less risky with a greater chance that at least some eggs will make it home. Under the one-trip strategy there is a 50 percent chance that no eggs will arrive home safely, whereas under the two-trip strategy the probability is only $\frac{1}{4}$ ($= \frac{1}{2} \times \frac{1}{2}$). This is why people prefer not to put all their eggs in one basket.

Diversification is a far more significant phenomenon than the basket-of-eggs example might imply. People seldom put all their wealth in a single asset; banks sharply limit the amount they will lend to any one borrower; and people would rather stand in a single line that feeds to many attendants at airline ticket counters than take the chance of getting in the slowest of several lines. These examples and many others show people's distaste for risk and the use of diversification as a means of reducing it.

Insurance

No fact attests more strongly to the prevalence of risk aversion than the size and diversity of the insurance industry in most developed countries. Each year in the United States, for example, people purchase about half a trillion dollars in life insurance protection, and probably twice that amount in insurance against casualty losses on homes, offices, automobiles, and so forth. These people are participating in an "unfair" game, because on average, they will receive far less in insurance benefits than the premiums they have paid. Insurance companies must pay for the costs of administering their policies out of premium income. People are willing to pay these costs (and thereby participate in an unfair game) because of the reduction in risk that insurance coverage provides.

Employment Decisions

Aversion to risk is also demonstrated in people's em-

Table 6.6
Average Annual Incomes in Independent and Salaried Professional Practice

	Salaried Practice	Independent Practice
Physicians (AMA survey, 1928)	$5,428	$6,499
Lawyers (New York County survey, 1933)	$4,316	$6,664

Source: M. Friedman and S. Kuznets, *Income from Independent Professional Practice* (New York: National Bureau of Economic Research, 1945), p. 299.

ployment choices. Jobs whose earnings are relatively uncertain will be unattractive to potential employees. Average earnings on these jobs may have to be higher than on jobs with fixed earnings to compensate for the risk of lower earnings. For example, Friedman and Kuznets[7] examined a number of surveys of professional employment that were conducted in the 1920s and 1930s. They concluded that people in independent practice earned considerably higher average incomes than those in a salaried practice. Table 6.6 illustrates a few of their findings. Although the authors attribute the income differences between independent and salaried practices to a number of factors (independent practitioners often have to buy their own equipment, for example), one reason for the differences was clearly the more risky nature of independent practice. The higher average incomes earned in independent practice can be seen in part as compensating for the risk.

To Think About

1. Why might some insurance be too expensive for even a very risk averse person to buy? Why, for example, is "first dollar" automobile collision insurance (that is, insurance with no deductible) very expensive? Why does no one buy it at this price? Can you think of other examples of risks that people take in their lives because buying insurance is too expensive?

2. Some risky assets tend to have returns that move together (stocks, for example, tend to rise and fall together) whereas other assets tend to move in opposite directions (gold and stocks are an example). How would a risk averse person make choices among such assets? Which assets would be substitutes for one another? Which would be complements?

---

[7]Milton Friedman and Simon Kuznets, *Income from Independent Professional Practice* (New York: National Bureau of Economic Research, 1945).

The individual is willing to pay up to $500 to avoid taking that bet. Risk aversion is the reason people purchase insurance of many types. They are willing to give up some income (the insurance premium) to avoid the possibility of large losses. Many other activities are also based on risk aversion motives, as "Applying Economics: Risk Aversion" shows.

The Search for Information

In a sense, all individual behavior in uncertain situations can be regarded as a response to a lack of information. If people knew that a coin was going to come up a head, or knew how their investments would fare next year, they would be better off. They may even be willing to pay for additional information to reduce uncertainty, and probably will do so as long as the expected gains from this information exceed its cost. For example, someone trying to decide whether or not to buy a used car may pay an impartial mechanic to evaluate the car's condition before buying it; someone wishing to buy a color television may check around to find the best price.

Better weather forecasting (paid for with tax dollars) undoubtedly has reduced the uncertainty in timing crop cultivation, and it has also mitigated the dangers of living on the Gulf coast. *Consumer Reports* magazine gives its subscribers detailed information on consumer goods, which presumably permits them to make more rational purchase decisions. "Applying Economics: The Value of Accurate Weather Forecasts to Raisin Growers" shows how increased information can reduce uncertainty to benefit producers of farm goods.

Government also may reduce the uncertainty in purchasing decisions both by providing consumers with testing information (such as mileage figures for cars) and by setting safety standards for certain products. Although such policies impose costs on consumers and on taxpayers, the benefits of those policies in terms of reduced risk may exceed these costs.

Economists have devoted considerable attention to studying how people gain information to reduce risk. The most thoroughly developed of these models involves people's job search activities. In looking for work, there is considerable uncertainty about where job openings are and what wages are offered. People looking for jobs must invest time and other resources to learn these things. Consumers searching for the best price on some item and football fans looking for a ticket to a sold-out Super Bowl game also need to invest time and other resources. We return to the implications of these activities for overall market performance in several places later in this book.

Summary

This chapter looks at three rather different applications of the notion that people make economic choices in a utility-maximizing way. Each of these applications shows how economists have tried to study a particular problem

APPLYING ECONOMICS

The Value of Accurate Weather Forecasts to Raisin Growers

Accurate weather forecasts are crucial to many situations in which decisions depend on the weather. People must make decisions about where to spend their vacations or whether to go to a baseball game; commuters must decide how they will get to work in bad weather; builders must schedule their outside work to take advantage of good weather; and ski slope operators must decide whether or not to turn on their artificial snow machines. One of the most important examples of the impact of the weather on production is agriculture, where anticipated rainfall affects a number of decisions, such as which crop to plant, when to harvest, and whether to use the sun or natural gas for crop drying. Although these decisions are subject to considerable uncertainty, the weather is very important in the economic calculations on which the decisions are based.

These calculations are particularly important in the raisin industry of the San Joaquin Valley in California. Raisins are produced by sundrying grapes in the early fall. If conditions for drying are expected to be unfavorable, the grapes can be crushed instead to produce wine, although this may be somewhat less profitable. A farmer who opts for drying raisins takes a considerable gamble because rain could virtually destroy the raisin crop (leaving the grapes with only a scrap value if sold to a distillery). Weather forecasting therefore plays a major role in growers' decisions: A fall forecast of rain could prompt many to sell their grapes for wine, whereas a sunny forecast would cause many farmers to try to make it through the required 21-day drying period for raisins.

In an important 1963 study, Lester Lave estimated the value that more accurate weather forecasts would have for raisin growers.[8] He first carefully outlined all of the relevant decisions that growers make as the fall harvest approaches and calculated how each decision depends on the expected weather. He then compared the expected profits under average (but uncertain) weather patterns with the profits that might be expected if the likelihood of rain could be accurately forecast over a three-week period. Using this procedure, Lave estimated that improved forecasting accuracy would increase raisin growers' profits by about $91 per acre. Applied to all acres planted in 1960, this figure yielded an estimate of over $20 million for the value of better weather information to the industry as a whole.[9] Even for this relatively small segment of the economy the value of information can be substantial.

To Think About

1. How can better weather forecasts make raisin growing more profitable? Better forecasts, after all, don't bring better weather, so why should it matter if growers know what the weather will be? How can better forecasts have any economic value at all?

2. Most weather forecasting in the United States is done by the U.S. Weather Service, a government agency. If weather forecasts are so valuable, why don't private firms buy their own forecasts just as they buy other productive services? What kinds of weather forecasts would you think would be most likely to be provided through private markets? Which kinds through the government?

---

[8]Lester B. Lave, "The Value of Better Weather Information to the Raisin Industry," *Econometrica*, January–April 1963, pp. 151–164.

[9]Lave also pointed out that the increased raisin production brought about through better information may cause raisin prices to fall, making this kind of aggregate estimate an overestimate for the industry as a whole. Lower prices would benefit consumers, however, so Lave's estimates may understate the social value of better forecasts.

in the theory of choice and each has many important implications for a number of economic subjects. The principal conclusions that can be drawn from these applications are:

- Voluntary trade can make both of the parties involved better off. The possibility for such mutually beneficial transactions occurs whenever two peoples' current consumption choices result in their having unequal marginal rates of substitution (MRS).
- The gains from trade may be unequally shared in any particular transaction. Generally, the closer the terms of trading are to an individual's MRS, the smaller will be that person's gains from trading.
- Construction of economic index numbers is a complex process that involves selecting weights to be used to add up different magnitudes. A primary reason that the construction of some index numbers is particularly difficult is that they seek to approximate individuals' preferences, which are essentially unmeasurable.
- In risky situations people will generally refuse fair bets. This risk aversion is a result of diminishing marginal utility of income (or wealth)—winning a fair bet offers less utility than the utility that is lost from losing the bet.
- All uncertainty can be regarded as a lack of information. People will be willing to pay for additional information that helps them to reduce uncertainty.

Problems

6.1 Backyard Jack has a yard full of trees and firewood, but cannot grow very much corn due to poor sunlight. Sunshine Steve, on the other hand, has wide open cornfields but little firewood to keep him warm. Jack starts out with 20 cords of firewood and only 5 bushels of corn and has a MRS (of firewood for corn) of $\frac{1}{3}$. Steve begins with 25 bushels of corn and only 10 cords of firewood and has a MRS of 2. How can both men be made better off through trade? Illustrate this situation with a graph.

6.2 The nation of Oskago is a rocky island whose inhabitants are particularly hardworking and adept fishermen. They are able to catch eight tons of fish per year, yet they can gather only four tons of coconuts per year. The going price for one coconut on the island is two fish. Nearby is the island paradise of Silveto whose lazy inhabitants catch only four tons of fish per year but gather eight tons of coconuts every year from the lush forests. On Silveto, the price of one fish is two coconuts. With the advent of lightweight boats, the possibility of virtually cost-free trade now exists. Should the two island nations trade products? Why or why not? Graph your results.

6.3 Assume that martini drinkers always use a ratio of 10 units of gin to 1 unit of vermouth when mixing their cocktails. Assuming they spend all their income on martinis, show that real income calculations for martini drinkers will be the same regardless of whether base year or current year price indices are used.

6.4 Suppose oil prices, natural gas prices, and coal prices always move together, with the price of a gallon of fuel oil being exactly equal to the price of 1,000 cubic feet of natural gas and 50 pounds of coal. Show that in this situation an index of fossil fuel (that is, oil, natural gas, and coal) prices will give the same estimate of inflation regardless of whether base year or current year quantities are used as weights.

6.5 The residents of Uurp consume only pork chops (X) and Coca Cola (Y). The utility function for the typical resident of Uurp is given by

$$\text{Utility} = U(X,Y) = \sqrt{X \cdot Y}.$$

In 1986 the price of pork chops in Uurp was \$1 each and Cokes were also \$1 each. The typical resident consumed 40 pork chops and 40 Cokes (saving is impossible in Uurp). In 1987 swine fever hit Uurp, and pork chop prices rose to \$4 with the Coke price remaining unchanged. At these new prices the typical Uurp resident consumed 20 pork chops and 80 Cokes.

a. Show that utility for the typical Uurp resident was unchanged between the two years.

b. Show that using 1986 prices would show an increase in real income between 1986 and 1987.

c. Show that using 1987 prices would show a decrease in real income between 1986 and 1987.

d. What do you conclude about the ability of these indices to measure changes in real income?

6.6 Suppose a person must accept one of three bets.

  ▪ Bet 1: Win \$100 with probability ½; lose \$100 with probability ½.
  ▪ Bet 2: Win \$100 with probability ¾; lose \$300 with probability ¼.
  ▪ Bet 3: Win \$100 with probability ⁹⁄₁₀; lose \$900 with probability ¹⁄₁₀.

a. Show that all of these are fair bets.

b. Graph each bet on a utility of income curve similar to Figure 6.4.

c. Explain carefully which bet will be preferred and why.

6.7 Show that if an individual's utility of income function is convex (rather than concave as shown in Figure 6.3), he or she will prefer fair gambles to income certainty and may even be willing to accept somewhat unfair gambles. Do you believe this sort of risk-taking behavior is common? What factors might tend to limit its occurrence?

6.8 A person purchases a dozen eggs and must take them home. Although making trips home is costless, there is a 50 percent chance that all of the eggs carried on one trip will be broken during the trip.

This person considers two strategies:

- Strategy one: Take all 12 eggs in one trip.
- Strategy two: Make two trips, taking 6 eggs in each trip.

a. List the possible outcomes of each strategy and the probabilities of these outcomes. Show that, on average, 6 eggs make it home under either strategy.
b. Develop a graph to show the utility obtainable under each strategy.
c. Could utility be improved further by taking more than two trips? How would the desirability of this possibility be affected if additional trips were costly?

*6.9 It is known that parking in an illegal space in downtown Podunk leads to a 50 percent chance of getting a $10 parking ticket.

a. Graph the individual's decision to park in this space. Show that, unless the space provides substantial convenience, the individual will not choose to park there.
b. Podunk is considering increasing its parking fine to $20. Show that this would reduce the utility of parking in the illegal space further.
c. The police chief of Podunk argues that increasing patrols to insure that any violator is caught (that is, to insure that there is a 100 percent likelihood of getting a $10 ticket if one parks in the illegal space) would be more effective at deterring illegal parking than increasing the fine. Would you agree? Graph your results.

*6.10 Ms. Fogg is planning an around-the-world trip. The utility from the trip is a function of how much she spends on it (Y) given by

$$U(Y) = \log Y.$$

Ms. Fogg has $10,000 to spend on the trip. If she spends all of it, her utility will be

$$U(10,000) = \log 10,000 = 4.$$

(In this problem we are using logarithms to the base 10 for ease of computation.)

a. If there is a 25 percent probability that Ms. Fogg will lose $1,000 of her cash on the trip, what is the trip's expected utility?
b. Suppose that Ms. Fogg can buy insurance against losing the $1,000 (say, by purchasing traveler's checks) at an "actuarially fair" pre-

---

*Denotes a problem that is rather difficult.

mium of $250. Show that her utility is higher if she purchases this insurance than if she faces the chance of losing the $1,000 without insurance.

c. What is the maximum amount that Ms. Fogg would be willing to pay to insure her $1,000?

d. Suppose that people who buy insurance tend to become more careless with their cash than those who don't, and assume that the probability of their losing $1,000 is 30 percent. What will be the actuarially fair insurance premium? Will Ms. Fogg buy insurance in this situation?

FIRMS, PRODUCTION, AND SUPPLY

Part 3 considers the production and supply of economic goods. The institutions that are engaged in this process are called "firms." They may be large, complex organizations, such as IBM or the U.S. Defense Department, or they may be quite small, such as "mom and pop" stores or self-employed farmers. The organizations may also have different goals—IBM may pursue maximum profits, while the U.S. Defense Department may be interested in the "protection" it can provide with the overall size of its budget. Whatever goals they pursue, all firms must make choices about what inputs they will use and the level of output they will supply. Part 4 looks at these choices.

To be able to produce any output firms must "hire" many inputs (labor, capital, natural resources, and so forth). These inputs, because they are scarce, have costs associated with their use. Our goal in Chapters 7 and 8 is to develop cost curves that relate these input costs to the level of the firm's output. In Chapter 7 we introduce the firm's "production function," which shows the relationship between inputs used and the level of output that results. Once the relationship between inputs and outputs is known, the costs of various input levels can be determined for corresponding levels of output, as shown in Chapter 8. By developing cost relationships from the underlying notion of production functions, we can more clearly see why cost curves might shift or how short-run and long-run costs might differ. An appendix to Chapter 8 uses a numerical example to show these results.

Chapter 9 then uses the cost curves developed in Chapter 8 to discuss firms' supply decisions. The primary model presented in the chapter is of a firm that seeks maximum profits given the market it faces. Several controversial issues that arise in connection with this assumption of profit maximization are briefly discussed. The chapter concludes with a detailed analysis of the supply decisions of profit-maximizing firms that will be used, with the analysis of demand from Part 2 to discuss price determination in Part 4.

The final chapter in Part 3, Chapter 10, looks at a few additional applications of the theory of the firm. The chapter is specifically concerned with the types of agreements (that is, "contracts") that exist between firms and their employees and managers. The study of such agreements has become a major area of interest to economists in recent years, and a general purpose of the chapter is to introduce you to some of this recent work. The chapter begins with a discussion of the relationship between employees and the firms they work for. It shows that both employees and firms will find it in their interest to establish relatively long-term commitments rather than settling for very short-term employment relationships. Having such relationships with their employees may change the ways firms behave in various situations. The hiring of managers poses similar issues for firms. In the second section of Chapter 10 we examine this relationship and show some of the problems that arise when the firm's owners must rely on hired managers to be their "agents" in making operating decisions. Finally we consider the market for firms themselves. We explore why one firm may wish to buy another one in order to obtain control of its operations. We show that these activities may restrict the kinds of agreements that firms may reach with employees and managers. The empirical examples in Chapter 10 show you how all of these topics are important to understanding issues of business behavior that appear on television and in newspapers every day. ▲

Production

Chapters 7 and 8 develop the relationship between the level of production in a firm and the input costs associated with that level of output. This description of costs provides the basis for our analysis of firms' supply decisions—the principal topic of Part 3. Chapter 7 begins this process with an analysis of the physical aspects of production. We show how economists conceptualize the relationship between the inputs a firm uses and the output it thereby obtains. Using this relationship, input costs can be associated with various output levels, a topic which is developed in Chapter 8.

Production Functions

Firm
Any organization that turns inputs into outputs.

Production function
The mathematical relationship between inputs and outputs.

The purpose of any **firm** is to turn inputs into outputs: General Motors combines steel, glass, workers' time, and hours of assembly line operation to produce automobiles; farmers combine their labor with seed, soil, rain, fertilizer, and machinery to produce crops; and colleges combine professors' time with books and (perhaps) hours of study to produce (perhaps) educated students. Because economists are interested in the choices that firms make to accomplish their goals, and because they wish to avoid many of the intricacies involved in actual production decisions, they have developed a rather abstract model of production. In this model the relationship between inputs and outputs is formalized by a **production function** of the form

$$Q = f(K, L, M \ldots),$$

[7.1]

157

where Q represents the output of a particular good[1] during a period, K represents the machine (that is, capital) use during the period, L represents hours of labor input, and M represents raw materials used. The form of the notation indicates the possibility of other variables affecting the production process. The production function, therefore, summarizes what the firm knows about mixing various inputs to yield output.

For example, this production function might represent a farmer's output of wheat during one year as being dependent on the amount of labor used on the farm, the quantity of machinery employed, the amount of land under cultivation, the amount of fertilizer and seeds used, and so forth. The function also shows that there are many different ways in which, say, 100 bushels of wheat could be produced. The farmer could use a very labor-intensive technique that would require only a small amount of mechanical equipment (as tends to be the case in China). The 100 bushels could also be produced using large amounts of equipment and fertilizer with very little labor (as in the United States). A great deal of land might be used to produce the 100 bushels of wheat with less of the other inputs (as in Brazil or Australia); or relatively little land could be used with great amounts of labor, equipment, and fertilizer (as in British or Japanese agriculture). All of these combinations are represented by the general production function in Equation 7.1. For any possible combination of land, equipment, labor, and other inputs, the function records the maximum wheat output that can be produced from those given inputs. The important question about the production function from an economic point of view is how the individual levels of Q, K, L, and M are chosen by the firm. We take this question up in detail in the next several chapters.

A Simplification

We simplify the production function here by assuming that the firm's production depends on only two inputs: capital (K) and labor (L). Hence, the simplified production function is now given by

$$Q = f(K,L). \qquad [7.2]$$

Our decision to focus on capital and labor is arbitrary. Most of our analysis here will hold true for any two inputs that might be investigated. For example, if we wished to examine the effects of rainfall and fertilizer on crop production, we could use those two inputs in the production function while holding other inputs (quantity of land, hours of labor input, and so on) constant. In the production function that characterizes a school system, we could examine

---

[1]*Output of a particular good* indicates that we are considering only productive processes that produce identical goods. For example, cheap shoes and good shoes are two different goods and, presumably, have different production functions. Sometimes this output for a firm is defined to include only its "valued added"; that is, the value of intermediate inputs used by the firm is excluded.

the relationship between the "output" of the system (say, academic achievement) and the inputs used to produce this output (such as teachers, buildings, and learning aids). The two general inputs of capital and labor are used here for convenience, and we frequently will show these inputs on a two-dimensional graph.

Marginal Physical Productivity

Marginal physical productivity
The additional output that can be produced by one more unit of a particular input while holding all other inputs constant.

A first question we might ask about the relationship between inputs and outputs is how much extra output can be produced by adding one more unit of an input to the production process. The **marginal physical productivity** of an input is defined as the quantity of extra output provided by employing one additional unit of that input while holding all other inputs constant. For our two principal inputs of capital and labor, the marginal physical product of labor is the extra output obtained by having one more worker—while holding the level of capital equipment constant. Similarly, the marginal physical productivity of capital is the extra output obtained by using one more machine while holding the number of workers constant. In mathematical terms:

$$\text{Marginal physical productivity of labor} = MP_L$$

$$= \frac{\text{Change in output}}{\text{Change in labor input}}. \qquad [7.3]$$

$\frac{\Delta Q}{\Delta L}$

As an application of this definition, consider the case of a farmer hiring one more person to harvest a crop while holding all other inputs constant. The extra output produced by this person is the marginal physical productivity of labor input. The concept is measured in physical quantities such as bushels of wheat, crates of oranges, or heads of lettuce. We might, for example, observe that 25 workers in a farm are able to produce 100 bushels of wheat per year, whereas 26 workers (with the same land and equipment) can produce 102 bushels. The marginal physical product of the 26th worker is 2 bushels per year.

Diminishing Marginal Physical Productivity

We might expect the marginal physical productivity of an input to depend on how much of that input is used. Workers, for example, cannot be added indefinitely to the harvesting of a given field (while keeping the amount of the equipment, fertilizer, and so forth fixed) without the marginal productivity eventually deteriorating. This possibility is illustrated in Figure 7.1. The relationship between the quantity of a particular input (labor) and total output is recorded in Graph a of Figure 7.1. At low levels of labor usage, output increases rapidly as additional labor is added. However, because *other inputs are held constant,* the ability of additional labor to generate additional output

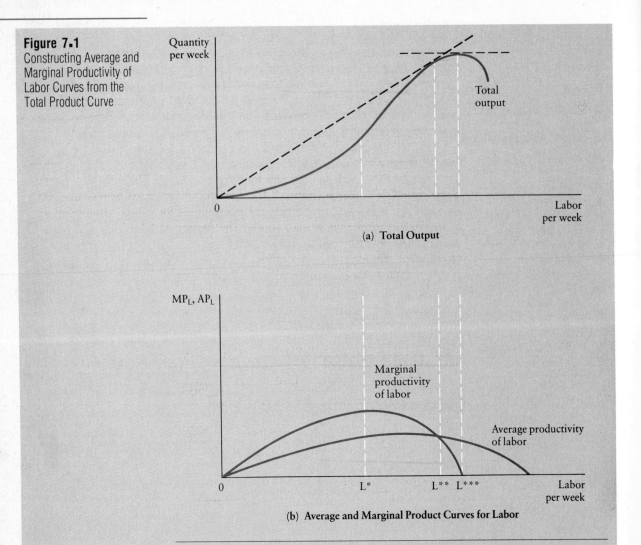

Figure 7.1
Constructing Average and
Marginal Productivity of
Labor Curves from the
Total Product Curve

Quantity per week

Total output

0   Labor per week

(a) Total Output

MP_L, AP_L

Marginal productivity of labor

Average productivity of labor

0   L^* L^{**} L^{***} Labor per week

(b) Average and Marginal Product Curves for Labor

These curves show how the average and marginal productivity of labor curves can be derived from the total output curve. The total output curve in Graph a represents the relationship between labor input and output, on the assumption that all other inputs are held constant. In Graph b, the slope of this curve shows the marginal productivity of labor (MP_L), and the slope of a chord joining the origin to a point on the TP_L curve gives the average productivity of labor (AP_L).

eventually begins to deteriorate. Finally, at L^{***} output reaches its maximum level. Any labor added beyond this point actually decreases output. Beyond L^{***} additional laborers get in each other's way to such an extent that total output begins to decline.

The total output curve in Graph a of Figure 7.1 shows graphically the assumption that labor's marginal physical productivity eventually declines as more labor is added to the production process while holding other inputs constant. This assumption is extremely important in economic analysis. If a firm continues to add workers to a production process, it must eventually run into diminishing returns. The inputs that are being held fixed (such as machinery or land) will eventually become "overutilized," and a decline in marginal productivity will set in. The nineteenth century philosopher Thomas Malthus argued that additional labor cannot be constantly added to a fixed supply of land without the productivity of labor in food production eventually beginning to diminish.[2] Since the quantity of land is, in the long run, absolutely fixed, Malthus predicted that the diminishing marginal productivity of labor would eventually mean that population growth would outpace the growth in food production (with not enough food for everyone). This led to economics being called the "dismal science." Most modern economists believe that Malthus did not adequately recognize the possibilities for capital equipment and technical advances that would prevent the decline of labor's productivity in agriculture. Nevertheless, the basic observation that the marginal productivity of labor (or any other factor) declines when *all other inputs* are held constant is still recognized as an empirically valid proposition.

Marginal Physical Productivity Curve

From the total labor productivity curve in Graph a of Figure 7.1, several other productivity curves can be constructed. The marginal physical product of labor is simply the slope of the total output curve, since this slope just shows how output expands as additional labor is added. In Graph b in Figure 7.1 the marginal product curve (MP_L) is drawn. This curve reaches a maximum at L^* and declines as labor input is added beyond this point. This movement is a reflection of the assumption of a diminishing marginal product of labor. MP_L is equal to 0 at the point L^{***} for which total output reaches a maximum. Beyond L^{***} further additions of labor input actually reduce output. Production will not take place beyond L^{***} since using more labor (which is presumably costly) will result in less output for the firm.

Average Physical Productivity

"Labor productivity" usually means average productivity. When it is said that a certain industry has experienced productivity increases, this is taken to mean that output per unit of labor input has increased. Although this concept of average productivity is not nearly so important in theoretical economics as is marginal productivity, it receives a great deal of attention in popular discussions. Because average productivity is easily measured (say, as so many bushels

[2]A somewhat facetious "proof" of the diminishing marginal productivity of labor input argues that if it were not true that marginal productivities diminish, the entire world food supply could be grown in a single flower pot if a sufficient quantity of labor were applied to the pot. Since this situation is obviously absurd, the marginal productivity of labor must, after some point, diminish.

of wheat per hour of labor input), it is often used as a measure of efficiency. It is a simple matter to derive average productivity relationships from the total product curve. This is also done in Figure 7.1. By definition the **average productivity** of any input (say, labor) is the ratio of total output produced to the quantity of the input employed. That is:

Average productivity
The ratio of total output produced to the quantity of a particular input employed.

$$\text{Average productivity of labor} = AP_L = Q/L. \qquad [7.4]$$

Geometrically, the value of the average productivity of labor for any quantity of labor input is the slope of the chord drawn from the origin in Graph a in Figure 7.1 to the relevant point on the total output curve. This is true since the slope of such a chord is simply Q/L. By drawing a series of chords through the origin to various points on the total output curve, the average product of labor curve (AP_L) can be constructed. This curve is shown in Graph b in Figure 7.1. It can be seen that the average and marginal productivities of labor are equal at L^{**}. For this level of labor input, the chord through the origin in Graph A in Figure 7.1 is just tangent to the total output curve. The average and marginal productivities of labor are equal.

Also at L^{**} the average productivity of labor is at its maximum value. This feature of the curve can be demonstrated as follows: for levels of labor input less than L^{**}, the marginal productivity of labor (MP_L) exceeds its average productivity (AP_L). Consequently, adding one more worker will raise the average production of all workers since the increased output from hiring this additional worker exceeds that produced by the average worker previously. A good example of this is a baseball team with a team batting average of .260 that acquires a .300 hitter: the team average would rise. For labor input greater than L^{**}, the average productivity of labor falls. Beyond L^{**}, labor's average productivity exceeds its marginal productivity, so average productivity is falling. Adding a worker to the production process causes output to rise by less than the average that previously prevailed. Consequently, the average productivity of labor will fall. In our baseball analogy, adding a .200 hitter to the team will indeed cause the team average to fall.

We have shown that to the left of L^{**} the AP_L curve is rising; to the right of L^{**} it is falling. Therefore, the average productivity of labor reaches its maximum value at L^{**}. Labor added beyond this point will cause the average productivity of labor to fall.

Physical Productivity Curves and the *Ceteris Paribus* Assumption

Figure 7.1 records all the available information about the way in which varying labor input (or any other input) affects output. It is important to remember the assumption that lies behind the construction of these curves: All possible inputs, other than labor, are being held constant at some specified levels. The marginal productivity curve records the *ceteris paribus* productivity of additional units of labor input, and the average productivity curve similarly records the *ceteris paribus* average productivity of various levels of labor input. If the firm were to hire more of some other input (say, more machines) all of the curves pictured in Figure 7.1 would move to new positions. For example, if a farmer were to double the land under cultivation and the use of machinery to work that land, we would expect both the marginal and the average productivity curves for labor to shift upward and to the right. With increased levels of complementary inputs more labor can be used before diminishing returns begin to appear.

The *ceteris paribus* assumption limits the application of the curves in Figure 7.1 to real-world production processes. Most firms change the levels of both labor *and* machines in response to changes in economic circumstances. We will therefore never observe a neat tracing of a single total productivity of labor curve, but rather a series of Q, L points that lie on a number of different curves. Before we describe a way of illustrating the entire production function that avoids this problem, it may be interesting to examine some productivity data from the real world in "Applying Economics: Average Productivity in Steel Production."

Isoquant Maps

Isoquant map
A contour map of a firm's production function.

Isoquant
A curve that shows the various combinations of inputs that will produce the same amount of output.

One way to picture the entire production function in two dimensions is to use its **isoquant map.** We can again use a production function of the form Q = f(K,L), using capital and labor as convenient examples of any two inputs that might happen to be of interest. How can we show the combinations of these inputs that would produce a given output level? An **isoquant** (from the Greek *iso*, meaning equal) can be used to show alternative combinations of capital and labor input that will produce a particular level of output. For example, all those combinations of K and L that fall on the curve labeled "Q = 10" in Figure 7.2 are capable of producing 10 units of output per period. This single isoquant records the many alternative ways of producing 10 units of output. One combination is represented by point A. We could use L_A and K_A to produce 10 units of output. Alternatively, we might prefer to use relatively less capital and more labor, and would therefore choose a point such as B. The isoquant clearly demonstrates the many different ways in which a firm can produce 10 units of output just as the indifference curves in Part 2 showed that many different bundles of goods yield the same utility.

There are infinitely many isoquants in the K-L plane. Each isoquant represents a different level of output. The isoquants record successively higher levels of output as we move out in a northeasterly direction. Presumably using more of each of the inputs will permit output to increase. Two other isoquants (for Q = 20 and Q = 30) are also shown in Figure 7.2. They record those combinations of inputs that can produce the specified level of output. You may notice the similarity between an isoquant map and the individual's indifference curve map discussed in Part 2. Both are "contour" maps. For isoquants, however, the labeling of the curves is measurable (an output of 10 units has a quantifiable meaning), and we are more interested in the shape of these curves than we were in the exact shape of indifference curves.

APPLYING ECONOMICS

Average Productivity in Steel Production

Table 7.1 reports data on the average productivity of labor in steel during a tumultuous period for the steel industry, 1970 through 1976. The data came from three producing areas: the United States, Japan, and the European Coal and Steel Community (ECSC). Entries in the table represent the output of steel (measured in metric tons) per 100 hours of labor input.

We can come to a number of interesting conclusions from the table. First, there is clear evidence of an upward trend in average productivity. Increasing amounts of capital used in steel production and improved steel-making technology (such as wider adoption of the basic oxygen process) probably accounted for this trend. During this period of significant change productivity rose much more rapidly in Japan than in the United States or in the ECSC, and that may also be related to Japan's more rapid adoption of new technologies. Economic problems of U.S. steelmakers during the 1980s and demands in the United States (and in Europe) for increased tariff protection against imported steel indicate that these productivity trends are of more than academic concern.

A final fact illustrated by the table concerns the behavior of labor productivity over the business cycle. Each of the producers saw its average productivity of labor in steel production fall during 1975—a year of worldwide recession. This pattern can better be explained as the reaction of steel firms to a downturn in demand than as a shift in the underlying productivity relationships. When orders for steel fall off (as they do in a recession) firms are reluctant to lay off workers immediately. Adopting a quick layoff policy would impose current costs on firms (such as having to make severance payments to laid-off workers) and might make it hard for the firms to hire their skilled workers back when demand conditions improve. Consequently, firms may "hoard" labor during temporary recessions (see Chapter 10). Since output (Q) falls and the work force (L) stays relatively constant, average productivity (Q/L) falls during

Table 7.1
Average Physical Productivity in Steel Production, 1970–1976, in Metric Tons of Finished Steel per 100 Labor-Hours

Year	United States	Japan	European Coal and Steel Community
1970	7.4	5.7	5.2
1971	7.9	5.6	5.2
1972	8.2	6.4	5.8
1973	9.3	8.0	6.4
1974	9.4	8.1	6.9
1975	8.1	7.5	6.7
1976	8.6	8.1	6.5

Source: Calculated from Council on Wage and Price Stability Report to the President on Prices and Costs in the United States Steel Industry, Washington, D.C., October 1977, Appendix Table No. 20.

such periods. In judging overall productivity trends in an industry (or in the entire economy) we must be careful not to put too much importance on short-term, cyclical movements.

To Think About

1. Some authors argue that Japan had an "advantage" in adopting new techniques for making steel because most of its older facilities were destroyed during World War II. Does this argument make sense? Are there reasons why a firm with older facilities might delay in adopting the best available technology?
2. Is the existence of older steel-making facilities in the United States a good reason for protecting the steel industry from open competition with the Japanese? Would such protection encourage U.S. steel firms to adopt the new techniques more quickly?

Rate of Technical Substitution

The slope of an isoquant shows how one input can be traded for another while holding the output constant. Examining the slope will give us some information about the technical possibilities for substituting labor for capital.

Figure 7.2
Isoquant Map

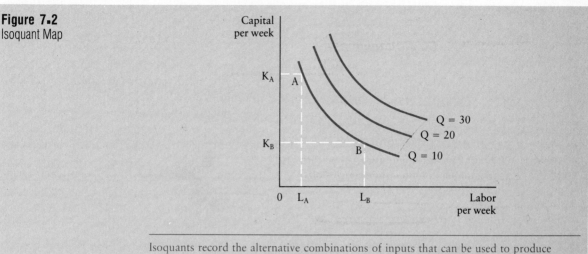

Isoquants record the alternative combinations of inputs that can be used to produce a given level of output. The slope of these curves shows the rate at which L can be substituted for K while keeping output constant. The negative of this slope is called the (marginal) rate of technical substitution (RTS). In the figure, the RTS is positive, and it is diminishing for increasing inputs of labor.

Marginal rate of technical substitution
The negative of the slope of an isoquant. This shows the amount by which capital input can be reduced while holding the output constant when one more unit of labor input is added.

Because of this, the slope of an isoquant (or, more properly, its negative) is called the **marginal rate of technical substitution (RTS)** of labor for capital. More precisely, the RTS is defined to be the amount by which capital input can be reduced while holding quantity produced constant when one more unit of labor input is used. Mathematically,

Rate of technical substitution = RTS (of L for K)
(of labor for capital)

$$= - \text{(Slope of isoquant)}$$

$$RTS = -\frac{\Delta K}{\Delta L}$$

$$= - \frac{\text{Change in capital input}}{\text{Change in labor input}}$$
(holding Q constant).

[7.5]

The particular value of this trade-off rate will depend not only on the level of output but also on the quantities of capital and labor being used. Its value depends on the point on the isoquant map at which the slope is to be measured. At a point such as A in Figure 7.2, relatively large amounts of capital can be given up if one or more units of labor are employed—at point A, the RTS is a high positive number. On the other hand, at point B the availability of an additional unit of labor does not permit a very large reduction in capital input, and the RTS is relatively small.

We can use the RTS concept to discuss the likely shape of a firm's isoquant map. Most obviously, it seems clear that the RTS should be positive—that is, each isoquant should have a negative slope. If the quantity of labor employed by the firm increases, the firm should be able to reduce capital input while keeping output constant. Since labor presumably has a positive marginal productivity, the firm should be able to get by with less capital input when more labor is used. If increasing labor actually required more capital to be used by the firm, it would imply that the marginal productivity of labor (or of capital[3]) is negative, and no firm would be willing to pay anything to hire an input with a negative marginal physical productivity. All isoquants that are actually observed should be negatively sloped to show the true trade-off between capital and labor input.

The isoquants in Figure 7.2 are drawn not only with a negative slope (as they should be) but also as convex curves. Along any one of the curves the RTS is *diminishing*. For a high ratio of K to L, the RTS is a large positive number indicating that a great deal of capital can be given up if one more unit of labor is employed. On the other hand, when a lot of labor is already being used, the RTS is low, signifying that only a small amount of capital can be traded for an additional unit of labor if output is to be held constant. This shape seems intuitively reasonable: The more labor (relative to capital) that is used, the less labor can substitute for capital. The diminishing RTS shows that a particular input can be pushed too far. Firms will not want to use "only labor" or "only machines" to produce a given level of output.[4] They will choose a more balanced input mix that uses at least some of each input. In Chapter 8 we will see exactly how an optimal (that is, minimum cost) mix of inputs might be chosen.

Returns to Scale

Because production functions represent tangible, measurable productive processes, economists pay considerable attention to the form of these functions. The shape and properties of a firm's production function are important for a

---

[3]This result can be shown formally by recognizing that the RTS is equal to the ratio of the marginal productivity of labor to the marginal productivity of capital. That is:

$$\text{RTS (of L for K)} = \frac{MP_L}{MP_K},$$

since this value of marginal productivities shows how L can be traded for K while holding Q constant. For example, if $MP_L = 2$ and $MP_K = 1$, the RTS will be 2, since one more unit of labor input can replace the production of two units of capital. Given this result, it is clear that if the RTS is negative (that is, if an isoquant has a positive slope) either MP_L or MP_K must be negative.

[4]An incorrect, but possibly instructive, argument (based on footnote 3 of this chapter) might proceed as follows. In moving along an isoquant more labor and less capital are being used. Assuming that each factor exhibits a diminishing marginal productivity, it might be argued that MP_L would decrease (since the quantity of labor has increased) and that MP_K would increase (since the quantity of capital has decreased). Consequently, the RTS (= MP_L/MP_K) should decrease. The fallacy in this argument is that *both* factors are changing together. It is not possible to make such simple determinations about changes in their marginal productivities, since the marginal productivity concept requires that all other inputs be held constant.

variety of reasons. Using such information, a firm may decide how its research funds might best be spent on developing technical improvements. We can also use the form of production functions to argue that laws prohibiting very large-scale firms would harm economic efficiency. The next two sections develop some terminology to aid in examining such issues.

The first important question we might ask about production functions is, how does the quantity of output respond to increases in all inputs together? For example, suppose all inputs were doubled. Would output also double, or is the relationship not quite so simple? This is an example of the **returns to scale** exhibited by a production function.

Returns to scale
The rate at which output increases in response to proportional increases in all inputs.

This concept has been of interest to economists ever since Adam Smith intensively studied (of all things) the production of pins in 1776. Smith identified two forces that come into play when all inputs are doubled (for a doubling of scale). First, a doubling of scale permits a greater "division of labor." Smith was intrigued by the skill of people who made only pin heads or pin shafts, or who stuck the two together. Efficiency might therefore increase—production might more than double—as greater specialization becomes possible.

Smith did not envision that these benefits to large-scale operations would always be available. He recognized that large productive enterprises may encounter inefficiencies in managerial direction and control if inputs are increased. Coordination of production plans for more inputs may become more difficult when there are many layers of management and many steps in the production process.

Which of these two effects of scale is more important is an empirical question. To investigate this question economists use a precise definition of returns to scale. A production function is said to exhibit *constant returns to scale* if a doubling of all inputs results in a precise doubling of output. If a doubling of all inputs yields less than a doubling of output, the production function is said to exhibit *decreasing returns to scale*. If a doubling of all inputs results in more than doubling output, the production function exhibits *increasing returns to scale*.

These three possibilities are illustrated in the three graphs of Figure 7.3. In each case production isoquants for Q = 10, 20, 30, and 40 are shown, together with a ray (labeled OA) showing a uniform expansion of both capital and labor inputs. Graph A illustrates constant returns to scale. There, as both capital and labor inputs are successively increased from 1 to 2, then 2 to 3, and then 3 to 4, output expands proportionally. That is, output and inputs move in unison. In Graph b, by comparison, the isoquants get further apart as output expands. This is a case of decreasing returns to scale—an expansion in inputs does not result in a proportionate rise in output. For example, the doubling of capital and labor inputs from 1 to 2 units is not sufficient to increase output from 10 to 20. That increase in output would require more than a doubling of inputs. Finally, Graph c illustrates increasing returns to scale. In this case the isoquants get closer together as input expands—a doubling of inputs is more than sufficient to double output. Large-scale operation would in this case appear to be quite efficient.

The types of scale economies experienced in the real world may, of course,

Figure 7.3
Isoquant Maps Showing
Constant, Decreasing, and
Increasing Returns to Scale

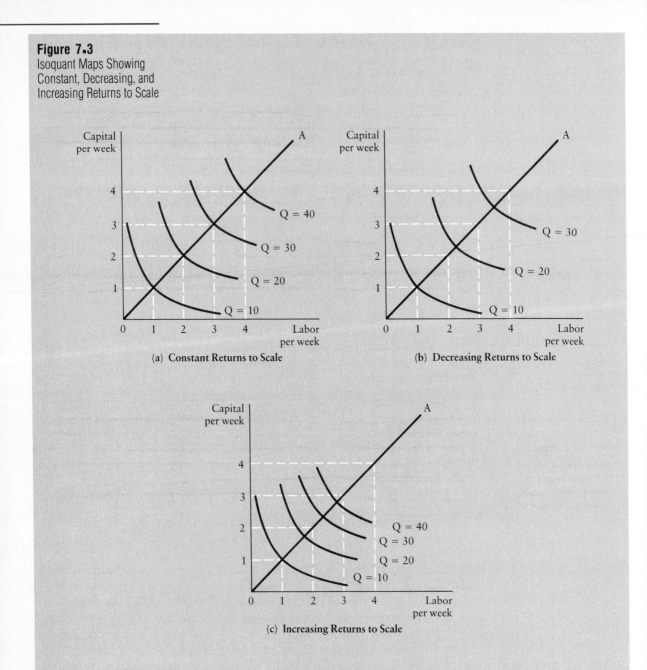

(a) **Constant Returns to Scale**

(b) **Decreasing Returns to Scale**

(c) **Increasing Returns to Scale**

In Figure 7.3a a proportionate expansion in both inputs leads to a similar proportionate expansion in output. This is constant returns to scale. In 7.3b an expansion in inputs yields a less than proportionate expansion in output, illustrating decreasing returns to scale. Figure 7.3c shows increasing returns to scale—output expands proportionately faster than inputs.

APPLYING ECONOMICS

Cargo Ships

Oceangoing cargo ships are a good illustration of the importance of the returns to scale concept for practical decision making as well as the complications that can arise in examining this concept closely. We can see why cargo ships might exhibit increasing returns to scale using a geometric example. Picture a ship as an empty cube. If the lengths of the four sides and top and bottom of the cube are doubled, its overall surface area will increase fourfold. The volume of the cube, on the other hand, will increase eightfold. A doubling of inputs (here the size of the ship's hull) will more than double its carrying capacity. Because other ship features such as power plants, staff, and control devices also probably exhibit increasing returns to scale, the cube analogy may not be very far from the truth. This result undoubtedly explains why very large oil tankers (up to 500,000 tons) are now used, for example, and it also explains why economies of scale occur in other forms of transportation such as oil and natural gas pipelines.

A closer examination of actual cargo ships reveals substantial problems with increases in size. Loading and unloading cargo from very large ships can be a difficult and costly process: larger cranes are needed, interior handling equipment must be used in the large holds, and goods must sometimes be moved substantial distances just to get them off the ship. The geometric allure of large ships must be tempered somewhat by logistical problems of cargo handling.

A 1978 study by J. O. Jansson and D. Shneerson illustrated these considerations quite clearly.[5] They showed that a 50 percent increase in the carrying capacity of a cargo ship on average increases the ship's capital cost by only about 25 percent. Ships' operating costs are increased even less (for example, a ship needs only one captain, no matter how large the ship is). On the other hand, the authors found that a 50 percent increase in carrying capacity tends to increase capital costs associated with cargo handling by nearly 90 percent, with similar cost increases in the operating of the handling equipment. Shipping firms must make very careful calculations in deciding how to trade off these advantages and disadvantages of very large-sized vessels.

To Think About
1. Why might the optimal size of a cargo ship change over time as economic conditions change? For example, what factors might have led oil companies to opt to build very large crude oil carriers (VLCCs) in the early 1970s whereas before they had used smaller vessels?
2. How would some of the issues discussed in connection with economies of scale in cargo ships apply to other methods of transportation such as railroads, trucking, or air cargo carriers? Can you think of examples where large-size carriers would be appropriate? How about applications where small sizes would be more efficient?

be rather complex combinations of these simple examples. A production function may, for example, exhibit increasing returns to scale over some output ranges and decreasing returns to scale over other ranges. Or some aspects of a good's production may illustrate scale economies, whereas other aspects may not. For example, the production of computer chips exhibits significant scale economies since the process of making chips can be highly automated. But the assembly of chips into electronic components is more difficult to automate and may exhibit few such scale economies. "Applying Economics: Cargo Ships" illustrates similar possibilities for the case of ocean shipping.

---

[5]J. O. Jansson and D. Shneerson, "Economies of Scale of General Cargo Ships," *Review of Economics and Statistics,* May 1978, pp. 291–296.

Input Substitution

Another important characteristic of a production function is how "easily" capital can be substituted for labor, or, more generally, any one input for another. This characteristic depends more on the shape of a single isoquant than on the whole isoquant map. So far we have assumed that a given output level can be produced with a variety of different input mixes—that is, we assumed firms could substitute labor for capital while keeping output constant. How easily that substitution can be made may, of course, vary. In some cases the substitution can be made easily and quickly in response to changing economic circumstances. In other cases firms may have little choice about the input combination they must use. Economists can measure this degree of substitution very technically, but for us to do so here would take us too far afield.[6] We can look at one special case in which input substitution is impossible, which will show us the kinds of problems in substitution that economists have noted.

Fixed-Proportions Production Function

Figure 7.4 demonstrates a case where no substitution is possible. This case is rather different from the ones we have looked at so far. Here the isoquants are L-shaped, indicating that machines and labor must be used in absolutely fixed proportions. Every machine has a fixed complement of workers that cannot be varied. For example, if K_1 machines are in use, L_1 workers are required to produce output level Q_1. Employing more workers than L_1 will not increase output with K_1 machines. (The Q_1 isoquant is horizontal beyond the point K_1, L_1). In other words, the marginal productivity of labor is 0 beyond L_1. On the other hand, using fewer workers would result in excess machines. If only L_0 workers were hired, for instance, only Q_0 units could be produced, but these units could be produced with only K_0 machines. When L_0 workers are hired, there is an excess of machines of an amount given by $K_1 - K_0$.

The production function whose isoquant map is shown in Figure 7.4 is called a **fixed-proportions production function.** Both inputs will be fully employed only if a combination of K and L that lies along the ray OA which passes through the vertices of the isoquants is chosen. Otherwise one input will be excessive in the sense that it could be cut back without restricting output. If a firm with such a production function wishes to expand, it must increase all inputs simultaneously so that none of the inputs are excessive.

The fixed-proportions production function has a wide variety of applications to real-world production techniques. Many machines do require a fixed

Fixed-proportions production function
A production function in which the inputs must be used in a fixed ratio to one another.

[6]Technically, the ease of input substitution is measured by the *elasticity of substitution,* which is defined as the ratio of the percentage change in K/L to the percentage change in the RTS along an isoquant. See K. J. Arrow, *et al.,* "Capital-Labor Substitution and Economic Efficiency," *Review of Economics and Statistics,* August 1961, pp. 225–250.

Figure 7.4
Isoquant Map with Fixed Proportions

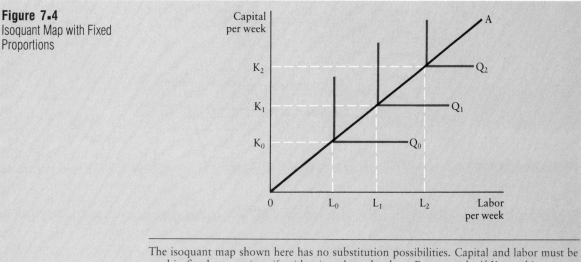

The isoquant map shown here has no substitution possibilities. Capital and labor must be used in fixed proportions if neither is to be redundant. For example, if K_1 machines are available, L_1 units of labor should be used. If L_2 units of labor are used there will be excess labor since no more than Q_1 can be produced from the given machines. Alternatively, if L_0 laborers were hired, machines would be in excess to the extent $K_1 - K_0$.

complement of workers; more than these would be excessive. For example, consider the combination of capital and labor required to mow a lawn. The lawn mower needs one person for its operation, and a worker needs one lawn mower in order to produce any output. Output can be expanded (that is, more grass can be mowed at the same time) only by adding capital and labor to the productive process in fixed proportions. Many production functions may be of this type, and the fixed-proportions model is in many ways appropriate for production planning.[7]

The Relevance of Input Substitutability

The ease with which one input can be substituted for another is of considerable interest to economists. We can use the shape of an isoquant map to see the relative ease with which different industries can adapt to the changing availability of productive inputs. For example, over the past hundred years there has been a great shift in the output of the American economy away from

---

[7]The lawn mower example points up another possibility. Presumably there is some leeway in choosing what size and type of lawn mower to buy. Any device, from a pair of clippers to a gang mower, might be chosen. Prior to the actual purchase, the capital-labor ratio in lawn mowing can be considered variable. Once the mower is purchased, however, the capital-labor ratio becomes fixed.

agricultural production and toward manufacturing and service industries. This shift moved certain factors of production, or inputs (notably labor), out of agriculture and into other industries. If production were relatively flexible in terms of input substitutability, the inputs formerly used in agriculture could be easily accommodated in the manufacturing and service industries. On the other hand, if production were closer to fixed proportions, the inputs might not be absorbed in exactly the proportions released by agriculture.

To make this example (unrealistically) simple, suppose that the capital to labor ratio in manufacturing is two to one; that is, it takes two machines to equip one worker. Suppose, on the other hand, that the capital to labor ratio in agriculture is one to one. If demand shifts so that agricultural production must be reduced and manufacturing output increased, problems will arise. The reduction in agricultural output will release capital and labor in the ratio of one to one. However, manufacturing can absorb capital and labor only in the ratio of two to one. It needs two machines from the agricultural sector in order to be able to employ one more worker. Half of the workers released by the agricultural sector would be unemployed. On the other hand, the released labor might easily have been absorbed if the capital-labor ratio in manufacturing had changed. To assess the effects on inputs of a shift in demand, we need to know how flexible production techniques are.

Some authors suggest that inflexibility in input substitution is a major concern for underdeveloped countries.[8] Since small, less developed countries are subject to rather sudden changes in the demand for the products they export, and since these countries are experiencing a movement of their labor forces from rural to urban areas, this lack of flexibility can cause serious problems. For example, the substantial unemployment in the urban areas of many less developed countries may be a direct result of an inability to substitute labor for capital in these countries' industries. Because these countries often must use capital equipment produced in the developed countries, this equipment may not be suited for the abundant labor supplies in the less developed world.

"Applying Economics: Energy and Capital" looks at the substitutability between two important inputs and how that substitutability affected the performance of the U.S. economy in the late 1970s.

Changes in Technology

A production function reflects the technical knowledge firms have about how to use inputs to produce outputs. When firms improve their production techniques, the production function changes. This kind of technical advancement occurs constantly as older, outmoded machines are replaced by more efficient ones that embody state-of-the-art techniques. Workers too are part of this technical progress as they become better educated and learn special skills for doing their jobs. Today, for example, steel is made far more efficiently than

[8]This problem was first explored in detail by R. S. Eckaus in "The Factor-Proportions Problem in Underdeveloped Areas," *American Economic Review,* September 1955, pp. 539–565.

Energy and Capital

One issue that has been of considerable recent interest to economists is the relationship between energy and capital in production. That interest was particularly sparked by the rapid increase in energy prices during the 1970s and concerns about firms' flexibility to respond to those increases. If energy and capital had a high degree of substitutability, firms could adapt rather quickly to rising energy prices by adopting more and better capital equipment that used less energy. On the other hand, if such substitutions were difficult, firms would have problems adapting to the increase in energy prices.

Studies of the relationship between capital and energy inputs during the 1970s suggested a third and even more damaging possibility: capital and energy may be complements in production. Some authors suggested that more sophisticated capital equipment would use more energy to operate, and that the only way firms could cope with increases in energy prices was to cut back on both capital and energy. A 1975 study by E. R. Berndt and D. O. Wood indicated this possibility was indeed true for many industries, and several later investigations reached similar conclusions.[9] The commonsense idea that energy and capital equipment are used jointly in production seems to be supported by these studies.

As an example of complementarity between capital and energy, consider the case of jet aircraft. Rapid increases in the price of jet fuel during the 1970s had a substantial influence on airlines' costs, making them think carefully about which planes to fly. Daily hours of use for fuel-inefficient versions of such planes as the 707, the DC8, and the DC9 were shortened or cancelled al-together. The airlines' use of capital was, at least over the short term, reduced significantly.

The idea that capital and energy are complements can also be used to explain the decline in labor productivity in the United States during the 1970s. Prior to 1973, average output per worker in the United States grew at about 2 to 2.5 percent per year. After 1973 (the year of the Arab oil embargo and the consequent rise in energy prices) productivity grew at less than 1 percent per year. A possible reason for this slower growth is that higher energy prices made use of some existing capital equipment uneconomical, and also reduced the demand for new machinery because of the complementary relationship between capital and energy. Both of these influences sharply reduced the amount of equipment that the typical employee had to work with, and thereby reduced his or her productivity. ("Applying Economics: The Productivity Decline of the 1970s" discusses some other reasons for this decline in growth.)

To Think About

1. Can you think of recent technical improvements in which capital and energy seem to substitute for each other? How about innovations in which capital and energy use seem to go together? How would changing energy prices affect the desirability of these different types of innovations?

2. How would you judge whether two inputs are substitutes or complements in production? What would be the problems in trying to develop a definition similar to those for substitute and complementary goods introduced in Chapter 4?

in the nineteenth century both because blast furnaces and rolling mills are better and because workers are better trained to use these facilities.

The production function concept and its related isoquant map are important tools for understanding the effect of technical change. Formally, technical progress represents a shift in the production function, such as that illustrated in Figure 7.5. In Figure 7.5 the isoquant Q_0 summarizes the initial state of technical knowledge. That level of output can be produced using K_0, L_0, or

---

[9]E. R. Berndt and D. O. Wood, "Technology, Prices, and the Derived Demand for Energy," *Review of Economics and Statistics*, August 1975, pp. 259–268.

Figure 7.5
Technical Change

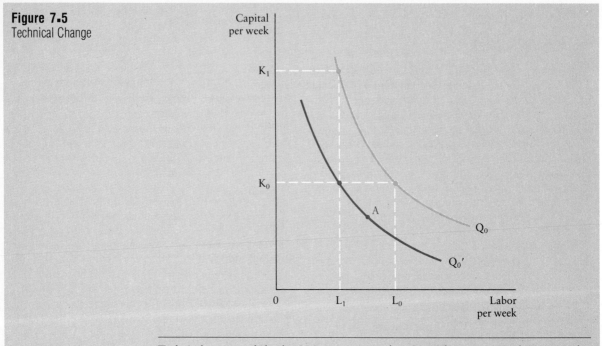

Technical progress shifts the Q_0 isoquant inward to Q'_0. Whereas previously it required K_0, L_0 to produce Q_0, now, with the same amount of capital, only L_1 units of labor are required. This result can be contrasted to capital-labor substitution in which the required labor input for Q_0 also declines to L_1 by using more capital (K_1).

any of a number of input combinations. With the discovery of new production techniques, the Q_0 isoquant shifts toward the origin—the same output level can now be produced using smaller quantities of inputs. If, for example, the Q_0 isoquant shifts inward to Q'_0, it is now possible to produce Q_0 with the same amount of capital as before (K_0) but with much less labor (L_1). It is even possible to produce Q_0 using both less capital and less labor than previously by choosing a point such as A. Technical change represents a real savings on inputs and (as we shall see in the next chapter) a reduction in the costs of production.

We can use Figure 7.5 to show an important distinction between true technical advancement and simple capital-labor substitution. With technical progress, the firm can continue to use K_0, but it produces Q_0 with less labor (L_1). The average productivity of labor rises from Q_0/L_0 to Q_0/L_1. Even in the absence of technical improvements the firm could increase the average productivity of labor by choosing to use K_1 units of capital. This substitution of capital for labor would also have caused the average productivity of labor to rise from Q_0/L_0 to Q_0/L_1. This rise would not mean any real improvement in the way goods are made, however. In studying productivity data, especially data on

The Productivity Decline of the 1970s

One important measure of the sluggish performance of the United States economy during the 1970s was its poor record of productivity growth. Some of that record's dimensions are reported in Table 7.2. The first row of the table shows annual rates of growth in total factor productivity over several periods since 1948. This productivity measure is close to our definition of technical progress. The data show a clear decline from an annual rate of growth of nearly 2 percent to much less than 1 percent in the 1973–1976 period. A similar decline was recorded for the growth in labor productivity (output per worker) during the period. The labor productivity growth figures exceed the total productivity figures because they also include the effects of higher capital-labor ratios. These figures have also been adjusted for the effects of the business cycle so that they are not abnormally influenced by the fall in output during the steep recession of 1974 and 1975.

Many explanations have been made for the productivity decline depicted in Table 7.2. One author found no fewer than 17 proposed explanations.[10] These range from fairly straightforward suggestions about lagging research and development spending and possible declines in opportunities for major new technical advances to more conjectural possibilities such as the notion that Americans "don't want to work hard any more."

Three specific explanations have interested economists the most. First is the question of whether the high rates of inflation during the 1970s contributed to poor productivity by making it more difficult for business managers to plan their production activities. A second related explanation focuses on changing energy prices during the period and how they affected business decision making (this explanation is discussed in "Applying Economics: Energy and Capital"). Finally, a number of authors have pointed to increasing government regulation of the economy (particularly in the environmental and health areas) as a possible cause of lagging productivity. Despite voluminous research, there is no generally agreed-upon explanation for the productivity decline

Table 7.2
Productivity Growth in Private Business, 1948–1979
(Annual Percentage Rate of Growth)

Productivity Measure	Period			
	1948–1957	1957–1968	1968–1973	1973–1979
Total factor productivity	1.90	1.85	1.50	0.34
Labor productivity	3.11	2.76	2.31	0.85

Sources: Total factor productivity: E. F. Denison, *Accounting for Slower Economic Growth: The United States in the 1970s* (Washington, D.C.: The Brookings Institution, 1979). The labor productivity figures are author computations based on data from the Bureau of Labor Statistics. All of the productivity statistics have been adjusted for effects of the business cycle.

during the 1970s. Because the early 1980s were characterized by a severe recession it is difficult to see if this poor performance continued. The second half of the decade will help to establish whether the 1970s productivity decline represents a long-term problem or only a temporary interruption in long-term growth.

To Think About
1. Explain why the figures for growth in total factor productivity in Table 7.2 are smaller than the figures for growth in labor productivity. Which of the measures do you think is more appropriate for judging improvements in technology? Which is better for judging how much workers should be paid?
2. How would you judge whether environmental and safety regulation played some role in the productivity decline of the 1970s? How would you evaluate the disadvantages of such a decline if it were possible to measure it? Shouldn't you include the benefits of the regulations (if any) in an overall assessment? How would you do that?

---

[10]See E. F. Denison, *Accounting for Slower Economic Growth: The United States in the 1970s* (Washington, D.C.: The Brookings Institution, 1979).

output per worker, we must be careful that the changes being observed represent technical improvements rather than capital-labor substitution. "Applying Economics: The Productivity Decline of the 1970s" illustrates this distinction.

Summary

Chapter 7 shows how economists conceptualize the process of production. We introduce the concept of the production function, which records the relationship between input use and output, and we show how this function can be illustrated with an isoquant map. Several features of the production function are explicitly discussed in the chapter:

- The marginal productivity of any input is the extra output that can be produced by adding one more unit of that input while holding all other inputs constant. The marginal productivity of an input declines as more of that input is used.
- The possible input combinations that a firm might use to produce a given level of output are shown on an isoquant. The slope of the isoquant is called the rate of technical substitution (RTS)—it shows how one input can be substituted for another while holding output constant.
- "Returns to scale" refers to the way in which a firm's output responds to proportionate increases in all inputs. If a doubling of all inputs causes output to more than double, there are increasing returns to scale. If such a doubling of inputs causes output to less than double, returns to scale are decreasing. The middle case, when output exactly doubles, is constant returns to scale.
- In some cases it may not be possible for the firm to substitute one input for another. In these cases, the inputs must be used in fixed proportions. Such production functions will have L-shaped isoquants and the marginal productivity of any one input will be zero.
- Technical progress will shift the firm's entire isoquant map. A given output level can be produced with fewer inputs.

Problems

7.1 Imagine that the production function for beer cans is given by:

$$Q = 6K + 4L$$

where

$$Q = \text{Output of beer cans per hour}$$

$$K = \text{Capital input per hour}$$

$$L = \text{Labor input per hour.}$$

a. Assuming capital is fixed at K = 6, how much L is required to produce 60 beer cans per hour? To produce 100 per hour?

b. Now assume that capital input is fixed at K = 8; what L is required to produce 60 beer cans per hour? To produce 100 per hour?

c. Graph the Q = 60 and Q = 100 isoquants. Indicate the points found in parts a and b. What is the RTS along the isoquants?

7.2 Frisbees are produced according to the production function:

$$Q = 2K + L$$

where

$$Q = \text{Output of frisbees per hour}$$

$$K = \text{Capital input per hour}$$

$$L = \text{Labor input per hour.}$$

a. If K = 10, how much L is needed to produce 100 frisbees per hour?

b. If K = 25, how much L is needed to produce 100 frisbees per hour?

c. Graph the Q = 100 isoquant. Indicate the points on that isoquant defined in parts a and b. What is the RTS along this isoquant? Explain why the RTS is the same at every point on the isoquant.

d. Graph the Q = 50 and Q = 200 isoquants for this production function also. Describe the shape of the entire isoquant map.

e. Suppose technical progress resulted in the production function for frisbees becoming

$$Q = 3K + 1.5L.$$

Answer parts a through d for this new production function and discuss how it compares to the previous case.

7.3 Digging clams by hand in Sunset Bay requires only labor input. The total number of clams obtained per hour (Q) is given by

$$Q = 100 \sqrt{L}$$

where L is labor input per hour.

a. Graph the relationship between Q and L.

b. What is the average productivity of labor in Sunset Bay? Graph this relationship and show that AP_L diminishes for increases in labor input.

c. It can be shown that the marginal productivity of labor in Sunset Bay is given by

$$MP_L = 50/\sqrt{L}.$$

Graph this relationship and show that $MP_L < AP_L$ for all values of L. Explain why this is so.

7.4 Contrast the concepts of diminishing returns to scale and diminishing marginal productivity. Can a production function exhibit constant returns to scale but still have diminishing productivities for *every* factor?

*7.5 Suppose the production function for widgets is given by

$$Q = KL - .8K^2 - .2L^2$$

where Q represents the annual quantity of widgets produced, K represents annual capital input, and L represents annual labor input.

a. Supposing K = 10, graph the total and average productivity of labor curves. At what level of labor input does this average productivity reach a maximum? How many widgets are produced at that point?

b. Again assuming that K = 10 and using the information that the MP_L curve is a straight line with an intercept of 10 (for L = 0), graph this curve. At what level of labor input does $MP_L = 0$?

c. Suppose capital inputs were increased to K = 20. How would your answers to parts a and b change?

7.6 Power Goat Lawn Company uses two sizes of mowers to cut lawns. The smaller mowers have a 24-inch blade and are used on lawns with many trees and obstacles. The larger mowers are exactly twice as big as the smaller mowers and are used on open lawns where maneuverability is not so difficult. The two production functions available to Power Goat are:

	Output per Hour (Square Feet)	Capital Input (# of 24″ Mowers)	Labor Input
Large Mowers	8,000	2	1
Small Mowers	5,000	1	1

a. Graph the Q = 40,000 square feet isoquant for the first production function. How much K and L would be used if these factors were combined without waste?

b. Answer part a for the second function.

---

*Denotes a problem that is rather difficult.

    c. How much K and L would be used without waste if half of the 40,000 square foot lawn were cut by the method of the first production function and half by the method of the second? How much K and L would be used if three-fourths of the lawn were cut by the first method and one-fourth by the second? What does it mean to speak of fractions of K and L?

    d. On the basis of your observations in part c, draw a Q = 40,000 isoquant for the combined production functions.

*7.7 The production of barstools (Q) is characterized by a production function of the form

$$Q = K^{1/2} \cdot L^{1/2} = \sqrt{K \cdot L}.$$

    a. What is the average productivity of labor and capital for barstool production (AP_L will depend on K, and AP_K will depend on L)?

    b. Graph the AP_L curve for K = 100.

    c. For this particular function it can be shown that $MP_L = \frac{1}{2} AP_L$, and $MP_K = \frac{1}{2} AP_K$. Using that information, add a graph of the MP_L function to the graph calculated in part b (again for K = 100). What is unusual about this curve?

    d. Sketch the Q = 10 isoquant for this production function.

    e. Using the results from part c, what is the RTS on the Q = 10 isoquant at the points: K = L = 10; K = 25, L = 4; and K = 4, L = 25? Does this function exhibit a diminishing RTS?

CHAPTER 8

Costs

Now that the concepts to describe the technical aspects of production have been developed, we can consider the costs associated with productive activities. This chapter answers two basic questions about costs. First, how should the firm choose its inputs to produce any given level of output as cheaply as possible? Second, how does this process of cost minimization differ between the short run and the long run? These questions are still technical in nature—we are not yet considering the crucial issue of how a firm chooses the level of output it will supply. We need to first develop the theory of costs to be able to understand the nature of the supply decision, which will be studied in Chapter 9.

Basic Concepts of Costs

Opportunity cost
The cost of a good or service as measured by the alternative uses that are forgone by producing the good or service.

At least three different concepts of costs can be distinguished: opportunity cost, accounting cost, and economic cost. For economists the most important of these is the **opportunity cost** (also called the *social cost*). Because resources are limited, any decision to produce some good means doing without some other good. When an automobile is produced, for example, an implicit decision has been made to do without 15 bicycles, say, that could have been produced using the labor, chrome, and glass that goes into the automobile. In this example the opportunity cost of one automobile is 15 bicycles. It is often inconvenient to express opportunity costs in terms of physical goods; we may sometimes choose monetary units instead. The price of a car may actually be based on the goods that were given up to produce it, and we could then say the opportunity cost of an automobile is $10,000 worth of other goods. This may not always be the case, however. The car may have been produced with resources that could not be usefully employed elsewhere, and the opportunity cost of its production would then be close to 0.

Accounting cost
The concept that goods or services cost what was paid for them.

Economic cost
The cost concept that goods or services cost the amount required to keep them in their present use: the amount that they would be worth in their next best alternative use.

Although the concept of opportunity cost is fundamental to all economic analysis, it may be too theoretical to be of practical usefulness to firms. Two other concepts of cost are directly related to the firm's choices: they are the accountant's concept and the economic concept of the firm's costs. **Accounting cost** stresses out-of-pocket expenses, historical costs of machines and depreciation related to them, and other bookkeeping entries. **Economic cost** (which draws, in obvious ways, on the idea of opportunity cost), on the other hand, is defined as the payment required to keep a resource in its present employment, or the remuneration that the resource would receive in its next best alternative use.

To look at how this definition might be applied in practice and how it differs from accounting ideas, we now consider the economic costs of three specific inputs: labor, capital, and the services of entrepreneurs.

Labor Costs

Wage rate (w)
The cost of hiring one worker for one hour.

Economists and accountants view labor costs in much the same way. To the accountant, expenditures on wages and salaries are current expenses and therefore are costs of production. Economists consider such payments as an *explicit cost*: labor services (worker-hours) are purchased at some hourly **wage rate** (what we will denote by w), and it is assumed that this rate is the amount that workers would earn in their next best alternative employment. There is a slight distinction in these views of labor costs in that accountants tend to stress the total wage bill, whereas economists look at the cost of hiring one more worker for an hour (w), but both these costs are measured in about the same way.

Capital Costs

Rental rate (v)
The cost of hiring one machine for one hour.

In the case of capital services (machine-hours), accounting and economic definitions of costs differ greatly. Accountants, in calculating capital costs, use the historical price of a particular machine and apply some (more or less) arbitrary depreciation rule to determine how much of that machine's original price to charge to current costs. For example, a machine purchased for $1,000 and expected to last 10 years might be said to "cost" $100 per year, in the accountant's view. Economists, on the other hand, regard the historical price of a machine as a "sunk cost" that is basically irrelevant to current production decisions. Instead, economists regard the *implicit cost* of a machine to be what someone else would be willing to pay for its use. Thus, the cost of one machine hour is the **rental rate** for that machine in the best alternative use. By continuing to use the machine itself, the firm is implicitly forgoing the rental rate someone else would be willing to pay for its use. We will use v to denote this

TC = wL + vK

rental rate for one machine hour. This is the rate that the firm must pay for the use of the machine for one hour regardless of whether the firm owns the machine (in which case it is an implicit cost) or rents the machine from someone else (in which case it is an explicit cost).

Entrepreneurial Costs and Economic Profits

Much of what accountants term profits would be called entrepreneurial costs by economists. Profits are what owners get to keep after paying all costs. If some payment is necessary to keep the owner in a particular business, economists would argue this is a cost of that business. For an economist, **economic profits** are the total revenues of a firm less total economic costs—including any opportunity costs incurred by the owner.

Economic profits
The difference between total revenue and total economic costs.

Profit = TR - TC

Indeed, if the owner of a firm earns only a nominal profit despite his or her great skills, an economist might conclude that the economic profits of the enterprise are zero or even negative. For example, many businesses earn only a small profit for their owners. A typical case might be a "mom and pop" gift shop that reported a profit of $5,000 per year. Economists would argue that the true profit of such a business is negative. The owners of the shop could earn a higher income if they were employed elsewhere, and this alternative earnings possibility should be counted as a cost of their being in the gift shop business. If, for example, the owners of the shop could earn $15,000 if they were employed elsewhere, economists would conclude that the economic profit of the shop is −$10,000. In this situation the accounting profits are positive whereas true economic profits are negative. In our analysis here we assume that entrepreneurial costs are part of labor costs, and that any excess of revenue over costs represents economic profits. "Applying Economics: Economic Costs of Homeowning" considers the economist's and the accountant's views of the cost of owning homes and shows how the differences may result in different assessments of the desirability of such ownership.

Cost-Minimizing Input Choice

Because of the assumptions we have made so far, the total costs for the firm are given by

$$\text{Total costs} = TC = wL + vK. \qquad [8.1]$$

In other words, total costs are given by the number of labor hours hired (L) times labor's wage (w), plus the number of machine hours hired (K) times capital's rental rate (v). The problem for the firm if it is to operate at minimal cost is to choose quantities of capital and labor so that total costs are minimized for *any* output level.

Economic Costs of Homeowning

In "Applying Economics: Federal Tax Benefits for Homeowners" in Chapter 5, we showed that special treatment of some expenses of homeowning under the federal income tax gives people a considerable incentive to own their homes rather than to rent. Although these tax (and other) benefits are very real, they should not be overstated. Consider, for example, the following claim: "Rent is just money down a rat hole: it will never be seen again. The same money spent on mortgage payments will build an investment. Once your mortgage is paid off, housing costs will be much cheaper."

Although this claim is frequently made (usually by prudent parents to their spendthrift children), it is simply wrong. It confuses the accountant's notion of the out-of-pocket costs of homeownership with the economic costs of that ownership. It is true that once a mortgage is paid off, out-of-pocket expenses are reduced. But someone who has a substantial investment in a house incurs an opportunity cost in terms of the interest these funds could have earned on some other investment. Even though this opportunity cost is implicit rather than explicit, it will still influence homeowning behavior.

Consider the relationship between owning and renting homes in southern California in the late 1970s. At that time a $100,000 home could be rented for about $1,000 per month, or $12,000 per year. The owner of this home might have incurred maintenance, taxes, and other expenses of $6,000 per year, so in terms of explicit costs, renting to someone else looks like a profitable enterprise. From this accounting point of view, renting the home out provides a profit of $6,000 per year to the owner (see Table 8.1). But had the owner been able to invest the $100,000 value of the house at the then prevailing bank interest rate of about 10 percent, this sum would have earned $10,000 per year in interest. That also is an opportunity cost of homeowning. Economic profits are therefore $-4,000$. From an economic perspective, renting a home to another person might more properly be viewed as a losing proposition for the owner.

Why should property owners in southern California have been willing to rent homes to someone else at a

Table 8.1

Alternative Views of the Profitability of Owning Rental Housing

Accounting View		Economic View	
Rental income	$12,000	Rental income	$12,000
Less:		Less:	
Costs (maintenance and depreciation)	6,000	Explicit costs (maintenance and depreciation)	6,000
Accounting profit	$ 6,000	Implicit costs (forgone interest)	10,000
		Loss before capital gain	$-4,000$
		Capital gain	5,000
		Economic profit	$1,000

loss? Because, at the time, they expected the value of the home to increase. Even a rather small annual rate of appreciation in house prices (say 5 percent) would have turned owning rental property into a profitable activity. The $5,000 capital gain on a $100,000 house would result in net economic profits of $1,000. In the 1980s, however, the prospects for home values to increase substantially are not so favorable, and rents have risen rather rapidly so as to cover owners' full economic costs.

To Think About

1. "Burning the mortgage papers" is a popular custom once the mortgage on a house has been paid off. Does paying off a mortgage have any economic significance? Should people try to get their mortgage paid off as quickly as possible? Is it better to live in a "debt-free" house?

2. Sometimes older people are said to be "house poor," meaning that too large a portion of their total assets is tied up in their house. What problems does being house poor pose for older people? Is there a cure for this problem?

Cost minimization → RTS = $\frac{w}{v}$ ($\frac{wages}{rent}$)

Intuitive Analysis

In order to minimize the cost of producing a given level of output, say Q_1, a firm should choose that point on the Q_1 isoquant for which the marginal rate of technical substitution (RTS) of L for K is equal to the ratio w/v. It should equate the rate at which K can be substituted for L in the productive process to the rate at which they can be traded in the market place. What if the firm chooses a different point on the isoquant? Suppose the firm is producing output level Q_1 using K = 10, L = 10, and the RTS is 2 at this point. Assume also that w = \$1, v = \$1, and hence that w/v = 1, which is unequal to the RTS of 2. At this input combination the cost of producing Q_1 is \$20, which is not the minimal input cost. Q_1 can also be produced using K = 8 and L = 11; the firm can give up two units of K and keep output constant at Q_1 by adding one unit of L. At this input combination the cost of producing Q_1 is only \$19. A proof similar to this one can be demonstrated any time the RTS and the ratio of the input costs differ. Therefore, we have shown that to minimize total cost the firm should produce where:

$$\text{RTS (of L for K)} = \frac{\text{Wage rate}}{\text{Rental rate for capital}} = \frac{w}{v}. \qquad [8.2]$$

Graphic Presentation

The cost-minimization principle is demonstrated graphically in Figure 8.1. The isoquant Q_1 shows all the combinations of K and L that are required to produce Q_1. We wish to find the least costly point on this isoquant. Using Equation 8.1 we can see that those combinations of K and L that keep total costs constant lie along a straight line with slope −w/v.[1] Consequently, all lines of equal total cost can be shown in Figure 8.1 as a series of parallel straight lines with slopes −w/v. Three lines of equal total cost are shown in Figure 8.1: $TC_1 < TC_2 < TC_3$. It is clear from the figure that the minimum total cost for producing Q_1 is given by TC_1 where the total cost curve is just tangent to the isoquant. The cost-minimizing input combination is L*, K*.

We have therefore shown that for a cost minimum the slope of the isoquant should equal −w/v. At that point of tangency the rate at which the firm is

---

[1] For example, if TC = \$100, Equation 8.1 would read 100 = wL + vK. Solving for K gives K = −w/vL + 100/v. Hence, the slope of this total cost line is −w/v and the intercept is 100/v (which is the amount of capital that can be purchased with \$100).

Figure 8.1
Minimizing the Costs
of Producing Q_1

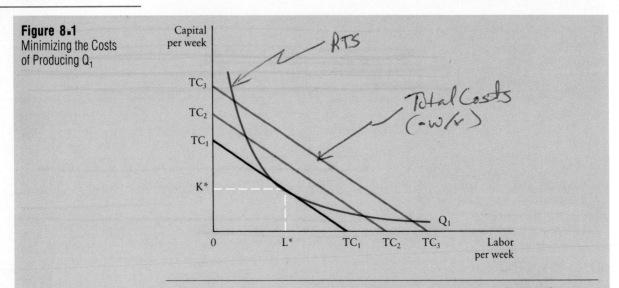

A firm is assumed to choose capital (K) and labor (L) to minimize total costs. The
condition for this minimization is that the rate at which L can be substituted for K (while
keeping $Q = Q_1$) should be equal to the rate at which these inputs can be traded in the
market. In other words, the RTS (of L for K) should be set equal to the price ratio w/v.
This tangency is shown here in that costs are minimized at TC_1 by choosing inputs K^*
and L^*.

technically able to trade L for K (the RTS) is equal to the rate at which the
firm can trade L for K in the market.[2]

Derived Demand for Inputs

Figure 8.1 shows the formal similarity between the firm's cost-minimization
problem and the individual's utility-maximization problem. In both cases we
took prices as fixed and derived the tangency conditions. In Chapter 4 we

---

[2]An alternative interpretation can be made using the result from note 3 of Chapter 7 that

$$RTS \text{ (of L for K)} = \frac{MP_L}{MP_K}.$$

Hence, using Equation 8.2,

$$\frac{MP_L}{MP_K} = \frac{w}{v},$$

or

$$\frac{MP_L}{w} = \frac{MP_K}{v}.$$

To minimize cost the firm should choose K and L so that the marginal productivity per dollar
spent is the same for all inputs used.

Figure 8.2
Firm's Expansion Path

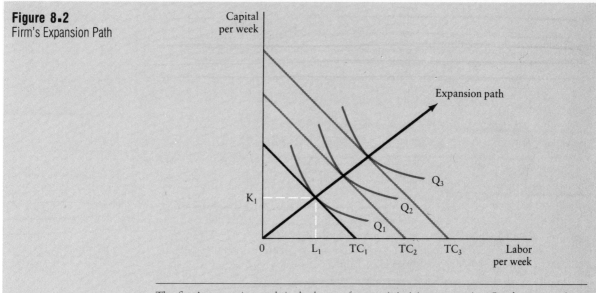

The firm's expansion path is the locus of cost-minimizing tangencies. On the assumption of fixed input prices, the curve shows how input use increases as output increases.

analyzed how the utility-maximizing choice of goods would change if a price were to change in order to construct the familiar downward-sloping demand curve. Can we do the same for the firm's demand for an input—could we change some input price (change the slope of the TC curves) and then trace out the effects of this price change on the quantity of the factor demanded?

The analogy to the individual's utility-maximization process can be misleading at this point. In order to analyze what happens to K^* as v changes, say, we also have to know what happens to output. The demand for K is a *derived demand* based on the demand for the firm's output. We cannot answer questions about K^* without looking at the market for the good being produced. This means that although the analogy to the theory of individual behavior is useful in pointing out basic similarities, it is not an exact analogy—the derivation of a firm's demand for an input is considerably more complex and is presented in Part 5.

The Firm's Expansion Path

We can perform an analysis such as the one we just performed for any level of output by a firm. For each Q we would find that input combination that minimizes the cost of producing Q. If input costs (w and v) remain constant for all amounts the firm chooses to use, we can easily trace out this locus of cost-minimizing choices, as shown in Figure 8.2. The ray OE records the cost-minimizing tangencies for successively higher levels of Q. For example, the minimum cost for producing output level Q_1 is given by TC_1, and inputs K_1

Figure 8.3
Factor Inferiority

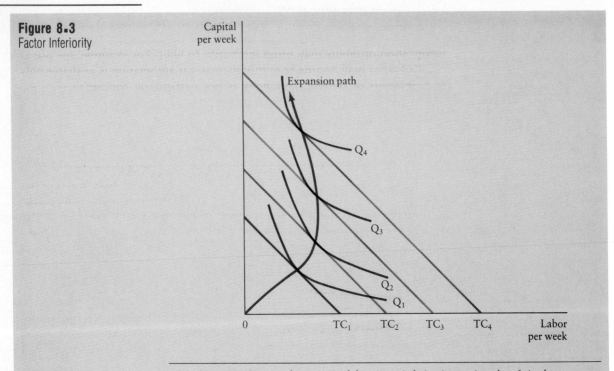

With this particular set of isoquants, labor is an inferior input since less L is chosen as output expands beyond Q_2. Such input inferiority is rare, however.

Expansion path
The locus of cost-minimizing input combinations a firm will choose to produce various levels of output (when the prices of inputs are held constant).

and L_1 are used. Other tangencies in the figure can be interpreted in a similar way. The locus of these tangencies is called the firm's **expansion path** because it records how input use expands as output expands while holding the prices of the inputs constant. As shown in Figure 8.3, the expansion path need not be a straight line. The use of some inputs may increase faster than others as output expands. Which inputs expand more rapidly will depend on the shape of the production isoquants.

Inferior Inputs

It would seem reasonable to assume that the expansion path will be positively sloped—that successively higher output levels will require more of both inputs. This assumption may not always be true, however, as Figure 8.3 illustrates. Increases of output beyond Q_2 actually cause the quantity of labor used to decrease. In this range labor would be said to be an *inferior input*—less is used as output expands. Inferior inputs are a theoretical possibility that may occur even when isoquants have their usual convex shape.

Much theoretical discussion has centered on the analysis of factor inferiority. Whether inferiority is likely to occur in real-world production functions is a difficult empirical question to answer. It seems unlikely that such comprehensive inputs as capital and labor could be inferior, but a less broad classification of inputs may bring inferiority to light. For example, the use of unskilled labor may decline as output increases if automation is available only for high levels of output. This book is not particularly concerned with the analytical complications of inferior inputs.

Cost Curves

The firm's expansion path shows how minimum-cost input use increases when the level of output expands, and allows us to see the relationship between output levels and total input costs. The cost curves that reflect this relationship are fundamental to the theory of supply. In Figure 8.4 four possible shapes for this cost relationship are illustrated. Graph a reflects a situation of constant returns to scale. In this case, as shown in Figure 7.3, output and required input use are proportional to one another. A doubling of output requires a doubling of inputs. Assuming input prices do not change, the relationship between output and total input costs is also directly proportional—the total cost curve is simply a straight line that passes through the origin (since no inputs are required if Q = 0).[3]

Graphs b and c in Figure 8.4 reflect the cases of decreasing returns to scale and increasing returns to scale, respectively. With decreasing returns to scale, successively larger quantities of inputs are required to increase output, and input costs rise rapidly as output expands, as shown by the convex total cost curve in Graph b. With increasing returns to scale, on the other hand, successive input requirements decline as output expands. In that case the total cost curve is concave, as shown in Graph c. In this case considerable cost advantages result from large-scale operations.

Finally, Graph d in Figure 8.4 demonstrates a situation in which the firm experiences ranges of both increasing and decreasing returns to scale. Such a situation might arise if the firm's production process required a certain "optimal" level of internal coordination and control by its managers. For low levels of output this control structure is underutilized, and expansion in output is easily accomplished. At these levels the firm would experience increasing returns to scale—the total cost curve is concave in its initial section. As output expands, however, the firm must add additional workers and capital equipment, which perhaps need entirely separate buildings or other production facilities. The coordination and control of this larger scale organization may be successively more difficult, and diminishing returns to scale may set in. The convex section of the total cost curve in Graph d reflects that possibility.

The four possibilities in Figure 8.4 illustrate most of the types of relation-

---

[3]A technical property of constant returns to scale production functions is that the RTS depends only on the ratio of K to L, not on the scale of production. For given input prices, the expansion path is a straight line and cost-minimizing inputs expand proportionally along with output. For an illustration, see the appendix to this chapter.

Figure 8.4
Possible Shapes of the
Total Cost Curve

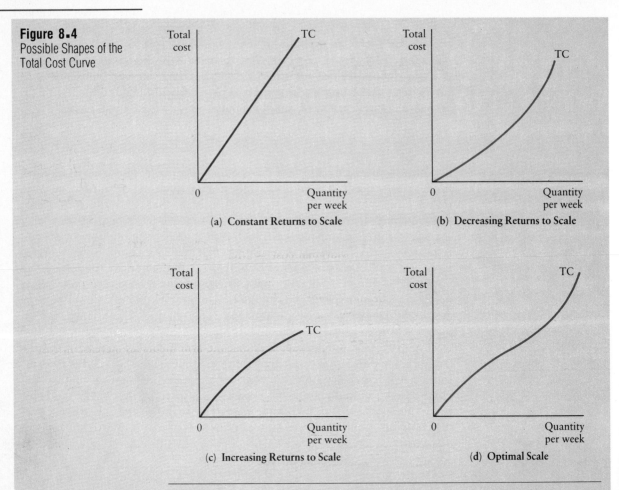

The shape of the total cost curve depends on the nature of the production function.
Graph a represents constant returns to scale: as output expands, input costs expand
proportionately. Graphs b and c show decreasing returns to scale and increasing returns
to scale, respectively. Graph d represents costs where there is an "optimal scale" of
operations for the firm.

ships between a firm's output and its input costs that arise from the desire to
minimize costs. The cost information shown in Figure 8.4 can also be depicted
on a per-unit-of-output basis. Although this depiction adds no new details to
the information implicit in the total cost curves, it will be quite useful when
we analyze the supply decision in Chapter 9.

Average cost
Total costs divided by
output—A common
measure of cost per
unit.

Average and Marginal Costs

Two per-unit-of-output cost concepts are average and marginal costs. **Average
cost** (AC) measures total costs per unit. Mathematically:

$$\text{Average cost} = AC = \frac{TC}{Q}. \qquad [8.3]$$

This is the per-unit-of-cost concept with which people are most familiar. If, for example, a firm has total costs of $100 in producing 25 units of output, it is quite natural to consider the cost-per-unit to be $4. Equation 8.3 reflects this common averaging process.

For economists, however, average cost is not necessarily the most meaningful cost-per-unit figure. In Chapter 1, we introduced Marshall's analysis of demand and supply. In his model of price determination, Marshall focused on the cost of the last unit produced since it is that cost that influences the supply decision. To reflect this notion of incremental cost, economists have developed the concept of **marginal cost** (MC). By definition then,

Marginal cost
The cost of producing one more unit of output.

$$\text{Marginal cost} = MC = \frac{\text{Change in TC}}{\text{Change in Q}}. \qquad \frac{\Delta TC}{\Delta Q} \qquad [8.4]$$

That is, as output expands, total costs increase, and the marginal cost concept measures this increase only *at the margin*. For example, if producing 24 units costs the firm $98, but producing 25 units costs it $100, the marginal cost of the 25th unit is $2: to produce that unit the firm incurs an increase in cost of only $2. This example shows that the average cost of a good ($4) and its marginal cost ($2) may be quite different. This possibility has a number of important implications for pricing and overall resource allocation.

Average and Marginal Cost Curves

Now that we have defined costs on a per-unit basis in several ways, we can show them graphically. Figure 8.5 compares average and marginal costs for the four total cost relationships shown in Figure 8.4. As Equation 8.4 makes clear, marginal costs are reflected by the slope of the total cost curve since (as we discussed in Chapter 2) the slope of any graph shows how the variable on the vertical axis (here total cost) changes for a unit change in the variable on the horizontal axis (here quantity). In Graph a of Figure 8.4 the total cost curve is linear—it has the same slope throughout. In this case, marginal cost (MC) is constant. No matter how much is produced, it will always cost the same to produce *one more unit*. The horizontal MC curve in Graph a of Figure 8.5 reflects this fact.

In the case of a convex total cost curve (Graph b in Figures 8.4 and 8.5), marginal costs are increasing. The total cost curve becomes steeper as output expands, so at the margin, the cost of one more unit is becoming greater. The MC curve in Graph b in Figure 8.5 is positively sloped.

For the case of a concave total cost curve (Graph c in Figures 8.4 and 8.5), this situation is reversed. Since the total cost curve becomes flatter as output

Figure 8.5
Average and Marginal
Cost Curves

Pencil is the shape of Total Cost Curves

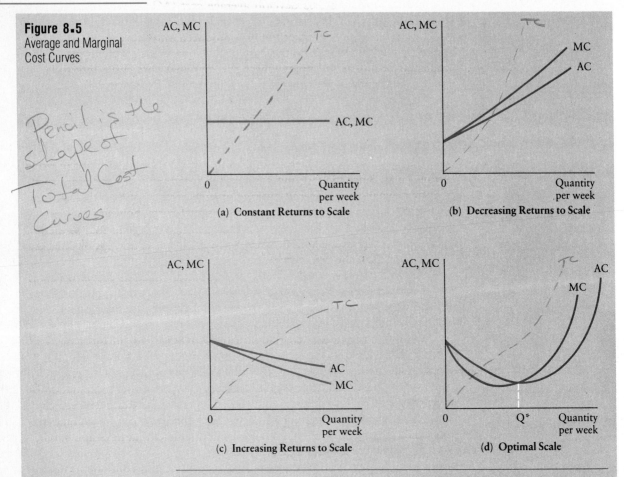

(a) Constant Returns to Scale

(b) Decreasing Returns to Scale

(c) Increasing Returns to Scale

(d) Optimal Scale

The average and marginal cost curves shown here are derived from the total cost curves in Figure 8.4. The shapes of these curves depend on the nature of the production function.

expands, marginal costs fall. The marginal cost curve in Graph c in Figure 8.5 has a negative slope.

Finally, the case of first concave, then convex total costs (Graph d in Figures 8.4 and 8.5) yields a U-shaped marginal cost curve. Initially marginal costs fall because the coordination and control mechanism of the firm is becoming more efficiently utilized. Diminishing returns to scale eventually appear, however, and the marginal cost curve turns upward. The MC curve in Graph d in Figure 8.5 reflects the general idea that there is some optimal scale of operation for the firm—if production is pushed too far, very high marginal costs will be the result. We will make this idea of optimal scale more precise as we study average costs.

It is relatively simple to develop average cost (AC) curves for each of the cases in Figure 8.5. The average and marginal cost concepts are identical for the very first unit produced. If the firm produced only one unit, both average and marginal cost would be the cost of that one unit. Graphing the AC relationship begins at the point where the marginal cost curve intersects the vertical axis. For Graph a in Figure 8.5, marginal cost never varies from its initial level. It always costs the same amount to produce one more unit, and AC must also reflect this amount. If it always costs a firm $4 to produce one more unit, both average and marginal costs are $4. Both the AC and MC curves are the same horizontal line in Graph a in Figure 8.5.

In the case of convex total costs, rising marginal costs also result in rising average costs. Since the last unit produced is becoming more and more costly as output expands, the overall average of such costs must be rising. Because the first few units are produced at low marginal costs, however, the overall average will always be somewhat less than the high marginal cost of the last unit produced. In Graph b in Figure 8.5 the AC curve is upward sloping, but it is always below the MC curve.

In the case of concave total costs, the opposite situation prevails. Falling marginal costs cause average costs to fall as output expands, but the overall average also reflects the high marginal costs of producing the first few units. As a consequence, the AC curve in Graph c in Figure 8.5 is negatively sloped and always lies above the MC curve. Falling average cost in this case is, as we shall see in Chapter 12, a principal force leading to relatively large-scale operations for firms with such increasing returns to scale technologies.

The case of a U-shaped marginal cost curve represents a combination of the above two situations. Initially falling marginal costs cause average costs to decline also. For low levels of output, the configuration of average and marginal cost curves in Graph d in Figure 8.5 resembles that in Graph b. Once the marginal costs turn up, however, the situation begins to change. So long as marginal cost is below average cost, average cost will continue to decline since the last good produced is still less expensive than the prior average. When MC < AC producing one more unit pulls AC down. Once the rising segment of the marginal cost curve cuts the average cost curve from below, however, average costs begin to rise. Beyond the point Q^* in Graph d in Figure 8.5, MC exceeds AC. The situation now resembles that in Graph c and AC must rise.[4] Average costs are being pulled up by the high cost of producing one more unit. Since AC is falling to the left of Q^* and rising to the right of Q^*, average costs of production are lowest at Q^*. Q^* represents in a sense an "optimal scale" for a firm whose costs are represented in Graph d in Figure 8.5. Later chapters show that this output level plays an important role in the

---

[4]An analogy may help here. If, on your most recent quiz (that is, your "marginal" quiz) you received a lower grade than your previous average, that average must be falling. On the other hand, if your most recent quiz score exceeded your previous average, the average must be rising. When the marginal and average grades are identical, your average will not change.

APPLYING ECONOMICS

The Measurement of Long-Run Costs

Long-run cost curves can be used to determine the appropriate scale of operation for various industries. Economists are particularly interested in estimating the output level (or range of levels) for which long-run average cost is as low as possible. Computing this level of output can show whether or not the industry in question is appropriate for the development of large-scale firms. If the point of minimum long-run average cost occurs at an output level that is small relative to the total industry output, economists would argue that it is efficient for such an industry to contain many small firms. For the American economy this observation has been made most often for the agricultural industry, where it appears that long-run average costs reach a minimum for farms of a relatively small size (400 to 800 acres). On the other hand, there are industries for which long-run average cost curves seem to be downward sloping over a broad range of output levels; the point of minimum average cost occurs at an output level that represents a substantial portion of total industry production.

Some General Findings on Long-Run Average Costs

Most studies of long-run cost curves have found that average costs decrease up to some particular output level and then remain relatively constant. These average cost curves have a modified "L" shape, such as that shown in Figure 8.6. The industries studied seem to exhibit "increasing returns to scale" up to some point, but there is no strong evidence that long-run average costs begin to rise after some point. Adam Smith's hypothesis about the difficulties of managing large-size firms does not appear to be strongly supported by the data in most cases.

Table 8.2 reports the results of representative studies of long-run average cost curves for six industries: banking, electric power, hospitals, life insurance, railroads, and trucking. Entries in the table represent the long-run average cost in an industry for a firm of a particular size (small, medium, or large) as a percentage of the minimal average cost firm in the industry. For example, the data for hospitals indicate that small hospitals have average costs that are about 29.6 percent greater than average costs for large ones. Hospitals, therefore, are one industry for which there do appear to be some cost

Figure 8.6
Long-Run Average Cost Curve Found in Many Empirical Studies

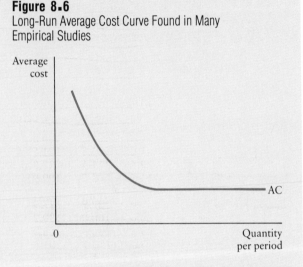

In most empirical studies the AC curve has been found to have this modified "L" shape. Average costs decline up to a point and then remain constant. There is no strong evidence that after some output level is reached, average costs start to rise.

advantages to larger-scale operations. Most other industries seem to be similar to that illustrated in Figure 8.6. Average costs are lower for medium and large firms than for smaller ones—that is, there appears to be a "minimum efficient scale" (termed, appropriately, MES in the field of industrial organization). In most cases, these cost advantages are not great, and for at least one case (trucking), smaller firms seem to operate with lower costs. There is no overwhelming evidence in Table 8.2 of substantial benefits to large-scale operations in general (of course, far more information has been gathered about cost curves than that reflected in Table 8.2). Two industries, railroads and refuse collection, are looked at in more detail here since findings about their long-run costs have important implications for government policies.

Railroad Costs

A 1960 study by George Borts looked at the long-run costs of 61 *class I* (large) American railway firms.[5] Borts

---

[5]G. Borts, "The Estimation of Rail Cost Functions," *Econometrica*, January 1960, pp. 108–131.

Table 8.2
Long-Run Average Cost Estimates for Six Industries
(Average Cost as a Percentage of Minimal Average Cost)

Industry	Firm Size		
	Small	Medium	Large
Commercial banking			
Demand deposits	116.1%	104.7%	100.0%
Installments loans	102.4	101.5	100.0
Electric power generation	113.2	101.0	101.5
Hospitals	129.6	111.1	100.0
Life insurance (Canada)	113.6	104.5	100.0
Railroads			
East	100.0	127.9	119.9
South	100.0	100.0	100.0
West	106.9	108.4	100.0
Trucking	100.0	102.1	105.6

Sources: Banking: F. W. Bell and N. B. Murphy, *Costs in Commercial Banking* (Boston: Federal Reserve Bank of Boston Research Report No. 41, 1968); Electric Power: L. H. Christensen and W. H. Greene, "Economies of Scale in U.S. Power Generation," *Journal of Political Economy,* August 1976, pp. 655–676; Hospitals: H. A. Cohen, "Hospital Cost Curves," in H. F. Klarman, ed., *Empirical Studies in Health Economics* (Baltimore: Johns Hopkins Press, 1970), pp. 279–293; Life Insurance: R. Geehan, "Returns to Scale in the Life Insurance Industry," *The Bell Journal of Economics,* Autumn 1977, pp. 497–516; Railroads: G. Borts, "The Estimation of Rail Cost Functions," *Econometrica,* January 1960, pp. 108–131; Trucking: R. Koenka, "Optimal Scale and the Size Distribution of American Trucking Firms," *Journal of Transport Economics and Policy,* January 1977, pp. 54–67.

defined the output of a railway to be either the number of cars loaded or the mean length of rail haul. Using either definition, he found that railways in the West exhibited slightly decreasing long-run average costs, but those in the East exhibited increasing average costs. Borts attributed this difference to the higher traffic density of the Eastern railroads, which led to higher costs of switching and yard operations.

More recently, excess capacity of railroads has been questioned. Because railroads are required to retain little-used lines by government agencies, they may not be minimizing long-run average costs—these railroads may be operating with too much capital given prevailing output levels. T. E. Keeler estimated a series of short-run cost curves for American railroads and used those cost curves (much as we do later in this chapter) to calculate a long-run cost curve.[6] He concluded that railroads currently possess an enormous amount of excess capacity (over 200,000 miles of track) and that a more appropriately sized rail network might save over $2.5 billion in annual operating costs.

If railroads were allowed to abandon the excess track and if smaller lines were allowed to merge, average costs might fall not only because of reduced capital costs but also because the remaining, larger railroads would exhibit some economies of scale. A 1981 paper found that the increase in haul lengths made possible by rail mergers in the 1960s and early 1970s provided substantial cost savings.[7] In years to come the U.S. rail network is likely to exhibit many similar consolidations if the railroads are deregulated.

Refuse Collection Costs
Refuse collection is a major municipal service carried out by both private and public enterprises. The question of scale economies plays an important role in deciding exactly how this service should be organized to achieve minimal costs. Two types of scale economies might be distinguished. First, using a number of refuse trucks may provide some reductions in average costs if it would reduce costs of maintenance facilities and allow purchasing of specialized equipment. A number of studies have found that these scale economies are relatively insignificant, however, and there seems to be little cost advantage to operating a large number of trucks.

A second, more important source of economies in refuse collection stems from customer density. As density increases, multiple pick-ups from a single stop become possible, and collection times (and costs) fall

(continued)

[6]T. E. Keeler, "Railroad Costs, Returns to Scale and Excess Capacity," *Review of Economics and Statistics,* May 1974, pp. 201–208.

[7]D. W. Caves, L. R. Christensen, and J. A. Swanson, "Productivity Growth, Scale Economies and Capacity Utilization in U.S. Railroads, 1955–74," *American Economic Review,* December 1981, pp. 994–1002.

dramatically. One study finds that each 10 percent increase in density of collection tonnage results in a 5 percent reduction in costs.[8]

These research findings on refuse collection costs have two implications for how the service might be organized. First, the absence of scale economies provides little support for the notion that collection should be done on a citywide basis. Contracting with several different firms instead would not result in increased costs. Second, offering exclusive contracts to service entire areas because of density economies (rather than permitting a totally free market with overlapping collection routes) should minimize overall average costs of refuse collection.

To Think About

1. Many of the industries listed in Table 8.2 seem to exhibit modest economies of scale. For one of these explain what you think the source of these economies is. That is, what is it about production in this industry that seems to be conducive to large-scale operations? Why doesn't this seem to apply to the trucking industry?
2. How would you interpret the notion that railroads (or any other industry) have "excess capacity?" What would the average and marginal cost curves for such a railroad look like? Should excess capacity be regarded as a short-run or a long-run concept?

theory of price determination. "Applying Economics: The Measurement of Long-Run Costs" looks at how long-run average costs can be used to determine which industries might find large-scale firms more appropriate. It also considers how the long-run average costs of two particular industries are affected by different methods of organization.

Distinction between the Short Run and the Long Run

It has been traditional in economics to distinguish between the **short run** and the **long run** for firms. These terms denote the length of time over which a firm may make decisions, and are useful in studying market responses to changed conditions. For example, if only the short run is considered, the firm may need to treat some of its inputs as fixed, because it may be technically impossible to change those inputs on short notice. If a time interval of only one week is involved, the size of a firm's physical plant would have to be treated as absolutely fixed. Similarly, an entrepreneur who is committed to a particular business in the short run would find it impossible (or extremely costly) to change jobs—in the short run, the entrepreneur's input to the production process is essentially fixed. Over the long run, however, neither of those inputs needs to be considered fixed, since a firm's plant size can be altered and an entrepreneur can indeed quit the business.

The distinction between the short run and the long run is the period over which some inputs are considered fixed and the longer period over which all inputs become variable. Making this distinction allows us to study the different types of decisions that a firm might make.

Short run
The period of time in which a firm must consider some inputs absolutely fixed in making its decisions.

Long run
The period of time in which a firm may consider all of its inputs to be variable in making its decisions.

---

[8]Peter Kemper and J. M. Quigley, *The Economics of Refuse Collection* (Cambridge, Mass.: Ballinger Publishing Company, 1976), p. 53.

Short-Run Production Function

Probably the easiest method (and the one we will use here) to introduce the distinction between the short run and the long run into our analysis of a firm's costs is to assume that one of the inputs is held constant in the short run. Specifically, we will assume that capital input is held constant at a level of K_1 and that (in the short run) the firm is free to vary only its labor input. The short-run production function now can be written as

$$Q = f(K_1, L). \tag{8.5}$$

This notation explicitly shows that capital input may not vary. The firm can change the level of Q only by altering its use of labor. We have already studied this possibility in Chapter 7, when we examined the marginal productivity of labor. Here we are interested in analyzing how changes in a firm's output level in the short run are related to changes in total costs. We can then contrast this relationship to the cost relationships studied earlier, in which both inputs could be changed.

A Note on Input Flexibility

Any firm obviously uses far more than two inputs in its production process. The level of some of these inputs may be changed on rather short notice. Firms may ask workers to work overtime, hire part-time replacements from an employment agency, or rent equipment (such as power tools or automobiles) from some other firm. Other types of inputs may take somewhat longer to be adjusted; for example, to hire new, full-time workers is a relatively time-consuming (and costly) process, and ordering new machines designed to unique specifications may involve a considerable time lag. At the most lengthy extreme, entirely new plants can be built, new managers may be recruited and trained, and raw material supplies can be discovered and extraction can be started. It would be impossible to cover all such variations of input types in any detail. Our analysis continues using only our two-input model holding the level of capital input fixed. This treatment should not be taken to imply that labor is a more flexible input than capital. We are considering only the distinction between fixed and variable inputs, and this approach enables us to do so. We could substitute any other inputs for capital and labor in the discussion that follows.

Short-Run Total Costs

Total cost for the firm continues to be given by

$$TC = vK + wL \tag{8.6}$$

for our short-run analysis, but now capital input is fixed at K_1. To denote this fact we will write

$$STC(K_1) = vK_1 + wL. \qquad [8.7]$$

The addition of the S to our notation makes it clear that we are analyzing short-run costs, and the notation also records the level of capital that is being held constant. The two types of input costs in Equation 8.7 are given special names. The term vK_1 is referred to as (short-run) **fixed costs**; since K_1 is constant, these costs will not change in the short run. If the firm has 20 machines that each rent for $500 per week, short-run fixed costs are $10,000 per week and cannot be varied. The term wL is referred to as (short-run) **variable costs**, since in our analysis labor input can indeed be varied in the short run. Using the terms $SFC(K_1)$ for short-run fixed costs and $SVC(K_1)$ for short-run variable costs, we have

Fixed costs
Costs associated with inputs that are fixed in the short run.

Variable costs
Costs associated with inputs that can be varied in the short run.

$$SFC(K_1) = vK_1$$
$$SVC(K_1) = vK_1 \qquad [8.8]$$

and therefore

$$STC(K_1) = SFC(K_1) + SVC(K_1). \qquad [8.9]$$

Short-run total costs are now classified as being either fixed or variable. How do short-run total costs change as the firm's output changes?

Short-Run Fixed and Variable Cost Curves

In the short run, fixed costs are obviously fixed. They do not change as the level of output changes. This relationship is shown in Graph a in Figure 8.7. The $SFC(K_1)$ curve is a horizontal line representing the cost of the fixed amount of capital being employed.

Graph b in Figure 8.7 records one possible relationship between short-run variable costs and output. Initially the marginal productivity of labor is assumed to rise as labor is added to the production process. The fixed input of capital is initially "underutilized," and labor's marginal productivity rises as the amount of labor available to work with this fixed amount of capital increases. Because the marginal product of labor is increasing, short-run variable costs rise less rapidly than output expands—in its initial section, the $SVC(K_1)$ curve is concave. Beyond some output level, say Q', however, the marginal product of labor will begin to decline. Because capital input is constant at K_1, the ability of labor to generate extra output will diminish; since the per-unit cost of labor is assumed to be constant, costs of production will begin to rise

Figure 8.7
Fixed and Variable Costs
in the Short Run

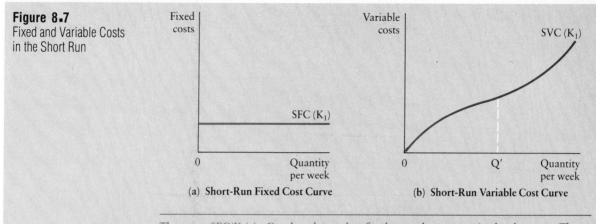

(a) **Short-Run Fixed Cost Curve**   (b) **Short-Run Variable Cost Curve**

The curve $SFC(K_1)$ in Graph a shows that fixed costs do not vary in the short run. They are determined by the fixed input of capital (here K_1) being used. Variable costs do change as the output increases. The shape shown in Graph b assumes that initially labor exhibits an increasing marginal productivity but that, after some point, the marginal productivity of labor diminishes, thus causing short-run costs to rise rapidly.

rapidly. Beyond Q' the $SVC(K_1)$ curve becomes convex to reflect this diminishing marginal productivity of labor. For output levels to the right of Q', existing capital inputs are now being "overutilized." The shape of the $SVC(K_1)$ curve in Graph b in Figure 8.7 is in general agreement with our hypotheses about the marginal productivity of labor in Figure 7.1. It is also quite similar to the case of U-shaped (long-run) marginal costs we discussed in the previous section.

Short-Run Total Cost Curve

We can now construct the short-run total cost curve by summing the two cost components in Figure 8.7. This total cost curve is shown in Figure 8.8, which has two important features. First, when output is 0, total costs are given by fixed costs, $SFC(K_1)$. Since capital input is fixed, it must be paid its rental rate even if no production takes place. The firm cannot avoid these fixed costs in the short run. Contrary to the long-run case, therefore, the STC curve does not pass through the origin. The firm can, of course, avoid all variable costs simply by hiring no labor. A second important feature of Figure 8.8 is that the shape of the curve is solely determined by the shape of the short-run variable cost curve. The way that changes in output affect costs is what determines the shape of the curve. Since fixed costs are constant, they play no role in determining the shape of the $STC(K_1)$ curve other than determining its zero-output intercept.

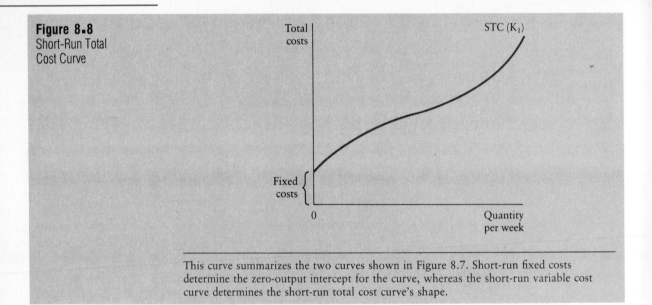

Figure 8.8
Short-Run Total
Cost Curve

This curve summarizes the two curves shown in Figure 8.7. Short-run fixed costs determine the zero-output intercept for the curve, whereas the short-run variable cost curve determines the short-run total cost curve's shape.

Input Inflexibility and Cost Minimization

The total costs shown in Figure 8.8 are not the minimal costs for producing the various output levels shown. Because we are holding capital fixed in the short run, the firm does not have the flexibility in input choice that was assumed when we discussed cost minimization and the related long-run cost curves earlier in this chapter. Rather, to vary its output level in the short run, the firm will be forced to use "nonoptimal" input combinations: the RTS will not be equal to the ratio of the input prices.

This is shown in Figure 8.9. In the short run, the firm can use only K_1 units of capital. To produce output level Q_0, it must use L_0 units of labor, L_1 units of labor to produce Q_1, and L_2 units to produce Q_2. The total costs of these input combinations are given by TC_0, TC_1, and TC_2 respectively. Only for the input combination K_1, L_1 is output being produced at minimal cost. Only at that point is the RTS equal to the ratio of the input prices. From Figure 8.9 it is clear that Q_0 is being produced with "too much" capital in this short-run situation. Cost minimization should suggest a southeasterly movement along the Q_0 isoquant indicating a substitution of labor for capital in production. On the other hand, Q_2 is being produced with "too little" capital, and costs could be reduced by substituting capital for labor. Neither of these substitutions is possible in the short run. However, over the long run the firm will be able to change its level of capital input and will adjust its input usage to the cost-minimizing combinations. This flexible case is discussed earlier in this chapter when we assumed that both labor and capital could be varied.

Figure 8.9
"Nonoptimal" Input
Choices Must Be Made
in the Short Run

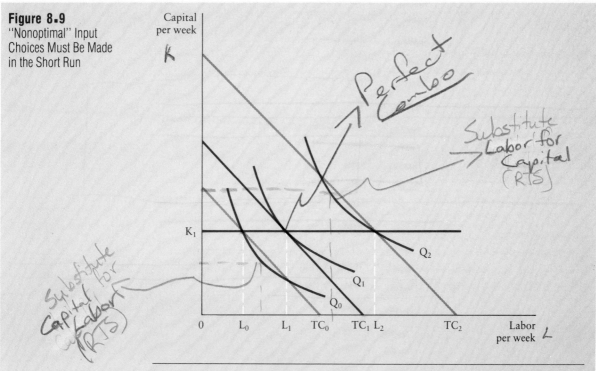

Because capital input is fixed at K_1 in the short run, the firm cannot bring its RTS into equality with the ratio of input prices. Given the input prices, Q_0 should be produced with more labor and less capital than it will be in the short run, whereas Q_2 should be produced with more capital and less labor than it will be.

The Relationship between Short-Run and Long-Run Total Costs

The inefficient nature of the short-run cost minimization process can also be illustrated using total cost curves. Figure 8.10 shows the long-run total cost curve (TC) corresponding to the fourth case of optimal scale in Graph d in Figure 8.4. To this graph we have added the short-run total cost curve associated with K_1 units of capital input—$STC(K_1)$—and the two short-run total cost curves for a somewhat smaller amount of capital, $STC(K_0)$, and a somewhat larger amount of capital, $STC(K_1)$.

The configuration of the curves in Figure 8.10 reflects many of the principles of cost minimization we have been discussing. The zero output intercept for the STC curves is higher for larger amounts of capital. Fixed costs are obviously greater when there is more capital for which rent must continue to be paid in the short run. The curves also reflect the cost penalties suffered by the firm in the short run. Each of the short-run cost curves lies above the long-

Figure 8.10
Relationships between
Short-Run and Long-Run
Total Costs

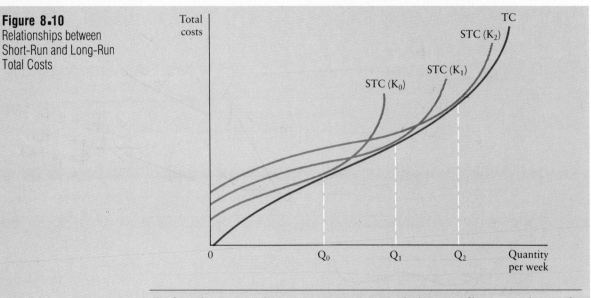

The firm's long-run total cost curve (TC) represents the lower profile (or "envelope") of its short-run total cost curves. Only when the capital stock is that which produces a given output at minimal cost will the short-run and long-run total costs be the same. Only at Q_1 is TC equal to $STC(K_1)$.

run curve at every output level but one.[9] Only for that level of output for which the available capital input is optimal (that is, output Q_1 when K_1 units of capital are employed—see Figure 8.9) do short-run and long-run costs agree. Elsewhere short-run costs are higher. A firm that wished to produce output level Q_2 in the long run, for example, would have to pay much higher costs if it tried to do so with K_1 units of capital than if it adjusted its capital stock to the optimal level K_2. The kind of information in Figure 8.10 gives firms another route to minimizing costs in the long run.

Per-Unit Short-Run Cost Curves

Using the short-run total cost curve already derived, we can easily derive the per-unit short-run cost curves related to it. As for the long run, we define

$$\text{Short-run average cost} = \text{SAC} = \frac{\text{STC}(K_1)}{Q} \qquad [8.10]$$

and

---

[9]The long-run total cost curve is technically termed an "envelope" of the various short-run total cost curves.

Figure 8.11
Short-Run Per-Unit
Cost Curves

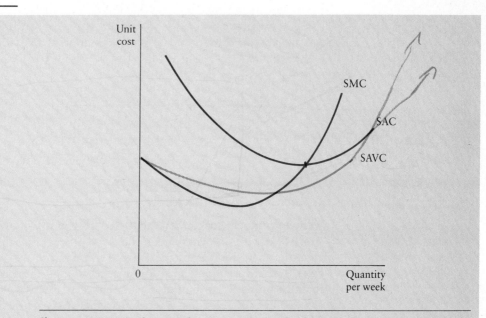

Short-run average and marginal cost curves are U-shaped because one input is held fixed in the short run. The figure illustrates short-run average variable costs (SAVC), which are also relevant to short-run production decisions.

$$\frac{\Delta STC}{\Delta Q}$$

$$\text{Short-run marginal cost} = SMC = \frac{\text{Change in } STC(K_1)}{\text{Change in } Q}. \qquad [8.11]$$

These short-run concepts are similar to those defined earlier for the long run in Equations 8.3 and 8.4 except that now they are based on total costs incurred with the level of capital input fixed at K_1. Because having capital fixed in the short run yields a total cost curve that is quite similar to the case of optimal scale of coordination and control discussed in connection with long-run costs, the resulting short-run average and marginal cost relationships will also be U-shaped here. These are illustrated in Figure 8.11.

As before, the curves not only are U-shaped, but the marginal cost curve (SMC) passes through the lowest point in the average cost curve (SAC) for exactly the same reason as in long-run curves. When SMC < SAC, average cost is falling since the last produced goods were relatively low in cost and lowered the average. Once SMC > SAC, however, the higher costs associated with successive increments of production pull up the average.

Although the SAC and SMC curves are used later in our discussion of price determination, one other short-run cost concept is important here. Recall from Equation 8.9 that short-run costs are categorized as being either "fixed" or "variable." That is,

$$STC = SFC + SVC. \qquad [8.12]$$

For simplicity we have omitted the notation of the level of capital being used. Using these two categories of short-run costs we can break down short-run average cost into fixed and variable components by dividing Equation 8.12 by Q. That is,

$$\frac{STC}{Q} = SAC = \frac{SFC}{Q} + \frac{SVC}{Q}$$

= Short-run average fixed cost   [8.13]

+ Short-run average variable cost

= SAFC + SAVC.

Short-run average variable cost (SAVC)
Total variable cost divided by quantity produced. These costs are avoidable if the firm produces no output.

Although the concept of average fixed cost is of little economic usefulness (since fixed costs never change), **short-run average variable cost (SAVC)** does enter the analysis on a few occasions. SAVC indicates the average "avoidable" costs that firms must incur to produce anything—these costs are avoidable if the firm produces no output. Avoidable costs clearly can affect firms' short-run production decisions. Average variable costs are similar to average total costs in our prior long-run analysis (in which no inputs were fixed): the SAVC and SMC curves have an identical configuration to that illustrated previously. SAVC always lies below SAC (the vertical difference being average fixed costs), but the two curves approach each other at high levels of output for which average fixed costs are quite small.[10]

Relationship between Short-Run and Long-Run Per-Unit Cost Curves

Implicit in the relationship between short-run and long-run total costs illustrated in Figure 8.10 is also a complex set of relations among the per-unit cost curves. Long-run average and marginal cost curves represent cost-minimizing solutions to an entire family of equivalent short-run curves (one for each possible level of capital input). Although it is possible to illustrate the precise relationship among all these curves, a detailed presentation is not essential here.[11] For firms with U-shaped long-run average and marginal cost curves, one particular set of relationships is useful to us.

---

[10]The SMC and SAVC curves in Figure 8.11 have the same zero-output intercept. The marginal cost and the average variable costs of the first unit produced in the short run are equal. The zero-output intercept for short-run average total costs is undetermined since for Q = 0, this is a positive number (fixed costs) divided by zero.

[11]Some of these relationships are illustrated by the numerical example in the appendix to this chapter.

Figure 8.12
Short-Run and Long-Run
Average and Marginal
Cost Curves at Optimal
Output Level

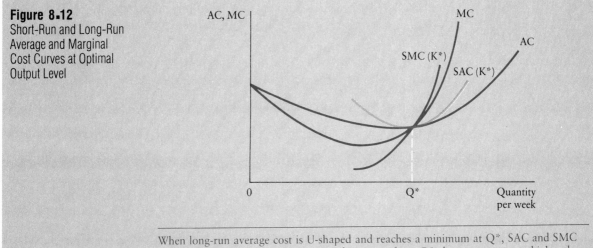

When long-run average cost is U-shaped and reaches a minimum at Q*, SAC and SMC will also pass through this point. For departures from Q* short-run costs are higher than long-run costs.

Figure 8.12 shows these cost relationships for such a firm. For this firm, long-run average costs reach a minimum at output level Q*, and as we have noted in several places, at this output level MC = AC. Also associated with Q* is a certain level of capital usage, K*. What we wish to do now is to examine the short-run average and marginal cost curves based on this level of capital input. We now look at the costs of a firm whose level of capital input is consistent with its minimum long-run average cost to see how costs vary in the short run as Q departs from its optimal level of Q*.

Our discussion about the total cost curves in Figure 8.10 shows that when the firm's level of capital input yields minimum costs for the output it wishes to produce, short-run and long-run total costs are equal. Average costs then are equal also. At Q*, AC is equal to SAC(K*). Figure 8.10 also shows that the short-run and long-run total cost curves are just tangent to each other at Q*. This means that at Q*, MC and SMC(K*) are also equal, since each represents the slope of the respective total cost curve. At Q* in Figure 8.12, the following equality holds:

$$AC = MC = SAC(K^*) = SMC(K^*). \qquad [8.14]$$

For movements away from Q*, short-run costs are higher than long-run costs. These higher per-unit costs reflect the inflexibility in the short run because some inputs are fixed. This inflexibility has important consequences for firms' short-run supply responses and for price changes in the short run.

"Applying Economics: Congestion Costs" shows one real-life case of how short-run costs rise rapidly as the traffic using roads and airports increases.

APPLYING ECONOMICS

Congestion Costs

One case in which the phenomenon of increasing short-run costs is obvious is traffic congestion. The demand placed on transportation facilities (for example, expressways) during peak travel hours can be viewed as an increase in output (vehicle miles) in the short run. Because some inputs (the size of the roadway) are held fixed when this output increases, we would expect that costs will rise. The primary increased cost will be increased time delays for travelers, although other costs (such as the costs of road maintenance) may increase as well. Anyone who has driven on a busy urban expressway at 8:00 A.M. or tried to land at a major airport at 4:00 P.M. knows that these costs can be substantial.

Some evidence on rising costs as a result of congestion is presented in Table 8.3. This table reports the marginal costs of automobile travel on San Francisco Bay area expressways and of landing at LaGuardia Airport in New York City. Both sets of figures are for the marginal costs incurred by producing one more "unit of output": one more vehicle mile or one more arriving flight, respectively. As the table shows, these costs increase markedly during the hours of peak travel demand. For both facilities, peak hour marginal costs are more than four times those incurred during off-peak hours. These data show that people who choose to travel during peak hours impose considerable costs (primarily in terms of time delays) on each other.

To Think About
1. Can you think of other examples of congestion costs? That is, are there other circumstances where a temporary need to expand output causes costs to rise rapidly? How about the opposite case of a temporary increase in output leading to lower costs? In your examples, do prices change temporarily to meet these temporary changes in costs? Can you explain the price movements you do see?
2. Economists have had a rather difficult time measuring increasing short-run marginal costs for many production processes. Suppose you wanted to make such a measurement. How would you proceed? How would you define "short-run increases in output"? How would you try to hold one or several inputs constant for the firm you were studying?

Table 8.3
Increasing Marginal Time Costs during Peak Travel Hours

	San Francisco Expressways		LaGuardia Airport	
Time Period	Marginal Costs per Vehicle Mile	Time of Day	Marginal Costs per Arriving Flight	Time of Day
Peak hours	38.1¢	7–8 AM, 5–6 PM	$1,025	3–5 PM
Near peak hours	8.9	6–7, 8–9 AM, 4–5, 6–7 PM	670	1–3, 5–7 PM
Off peak hours	7.7	Other times	$0–$200	Other times

Sources: Expressways: T. E. Keeler and K. A. Small, "Optimal Peak-Load Pricing, Investment, and Service Levels on Urban Expressways," *Journal of Political Economy*, February 1977, pp. 1–26; figures are calculated from equation 16 and from Table 5, p. 18. LaGuardia airport: A. Carlin and R. F. Park, "Marginal Cost Pricing of Airport Runway Capacity," *American Economic Review*, June 1970, pp. 310–319. Figures are averaged from Table 2, p. 314.

Shifts in Cost Curves

We have shown how the cost curves for a firm's output are derived from its cost-minimizing expansion path. Any change in economic conditions that affects this expansion path will also affect the shape and position of the cost curves. Two kinds of economic changes are likely to have such effects: changes in input prices and technological innovations.

Changes in Input Prices

A change in the price of an input will tilt the firm's total cost lines and alter its expansion path. A rise in wage rates will, for example, cause firms to produce any output level using relatively more capital and relatively less labor. To the extent that a substitution of capital for labor is possible (remember substitution possibilities depend on the shape of the isoquant map), the entire expansion path of the firm will rotate toward the capital axis. This movement in turn implies a new set of cost curves for the firm. A rise in the price of labor input has caused the entire relationship between output levels and costs to change. Presumably all cost curves would be shifted upward, and the extent of the shift would depend both on how "important" labor is in production and on how successful the firm is in substituting other inputs for labor.

One historical example of the effects of changing input prices on cost curves is the effect of the opening of major coal fields in Pennsylvania and West Virginia in the nineteenth century on the cost curves of iron producers. The development of the new fields sharply reduced the price of coal. Iron producers consequently substituted coal for wood as a fuel. The cost curves for iron output shifted downward in response to the substitution. This downward shift in costs had important implications for the price of iron, which also fell (we analyze this type of effect precisely in Chapter 11).

Technological Innovation

New technologies can also have important effects on cost curves. Since technical advances alter a firm's production function (as discussed in Chapter 7), isoquant maps will shift as well as the firm's expansion path when technology changes. For example, an advance in knowledge might simply shift all isoquants toward the origin, with the result that any output level could then be produced with a lower level of input and a lower cost. Alternatively, technical change might be "biased" in that it might save only on the use of one input ("automation" saves only on labor costs, for instance). Here again the end result would be to alter isoquant maps, shift expansion paths, and finally affect the shape and location of a firm's cost curves.

Although this section does not analyze cost curve shifts in great detail, you should be able to see how such an analysis would be done. Only by carefully sorting out the effects of technical change from those of input price changes can we understand the reasons for such shifts. This understanding is important if we are to analyze why supply conditions in an industry might change. This effect of technological change in a real-world situation is discussed in "Applying Economics: Power Looms and the Growth of New England Textile Production."

APPLYING ECONOMICS

Power Looms and the Growth of New England Textile Production

One of the most dramatic economic events in the history of the United States was the adoption of the power loom by the New England textile industry following the War of 1812. First developed by Francis Cabot Lowell in Boston in 1814, the designs for these looms were based on looms operating in Lancashire, England. As experience with the new technology expanded and the looms were adapted to American conditions, costs of textile production fell rapidly. Between 1815 and 1823 it is estimated that average total costs of cotton textile production were halved. These declines continued into the 1830s and 1840s with average costs falling by another 30 to 50 percent as firms adapted more completely to the new technology.[12] Prices of textiles fell along with these cost declines, and the quantity of cloth produced expanded greatly. Between 1815 and 1826 output of the New England cotton industry expanded by a factor of 40. This growth was in large measure responsible for the early economic growth of the new nation. By 1870 the economy of New England had greatly transformed from an agricultural one to one based on manufactur-

ing, and the industrial revolution in the New World was under way.

To Think About

1. For many years the British tried to keep their textile production techniques a secret so that they could enjoy cost advantages over other producers. Were they successful in this? What would have prevented the British from obtaining significant advantages from their technology? What forces would be at work tending to spread the information to other countries? Do you remember from your high school history course how the British technology came to America?

2. Probably the most dramatic recent example of technology lowering costs is in the field of consumer electronics. (Calculators, stereos, and video recorders are some important cases.) Use the concepts of this chapter to explain why costs fell so rapidly for these goods. What specific changes in technology had the most important effect on costs?

Summary

This chapter shows how to construct the firm's cost curves. These curves show the relationship between the amount that a firm produces and the costs of the inputs required. In later chapters we will see how these curves are important building blocks for developing the theory of supply. The primary results of this chapter were:

- To minimize the cost of producing any particular level of output, the firm should choose a point on the isoquant for which the rate of technical substitution (RTS) is equal to the ratio of the inputs' market prices.
- By repeating this cost minimization process for every possible level of output, the firm's expansion path can be constructed. This shows the minimum cost way of producing any level of output. The firm's total cost curve can be calculated directly from the expansion path.

---

[12]These figures are taken from R. B. Zevin, "The Growth of Cotton Textile Production after 1815," in R. W. Fogel and S. L. Engerman, eds., *The Reinterpretation of American Economic History* (New York: Harper and Row, 1971).

- The two most important unit cost concepts are average cost (that is, cost per unit of output) and marginal cost (that is, the incremental cost of the last unit produced). Average and marginal cost curves can be constructed directly from the total cost curve. The shape of these curves depends on whether the firm's production function exhibits increasing, decreasing, or constant returns to scale.

- Short-run cost curves are constructed by holding one of the firm's inputs constant in the short run. These short-run costs will not generally be the lowest cost the firm could achieve if all inputs could be adjusted. Short-run costs also increase rapidly as output expands because the inputs that can be adjusted experience diminishing marginal productivities.

- Cost curves will shift to a new position whenever the prices of inputs change. Improvements in production techniques will also shift cost curves since the same output can then be produced with fewer inputs.

Problems

8.1 A widget manufacturer has an infinitely substitutable production function of the form

$$Q = 2K + L.$$

a. Graph the isoquant maps for $Q = 20$, $Q = 40$, and $Q = 60$. What is the RTS along these isoquants?

b. If the wage rate (w) is $1 and the rental rate on capital (v) is $1, what cost-minimizing combination of K and L will the manufacturer employ for the three different production levels in part a? What is the manufacturer's expansion path?

8.2 Show that for the production function in Problem 8.1, the cost-minimizing input ratio may require the use of only capital or only labor. In such a situation what will be the firm's expansion path? What will the shape of its marginal and average cost curves depend on? How will these cost curves shift as the price of the input that is utilized rises?

8.3 Is it possible that isoquants might have positive slopes? How would you interpret this possibility? Show that positively sloped sections of isoquants will never be observed because they do not represent cost-minimizing positions.

8.4 Trapper Joe, the fur trader, has found that his production function in acquiring pelts is given by:

$$Q = 2\sqrt{H}$$

where

Q = the number of pelts acquired in a day and
H = the number of hours Joe's employees
spend hunting and trapping in one day.

Joe pays his employees $8 an hour.

a. Calculate Joe's total and average cost curves (as a function of Q).
b. What is Joe's total cost for the day if he acquires four pelts? Six pelts? Eight pelts? What is Joe's average cost per pelt for the day if he acquires four pelts? Six pelts? Eight pelts?
c. Graph the cost curves from part a and indicate the points from part b.

8.5 A firm producing hockey sticks has a production function given by

$$Q = 2\sqrt{K \cdot L}.$$

In the short run, the firm's amount of capital equipment is fixed at K = 100. The rental rate for K is v = $1, and the wage rate for L is w = $4.

a. Calculate the firm's short-run total cost curve. Calculate the short-run average cost curve.
b. The firm's short-run marginal cost curve is given by SMC = Q/50. What is the STC, SATC, and SMC for the firm if it produces twenty-five hockey sticks? Fifty hockey sticks? One hundred hockey sticks? Two hundred hockey sticks?
c. Graph the SATC and the SMC curves for the firm. Indicate the points found in part b.
d. Where does the SMC curve intersect the SATC curve? Explain why the SMC curve will always intersect the SATC at its lowest point.

*8.6 Professor Smith and Professor Jones are going to produce a new introductory textbook. As true scientists they have laid out the production function for the book as:

$$Q = S^{1/2}J^{1/2}$$

where Q = the number of pages in the finished book, S = the number of working hours spent by Smith, and J = the number of hours spent working by Jones.

Smith values his labor at $3 per working hour. He has spent 900 hours preparing the first draft. Jones, whose labor is valued at $12 per working hour, will revise Smith's draft to complete the book.

a. How many hours will Jones have to spend to produce a finished book of 150 pages? Of 300 pages? Of 450 pages?
b. What is the marginal cost of the 150th page of the finished book? Of the 300th page? Of the 450th page?

─────────────────────

*Denotes problems that are rather difficult.

*8.7   An enterprising entrepreneur purchases two firms to produce widgets. Each firm produces identical products and each has a production function given by

$$Q_i = \sqrt{K_i \cdot L_i}$$
$$i = 1, 2.$$

The firms differ, however, in the amount of capital equipment each has. In particular, firm 1 has $K_1 = 25$, whereas firm 2 has $K_2 = 100$. The marginal product of labor is $MP_L = 5/(2\sqrt{L})$ for firm 1, and $MP_L = 5/\sqrt{L}$ for firm 2. Rental rates for K and L are given by $w = v = \$1$.

   a.   If the entrepreneur wishes to minimize short-run total costs of widget production, how should output be allocated between the two firms?
   b.   Given that output is optimally allocated between the two firms, calculate the short-run and total average cost curves. What is the marginal cost of the 100th widget? The 125th widget? The 200th widget?
   c.   How should the entrepreneur allocate widget production between the two firms in the long run? Calculate the long-run total and average cost curves for widget production.
   d.   How would your answer to part c change if both firms exhibited diminishing returns to scale?

8.8   Suppose a firm's production function requires it to use capital and labor in a fixed ratio of two workers per machine to produce 10 units and that the rental rates for capital and labor are given by $v = 1$, $w = 3$.

   a.   Calculate the firm's long-run total and average cost curves.
   b.   Suppose K is fixed at 10 in the short run. Calculate the firm's short-run total and average cost curves. What is the marginal cost of the 10th unit? The 25th unit? The 50th unit? The 100th unit?

*8.9   In a famous article by Jacob Viner, "Cost Curves and Supply Curves," *Zeitschrift fur Nationalokonomie*, September 1931, pp. 23–46, Viner criticized his draftsman because he could not draw a family of short-run average cost curves whose points of tangency with the long-run average cost curve were also the minimum points on each SAC curve. The draftsman protested that such a drawing was impossible to construct. Whom would you support in this debate? Are there cases in which either might be correct?

8.10   A stuffed wombat manufacturer determined that the lowest average production costs were achieved when eight wombats were produced at an average cost of $1,000 each. If the marginal cost curve is a straight line intersecting the origin, what is the marginal cost for producing the ninth wombat?

APPENDIX TO CHAPTER 8

NUMERICAL EXAMPLE OF A PRODUCTION FUNCTION AND ITS COST CURVES

This appendix looks at a simple numerical example of a production function and its associated cost curves. The example illustrates in detail the precise way in which cost curves are derived from production functions. The appendix may help you understand how the two concepts are related. The example we have chosen is not necessarily a realistic one, but it does reflect features found in many actual situations.

The Production Function

For our simple example we assume that the firm Hamburger Heaven is in the business of producing exquisite hamburgers using grills (that is, capital, K) and hours of workers' time (L). We assume that the production function for burgers is given explicitly by

$$\text{Burgers per hour} = Q = 10\sqrt{K \cdot L}. \qquad [\text{8A.1}]$$

Table 8A.1 shows that this production function exhibits constant returns to scale.[1] As grills and workers are increased proportionately, hourly hamburger output also increases in the same proportion.

Table 8A.1
Production of Hamburgers Exhibits Constant Returns to Scale

Grills	Workers	Hamburgers per Hour
1	1	10
2	2	20
3	3	30
4	4	40
5	5	50
6	6	60
7	7	70
8	8	80
9	9	90
10	10	100

---

[1]This production function can also be written as $Q = 10K^{1/2}L^{1/2}$. That particular form is one example of what is called a Cobb-Douglas production function (after its discoverers). Such a function will exhibit constant returns to scale whenever the exponents of K and L sum to 1.

Table 8A.2

Total Output, Marginal and Average Productivity for Workers with Four Grills

Workers	Grills	Hamburgers per Hour	MP_L	AP_L
1	4	20.0		20.0
2	4	28.3	8.3	14.2
3	4	34.6	6.3	11.5
4	4	40.0	5.4	10.0
5	4	44.7	4.7	8.9
6	4	49.0	4.3	8.2
7	4	52.9	3.9	7.6
8	4	56.6	3.7	7.1
9	4	60.0	3.4	6.7
10	4	63.2	3.2	6.3

Marginal and Average Productivities

Tables 8A.2 and 8A.3 show the total productivity of labor, the marginal productivity of labor, and the average productivity of labor for two possible grill configurations Hamburger Heaven might use—four grills and nine grills. Two features of those tables are immediately clear. First, the marginal productivity and average productivity of labor both decline in each table as the quantity of labor hired increases. This is a reflection of the fact that the number of grills (that is, capital) is held constant in the tables. Although when both factors are increased together the production function exhibits constant returns to scale, holding grills constant causes workers to exhibit a diminishing marginal productivity. Because the marginal productivity is falling, the average is falling also. Since an extra worker produces fewer hamburgers than the average number of hamburgers per worker output that previously prevailed, hiring this extra worker causes the overall average to fall.

Table 8A.3

Total Output, Marginal and Average Productivity for Workers with Nine Grills

Workers	Grills	Hamburgers per Hour	MP_L	AP_L
1	9	30.0		30.0
2	9	42.4	12.4	21.2
3	9	52.0	9.6	17.3
4	9	60.0	8.0	15.0
5	9	67.1	7.1	13.4
6	9	73.5	6.4	12.3
7	9	79.4	5.9	11.3
8	9	84.8	5.4	10.6
9	9	90.0	5.2	10.0
10	9	94.9	4.9	9.5

A second feature to note about the tables is that the marginal and average productivities of labor are all higher in Table 8A.3 than they are in Table 8A.2. This simply shows that the workers in the latter table have a larger number of grills to work with than do those in the former. Even though the marginal productivity of labor declines in both cases, labor is more productive in Table 8A.3 because it has more capital input with which to make hamburgers—there is less crowding around the grills in Table 8A.3 than in Table 8A.2.

The Isoquant Map

As a final example of using this simple production function, we shall construct its isoquant map. Of course, there are infinitely many isoquants that might be drawn (one for each conceivable output level), but we will consider only two—for 40 hamburgers per hour and for 100 hamburgers per hour.

For the 40-hamburger isoquant, we are interested in those combinations of K and L for which

$$40 = 10\sqrt{K \cdot L}. \qquad [8A.2]$$

Manipulating this expression, we get

$$16 = K \cdot L \qquad [8A.3]$$

or

$$K = \frac{16}{L}. \qquad [8A.4]$$

Holding hamburger output constant implies a relationship that shows potential tradeoffs between grills and workers. We can graph that relationship. In Table 8A.4 we have calculated the number of grills that combine with integral values of L (from 1 to 10) to produce 40 hamburgers (of course it makes no sense to speak of fractions of grills, but then again, this example is far-fetched anyway). For each of these input combinations we have also calculated the RTS as the ratio of the change in capital input to the change in labor input. From this information, the 40 hamburger isoquant can be constructed in Figure 8A.1. This isoquant clearly shows those combinations of grills and workers that produce 40 hamburgers. As demonstrated by Table 8A.5, the isoquant exhibits a diminishing RTS (of L for K) and resembles those drawn in Chapters 7 and 8.

Table 8A.5 for the 100 hamburger per hour isoquant is constructed in an identical manner. By an algebraic manipulation similar to that shown previ-

Table 8A.4
Construction of the 40
Hamburger per Hour
Isoquant

Workers (L)	Grills (K)	ΔL	−ΔK	$RTS = \dfrac{-\Delta K}{\Delta L}$
1	16.0	1		
2	8.0	1	8	8
3	5.3	1	2.7	2.7
4	4.0	1	1.3	1.3
5	3.2	1	0.8	0.8
6	2.7	1	0.5	0.5
7	2.3	1	0.4	0.4
8	2.0	1	0.3	0.3
9	1.8	1	0.2	0.2
10	1.6	1	0.2	0.2

Figure 8A.1
Graph of the 40 and 100
Hamburger per Hour
Isoquants for Hamburger
Heaven

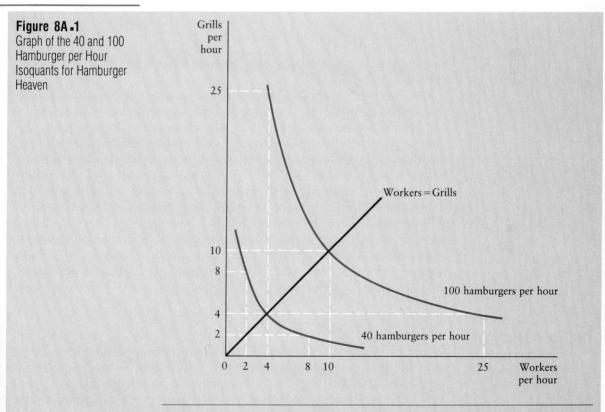

These isoquants are taken directly from Tables 8A.4 and 8A.5. They show those combinations of grills and workers that can produce 40 and 100 hamburgers per hour respectively. The isoquants clearly display a diminishing RTS.

Table 8A.5
Construction of the 100 Hamburger per Hour Isoquant

Workers (L)	Grills (K)	ΔL	−ΔK	RTS = $\dfrac{-\Delta K}{\Delta L}$
1	100.0	1		
2	50.0	1	50.0	50.0
3	33.3	1	16.7	16.7
4	25.0	1	8.3	8.3
5	20.0	1	5.0	5.0
6	16.7	1	3.3	3.3
7	14.3	1	2.4	2.4
8	12.5	1	1.8	1.8
9	11.1	1	1.4	1.4
10	10.0	1	1.1	1.1

ously it is an easy matter to calculate that those combinations of K and L that can produce 100 hamburgers per hour satisfy the relation

$$K = \frac{100}{L}. \tag{8A.5}$$

Some of those combinations are also shown in Figure 8A.1. Again the isoquant exhibits a diminishing RTS.

One useful fact illustrated by these two isoquants is that the RTS depends only on the ratio of K to L, not on the scale of production. This is true for any constant returns to scale production function. For example, with the four grills on the 40 hamburger isoquant, four workers are employed per hour and the RTS is also approximately 1. Similarly, on the 100 hamburger per hour isoquant, with 10 grills, 10 workers are required, and the RTS is also approximately 1. This example shows that for a constant returns to scale production function the isoquants are simply radial blowups of one another—the RTS depends only on the ratio of grills (K) to workers (L). The RTSs do not agree exactly in the tables, but this results from the fact that we are studying "large" changes in K and L rather than the very small changes that are actually required by the definition of the RTS. If we had calculated such minute changes, the RTSs would agree exactly.

Cost Minimization

In order to discuss Hamburger Heaven's cost minimizing input choices, we must know the costs of capital and labor. Suppose that the firm rents its grills from a grill leasing firm at $1 per hour. Suppose also that workers are hired at $1 per hour (Hamburger Heaven pays little attention to the minimum wage law). Total costs are given by

$$TC = \$1 \cdot K + \$1 \cdot L. \tag{8A.6}$$

Table 8A.6
Costs of Producing 40 Hamburgers per Hour Using Various Combinations of Inputs

Workers	Grills	Total Cost
1	16.0	$17.00
2	8.0	10.00
3	5.3	8.30
4	4.0	8.00
5	3.2	8.20
6	2.7	8.70
7	2.3	9.30
8	2.0	10.00
9	1.8	10.80
10	1.6	11.60

Suppose the firm wants to minimize the total costs of producing 40 hamburgers per hour. There are many possible ways of producing 40 hamburgers, and all of those possible combinations lie on the isoquant shown in Figure 8A.1. The first two columns of Table 8A.6 repeat some of this information about grills and workers that can produce 40 hamburgers per hour that appears in Table 8A.5. In the third column of Table 8A.6, we have computed the total costs of each of those input combinations. As Table 8A.6 makes clear, the cost-minimizing way to produce 40 hamburgers per hour is by using four grills and four workers. These will cost $8, and this is the lowest cost attainable. That this is the cost-minimizing input combination should have been obvious from our previous discussion in which we showed that the RTS on the 40 hamburger per hour isoquant is 1 for this input combination. This is exactly the ratio of the wage rate (w) to the rental rate of capital (v). At this point the RTS is equal to the ratio of the inputs prices, and this is what must be true for cost minimization.

A Graphic Proof

In Figure 8A.2 we have redrawn the 40 hamburger per hour isoquant together with the TC = $8 line. For four grills and four workers total costs are indeed $8, and all other input combinations capable of producing 40 hamburgers per hour cost more than $8. It should also be clear from the figure that had the ratio of labor to capital costs been other than 1, some other capital-labor combination would have been chosen. For example, if the wage had been $2 per hour instead of $1, the ratio w/v would be 2; Hamburger Heaven would have used more grills and fewer workers to produce 40 hamburgers per hour. This new input price ratio would cause the firm to use about 2.8 worker hours and 5.6 grills to produce 40 hamburgers per hour most cheaply. Total costs would then be $11.20 [= $2 · (2.8) + $1 · (5.6)], which is the lowest level of costs attainable given the new input prices.

Figure 8A.2
Cost-Minimizing Input
Choice for 40 Hamburgers
per Hour

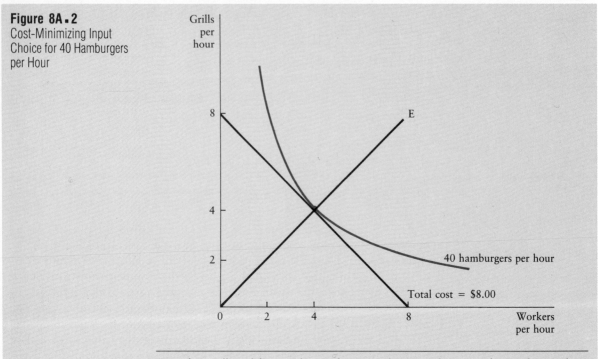

Using four grills and four workers is the minimal cost combination of input that can be used to produce 40 hamburgers per hour. For this input choice, the RTS is equal to the factor price ratio w/v. In other words, the slope of the 40 hamburgers per hour isoquant with four grills and four workers is − 1.

The Expansion Path

If wage rates and grill rental rates don't change, it is easy to construct Hamburger Heaven's expansion path. We have already shown that if w = $1 and v = $1, then the cost-minimizing input choice is four grills and four workers, because at this point the RTS is equal to the input price ratio. We also know that for a constant returns to scale production function (such as the one we are using) the RTS depends only on the ratio of the two inputs, not on the scale of production. Consequently the RTS will always be 1 when equal numbers of grills and workers are used. Since w/v is also always equal to 1, the desire to minimize costs will result in the firm always using grills and workers in a ratio of 1:1. The firm's expansion path is then just the ray through the origin along which grills and workers are used in equal amounts. This ray is labeled OE in Figure 8A.2. Table 8A.7 calculates this expansion path for output levels ranging from 10 to 100 hamburgers per hour. It also computes the (minimum) total cost for producing each of these output levels. The table clearly reflects the constant returns to scale nature of the production function—total costs are exactly proportional to hamburger output. Along the expansion path, hamburgers always cost exactly $.20 each.

Table 8A.7
Expansion Path for
Hamburger Heaven

Hamburgers per Hour	Workers	Grills	Total Cost
10	1	1	$ 2.00
20	2	2	4.00
30	3	3	6.00
40	4	4	8.00
50	5	5	10.00
60	6	6	12.00
70	7	7	14.00
80	8	8	16.00
90	9	9	18.00
100	10	10	20.00

Long-Run Cost Curves

Given the information in Table 8A.7, it is a simple matter to graph Hamburger Heaven's long-run total cost curve. As Graph a in Figure 8A.3 shows, this total cost curve is a straight line that passes through the origin. This is another reflection of the constant returns to scale in this example. The slope of the total cost curve is 0.20, indicating that marginal (and average) costs are always

Figure 8A.3
Total, Average, and
Marginal Cost Curves

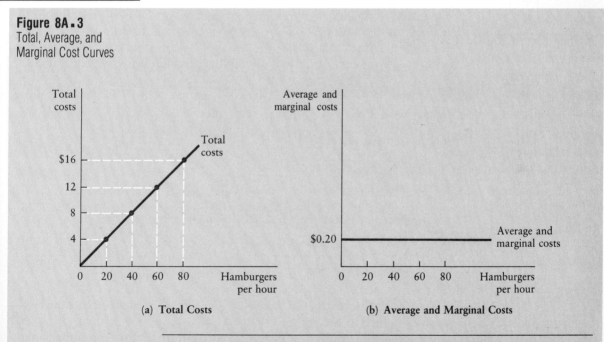

(a) **Total Costs**   (b) **Average and Marginal Costs**

The total cost curve is simply a straight line through the origin reflecting constant returns to scale. Long-run average and marginal costs are constant at $.20 per hamburger.

Table 8A.8
Short-Run Total Costs for
Hamburger Heaven with
Four Grills

Hamburgers per Hour	Grills	Workers	Short-Run Total Costs
10	4	0.25	$ 4.25
20	4	1.00	5.00
30	4	2.25	6.25
40	4	4.00	8.00
50	4	6.25	10.25
60	4	9.00	13.00
70	4	12.25	16.25
80	4	16.00	20.00
90	4	20.25	24.25
100	4	25.00	29.00

$.20 per hamburger. Hence, the long-run average and marginal cost curves are the same horizontal line as shown in Graph b in Figure 8A.3. No matter how much is produced, if Hamburger Heaven has complete flexibility in choosing the mix of grills and workers it uses, the firm can produce all the hamburgers it wants at $.20 each.

Short-Run Cost Curves

To analyze short-run costs, assume that Hamburger Heaven's cooking facilities are fixed at four grills. Short-run fixed costs are $4 per hour—$1 rental for each grill used. Variable costs are w · L—the total cost of paying the number of workers hired. The short-run relationship between Q and L is

$$Q = 10\sqrt{4 \cdot L} = 20\sqrt{L}$$

or

$$L = \frac{Q^2}{400}. \qquad [8A.7]$$

In the short run Hamburger Heaven's total costs are given by:

$$TC = 4 + wL = 4 + \frac{Q^2}{400} \qquad [8A.8]$$

which shows the relationship between Q and total costs when cooking facilities are limited to four grills

In Table 8A.8 we have calculated short-run total costs for output levels ranging from 10 to 100 hamburgers. It is important to notice two features of Table 8A.8. First, total costs increase rapidly as more hamburgers are grilled.

Table 8A.9
Short-Run Average and
Marginal Costs for
Hamburger Heaven
with Four Grills

Hamburgers per Hour	Short-Run Total Cost	Short-Run Average Cost	Short-Run Marginal Cost
10	$ 4.25	$0.425	
20	5.00	0.250	$0.075
30	6.25	0.208	0.125
40	8.00	0.200	0.175
50	10.25	0.205	0.225
60	13.00	0.217	0.275
70	16.25	0.232	0.325
80	20.00	0.250	0.375
90	24.25	0.269	0.425
100	29.00	0.290	0.475

This is a reflection of the diminishing marginal productivity of cookers when they are increasingly crowded around the four available grills. A second, related observation is that all but one of the entries in the table exceed those for long-run costs in Table 8A.7. The fact that grills are fixed at four causes all the input combinations except K = 4, L = 4 to be more costly than if both inputs can be adjusted. Only when the "correct" amount of labor (here four workers per hour) is being used with the available facilities to produce 40 hamburgers per hour will costs be truly minimized. A comparison of the tables indicates the kinds of adjustments that a firm would like to make in the long run when all inputs become variable.

Short-Run Average and Marginal Costs

Table 8A.9 uses the total cost information from Table 8A.8 to calculate short-run average and marginal costs. So long as marginal costs are below average costs, average costs decline. Average costs decline from $.425 per hamburger to $.20 each as output expands from 10 to 40 burgers per hour.[2] For expansions beyond 40 per hour, however, marginal costs exceed average costs; therefore average costs rise. At output levels of 100 or more hamburgers per hour, average and marginal costs are rising quite rapidly. During the lunch time rush, Hamburger Heaven gets so crowded and the workers get so harried that the spoilage and other costs rise rapidly.

---

[2]Again, here the marginal cost figures do not reflect small changes as they should. Rather, for pedagogic purposes, marginal costs have been recorded for rather large changes in output (10 hamburgers per hour). For this reason, marginal and average costs are not equal at the minimum point of the SATC curve (that is, at 40 hamburgers per hour). Had the figures been computed for small changes, SATC and SMC would be identical ($.20) at 40 hamburgers per hour. This is shown in Figure 8A.3.

Figure 8A.4
Short-Run, Total, Average,
and Marginal Cost Curves
When Four Grills Are Used

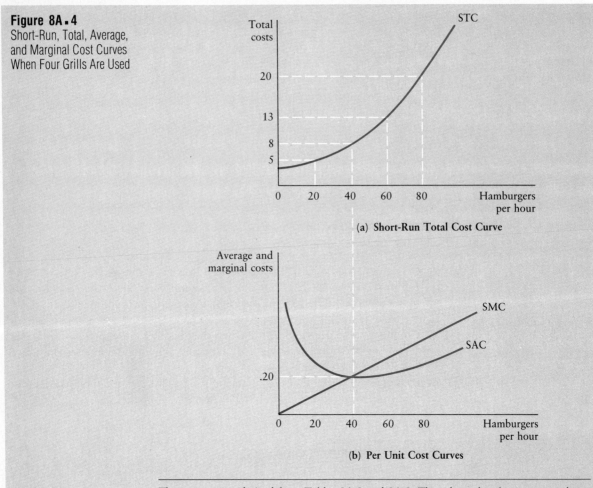

(a) **Short-Run Total Cost Curve**

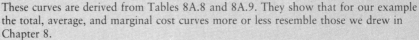

(b) **Per Unit Cost Curves**

These curves are derived from Tables 8A.8 and 8A.9. They show that for our example the total, average, and marginal cost curves more or less resemble those we drew in Chapter 8.

Graphs of the costs recorded in Tables 8A.8 and 8A.9 are presented in Figure 8A.4. The total cost curve is a rapidly increasing function of Q with an intercept of $4 (this reflects the fixed cost of the four grills).[3] The average cost curve in the figure has the familiar U shape and reaches a minimum at 40 hamburgers per hour. The marginal cost curve passes through this minimum and, in this example, is simply a straight line. All of the curves in Figure 8A.4 clearly show the effect that holding cooking facilities fixed in the short run has on costs. Since producing extra hamburgers can only be accomplished

---

[3]Technically, the cost function is a quadratic equation since it involves terms in Q^2.

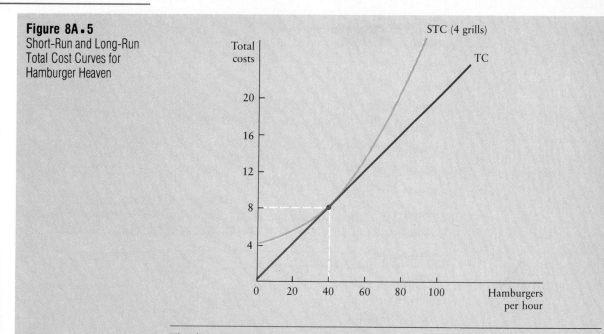

Figure 8A.5
Short-Run and Long-Run
Total Cost Curves for
Hamburger Heaven

The short-run total cost curve when four grills are used lies above the long-run total cost curve except at an output level of 40 hamburgers per hour. At that output level, the constant number of grills (four) is also appropriate for long-run cost minimization. Hence at that output level, the short-run and long-run total cost curves are tangent.

by hiring more workers, this process runs into diminishing marginal productivities, and costs rise rapidly.

Relationship of Long-Run and Short-Run Cost Curves

Figure 8A.5 is a combined graph of the information on short-run and long-run total costs. As in Figure 8A.3, the TC curve is a straight line. The STC curve for four grills is tangent to the TC curve at an output of 40 hamburgers per hour since that is an appropriate level of output when Hamburger Heaven opts for four grills. The vertical axis intercepts of the STC curve reflect fixed costs of $4. In the long run, there are no fixed costs; the TC curve passes through the origin.

Finally, Figure 8A.6 depicts the short-run and long-run average and marginal cost curves for Hamburger Heaven. This configuration of curves resembles that which was shown in Chapter 8 for the general theoretical case. Again, the curves show that per unit costs may rise rapidly in the short run even though the long-run marginal cost curve is horizontal. Only at the appropriate output levels are short-run and long-run average costs equal.

Figure 8A.6

Short-Run and Long-Run Average and Marginal Cost Curves for Hamburger Heaven

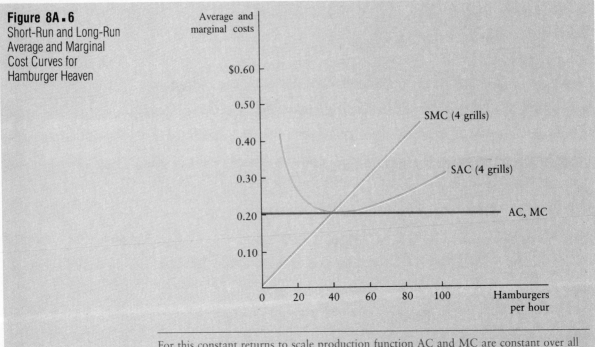

For this constant returns to scale production function AC and MC are constant over all ranges of output. Since w = v = $1, this constant average cost is $.20 per unit. The short-run average cost curve does, however, have a general U shape since the number of grills is held constant. The SAC curve is tangent to the AC curve at an output of 40 hamburgers per hour.

Summary

This analysis of our trivial hamburger example shows how, once input costs are known, all of Hamburger Heaven's cost curves can be derived directly from its production function. Because of the cost minimization assumption it is always possible to obtain information about a firm's cost curves from its production function and vice versa. Of course, the mathematics associated with such a process may not always be so simple as in the example presented here, but the approach used would be identical. In empirical studies of production this relationship between the two concepts is frequently used to derive important conclusions about the nature of production in various industries.

CHAPTER 9

Profit Maximization and Supply

Chapter 8 looks at how firms minimize costs for any level of output they may choose. This chapter now focuses on determining what level of output they will choose to produce. Before we investigate that decision, we discuss briefly the nature of firms themselves and how their output choices might be analyzed.

Nature of Firms

As we pointed out in Chapter 7, a firm is a collection of people who turn inputs into outputs. Different individuals supply different types of inputs, such as workers' skills and types of capital equipment, to the output process, and they expect to receive some type of reward for doing so.

The contractual relationships among these providers of inputs in a firm may be quite complicated. Each provider agrees to devote his or her input to production activities under a set of understandings about how the input is to be used and what benefit the provider will receive. In some cases these contracts are explicit. Workers often negotiate contracts that specify in considerable detail what hours are to be worked, what rules of work are to be followed, and what rate of pay is to be received. Similarly, capital owners invest in a firm under a set of explicit legal principles about how the capital will be used and the compensation the owners will receive. Even with these formal arrangements, there are many implicit relationships between the providers of inputs to a firm, such as the relationship between managers and workers in following certain procedures in making production decisions about who has the authority to do what. Workers have numerous implicit understandings about how work tasks are to be shared. Capital owners may delegate much authority to managers and workers to make decisions on their behalf (General Motors shareholders are, for example, never involved in how assembly-line equipment will be used, though they technically own it). All of these explicit and implicit relationships among providers change through time in response to experiences and to events external to the firm. Much as a basketball team will try out new plays and defensive strategies, so too firms will alter the nature of their internal organizations in order to achieve better long-run results.[1]

Firms' Goals

These complicated relationships among the providers of inputs in a firm pose some problems for economists who wish to develop theoretical generalizations about how firms behave. In our study of demand theory, it made some sense to talk about choices by a rational consumer because we were examining decisions by only a single person. But for firms, many people may be involved in decisions and any detailed study of such decisions may quickly become deeply mired in the subjects of psychology, sociology, and group dynamics.

Although some economists have adopted an "organizational behavior" approach to studying firms' decisions, that approach can be too cumbersome for general purposes. Rather, most economists treat the firm as a single decision-making unit to sweep away all the complicated behavioral issues about relationships among employees and capital owners. This approach often assumes that firms' decisions are made by a single dictatorial manager who rationally pursues some goal. At times we discuss the complexities of actual decision-making procedures within firms to show how they influence the managers' abilities to achieve the desired goals, but for the most part, we assume that the manager can exercise a relatively free hand. The questions that are of central concern here is what goals might be pursued by the manager, and how those goals will influence observed firm behavior. In Chapter 10 we will look at some additional issues about the relationships among the various people who comprise a firm.

Profit Maximization

The major part of this chapter studies firms that pursue the goal of achieving the largest economic profits possible. That is, the firm seeks to make the difference between its total revenues and its total economic costs as large as possible. We are using economic concepts of costs and profits in this assumption about firm behavior. Accounting profits are relevant to questions about how the firm is taxed ("Applying Economics: What Does the U.S. Corporate Profits Tax Actually Tax?" shows this relationship) but, as we will show, maximizing economic profits is the fundamental goal motivating actual behavior.

The assumption that firms seek maximum economic profits has a long history in economic literature. Analyses based on this assumption can yield

---

[1]For an elaboration of these points see K. J. Arrow, *The Limits of Organization* (New York: Norton, 1974). The subject of implicit contracts is taken up in more detail in Chapter 10.

What Does the U.S. Corporate Profits Tax Actually Tax?

A corporate income (or profits) tax was first introduced into the United States in 1909—about four years before the personal income tax was put into effect. In 1985 corporate income tax revenues amounted to more than $60 billion, or approximately 9 percent of total federal tax collections. To many people this tax seems a natural complement to the personal income tax. Since under U.S. law corporations share many of the same rights as do individuals, it might seem only reasonable that corporations should be taxed in a similar way. Some economists, however, feel that the corporate profits tax seriously distorts the allocation of resources, primarily because of its failure to use an economic concept of profits under the tax law.

A large portion of what are defined as corporate profits under the tax laws are in fact a normal return to shareholders for the equity funds they have invested in corporations. These shareholders might expect such a return from any other investment they might have made, such as depositing their funds in a bank. This portion of corporate profits should be considered an economic cost of business since it reflects what owners have forgone by making an equity investment. If this cost were added to other corporate costs, their correctly defined economic profits would be reduced substantially.

The corporate profits tax is not so much as a tax on profits as it is a tax on the equity investments of corporate shareowners. Such taxation may have two consequences. First, corporations will find it more attractive to finance new capital investments through loans and bond offerings (whose interest payments are an allowable cost) than through new stock issues (whose implicit costs are not an allowable cost under the tax law). Second, investors will be less willing to invest in corporate businesses than in noncorporate ones, which are not subject to the corporate profits tax, and which therefore may pay a higher return to the investor. A number of economists have found that both these distortionary effects are rather large and have suggested ways in which the corporate profits tax might be changed so as to reduce them.[2]

To Think About

1. Would the defects of the corporate profits tax be cured by taxing only economic profits? How could this be achieved in practice? Is it possible to redefine accounting concepts of costs to reflect economic concepts?
2. A popular slogan of some tax reformers is "Corporations don't pay taxes, people do." Do you agree? If so, why do we have a separate corporate tax? Which "people" end up paying the tax?

interesting theoretical results and also can explain the decisions of actual firms about how much output to supply and which inputs to hire. Most of this chapter is concerned with these results. We also briefly survey some of the controversy over the profit-maximization assumption and describe a few alternative assumptions that have been proposed.

Profit Maximization and Marginalism

If firms are strict profit maximizers, they will make decisions in a marginal way. The manager-owner will adjust the variables under his or her control until it is impossible to increase profits further. The manager looks, for ex-

---

[2]See C. E. McClure, *Must Corporate Income Be Taxed Twice?* (Washington, D.C.: Brookings Institution, 1979).

ample, at the incremental (or marginal) profit from producing one more unit of output, or the additional profit from hiring one more laborer. So long as this incremental profit is positive, the firm will produce the extra output or hire the extra laborer. When the incremental profit of an activity becomes zero, the manager has pushed the activity far enough and it would not be profitable to go farther.

The Output Decision

We can show this relationship between profit maximization and marginalism by looking at the output level that a firm will choose to produce in attempting to obtain maximum economic profits. First we must describe these profits. A firm sells some level of output, Q, and from these sales the firm receives its revenues, R(Q). The amount of revenues received obviously depends on how much output is sold and on what price it is sold for. That is, R(Q) is P · Q where P is the market price of the good. For the moment, however, it is easiest to regard revenues as simply a general function of Q. Similarly, in producing Q certain economic costs are incurred, TC(Q), and these also will depend on how much is produced. Profits (π) are therefore defined as:

$$\pi = R(Q) - TC(Q). \tag{9.1}$$

In deciding how much output, Q, to produce, the firm will choose the amount for which economic profits are as large as possible. This process is illustrated in Figure 9.1. There the curve TC(Q) is drawn with the same general shape as the total cost curves we introduced in Chapter 8. The curve R(Q), which represents total revenue, is drawn so that greater revenues are provided from selling more output.[3] We can calculate profits by looking at the vertical distance between the R(Q) and TC(Q) curves, and profits are shown explicitly in the bottom panel of the figure. It is clear that profits reach a maximum at Q*. For outputs either larger or smaller than Q*, profits are lower than they are at Q*. We wish to examine those conditions that must hold at Q* for maximum profits.

The Marginal Revenue/Marginal Cost Rule

For output levels below Q* an increase in output brings in more in additional revenue than producing these additional output costs. A firm interested in

---

[3]We examine the exact shape of the R(Q) curve when we reintroduce demand curves. For the moment, the curve R(Q) is drawn so that increasing output leads to increasing revenues. In the case where the firm's decisions do not affect price, the R(Q) curve would be a straight line with slope given by this price.

Figure 9.1
Marginal Revenue Must
Equal Marginal Cost for
Profit Maximization

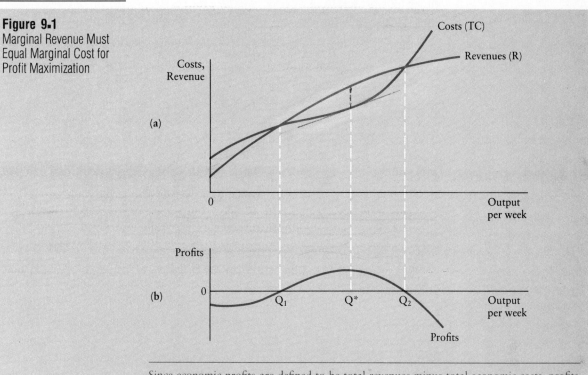

Since economic profits are defined to be total revenues minus total economic costs, profits reach a maximum when the slope of the revenue function (marginal revenue) is equal to the slope of the cost function (marginal cost). In the figure this occurs at Q*. Profits are zero at both Q_1 and Q_2.

maximizing profits would never stop short of Q*. If a firm decided to increase output level beyond Q* it would reduce its profits. The additional revenues from increasing Q would fall short of the additional costs incurred in expanding output. We have shown that at Q* the additional costs of producing an infinitesimal amount more are exactly equal to the additional revenues that this extra output will bring in. Economists would say that at Q*, *marginal cost* (we have already met this concept in Chapter 8) is equal to **marginal revenue** (the extra revenue provided by the sale of one more unit), which indicates profit maximization.[4] In order to maximize profits, a firm should produce that output level for which the marginal revenue from selling one

Marginal revenue
The extra revenue a firm receives when it sells one more unit of output.

_____

[4]Another way of seeing this result uses geometry. The distance between any two curves is greatest when the slopes of the curves are equal—if the slopes aren't equal, you can get closer or farther apart by moving one way or the other. For the R(Q) and C(Q) curves, this geometric fact again proves that profits are maximized when marginal revenue equals marginal cost.

more unit of output is exactly equal to the marginal cost of producing that unit of output. More succinctly,

$$\text{Marginal revenue} = \text{Marginal cost} \qquad [9.2]$$

or

$$MR = MC. \qquad [9.3]$$

This principle is so important for the theory of the firm (and for the analysis of supply) that it deserves further elaboration. A firm might determine its maximum profits conceptually starting at an output level of zero and increasing output one unit at a time. So long as marginal revenue exceeds marginal cost, the firm should continue to increase output because each additional unit it produces will add something to its profits. The firm can, however, push things too far. Eventually marginal costs will start to rise. As soon as they equal marginal revenue, the firm has gone far enough. Further increases in output would reduce profits since the cost of producing more output would exceed the revenue it brings in. In each period the firm can conduct a similar conceptual experiment and thus decide on a profit-maximizing output level.

Marginalism in Input Choices

Although we have so far developed a firm's marginal decision rules as they relate to output choices, we can make a similar argument for input choices as well. Hiring additional labor, for example, entails some increase in costs, and a profit-maximizing firm should balance the additional costs against the extra revenue brought in by selling the output produced by the extra labor. A similar analysis holds for the firm's decision on the number of machines to rent. Additional machines should be hired only so long as their marginal contributions to profits are positive. As the marginal productivity of machines begins to decline, the ability of machines to yield additional revenue also declines. The firm will eventually reach a point at which the marginal contribution of an additional machine to profits is exactly zero; the firm should not expand the rental of machines beyond this point. In Chapter 14 we will see how this application of marginalism leads to a theory of input demand. For the moment, our attention is centered on a firm's output choice and on the profit-maximizing condition: Marginal revenue equals marginal cost. Since we have already discussed the concept of marginal cost in detail, we now analyze the notion of marginal revenue.

Marginal Revenue

It is the revenue from selling one more unit of output that is relevant to the profit-maximizing firm. If a firm can sell all it wishes without affecting market price (that is, if the firm is a **price taker**), the market price will indeed be the

Price taker
A firm or individual whose decisions regarding buying or selling have no effect on the prevailing market price of a good or service.

extra revenue obtained from selling one more unit. Phrased in another way, if a firm's output decisions will not affect market price, marginal revenue is equal to price. We can easily demonstrate this result. Suppose a firm were selling 50 widgets at $1 each. Then total revenues would be $50. If selling one more widget does not affect price, that additional widget will also bring in $1, and total revenue will rise to $51. Marginal revenue from the 51st widget will be $1 (= $51 − $50). For a firm that does not affect market price we therefore have:

$$MR = P. \quad \text{if a price taker} \quad [9.4]$$

Marginal Revenue for a Downward-Sloping Demand Curve

A firm may not always be able to sell all it wants at the prevailing market price. If it faces a downward-sloping demand curve for its product, it can sell more only by reducing its selling price. In this case marginal revenue will be less than market price. To see why, assume that the sale of the 51st widget causes market price to fall to $.99. Total revenues are now $50.49 (= $.99 × 51) and the marginal revenue from the 51st widget is only $.49 (= $50.49 − $50). Even though the 51st widget sells for $.99, the extra revenue obtained from selling the widget is a net gain of only $.49 (a $.99 gain on the 51st widget less a $.50 reduction in revenue from the first 50). When selling one more unit causes market price to decline, marginal revenue is less than market price:

$$MR < P. \quad [9.5]$$

Firms that must reduce their prices to sell more of their products (that is, firms facing a downward-sloping demand curve for their products) must take this fact into account in deciding how to obtain maximum profits.

A Numerical Example

The result that marginal revenue is less than price for a downward-sloping demand curve is illustrated with a numerical example in Table 9.1. There we have recorded the quantity of tape cassettes demanded per week (Q), their price (P), total revenues from cassette sales (P · Q), and marginal revenue (MR) for a simple linear demand curve of the form

$$Q = 10 - P. \quad [9.6]$$

Total revenue from tape sales reaches a maximum at Q = 5, P = 5. For Q > 5, total revenues decline. Increasing tape sales beyond 5 per week actually causes marginal revenue to be negative.

Table 9.1
Total and Marginal
Revenue for Cassette Tapes
$(Q = 10 - P)$

Price (P)	Quantity (Q)	Total Revenue (P · Q)	Marginal Revenue (MR)
$10	0	$ 0	
9	1	9	$ 9
8	2	16	7
7	3	21	5
6	4	24	3
5	5	25	1
4	6	24	−1
3	7	21	−3
2	8	16	−5
1	9	9	−7
0	10	0	−9

In Figure 9.2 we have drawn this hypothetical demand curve. We can use the figure to illustrate the marginal revenue concept. Consider, for example, the extra revenue obtained if the firm sells four tapes instead of three. When output is three, the market price per tape is $7 and total revenues (P · Q) are $21. These revenues are shown by the area of the rectangle OP*AQ*. If the firm instead produces four tapes per week, price must be reduced to $6 to sell this increased output level. Now total revenue is $24, illustrated by the area of the rectangle OP**BQ**. A comparison of the two revenue rectangles shows why the marginal revenue obtained by producing the fourth tape is less than its price. The sale of this tape does indeed increase revenue by the price at which it sells ($6). Revenue increases by the area of the light gray rectangle in Figure 9.2. But to sell the fourth tape, the firm must reduce its selling price from $7 to $6 on the first three tapes sold per week. That price reduction causes a fall in revenue of $3, shown as the area of the dark gray rectangle in Figure 9.2.

The net result is an increase in revenue of $3 ($6 − $3) rather than the gain of $6 that would be assumed if only the sale of the fourth tape is considered in isolation. The marginal revenue for other points in this hypothetical demand curve could also be illustrated. In particular, if you draw the case of a firm producing eight tapes instead of seven, you will see that marginal revenue at that level of output is negative.

Marginal Revenue and Price Elasticity

In Chapter 5 we introduce the concept of the price elasticity of demand $(e_{Q,P})$, which we defined as

$$e_{Q,P} = \frac{\text{Percent change in Q}}{\text{Percent change in P}}. \qquad [9.7]$$

Figure 9.2
Illustration of Marginal
Revenue for the Demand
Curve for Cassette Tapes
(Q = 10 − P)

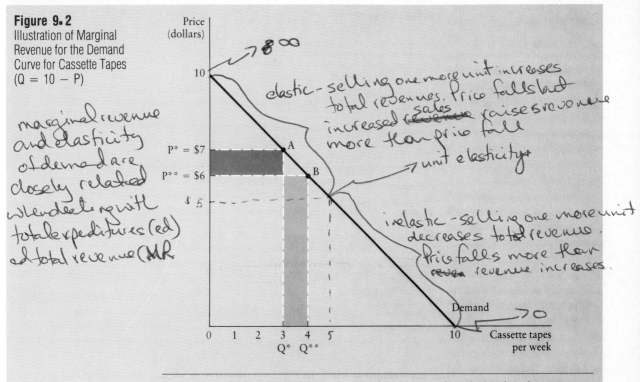

marginal revenue and elasticity of demand are closely related when dealing with total expenditures (ed) ed total revenue (MR

→ 8 ∞

elastic - selling one more unit increases total revenues. Price falls but increased sales raise revenue more than price fall

→ unit elasticity

inelastic - selling one more unit decreases total revenue. Price falls more than revenue increases.

For this hypothetical demand curve, marginal revenue can be calculated as the extra revenue from selling one more tape. If the firm sells four tapes instead of three, for example, revenue will be $24 rather than $21. Marginal revenue from the sale of the fourth tape is therefore $3. This represents the gain of $6 from the sale of the fourth tape *less* the decline in revenue of $3 as a result of the fall in price for the first three tapes from $7 to $6.

We also showed that the price elasticity of demand provides some information about how total expenditures (P · Q) change when price changes. A fall in price will increase total expenditures if demand is elastic ($e_{Q,P} < -1$), but such a fall will decrease total expenditures if demand is inelastic ($e_{Q,P} > -1$).

Marginal revenue is concerned with changes in quantity, not price. However, since for a negatively sloped demand curve increases in Q imply decreases in P, it is clear that the concepts of marginal revenue and price elasticity are closely related. In particular, attempting to sell one more unit may require a firm to reduce its price slightly. What will happen to total revenues (that is, to total expenditures P · Q) depends on the elasticity of demand. From our previous discussion it is easy to see that if demand is elastic, selling one more unit will increase revenues: the marginal revenue of the last unit sold will be positive. Since demand is price responsive, selling one more unit will necessitate only a "small" fall in price; consequently total revenues will increase. On the other hand, if demand is inelastic the firm will have to reduce the price

Table 9.2
Relationship Between
Marginal Revenue
and Elasticity

Demand Curve	Marginal Revenue
Elastic ($e_{Q,P} < -1$)	$MR > 0$
Unit elastic ($e_{Q,P} = -1$)	$MR = 0$
Inelastic ($e_{Q,P} > -1$)	$MR < 0$

substantially to be able to sell one more unit of output. This price decline will be so large that total revenues will be reduced by the sale: marginal revenue now is negative.[5] As an intermediate case, demand might be of unitary elasticity ($e_{Q,P} = -1$), in which case total revenues are constant. Selling one more unit will bring about a price decline of the exact magnitude necessary to keep $P \cdot Q$ constant. In that case the marginal revenue from the sale of one more unit is zero.

These relationships between marginal revenue and elasticity are summarized in Table 9.2. More generally, it can be shown that

$$MR = P\left(1 + \frac{1}{e_{Q,P}}\right) \qquad [9.8]$$

and all of the relationships in Table 9.2 can be derived from this basic equation.[6] For example, if demand is elastic ($e_{Q,P} < -1$), Equation 9.8 shows that MR is positive. Indeed, if demand is infinitely elastic ($e_{Q,P} = -\infty$) MR will equal price since, as we showed before, the firm is a price taker and cannot affect the price it receives.

As another use of Equation 9.8, suppose that a firm knew that the elasticity of demand for its product was -2. It might derive this figure from historical data that show that a 10 percent decline in price has usually led to an increase in sales of about 20 percent. Now assume that the price of the firm's output is $10 per unit and the firm wishes to know how much additional revenue the sale of one more unit of output would yield. The additional unit of output will not yield $10 since the firm faces a downward-sloping demand curve: To sell the unit requires a reduction in its overall selling price. The firm can, however, use Equation 9.8 to calculate that the additional revenue yielded by the sale will be $5 [$= \$10 \cdot (1 + 1/-2) = \$10 \cdot 1/2$]. The firm will produce

---

[5]So long as marginal costs are positive a profit-maximizing firm will not produce at a point on the demand curve for which demand is inelastic. In such a case, marginal revenue (negative) could not be equated to marginal cost (positive). In Chapters 12 and 13 we use this observation to show how the elasticity of demand may reflect something about market structure.

[6]The proof requires calculus. See Walter Nicholson, *Microeconomic Theory: Basic Principles and Extensions*, 3d ed. (Hinsdale, Ill.: Dryden Press, 1985), p. 174.

Figure 9.3
Marginal Revenue Curve
Associated with a
Demand Curve

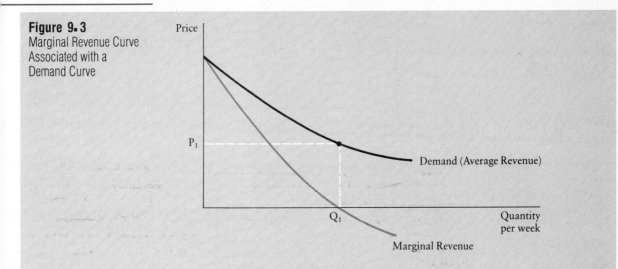

Since the demand curve is negatively sloped, the marginal curve will fall below the demand ("average revenue") curve. For output levels beyond Q_1, marginal revenue is negative. At Q_1 total revenue ($P_1 \cdot Q_1$) is a maximum; beyond this point additional increases in Q actually cause total revenues to fall because of the related declines in price.

this extra unit if marginal costs are less than \$5; that is, if MC < \$5, profits will be increased by the sale of one more unit of output. Although firms in the real world may use more complex means to decide on the profitability of increasing sales (or of lowering prices), our discussion here illustrates the logic these firms must use. They must recognize how changes in quantity sold affect price (or vice versa) and how these price changes affect total revenues.

Marginal Revenue Curve

Any demand curve has a marginal revenue curve associated with it. It is sometimes convenient to think of a demand curve as an *average revenue curve* in that it shows the revenue per unit (in other words, the price) yielded by alternative output choices. The marginal revenue curve, on the other hand, shows the extra revenue provided by the last unit sold. In the usual case of a downward-sloping curve, the marginal revenue curve will lie below the demand curve since at any level of output, marginal revenue is less than price.[7] In Figure 9.3 we have drawn such a curve together with the demand curve from which it was derived. For output levels greater than Q_1 marginal revenue

---

[7]If demand is infinitely elastic (that is, if the demand curve is a horizontal line at some price), the average and marginal revenue curves coincide. Selling one more unit has no effect on price; therefore marginal and average revenue are equal.

Profit Maximization and Airline Deregulation

Under the Airline Deregulation Act of 1978, a variety of legal restrictions on the operations of U. S. airlines were to be gradually phased out. Regulation of airline fares was reduced or eliminated entirely and rules governing the assignment of airline routes were relaxed significantly. These dramatic changes in the legal environment under which airlines operated provided economists with an ideal opportunity to observe how firms respond to altered circumstances. In general, these responses were quite consistent with the profit maximization hypothesis.

A clear example of the airlines' attention to marginal revenue was their development of new fare structures following deregulation. Prices for standard coach fares dropped relatively little since these fares are usually utilized by people traveling on business who have relatively inelastic demands. Little, if any, extra revenue would have been brought in by trying to lure additional coach fare passengers into flying. For special discount fares, it was an entirely different story, however. These fares were generally targeted at people with highly elastic travel demands (tourists, families traveling together, and so forth). In this case, large price reductions increased passenger demand significantly, thereby improving the passenger levels on many flights. Overall the increased use of discount fares resulted in a 17 percent decline in the average price per passenger-mile flown.[9] The structure of the price declines insured that they generated far more additional revenue for the airlines than would have an across-the-board fare cut of a similar magnitude. Whether airlines can continue such price discrimination in the

new, more competitive environment is open to question, however.

The airlines' attention to marginal cost in response to deregulation also reflected what might have been expected on the basis of the profit maximization hypothesis. Their fleets of aircraft could not be changed significantly in the short run, so airlines altered their route structures to coincide with those aircraft they already had. Service in many small communities (previously required under Civil Aeronautics Board regulation) was curtailed. Flight lengths were generally brought into greater correspondence with the optimal operating characteristics of the aircraft. Finally, slackening in the growth of air traffic in 1979–1980 left many airlines with excess capacity in their "wide-bodied" aircraft (747s, DC-10s, and L1011s). Since marginal costs of carrying additional passengers on such flights were quite low, fare discounting was aimed particularly toward these flights.

To Think About
1. Some critics of airline deregulation have charged that it has led to an airline industry of uncertain financial health and has caused airlines to skimp on safety-related maintenance to keep costs down. How would a determined advocate of deregulation respond to these charges?
2. How do you think airline employees (pilots, cabin attendants, luggage handlers, and so forth) feel about deregulation? Might employees of United Airlines or American Airlines feel differently than People's Express employees?

is negative. As Q increases from 0 to Q_1, total revenues (P · Q) increase. However, at Q_1 total revenues (P · Q) are as large as possible; beyond this output level, price falls proportionately faster than output rises.[8]

In Chapter 5 we talked in detail about the possibility of a demand curve's

---

[8]Another way of saying this is that beyond Q_1 demand is inelastic. See our discussion of elasticity along a linear demand curve in Chapter 5.

[9]This figure and much of the analysis in this example are based on J. R. Meyer *et al.*, *Airline Deregulation—The Early Experience* (Boston: Auburn House, 1981).

shifting because of changes in factors other than price that go into determining individuals' choices. Whenever a demand curve shifts, its associated marginal revenue curve also shifts. This should be obvious since a marginal revenue curve cannot be calculated without referring to a specific demand curve. In later analysis we will have to keep in mind the kinds of shifts that marginal revenue curves might make when we talk about changes in demand.

Some economists doubt that firms are able to make calculations about marginal revenue with any degree of accuracy. For this and other reasons, there is considerable controversy over the precise meaning of the profit maximization hypothesis. Before examining that controversy, "Applying Economics: Profit Maximization and Airline Deregulation" shows the importance of profit maximization to at least one industry's behavior.

Controversy over the Profit Maximization Hypothesis

The so-called "marginalist controversy," although usually dormant in the economics profession, occasionally has a revival that spurs a wide variety of theoretical and empirical research.[10] There are three broad types of attacks on the marginalist, profit-maximizing approach to firm behavior: (1) the profit maximization approach is too simple; (2) there exist alternative, equally simple hypotheses that can better explain what firms do; and (3) real-world firms do not have suitable information to be able to maximize profits, nor would they particularly want to maximize profits if they had such information. Because we are investigating only simple theories of firm behavior here, we will not pursue the first criticism. The second criticism is dealt with later in this chapter, where some other simple motives that have been proposed as substitutes for profit maximization are mentioned. This section summarizes the arguments of the third type.

Evidence on Profit Maximization

The empirical evidence on whether firms maximize profits is ambiguous. As we mentioned in Chapter 1, when firms answer questionnaires, they seldom rank profits as their only goal. Similarly they often deny having enough information to make precise marginal choices. On the other hand, economists have found the profit maximization hypothesis to be extremely accurate in predicting certain aspects of firms' behavior. For example, many firms seem eager to enter into the most profitable industries, and some of the larger, stagnant firms seek to diversify to increase profitability. Many firms have also adopted a "profit center" form of organization in which managers are judged by the profits their divisions earn.

---

[10]Perhaps the most interesting of these debates over the goals of the firm was conducted by R. A. Lester and Fritz Machlup in the *American Economic Review* during the years 1946 and 1947.

Some of the attempts to reconcile this ambiguous evidence about profit maximization center on the question of the role of assumptions in economics. Milton Friedman and others argue that one cannot judge the assumption of profit maximization either by *a priori* logic or by asking firms what they do. They feel the ultimate test is the predictive ability of the hypothesis. As discussed in Chapter 1 Friedman made the analogy of the expert pool player who has no knowledge of the rules of physics that determine the movements of the balls on the table. Friedman argued that this ignorance on the part of the player does not prevent an observer from accurately predicting the player's behavior by applying physical principles.[11] Just as Molière's Monsieur Jourdain spoke prose all his life without knowing it, firms may in fact maximize profits despite their protests that they have no such intentions.

Survivorship Principle and the Market for Firms

A second set of reasons why economists tend to favor profit maximization as an explanation of firm behavior concerns competitive pressures. Profits represent a return to the owners of a firm. If the firm does not make the largest profits possible, owners may take their assets elsewhere. Indeed, in Chapter 11 we will see that competition itself can force all firms in an industry to operate with, at most, zero economic profits. If a firm opts not to follow the marginal rules, it will lose money. In that event, the owner will be even more likely to close down. Those firms that survive in such an environment will be those that do maximize profits. The **survivorship principle** states that we are likely to find only profit-maximizing firms in competitive markets.

Survivorship principle
The idea that in competitive markets, only profit-maximizing firms are likely to survive.

Related to this principle is the fact that firms themselves can be bought and sold. Any firm that is not making maximum profits with its existing assets is a tempting target for an investor who believes he or she can do better. Just as for any economic goods, firms will gravitate toward those buyers who can do the most with them. This "market for corporate control" provides another force that encourages profit-maximizing behavior. The study of this market is one of the major new areas of research in the economics of business behavior, and we examine it in a bit more detail in the next chapter.

Alternatives to Profit Maximization

The debate over whether firms have enough information actually to maximize profits has caused economists to examine a number of other possible goals that may not be so hard for firms to achieve. Two of these are *revenue maximization* and *markup pricing*.

---

[11]See Milton Friedman, "The Methodology of Positive Economics," in *Essays in Positive Economics* (Chicago: University of Chicago Press, 1953).

Figure 9.4
A Comparison of Profit
Maximization and Revenue
Maximization

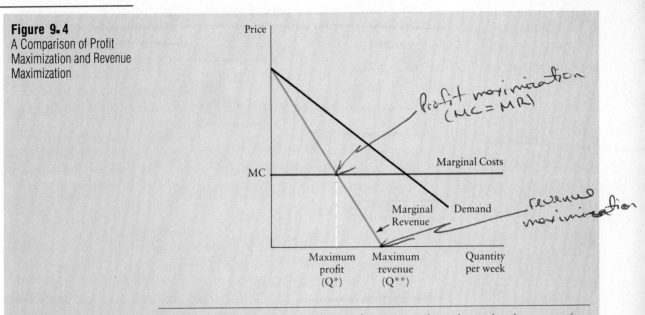

For simplicity we assume that each unit of output can always be produced at a cost of
MC. A profit-maximizing firm will therefore produce output level Q*, for which MR =
MC. If the firm pursues the goal of revenue maximization, however, it would proceed to
output level Q**, since at this level of output marginal revenue is zero.

Revenue Maximization

Revenue maximization
A goal for firms in
which they work to
maximize their total
revenue rather than
profits.

One alternative goal to profit maximization for firms, that of **revenue maximization,** was first proposed by William J. Baumol.[12] In his consulting work,
Baumol noticed that most managerial incentives are tied to increases in sales
revenues rather than to profits. For example, higher salaries are paid to the
managers of the largest corporations (with the highest dollar volume of sales)
than to the managers of the most profitable ones. Other pieces of evidence
also suggested to Baumol that revenue maximization might be the most important goal for firms. Often a firm's success is judged by the share of the
market it commands. Firms that dominate the market may have a number of
advantages over other firms, such as better credit with banks or greater consumer recognition of products.[13]

Figure 9.4 shows that a strictly revenue-maximizing firm would produce

---

[12]A clear statement of this hypothesis is found in Chapter 6 of William J. Baumol, *Business
Behavior, Value and Growth,* rev. ed. (New York: Harcourt, Brace & World, 1967).

[13]It has also been suggested that maintaining market share is a reasonable long-run profit-maximizing strategy in an uncertain market environment.

that quantity of output for which marginal revenue equals zero—the quantity Q^{**}. Output will be expanded so long as any additional revenue is obtainable. Baumol suggests that a firm may not go this far in pursuing sales volume to the exclusion of any consideration of cost, however. Instead, the firm's owners may require that some minimum amount of profits be earned. Baumol's firm would probably produce some quantity between that which a profit maximizer would (Q^* in Figure 9.4) and that which a revenue maximizer would (Q^{**} in Figure 9.4).

An appropriate real-life example of how authors may be interested in maximizing revenues is found in "Applying Economics: Textbook Royalties."

Markup Pricing

Markup pricing
Determining the selling price of a good by adding a percentage to the cost of producing it.

Many firms use neither the terminology nor the analytical techniques that we have introduced in this chapter. Even if firms do profess to seek profits, their methods to do so may be considerably different than our analysis describes. The most common management technique to seek profits is **markup pricing**. This section compares this technique to the profit-maximization model we have developed.

The markup pricing technique works as follows. Management first computes the average total cost of producing some "normal" level of output. To this cost it then adds a profit markup to arrive at the good's selling price. Usually the profit markup is a fixed percentage of average costs, which means that the selling price is some multiple of average cost. With a markup of 50 percent, for example, firms would price their goods at 1.5 times average total cost. Unlike a revenue-maximizing firm, the firm that uses a markup pricing strategy is obviously paying some attention to costs. Is this firm actually maximizing profits?

A first distinction between profit maximization and markup pricing is that the former requires firms to use marginal cost in their calculations whereas the latter requires them to use average total cost. As we show in Chapter 8, if a firm is producing at the low point of its average total cost curve, average and marginal costs are equal. Markup pricing and profit maximization, at least with regard to the cost side of the calculation, may not be very different in this case, especially if firms have long-run average total cost curves that are horizontal over a broad range of output levels, as shown in Figure 8.6.

A second principal difference between profit-maximizing behavior and markup pricing is that markup pricing seems to take no account of demand. A profit maximizer must, as we have shown, consider the marginal revenue from selling one more unit of output. A firm using a markup over average cost would appear to make no such consideration. Only if firms' markup were in some way influenced by demand would this not be the case.

Several observations suggest that firms do indeed consider demand in deciding on a markup. For example, convenience stores have much higher markups on specialty or emergency items, such as deli foods or cold remedies, than they do on everyday items such as milk or soft drinks that can be bought

APPLYING ECONOMICS

Textbook Royalties

Most authors (including the author of this textbook) receive royalties based on total book sales. Royalty rates usually range between 10 and 20 percent of the sales price of a book, although some particularly popular authors may be able to negotiate a higher rate. Because royalties are a fixed fraction of total sales, authors would like their publishers to price their books in such a way as to maximize total sales revenue. That is, the authors would prefer the price to be set so that the quantity demanded will be that quantity for which marginal revenue is zero.

Publishers, on the other hand, may not agree with their authors. They may wish to price their books so that the quantity demanded is the quantity for which marginal revenue is equal to marginal cost. As Figure 9.4 illustrates, this will usually result in a higher price for the book and a lower quantity sold than authors would prefer. Unfortunately from the authors' point of view, publishers set prices and make output decisions, so profit maximization rather than sales maximization is usually stressed. Even though authors may make more per book, they lose out because they do not sell so many at a high price. You may also have to pay a higher price for my book as a result.

The conflict between authors and publishers can be seen in their wishes about inputs as well. Authors prefer publishers to invest additional resources to sell books so long as those resources yield any new sales, regardless of what these resources cost the publishers. Authors prefer elaborate sales efforts, large customer service departments, and special book features (such as elaborate graphic devices). Publishers, on the other hand, want to use these devices only if the additional revenues they generate will exceed the cost of the devices. The publishers may employ rather small sales forces; they may skimp to some extent on customer services by filling orders slowly (because of a small staff) or by holding rather small inventories; and they may adopt rather drab book formats if they are less expensive to produce. Profit maximization means that the publishers will want only those features that are worth to them in extra revenues what the features cost.

To Think About

1. If the conflict between authors and publishers is so great and publishers always win, why don't authors negotiate for a share of profits? In what sense are sales-related royalties desirable for authors?

2. Can you think of other situations in which different participants in the production process may have different motives? Might owners and managers of firms have similar conflicts? How about patients and doctors? (See Chapter 10 for a discussion.)

anywhere. Hot dogs sold at ball games or amusement parks usually have a higher price than hot dogs sold by street vendors, which probably reflects the greater choices available to consumers of the street vendors' hot dogs. If firms using a markup pricing strategy are profit maximizers, the markup would be higher for goods that are inelastically demanded.[14] "Applying Economics:

not many substitutes

---

[14]A precise analysis of this result would use Equation 9.8 together with the MR = MC rule:

$$MC = MR = P\left(1 + \frac{1}{e}\right)$$

where e is the price elasticity of demand. Hence

$$\frac{P}{MC} = \text{Markup} = \frac{e}{1 + e}.$$

If $e > -1$ demand is inelastic, and MR cannot be equal to MC; we need only examine elastic cases where $e < -1$. If demand is infinitely elastic ($e = -\infty$), then P/MC = 1 and there is no markup. As e gets closer to -1, the markup increases.

APPLYING ECONOMICS

Actual Markup Pricing Behavior

Most available evidence concludes that major corporations take demand into account in their pricing policies. For example, in their study of the pricing policies of U.S. Steel Corporation, Kaplan, Dirlam, and Lanzillotti found that the markup on steel products varied inversely with the elasticity of demand for these products. Margins were high on steel rails, for example, since this was a product line in which U.S. Steel faced little competition. On the other hand, margins were low on stainless steel and tin plate, since these are products for which competition from aluminum and lumber producers was strong. The authors found similar results for many major corporations, including E. I. Du Pont de Nemours, Standard Oil Company of New Jersey, and Aluminum Company of America.[15] In all of them, target profit margins seemed to be related to the elasticity of demand, just as profit maximization requires. In a study of Danish firms, B. Fog also found that target profit margins vary with demand conditions. He reports that many companies respond to questions about how profit margins are set by noting they will "charge what the traffic will bear" or the "market conditions determine the price."[16] In other words, markups are determined in a profit-maximizing way.

In their study of retailing, R. M. Cyert and J. G. March spent considerable effort analyzing the feedback from the market for the pricing of a product. Even though the firm may set prices and profit margins without considering demand, the subsequent reaction of the market (which provides information on the true demand situation) causes the firm to adjust its prices accordingly. Cyert and March apply their model to a department store's markdown policy and conclude that the prices of items are adjusted over time to meet demand conditions.[17] Any experienced bargain hunter knows that retailers adjust the prices of unpopular items downward much more rapidly than they reduce the prices of "hot" items. Price changing such as this is consistent with the notion that markups are set with profit maximization goals in mind.

To Think About

1. Profit markups are much higher in the prescription drug industry than in the fast food industry. Is this consistent with profit-maximizing behavior?

2. If firms are profit maximizers, how should they vary their profit markups over the business cycles as the demand for a product changes? Does the evidence on profits during recessions support this notion?

Actual Markup Pricing Behavior" shows that there is some evidence to support this possibility.

Short-Run Supply by a Price-Taking Firm

Short-run supply decisions by a price-taking firm are our final and most important illustration of the profit-maximizing assumption. Our analysis here leads directly into the study of market supply and price determination that

---

[15]A. D. H. Kaplan, J. B. Dirlam, and R F. Lanzillotti, *Pricing in Big Business: A Case Approach* (Washington, D.C.: Brookings Institution, 1958), pp. 172–174.

[16]B. Fog, *Industrial Pricing Policies* (Amsterdam: North-Holland Publishing Co., 1960), p. 104. See especially Chapter 6.

[17]R. M. Cyert and J. G. March, *A Behavioral Theory of the Firm* (Englewood Cliffs, N.J.: Prentice-Hall, 1963), Chapter 7.

Figure 9.5
Short-Run Supply Curve
for a Price-Taking Firm

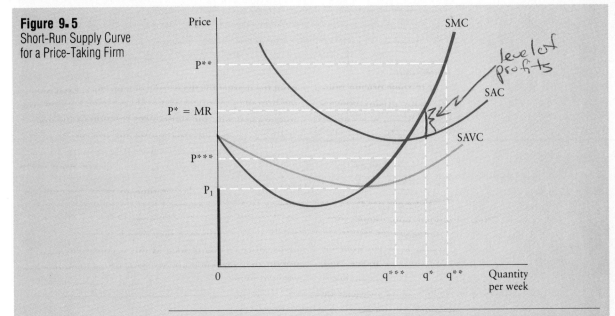

In the short run a price-taking firm will produce the level of output for which SMC = P. At P*, for example, the firm will produce q*. The SMC curve also shows what will be produced at other prices. For prices below SAVC, however, the firm will choose to produce no output. The heavy blue lines in the figure represent the firm's short-run supply curve.

we take up in the next part. Here we focus only on the profit-maximizing decisions of a single firm.

Profit-Maximizing Decision

By definition, a price-taking firm has no effect on the price it receives for its product. In this case, as we show earlier in this chapter, market price is also the marginal revenue from selling one more unit. No matter how much the firm sells, its decisions have no effect on this price. Under these assumptions the firm's desire to maximize profits then dictates that it should produce that quantity for which marginal cost equals price. The short-run marginal cost curve is relevant to this decision in the short run.

Figure 9.5 shows the individual firm's short-run decision. The market price is given by P*. The demand curve facing the firm is therefore a horizontal line through P*. This line is labeled P* = MR to remind us that an extra unit always can be sold by this price-taking firm without affecting the price. Output level q* provides maximum profits, since at q* price is equal to short-run marginal cost.[18] The fact that profits are positive can be seen by noting that at q* price exceeds average costs. The firm earns a profit on each unit sold. If price were below average cost (as is the case for p***) the firm would have a loss on each unit sold. If price and average cost were equal, profits would be zero.

A geometric proof that profits are a maximum at q* would proceed as follows. For output levels slightly less than q*, price (P*) exceeds short-run marginal cost. Reducing output below q* would cut back on revenues more than on costs, and profits would fall. For output levels greater than q*, marginal costs exceed P*. Producing more than q* would now cause costs to rise more rapidly than revenues, and again profits would fall. This means that if a firm produces either more or less than q*, its profits will be lowered. Only at q* are profits at a maximum. Notice that at q* the marginal cost curve has a positive slope. This is required if profits are to be a true maximum. If P = MC on a negatively sloped section of the marginal cost curve, this is not a point of maximum profits, since increasing output would yield more in revenues (price times the amount produced) than this production would cost (marginal cost would decline if the MC curve had a negative slope). Consequently, profit maximization requires both that P = MC and that at this point marginal cost be increasing.

The Firm's Supply Curve

The positively sloped portion of the short-run marginal cost curve is the short-run supply curve for this price-taking firm, since the curve shows how much the firm will produce for every possible market price. At a higher price of P**, for example, the firm will produce q** since it will find it in its interest to incur the higher marginal costs q** entails. With a price of P***, on the other hand, the firm opts to produce less (q***) since only a lower output level will result in lower marginal costs to meet this lower price. By considering all possible prices that the firm might face, we can see by the marginal cost curve how much output the firm should supply at each price.

For very low prices we have to be careful about this conclusion. Should market price fall below P_1, the profit-maximizing decision would be to produce nothing. Prices less than P_1 do not cover variable costs. There will be a loss on each unit produced in addition to the loss of all fixed costs. By shutting down production, the firm still must pay fixed costs, but it avoids the losses incurred on each unit produced. Since, in the short run, the firm cannot close down and avoid all costs, its best decision is to produce no output. On the other hand, a price only slightly above P_1 means the firm should produce some

---

[18]Here we use a lower case q to denote the firm's output. In Chapter 11, the upper case Q is used to denote the output of the industry as a whole. Here, and throughout Parts 4–6, firms' supply will be shown in color in graphs.

output. Even though profits may be negative (which they will be if price falls below short-run average total costs—the case at P^{***}), so long as variable costs are covered, the profit-maximizing decision is to continue production. Fixed costs must be paid in any case, and any price that covers variable costs will provide revenue as an offset to the fixed costs.[19]

For prices above P_1 the firm's short-run marginal cost curve shows how much output will be supplied. The price P_1 represents a **shutdown price**, however. If price falls below that level, nothing will be produced. The bold segment of the vertical axis up to P_1 reflects these zero-output decisions. Chapter 11 makes considerable use of this short-run supply curve for price-taking firms.

"Applying Economics: The Demise of OPEC and Drilling for Oil in the United States" illustrates the kinds of effects that changing prices can have on firms' willingness to incur various levels of marginal cost.

Shutdown price
The price below which the firm will choose to produce no output in the short run. Equal to minimum average variable cost.

Summary

In this chapter we examine the assumption that firms seek to achieve maximum profits in making their decisions. Although some questions have been raised about whether firms have all of the information that would be required to make such decisions, we show that there is much available evidence to support this approach to analyzing firm behavior. We also describe how a variety of market pressures may enforce profit maximization by firms. The profit maximization assumption seems to provide a good foundation for our study of firm behavior. A number of conclusions follow from this assumption.

- In making output decisions a firm should produce the output level for which marginal revenue equals marginal cost. Only at this level of production is the cost of extra output, at the margin, exactly balanced by the revenue it yields.
- Similar marginal rules apply to the hiring of inputs by profit-maximizing firms. These are examined in Part 5.
- For a firm facing a downward-sloping demand curve, marginal revenue will be less than price. In this case the marginal revenue curve will lie below the market demand curve.
- The techniques of analyzing profit-maximizing firms can also be used to study firms that use other strategies, such as revenue maximization or markup pricing. In some cases, pursuit of such other strategies may also be consistent with profit maximization.

---

[19]Some algebra may clarify matters. Since we know total costs equal the sum of fixed and variable costs:

$$TC = FC + VC,$$

profits are given by

$$\pi = TR - TC = P \cdot Q - FC - VC.$$

If $Q = 0$, variable costs are zero, so

$$\pi = -FC,$$

so the firm will only produce if $\pi > -FC$. But that means that

$$P \cdot Q > VC \text{ or } P > VC/Q = AVC.$$

The Demise of OPEC and Drilling for Oil in the United States

Beginning in the early 1970s the Organization of Petroleum Exporting Countries (OPEC) came to exercise a dramatic effect on the world pricing of crude oil. Between 1971 and 1980 world oil prices increased more than 800 percent. In real inflation-adjusted terms the increase was somewhat less spectacular, but still amounted to a threefold increase in the relative price of crude oil. For oil well drillers throughout the world this price increase provided a clear signal to produce more. In the United States, for example, even though the influence of OPEC was softened a bit by domestic price controls and restrictions on imports, drilling increased dramatically. As Table 9.3 shows, the number of wells drilled more than tripled between 1971 and 1980. Increasingly these additional wells were drilled in high-cost locations (for example, in deep water offshore or in difficult environments such as Alaska). The data in Table 9.3 also show that the wells were drilled to a somewhat greater average depth, further illustrating the willingness of firms to incur higher marginal costs to produce crude oil.

Table 9.3
World Oil Prices and Oil Well Drilling Activity in the United States

	World Price per Barrel	Real Price per Barrel[a]	Number of Wells Drilled	Average Depth (ft.)
1973	3.89	3.04	9,705	3,946
1981	31.77	11.78	38,725	4,183
1984	24.59	8.44	16,276	3,918

Source: Statistical Abstract of the United States, 1985.
[a]World price divided by the Producer Price Index (1967 = 100).

The steep recession of 1982 and 1983, combined with vast new supplies of crude oil becoming available (in the North Sea and Mexico, for example), put considerable pressure on the OPEC pricing structure. By 1984 nominal crude oil prices had declined by about 25 percent from their highest levels. In real terms the decline was even sharper. U.S. drillers were quick to respond to these changed circumstances. As Table 9.3 shows, 25 percent fewer wells were drilled in 1984 than in 1981, and those wells that were drilled were not quite as deep as had previously been the case. Clearly domestic drillers responded to lower prices by no longer incurring very high marginal costs.

The decline in drilling activity in 1983 and 1984 posed significant problems for suppliers to the oil drilling industry. For example, producers of high strength oil pipe in Texas and Louisiana suffered huge financial losses as they were not able to sell enough pipe to keep their factories fully utilized. Similarly, firms in the business of supplying oil drilling teams with everything from food and clothing to candy and VCR movies found that there was little work to be had. Many filed for bankruptcy during the period. The decline in crude oil prices in the mid-1980s, which was greeted with enthusiasm by consumers and industrial users of oil, had very negative consequences for some groups.

To Think About
1. Are U.S. producers of crude oil accurately described as price takers? How many companies are there in this industry? Is a firm such as Exxon too large to be a price taker? Perhaps you'll need to look up some data on the oil industry to resolve these issues.
2. This example shows that there are many kinds of margins to consider in connection with marginal cost (for example, location and depth of drilling). What are some of the other factors that may influence the marginal cost of drilling for oil? Can you think of examples in other industries of how increasing marginal costs might occur along several dimensions?

- A firm whose decisions have no effect on the price of its product (a price taker) will maximize profits where price equals marginal cost. The marginal cost curve will be the supply curve for such a firm. If price falls below short-run average variable costs, however, the firm will choose to shut down and produce no output.

Problems

9.1 John's Lawn Mowing Service is a small business that acts as a price taker (MR = P). The prevailing market price of lawn mowing is $20 per acre. John's costs are given by

$$\text{Total cost} = .1q^2 + 10q + 50$$

$$\text{Marginal cost} = .2q + 10$$

where q = the number of acres John chooses to mow in a day.

    a.   How many acres should John choose to mow in order to maximize profit?

    b.   Calculate John's maximum daily profit.

    c.   Graph these results and label John's supply curve.

9.2 Widgets International faces a demand curve given by

$$Q = 10 - P$$

and has a constant marginal and average cost of $3 per widget produced. Complete the following table for the various production levels.

Q	P	TR (= P · Q)	MR	MC	AC	TC	π = TR − TC
1							
2							
3							
4							
5							
6							
7							
8							
9							
10							

How many widgets will the firm produce in order to maximize profits? Explain briefly why this is so.

9.3 Suppose a farmer can sell all the corn that he or she can produce at a price of P. Show the total revenue curve for the farmer and demonstrate geometrically (using a graph similar to Figure 9.1) that in this case the profit-maximizing output level occurs where marginal cost is equal to P.

9.4 Would a lump-sum profit tax affect the profit-maximizing quantity of output? How about a proportional tax on profits? How about a tax assessed on each unit of output?

9.5 Suppose that a firm faces a demand curve which has a constant elasticity of −2. This demand curve is given by:

$$Q = 256/P^2.$$

Suppose also that the firm has a marginal cost curve of the form

$$MC = .001Q.$$

a. Graph these demand and marginal cost curves.
b. Calculate the marginal revenue curve associated with the demand curve; graph this curve. (Hint: Use Equation 9.8 for this part of the problem.)
c. At what output level does marginal revenue equal marginal cost?

9.6 Suppose a firm faces the following demand curve:

$$Q = 60 - 2P.$$

a. Calculate the total revenue curve for the firm (in terms of Q).
b. Using a tabular revenue proof, show that the firm's MR curve is given by $MR = 30 - Q$.
c. Assume also that the firm has a MC curve given by $MC = .2Q$. What output level should the firm produce to maximize profits?
d. Graph the demand, MC, and MR curves and the point of profit maximization.

9.7 A firm faces a demand curve given by:

$$Q = 100 - 2P.$$

Marginal and average costs for the firm are constant at $10 per unit.

a. Use a graphic or tabular proof to show that, for this demand curve, $MR = 50 - Q$.
b. What output level should the the firm produce to maximize profits? What are profits at that output level?
c. What output level should the firm produce to maximize revenues? What are profits at that output level?
d. Suppose the firm wishes to maximize revenues subject to the constraint that it earn $12 in profits for each of the 64 machines it employs. What level of output should it produce?
e. Graph your results.

*9.8 Universal Widget produces high quality widgets at its plant in Gulch, Nevada, for sale throughout the world. The cost function for total widget production (Q) is given by

----

*Denotes a rather difficult problem.

$$\text{Total costs} = .25Q^2.$$
$$\text{Marginal costs} = .50Q.$$

Widgets are demanded only in Australia (where the demand curve is given by $Q = 100 - 2P$ and $MR = 50 - Q$) and Lapland (where the demand curve is given by $Q = 100 - 4P$ and $MR = 25 - 2Q$). If Universal Widget can control the quantities supplied to each market, how many should it sell in each location in order to maximize total profits?

CHAPTER 10

Further Applications of the Theory of the Firm

Our analysis of the firm and its decisions in Chapter 9 is based on a very simple model in which the manager chooses levels of inputs and outputs with the sole goal of obtaining maximum profits. In this chapter we move beyond this simple model by looking more closely at the internal operations of firms. We focus on the kinds of contracts that exist between firms and their workers and between firms and managers in order to provide a somewhat more detailed picture of how firms operate. The topics in this chapter represent some of the most important areas of current research in economics. Many economists believe that in order to understand such diverse topics as persistent unemployment, worker productivity, and corporate takeovers, a necessary first step is to develop a better understanding of the firm itself. A major purpose of this chapter, then, is to introduce some of the recent work related to these topics.

Contracts within Firms

As we discussed briefly in Chapter 9, a firm is an organization that produces economic goods. In that process the activities of workers, managers, and suppliers of capital must be coordinated and controlled. This is accomplished through a series of contracts among these parties. In some cases the contracts may be explicitly written down—for example, the contract between the United Automobile Workers and General Motors runs hundreds of pages. In many other instances, however, contracts may be in the form of implicit understandings about what the terms of employment are. Even though such contracts are not on paper, they may be very effective in assuring that the rights and responsibilities of the various parties are followed.

The modern study of the theory of the firm is primarily a study of these various contracts. The firm itself is the legal entity (in the United States, legally firms are treated as individuals) that usually represents one side of the contract, and workers, managers, and capital suppliers represent the other side. The problem these parties face is to develop contracts that are desirable to everyone concerned. For example, contracts with workers must be desirable from the workers' point of view in terms of the wages paid and the working conditions provided, and desirable from the firm's point of view in terms of providing incentives for the workers to perform in a productive way. Creating such contracts may be a costly and tedious process even when nothing has to be explicitly written down. And the final solutions adopted may, at first glance, seem unusual or even counterproductive. But the contracting process is necessary for any firm.

This chapter discusses three related topics that apply the traditional theory of the firm to contractual relations. First, we examine the firm's contracts with its workers and show why both parties will find it in their interest to establish rather long-term relationships. Then we look at managerial contracts and describe the "agent" problem that arises because managers and capital owners may have different goals in making decisions about firms' operations. Finally, we will look at the market for firms themselves (the market for corporate control) and show how this market may help to insure that the various contractual provisions established by firms will result in cost-minimizing behavior.

Contracts with Workers

Only about 20 percent of American workers are represented by unions with collective bargaining agreements. The fraction of workers covered by such formal arrangements is somewhat higher in other western countries, but even in these other countries most workers are not subject to this sort of explicit contract. Still, virtually all employees have clear understandings with their employers about what their duties are and how they will be paid. In Chapter 14 we examine the theory of how wage levels are determined. Here we are not interested in the wage itself, but rather focus on explicit and implicit employment contracts and show how they may affect the firms' costs and its supply decisions.

Job-Specific Skills and Long-Term Contracts

As workers hold a job longer, they learn to do it better. Anyone who has ever started a new job knows the feeling of being confused and perplexed when trying to fit into a new employment situation. A new worker's productivity may be negative for the first few weeks as he or she asks so many questions and makes so many mistakes that total firm output may actually decline for awhile. Even after the chaos of orientation has ended, new workers may not be very productive until they learn what the job entails and how they can work most effectively with those around them. In economic terms, any new worker must learn a set of **job-specific skills** and that learning process will be time-consuming and costly.

Job-specific skills
Skills learned on a job about how to do that specific job better.

Figure 10.1
With Implicit Contracts, Output and Hiring Decisions May Be Less Flexible

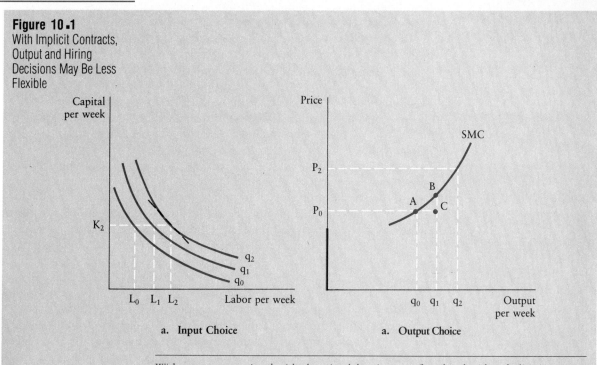

a. **Input Choice**

a. **Output Choice**

With no costs associated with changing labor input, a firm faced with a decline in price from P_2 to P_0 would reduce output from q_2 to q_0 and reduce labor input from L_2 to L_0. If there were an implicit contract between the workers and the firm, hiring might only fall to L_1, and output to q_1. This would still be the most profitable output level since costs associated with reducing labor input to L_0 would exceed profits lost at q_1 (area ABC).

Firms wish to reduce these costs as much as possible. The most direct way to do that is to adopt policies that encourage workers to stay with the firm. In Chapters 7 through 9 we were not concerned with this issue. Nothing in those chapters would have prevented a firm from hiring a different set of workers every hour so long as they all could be hired at the prevailing wage rate. In fact, however, such employee turnover would be very costly for firms both because of the expenses involved in hiring new employees (such as the paperwork) and because of the low productivity of new employees. Instead, firms will try to develop a longer-term relationship with their employees.

Effects on Employment Decisions

One consequence of such a long-term employment policy is that firms will be reluctant to vary the number of workers they hire in response to temporary fluctuations in the demand for their products. They may make short-run decisions that are not exactly the same as those we examined in Chapters 8 and 9. Figure 10.1 illustrates such a situation. Graph a of this figure shows a price-taking firm's isoquant map, and Graph b shows its short-run supply (and marginal cost) curve. Initially, the firm faces a market price of P_2 for its output and opts to produce at a level of q_2 per week as shown in Graph b. Assuming the firm has been producing q_2 for some time, it will have adjusted both its capital and labor inputs to their cost-minimizing levels K_2, L_2. These are shown in Graph a.

Suppose now that the market price of this firm's product falls temporarily to P_0—perhaps because a recession temporarily reduces the demand for most goods. How will the firm respond to this decline? According to our discussion in Chapter 9, the firm would reduce output to q_0 and reduce its hiring of labor to L_0 since capital is fixed at K_2 in the short run. Under our previous assumptions, this temporary cutback in hiring could be accomplished by the firm with no special problems.

If workers have unique job-specific skills, however, reducing employment in this way may be costly for the firm. Once a worker is laid off, he or she may seek another job. Job-specific skills already acquired would be lost to the firm making the layoff. Even if the worker ultimately is hired back by this firm once the price returns to P_2, he or she may still need to readjust to the work process. For these reasons, the firm may hesitate to reduce employment immediately in response to temporary declines in demand. It may, instead, reassign workers to nonproduction activities (for example, cleaning up the stock room or doing preventive maintenance on machines), or it may continue to produce and add the surplus goods to inventory. The firm might also change work schedules, as discussed in "Applying Economics: Short-Time Compensation and Layoffs."

In all of these cases the nature of the explicit or implicit contracts between workers and firms make employment decisions far more complicated than our previous models assumed. A reduction of labor input to L_0 in Figure 10.1 may therefore be very costly, and some more modest steps might be taken. The firm could, for example, reduce hiring to L_1 and produce output level q_1. Such an output level would not provide maximum profits under our previous analysis of supply (see Graph b of Figure 10.1), but it may be more profitable than q_0 once all the costs associated with changing labor input are taken into account—that is, if the costs of reducing labor further exceed the lost profits with output level q_1 rather than q_0 (area ABC). Consequently, the firm's short-run supply (and hiring) decisions may be less responsive to temporary price changes than our simple models in Chapter 9 suggest.

Other Effects of Implicit Contracts

Long-term implicit contracts may affect other aspects of the worker-firm relationship. Both parties may find it attractive to adopt incentive schemes that encourage workers to stay with a firm rather than to switch jobs in response to other opportunities. Seniority-based wage systems are probably the most important example of the way in which workers are rewarded for staying with a firm. The widespread use of such systems, rather than compensation based

Short-Time Compensation and Layoffs

When firms need to reduce the labor they employ, they have two options: they may reduce the number of hours each employee works, or they may lay off some employees completely. During recessions firms use both of these methods to adjust their labor input. Firms in the United States seem more willing to use layoffs than do firms in other countries such as West Germany or Japan where hours reductions are much more common.

This "layoff prone" nature of the United States economy has been a concern to many economists both because of the problems that unemployment poses for laid-off workers and because of the inefficiencies that layoffs may cause. When employees are laid off they may seek other jobs and may, if the layoff lasts for a while, lose some of their job skills. Rehiring workers following layoffs can be a costly process for the firm. Many of these inefficiencies could be avoided if firms reduced hours of work during recessions, which would keep the employment relationship largely intact.

One policy that has been suggested to encourage employees and employers to choose hours reductions instead of layoffs is for workers on short time to receive unemployment benefits for the hours they do not work. Under the rules that prevail in most states unemployment benefits can be collected only if the worker is completely laid off. Some economists believe this policy encourages layoffs rather than hour reductions. A change in unemployment insurance laws would reverse this result.

California was the first state to adopt a short-time compensation provision in its unemployment insurance law in 1977, and since that time, several other states have followed. A study of the 1982–1983 recession found that firms that used short-time benefits reduced their layoffs by about 15 percent over what they would have been without the program.[1] For the relatively few firms that used it, the program did seem to be effective in preserving the long-term employment relationship for some workers. As the program becomes more widely understood, its use in future recessions may be even more substantial.

To Think About

1. Why should firms care whether or not their employees receive unemployment insurance benefits? Can't they make decisions on how to reduce their work forces without thinking about the workers' well-being? What does this example suggest about the relationship between employers and employees?

2. Unemployment insurance is financed by a tax on employers. In some cases tax rates are adjusted to reflect a firm's unemployment experiences. Would the way in which such rates are calculated have an effect on how firms react to a decline in their labor requirements?

exclusively on an individual worker's productivity, illustrates how workers and firms are bound together as a team to develop an efficient overall organization of production.

Special types of nonwage compensation are also used to achieve this result. Pension benefits are usually based on length of service and often depend on the financial success of the firm as well. Some firms use bonus payments as a way of supplementing wages. This practice is quite common in Japan, as discussed in "Applying Economics: Wage Bonuses in Japan". Some authors

---

[1] For a summary, see Stuart Kerachsky, Walter Nicholson, Edward Cavin, and Alan Hershey, "Work Sharing Programs: An Evaluation of Their Use," *Monthly Labor Review*, May 1986, pp. 31–33.

APPLYING ECONOMICS

Wage Bonuses in Japan

Employment relations in Japan have several unique features that clearly reflect the long-term nature of labor contracts. Under the *Nenko* system some workers are assured of more or less permanent employment together with promotions and wage increases based almost exclusively on years of service with the firm. Such an arrangement cements the relationship between employees and employers and gives each an interest in the other's well-being. To increase those incentives further, Japanese workers under the *Nenko* system are often paid semiannual bonuses based on their firm's performance. These bonuses can be quite large, sometimes amounting to one-fourth or more of the total annual earnings.

Although some authors view the *Nenko* system as a development of Japanese cultural traditions, the more common view among economists is that the system arose during rapid industrialization in Japan and reflects an efficient implicit contract between employees and employers. Payment of bonuses is consistent with this latter view. The bonuses can be regarded as a method by which workers and employers share in the firm's success. With such bonuses workers are given strong incentives to accumulate the kinds of job-specific skills that will be most useful to the firm.

A recent empirical study of the Japanese bonus system found substantial evidence to support this interpretation.[2] Examining information from 647 different industries, the author concluded that bonuses tended to be higher in precisely those industries for which job-specific skills seemed to be most important. Bonuses also tended to be higher in industries (such as machinery production) that are very sensitive to the business cycle. This finding is consistent with the importance of job-specific skills since the productivity of highly skilled workers may be more volatile in such industries. What appears to be a cultural aspect of the Japanese economy may be a response to the universal problem of developing efficient labor contracts.

To Think About

1. How are the three components of the *Nenko* system (lifetime employment, seniority based on wages, and annual bonuses) connected? Why might all the features be required to assure an efficient overall contract? How would omission of one of the components affect the joint behavior of workers and firms?

2. Many college professors (perhaps yours) have tenure, which assures them lifetime employment at their institution. In what ways is this an efficient labor contract? Do both professors and the university gain from it? How does academic tenure differ from the Japanese *Nenko* system? Can you think of reasons for such differences?

argue that such bonuses give workers a more direct stake in the success of their firms. Employee stock ownership plans (ESOPs) may serve a similar function of encouraging workers to be more productive in their current jobs by giving them a stake in the financial success of the firm.

These possible outcomes of the implicit contract between workers and the firm suggest that, at least in some cases, long-term employees will be paid more than it would cost the firm to hire replacements for them. In the interest of maintaining a long-term productive arrangement, the firm will pay an **ef-**

---

[2]Masanori Hashimoto, "Bonus Payments, On-the-Job Training, and Lifetime Employment in Japan," *Journal of Political Economy,* October 1979, pp. 1086–1104.

Efficient wage
A wage above the market wage paid to encourage a worker to remain with a firm.

ficient wage higher than the prevailing market wage, w.[3] By itself, such an action would tend to raise costs, but if it succeeds in developing a more efficient enterprise, it may in fact reduce costs. The effect on the marginal cost curve illustrated in Figure 10.1 is therefore indeterminate. Economists are only beginning to be able to measure the relative importance of these effects and to explore their consequences for a number of important economic questions.[4]

Contracts with Managers

Agent
The role of making economic decisions for another party, such as the manager of a firm being hired to act for the owner.

In Chapter 9 we tend to treat the owner of a firm (that is, the owner of the firm's capital) and the manager of that firm as being the same person. This treatment makes the assumption of profit-maximizing behavior believable—a person who maximizes the profits in a firm that he or she owns will succeed in making as much income as possible from this ownership. The process of profit maximization is consistent with the process of utility maximization we studied in Part 2.

For many firms, however, managers do not actually own the firm for which they work. Rather, there is a separation between the ownership of the firm and the control of its behavior by hired managers. In this case, a manager acts as an **agent** for the owner. Do agents perform in the ways that owners want—that is, do they maximize profits?

Conflicts in the Agent Relationship

Adam Smith understood the basic conflict between owners and managers. In *The Wealth of Nations* he observed that "the directors of . . . companies, being the managers of other people's money than of their own, it cannot well be expected that they should watch over it with the same anxious vigilance with which [owners] watch over their own."[5] From this observation Adam Smith then went on to look at the behavior of such famous British institutions as the Royal African Company, the Hudson's Bay Company, and the East India Company to illustrate some of the consequences of management by nonowners. His observations provide an important starting point for the study of modern firms.

---

[3]One of the first economists to propose this efficient wage hypothesis was Joseph Stiglitz in "Wage Determination and Unemployment in L.D.C.'s: The Labor Turnover Model," *Quarterly Journal of Economics*, May 1974, pp. 194–227.

[4]Some of the most important questions center on the level of unemployment and the business cycle. For a brief survey, see Janet L. Yellen, "Efficiency Wage Models of Unemployment," *American Economic Review*, May 1984, pp. 200–205.

[5]Adam Smith, *The Wealth of Nations*, 1776 Cannan Edition (New York: Modern Library, 1937), p. 700.

Figure 10.2
Incentives for a Manager
Acting as an Agent for a
Firm's Owners

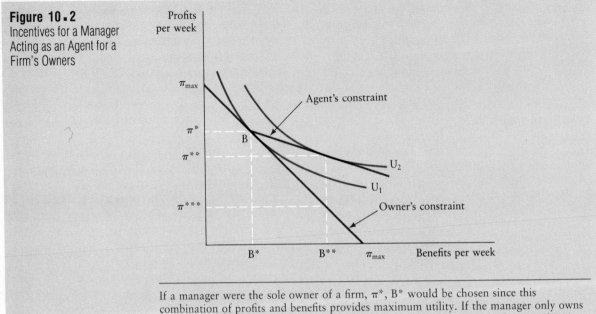

If a manager were the sole owner of a firm, π^*, B^* would be chosen since this combination of profits and benefits provides maximum utility. If the manager only owns one-third of the firm, however, the perceived budget constraint will be flatter and B^{**}, π^{**} will be chosen.

The principal issue raised by the use of manager-agents is illustrated in Figure 10.2. That figure shows the indifference curve map of a manager's preferences between the firm's profits (which are of primary interest to the owners) and various benefits (such as fancy offices or travel in the corporate jet or helicopter) that accrue mainly to the manager.[6] This indifference curve map has the same shape as in Part 2 on the presumption that both profits and benefits provide utility to the manager.

To construct the budget constraint that the manager faces in seeking to maximize his or her utility, assume first that the manager is also the owner of this firm. If the manager chooses to have no special benefits from the job, profits will be π_{max}. Each dollar of benefits received by the manager reduces these profits by one dollar. The budget constraint will have a slope of -1, and profits will reach zero when benefits total π_{max}.

Given this budget constraint, the owner-manager maximizes utility by opting for profits of π^* and benefits of B^*. Profits of π^*, while less than π_{max}, still represent maximum profits in this situation since any other owner-manager would also wish to receive B^* in benefits. That is, B^* represents a true

---

[6]Figure 10.2 is based on one presented in Michael C. Jensen and William H. Meckling, "Theory of the Firm: Managerial Behavior, Agency Costs and Ownership Structure," *Journal of Financial Economics,* October 1976, pp. 305–360.

cost of doing business, and given these costs, the firm's manager really does maximize profits.

Now suppose that the manager is not the only owner of this firm. Instead, assume that, say, one-third of the capital of the firm is owned by the manager and the other two-thirds are owned by outside investors who play no role in operating the firm. In this case the manager will act as if he or she no longer faces a budget constraint that requires sacrificing one dollar of the profits for each dollar of benefits. Now a dollar of benefits costs the manager only \$.33 in profits, since the other \$.67 is effectively paid by the other owners in terms of reduced profits on their investment. Although the new budget constraint continues to include the point B*, π* (since the manager could still make the same decision a sole owner could), for benefits greater than B* the slope of the budget constraint is only $-\frac{1}{3}$—profits on the manager's portion of the business decline by only \$.33 for each dollar in benefits received. Given this new budget constraint, the manager would choose point B**, π** to maximize his or her utility. Being only a partial owner of the firm causes the manager to choose a lower level of profits and a higher level of benefits than would be chosen by a sole owner.

Point B**, π** is not really attainable by this firm. Although the cost of one dollar of benefits appears to be only \$.33 in profits for the manager, in reality, of course, the benefits cost one dollar. When the manager opts for B** in benefits, the loss in profits is greater for the firm as a whole than for him or her personally. The firm's owners are harmed by having to rely on an agency relationship with the firm's manager. It appears that the smaller the fraction of the firm that is owned by the manager, the greater the extent of distortions that will be induced by this relationship.

The situation illustrated in Figure 10.2 is representative of a variety of principal-agent problems that arise in economics. Whenever one person (the principal) hires another person (the agent) to make decisions, the motivation of this agent must be taken into account since the agent may make different decisions than would the principal. Examples of this relationship occur not only in the management of firms, but also in such diverse applications as hiring investment advisors (do they really put their clients' interests first?); relying on an automobile mechanic's assessment in ordering repairs; and buying a friend's clothes for him or her. In "Applying Economics: The Physician-Patient Relationship," we examine one of the most important agency relationships and show that, as for the owner-manager problem, relying on the advice of doctors may create significant distortions in the allocation of resources.

Reactions of Owners and the Development of Management Contracts

The firm's owners would be unlikely to take the kind of behavior illustrated in Figure 10.2 lying down. They are being forced to accept lower profits than might be earned on their investments in exchange for manager-oriented benefits that provide no value to them personally. What can they do? Most obviously, they can refuse to invest in the firm if they know the manager will

APPLYING ECONOMICS

The Physician-Patient Relationship

When people are sick they often have very little idea of what is wrong or what the most promising treatment is. They may place themselves under a physician's care in the belief that the physician is better qualified to make decisions about the proper course of action. The physician acts as an agent for the patient. For many treatments (such as prescription drugs or surgery) the physician offers the only access to treatment—even fully informed people cannot prescribe drugs or perform surgery for themselves if they are not physicians.

There are several reasons why a physician acting as an agent for a patient may not choose exactly what a fully informed patient would choose. The physician generally pays none of the bills—to the physician the price of anything prescribed is essentially zero. Indeed, since the physician may in many instances also be the provider of care, he or she may even benefit from the services prescribed. This effect is reinforced by medical insurance, which further encourages the physician to prescribe services, since the patient may not pay directly for them either. Finally, the growth of malpractice claims in recent years has led physicians to practice "defensive medicine"—ordering more tests than required to protect themselves against possible law suits.

All of these aspects of the agent relationship between physicians and patients suggest that more medical care will be chosen by physicians for their patients than the

patients would choose for themselves. A number of studies have gathered evidence on physician-induced demand, and most have reported relatively small but significant effects. For example, a 1978 study of surgery by Victor Fuchs found that the more surgeons there were in a given geographic area, other things being equal, the more surgical operations were performed.[7] According to his estimates each 10 percent increase in the ratio of surgeons to population resulted in a 3 percent increase in operations. The effects of physician-induced demand seemed especially strong in regions where people were less educated—perhaps because less educated patients were less likely to argue with their physician about the treatment prescribed.

To Think About
1. Isn't the notion of physician-induced demand inordinately cynical? Aren't physicians under such strong moral constraints in what they do that it is unlikely many would make decisions that were not in a patient's best interest? Can you think of other factors that might control the extent of physician-induced demand?
2. If surgeons really can increase the demand for operations, which kinds of operations do you think would be most affected? How would you decide which were unnecessary? Can you think of any examples from your own experiences?

behave in this manner. In such a case the manager would have two options. First, he or she could go it alone, financing the company completely with his or her own funds. The firm would then return to the owner-manager situation in which B^*, π^* is the preferred choice of benefits and profits. Alternatively, the manager may obtain outside financing to operate the firm if the operation is too expensive to finance alone. In this case the manager has to work out some sort of contractual arrangement with would-be owners to get them to invest.

One possible contract would be for the manager to agree to finance all of the benefits received out of his or her share of the profits. This would make

---

[7]Victor Fuchs, "The Supply of Surgeons and the Demand for Operations," *Journal of Human Resources*, Volume XIII supplement, 1978, pp. 35–56.

Figure 10.3
Possible Managerial
Contracts

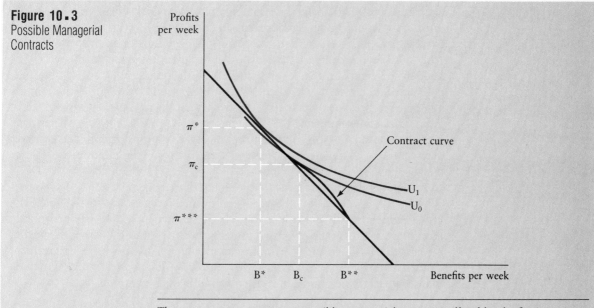

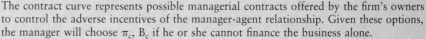

The contract curve represents possible managerial contracts offered by the firm's owners to control the adverse incentives of the manager-agent relationship. Given these options, the manager will choose π_c, B_c if he or she cannot finance the business alone.

would-be owners happy (since they would get the same level of profits no matter how many benefits the manager chose). However, if the manager persists in choosing B^{**}, he or she will receive only π^{***} in profits. This will yield a very low level of utility—lower than the manager would get if the would-be owners would provide funds without strings attached (U_2) but also lower than what the manager would get as the sole owner (U_1). In this situation, a manager who succumbed to the desire for benefits seemingly created by the agency relationship would actually be made worse off.

Writing a contract under which managers pay completely for benefits out of their share of the profits is probably impossible for owners to do. Enforcing the provisions of such a contract would require constant supervision of the manager's activities—something the owners would prefer not to do since that would force them into a managerial role. Instead, they may try to develop less strict contracts that give managers an incentive to economize on benefits and thereby pursue goals closer to pure profit maximization. By offering such contract options as profit-sharing bonuses, stock option plans, and company-financed pensions, the owner may be able to give managers an incentive to be careful about the benefits they choose to take.

Graphing actual complex contract provisions such as stock options is impossible. A simplified view of this contracting process is illustrated in Figure 10.3. The contract curve shows the relationship between benefits the manager receives and the amount of the firm's profits he or she is allowed to keep.

This curve lies outside the sole owner budget constraint since owners recognize that they cannot make managers pay completely for their benefits because that would involve too much supervision. However, the slope of the contract curve is steeper than the agent's budget constraint shown in Figure 10.2 because the contract's provisions do require a significant financial sacrifice by managers for the benefits they take. Given these contractual offerings, the manager chooses B_c, π_c as the best of the options available. Although this outcome requires the owners to sacrifice some of the profits they would receive if the firm were operated by a manager who behaved like a sole owner, it is preferable to a situation in which the manager is a pure agent. The contract may represent a trade-off of some profit dollars for the assurance of better management performance.

As with labor contracts, the development of management contracts requires considerable give-and-take between the parties (owners and managers). The final agreement will be a compromise between owners' desires to incorporate incentives to encourage profit-maximizing behavior and the costs involved in writing the contract and monitoring that behavior. Real-world management contracts may be quite complex. In "Applying Economics: Stock Purchase Plans" we examine one feature often found in such contracts.

The Market for Firms

So far we have discussed labor and management contracts as evolving from bargaining between the parties involved with the firm. Now we take a somewhat broader view by considering the outside market pressures that affect these settlements. Specifically, we focus on the market for firms themselves—what has come to be termed "the market for corporate control" in recent economic discussions. Our general goal is to show how the workings of this market help to weed out inefficient, high-cost contractual arrangements within firms.

Two other types of market pressures on firms should be mentioned. First, any firm must be attentive to the markets for the inputs it hires. Labor contracts that are distinctly inferior to those offered elsewhere will make it impossible for the firm to attract workers. Similarly, inferior management contracts will severely restrict the firm's ability to attract the managers it wishes to hire. The economic operations of these markets is a topic we take up in Part 5. Second, firms must be attentive to the market for their product. If the firm's costs are too high, it may not be able to compete effectively with other producers. Competition in the product market provides a powerful regulator of firms' behavior, and we study that topic extensively in Part 4.

Profit Opportunities in the Market for Firms

The possible attractions of a would-be buyer of a firm are illustrated in Figure 10.4. The firm's short-run average and marginal cost curves are given by SAC

Stock Purchase Plans

An obvious way for a firm's owners to encourage managers to seek maximum profits is to give the managers a financial stake in the success of the business. For public corporations that amounts to encouraging managers to own common stock. Many corporations have rather elaborate stock ownership incentives, especially for their top managers who are most involved in decision making.

Examining the consequences of various stock plans on managers' decisions is a complicated process because such plans serve other goals as well. Many plans, such as stock options, offer personal tax benefits to the manager—they are a lower cost way of paying the manager (as opposed to taxable wages) whether or not they provide any incentive to maximize the firm's profits. Direct stock purchase plans, under which managers can buy shares at, say, 85 percent of market price with borrowed funds and no brokerage commissions, offer few direct tax advantages. The incentive effects of stock ownership can be examined in a relatively simple case.

A 1985 study of 130 stock purchase plans provides some evidence of these effects.[8] On average, these plans offered about 8 percent of the corporation's stock to its managers at a discount of 12 to 15 percent from market price. Practically all of the plans allowed the shares to be bought with borrowed funds, usually with the managers paying very low interest rates.

Judging by the stock market's reaction, these plans were quite successful in encouraging managers' performance. Following announcement of the plans, the value of the firm's shares tended to rise by about 3 percent over the general market trend. Stock purchase plans for top managers were more effective in prompting such a price rise than were more broadly based plans—perhaps because investors believed that it was more important to have top managers own a portion of the company. In this way major management decisions were brought into closer accord with those favored by the owners of the firm.

To Think About

1. Why do owners have to worry about incentives for management performance? Why don't corporate directors just fire managers who aren't doing a satisfactory job? Doesn't the whole concern with managers' performance reflect a lack of attention by the corporation's directors?
2. If direct stock ownership by managers is desirable, why not require it as a condition of employment? What would be the effects of such a requirement? Would such a requirement necessarily be best for the firm in terms of overall efficiency of operations?

and SMC.[9] With a market price of P* this firm will produce q* and, since price exceeds average cost, earn a modest profit.

Assume now that a would-be buyer believes that this firm is currently rather inefficient and could be operated at lower cost by a new management team. Specifically, assume this buyer believes that the firm could be operated with costs given by SAC' and SMC' if it were under new management. With these new costs, profits would be given by area P*E'BC' instead of P*EAC. Such larger profits offer a major incentive for the potential buyer to proceed with plans to purchase the firm. If the firm is privately owned, an offer may be

---

[8]Sanjai Bhagat, James A. Brickley, and Ronald C. Lease, "Incentive Effects of Stock Purchase Plans," *Journal of Financial Economics,* June 1985, pp. 195–215.

[9]Figure 10.4 uses short-run curves because our discussion in Chapter 11 will show that cost inefficiencies are substantially eliminated over the longer term by competition in the market for goods.

Figure 10.4
Inefficient Costs Make the
Firm a Takeover Candidate

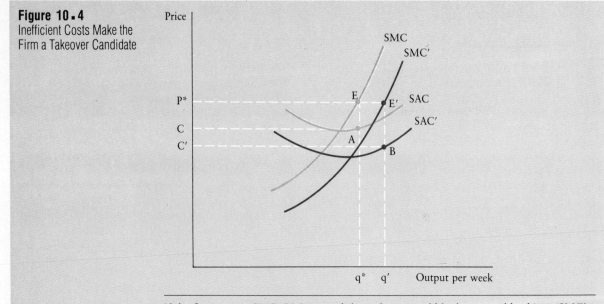

If the firm's costs (SMC, SAC) exceed those that a would-be buyer could achieve (SMC', SAC'), the firm may be acquired provided the increase in profits exceeds the costs of the acquisition.

made directly to these owners. On the other hand, if ownership of the firm is spread widely over a large number of shareholders, the buyer may make a public offer to these shareholders. In "Applying Economics: Corporate Raiders," we take a brief look at some of the more spectacular recent examples of such takeover efforts.

Buying an entire firm is a more complex transaction than buying a loaf of bread, for example. Often considerable capital may be required to make the transaction, necessitating complex borrowing arrangements with banks and the accompanying legal formalities. Takeovers may also involve some explicit short-term costs, such as relocating a firm's headquarters or highly skilled employees leaving because they oppose the change. Existing management may make the purchase of their firm difficult by adopting various defensive ploys such as rigging the voting by shareholders or enlisting the government's assistance in opposing the takeover. As a result of these costs, it might be expected that only purchases that are quite profitable would proceed. Situations in which potential buyers would obtain only minor cost improvements over existing management would not produce sufficiently higher short-run profits to warrant incurring these costs. Instead, the normal workings of the marketplace (as we take up in the next part) will insure that such inefficiencies are reduced over the long run.

Evidence from merger and takeover activity in the late 1970s is consistent with this view. One extensive review of the research on this topic finds that shareholders of firms that were acquired in this way experienced an increase

Corporate Raiders

"Corporate raiders" are individual investors who seek to take over the management of specific target firms primarily by using borrowed funds. In recent years formerly obscure investors such as T. Boone Pickens, Carl Icahn, David Murdock, and Victor Posner have become widely known as their aggressive pursuit of various firms has made front-page news. The principal objection to these raiders appears to be the fear that they will loot the target company—that they are solely interested in making a quick profit and will then leave the company in shambles.

Both economic logic and the actual evidence contradict this villainous view of corporate raiders. In theoretical terms, raiders have no reason to destroy a firm. Presumably they are purchasing a firm's assets because they believe the assets are worth more than currently valued in the market. If the raider were really set on destroying the firm, some other potential buyer would step in to prevent this from happening.

An alternative view is that corporate raiders are performing a useful function by identifying poorly managed firms and promoting new management practices. For example, some observers argue that the persistent raids of T. Boone Pickens on various major oil companies had the effect of making these firms think of themselves as two different businesses—owners of oil-producing properties and refiners of crude oil. By recognizing that many oil companies were poorly managing their crude oil reserves, Pickens was able to find a route to profitable acquisitions.[10]

A 1985 study of the activities of six infamous corporate raiders by Clifford Holderness and Dennis Sheehan reaches a similar conclusion.[11] Here the authors show that announcement of stock purchases by these six influential investors significantly raised the market value of the target firms' shares, a finding inconsistent with the raider notion. The authors then examine possible reasons for this market reaction and conclude that a major portion can be attributed to the investors' ultimate involvement in managing the company. That is, the value of the corporation was increased by the raider's activities in some measure because the raider represented the promise of better management.

Once raiders acquire a firm, they aren't just passive investors. They often move into the new firm and "clean house" by firing unproductive managers and selling unprofitable assets. It is no wonder that managers adopt all kinds of strategies to ward off such changes.

To Think About

1. Why do takeovers by corporate raiders seem to be more controversial than takeovers by other firms (that is, mergers)? Do the raiders have different motives? Would raiders who don't know the business be less successful managers than firms that do? Couldn't a raider just hire better managers for the firms they acquire?
2. Should the government seek to control takeover activity more closely? What would be the gains from such closer scrutiny? What would be the economic losses from prohibiting certain takeovers?

in the value of their investments of 20 to 30 percent.[12] Unsuccessful takeover attempts, on the other hand, actually resulted in a small loss for existing shareholders, perhaps because managers spent real resources fighting off the takeover.

---

[10]For a discussion of this case and several other issues related to the market for corporate control, see U.S. Council of Economic Advisors to the President, "The Market for Corporate Control," Chapter 6 in *Economic Report of the President, 1985* (Washington, D.C.: U.S. Government Printing Office, 1985), pp. 187–216.

[11]Clifford G. Holderness and Dennis P. Sheehan, "Raiders or Saviors? The Evidence on Six Controversial Investors," *Journal of Financial Economics,* December 1985, pp. 555–579.

[12]Michael C. Jensen and Richard S. Ruback, "The Market for Corporate Control: The Scientific Evidence," *Journal of Financial Economics,* March 1983, pp. 5–50.

It is possible that some of these gains from successful takeovers represent factors other than the lower operating costs illustrated in Figure 10.4. For example, as we discuss in Chapter 12, some of these gains may reflect monopoly profits that are garnered by the larger firms that result from a merger. But such monopoly gains probably occur in only a few cases, and these mergers are extensively regulated by antitrust law. It seems likely that a substantial portion of shareholders' profits do reflect some types of improved management efficiencies. The continuing strength of takeover activity in the United States indicates that the market for firms may be an important source of improvement in the overall performance of the U.S. economy.

Summary

This chapter surveys some recent topics in the theory of the firm. The main purpose of this survey is to show how the traditional theory can be applied to a number of new and exciting topics. The principal conclusions from this examination were:

- Firms can be regarded as comprising a set of contracts among workers, capital owners, and managers.
- Contracts with workers will reflect the firm-specific skills that are developed on the job. They prompt long-term relationships and deter extensive short-term turnover of employees.
- Managers must act as agents for the firm's owners. In their decisions as managers they may pursue some goals that are costly to owners by reducing their profits.
- Management contracts will be structured to control these agency problems. Such contracts may be costly for owners to develop and enforce.
- The market for firms will operate to insure that the firm's contracts are relatively efficient ones. High-cost, inefficient firms may be acquired by another owner if the profits from such an acquisition exceed the costs involved in making the acquisition.

Problems

10.1 How do costs associated with hiring new employees affect the marginal revenue—marginal cost rule for profit maximization? Explain carefully why this effect might depend on whether short-run or long-run marginal costs are used. Why might a firm respond differently to temporary and permanent changes in the price of its product?

*10.2 One way of modeling the way firms adjust their work forces is to use a "stock-adjustment model" that assumes the change in labor hired be-

---

*Denotes a rather difficult problem.

tween week t − 1 and week t $(L_t - L_{t-1})$ is a fraction of the difference between what the firm wants to hire (L^*_t) and what it hired last week (L_{t-1}). That is

$$L_t - L_{t-1} = k(L^*_t - L_{t-1})$$

where k is some fraction less than one.

Suppose that a taxidermy shop has a short-run production function given by

$$q = \sqrt{L}$$

where q is the number of animals stuffed per week and L is hours of labor hired per week. Assume that the wage rate is $1 per hour and that short-run total costs are given by

$$STC = 200 + 10q^2.$$

Short-run marginal costs are given by

$$SMC = 20q.$$

a. If the market price of q is $200 each, how many will be produced and how many workers will the firm wish to hire each week?
b. Suppose the firm starts in week 0 with 50 hours of workers' time used per week. If k = 1/2, how many workers will be hired in week 1? How many animals will be stuffed?
c. Answer part b for week 2.
d. Graph the firm's output and labor hiring decisions for weeks 0 to 5.
e. How many weeks will it take for the firm to get within one hour of the desired labor input?

10.3 Suppose the production function for high quality brandy is given by

$$q = \sqrt{K \cdot L}$$

where q is the output of brandy per week and L is labor hours per week. In the short run, K is fixed at 100, so the short-run production function is

$$q = 10 \sqrt{L}.$$

a. If capital rents for 10 each and wages are $5 per hour, show that short-run total costs are

$$STC = 1000 + .05q^2.$$

b. Given the short-run total cost curve in part a, short-run marginal costs are given by

$$SMC = .1q$$

With this short-run marginal cost curve, how much will the firm produce at a price of $20 per bottle of brandy? How many labor hours will be hired per week?

c. Suppose that during recessions, the price of brandy falls to $15 per bottle. With this price, how much would the firm choose to produce and how many labor hours would be hired?

d. Suppose that the firm believes that the fall in the price of brandy will last for only one week, after which it will wish to return to the level of production in part a. Assume also that for each hour that the firm reduces its work force below that described in part a, it incurs a cost of $1. If it proceeds as in part c, will it earn a profit or a loss? Explain.

e. Is there some level of hiring other than that described in part c that will yield more profits for the firm during the temporary recession?

10.4 Why would firms pay more than the existing market wage to retain their employees? How might workers who are not employees of the firm respond to such high wages? Could higher than market wage rates continue to be paid over the long term?

10.5 Figure 10.2 assumes that the manager owns one-third of the firm. How would the situation change if a smaller fraction were owned? Suppose, for example, the manager owned none of the firm; what would his or her preferred mix of profits and benefits be? Explain your result carefully and indicate whether you think it is a reasonable outcome.

10.6 Managers often receive liberal severance pay provisions in their contracts (these are sometimes called "golden parachutes"). Why would owners opt for such provisions? Once a manager is fired, he or she no longer can affect profits, so why should owners pay managers anything in such a situation?

10.7 United Frisbee produces high quality, jeweled frisbees. The firm's short-run total costs are given by

$$STC = .01q^2 + 10,000$$

where q is the quantity of frisbees produced per week. Marginal costs are given by

$$SMC = .02q.$$

a. Suppose United can sell its frisbees at $30 each. How many will be produced and what will weekly profits be?

b.   Suppose Ted Turnover, a famous corporate raider, can operate United at three-fourths the costs of the current management. What would the costs of the firm be in this situation?

 If frisbee prices remain at $30, how many would be produced and what would profits be?

c.   How much more would Ted be willing to pay for United than would another buyer who could not achieve these cost efficiencies?

PRICING OF GOODS

Parts 1 through 3 discuss people's demands and firms' costs. This part now brings these two strands of analysis together to discuss how the prices of goods are determined. In many respects our analysis here is simply an elaboration of Marshall's supply and demand model first mentioned in Chapter 1. A principal purpose of this part is to make that model more precise.

There are several assumptions that underlie our analysis in Part 4. First, we look at the market for only one good. We are consciously ignoring the secondary effects that spread through the economy whenever conditions in one market change. When the price of bread rises, for example, workers' real incomes are reduced, and they may press for higher wages. These higher wages may then increase bread makers' costs, resulting in a further increase in the price of bread. We wish to hold these "feedback" effects constant for the time being. Our analysis is therefore of a partial equilibrium nature; we will study general equilibrium in Part 6.

Second, we assume that a large number of people demand the good under examination. Although the actions of demanders as a group have a great deal to do with the market price of a good, we assume here that no one person can affect the market price by his or her own actions. Each person takes the price of the good as given. There is nothing he or she can do about the price except to adjust consumption patterns. This assumption is made throughout Part 2, and the analysis of individual and market demand carries over here.

While this assumption of individual impotence may be true for the demand side of a large and complex economy, the same assumption cannot be made about the supply side of the market. Many goods are produced by only a few sellers. The behavior of General Motors, for example, certainly has an effect on the price of cars, so it would be a mistake to assume that firm is a price taker. Part 4 looks at the differences in the behavior of markets characterized by "one," "few," or "many" sellers.

In this introductory section we need to develop some vocabulary to use in our discussions of various types of markets. This vocabulary is summarized in a glossary at the end of the section. First, we discuss the notion of product differentiation and show that it is important to distinguish between the markets for homogeneous and for differentiated products. Next, we discuss how markets work. Then we turn to some definitions of specific market types. A final section of this introduction presents an overview of Part 4.

Homogeneous and Differentiated Goods

In order to analyze pricing in the goods market we must first describe what is meant by *good* and *market*. For example, how precisely is the term *good* defined? Possible definitions extend from the very general ("consumption," "investment") to the uniquely specific ("1 pound of 10X confectioner's cane sugar bought at 9 A.M. on January 21, 1987, in Amherst, Massachusetts"). Obviously, neither of these extreme definitions is useful for studying pricing. The first is too general: people's and firms' decisions about total consumption are in reality a multitude of decisions on more specifically defined goods such as toothpaste, toasters, or milling machines. If we used an aggregate definition we would obscure any understanding of market interactions. The second very specific type of definition is also not very useful because it represents a unique transaction that will never again take place. Clearly some middle ground must be chosen, which will depend on the interests of the investigator.

Economists define goods as either "homogeneous" or "differentiated." All suppliers of a **homogeneous good** produce the identical good. People are indifferent about which firm they will buy a homogeneous good from since every firm produces the same item. Assuming perfect knowledge and costless mobility of goods, the market for this kind of good must obey the **law of one price.** All trades of the good between seller and buyer must be conducted at the same price. If the price for a homogeneous good were to differ among firms, everyone would flock to the less expensive seller, which is why only a single price can prevail. Examples of relatively homogeneous goods might include steel girders, concrete pipe, work clothes, gasoline, most farm products, and many consumer electronics.[1]

For **differentiated goods,** on the other hand, it does make a difference which firm the individual buys from. These goods are not identical (although the differences may not be too great), and firms may strive to differentiate their products from those of their competitors. Most consumer goods fall in this category, which creates some problems in defining exactly what we mean by a particular good. For example, suppose we wished to study the demand for automobiles. Should station wagons be included? How about jeeps? Or pickup trucks? Or taxis? Even in the category of what are usually considered automobiles, there is a huge variation of possible models—sedans, sportscars, luxury models, compacts, and so forth. Should all these be considered the same basic good—an automobile?

To be able to explain the factors that influence pricing, we must simplify what we mean by a good. We assume that it is possible to delimit a well-defined good and its respective market. Homogeneous goods, because they can be most easily handled, occupy the major portion of our analysis, but we do occasionally discuss the complications presented by differentiated products.

Organization of Markets

A **market** is a hypothetical place where the producers of a good (suitably defined) get together with the buyers to haggle about price.[2] In order to analyze the behavior of the agents entering into these bargains, we must look at matters from their point of view. The buyer's point of view is simple. Buyers are generally so numerous that any one of them can have no effect on the outcome of the price-setting process. Each is a price taker who is forced to accept the price that the market dictates. The actual quantities that any one buyer (and buyers as a group) will demand depends on this price.

The way a firm looks at the market is not so simple. If there are so many firms that any particular one of them must accept the price of its product as given by the market, then the firms face a horizontal demand curve. Each firm can sell all it wants at the prevailing price because its own actions have no effect on price. In this case, as we showed in Chapter 9, the firm as well as the buyer is a price taker.

At the other extreme, a firm that is the only producer of some good faces the entire market demand. Its actions will obviously affect price. If the market demand curve is downward sloping it will have to charge a lower price to get people to buy a high level of output than it would if it produced less.

Between these two extremes of many sellers and only one seller of a product lies the case of a market with a few sellers. In that case it is difficult to say exactly what kind of a demand curve the firms face. Each firm's actions will have some effect on price, so it is not a price taker. On the other hand, its competitors are also absorbing some of the total demand for the product, so the total market demand curve is not relevant either. The demand curve facing the firm in a market with a few sellers is therefore uncertain. The firm must make decisions while being in some ignorance about what its competitors will do. Analyzing firm behavior in such situations raises challenging and interesting problems.

---

[1]Even for some of these goods, firms make valiant efforts to differentiate their products by providing "service" or "brand identification."

[2]This is, of course, a simplification. In reality, most trading is through middlemen, such as supermarkets, department stores, trading companies, or automobile dealerships. The buyer of a good purchases the services of these middlemen with the actual product.

Types of Markets

To be able to study pricing in the market for a good, we must first ask how the market is organized. Our approach to explaining a firm's actions depends on how many other firms are in the market. It will depend on the type of demand curve that faces the firm. Markets are usually classified by whether there are many, few, or one producer. A cross-classification is also made about whether the good produced is homogeneous or differentiated. These classifications give us six possible market types (although we will see below that one of these is not used). The economic names of these market types are shown in Table IV.1 and each is discussed below.

Perfect Competition

A market in **perfect competition** is characterized by a large number of firms that produce a homogeneous good. None of the firms is large relative to the market as a whole. Each firm in a perfectly competitive market operates as if it were faced by a horizontal (that is, infinitely elastic) demand curve. Its individual decisions on output will not affect market price. Entry into the market or industry by other firms is assumed to be costless. In the long run, new firms will be able to enter the market in response to opportunities for profit. Perfect competition is the prototype for a major portion of economic analysis. Although it is difficult to identify a market that is perfectly competitive as strictly defined here, close examples are the markets for most agricultural crops. Many other markets can also be understood using the perfectly competitive model, and we investigate that model in detail in Part 4.

Monopolistic Competition

A market characterized by a large number of producers of slightly different goods is termed **monopolistic competition**.[3] Although each firm in this market is small relative to

Table IV.1
Market Types

Number of Firms	Type of Product	
	Homogeneous	Differentiated
Many	Perfect competition	Differentiated or monopolistic competition
Few	Homogeneous oligopoly	Differentiated oligopoly
One	Monopoly	(Not used)

total demand, because it sells a slightly different product than the other firms the price it receives is affected by its actions. These firms face a negatively sloped demand curve. Each firm in this market must be careful in its decisions, however, because there are many close substitutes for its product that are offered by competitors. Entry into the monopolistically competitive market is assumed to be costless, and it is presumed that new firms will be brought into the market by the prospect of profits. An example of a monopolistically competitive market is provided by gasoline stations. There are many small firms in this industry, but the product of each is slightly different from that of its competitors both because of location of the station and because each station sells a (very) slightly different product. Because of the large number of firms, there are clear limits on the ability of any one of them to raise the price of its product significantly above prices prevailing elsewhere.

Homogeneous Oligopoly

A market in which relatively few firms produce a homogeneous product is termed a **homogeneous oligopoly**.[4] A

---

[3]The term "monopolistic competition" was made widely known by Edward Chamberlin in *The Theory of Monopolistic Competition* (Cambridge, Mass.: Harvard University Press, 1933).

[4]The meaning of *few* here is necessarily ambiguous and will vary from case to case. Entry into the market by others can be assumed to be either impossible or relatively costly. If the latter assumption is made (as would usually be the case), then those firms already in the market will not only pay attention to the actions of their rivals but they may also adopt strategies that discourage other firms from entering the market.

firm in this market can, because it produces a large share of the total output, have some effect on the price it will receive. However, the precise demand curve one firm faces is difficult to determine. This is so not only because there are close substitutes (indeed, the identical product) being produced by others, but also because the firm must explicitly take account of how its competitors will react to any decisions that it makes. This feature of the market makes decision making in oligopoly markets subject to great uncertainties. Consequently, the analysis of these markets has a certain lack of precision and an absence of definitive results. Nonetheless, since numerous markets (steel, aluminum, glass, and chemicals, to name a few) can be classified as homogeneous oligopolies, such studies are extremely important to any understanding of the details of how any advanced market economy works.

Differentiated Oligopoly

Most ordinary consumer products (toothpaste, soft drinks, frozen food, automobiles—the list is almost endless) are produced in markets that can be described as **differentiated oligopolies:** there are a relatively few firms that each produce a slightly different product. All of the comments made about homogeneous oligopoly markets also apply to the differentiated oligopoly. In this type of market, firms have the additional strategy of making their products different from those of their competitors. Whereas it may be hard to impart a special identity to brands of concrete pipe, this is not the case for deodorants or toothpastes. For these products, much effort goes into developing "product identification" and "brand loyalty." Any economic model that seeks to explain behavior in differentiated oligopoly markets must take into account these additional choices open to these firms.

Monopoly

A **monopoly** market is one in which there is only a single supplier. This single firm, then, faces the entire market demand. It has relative freedom in its pricing policies because there are no other firms about which to worry. The monopoly is in general competition for the consumer's dollar, but this does not lead to the great uncertainties that are present in oligopolies. Entry into a monopoly market is difficult, perhaps even impossible. Nonetheless,

most monopolies are aware of the possibility of entry and may adopt strategies that make it more difficult. For example, companies that obtain monopoly power in a market by owning patents may not strive for huge profits for fear of attracting successful imitators.

Overview of Part 4

In Part 4 we do not investigate all of these market types in detail. This part centers its attention on the polar cases of perfect competition and monopoly since most real-world markets are a mixture of these two types. Chapter 11 discusses the theory of perfectly competitive pricing. In the short run, the number of firms in an industry is fixed. No entry by new firms is possible. The supply curve for the industry is simply the sum of each firm's supply curve as we derived in Chapter 9. Combining this market supply curve with the market demand curve from Chapter 5 yields Marshall's familiar "cross" diagram. This is the model most often used in supply and demand analysis. In the long run, new firms are lured into competitive markets by the availability of profits; the entry of these new firms then changes supply conditions. This entry makes long-run supply considerably more flexible than short-run supply.

Our examination of these possibilities for entry completes the perfectly competitive model. This model provides not only a complete view of a simplified theoretical model, but it also provides an excellent starting place for the analysis of real-world markets. Only by understanding how demand, costs, and the possibility of entry by new firms interact in a simple model can we understand how those factors may affect pricing in real-world circumstances. In the appendix to Chapter 11 we discuss how prices arrive at their equilibrium levels in competitive markets.

In Chapter 12 we take up the theory of monopoly. The primary purpose of the chapter is to illustrate the misallocation of resources that monopolies may bring about. The chapter also discusses some ways in which this misallocation might be measured and analyzes both theoretical and practical problems in regulating monopolies.

Chapter 13 provides a brief introduction to the ways economists analyze markets with relatively few suppliers. Drawing on material discussed in Chapters 11 and 12, we show how behavior in these oligopolies can be contrasted to that predicted by the competitive and monopoly models. The strategic relationships among the firms in an oligopoly are also discussed. The appendix to Chapter 13 discusses a few simple numerical models of interfirm strategy and game theory that have been developed.

In short, Part 4 is about the general ways in which supply and demand factors determine the prices that firms receive for their products. Although markets may diverge from the perfectly competitive "ideal," a natural place to start any analysis is by quantifying demand and cost conditions. As we will see, the insights provided by even a cursory examination of these conditions can be great. ▲

Homogeneous good
A good that is identical from producer to producer.

Law of one price
All trades between sellers and buyers for the same good are conducted at one price.

Differentiated good
A good that differs from producer to producer.

Market
A hypothetical "place" where buyers and sellers determine the price of a good.

Perfect competition
A market in which there are assumed to be a large number of buyers and sellers for a good who do not individually affect the good's price. Entry into the market is assumed to be costless.

Monopolistic competition
A market in which a number of producers offer slightly different goods. Entry into the market is assumed to be costless.

Homogeneous oligopoly
A market in which relatively few firms produce a homogeneous good.

Differentiated oligopoly
A market in which relatively few firms produce a differentiated good.

Monopoly
A market in which there is only one seller of a good.

CHAPTER 11

Pricing in Perfectly Competitive Markets

This chapter discusses perfectly competitive price determination. The theory we develop here is an elaboration of Marshall's supply and demand analysis that we introduced in Chapter 1. We show how equilibrium prices are established and describe some of the factors that may tend to change such prices. In its final and complete form the competitive model we develop here is the most basic model of pricing used by economists. It provides a standard against which actual market performance can be measured.

Timing of a Supply Response

Supply response
The change in quantity of output in response to a change in demand conditions.

In the analysis of pricing it is important to decide the length of time that is to be allowed for a **supply response** to changing demand conditions. The establishment of equilibrium prices will be different if we are talking about a very short period of time during which supply is essentially fixed and unchanging or if we are envisioning a very long-run process in which it is possible for entirely new firms to enter an industry or market. For this reason, it has been traditional in economics to discuss pricing in three different time periods: (1) the very short run, (2) the short run, and (3) the long run. While it is not possible to give these terms an exact time length, the essential distinction among them concerns the nature of the supply response that is assumed to be possible. In the *very short run* there can be no supply response—quantity supplied is absolutely fixed. In the *short run*, existing firms may change the quantity they are supplying, but there can be no entry into the industry by new firms. In the *long run*, firms can further change the quantity supplied and completely new firms may enter an industry; this produces a very flexible supply response. This chapter discusses each of these different types of responses.

Pricing in the Very Short Run

Market period
A short period of time during which quantity supplied is fixed.

Equilibrium price
The price at which the quantity demanded by buyers of a good is equal to the quantity supplied of the good by sellers.

In the very short run or **market period,** there is no supply response. The goods are already "in" the marketplace and must be sold for whatever the market will bear. In this situation price acts to ration demand. The price will adjust to clear the market of the quantity that must be sold during the very short run. Although the market price may act as a signal to producers in future periods, it does not perform such a function in the very short run since current period output cannot be changed. Figure 11.1 pictures this situation. Market demand is represented by the curve D. Supply is fixed at Q^*, and the price that clears the market is P_1. At P_1 people are willing to take all that is offered in the market. Sellers want to dispose of Q^* without regard to price (for example, the good in question may be perishable and will be worthless if not sold immediately). The price P_1 balances the desires of demanders with the desires of suppliers. For this reason it is called an **equilibrium price.** In Figure 11.1, a price in excess of P_1 would not be an equilibrium price since people would demand less than Q^* (remember firms are always willing to supply Q^* no matter what the price). Similarly, a price below P_1 would not be an equilibrium price since people would then demand more than Q^*. P_1 is the only equilibrium price possible when demand conditions are those represented by the curve D.

Shifts in Demand: Price as a Rationing Device

If the demand curve in Figure 11.1 shifted outward to D' (perhaps because incomes increased, or because the price of some substitute increased), P_1 would no longer be an equilibrium price. With the demand curve D', far more than Q^* is demanded at the price P_1. Some people who wish to make purchases at a price of P_1 would find that not enough of the good is now available to meet the increase in demand. In order to ration Q^* among all demanders, the price would have to rise to P_2. At that new price, demand would again be reduced to Q^* (by a movement along D' in a northwesterly direction as the price rises). Hence the price rise would restore equilibrium to the market. The curve labeled S (for "supply") in Figure 11.1 shows all the equilibrium prices for Q^* for any conceivable shift in demand. The price must always adjust to ration demand to exactly what firms are willing to supply. These price adjustments can be quite frequent (changing even on a minute-to-minute basis), as "Applying Economics: Fish Auctions" shows.

Applicability of the Very Short-Run Model

The model of the very short run is not particularly useful for most markets. While the theory may adequately apply to some situations where goods are perishable (such as fish auctions), the far more common situation involves some degree of supply response to changing demand. It is usually presumed

Figure 11.1
Pricing in the Very
Short Run

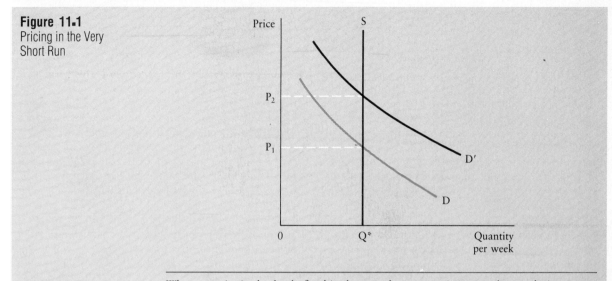

When quantity is absolutely fixed in the very short run, price acts only as a device to ration demand. With quantity fixed at Q*, price P_1 will prevail in the marketplace if D is the market demand curve. At this price, individuals are willing to consume exactly that quantity available. If demand should shift upward to D', the equilibrium price would rise to P_2.

that a rise in price will bring additional quantity into the market. The next section looks at why firms would increase their output levels in the short run in response to a price increase.

Before beginning that analysis, we should understand that increases in quantity supplied need not come only from increased production. In a world in which some goods are durable (that is, last longer than a single market period), current owners of these goods may supply them in increasing amounts to the market as price rises. For example, even though the supply of Rembrandts is absolutely fixed, we would not draw the market supply curve for these paintings as a vertical line, such as that shown in Figure 11.1. As the price of Rembrandts rises, people (and museums) become increasingly willing to part with them. From a market point of view, the supply curve for Rembrandts will have an upward slope even though no new production takes place. A similar analysis would follow for many types of durable goods, such as antiques, used cars, back issues of the *National Geographic,* or corporate shares, all of which are in nominally fixed supply. We are more interested here in examining how demand and production are related, and do not analyze other causes of increased supply in detail.

Short-Run Supply

In analysis of the short-run the number of firms in an industry is fixed. It is assumed that firms are not flexible enough either to enter or to leave a given

APPLYING ECONOMICS

Fish Auctions

An important example of pricing in the very short run is provided by auctions. In most cases the goods put up for bid at an auction must all be sold. Supply is fixed, and price acts only to allocate the available goods among auction participants. When the goods being auctioned are perishable, market period analysis is even more directly relevant, since auctioneers cannot adopt "reservation prices" and hold back goods that do not attain such prices. Instead they must sell for whatever price the market will bear.

Auctions for freshly caught fish are a particularly widespread illustration of this type of transaction. Such auctions are conducted in practically every major fishing city in the world. Although the particular customs of these auctions differ among nations, the procedures are very similar. First, the auctions are conducted quickly. Since fish must be sold to the final users rapidly to remain fresh, there is no time for middlemen to engage in lengthy haggling about prices. Formal, and rather frantic, auction methods have been developed. Second, although a variety of these auction methods are in use, all arrive at equilibrium prices rather accurately. For example, the three most widely used bidding systems (the English ascending bid system, the Dutch descending bid system, and the Japanese simultaneous bid system) all seem to result in about the same prices being reached.

A final similarity among fish (and other) auctions throughout the world is the importance of market participants knowing the total quantity being sold. Since rather small differences in quantity supplied can result in great differences in the final prices agreed upon, market participants must know what the true situation is if they are to avoid serious mistakes. For example, a common practice in Manila and other Far East fish markets is for fishermen to unload only part of their day's catch at first to make it appear that supply will be small in hopes that higher prices will be bid. Of course buyers are generally aware of the possibility of misinformation and may employ elaborate networks of spies to find out the true situation.

To Think About

1. Why do auctions succeed in arriving at equilibrium prices? If price starts well below equilibrium, as in the American bidding system, why does the supply and demand model predict that price must rise to its equilibrium level before bidding stops?
2. Is there really no possibility of supply responses to changing auction prices? Can you think of ways that additional fish might be brought to market on short-term notice if prices proved to be unexpectedly favorable?

---

industry. However, the firms presently in the industry are able to adjust the quantity they are producing in response to changing prices. Because there are a large number of firms producing a homogeneous good, each firm will act as a price taker. The model of short-run supply by a price-taking firm in Chapter 9 is appropriate to use here. That is, each firm's short-run supply curve is simply the positively sloped section of its short-run marginal cost curve above minimum average variable cost. Using this model to record individual firms' supply decisions, we can add up all of these decisions into a single market supply curve.

Construction of a Short-Run Supply Curve

horizontal ←

The quantity of a good that is supplied to the market during some period is the sum of the quantities supplied by each firm. Since each firm considers the

Figure 11.2
Short-Run Market
Supply Curve

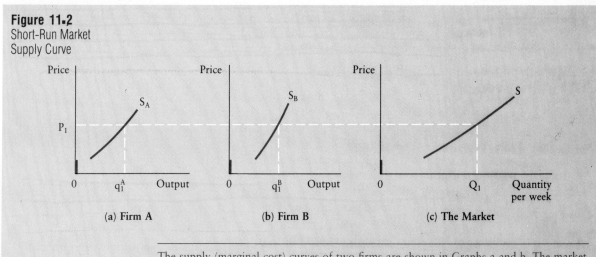

The supply (marginal cost) curves of two firms are shown in Graphs a and b. The market supply curve in Graph c is the horizontal sum of these curves. For example, at P_1, firm A supplies q_1^A, firm B supplies q_1^B, and total market supply is given by $Q_1 = q_1^A + q_1^B$.

market price in deciding how much to produce, the total supplied to the market will also depend on price. This relationship between market price and quantity supplied is called a **short-run supply curve**.

Figure 11.2 illustrates the construction of the curve. For simplicity we assume only two firms, A and B. The short-run supply (that is, marginal cost) curves for firms A and B are shown in Graphs a and b. The market supply curve shown in Graph c is the horizontal sum of these two curves. For example, at a price of P_1, firm A is willing to supply q_1^A, and firm B is willing to supply q_1^B. At this price the total supply in the market is given by Q_1, which is equal to $q_1^A + q_1^B$. The other points on the curve are constructed in an identical way. Because each firm's supply curve slopes upward, the market supply curve will also slope upward. This upward slope reflects the fact that short-run marginal costs increase as firms attempt to increase their outputs. They will be willing to incur these higher marginal costs only at higher market prices.

Short-run supply curve
The relationship between market price and quantity supplied of a good in the short run.

Slope of the Supply Curve

Although the construction in Figure 11.2 uses only two firms, actual market supply curves represent the summation of many firms' supply curves. Again the market supply curve will have a positive slope because of the positive slope in each firm's underlying marginal cost curve. This market supply curve summarizes the short-run diminishing returns experienced by all firms, the prices of the inputs they use, and the profit-maximizing decisions that each firm makes.

[margin note: Reasons for positive slope of supply curve:
① marginal costs increase as output increases
② as output increase scarce input prices rise.]

There is a second reason why the short-run supply curve may have a positive slope. Although each firm takes input prices as given in making its decisions, those prices may not remain constant, as output for the industry as a whole expands. It is possible that increases in industry output will increase the demand for scarce inputs, thereby bidding up the prices of those inputs. For example, expansion of the professional sports leagues in the 1960s had the effect of bidding up players' salaries, and that raised teams' costs. Similarly, major increases in oil well drilling in the late 1970s (as discussed in "Applying Economics: The Demise of OPEC and Drilling for Oil in the United States" in Chapter 9) resulted in substantially increased demand for steel pipe and well testing equipment, whose prices then rose significantly. Marginal costs of drilling also rose accordingly. These types of effects are termed *interaction effects*—they arise when expanding output raises all firms' marginal costs. When these effects are present, the short-run market supply curve may be more steeply sloped than a simple summation of firms' marginal cost curves would suggest. Expansion in output raises firms' marginal costs both because of diminishing marginal productivity and because rising input prices may increase overall costs. The short-run supply curve summarizes both effects and as we show in the next section, using that curve lets us see how these factors interact with market demand to determine price.

Short-Run Price Determination

[margin note: Functions of price:
① how much to produce P = MC
② rations demand => how much to buy.]

We can now combine demand and supply curves to demonstrate how equilibrium prices are established in the short run. Figure 11.3 shows this process. In Graph b, the market demand curve D and the short-run supply curve S intersect at a price of P_1 and a quantity of Q_1. This price-quantity combination represents an equilibrium between the demands of individuals and the supply decisions of firms—there is a precise balancing of the forces of supply and demand. What firms supply at this point is exactly what people want to buy. Equilibrium will tend to persist from one period to the next unless one of the factors underlying the supply and demand curves should change.

Here the equilibrium price P_1 serves two important functions. First, this price acts as a signal to producers about how much should be produced. In order to maximize profits, firms will produce that output level for which marginal costs are equal to P_1. In the aggregate, then, production will be Q_1. A second function of the price is to ration demand. Given the market price of P_1, utility-maximizing individuals will decide how much of their limited incomes to spend on the particular good. At a price of P_1, total quantity demanded will be Q_1, which is precisely the amount that will be produced. This is what economists mean by an equilibrium price-quantity combination. No other P,Q combination represents such a balancing of supply and demand.

The implications of the equilibrium price (P_1) for a typical firm and for a typical person are shown in Graphs a and c, respectively. For the typical firm, the price P_1 will cause an output level of q_1 to be produced. The firm earns a small profit at this particular price because price exceeds short-run average total cost. The initial demand curve d for a typical person is shown in Graph

Figure 11.3
Interactions of Many
Individuals and Firms
Determine Market Price
in the Short Run

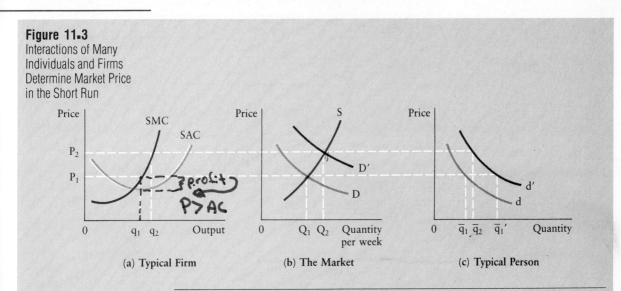

(a) **Typical Firm**   (b) **The Market**   (c) **Typical Person**

Market demand curves and market supply curves are each the horizontal sum of
numerous components. These market curves are shown in Graph b. Once price is
determined in the market, each firm and each individual treat this price as fixed in their
decisions. If the typical person's demand curve shifts to d′, market demand will shift to
D′; in the short run, price will rise to P₂.

c. At a price of P_1, this person demands $\bar{q}_1$. Adding up the quantities that each
person demands at P_1 and the quantities that each firm supplies shows that
the market is in equilibrium. The market supply and demand curves are a
convenient way of doing that addition.

Effect of an Increase in Market Demand

To study the nature of the short-run supply response, we can assume that
many people decide they want to buy more of the good in Figure 11.3. The
typical person's demand curve shifts outward to d′ and the entire market
demand curve will shift. Graph b shows the new market demand curve, D′.
The new equilibrium point is P_2, Q_2: at this point, supply-demand balance is
reestablished. Price has now increased from P_1 to P_2 in response to the demand
shift. The quantity traded in the market has also increased from Q_1 to Q_2.

The rise in price in the short run has served two functions. First, as shown
in our analysis of the very short run, it has acted to ration demand. Whereas
at P_1 a typical individual demanded $\bar{q}_1'$, now at P_2 only $\bar{q}_2$ is demanded.

The rise in price has also acted as a signal to the typical firm to increase
production. In Graph a the typical firm's profit-maximizing output level has
increased from q_1 to q_2 in response to the price rise. That is what economists
mean by a *short-run supply response*: an increase in market price acts as an

Table 11.1
Reasons for a Shift in
Demand or Supply Curve

Demand	Supply
Shifts outward (→) because: • Income increases (↑) • Price of substitute rises (↑) • Price of complement falls (↓) • Preferences for good increase (↑)	Shifts outward (→) because: • Input prices fall (↓) • Technology improves (↑)
Shifts inward (←) because • Income falls (↓) • Price of substitute falls (↓) • Price of complement rises (↑) • Preferences for good diminish (↓)	Shifts inward (←) because • Input prices rise (↑)

inducement to increase production. Firms are willing to increase production (and to incur higher marginal costs) because price has risen. If market price had not been permitted to rise (suppose, for example, government price controls were in effect), firms would not have increased their outputs. At P_1 there would have been an excess (unfilled) demand for the good in question. If market price is allowed to rise, a supply-demand equilibrium can be reestablished so that what firms produce is again equal to what people demand at the prevailing market price. At the new price P_2, the typical firm has also increased its profits. This increased profitability in response to rising prices is important to our discussion of long-run pricing later in this chapter.

Shifts in Supply and Demand Curves

In previous chapters we analyze many of the reasons why either demand or supply curves might shift. Some of these reasons are summarized in Table 11.1. You may wish to review the material in Chapter 5, "Market Demand," and Chapter 8, "Costs," to see why these changes shift the various curves. These types of shifts in demand and supply occur frequently in real-world markets. When either a supply curve or a demand curve does shift, equilibrium price and quantity will change. This section looks briefly at the relative magnitudes of such changes, and we also show how the outcome depends on the shapes of the curves.

Short-Run Supply Elasticity

Some terms used by economists to describe the shapes of demand and supply curves need to be understood before we can discuss these shifts. We have already introduced the terminology for demand curves in Chapter 5. There we introduced the concept of the price elasticity of demand, which shows how the quantity demanded responds to changes in price. When demand is elastic, changes in price have a major impact on quantity demanded. In this case of inelastic demand, however, a price change does not have very much effect on what people choose to buy. Firms' short-run supply responses can be described along the same lines. If an increase in price causes firms to supply significantly more output, we say that the supply curve is "elastic" (at least in the range currently being observed). Alternatively, if the price increase has only a minor effect on the quantity firms choose to produce, supply is said to be inelastic. More formally:

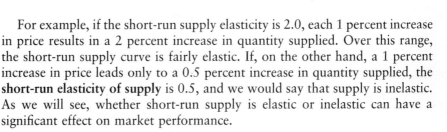

$$\text{Short-run supply elasticity} = \frac{\text{Percent change in quantity supplied in short run}}{\text{Percent change in price}}. \tag{11.1}$$

For example, if the short-run supply elasticity is 2.0, each 1 percent increase in price results in a 2 percent increase in quantity supplied. Over this range, the short-run supply curve is fairly elastic. If, on the other hand, a 1 percent increase in price leads only to a 0.5 percent increase in quantity supplied, the **short-run elasticity of supply** is 0.5, and we would say that supply is inelastic. As we will see, whether short-run supply is elastic or inelastic can have a significant effect on market performance.

Short-run elasticity of supply
The percent change in quantity supplied in the short run in response to a 1 percent change in price.

Shifts in Supply Curves and the Importance of the Shape of the Demand Curve

A shift inward in the short-run supply curve for a good might, for example, result from an increase in the prices of the inputs used by firms to produce the good. Whatever the cause of the shift, its effect on the equilibrium levels of P and Q will depend on the shape of the demand curve for the product. Figure 11.4 illustrates two possible situations. The demand curve in Graph a is relatively price-elastic; that is, a change in price substantially affects the quantity demanded. For this case, a shift in the supply curve from S to S' will cause equilibrium prices to rise only moderately (from P to P'), whereas quantity is reduced sharply (from Q to Q'). Rather than being "passed on" in higher prices, the increase in the firms' input costs is met primarily by a decrease in quantity (a movement down the firms' marginal cost curves) with only a slight increase in price.[1]

This situation is reversed when the market demand curve is inelastic. In Graph b in Figure 11.4, a shift in the supply curve causes equilibrium price to rise substantially but quantity is little changed, because people do not reduce their demands very much if prices rise. Consequently, the shift upward in the

---

[1]Notice, for example, that on the supply curve S', the marginal cost of producing output level Q is considerably higher than the marginal cost of producing Q'.

Figure 11.4
Effect of a Shift in the
Short-Run Supply Curve
Depends on the Shape of
the Demand Curve

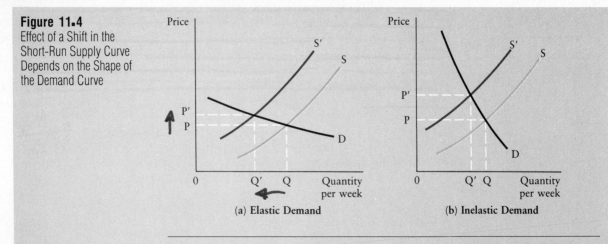

(a) Elastic Demand

(b) Inelastic Demand

In Graph a the shift inward in the supply curve causes price to increase only slightly, whereas quantity contracts sharply. This results from the elastic shape of the demand curve. In Graph b the demand curve is inelastic; price increases substantially with only a slight decrease in quantity.

supply curve is passed on to demanders almost completely in the form of higher prices.

Shifts in Demand Curves and the Importance of the Shape of the Supply Curve

We can also show that a given shift in a market demand curve will have different implications for P and Q depending on the shape of the short-run supply curve. Two illustrations are shown in Figure 11.5. In Graph a the supply curve for the good in question is relatively inelastic. As quantity expands, firms' marginal costs rise rapidly, giving the supply curve its steep slope. In this situation, a shift outward in the market demand curve (caused, for example, by an increase in income) will cause prices to increase substantially. On the other hand, the quantity increases only slightly. The increase in demand (and in Q) has caused firms to move up their steeply sloped marginal cost curves. The accompanying large increase in price serves to ration demand. There is little response in terms of quantity supplied. Such a sharp price response to an increase in demand is illustrated in "Applying Economics: The Russian Wheat Deal and Its Aftermath."

Graph b in Figure 11.5 shows a relatively elastic short-run supply curve. This kind of curve would occur for an industry in which marginal costs do not rise steeply in response to output increases. For this case an increase in demand produces a substantial increase in Q. However, because of the nature

Figure 11.5
Effect of a Shift in the Demand Curve Depends on the Shape of the Short-Run Supply Curve

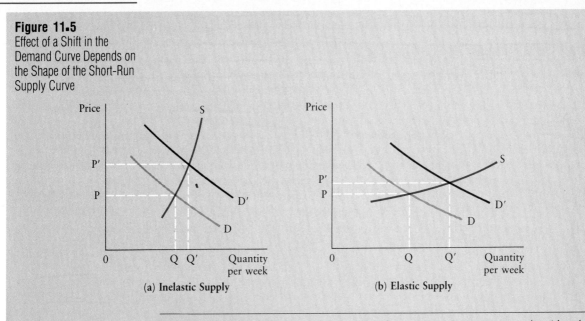

(a) Inelastic Supply

(b) Elastic Supply

In Graph a supply is inelastic; a shift in demand causes price to increase greatly with only a small increase in quantity. In Graph b, on the other hand, supply is elastic; price rises only slightly in response to a demand shift.

of the supply curve, this increase is not met by great cost increases. Consequently, price rises only moderately.

These examples again demonstrate Marshall's observation that demand and supply together determine price and quantity. As we demonstrated in Chapter 1, just as it is impossible to say which blade of a scissors does the cutting, so too is it impossible to attribute price solely to demand or to supply characteristics. Rather, the effect that shifts in either a demand curve or a supply curve will have depends on the shapes of both of the curves. In predicting the effects of shifting supply or demand conditions on market price and quantity in the real world, this simultaneous relationship must be considered.

Numerical Illustration

Supply and demand equilibrium and possible changes in that equilibrium can be illustrated with a simple numerical example. Suppose, as we did in Chapter 9, that the quantity of cassette tapes demanded per week (Q) depends on the price of tapes (P) according to the simple relation

$$\text{Demand: } Q = 10 - P. \qquad [11.2]$$

APPLYING ECONOMICS

The Russian Wheat Deal and Its Aftermath

On July 8, 1972, the Soviet Union announced it would purchase 400 million bushels of wheat from the United States—nearly one-fourth of total annual U.S. wheat production. Although problems with Soviet wheat production were known prior to the announcement (and indeed they generally persist to this day), the size of the proposed sale caught both wheat farmers and middlemen in the wheat market by surprise. Because the short-run supply of wheat is relatively price inelastic, prices rose rapidly. At the end of June, the price of hard winter wheat (which figured predominantly in the sale) was about $1.60 per bushel. By mid-September the price had risen to $2.25 per bushel—more than a 40 percent increase over only slightly more than two months. This dramatic price rise brought forth a variety of charges of profiteering by grain traders and of improprieties by officials who may have known about the sale beforehand. It also resulted in windfall gains for those farmers who had waited to sell their crops, and hard feelings from those farmers who happened to have sold before the announcement.

The Russian wheat deal of 1972 had important consequences for the longer run as well. As a result of the sharp run-up in wheat prices, farmers increased their planting of wheat significantly. Acres harvested rose by nearly 50 percent from 43 million acres in the 1970–1971 growing season to over 65 million acres in the 1974–1975

growing season. This expansion in supply is precisely the kind of response to increasing price that might have been expected in the long run. (It resulted in a gradually declining wheat price over the next several years as the market adjusted toward a new equilibrium.) The 1972–1973 experience also resulted in a long-term wheat purchasing agreement between the United States and the Soviet Union signed in 1975. A stated purpose of the agreement was to regularize grain trade between the two countries and thereby lead to "fewer surprises" in the future. Given the recurrent problems with Soviet harvests and the interconnectedness of the world's grain markets, however, the agreement probably had only limited effectiveness in that regard, since any shortfall in Soviet production continued to exert an effect on world (and U.S.) wheat prices.[2]

To Think About
1. Suppose the Soviets had decided to buy their wheat from Canada or Australia only. Would U.S. prices have been affected as much as they actually were? Is the wheat market a national or a world market?
2. One purpose of the long-term wheat deal with the Soviets was to "regularize" grain trade. Would farmers be better off (with higher revenues) under such a system or under one in which the same total quantity is bought, but at erratic and unexpected intervals?

Suppose also that the short-run supply curve for tapes is given by

$$\text{Supply: } Q = P - 2, \text{ or} \qquad [11.3]$$
$$P = 2 + Q.$$

Figure 11.6 graphs these equations. As before, the demand curve (labeled D in the figure) intersects the vertical axis at $P = 10$. At higher prices no tapes are demanded. The supply curve (labeled S) intersects the vertical axis at $P = 2$. This is the shutdown price for firms in the industry—at a price lower than

---

[2]For a discussion see C. B. Luttrell, "Grain Export Agreements—No Gains, No Losses," *Federal Reserve Bank of St. Louis Review*, August/September 1981, pp. 23–29.

Figure 11.6
Demand and Supply
Curves for Cassette Tapes

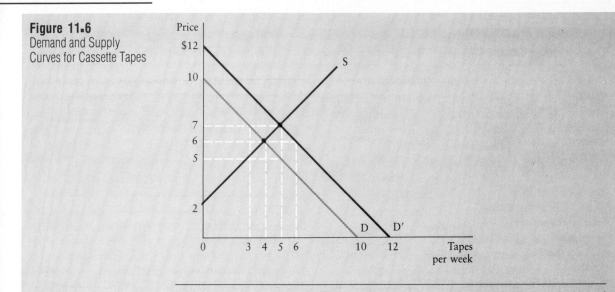

With the curves D and S, equilibrium occurs at a price of $6. At this price people demand four tapes per week, and that is what firms supply. When demand shifts to D', price will rise to $7 to restore equilibrium.

$2 no tapes will be produced. As Figure 11.6 shows, these supply and demand curves intersect at a price of $6 per tape. At that price people demand four tapes per week, and firms are willing to supply four tapes per week. This equilibrium is also illustrated in Table 11.2, which shows the quantity of tapes demanded and supplied at each price. Only when P = 6 do these amounts agree. At a price of $5 per tape, for example, people want to buy five tapes per week, but only three will be supplied: there is an excess demand of two tapes per week. Similarly, at a price of $7 per tape there is an excess supply of two tapes per week.

If the demand curve for tapes were to shift outward, this equilibrium would change. For example, Figure 11.6 also shows the demand curve D', whose equation is given by

$$Q = 12 - P. \qquad [11.4]$$

With this new demand curve, equilibrium price rises to $7 per tape, and quantity also rises to five tapes per week. This new equilibrium is confirmed by the entries in Table 11.2, which show that this is the only price that clears the market given the new demand curve. For example, at the old price of $6 there is now an excess demand for tapes, since the amount people want (Q = 6) exceeds what firms are willing to supply (Q = 4). The rise in price from $6 to $7 restores equilibrium both by prompting people to buy fewer tapes and by encouraging firms to produce more.

Table 11.2
Supply and Demand Equilibrium in the Market for Cassette Tapes

	Supply	Demand	
Price	$Q = P - 2$ Quantity Supplied (Tapes per Week)	Case 1 $Q = 10 - P$ Quantity Demanded (Tapes per Week)	Case 2 $Q = 12 - P$ Quantity Demanded (Tapes per Week)
$10	8	0	2
9	7	1	3
8	6	2	4
7	5	3	5
6	4	4	6
5	3	5	7
4	2	6	8
3	1	7	9
2	0	8	10
1	0	9	11
0	0	10	12

☐ New equilibrium.
☐ Initial equilibrium.

The Long Run

In long-run pricing in perfectly competitive markets, supply responses are considerably more flexible than in the short run for two reasons. First, long-run cost curves reflect the greater input flexibility that firms have in the long run. Second, the long run also allows for firms' entry into and exit from an industry in response to profit opportunities. These actions have important implications for pricing. We begin our analysis of these various effects with a description of the long-run equilibrium for a competitive industry. Then, as we did for the short run, we will show how supply and prices change when conditions change. Later in the chapter we show several illustrations of how the competitive model of long-run supply can be applied.

Equilibrium Conditions

A perfectly competitive market is in equilibrium when no firm has an incentive to change its behavior. Such an equilibrium has two components: firms must be content with their output choices (that is, they must be maximizing profits), and they must be content to stay in (or out of) the industry. We discuss each of these components separately.

Profit Maximization

As before, we assume that firms seek maximum profits. Because each firm is a price taker, profit maximization requires that the firm produce where price

[handwritten note at top: note: monopolies produce where MC < P thus creating inefficiency ⇒ ch. 17 p 521.]

is equal to (long-run) marginal cost. This first equilibrium condition, P = MC, shows both the firm's output choice and its adaptation of inputs to minimize costs in the long run.

Entry

We must also consider a second feature of long-run equilibrium: the possibility of the entry of entirely new firms into the industry, or the exit of existing firms from the industry. The perfectly competitive model assumes that there are no special costs of entering and exiting an industry.[3] Consequently, new firms will be lured into any market in which (economic) profits are positive. Similarly, firms will leave any industry in which profits are negative. The entry of new firms will cause the short-run industry supply curve to shift outward, since there are now more firms producing than there were previously. Such a shift will cause market price (and industry profits) to fall. The process will continue until no firm contemplating entering the industry would be able to earn an economic profit.[4] At that point, entry by new firms will cease, and there will be an equilibrium number of firms in the industry. When the firms in an industry suffer short-run losses, some firms will choose to leave the industry, causing the supply curve to shift to the left. Market price will then rise, restoring profitability to those firms remaining in the industry.

Long-Run Equilibrium

For the purposes of this chapter we assume that all the firms in an industry have identical cost curves; that is, we assume that there are no special resources or technologies controlled by any one firm.[5] Because all firms are identical, the equilibrium long-run position requires every firm to earn exactly zero economic profits. In graphic terms, long-run equilibrium price must settle at the low point of each firm's long-run average total cost curve. Only at this point do the two equilibrium conditions hold: P = MC (which is required for profit maximization) and P = AC (which is the required zero profit).

[handwritten note at left: when price is at low point of AVC: ① P = MC ② P = AC]

These two equilibrium conditions have rather different origins. Profit maximization is a goal of firms. The P = MC rule reflects our assumptions about firms' behavior and is similar to the output decision rule used in the short

---

[3]In Chapter 12 we discuss some barriers to entry that may make this assumption inappropriate in certain situations.

[4]Remember, we are using the economic definition of profits here. These profits represent the return to the owner of a business in excess of that which is strictly necessary to keep him or her in the business.

[5]The important case of firms having different costs is discussed in Chapter 14. In that chapter we see that very low-cost firms can earn positive, long-run profits.

run. The zero-profit condition is not a goal for firms. Firms would obviously prefer to have large profits. The long-run operation of the market, however, forces all firms to accept a level of zero economic profits (P = AC) because of the willingness of firms to enter and to leave an industry. While the firms in a perfectly competitive industry may either earn positive or negative profits in the short run, in the long run only a level of zero profits will prevail.[6]

Long-Run Supply: Constant Cost Case

Constant cost industry
An industry in which the entry or exit of firms has no effect on the cost curves of the firms in the industry.

Before we can discuss long-run pricing in detail, we must make some assumption about how the entry of new firms into an industry affects the costs of inputs. The simplest assumption is that entry has no effect on the costs of those inputs. Under this assumption, no matter how many firms enter or leave an industry, every firm will retain the same set of cost curves with which it started. There are many important cases about which this constant input cost assumption may not be made, which we analyze later. For the moment, however, we wish to examine the equilibrium conditions for a **constant cost industry.**

Market Equilibrium

Figure 11.7 demonstrates long-run equilibrium for a constant cost industry. For the market as a whole, in Graph b, the demand curve is labeled D and the short-run supply curve is labeled S. The short-run equilibrium price is therefore P_1. The typical firm in Graph a will produce output level q_1, since at this level of output price is equal to short-run marginal cost (SMC). In addition, with a market price of P_1, output level q_1 is also a long-run equilibrium position for the firm. The firm is maximizing profits since price is equal to long-run marginal cost (MC). When all possible variations in inputs are considered, q_1 remains the optimal level of output for a profit-maximizing firm. There is a second long-run equilibrium property shown in Graph a in Figure 11.7: Price is equal to long-run average total costs (AC). Consequently, economic profits are zero and there is no incentive for firms either to enter or to leave the industry.

The market shown in Figure 11.7 is in both short-run and long-run equilibrium. Firms are in equilibrium because they are maximizing profits, and the number of firms is stable because economic profits are zero. This equilibrium will tend to persist until either supply or demand conditions change.

---

[6]These equilibrium conditions also point out what seems to be, somewhat imprecisely, an "efficient" aspect of the long-run equilibrium in perfectly competitive markets. The good under investigation will be produced at minimum average cost. We consider the issue of efficiency in more detail in Chapter 17.

Figure 11.7
Long-Run Equilibrium for
a Perfectly Competitive
Industry: Constant
Cost Case

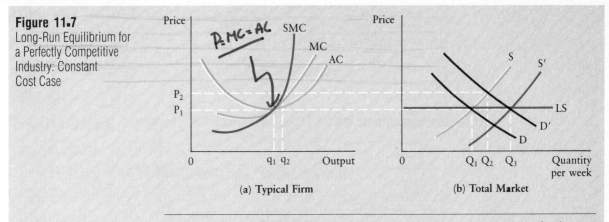

(a) **Typical Firm**   (b) **Total Market**

An increase in demand from D to D′ will cause price to rise from P_1 to P_2 in the short run. This higher price will create profits in the industry and new firms will be drawn into the market. If the entry of these new firms has no effect on the cost curves of the firms in the industry, new firms will continue to enter until price is pushed back down to P_1. At this price economic profits are zero. The long-run supply curve LS will therefore be a horizontal line at P_1. Along LS, output is increased by increasing the number of firms that each produce q_1.

A Shift in Demand

Suppose now that the market demand curve shifts outward to D′. If S is the relevant short-run supply curve for the industry, then in the short run, price will rise to P_2. The typical firm will, in the short run, choose to produce q_2, and will earn profits on this level of output. In the long run, these profits will attract new firms into the market. Because of the constant cost assumption, this entry of new firms will have no effect on the typical firm's cost curves. The additional inputs needed by these new firms can be hired without driving up their prices. New firms will continue to enter the market until price is forced down to the level at which there are again no pure economic profits. The entry of new firms will therefore shift the short-run supply curve to S′ where the equilibrium price (P_1) is re-established. At this new long-run equilibrium, the price quantity combination P_1, Q_3 will prevail in the market. The typical firm will again produce at output level q_1, although now there will be more firms than there were in the initial situation.

Long-Run Supply Curve

By considering many such shifts in demand, we can examine long-run pricing in this industry. Our discussion suggests that no matter how demand shifts, economic forces will come into play that cause price always to return to P_1.

All long-run equilibria will occur along a horizontal line at P_1. Connecting these equilibrium points gives the long-run supply response of the industry. This long-run supply curve is labeled LS in Figure 11.7. For a constant cost industry of identical firms, the long-run supply curve is a horizontal line at the low point of the firms' long-run average total cost curves.

An Illustration Using the Model: Tax Incidence Theory

This model of long-run pricing can be used to examine the important question of who actually pays various taxes. Consider a *specific tax* of a fixed amount per unit on a firm's production. This is a cost per unit of output that appears to be paid by the firm to the government. If a per-unit tax of t dollars is levied, the average and marginal cost curves of the firm are shifted upward by t. There is, however, another more convenient way of analyzing this tax here. The demand curve relevant to an industry's behavior is in fact an aftertax demand curve. A specific tax merely shifts the demand curve that is relevant to the firms in the industry downward by the amount t. Any quantity that is produced will sell at some market price P, but the aftertax revenue received by firms in the industry will be $P - t$. The aftertax demand curve is labeled D′ in Figure 11.8. This is the demand curve on which industry output decisions will be based, although the market price of any output produced will still be determined by the original market demand curve D.

The initial equilibrium in the market is given by the intersection of the long-run supply curve (LS) and the market demand curve. At this point, market price is P_1, the quantity exchanged in the market is Q_1, and the typical firm will produce output level q_1. With the imposition of the tax, the aftertax demand curve becomes D′. In the short run, industry output will be determined by the intersection of the curve D′ with the industry short-run supply curve S. This intersection occurs at output level Q_2 and price P_2. The aftertax price received by the firm is now P_2, and the typical firm (assuming P_2 exceeds average variable cost) will produce output level q_2. In the market, total output Q_2 will sell for P_3. Notice that $P_3 - P_2 = t$. In the short run, then, the tax is borne partially by consumers of the good (market price has risen from P_1 to P_3) and partially by firms in the industry who are operating at a short-term loss.

In the long run, firms will not continue to operate at a loss. Some firms will leave the industry bemoaning the role of an oppressive government in bringing about their downfall. The industry short-run supply curve will shift leftward as fewer firms remain in the market. A new long-run equilibrium will be established at Q_3 where the after-tax price received by firms still in the industry enables them to earn exactly zero in economic profits. Those firms left in the industry will return to producing output level q_1. The price paid by individuals in the market will now be P_4. In the long run the entire amount of the tax has been shifted into increased prices. Even though the firm ostensibly "pays" the tax, in fact the burden is borne by consumers.

Figure 11.8
Effect of the Imposition of a Specific Tax on a Perfectly Competitive, Constant Cost Industry

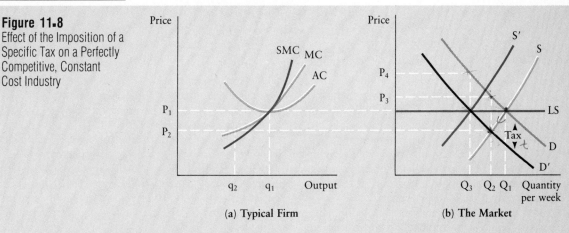

(a) Typical Firm   (b) The Market

A specific commodity tax of amount t lowers the aftertax demand curve to D′. With this "new" demand curve Q_2 will be produced in the short run at an aftertax price of P_2. The market price will be P_3. In the long run, firms will leave the industry, and the aftertax price will return to P_1. The entire amount of the tax is shifted onto consumers in the form of a higher market price (P_4).

Tax incidence theory
The study of the final burden of a tax after considering all market reactions to it.

This analysis is perhaps the simplest example of **tax incidence theory**. It clearly shows that in order to determine who ultimately pays a tax, it is necessary to investigate long-run market responses. It would be incorrect to assume that whoever pays the tax to the government always bears the burden of the tax. A careful analysis of the supply and demand influences is required. "Applying Economics: Cigarette Taxes" shows this very clearly for the case of cigarette taxes.

Shape of the Long-Run Supply Curve

In the previous section we point out that, contrary to the short-run case, long-run analysis has very little to do with the shape of the marginal cost curve. Rather, the zero-profit condition centers attention on the low point of the long-run average cost curve as the factor most relevant to long-run price determination. In the constant cost case the position of this low point does not change as new firms enter or leave the industry. Consequently, only one price can prevail in the long run regardless of how demand shifts. The long-run supply curve is horizontal at this price. Once the constant cost assumption is abandoned, this need not be the case. If the entry of new firms causes average costs to rise, the long-run supply curve will have an upward slope. On the other hand, if entry causes average costs to decline it is even possible for the long-run supply curve to be negatively sloped. We now discuss these possibilities.

APPLYING ECONOMICS

Cigarette Taxes

Most states impose excise taxes on cigarette sales, usually these are specific taxes of a certain amount per pack. Our discussion of specific taxes suggests that virtually all these taxes will be passed on to consumers in the form of higher cigarette prices. The long-run supply curve for cigarettes in any state is nearly horizontal since increases in sales in a single state will not increase industry costs significantly. Demand for cigarettes, on the other hand, is relatively price inelastic. Higher prices can be passed on to consumers without large changes in quantity demanded. Figure 11.8 probably represents the situation for state cigarette taxes fairly accurately.

Several studies of cigarette pricing have confirmed this theoretical prediction. For example, in 1981 Sumner and Ward found that about 93 percent of any change in a state's tax rate was quickly reflected in cigarette prices.[7] One reason suggested by the authors for the fraction not being exactly 100 percent (as predicted by our theory) is that additional consumers may choose to

shop across state borders for their cigarettes when state tax rates change (many Massachusetts residents buy their cigarettes in New Hampshire, for example).

Another possible explanation is that under a specific tax, suppliers have an incentive to substitute quality for quantity in their activities, since only quantity is taxed. In the cigarette example, sellers may provide better service or more attractive displays. In the process, they will raise their costs and their prices and sell fewer packs of cigarettes. This may be the profit-maximizing response to the tax.[8]

To Think About
1. Why do governments tax cigarettes so highly? Is it to discourage smoking, or because the inelastic demand for cigarettes makes the tax a good revenue raiser?
2. Could a local government impose a stiff tax on cigarettes if other local governments did not? Might a modest tax raise more revenues than a large one?

[handwritten margin notes:]
reasons for
① competition of scarce inputs
② external costs on existing firms
③ strains on gov't services.

The Increasing Cost Industry

There are several reasons why the entry of new firms may cause the average cost of all firms to rise. New firms may compete for scarce inputs, thus driving up their prices. New firms may impose external costs on existing firms (and on themselves) in the form of air or water pollution. And new firms may place strains on governmental services (police forces, sewage treatment plants, and so forth), and these may show up as increased costs for all firms.

Figure 11.9 demonstrates market equilibrium in an **increasing cost industry**. The initial equilibrium price is P_1. At this price the typical firm in Graph a produces q_1 and total industry output, shown in Graph c, is Q_1. Suppose that the demand curve for the industry shifts outward to D'. In the short run, price will rise to P_2, which is where D' and the industry's short-run supply curve

Increasing cost industry
An industry in which the entry of firms increases the costs of the firms in the industry.

---

[7]M. T. Summer and R. Ward, "Tax Changes and Cigarette Prices," *Journal of Political Economy*, December 1981, pp. 1261–1265.

[8]For an example of how this differs from that of a tax on the *value* of sales, see Yoram Barzel, "An Alternative Approach to the Analysis of Taxation," *Journal of Political Economy*, December 1976, pp. 1177–1197.

Figure 11.9
An Increasing Cost Industry has a Positively Sloped Long-Run Supply Curve

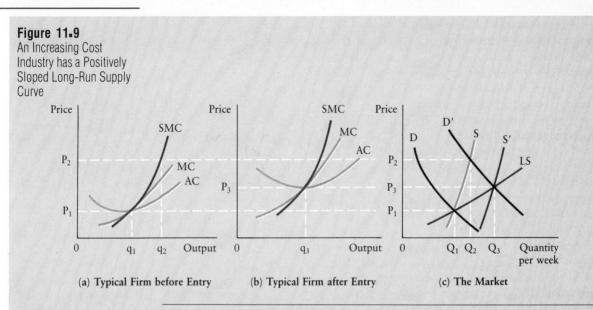

(a) **Typical Firm before Entry**   (b) **Typical Firm after Entry**   (c) **The Market**

Initially the market is in equilibrium at P_1, Q_1. An increase in demand (to D′) causes price to rise to P_2 in the short run, and the typical firm produces q_2 at a profit. This profit attracts new firms into the industry. The entry of these new firms causes costs to rise to the levels shown in Graph b. With this new set of curves, equilibrium is re-established in the market at P_3, Q_3. By considering many possible demand shifts and connecting all the resulting equilibrium points, the long-run supply curve LS is traced out.

(S) intersect. At this price, the typical firm will produce q_2 and will earn a substantial profit. This profit attracts new entrants into the market and shifts the short-run supply curve outward.

Suppose that the entry of new firms causes the cost curves of all firms to rise. The new firms may compete for scarce inputs and thereby drive the prices of these inputs up. A typical firm's new (higher) set of cost curves is shown in Graph b of Figure 11.9. The new long-run equilibrium price for the industry is P_3 (here P = MC = AC), and at this price Q_3 is demanded. We now have two points (P_1, Q_1, and P_3, Q_3) on the long-run supply curve.[9] All other points on the curve can be found in an analogous way by considering all possible shifts in the demand curve. These shifts would trace out the long-run supply curve LS. Here LS has a positive slope because of the increasing cost nature of the industry. The LS curve is somewhat flatter than the short-run supply curves, which indicates the greater flexibility in supply response that is possible in the long run.

---

[9]Figure 11.9 also shows the short-run supply curve associated with the point P_3,Q_3. This supply curve has shifted to the right because there are more firms producing now than initially.

Figure 11.10
Price Controls Inhibit
Supply Responses

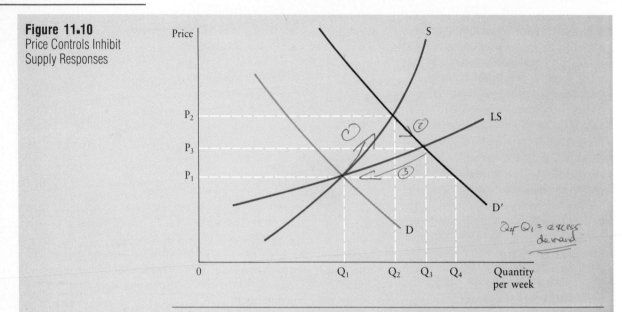

This market is initially in equilibrium at P_1, Q_1. A shift in demand to D' would cause price to rise to P_2 in the short run and to P_3 in the long run. Quantity would increase to Q_2 and Q_3, respectively. Price controls that held price at P_1 would inhibit this process since firms would continue to supply Q_1. At P_1 there is a long-run shortage given by $Q_4 - Q_1$.

Price Controls and Shortages

In our analysis of competitive pricing in the long run, price increases play the crucial role of providing firms with the incentive to increase production in response to increases in demand. Governmental or other controls over prices may short-circuit this process and deter any long-run supply responses. That possibility is illustrated in Figure 11.10. Initially the market is in equilibrium at the point P_1, Q_1 where the market demand curve D and the long-run supply curve LS intersect. Consider the reaction to a shift in the market demand curve to D'. In the absence of price controls, price would rise to P_2 in the short run, and firms would increase output to Q_2. Supply would increase further to Q_3 in the long run as new firms enter the industry in response to profit possibilities. Imposition of price controls prevents both of these supply responses. If price is not allowed to rise above P_1, firms will continue to produce Q_1 even though demand has increased. At a price of P_1 individuals demand Q_4 (with the demand curve D'), but only Q_1 is produced. There is now a shortage in the market, given by the distance $Q_4 - Q_1$. That shortage will persist so long as price controls retard supply response. The shortage is exacerbated by the fact that more is demanded at the artificially low controlled price (Q_4) than would be demanded at the long-run market clearing price (Q_3).

Rent Controls

During World War II, many American cities adopted controls on rent in order to stop rising housing prices that were occurring as a result of increased demand. Many cities (notably New York) and several European countries still maintain such controls. These are usually rationalized on the grounds that landlords (who are assumed to be rich) should not be allowed to exploit tenants (who are assumed to be poor). Without examining the facts behind such asserted principles of equity, the economic implications of controls are clearly predicted by the competitive model: shortages will result.

Table 11.3 provides some evidence on shortages in the city of Stockholm during the 1950s. The data report the average period in months that families had to wait for an apartment. The data show that this period lengthened greatly during the 1950s as postwar increases in income sharply increased the demand for housing and rent controls retarded long-run supply responses. Existing tenants may have benefited from lower rents, but substantial costs were imposed on families who had to wait more than three years to find a place of their own in which to live.

The effects of rent controls may show up in many other ways. In addition to the shortfall in the quantity of housing, the quality of housing may also deteriorate as landlords find it unprofitable to make repairs. For example, one study found that repair expenditures in 1967 on rent-controlled apartments in New York City averaged only about one-half of the expenditures on similar apartments that were not subject to rent controls.[10] Elective repairs (that is, those in excess of minimal requirements for health and safety) were particularly unlikely to be made in the rent-controlled apartments. Indeed, the effects of rent control on the condition of some New York City apartments have caused some economists to compare their condition to the devastation caused by bombing in World War II. Finally, tenants of rent-controlled apartments may sometimes take advantage of their possession of a good for which there is excess demand. It is a common practice in some cities, for example, to require that new tenants pay key money to existing tenants for the right to take over their leases. Rent-controlled apartments are also passed down among family members as if they were valuable heirlooms.

To Think About
1. Why do communities vote for rent controls if their effects are so negative? Who gains from the controls? Do losers from rent control have as much political clout as the gainers?
2. Some cities with rent control also provide for "vacancy decontrol"—that is, rents can be raised on vacated apartments. How might existing tenants respond to such provisions? What would you expect to happen to the number of vacancies?

Table 11.3
Waiting Time in Months for an Apartment in Stockholm

Year	Wait	Year	Wait
1950	9	1955	23
1951	15	1956	30
1952	21	1957	35
1953	24	1958	40
1954	26		

Source: S. Rydenfelt, "Rent Control Thirty Years On" in *Verdict on Rent Control* (London: Institute for Economic Affairs, 1972), p. 65.

The model depicted in Figure 11.10 makes two predictions about the impact of price controls: (1) they will cause shortages; and (2) they will result in somewhat lower prices for those who are able to buy the good (for the increasing cost case illustrated in the figure). "Applying Economics: Rent Con-

---

[10]George Sternlieb, *The Urban Housing Dilemma* (New York: Housing and Development Administration, 1972), p. 202.

trols" looks at the important case of rent control, where these predictions have been proved accurate.

Long-Run Supply Elasticity

As we have just shown, the long-run supply curve for an industry is constructed by considering all possible shifts in the demand curve for the product. In order to predict the effects that such increases in demand will have on market price, it is therefore important to know something about the shape of the supply curve. A convenient measure for summarizing the shape of long-run supply curves is the **long-run elasticity of supply**. This concept records how proportional changes in price affect the quantity supplied, once all long-run adjustments have taken place. More formally:

Long-run elasticity of supply
The percent change in quantity supplied in the long run in response to a 1 percent change in price.

$$\text{Long-run elasticity of supply} = \frac{\text{Percent change in quantity supplied in long run}}{\text{Percent change in price}}. \quad [11.5]$$

An elasticity of 10, for example, would indicate that a 1 percent increase in price would result in a 10 percent increase in the long-run quantity supplied. We would say that long-run supply is very price elastic: the long-run supply curve would be nearly horizontal. A principal implication of such a high price elasticity is that long-run equilibrium prices would not increase very much in response to outward shifts in the market demand curve.

A small supply elasticity would have a quite different implication. If the elasticity were only 0.1, for example, a 1 percent increase in price would increase quantity supplied by only 0.1 percent. In other words, the supply curve would be nearly vertical, and shifts outward in demand would result in rapidly rising prices without significant increases in quantity. "Applying Economics: Long-Run Supply Elasticities" describes some evidence about the supply situation in various industries.

The Decreasing Cost Industry

Not all industries must exhibit constant or increasing costs. In some cases entry may reduce costs. The entry of new firms may provide a larger pool of trained labor to draw from than was previously available, which would reduce the costs of hiring new workers. The entry of new firms may also provide a "critical mass" of industrialization that permits the development of more efficient transportation, communications, and financial networks. Whatever the exact nature of the cost reductions, the final result is illustrated in the three panels of Figure 11.11. The initial market equilibrium is shown by the price quantity combination P_1, Q_1 in Graph c. At this price the typical firm in Graph a produces q_1 and earns exactly zero in economic profits. Now suppose market demand shifts outward to D'. In the short run, price will increase to P_2, and

Long-Run Supply Elasticities

Table 11.4 reports a number of long-run supply elasticity estimates that have been gathered from a variety of sources. Many of these concern natural resources, since economists have from the time of Thomas Malthus been interested in the effects of increasing demand for resources on their price. Other estimates are for agricultural crops and for housing. The implications of some of these numbers are discussed here.

Agricultural Production

The estimated elasticities for agricultural products are "acreage elasticities." They reflect how acres planted in a particular crop respond to that crop's price. Assuming a constant yield per acre, we can translate them directly

Table 11.4
Selected Estimates of Long-Run Supply Elasticities

Industry	Elasticity
Agricultural acreage:	
Cotton	0.67
Wheat	0.93
Corn	0.18
Aluminum	Nearly infinite
Chromium	0–3
Coal (eastern reserves)	15–30
Natural gas (U.S. reserves)	0.20
Oil (U.S. reserves)	0.76
Urban housing:	
Density	5.3
Quality	3.8

Sources: Agricultural acreage: M. Nerlove, "Estimates of the Elasticities of Supply of Selected Agricultural Commodities," *Journal of Farm Economics,* May 1956, pp. 496–509; Aluminum and chromium: estimated from *Critical Materials Commodity Action Analysis* (Washington, D.C.: U.S. Department of the Interior, 1975); Coal: estimated from M. B. Zimmerman, "The Supply of Coal in the Long Run: The Case of Eastern Deep Coal" (Cambridge, Mass.: MIT Energy Laboratory Report No. MITEL 75-021, September 1975); Natural gas: based on estimate for oil (see text). See also J. D. Khazzoom, "The FPC Staff's Econometric Model of Natural Gas Supply in the United States," *The Bell Journal of Economics and Management Science,* Spring 1971; Oil: E. W. Erickson, S. W. Millsaps, and R. M. Spann, "Oil Supply and Tax Incentives," *Brookings Papers on Economic Activity,* 1974, pp. 449–478; Urban housing: B. A. Smith, "The Supply of Urban Housing," *Journal of Political Economy,* August 1976, pp. 389–405.

into the supply-elasticity concept. All of the reported elasticities are relatively low (less than 1.0). But all are positive, indicating that increases in prices do lead to increases in output. Of course, increases in agricultural output in recent years have come about mainly from improved technology. The data show that higher prices also lead to more land being planted.

Natural Resources

Two different types of supply elasticity are reported for natural resources in Table 11.4. For aluminum and chromium the data refer to the relationship between annual production and market price. They show that the long-run supply of aluminum is nearly infinitely elastic at current market prices. This results from the fact that alumina deposits are easy to obtain using current technology. The supply elasticity for chromium is considerably lower—primarily because it would require a large price increase to make most existing deposits economically attractive. For coal, natural gas, and oil, supply elasticities refer to the responsiveness of available reserves to price. The data show that coal reserves are far more price responsive than are oil and natural gas reserves. That result derives primarily from geology: greater reserves of coal are easily within the reach of current mining methods than is the case for oil.

Housing

The final estimates in Table 11.4 refer to two aspects of the supply of urban housing. They show that "more housing" can be produced in two ways: by increasing residential density while holding quality constant; and by increasing quality while holding density constant. Both of these output measures seem to be reasonably responsive to price. That is, increases in the demand for housing will not result in sharply increased costs and prices in the long run.

To Think About

1. What does it mean to say some natural resources are "scarcer" than others? How is the notion of supply elasticity related to the more commonsense notion of scarcity?
2. The coal and oil supply elasticities in this example refer to finding reserves. How is this activity related to firms' decisions on how much coal or oil to produce from these reserves?

Figure 11.11
A Decreasing Cost Industry
Has a Negatively Sloped
Long-Run Supply Curve

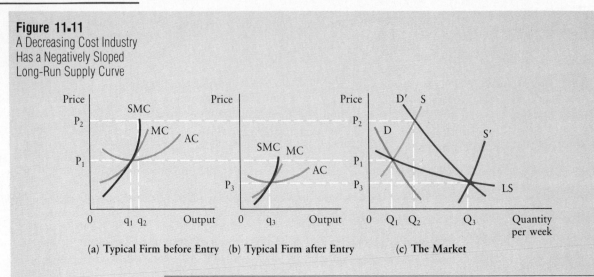

(a) **Typical Firm before Entry**   (b) **Typical Firm after Entry**   (c) **The Market**

Initially the market is in equilibrium at P_1, Q_1. An increase in demand to D' causes price to rise to P_2 in the short run, and the typical firm produces q_2 at a profit. This profit attracts new firms to the industry. If the entry of these new firms cause costs to fall, a set of new cost curves might look like those in Graph b. With this new set of curves, market equilibrium is re-established at P_3, Q_3. By connecting such points of equilibrium, a negatively sloped long-run supply curve LS is traced out.

Decreasing cost industry
An industry in which
the entry of firms de-
creases the costs of the
firms in the industry.

the typical firm will produce q_2. At this price level, positive profits are earned. These profits cause new firms to enter the market. If this entry causes costs to decline, a new set of cost curves for the typical firm might resemble those in Graph b. Now the new equilibrium price is P_3. At this price, Q_3 is demanded. By considering all possible shifts in demand, the long-run supply curve LS can be traced out. For this **decreasing cost industry** the long-run supply curve has a negative slope.

Infant Industry Case for Tariff Protection

Industries in underdeveloped countries frequently exhibit high production costs. They must absorb the expense of training workers, contend with a poor internal monetary system, and make do with poorly developed transportation facilities and inefficient public utilities. Faced with these costs, such industries frequently cannot compete at prevailing world prices. For example, the cost curves for the firms in an underdeveloped economy might resemble those in Graph a in Figure 11.12. Since the minimum point on the AC curve (P_1) exceeds the world price (P_w), a policy of free trade will cause the good in question to be imported, and a domestic industry will not develop.

   In an effort to protect their industries, many underdeveloped countries adopt tariffs that raise the price for imports above P_1. Given the shield of the tariff,

Figure 11.12
Infant Industry Argument
for Tariff Protection

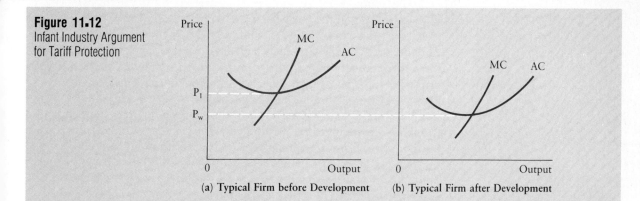

(a) Typical Firm before Development (b) Typical Firm after Development

The firms in an underdeveloped country may have high costs, as shown in Graph a. The firms cannot compete at world prices (P_w). A tariff that raises price above P_1 will permit the firms to sell in the domestic market, and their growth may bring about the development of a more efficient economic network. That development may lower firms' costs so that they may now compete at the world price without tariff protection.

the domestic industry can now sell in its home market. If this were the end of the story, many economists would object to the imposition of the tariff on the grounds that residents of the country are being forced to pay more for the good than would be necessary in a free trade situation. However, it is possible that temporarily protecting the infant industry will permit the development within the country of a better-trained labor force and the construction of more efficient transportation, communication, and utility facilities. If that happens (as it did in the early history of the United States when textile products were protected), cost curves in the industry may be lowered so that firms may eventually compete in world markets. Such a lowering of costs is shown in Graph b in Figure 11.12. Once costs have been reduced, the tariff can be removed, having served its purpose of nurturing the domestic industry. Of course, if costs never decline, the tariff will only have protected an inefficient domestic industry, so a country should be careful in choosing such a policy.[11]

Summary

The model of pricing in perfectly competitive markets that we present in this chapter is probably the most widely used economic model. Even when markets do not strictly obey all of the assumptions of perfect competition, it is still frequently possible to use that model as a reasonable approximation of how such markets work. Some of the basic features of the perfectly competitive model that are highlighted in this chapter are:

- The short-run supply curve in a perfectly competitive market represents the horizontal sum of the short-run supply curves for many price-taking firms. The upward slope of the short-run supply curve reflects these firms' increasing short-run marginal costs.
- Equilibrium prices are determined in the short run by the interaction of the short-run supply curve with the market demand curve. At the equilibrium price, firms are willing to produce precisely the amount of output that people want to buy.
- Shifts in either the demand curve or the supply curve will change the equilibrium price. The extent of such a change depends on the particular shape of the two curves.
- Economic profits will attract entrants into a perfectly competitive market in the long run. This entry will continue until economic profits are reduced to zero. At that point, the market price will equal long-run average cost, and each firm will be operating at the low point of its long-run average cost curve.
- Entry of new firms may have an effect on the cost of firms' inputs. In the constant cost case, however, input costs are not affected, so the long-run supply curve is horizontal. If entry raises input costs, the long-run supply curve is upward sloping. If entry reduces such costs, the long-run supply curve is downward sloping.

Problems

11.1 Suppose the daily demand curve for flounder at Cape May is given by

$$Q_D = 1,600 - 600P$$

where Q_D is demand in pounds per day and P is price per pound.

a. If fishing boats land 1,000 pounds one day, what will the price be?
b. If the catch were to fall to 400 pounds, what would the price be?
c. Suppose the demand for flounder shifts outward to

$$Q'_D = 2,200 - 600P.$$

How would your answers to parts a and b change?
d. Graph your results.

11.2 Suppose, as in Problem 11.1, the demand for flounder is given by

$$Q'_D = 1,600 - 600P,$$

but now assume that Cape May fishermen can, at some cost, choose to sell their catch elsewhere. Specifically, assume that the amount they will sell in Cape May is given by

$$Q_S = -1,000 + 2,000P \text{ for } Q_S \geq 0$$

where Q_S is the quantity supplied in pounds and P is the price per pound.

a. At least what will the price of flounder have to be if any is to be supplied to the Cape May market?
b. Given the demand curve for flounder, what will the equilibrium price be?
c. Suppose now, as in Problem 11.1, demand shifts to

$$Q'_D = 2,200 - 600P.$$

What will be the new equilibrium price?
d. Explain intuitively why price will rise by less in part c than it did in Problem 11.1.
e. Graph your results.

11.3 A perfectly competitive market has 1,000 firms. In the very short run each of the firms has a fixed supply of 100 units. The market demand is given by

$$Q = 160,000 - 10,000P.$$

a. Calculate the equilibrium price in the very short run.
b. Calculate the demand schedule facing any one firm in the industry. Do this by calculating what the equilibrium price would be if one of the sellers decided to sell nothing or if one seller decided to sell 200 units. What do you conclude about the effect of any one firm on market price?

11.4 Assuming the same conditions as in Problem 11.3, suppose now that in the short run each firm has a supply curve that shows the quantity the firm will supply (q_i) as a function of market price. The specific form of this supply curve is given by

$$q_i = -200 + 50P.$$

Using this short-run supply response, supply new solutions to parts a and b in Problem 11.3. Why do you get different solutions in this case?

11.5 Widgets, Inc. is a small firm producing widgets. The widget industry is perfectly competitive; Widgets, Inc. is a price taker. The short-run total cost curve for Widgets, Inc. has the form:

$$STC = \tfrac{1}{3}q^3 + 10q^2 + 100q + 48$$

and the short-run marginal cost curve is given by:

$$SMC = q^2 + 20q + 100.$$

a. Calculate the firm's short-run supply curve with q (the number of widgets produced per day) as a function of market price (P).
b. How many widgets will the firm produce if the market price is P = 121? P = 169? P = 256? (Assume variable costs are covered.)
c. How much profit will Widgets, Inc. make when P = 121? P = 169? P = 256?

11.6 Suppose there are one hundred identical firms in a perfectly competitive notecard industry. Each firm has a short-run total cost curve of the form:

$$STC = \tfrac{1}{300}q^3 + 0.2q^2 + 4q + 10,$$

and marginal cost is given by

$$SMC = .01q^2 + .4q + 4.$$

a. Calculate the firm's short-run supply curve with q (the number of crates of notecards) as a function of market price (P).
b. On the assumption that there are no interaction effects between costs of the firms in the industry, calculate the industry supply curve.
c. Suppose market demand is given by Q = −200P + 8,000. What will be the short-run equilibrium price-quantity combination?
d. Suppose everyone starts writing more research papers, and the new market demand is given by Q = −200P + 10,000. What is the new short-run price-quantity equilibrium? How much profit does each firm make?

*11.7 Suppose there are 1,000 identical firms producing diamonds and that the total cost curve for each firm is given by:

$$C = q^2 + wq$$

and marginal cost is given by:

$$MC = 2q + w$$

(where q is the firm's output level and w is the wage rate of diamond cutters).

a. If w = 10, what will be the firm's (short-run) supply curve? What is the industry's supply curve? How many diamonds will be produced at a price of 20 each? How many more diamonds would be produced at a price of 21?

b. Suppose that the wages of diamond cutters depend on the total quantity of diamonds produced and the form of this relationship is given by

$$w = .002Q$$

(where Q represents total industry output, which is 1,000 times the output of the typical firm). In this situation show that the firm's marginal cost (and short-run supply) curve depends on Q. What is the industry supply curve? How much will be produced at a price of 20? How much more will be produced at a price of 21? What do you conclude about the shape of the short-run supply curve?

11.8 Wheat is produced under perfectly competitive conditions. Individual wheat farmers have U-shaped, long-run average cost curves that reach a minimum average cost of $3 per bushel when 1,000 bushels are produced.

a. If the market demand curve for wheat is given by

$$Q_D = 2,600,000 - 200,000P$$

where Q_D is the number of bushels demanded per year and P is the price per bushel, in long-run equilibrium what will be the price of wheat? How much total wheat will be demanded? How many wheat farms will there be?

b. Suppose demand shifts outward to

$$Q_D = 3,200,000 - 200,000P.$$

If farmers cannot adjust their output in the short run, (that is, suppose the SMC curve is vertical), what will market price be with this new demand curve? What will the profits of the typical farm be?

c. Given the new demand curve described in part b, what will be the new long-run equilibrium? (That is, calculate market price, quantity of wheat produced, and the new equilibrium number of farms in this new situation.)

d. Graph your results.

*11.9 Gasoline is sold through local gas stations under perfectly competitive conditions. All gas station owners face the same long-run average cost curve given by:

$$AC = .01q - 1 + 100/q$$

and the same long-run marginal cost curve given by:

$$MC = .02q - 1$$

where q is the number of gallons sold per day.

a. Assuming the market is in long-run equilibrium, how much gas will each individual owner sell per day? What is the long-run average cost and marginal cost at this output level?

b. The market demand for gasoline is given by:

$$Q_D = 2,500,000 - 500,000P$$

where Q_D is the number of gallons demanded per day and P is the price per gallon. Given your answer to part a, what will be the price of gasoline in long-run equilibrium? How much gasoline will be demanded and how many gas stations will there be?

c. Suppose that because of the development of solar powered cars, the market demand for gasoline shifts inward to

$$Q_D = 2,000,000 - 1,000,000P.$$

In long-run equilibrium, what will be the price of gasoline, how much total gasoline will be demanded, and how many gas stations will there be?

d. Graph your results.

11.10 A specific tax imposed on a competitive, decreasing-cost industry will, in the long run, raise market price by more than the amount of the tax. Show why this is so and explain your result intuitively.

*11.11 A perfectly competitive painted necktie industry has a large number of potential entrants. Each firm has an identical cost structure such that long-run average cost is minimized at an output of 20 units ($q_i = 20$). The minimum average cost is $10 per unit. Total market demand is given by:

$$Q = 1,500 - 50P.$$

a. What is the industry's long-run supply schedule?

b. What is the long-run equilibrium price (P^*)? The total industry output (Q^*)? The output of each firm (q_i^*)? The number of firms? The profits of each firm?

c. The short-run total cost curve associated with each firm's long-run equilibrium output is given by:

$$C = .5q^2 - 10q + 200$$

where MC = q − 10. Calculate the short-run average and marginal cost curves. At what necktie output level does short-run average cost reach a minimum?

d. Calculate the short-run supply curve for each firm and the industry short-run supply curve.

e. Suppose now painted neckties become more fashionable and the market demand function shifts upward to Q = 2,000 − 50P. Using this new demand curve, answer part b for the very short run when firms cannot change their outputs.

f. In the short run, use the industry short-run supply curve to recalculate the answers to part b.

g. What is the new long-run equilibrium for the industry?

*11.12 Suppose the demand for stilts is given by:

$$Q = 1,500 - 50P$$

and that long-run total operating costs of each stilt-making firm in a competitive industry are given by

$$TC = .5q^2 - 10q$$

where MC = q − 10.

Entrepreneurial talent for stilt making is scarce. The supply curve for entrepreneurs is given by

$$Q_s = .25w$$

where w is the annual wage paid.

Suppose also that each stilt firm requires one (and only one) entrepreneur (the quantity of entrepreneurs hired is equal to the number of firms). Long-run total cost for each firm are given by

$$C = .5q^2 - 10q + w.$$

a. What is the long-run equilibrium quantity of stilts produced? How many stilts are produced by each firm? What is the long-run equilibrium price of stilts? How many firms will there be and how many entrepreneurs will be hired? What is their wage?

b. Suppose the demand for stilts shifts outward to

$$Q = 2,428 - 50P.$$

Answer the questions posed in part a.

c. Sketch your results. Show the approximate shape of the long-run supply curve. Why does the curve have this shape?

MARKET ADJUSTMENTS AND TRANSACTION COSTS

In Chapter 11 we discuss a number of examples of what is called *comparative statics analysis*. The conditions of supply-demand equilibrium for a particular situation are illustrated, and then we ask what new equilibrium would emerge as a result of changed conditions. There is always the implicit assumption that price and quantity would move promptly to their new short-run equilibrium levels whenever a movement from one equilibrium to another was necessary.[1] How is it that suppliers and demanders are able to settle on a new equilibrium price? The only information available to them must come from the market, and no trading is permitted except at equilibrium prices. It is therefore hard to envision exactly how a new equilibrium is established. This appendix discusses how economists have attempted to model the way markets adjust to changing circumstances and how various transactions costs may slow that adjustment process.

Adjustment Processes: Basic Concepts

The problem we investigate here can be stated most precisely in a mathematical way. Consider a demand function in which quantity depends on price, $D(P)$, and a short-run supply function in which quantity also depends on price, $S(P)$. An equilibrium price, P^*, is one for which:

$$D(P^*) = S(P^*). \qquad [11A.1]$$

That is, at P^* the quantity demanded is equal to the quantity supplied.

Suppose that the price starts at some arbitrary price P_0 (perhaps this was an equilibrium before conditions changed, but that is not a necessary condition of the problem). Are there economic forces that cause the market price to move from P_0 to P^*? Related to this basic question are several others, such as: How long will it take for price to get to P^*? Will prices "midway" between P_0 and P^* be observed in the market? What meaning are we to assign to any nonequilibrium prices that do occur? Only the initial question is answered in any detail; the others are discussed briefly at the end of this appendix.

---

[1]This appendix discusses only the establishment of short-run equilibrium prices. Since the working of markets in the long run is a succession of short-run equilibria, the analysis to be presented is also relevant to that case.

The Impartial Auctioneer

To explain the movement of price to its equilibrium level, economists have relied on the fictitious notion of an *impartial auctioneer*. The auctioneer is charged with calling out prices and recording the actions of buyers and sellers. Only when the auctioneer calls a price for which the quantity demanded is identical to that which is supplied will trading be permitted.[2] Presumably the auctioneer will use information about the market supply and demand curves to guide these pricing decisions, but precise rules for this operation are seldom spelled out.

There have been numerous attempts to give this fictional concept of an auctioneer a behavioral interpretation. One such interpretation is the idea of *recontracting*. Buyers and sellers are assumed to enter into provisional contracts before the exchange of goods actually takes place. Each of these provisional contracts is voided if it is discovered that at the agreed upon price the market is not in equilibrium. Only when market clearing prices for all markets are discovered will exchange take place. Recontracting is then a form of haggling over price.

Walrasian Price Adjustment

A second suggestion, which is similar to recontracting, was proposed by Leon Walras in the nineteenth century. In this scheme equilibrium prices are a goal toward which the market struggles. Changes in price are motivated by information from the market about the degree of **excess demand** at any particular price.[3] It is assumed price will increase if there is positive excess demand, and decrease if excess demand is negative (that is, if supply exceeds demand).

Excess demand
The extent to which quantity demanded exceeds quantity supplied at a particular price.

Figure 11A.1 shows the Walrasian process of adjustment schematically. For the supply and demand curves shown in the figure, P* is an equilibrium price. For prices less than P*, there will be an excess demand for this good. At such bargain prices, people will demand more than firms would be willing to supply. Crowds will descend on stores and buy all of this good off the shelves. Walras assumed that this behavior would be translated in the market into an increase in price and this increase in price will serve to equilibrate supply and demand. In Figure 11A.1 the upward-pointing arrow indicates the movement in price in response to excess demand. A similar argument follows for prices

---

[2]Real-world analogies to this notion are rare. One interesting Middle Eastern custom has an auctioneer sit between buyer and seller holding the hand of each. The auctioneer calls off prices and the buyer and seller indicate their willingness to trade at these prices by pressing the hand of the auctioneer. When both parties agree to a price, the auctioneer announces that the trade has been completed.

[3]Leon Walras, *Elements of Pure Economics*, translated by William Jaffe (Homewood, Ill.: Irwin, 1954).

Figure 11A.1
Walrasian Price
Adjustment

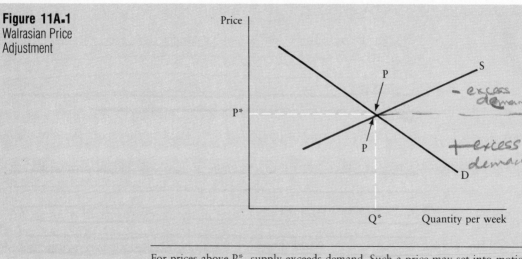

For prices above P*, supply exceeds demand. Such a price may set into motion a chain of events that causes price to fall. For prices less than P*, the quantity demanded exceeds that supplied. In reaction, price may rise.

Walras = price
Marshall = demand

above P*. At such prices, the quantity supplied will exceed that which is demanded. Firms will be producing more than individuals demand, and the inventory of the good will begin to accumulate in the firms' warehouses. Eventually, this will lead to a fall in price that will again equilibrate supply and demand. The downward-pointing arrow in the figure indicates that result.

Marshallian Quantity Adjustment

The Walrasian adjustment process views price as the motivating force in the adjustment of markets to equilibrium. Individuals and firms respond to price changes by moving along their respective demand and supply curves until an equilibrium price-quantity combination is reached. A somewhat different picture of the adjustment process was suggested by Alfred Marshall in his classic *Principles of Economics*.[4] Marshall theorized that individuals and firms adjust quantity in response to imbalances in demand and supply, and that price changes follow from these changes in quantity. Movements in quantity toward equilibrium are motivated by discrepancies between the price individuals are willing to pay and what firms wish to receive. When those two figures coincide, quantity adjustment ceases.

[4]Alfred Marshall, *Principles of Economics*, 8th ed. (London: Macmillan, 1920), pp. 287–288.

Figure 11A.2
Marshallian Quantity
Adjustment

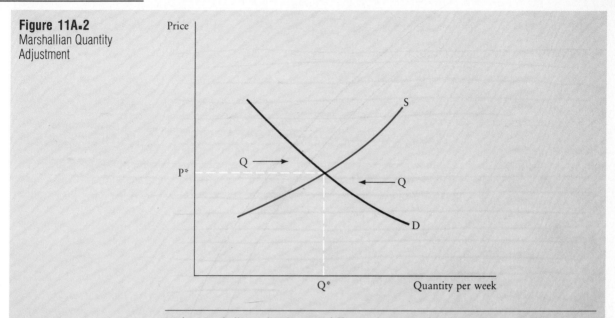

Under Marshallian adjustment, a difference between what demanders are willing to pay and what suppliers require sets up incentives for economic agents to alter output levels. If demand price exceeds supply price, Q will rise. If supply price exceeds demand price, Q will fall. The adjustment mechanism shown in the figure is stable, since Q converges to Q*.

Quantity adjustment is illustrated in Figure 11A.2. For quantities below equilibrium (Q*), what individuals are willing to pay exceeds what firms require to cover their marginal costs. Quantity produced and consumed therefore increases. For quantities above equilibrium, marginal costs exceed what demanders are willing to pay, which provides incentives for quantity reduction. As was the case for the price-adjustment mechanism, the Marshallian mechanism pictured in Figure 11A.2 implies that the price-quantity equilibrium is a stable one. Starting from any initial position, forces come into play that move economic agents toward equilibrium. The precise mechanism by which the movement comes about, however, differs between the Walrasian and Marshallian models.

The Importance of Economic Factors in the Adjustment Process

Movement to an equilibrium price-quantity combination will usually involve changes in both price and quantity. The important questions concern which of those variables is adjusted by economic agents, and how do these agents perceive the need to make such adjustments. Although studying this issue in depth would take us beyond the scope of this book, the general approach to be followed is clear. Any theory of the adjustment process must focus on the

Dispersion of Retail Gasoline Prices

Imperfect information and transaction costs may result in market situations that appear to be out of equilibrium, but in fact are quite stable. One example is the widely differing prices in a market for a seemingly homogeneous product. When information is costly, a potential buyer may choose not to check all the possible sellers for the lowest price, but may instead adopt relatively simple low cost search procedures such as shopping at a customary outlet. In this situation then, market forces that tend to assert the law of one price will be weakened, and a degree of dispersion (that is, price differences among sellers) can persist indefinitely.[5]

An illustration of this sort of situation is provided in a 1976 study of gasoline prices by Howard Marvel.[6] In that study the author examined the dispersion of prices for regular grade gasoline in 20 U.S. cities. He found the average observed price range within the cities was nearly five cents per gallon, and in some instances, ranges as wide as twenty cents per gallon seemed quite compatible with market equilibrium.

Perhaps more interestingly, Marvel found the degree of price dispersion in particular cities seemed to be associated with the costs and benefits of price information to consumers. For example, cities in which gasoline use was relatively greater tended to have less price disper-

sion possibly because drivers in such cities had greater incentives to seek out low prices. Similarly, cities that required gas stations to post prices that were readable from the highway tended to have smaller price dispersions, probably because such price posting provided simple price information to passing motorists. Though not studied in the Marvel study, price advertising has been found to have a similar effect on reducing dispersions in eyeglass prices, lawyer's fees, and prescription drug prices. Because search costs to potential buyers are reduced through price advertising, a smaller spread in equilibrium market prices will result.

To Think About

1. Some groups such as lawyers and pharmacists argue that price advertising is nonprofessional and should be banned. What are the effects of such bans? Would readily available price information improve demander welfare? Can you think of any harm that might be caused?
2. Think of a consumer product, such as a color television. Do you know what price you would have to pay for this today? Would you pay different prices to different sellers? How would you find out what prices actually are?

costs to demanders and suppliers of changing their behavior. Those costs derive both from problems associated with gathering information about the true supply-demand configuration and from difficulties in adapting to this new information once it is acquired. We now turn to examine these costs.

| Transaction Costs and Market Adjustments | Many economists believe that markets are usually out of equilibrium. Demand and supply curves constantly shift as preferences and costs change, and markets never have a chance to adjust completely to a particular supply-demand |

---

[5]For an elegant theoretical analysis of price searching and price dispersions, see G. J. Stigler, "The Economics of Information," *Journal of Political Economy*, June 1961, pp. 213–225.

[6]Howard Marvel, "The Economics of Information and Retail Gasoline Price Behavior," *Journal of Political Economy*, October 1976, pp. 1033–1059.

Transactions costs
Costs involved in making market transactions and in gathering information with which to make those transactions.

configuration. In explaining why markets do not adjust immediately to changing conditions, economists have tended to stress **transaction costs**. Bringing suppliers and demanders together is not so simple a process as the Marshallian diagram suggests. There may be significant costs involved. Such costs not only consist of the direct costs of finding a place in which to transact business but, more important, they also include the costs to the participants of gaining information about the market. For demanders, all prices are not perfectly known. Rather, they must invest some time in search procedures that permit them to learn market prices. "Applying Economics: Dispersion of Retail Gasoline Prices" looks at one aspect of this search process.

Suppliers face similar costs in making transactions. The most important of these is the need to find out something about the demand for their product. Since production takes time, the absence of such information can lead to serious mistakes in the quantity a firm chooses to produce. Firms must also consider the random nature of demand over a short period. For example, no retailer knows exactly when he or she will sell shirts of particular sizes. One of the costs incurred in selling shirts is the cost of maintaining an inventory and making adjustments in that inventory.

The competitive assumption of zero transaction costs is not likely to be fulfilled in the real world. Although supply and demand analysis provides information about equilibrium prices and about the direction of change in prices, various costs will prevent markets from adjusting promptly. Consequently we should observe in the real world examples of not only the systematic influence of supply and demand but also *disequilibria* caused by transaction costs. Here we shall discuss three brief illustrations.

Unemployment

Probably the most important example of market disequilibrium is the persistently high level of unemployment in the American economy.[7] If a simple supply-demand model adequately represented the labor market, there would be little unemployment. The wage rate would be adjusted to ensure that every worker who wanted to work would be able to get a job. This does not happen, however, because there is always some frictional unemployment. Demands for labor are constantly shifting, and workers released by one firm will take time to find a job at another firm. Similarly, new workers enter the labor force and spend time searching for a job. Finally, workers may voluntarily quit one job in order to look for a better one. All these factors cause a temporary mismatch

---

[7]See, for example, Amen Alchian, "Information Costs, Price, and Resource Unemployment," in Edmund Phelps *et al.*, ed., *Microeconomics, Foundations of Employment and Inflation Theory* (New York: Norton, 1970), pp. 27–52.

between the supply of labor and the demand for labor, which shows up in the unemployment statistics.[8]

Inventory Behavior

Similar results occur in the supply and demand for industrial products. An increase in demand, for example, may not always lead to an adjustment in price. Rather, the demand shift will first show up in firms' inventory positions. As inventories are depleted, firms may adjust prices upward toward the new supply-demand equilibrium. Inventory fluctuations and lags in price adjustments are therefore an important type of market disequilibria. These may result from transaction costs. It is costly for a firm to analyze the demand for its product precisely, and watching inventory levels may be a relatively inexpensive method for doing so. As we show in Chapter 10, changing input levels also may be costly, which may keep firms from making input adjustments until some threshold level is passed. One example of this is the tendency of firms to hoard labor in the initial phase of a recession in order to reduce special costs associated with laying off workers.

Queueing

A final important sign of market disequilibrium is queueing. Waiting lines for doctor appointments, ski lifts, and theater tickets reflect a failure of price to respond to short-run demand fluctuations. In the long term, some adjustment in price (or perhaps the entry of new firms) would be expected. However, in the short run, queues reflect the inability of price to act as an effective rationing device.

Transaction Costs and Market Equilibrium

Transaction costs associated with acquiring information can have major effects on market equilibria. In extreme situations, high information costs may even prevent all trading from occurring. Direct trading between individuals seldom occurs for items such as jewelry, precious metals, or works of fine art where a degree of expertise is required to determine authenticity. Buyers and

---

[8]This frictional unemployment might be differentiated from unemployment that arises from a lack of "aggregate" demand. This latter type of unemployment is usually studied in macroeconomics courses and is not analyzed here. The microeconomic determinants of such "Keynesian" unemployment are not well understood. Some authors, in fact, believe that Keynesian economics should be interpreted as a short-run, disequilibrium model of competitive markets in which information is low and transaction costs are high. See, for example, A. Leijonhufvud, *On Keynesian Economics and the Economics of Keynes* (London: Oxford University Press, 1968), especially pp. 67–80.

sellers of such products usually call in experts to act as middlemen, even though this results in extra expense. Similarly, relatively high transaction costs may explain the absence of well-developed markets for television set rentals since sellers may find it difficult to assure proper use of the set.

Even when information costs are not prohibitive, the existence of such costs may lead to the development of many institutions to economize on them, thereby creating changes in underlying market situations. The widespread popularity of *Consumer Reports* and other buyer information services, for example, clearly reflects this demand. And the availability of information through these sources probably has a significant impact on what specific goods are actually purchased.

Asymmetric Information and the "Lemons" Problem

Asymmetric information
A situation in which buyers and sellers have different amounts of information about a market transaction.

A particularly intriguing problem involving information costs may occur when the parties to a transaction possess significantly different (**asymmetric**) amounts of **information**. Since this situation was first examined in detail for the case of used cars by George Akerlof, it is sometimes called the "lemons" problem.[9] Suppose used cars are of two types (good cars and lemons) and only the owner of a car knows for certain into which category that vehicle falls. Since buyers cannot differentiate between good cars and lemons, all used cars of a particular type will sell for the same price—somewhere between the true worth of the two types. The owner of a car will choose to keep his or her car if it is a good one (since a good car is worth more than the prevailing market price), but will sell the car if it is a lemon (since a lemon is worth less than the market price). Consequently, only lemons will be brought to the used car market, and the quality of cars traded will deteriorate. Of course, this erosion in quality may be retarded by trustworthy used car dealers or by development of car buying expertise by the general public. But anyone who has ever shopped for a used car knows the problem of potential lemons is a very real one.

Whether the lemons problem is a pervasive one is unclear. Some authors claim it is important in any situation where sellers have special information not readily available to buyers. Such markets might include medical services (where advice from quacks may come to predominate in the absence of regulation), investment advice (since all good investment advisors should be already wealthy with no need to sell their advice to the public), and low skilled employment (where workers who know they are particularly able will seek out better jobs, leaving only unqualified workers to fill available slots). In all of these instances, however, buyers have a substantial incentive to gather information on the services they are buying, so long-run quality deterioration is not a forgone conclusion.

---

[9]G. A. Akerlof, "The Market for 'Lemons': Quality Uncertainty and the Market Mechanism," *Quarterly Journal of Economics*, August 1970, pp. 488–500.

The Time Path of Market Adjustment and the Cobweb Model

In addition to studying the role of transaction costs in market adjustments, economists have spent considerable effort in analyzing the actual time paths through which adjustments occur. As a simple illustration we will examine the **cobweb model** of market adjustment, which, though based on a number of overly simple assumptions, may be generally indicative of how some markets achieve equilibrium.

Supply-Demand Assumption

To begin our analysis, suppose that firms' supply decisions in a particular period (t) depend only on the price that prevailed in the previous period (t − 1):

$$\text{Supply in period t} = Q_t^S = a + bP_{t-1}. \qquad [11A.2]$$

For example, this equation may represent the supply decision of farmers planting a crop. At the time the crop is planted only the previous year's price is known. Farmers must make their decisions based on that price. Once the crop is harvested, it represents the current year's supply. The supply will not, however, respond to the current year's price. The total quantity supplied is sold in the market for whatever it will bring. Market demand depends on current price:

$$\text{Demand in period t} = Q_t^D = c - dP_t, \qquad [11A.3]$$

and equilibrium in the market at time t necessitates that

$$Q_t^S = Q_t^D. \qquad [11A.4]$$

This view of the market assumes the following sequence of events: Firms decide how much they will produce by referring to the previous period's price (P_{t-1}). They produce this output during the current period and sell it in the market for what demanders are willing to pay. Demanders then bid for this output (perhaps in auctions); in so doing they establish the current market price (P_t). This price enters into firms' production decisions in period $t + 1$. In this way there is a lagged response of suppliers to the actions of demanders in determining price.

A Graphic Analysis

Figure 11A.3 illustrates the working of the cobweb model. There P* is an equilibrium price because the quantity demanded at this price is exactly equal

Figure 11A.3
Cobweb Model of Price
Determination

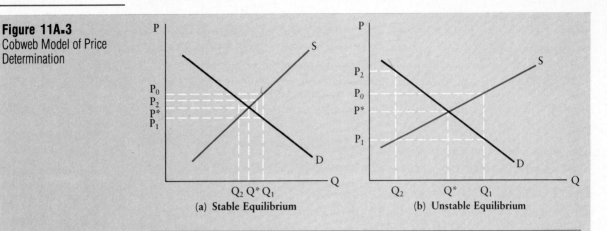

(a) Stable Equilibrium   (b) Unstable Equilibrium

The cobweb model of lagged response to price by firms provides a simple theory of
market adjustment. Whether prices will approach an equilibrium level will depend on the
relative slopes of the demand and supply curves. In the configuration shown in Graph a,
convergence will take place, whereas in Graph b, it will not. A third possibility (not
shown) would be for the supply and demand curves to have slopes such that the price
perpetually oscillates at about P^*.

to the quantity supplied.[10] The price P^* can persist from one period to the
next since firms, by referring to the previous period's price (which is also P^*),
produce Q^*, this is what demanders are willing to buy at P^* in the current
period.

We can see why this model is called the "cobweb" by analyzing the sequence of events that follows if price starts from a nonequilibrium position.
Suppose that price starts at P_0, and consider Graph a in Figure 11A.3. In
period 1, firms will produce output level Q_1 by referring to P_0. For example,
P_0 might represent the average price of wheat from the 1986 grain harvest,
and farmers use this information to decide the number of acres to be planted
in 1987. Once Q_1 is produced, however, it must be sold in the market for
whatever it will bring. Since Q_1 represents a relatively large output level, a
low price must prevail in the market in period 1 (call this price P_1) to get
demanders to buy this amount. In the grain harvest example, the price of
wheat will fall substantially in 1987 from its 1986 level because of the over-
production in 1986.

In period 2, firms will base their output decisions on P_1. They will therefore
produce a relatively low output level (Q_2). Demanders will bid for this output
level and will drive the market price up to P_2. This price will then affect firms'
output decision in period 3. As we can see in Figure 11A.3, this process will
proceed until price converges to its equilibrium level at P^*. Over time, price

---

[10]Simple algebra can be used to solve Equations 11A.2 and 11A.3 for $P^* = (c - a)/(b + d)$.

APPLYING ECONOMICS

Speculation

One of the most important attempts of suppliers and demanders to predict the direction of price movements is that of speculation. When some people believe there are good reasons for the price of a commodity to move in a particular direction, they may try to profit from such a movement. For example, if speculators believed that the price of a crop were going to move from P_1 to P_2 during the next period in Fig. 11A.3, they might demand more of the crop this period hoping to make windfall profits out of the price rise. Similarly, if speculators expected a fall in price they might sell all of the crop in their possession (or even sell short crops they did not currently own), hoping to replenish their supplies later at the expected lower price. In general, it might be thought that such actions by speculators would help to bring markets into supply-demand equilibrium. Because speculators will find it profitable to acquire information about true supply-demand conditions in the market, they will maximize profits by taking actions that move the market toward equilibrium. This may dampen the natural fluctuations in market prices (such as those in the cobweb model).

Although speculation might, in the long run, help to stabilize equilibrium market prices, it is possible that in the short run it may lead to wide market gyrations. We examine two particularly spectacular cases here.

Tulipomania

Following the spread of a tulip virus in Holland during the 1630s a wide variety of new bulbs were developed.[12] Because there were no existing markets for these new bulbs, prices fluctuated widely. By 1634, speculating on price movements in bulbs had become a major preoccupation of the Dutch upper class and tulip trading had started on the stock exchanges in Amsterdam and Rotterdam. Throughout 1635 and 1636, speculators pushed the price of rare bulbs ever higher with the hope of making profits on their purchases. At the height of the trading frenzy, some particularly prized bulbs sold for as much as the equivalent of $10,000. This is clearly an example of speculators having a short-run destabilizing effect as bulb prices departed greatly from underlying supply-demand conditions. As might have been ex-

---

Stable equilibrium
A situation in which market forces cause price to move to its equilibrium level.

Unstable equilibrium
A situation in which market forces cause price to move away from its equilibrium level.

therefore moves from P_0 to P^* because of the way in which supply and demand interact in the market. The price P^* is therefore a **stable equilibrium**.

The interaction we have outlined does not necessarily lead to an equilibrium price. Graph b of Figure 11A.3 shows a set of supply and demand curves for which the supply curve is somewhat flatter than that in the previous example. By starting at a price of P_0 in Graph b, an argument similar to that we used for Graph a shows that price will oscillate in wider and wider movements away from P^*. You can follow the sequence of events by which market price moves from P_0 to P_1 to P_2. As Figure 11A.3 clearly shows, the price P^* is an **unstable equilibrium**. The workings of supply and demand will not suffice to move price to P^* with this particular configuration of supply and demand curves.[11] Since real-world prices probably do not oscillate as wildly as those

---

[11]Technically it can be shown that, for the linear demand curves used in this example, P^* is stable if $b/d < 1$ and unstable if $b/d > 1$. For stability, then, the supply curve must be more steeply sloped than the demand curve. In the intermediate case where $b/d = 1$, price will constantly oscillate between a price above P^* and one below P^*.

[12]For a discussion of this episode together with some fascinating photographs see T. Berger, "Tulipomania Was No Dutch Treat to Gambling Burghers," *Smithsonian*, April 1977, pp. 70–77.

pected, "tulipomania" was short-lived. In 1637 the market price of bulbs fell sharply, and speculators moved rapidly to liquidate their stocks. Although the market for bulbs rapidly returned to relatively stable conditions, Dutch courts were clogged for many years with lawsuits that resulted from the debacle.

Sugar

A more recent (though less spectacular) example of destabilizing speculation of this type occurred in the market for sugar in 1974. Prices of sugar rose from about 10 cents per pound in late 1973 to over 72 cents per pound in November 1974. Although some part of that movement can probably be explained by shifting supply and demand conditions (crops were poor in some countries and the demand for sugar is relatively price inelastic) a major portion of the increase can be attributed to speculation.[13] At the time of the sugar price increase there was widespread hoarding of sugar by firms and households in anticipation of further price increases. In

addition, the 1973 oil embargo created a shortage mentality that caused incautious extrapolations of short-run price movements. Again, it proved impossible for market price to depart forever from its underlying supply-demand equilibrium. By 1977 sugar prices were below their 1973 levels and Congress debated ways to aid U.S. sugar producers.

To Think About

1. "Buy cheap, sell dear" is a basic principle that should yield speculators long-term profits. Use a simple supply and demand graph to show why this is so. Use the graph also to show why such speculation may help price to adjust to its equilibrium level.
2. To many people, "speculators" are undesirable, almost criminal. For a speculative good such as common stocks or foreign exchange, how would you differentiate between "speculators" and "investors"? Do they have different motives? Do they perform different economic functions?

in Graph b, we must conclude that either most real-world markets have a supply-demand pattern that resembles Graph a or the real world is characterized by a more complex model than those depicted by the cobweb model.

This model is an obvious oversimplification of reality. It would take a peculiar lack of sophistication on the part of buyers and sellers to accept a regularly oscillating price for long, and some kinds of adjustments based on people's expectations of prices are bound to be made. That is, the market participants may eventually figure out what the equilibrium price is and move to that point without further fluctuations. We do not study that learning process here. "Applying Economics: Speculation" does illustrate some situations where rather wild price movements have been observed.

Summary

This appendix illustrates some of the problems involved in markets adjusting to equilibrium when transactions are costly. None of these problems invali-

---

[13]For a discussion, see Council on Wage and Price Stability," Staff Report on Sugar Prices" (Washington, D.C.: U.S. Government Printing Office, May 1975).

dates the analysis developed in Chapter 11 since, as we have shown, demand and cost conditions will always exert a major influence on market outcomes. But the analysis here does suggest that transaction costs can play important roles in affecting the ways markets adjust to changing conditions and in determining the actual time path of adjustment. Our principal conclusions from this examination are:

- Equilibrium can be achieved either through price or quantity adjustments. Transaction costs will determine which method is used.
- Lack of information is a primary reason for transaction costs. In some cases, such as the lemons problem, this lack of information can cause markets to perform poorly.
- With imperfect information, disequilibrium prices may occur. Usually prices will move toward equilibrium over time, but on occasion markets may have unstable equilibrium prices.

CHAPTER 12

Pricing in Monopoly Markets

The market for a good is described as a monopoly if there is only one producer of the good.[1] This single firm faces the entire market demand curve. Using its knowledge of this demand curve, the monopoly makes a decision on how much to produce. Unlike the perfectly competitive firm's output decision (which has no effect on market price), the monopoly output decision will completely determine the good's price. In this sense monopoly markets are the opposite, polar case from perfectly competitive ones. Of course, even though a monopoly has far more market power than a competitive firm, it is not all-powerful. It cannot sell all it wants at whatever price it chooses. The monopoly still must contend with the demand curve for its product and must recognize that it can sell more only by lowering its price. Still, it can choose to operate at any point along the market demand curve that it wishes, so it has considerably more discretion than a price-taking firm.

Causes of Monopoly

Barriers to entry
Factors that prevent new firms from entering a market or industry.

The reason monopolies exist is that other firms find it unprofitable or impossible to enter the market. **Barriers to entry** are the source of all monopoly power. If other firms could enter the market, there would, by definition, no longer be a monopoly. There are two general types of barriers to entry: technical barriers and legal barriers.

---

[1]No monopoly is totally without competition. The good in question will always have some substitutes available, if only because it is in competition for the consumer's dollar.

Technical Barriers to Entry

A primary technical barrier to entry is that the production of the good in question may exhibit decreasing average cost over a wide range of output levels. That is, relatively large-scale firms are more efficient than small ones. In this situation one firm may find it profitable to drive others out of the industry by price cutting. Similarly, once a monopoly has been established, entry by other firms will be difficult because any new firm must produce at relatively low levels of output and therefore at relatively high costs.

The range of declining average costs need only be "large" relative to the market in question. Declining costs on some absolute scale are not necessary. For example, the manufacture of concrete does not exhibit declining average costs over a broad range of output when compared to the total U. S. market. However, in any particular small town, declining average costs may permit a concrete monopoly to be established. The high costs of transporting concrete tend to create local monopolies for this good.

Another technical basis of monopoly is special knowledge of a low-cost method of production. In this case the problem for the monopoly fearing entry by other firms is to keep this technique uniquely to itself. When matters of technology are involved this may be extremely difficult, unless the technology can be protected by a patent, (discussed below). Ownership of unique resources (such as mineral deposits or land locations) or the possession of unique managerial talents may also be a lasting basis for maintaining a monopoly.[2]

Legal Barriers to Entry

Many pure monopolies are created as a matter of law rather than as a matter of economic conditions. One important example of a government-granted monopoly position is the legal protection provided by a patent. Xerox machines and Polaroid cameras are just two notable examples of goods that would-be competitors may be prevented from copying by patent law. Because the basic technology for these products was assigned by the government to only one firm, a monopoly position was established. The rationale of the patent system, originally put forth by Thomas Jefferson, is that it makes innovation more profitable and therefore encourages technical advancement.

---

[2]"High costs" of entry into a market are sometimes mentioned as a basis for monopoly. Whereas there are probably cases in which this is correct, it is important to be careful in distinguishing these cases. If there were perfect capital markets, a firm would enter a market so long as the present discounted value of future profits exceeded the fixed costs of entry, since it could borrow these costs and repay the loan out of profits.

Whether or not the benefits of such innovative behavior exceed the costs of creating monopolies is an open question.[3]

A second example of a legally created monopoly is in the awarding of an exclusive franchise or license to serve a market. These are awarded in cases of public utility (gas and electric) services, communication services, the post office, some airline routes, some television and radio station markets, and a variety of other businesses. The argument usually put forward in favor of creating these monopolies is that having only one firm in the industry is more desirable than open competition.

There are several reasons given for the desirability of such policies. In some cases it is argued that the firm is a *natural monopoly:* Average cost is diminishing over a broad range of output levels, and minimum average cost can be achieved only by organizing the industry as a monopoly. The public utility and communications industries are representative of these so-called natural monopolies. It seems unnecessary to have two overlapping local telephone or electricity distribution systems when one will do quite satisfactorily. Other cases of government franchises (certain airline routes, the post office) do not appear to be natural monopolies, and the reasons for creating monopolies in these cases are less clear.

In some instances it is argued that restrictions on entry into some industries are needed to assure adequate quality standards (licensing of physicians, for example) or to prevent environmental harm (franchising businesses in the national parks). In many cases there are sound reasons for such entry restrictions, but in some cases, as "Applying Economics: Entry Restriction by Licensing: Raising the Price of Clean Clothes" shows, the reasons are obscure, and the restrictions act mainly to limit the competition faced by existing firms.

Profit Maximization

In order to maximize profits, a monopoly will choose to produce that output level for which marginal revenue is equal to marginal cost. Since the monopoly, in contrast to a perfectly competitive firm, faces a negatively sloped market demand curve, marginal revenue will be less than market price. To sell an additional unit, the monopoly must lower its price on all units to be sold in order to generate the extra demand necessary to absorb this marginal unit. In equating marginal revenue to marginal cost, the monopoly will produce an output level for which price exceeds marginal cost. This feature of monopoly pricing is the primary focus of our analysis of the distorting effect of a monopoly on resource allocation later in this chapter.

---

[3]Some economists have argued that inventors should be rewarded directly by the government and that the invention should then be made available to all firms at no cost. Ideally the prize to inventors would provide the incentive that the patent system currently provides without creating the monopolies that arise under patents. In practice, however, it would be very difficult to decide how much a particular invention is "worth."

Entry Restriction by Licensing: Raising the Price of Clean Clothes

State governments license many occupations and impose stiff legal penalties on people who practice the business without a license. The principal reason usually stated for such licensing is to assure the safety and quality of the service provided. Using this rationale, states have licensed physicians, dentists, optometrists, and a variety of other occupations. For many of these occupations licensing seems warranted—no one wants to be treated by a quack when he or she is seriously ill. However, in some cases, the urge to license may go too far. In California, for example, it has been estimated that more than 25 percent of the work force is licensed by 52 different regulatory boards.[4] Occupations such as embalmers, guide dog trainers, appliance repairers, and golf course designers are all licensed, though consumer gains in terms of quality or safety from such licensing seem to be unlikely.

An alternative explanation for licensing is that existing firms find it in their interest to promote entry restrictions to preserve the market for themselves. A good illustration is provided by dry cleaners in California. In order to enter the business, a would-be cleaner must pass examinations in a variety of specialties (fur cleaning, hat renovating, spot removal, and so forth).

In order to take such exams, one must usually attend a dry cleaning "school" and even then, pass rates tend to be very low. Those who try to skirt this process and take in some laundry on the side face stiff fines and even jail sentences for "practicing" dry cleaning without a license.

Whether Californians have cleaner clothes than the rest of us as a result of all this is unclear. Several studies have found that citizens of that state do pay more for their cleaning and that profits in the industry are higher than in other states. It is no wonder that existing dry cleaning firms are the staunchest defenders of continued regulation by the Board of Fabric Care.

To Think About

1. Can you think of good reasons for regulating entry into the dry cleaning business? Is licensing needed to assure quality? How would you judge quality for businesses that aren't licensed?
2. One argument for licensing is that consumers don't have adequate information to judge quality for themselves. Does this apply to dry cleaning? Embalming? How about getting medical care? In what ways is this latter product different from the others?

The profit-maximizing output level for a monopoly is given by Q^* in Figure 12.1.[5] For that output, marginal revenue is equal to marginal costs, and profits are maximized. If a firm produced slightly less than Q^*, profits would fall, since the revenue lost from this cutback (MR) would exceed the decline in production costs (MC). A decision to produce more than Q^* would also lower profits since the additional costs from increased production would exceed the

---

[4]This example is based on David Kirp and Eileen Soffer, "Taking Californians to the Cleaners," *Regulation*, September/October 1985, pp. 24–26. The puns in the article are highly recommended.

[5]In Figure 12.1, and in the other diagrammatic analysis of this chapter, no distinction is made between the behavior of a monopoly in the short run and in the long run. The analysis is the same in both cases, except that different sets of cost curves would be used depending on the possibilities for adjustment that are assumed to be feasible for the firm. Notice though that in the long run, a monopoly will not in general choose that level of capital output for which long-run average cost is a minimum. The only situation in which this would occur would be if MR and MC happened to intersect at the low point of the AC curve.

Figure 12.1
Profit Maximization and
Price Determination in a
Monopoly Market

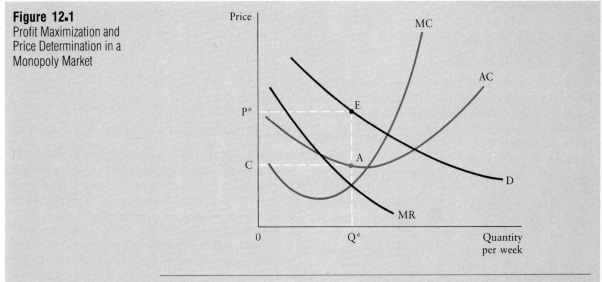

A profit-maximizing monopolist produces that quantity for which marginal revenue is equal to marginal cost. In the diagram this quantity is given by Q*, which will yield a price of P* in the market. Monopoly profits can be read as the rectangle P*CAE.

extra revenues from selling the extra output. Consequently, profits are at a maximum at Q*, and a profit-maximizing monopoly will choose this output level.

Given the monopoly's decision to produce Q*, the demand curve D indicates that a market price of P* will prevail. This is the price that demanders as a group are willing to pay for the output of the monopoly. In the market, an equilibrium price-quantity combination of P*,Q* will be observed.[6] This equilibrium will persist until something happens (such as a shift in demand or a change in costs) to cause the monopoly to alter its output decision.

Monopoly Supply Curve

In the theory of perfectly competitive markets we presented earlier, it was possible to speak of an industry supply curve. We constructed this curve by allowing the market demand curve to shift and observing the supply curve

---

[6]This combination will be on an elastic section of the demand curve. This will be true because MC is positive so for a profit maximum MR must also be positive. But, if marginal revenue is positive, demand must be elastic, as we showed in Chapter 9 (see especially Equation 9.8). One conclusion to be drawn is that industries that are estimated to operate along an inelastic portion of the demand curve for their product are not exercising strong monopoly power.

APPLYING ECONOMICS

Deregulation and the Value of Stock Exchange Seats

The value of a monopoly firm to a would-be buyer depends on the value of the profits the firm is able to generate. The profits depend on the location of the demand curve for the monopolist's product. Shifts in demand can affect potential profits and the market value of the monopoly itself. Table 12.1 illustrates this for seats on the New York Stock Exchange.

The prices of these seats have fluctuated widely over time. They reached their peak value in 1929 in response to the huge stock trading activity (and brokerage profits) in that year. Prices were relatively low throughout the Depression and during World War II. In the 1960s, trading activity in stocks picked up, which was again reflected in the market value of exchange seats. Although trading volume continued to be high in the 1970s, a number of factors reduced monopoly profits available from New York Stock Exchange membership. Most important was that a growing proportion of stock trades were made off the New York Stock Exchange, as improved methods of communication reduced the need for a central marketplace. In a related development, after several years of prodding by the Securities and Exchange Commission, the New York Stock Exchange eliminated fixed commission rates on May 1, 1975. The sales price for exchange memberships reflected these pro-competition developments, and by 1977 had fallen to less than one-tenth of the price in 1929. That contrast is even more dramatic when we remember that the overall price level increased more than fourfold between 1929 and 1977.

Table 12.1
Changing Values of Monopoly Rights:
Stock Exchange Seats

Year	Price of an Exchange Seat in Thousands of Dollars
1905	$ 72
1925	99
1929	625
1945	49
1960	135
1970	130
1975	55
1977	42

Source: The New York Stock Exchange Fact Book, 1976 (New York: The New York Stock Exchange, 1976), pp. 58 and 82. 1977 data supplied by the author. All prices are the lowest bid price in a given year.

that was traced out by the series of equilibrium price-quantity combinations. This type of construction is not possible for monopoly markets. With a fixed market demand curve, the supply "curve" for a monopoly will be only one point—namely, that quantity for which MR = MC. If the demand curve should shift, the marginal revenue curve would shift along with it, and a new profit-maximizing output would be chosen. However, to connect the resulting series of equilibrium points would have little meaning and would not represent a supply curve. The set of points might have a very strange shape, depending on how the market demand curve's elasticity (and its associated MR curve) changed as the curve was shifted outward. In this sense the monopoly firm has no well-defined supply curve. Instead, each demand curve represents a unique profit-maximizing opportunity for a monopoly, and each has to be studied independently.

Table 12.2
Average Stock Commission Rates in Cents per Share
(Constant 1975 Dollars)

	Institutional Trades	Individual Trades
1975	27.6¢	32.6¢
1976	18.0	30.3
1977	14.2	28.9
1978	11.5	27.3

Source: Calculated from S. M. Tinic and R. R. West, "The Securities Industry under Negotiated Commissions: Changes in the Structure and Performance of New York Stock Exchange Member Firms," *The Bell Journal of Economics,* Spring 1980, p. 36. Institutional data refer to trades of 1,000–9,999 shares; individual data refer to trades of 200–999 shares.

Results of the "May Day" deregulation of the securities industry were also reflected in brokerage commissions. Table 12.2 records the trend in brokerage commission rates (in 1975 prices) for the three years following the 1975 decision. For institutional trading, the rates fell dramatically—by 1978 they stood at about 30 percent of their pre–May Day level. For individual rates, some modest declines were also apparent, though in this case the costs of handling individual accounts probably slowed the decline. Prior to deregulation, high institutional brokerage rates tended to shield individuals from some costs of the brokerage services they received (research on stocks, for example), whereas following deregulation, this subsidization no longer existed. Still the decline in brokerage rates occurred on an across-the-board basis, and it is not surprising that the value of the right to trade on the New York Stock Exchange dropped significantly.

To Think About
1. Prior to "May Day," 1972, many brokers argued that restrictions on entry were necessary to maintain an "orderly central market" for stocks. Would free entry into the brokerage business lead to more unstable stock prices? What have been the results in the years since deregulation?
2. Can you think of other monopoly rights that are traded in the market (for example, what kinds of licenses are bought and sold)? How are such rights created? Who usually gets the proceeds from their sale?

Monopoly Profits

Economic profits earned by the monopolists can be read directly from Figure 12.1. These are shown by the rectangle P*CAE and again represent the profit per unit (price minus average cost) times the number of units sold. These profits will be positive when, as in the figure, market price exceeds average total cost. Since no entry is possible into a monopoly market, these monopoly profits can exist even in the long run. For this reason some authors call the profits that a monopoly earns in the long run **monopoly rents**. These profits can be regarded as a return to the factor that forms the basis of the monopoly (such as a patent, a favorable location, or the only liquor license in town). Some other owner might be willing to pay that amount in rent for the right to operate the monopoly and obtain its profits. "Applying Economics: Dereg-

Monopoly rents
The profits that a monopoly earns in the long run.

ulation and the Value of Stock Exchange Seats" shows that these rights can be quite valuable. This value can also erode immediately if the firm's monopoly profits are threatened.

What's Wrong with Monopoly?

Firms that have a monopoly position in a market are frequently damned for a variety of reasons. It has been argued that monopolies earn excess profits; give poor, unresponsive service; exploit their employees; stifle technical progress; and distort the allocation of resources. Although each of these complaints undoubtedly has some truth to it, only two are discussed here: the profitability of monopoly and the effect of monopoly on resource allocation. Some of the other arguments are investigated in other sections of this chapter.

Profitability

Since perfectly competitive firms earn no pure profits in the long run, a firm with a monopoly in a market can earn higher profits than if the market were competitive. This does not imply, however, that monopolies necessarily earn huge profits. Two equally strong monopolies may differ greatly in their profitability. It is the ability of monopolies to raise price above *marginal* cost that reflects their monopoly power. Since profitability reflects the difference between price and *average* cost, profits are not necessarily a sign of monopoly power.

Figure 12.2 exhibits the cost and demand conditions for two firms with essentially the same degree of monopoly power (that is, the divergence between price and marginal cost is the same in both panels). The monopoly in Graph a earns a high level of profits, whereas the one in Graph b actually earns zero in profits since market price equals average cost. Excess profitability is not inevitable, even for a strong monopoly.

More than the size of monopoly profits, people are likely to object to the distribution of these profits. If the profits go to relatively wealthy owners at the expense of less well-to-do consumers, there may be valid objections to monopoly profits no matter what their size. It may not necessarily be the case that profits from a monopoly always go to the wealthy. For example, consider the decision of Navajo blanket makers to form a monopoly to sell their products to tourists at the Grand Canyon. In this situation the monopoly profits make income distribution more equal by transferring income from more wealthy tourists to low income Navajos.

Distortion of Resource Allocation

Economists (who tend to worry about such matters) raise a second objection to monopolies: that their existence distorts the allocation of resources. Mo-

Figure 12.2
Monopoly Profits Depend on the Relationship between the Demand and Average Cost Curves

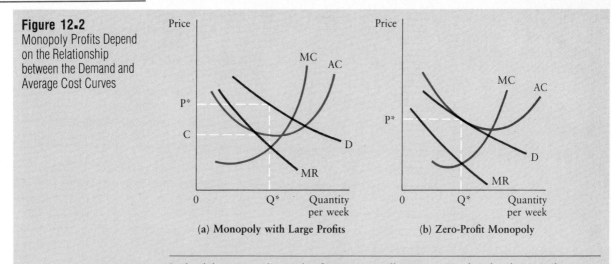

(a) Monopoly with Large Profits

(b) Zero-Profit Monopoly

Both of the monopolies in this figure are equally "strong" in that they have similar divergences between market price and marginal cost. However, because of the location of the demand and average cost curves, it turns out that the monopoly in Graph a earns high profits, whereas that in Graph b earns no profits. The size of profits is not a measure of the strength of a monopoly.

nopolies intentionally restrict their production in order to maximize profits. The discrepancy between price and marginal cost shows that at the monopoly's profit-maximizing output level consumers are willing to pay more for an extra unit of output than it costs to produce that output. From a social point of view, output is too low.

Figure 12.3 illustrates this observation by comparing the output that will be produced in a market characterized by perfect competition with the output that will be produced in the same market when there is only one firm in it. The figure assumes that the monopoly produces under conditions of constant marginal cost and that the competitive industry also exhibits constant costs with the same minimum long-run average cost as the monopolist—an assumption we question in the next section. In this situation a perfectly competitive industry would choose output level Q^*, where long-run supply and demand intersect. At this point price is equal to average and marginal cost. A monopoly would choose output level Q^{**}, for which marginal revenue is equal to marginal cost. The restriction in output $(Q^* - Q^{**})$ is then some measure of the allocation harm done by monopoly. Because of the way in which the market is organized, fewer resources are being devoted to the production of the good than the demand curve warrants. People would be willing to pay P^{**} for additional output, which would only cost MC. However, the monopolist's market control and desire to maximize profits prevent the additional resources from being drawn into the industry to fill this demand.

As an admittedly inane example of this distortion, suppose a local hamburger joint has a monopoly in the production of chili dogs because its cook

Figure 12.3
Differential Effects of
Perfect Competition and
Monopoly in a Market

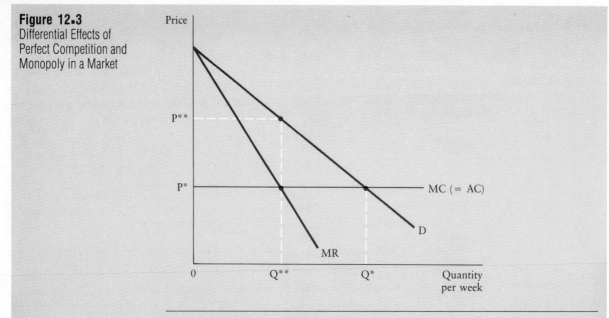

A perfectly competitive industry would produce output level Q*, for which price equals marginal (and long-run average) cost. A monopoly, by recognizing the downward slope of the demand curve, would produce Q** where marginal revenue equals marginal cost. This output reduction is a measure of the allocational cost of monopolies. In some cases it may be possible to place a value on this loss in output.

is the only one in town capable of concocting them. To maximize profits the owner of the monopoly restricts chili dog output to a point at which each dog sells for $2, but, at the margin, costs only $1 in terms of ingredients and the cook's time. Why is this inefficient? Because the well-being of both the cook and chili dog consumers could be improved by further trading. If the cook agreed to sell chili dogs at $1.50 to people who came around to the back door, overall welfare would be improved. Consumers would be better off (since they save $.50 per dog) and the cook would be better off (by effectively getting a higher wage). Of course, the monopoly owner would prevent these illicit sales since they would undercut the profits being made. But, the fact that there exists such unexploited mutually beneficial trading opportunities is clear evidence that resources (here the cook's time) are not being used efficiently.

Measuring Monopolistic Distortions

Monopolies cause an artificial restriction in output and thereby distort the allocation of resources. To put a dollar figure on this distortion, economists have devised a way of measuring how much the total output of a good is "worth" to the people who buy it. By using such a measure, it is possible to

Figure 12.4
Consumer's Surplus

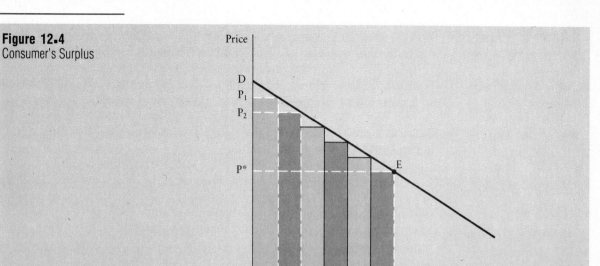

A perfect price discriminator could collect a total revenue of DOQ*E for output level Q*. Because most goods sell at a single price, however, consumers pay only P*OQ*E. Consequently, consumers receive a "surplus" given by area DP*E.

place an approximate cost on the output restrictions brought about by a monopoly.

Perfect Price Discrimination

Perfect price discrimination
Selling a good one unit at a time for the maximum amount demanders will pay.

In Figure 12.4 we have drawn a downward-sloping demand curve for a good. Suppose that Q* is currently being consumed. We wish to measure the total value of Q* to consumers. One way to determine this value is to ask how much in total revenues a firm that practiced **perfect price discrimination** could collect for Q*. If the market were organized so that the producer could dole out one unit at a time to that consumer who would pay the highest price for that unit, we wish to know how much in total revenue would be collected. This will be our measure of the total value of Q*; it represents the maximum amount that can be collected from consumers in exchange for Q* units of output.

Figure 12.4 illustrates the perfect price discrimination procedure. If the producer initially puts Q_1 on the market, it will bring a price of P_1; total revenues will be given by the area of the rectangle P_1,Q_1. After this sale, the producer can put some more of the good on sale ($Q_2 - Q_1$). This additional amount will have a price of P_2, and total revenues are given by the rectangle $P_2, Q_2 - Q_1$. Continuing in this manner, the producer can eventually collect a total revenue equal to the area under the demand curve from $Q = 0$ to $Q = Q^*$. This total revenue (given by $D0Q^*E$ in Figure 12.4) is the total value that people place on output level Q^*: It is the *maximum amount* that consumers would be willing to pay for Q^* rather than be without it.

Consumer Surplus

It is practically never possible for a producer to practice the kind of perfect price discrimination that we have just described. Most firms cannot successfully discriminate in the price they charge different buyers, and firms are therefore unable to charge the maximum amount each person will pay. Rather, the firm will usually treat all buyers as a group and sell its output at a single price to this group. A firm that is faced by the demand curve D in Figure 12.4 will, if it sells Q^* without practicing discrimination among buyers, obtain a price of P^* on the sale. It is the marginal buyer who determines this price. Intramarginal buyers (perhaps those who were, say, willing to pay P_1 for an output of Q_1) receive a "bonus" through the workings of the market. They can buy the good at a lower price than if the firm practiced perfect price discrimination. This bonus is called **consumer surplus** and can also be seen in Figure 12.4. If the firm adopts a one-price policy, consumers will pay total revenues of P^*0Q^*E for the output they buy. However, as we have shown, the total value of this output is given by $D0Q^*E$. Consequently, because of the one-price policy, consumers receive a bonus; the value of this bonus is given by the triangle DP^*E. This is the difference between the total value of Q^* and what individuals actually pay for it. It is this triangle that is termed consumer surplus.[7]

Now that we have shown how to measure the benefits that consumers derive from consuming a particular output level, we can evaluate the restriction in output by a monopoly. We now show that the monopolization of a market leads to a loss of consumer surplus, and how this loss can be measured.

Consumer surplus
The difference between the total revenue that would be collected under perfect price discrimination and the amount actually paid by consumers.

Monopolistic Effect on Allocation and Distribution

Figure 12.3 demonstrates the nature of the output reduction brought about by the monopolization of a market. Now we can use the notion of consumer

---

[7]For a more rigorous discussion of the concept of consumer's surplus, see R. C. Willig, "Consumer Surplus without Apology," *American Economic Review*, September, 1976, pp. 589–597. Using the notion of consumer's surplus, it has sometimes been claimed that perfect discrimination may be desirable. By being a perfect discriminator a firm is able to expropriate all (or almost all) the "value" of its product. If perfect price discrimination were possible, therefore, the good might be provided even though cost considerations could prevent its being provided if the firm had to obey a one-price pricing policy. For example, it might be argued that the ability of small-town doctors to practice price discrimination among their patients is beneficial because otherwise there would be no medical service at all.

Figure 12.5
Allocational and
Distributional Effects
of Monopoly

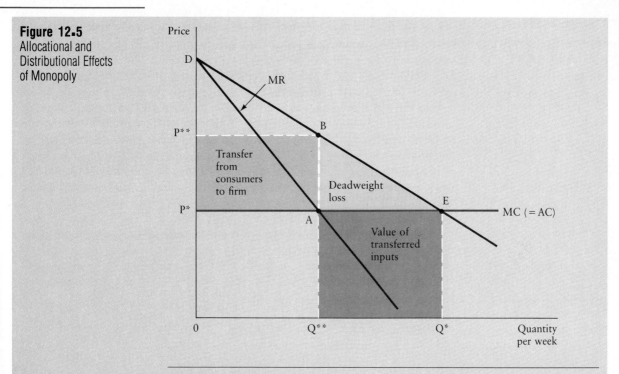

This figure is based on Figure 12.3 to show the effects of monopolization. Consumer expenditures and productive inputs worth $AQ^{**}Q^*E$ are reallocated into the production of other goods. Consumer surplus equal to $P^{**}P^*AB$ is transferred into monopoly profits. There is a deadweight loss given by BAE.

surplus to place a value on that reduction. Figure 12.5 uses our previous illustration of the output restriction by a monopoly. When the market is competitively organized, Q^* is produced at a price of P^*. The total value to consumers of this output level in Figure 12.5 is given by the area under the demand curve (that is, by area $D0Q^*E$), for which they pay P^*0Q^*E. Total consumer surplus is given by the triangle DP^*E. Under a monopoly only Q^{**} is produced, and the price of this output is P^{**}. The restriction in output has had several effects. The total value of this good that consumers receive has been reduced in Figure 12.5 by the area $BQ^{**}Q^*E$. This reduction is not a total loss, however, since consumers previously had to pay $AQ^{**}Q^*E$ for these goods, and they may now spend this money elsewhere. Since the monopoly produces less, it needs to hire fewer inputs. These released inputs will be used to produce those other goods that consumers buy. The loss of consumer surplus given by the area BAE is, however, an unambiguous reduction in welfare as a result of the monopoly. Some authors refer to triangle BAE as the **deadweight loss** from a monopoly. It is the best single measure of the allocational harm caused by monopoly.

Deadweight loss
A loss of consumer
surplus that is not
transferred to another
economic actor.

In addition to the allocational effect of monopolization of a market, there is a distributional effect which can also be seen in Figure 12.5. At the monopoly's output level of Q**, there exist monopoly profits given by the area P**P*AB. In the case of perfect competition this area was a part of the consumer's surplus triangle. If the market is a monopoly, that portion of a consumer's surplus is transferred into monopoly profits. The area P**P*AB in Figure 12.5 does not necessarily represent a loss of social welfare. It does measure the redistributional effects of a monopoly, and these may be undesirable. In order to make such an assessment, however, we would have to introduce an explicit concept of equity so that the welfare of the firm's owners and consumers could be compared. Concepts of equity are not necessary to demonstrate the nature of the allocational loss represented by area BAE. That is an unambiguous loss from the monopolization of the market. If the market were competitive, output would expand to Q*, and overall welfare would increase by the extent of this area.

Monopolists' Costs

Our analysis has assumed that monopolists and competitive firms have essentially the same costs of production. A slightly deeper analysis may suggest this in fact may not be the case. Monopoly profits, after all, provide a tantalizing target for firms, and they may spend real resources to achieve those profits. They may, for example, adopt extensive advertising campaigns or invest in ways of differentiating their product to erect barriers to entry against other firms and hence obtain monopoly profits. Similarly, firms may seek special favors from the government in the form of tariff protection, restrictions on entry through licensing, or favorable treatment from a regulatory agency. Costs associated with these activities (such as lobbyists' salaries, legal fees, or "public service" advertising) may make monopolists' costs exceed those in a competitive industry.

The possibility that costs may be different (and presumably higher) for a monopolist than for a firm in a competitive industry creates some complications for theory and measurement of monopolistic distortions of the allocation of resources. In this case, some potential monopoly profits will be dissipated into monopoly-creating costs, and it is possible that some of those costs (advertising, for example) may even shift the demand curve facing the producer. Such effects seriously complicate Figure 12.5, and we will not analyze them in detail here.[8] "Applying Economics: Social Costs of Monopoly in the United States" shows how the costs induced by monopoly-seeking activities may have a major impact on the estimated degree of the economic harm that monopolies do.

---

[8]For a relatively simple treatment see R. A. Posner, "The Social Costs of Monopoly and Regulation," *Journal of Political Economy,* August 1975, pp. 807–827. Posner also makes the interesting point that social costs of crime (such as robbery) may be, as for the case of monopoly, understated unless the resources invested in crime prevention are also taken into account.

APPLYING ECONOMICS

Social Costs of Monopoly in the United States

Arnold Harberger was one of the first economists to use the kind of analysis we have been discussing to estimate the allocational losses from monopolization of markets in the U.S. economy.[9] Harberger's method was rather simple. First, he assembled cost and profit data for 73 different industries. For each industry he estimated the percent by which price exceeded average cost. This is equivalent to measuring the distance $P^{**} - P^*$ in Figure 12.5. For example, Harberger found that prices in the cement industry exceeded average costs by 8.4 percent. Next, Harberger calculated the expansion in demand $(Q^* - Q^{**})$ that would occur by lowering prices to the competitive level. By assuming an elasticity of demand for cement of -1.0, the quantity of cement demanded would be increased by 8.4 percent if competitive prices prevailed. Using those two figures, he then calculated the area of the triangle BAE [$= \frac{1}{2} \times (P^{**} - P^*) (Q^* - Q^{**})$] as a measure of the welfare loss from monopoly. For the case of cement, this loss amounted to $420,000 for the period under investigation (1924–1928). Making similar calculations for the other 72 industries in his sample, Harberger concluded that the total welfare loss from monopolies was about $150 million. This amounted to about 0.1 percent of gross national product during the period. Most more recent studies have arrived at similar estimates. Although monopoly losses may be relatively large in some industries, in comparison to the overall output of the economy they are rather small.

Some economists believe these types of calculations substantially understate the social costs of monopoly because they take no account of possible differences in costs between monopolies and competitive firms. Taking account of such differences, it is claimed, may substantially reverse the notion that the allocational costs

of monopoly are small. For example, a 1978 study by K. Cowling and D. C. Mueller estimated the portion of firms' costs that went toward creating monopoly profits.[10] From those estimates the authors calculated that monopolistic distortions may have represented as much as 13 percent of U.S. GNP in 1973. Estimates of such distortions were particularly large for automobile companies (they amounted to more than $1 billion for General Motors) and for household products companies (nearly $500 million each for Unilever and Procter & Gamble). The estimates are controversial because of the necessary arbitrariness in deciding which costs are really directed toward creating a monopoly position. For example, Cowling and Mueller included *all* advertising costs in that category, though they admit that some portion of these expenditures is probably unrelated to monopolistic goals. Despite this arbitrariness, the estimates illustrate the potential importance of the allocational effects of monopolies in situations where they may have significant effects on production costs.

To Think About

1. If the social cost of monopoly is so small (about 0.1 percent of GNP), why does the U.S. government spend so much on antimonopoly regulation through the Federal Trade Commission and the Department of Justice? Is the extent of such efforts misplaced, or does it seek goals (that is, preventing monopoly profits) other than just improving the allocation of resources?

2. The notion that monopolies may make expenditures in order to achieve monopoly profits has applications in other fields as well. Can you think of other ways in which firms may make "rent seeking" expenditures in order to obtain favorable market positions for themselves?

---

[9]Arnold Harberger, "Monopoly and Resource Allocation," *American Economic Review,* May 1954, pp. 77–87.

[10]K. Cowling and D. C. Mueller, "The Social Cost of Monopoly Power," *Economic Journal,* December 1978, pp. 727–748.

Table 12.3

Effects of Monopolization on the Market for Cassette Tapes

Price	Quantity (Tapes per Week)	Total Revenue	Marginal Revenue	Average and Marginal Cost	Under Perfect Competition	Under Monopoly	Monopoly Profits
$9	1	$ 9	$9	$3	$ 6	$ 3	$ 3
8	2	16	7	3	5	2	3
7	3	21	5	3	4	1	3
6	4	24	3	3	3	0	3
5	5	25	1	3	2	—	—
4	6	24	− 1	3	1	—	—
3	7	21	− 3	3	0	—	—
2	8	16	− 5	3	—	—	—
1	9	9	− 7	3	—	—	—
0	10	0	− 9	3	—	—	—
				Totals	$21	$6	$12

The column headers group as: **Demand Conditions** (Price, Quantity, Total Revenue, Marginal Revenue) and **Consumer Surplus** (Under Perfect Competition, Under Monopoly, Monopoly Profits).

▨ Competitive equilibrium
▨ Monopoly equilibrium

A Numerical Illustration of Deadweight Loss

As a numerical illustration of the types of calculations made by economists in studying the effects of monopoly, consider again the example of cassette tape sales introduced in Chapter 9. Table 12.3 repeats some of the information about this market originally presented in Table 9.1. Assume now that tapes have a marginal cost of $3 per tape. Under a situation of marginal cost pricing, tapes would also sell for $3 each, and as Table 12.3 shows, seven tapes per week would be bought. Consumer surplus can now be computed as the amount people were willing to pay for each tape less what they actually pay ($3). For example, someone who was willing to pay $9 for the first tape sold only paid $3. He or she received a consumer surplus of $6. The sixth column of Table 12.3 makes a similar computation for each level of output from one to seven tapes. As the table shows, total consumer surplus is $21 per week when price is equal to marginal cost.

Suppose now that the tape market is monopolized by a single local merchant with a marginal cost of $3. This profit-maximizing firm will supply four tapes per week since at this level of output marginal revenue equals marginal cost. At this level of sales, price will be $6 per tape, profit per tape will be $3, and the firm will have total profits of $12. These profits represent a transfer of what was previously consumer surplus for the first four buyers of tapes. The seventh column of Table 12.3 computes consumer surplus figures for the monopolized situation. With a price of $6, for example, the buyer of the first tape now receives a consumer surplus of only $3 ($9 − $6)—the other $3 he or she enjoyed under marginal cost pricing has been transferred into $3 of profits for the monopoly. As Table 12.3 shows, total consumer surplus under the monopoly amounts to only $6 per week. When combined with the monopolist's profits of $12 per week, it is easy to see that there is now a deadweight loss of $3 per week ($21 − $18). Some part of what was previously consumer surplus has simply vanished with the monopolizing of the market.

Market Separation and Price Discrimination

Price discrimination
The practice of charging different prices for a good in different markets.

A firm may have a monopoly position in two different markets for the same good. If these markets are effectively separated so that buyers cannot shift their purchasing from one market to the other, the monopolist may be able to increase profits and reduce consumer surplus further by practicing **price discrimination.** The profit-maximizing decision would be to produce that quantity in each market for which marginal revenue equals marginal cost. This may lead to different prices for the same good in the two markets. If the markets can be kept separate by the monopoly, these price differences can persist even though they are unrelated to actual production costs.

A Graphic Analysis

Such a discriminating situation is shown graphically in Figure 12.6. The figure is drawn so that the market demand and marginal revenue curves in the two markets share the same vertical axis, which records the price charged for the good in each market. For simplicity the figure also assumes that marginal cost is constant over all levels of output. The profit-maximizing decision for the monopoly is to produce Q_1^* in the first market and Q_2^* in the second market; these output levels obey the MR = MC rule for each market. The prices in the two markets will then be P_1 and P_2, respectively. It is clear from the figure that the market with the more inelastic demand curve will have the higher price.[11] The price-discriminating monopolist will charge a higher price in that market in which quantity purchased is less responsive to price changes. Although the analysis in Figure 12.6 assumes that marginal costs are constant, an identical result would hold in the more realistic case of increasing marginal costs. The price discriminator would charge higher prices in the market in which demand is less elastic.

Conditions for Successful Price Discrimination

Whether a monopoly is successful in price discrimination depends critically on its ability to keep markets separated. In some cases, that separation may

---

[11]*Proof:* Since MR = $P(1 + 1/e)$, $MR_1 = MR_2$ implies $P_1(1 + 1/e_1) = P_2(1 + 1/e_2)$. If $e_1 > e_2$ (if the demand in market 1 is less elastic), then P_1 must exceed P_2 for this equality to hold.

Figure 12.6
Separated Markets Raise
the Possibility of Price
Discrimination

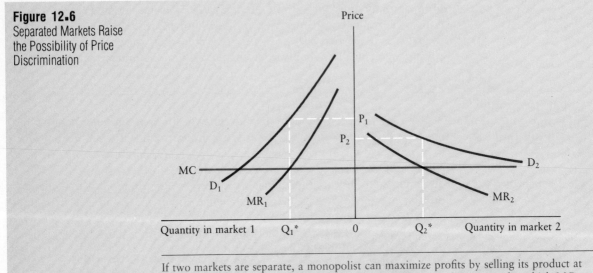

If two markets are separate, a monopolist can maximize profits by selling its product at different prices in the two markets. The firm would choose that output for which MC = MR in each of the markets. The diagram shows that the market that has a less elastic demand curve will be charged the higher price by the price discriminator.

be geographic. For example, book publishers tend to charge higher prices in the United States than abroad since foreign markets are more competitive and subject to illegal copying. In this case the oceans enforce market separation since few people would travel abroad simply to buy books. Such a discriminatory policy would not work if transportation costs were low, however. As chain stores that charge different prices in different parts of town have discovered, people will flock to where the bargains are.

Price discrimination by time of sale may also be possible. For example, tickets to late night or afternoon showings of motion pictures are usually cheaper than to evening shows. Discriminating against those who wish to attend prime-time shows succeeds because the good being purchased cannot be resold later. A firm that tried to sell toasters at two different prices during the day might discover itself to be in competition with savvy customers who bought when the price was low and undercut the firm by selling to other customers during high price periods. If customers themselves can alter when they shop, a discriminatory policy may not work. A firm that offers lower post-Christmas prices may find its pre-Christmas business facing stiff competition from those sales.

Finally, of course, the practice of price discrimination requires monopoly power. Because the discriminator chooses an output level for which price exceeds marginal (and perhaps average) cost, potential competitors may be encouraged to enter the market. Prior to deregulation, for example, airlines practiced a number of discriminatory policies in their pricing. The goal of such policies as advance ticket purchase requirements and minimum stay provisions was to differentiate between business travelers (who had relatively inelastic demands) and discretionary travelers. The large profits made from business travel could not persist in an era of greater competition as new airlines sought to enter this market.

The practice of price discrimination is subject to a number of constraining influences. Still, there are many situations where buyers pay different prices for the same product. Some of these may involve quite intricate pricing strategies, as "Applying Economics: Pricing at Disneyland" illustrates.

Regulation of Monopolies

The regulation of monopolies is an important subject in applied economic analysis. The utility, communications, and transportation industries are highly regulated in most countries, and devising regulatory procedures that cause these industries to operate in a desirable way is an important practical problem. Here we look at a few aspects of the regulation of monopolies that relate to pricing policies.

Marginal Cost Pricing and the Natural Monopoly Dilemma

By analogy to the perfectly competitive case, many economists believe that it is important for the prices charged by regulated monopolies to accurately reflect marginal costs of production. In this way the deadweight loss from monopolies is minimized. The principal problem raised by an enforced policy of marginal cost pricing is that it may require natural monopolies to operate at a loss.

Natural monopoly
A firm that exhibits diminishing average cost over a broad range of output levels.

Natural monopolies, by definition, exhibit decreasing average costs over a broad range of output levels. The cost curves for such a firm might look like those shown in Figure 12.7. In the absence of regulation the monopoly would produce output level Q_A and receive a price of P_A for its product. Profits in this situation are given by the rectangle P_ACBA. A regulatory agency might set a price of P_R for this monopoly. At this price, Q_R is demanded, and the marginal cost of producing this output level is also P_R. Consequently, marginal cost pricing has been achieved. Unfortunately, because of the declining nature of the firm's cost curves, the price P_R (= marginal cost) falls below average costs. With this regulated price the monopoly must operate at a loss of GP_REF. Since no firm can operate indefinitely at a loss, this poses a dilemma for the regulatory agency: Either it must abandon its goal of marginal cost pricing, or the government must subsidize the monopoly forever.

Two-Tier Pricing Systems

One way out of the marginal cost pricing dilemma is a two-part pricing system. Under this system the monopoly is permitted to charge some users a high price

Pricing at Disneyland

Disneyland and Disney World are unique entertainment attractions. Amusement park aficionados (including this author) agree there are few, if any substitutes for these products, and therefore the Disney company occupies a potentially strong monopoly position in its pricing decisions. Given this position, it is not surprising that Disney adopts a bewildering array of price policies, all presumably with the purpose of converting available consumer surplus into profits.

Not only does the firm use a variety of group discounts, time-of-year pricing differentials, and reduced prices for children of various ages, but until recently it used a complicated multipart pricing schedule for its rides.[12] Under that schedule, Disneyland patrons had to purchase a "passport" containing a ticket for admission to the park together with coupons for admission to the rides themselves. Contents of a typical passport are summarized in Table 12.4 as well as the prices of individual tickets for each type of ride. The company enjoyed a great deal of pricing flexibility with this passport arrangement. It could vary the basic price of a passport, it could vary the composition of tickets contained in a passport, it could redefine which ride requires which ticket, and it could alter the prices of extra tickets. In short, the passport pricing method provided the firm with myriad opportunities to increase profits through price discrimination among different types of buyers.

For example, the passport composition seems to have been designed to appeal to a large number of buyers without overly straining the capacity of any one ride. For example, the number of "E" ride tickets seems to be carefully chosen both to allow passport purchasers to ride most of the major attractions without permitting second rides, except at additional cost. The lesser attraction tickets in the passport spread patrons around the park. Finally, and perhaps most interesting, the price of extra tickets for rides were quite high (certainly well above marginal cost). This pricing policy is consistent with the low price elasticity of patrons for extra rides once they are already at the park.

Disney's passport pricing schedule posed problems for the parks. Most importantly, labor costs were substantially higher under such a system (since many ticket collectors and salespersons are needed) than under a single price admission policy, followed at many other amusement parks (Great Adventure and Busch Gardens, for example). Recently, Disney has moved away from individual tickets for rides and toward a single entry fee. This single fee still provides the company with opportunities for price discrimination, such as charging reduced prices for multiday tickets and lower rates for local residents than for tourists. The company still appears to be following the profit motive.

To Think About

1. If you have been to Disneyland or Disney World, can you remember other examples of price discrimination? How is food priced? How about hotel accommodations? Can you explain why the company might adopt seasonal price differentials?

2. The former Disney pricing scheme is formally termed a two-part pricing schedule. Can you think of other examples of situations where customers are charged a flat fee for basic service and extra fees for additional services? How do these various fees relate to marginal costs?

Table 12.4 Structure of a Typical Disneyland Passport

Item	Example	Number of Tickets in Passport	Price of Extra Ticket
Admission to park	—	1	$4.00
"A" ride	Toddler Rides, Shooting Gallery	2	.25
"B" ride	Dumbo, Train	3	.50
"C" ride	Peter Pan's Flight, Mr. Toad's Wild Ride	3	.75
"D" ride	Tom Sawyer's Island, Autopia	2	1.00
"E" ride	Space Mountain, Haunted Mansion	5	1.50

Source: Author's 1978 passport. *Note:* As discussed in this example, Disneyland now has a single price admission policy.

---

[12]For an analytical treatment of these points see W. Y. Oi, "A Disneyland Dilemma: Two-Part Tariffs for a Mickey Mouse Monopoly," *Quarterly Journal of Economics,* February 1971, pp. 77–96.

Figure 12.7
Price Regulation for a
Natural Monopoly

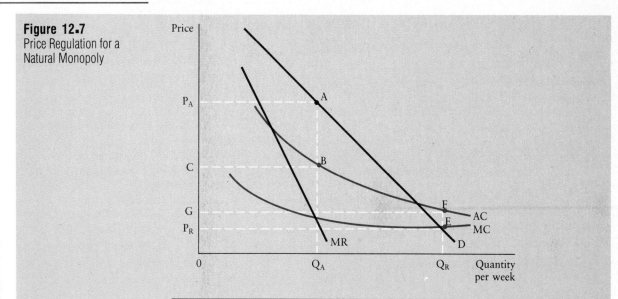

Because natural monopolies exhibit decreasing average cost, marginal costs fall below
average cost. Enforcing a policy of marginal cost pricing will entail operating at a loss. A
price of P_R, for example, will achieve the goal of marginal cost pricing but will necessitate
an operating loss of GP_REF.

while maintaining a low price for "marginal" users. In this way the demanders
paying the high price in effect subsidize the losses of the low-price customers.

Such a pricing scheme is shown in Figure 12.8. Here the regulatory commission has decided that some users will pay a relatively high price, P_1. At
this price, Q_1 is demanded. Other users (presumably those who would not
buy the good at the P_1 price) are offered a lower price, P_2. This lower price
generates additional demand of $Q_2 - Q_1$. Consequently, a total output of Q_2
is produced at an average cost of A. With this two-part pricing system, the
profits on the sales to high-price demanders (given by the rectangle P_1ABG)
balance the losses incurred on the low-priced sales (BCEF). Furthermore, for
the "marginal user," the marginal cost pricing rule is being followed: It is the
"intramarginal" user who subsidizes the firm so that it does not operate at a
loss.

Although it may not in practice be so simple to establish pricing schemes
that maintain marginal cost pricing and cover operating costs, many regulatory commissions do use multipart price schedules that intentionally discriminate against some users to the advantage of others. "Applying Economics:
Electricity Pricing" discusses one example of this type of pricing.

Electricity Pricing

Many regulated electric utilities follow a declining block pricing schedule such as that illustrated in Table 12.5. One intention of such a schedule is to approximate the theoretical goals illustrated in Figure 12.8. That is, the marginal price of electricity is an approximation to the marginal cost of producing it.

One particularly interesting example of this type of policy is time-of-day pricing of electricity. The purpose of such pricing is to shift electricity use during peak periods to off-peak hours. Such a policy has been fol-

lowed in France for many years under the "Green Tariff" in which electricity during peak winter hours costs four times as much as electricity during more normal periods. In the United States, local utility companies in at least 10 locations have experimented with such rates, although none has implemented the rates across its entire system. In general, these companies have found that users will shift their electricity use in response to peak hour price premiums, but the elasticities involved are fairly low.[13] Whether the expense required to install time-of-day electric meters would yield a sufficient payoff in terms of peak load leveling remains an open question.

To Think About

1. Can you think of other regulated monopolies where marginal cost pricing might make sense? For phone service, for example, what would marginal cost pricing require? Do actual phone rates seem to follow such principles?
2. The electric industry is really a combination of two industries: power generation and power distribution. Are both of these natural monopolies? If not, are there ways in which competition might be introduced?

Table 12.5
Typical Monthly Residential Electricity Rate Schedule Showing Declining Block Structure

Amount of Electricity Used	Price
First 12 kilowatt-hours	$2.25
Next 338 kilowatt-hours	.0455 per kilowatt-hour
Next 650 kilowatt-hours	.0260 per kilowatt-hour
Over 1,000 kilowatt-hours	.0200 per kilowatt-hour

Source: Author's electric bill.

Rate of Return Regulation

Another approach to setting the price charged by a natural monopoly that is followed in many regulatory situations is to permit the monopoly to charge a price above marginal cost that will earn a "fair" rate of return on investment. Much analytical effort is then spent on defining the "fair" rate and on developing how it might be measured. From an economic point of view some of the most interesting questions about this procedure concern how the regulatory activity affects the firm's decisions. If, for example, the rate of return allowed to firms exceeds what the firm might earn under competitive circumstances, the firm will have an incentive to use relatively more capital input than needed to truly minimize costs. If regulators typically delay in making

---

[13]See *Forecasting and Modeling Time-of-Day and Seasonal Electric Demands* (Palo Alto, Calif.: Electric Power Research Institute, 1977).

Figure 12.8
Two-Part Pricing Schedule

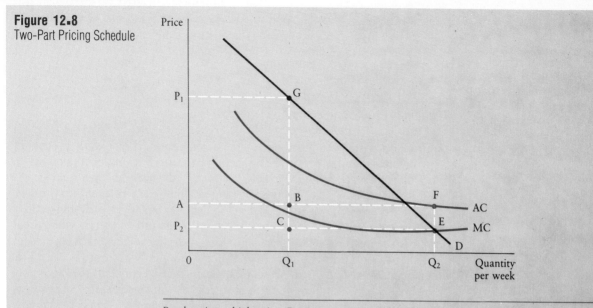

By charging a high price (P_1) to some users and a low price (P_2) to others, it may be possible for a regulatory commission to: (1) enforce marginal cost pricing, and (2) create a situation where the profits from one class of user (P_1ABG) subsidize the losses of the other class (BCEF).

rate decisions, firms may be given incentives to minimize costs that would not otherwise exist since they cannot immediately recover their costs through higher rates. Although it is possible to develop a formal analysis of all of these possibilities, we do not do so here.[14]

Benefits of Monopoly

Our analysis in this chapter makes two arguments against monopoly. The first concludes that the allocational effects of monopoly are harmful: Too few resources are devoted to the production of a good for which the supply is monopolized. The second argument is somewhat more ambiguous but is probably more important from a policy perspective: Monopolies have undesirable distributional effects. Monopolies may make long-run profits, and these profits may accrue to relatively rich owners at the expense of relatively poor consumers. This consideration of the distributional fairness of monopolies reinforces the allocational argument and provides the basis for the notion that monopolies are an unambiguous evil. This simple conclusion is questioned by

---

[14]For a detailed treatment see E. E. Bailey, *Economic Theory of Regulatory Constraint* (Lexington, Mass.: D. C. Heath, 1973).

some economists. For example, J. A. Schumpeter stressed the beneficial role that monopoly profits can play in the process of economic development.[15] This section briefly reviews some of the possible beneficial aspects of monopoly that have been suggested.

Monopoly Profits and Economic Growth

Authors discussing the possible benefits of monopoly tend to take a dynamic view of the economic process. They emphasize innovation and the ability of particular types of firms to achieve technical advances. In this context, the profits that monopolistic firms earn play an important role. Profits provide the funds to invest in research and development. Whereas perfectly competitive firms must be content with a normal return on invested capital, monopolies have the surplus funds to undertake the risky process of research. More important, perhaps, the possibility of attaining a monopoly position, or the desire to maintain such a position, provides an important incentive to the monopoly to keep one step ahead of potential competitors. Innovations in new products and cost-saving production techniques may be integrally related to the possibility of monopolization. Without a monopoly position, the full benefits of innovation could not be obtained by the innovating firm.

Monopoly and Cost Saving

Schumpeter stresses that the monopolization of a market may make it less costly for a firm to plan its activities. Being the only source of supply for a product eliminates many of the contingencies that a firm in a competitive market must face. For example, a monopoly may not have to spend as much on selling expenses (such as advertising, brand identification, or visiting retailers) as would be the case in a more competitive industry. Similarly, a monopoly may know more about the specific demand curve for its product and may more readily adapt to changing demand conditions.

Of course, whether or not any of these purported benefits of monopolies outweigh their allocational and distributional disadvantages is an open question. Generally, economists have not been sufficiently convinced about the benefits of monopoly to favor deliberate creation of monopoly power through licensing or other barriers to entry.

---

[15]J. A. Schumpeter, *Capitalism, Socialism, and Democracy*, 3d ed. (New York: Harper & Row, 1950), especially Chapter 8.

Summary

A market in which there is a single seller is called a "monopoly." In a monopoly situation the firm faces the entire market demand curve. Contrary to the case of perfect competition, the monopoly's output decision will completely determine market price. The major conclusions of our investigation of pricing in monopoly markets are:

- The profit-maximizing monopoly will choose an output level for which marginal revenue is equal to marginal cost. Since the firm faces a downward sloping demand curve, market price will exceed both marginal revenue and marginal cost.
- The divergence between price and marginal cost is a sign that the monopoly causes resources to be allocated inefficiently. Buyers are willing to pay more for one more unit of output than it costs the firm to produce it, but the monopoly prevents this beneficial transaction from occurring.
- Because of barriers to entry, a monopoly may earn positive long-run economic profits. These profits may have undesirable distributional effects.
- A monopoly may adopt a policy of price discrimination among buyers if it can successfully separate those buyers into different markets. Prices will be higher in markets with less elastic demand.
- Governments may choose to regulate the prices charged by monopolies. In the case of a natural monopoly (for which average costs decline over a broad range of output) this poses a dilemma. The regulatory agency can opt for marginal cost pricing (in which case the monopoly will operate at a loss) or for average cost pricing (in which case an inefficient quantity will be produced).

Problems

12.1 A monopolist can produce at constant average and marginal costs of $AC = MC = 5$. The firm faces a market demand curve given by $Q = 53 - P$. The monopolist's marginal revenue curve is given by $MR = 53 - 2Q$.

a. Calculate the profit-maximizing price-quantity combination for the monopolist. Also calculate the monopolist's profits.

b. What output level would be produced by this industry under perfect competition (where price = marginal cost)?

c. Calculate the consumer surplus obtained by consumers in part b. Show that this exceeds the sum of the monopolist's profits and consumer surplus received in part a. What is the value of the "deadweight loss" from monopolization?

12.2 A monopolist faces a market demand curve given by

$$Q = 70 - P.$$

The monopolist's marginal revenue curve is given by

$$MR = 70 - 2Q.$$

a. If the monopolist can produce at constant average and marginal costs of AC = MC = 6, what output level will the monopolist choose in order to maximize profits? What is the price at this output level? What are the monopolist's profits?
b. Assume instead that the monopolist has a cost structure where total costs are described by

$$TC = .25Q^2 - 5Q + 300$$

and marginal cost is given by

$$MC = .5Q - 5.$$

With the monopolist facing the same market demand and marginal revenue, what price-quantity combination will be chosen now to maximize profits? What will profits be?
c. Assume now that a third cost structure explains the monopolist's position with total costs given by

$$TC = .333Q^3 - 26Q^2 + 695Q - 5,800$$

and marginal costs given by

$$MC = Q^2 - 52Q + 695.$$

Again, calculate the monopolist's price-quantity combination that maximizes profits. What will profits be? (Hint: set MC = MR as usual and use the quadratic formula or simple factoring to solve the second order equation for Q.)
d. Graph the market demand curve, the MR curve, and the three marginal cost curves from parts a, b, and c. Notice that the monopolist's profit-making ability is constrained by (1) the market demand curve it faces (along with its associated MR curve), and (2) the cost structure underlying production.

12.3 A single firm monopolizes the entire market for widgets and can produce at constant average and marginal costs of

$$AC = MC = 10.$$

Originally, the firm faces a market demand curve given by

$$Q = 60 - P$$

and a marginal revenue curve given by

$$MR = 60 - 2Q.$$

a. Calculate the profit-maximizing price-quantity combination for the firm. What are the firm's profits?

b. Now assume that the market demand curve shifts outward (becoming steeper) and is given by

$$Q = 45 - .5P$$

with the marginal revenue curve given by

$$MR = 90 - 4Q.$$

What is the firm's profit-maximizing price-quantity combination now? What are the firm's profits?

c. Instead of the assumptions of part b, assume that the market demand curve shifts outward (becoming flatter) and is given by

$$Q = 100 - 2P$$

with the marginal revenue curve given by

$$MR = 50 - Q.$$

What is the firm's profit-maximizing price-quantity combination now? What are the firm's profits?

d. Graph the three different situations of parts a, b, and c. Using your results, explain why there is no supply curve for a monopoly.

12.4 Suppose that the market for hula hoops is monopolized by a single firm.

a. Draw the initial equilibrium for such a market.

b. Suppose now that the demand for hula hoops shifts outward slightly. Show that, in general (contrary to the competitive case), it will not be possible to predict the effect of this shift in demand on the market price of hula hoops.

c. Consider three possible ways in which the price elasticity of demand might change as the demand curve shifts—it might increase, it might decrease, or it might stay the same. Consider also that marginal costs for the monopolist might be rising, falling, or constant in the range where MR = MC. Consequently there are nine different combinations of types of demand shifts and marginal cost slope configurations. Analyze each of these to determine for which it is possible to make a definite prediction about the effect of the shift in demand on the price of hula hoops.

*12.5 Suppose a company has a monopoly on a game called *Monopoly* and faces a demand curve given by

$$Q_T = 100 - P$$

and a marginal revenue curve given by

$$MR = 100 - 2Q_T$$

where Q_T equals the combined total number of games produced per hour in the company's two factories ($Q_T = q_1 + q_2$). If factory 1 has a marginal cost curve given by

$$MC_1 = q_1 - 5$$

and factory 2 has a marginal cost curve given by

$$MC_2 = .5q_2 - 5,$$

how much total output will the company choose to produce and how will it distribute this production between its two factories in order to maximize profits?

*12.6 Suppose a monopoly can produce any level of output it wishes at a constant marginal (and average) cost of $5 per unit. Assume that the monopoly sells its goods in two different markets that are separated by some distance. The demand curve in the first market is given by

$$Q_1 = 55 - P_1$$

and the curve in the second market is given by

$$Q_2 = 70 - 2P_2.$$

If the monopolist can maintain the separation between the two markets, what level of output should be produced in each market and what price will prevail in each market? What are total profits in this situation?

How would your answer change if it only cost demanders $5 to transport goods between the two markets? What would be the monopolist's new profit level in this situation? How would your answer change if transportation costs were 0?

(Hint: Show that for a downward-sloping linear demand curve, profits are maximized when output is set at $Q^*/2$, where Q^* is the output level that would be demanded when $P = MC$. Use this result to solve the problem.)

12.7 Use the concept of consumer surplus to show that imposition of a specific tax in a perfectly competitive industry involves a deadweight loss similar to that shown for the case of a monopoly.

12.8 Suppose a perfectly competitive industry can produce widgets at a constant marginal cost of $10 per unit. Once the industry is monopolized, marginal costs rise to $12 per unit because $2 per unit must be paid to lobbyists to retain the widget producers' favored position. Suppose the market demand for widgets is given by

$$Q_D = 1,000 - 50P$$

and the marginal revenue curve by

$$MR = 20 - Q/25.$$

    a. Calculate the perfectly competitive and monopoly outputs and prices.

    b. Calculate the total loss of consumer surplus from monopolization of widget production.

    c. Graph your results.

CHAPTER 13

Pricing in Imperfectly Competitive Markets

This chapter discusses the theory of pricing in markets that fall between the polar extremes of perfect competition and monopoly. Although no single model can be used to explain all possible forms of imperfect competition, we look at a few of the basic elements that are common to many of the models in current use. To that end we focus on three specific topics: (1) pricing of homogeneous goods in markets in which there are relatively few firms; (2) product differentiation in these markets; and (3) how entry and exit possibilities affect long-run outcomes in imperfectly competitive markets.

In a sense, Chapter 13 concerns how the stringent assumptions of the perfectly competitive model can be relaxed and what the results of changing those assumptions are. For this study, the perfectly competitive model provides a useful benchmark, since departures from the competitive norm may involve efficiency losses similar to those described in the previous chapter in connection with monopolistic markets. Two specific criteria we use in this comparison are (1) whether prices under imperfect competition equal marginal costs and (2) whether, in the long run, production occurs at minimum average cost. As we will see, imperfectly competitive markets often lack one or both of these desirable features of perfect competition.

Because the theory of imperfect competition does not yield the precise and well-defined results that the theories of perfect competition and monopoly do, much of the literature on the subject is descriptive and empirical rather than strictly analytical. The field of "industrial organization" has grown rapidly in recent years and provides a number of insights into behavior in complicated real-world situations. The final sections of this chapter offer a brief glimpse of some of this research into industrial organization.

Pricing of Homogeneous Goods

This section looks at the theory of pricing in markets in which relatively few firms produce a single homogeneous good. As before, we assume that the market is perfectly competitive on the demand side; that is, there are assumed to be many demanders, each of whom is a price taker. We also assume that there are no transactions or informational costs, so that the good in question obeys the law of one price and we may speak unambiguously of *the* price of the good. (Later in this chapter we relax this assumption to consider product differentiation.) In this section we also assume that there are a fixed small number of identical firms. The appendix to this chapter considers a simple numerical example of a market with exactly two firms, but our analysis here is not restricted to any specific number since the method of analysis does not, for the most part, depend on the number of firms. Later in this chapter we allow the number of firms to vary through entry and exit in response to profitability.

Quasicompetitive Model

Quasicompetitive model
A model of oligopoly pricing in which each firm acts as a price taker.

The possible outcomes for prices when there are few firms is uncertain—they depend on how the firms react to competitors' activities. At one extreme is what we might call a **quasicompetitive model.** In this case each firm acts as a price taker. For example, a new gas station operator would be a price taker if he or she assumed that opening the station would not affect the local price of gasoline either directly (because the local supply hasn't increased very much) or indirectly (because nearby stations will not change their prices in the face of the new competition). The price taker assumption may not always be valid, especially in volatile, cutthroat markets such as gasoline sales. But this (perhaps naive) assumption is a useful place to start.

If a firm acts as a price taker, it will, as before, produce where price equals long-run marginal cost. The market solution in this case will resemble a competitive one even though there may be relatively few firms involved. Figure 13.1 shows a particularly simple market solution of this type. The figure assumes that marginal cost (and average cost) is constant for all output levels. Consequently, market price (P_C) must equal this marginal cost. Under this quasicompetitive solution Q_C will be produced and market equilibrium will occur at point C. This equilibrium represents the highest quantity and lowest price that can prevail in the long term with the demand curve D. A price lower than P_C would not cover firms' average cost, so it would not be sustainable in the long run.

Cartel Model

The assumption of price-taking behavior may be particularly inappropriate in oligopolistic industries in which each firm's decisions have an effect on price.

Figure 13.1
Pricing under Imperfect
Competition

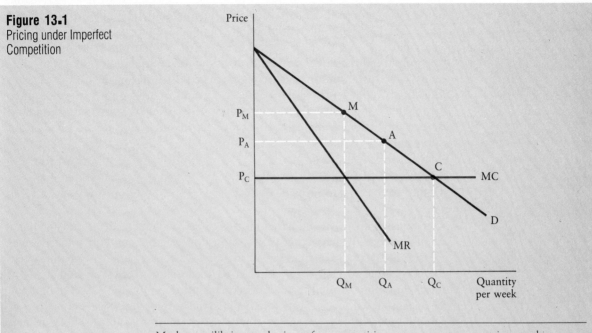

Market equilibrium under imperfect competition can occur at many points on the demand curve. In this figure (which assumes that marginal costs are constant over all output ranges), the quasicompetitive equilibrium occurs at point C and the cartel equilibrium at point M. Many solutions (such as A) may occur between points M and C, depending on the specific assumption made about firms' strategic interrelationships.

Cartel model
A model of oligopoly pricing in which firms coordinate their decisions to act as a multiplant monopoly.

An alternative assumption here would be that firms as a group recognize that they can affect price and coordinate their decisions to achieve monopoly profits. This case can be described by a **cartel model** in which the cartel acts as a multiplant monopoly and produces in each of its "plants" (that is, in each firm in the cartel) where marginal revenue equals marginal cost. Assuming, as before, that these marginal costs are equal and constant for all firms, the output choice is indicated by point M in Figure 13.1. Because this coordinated plan requires a specific output level for each firm, the plan also dictates how monopoly profits earned by the cartel are to be shared by its members. In the aggregate, these profits will be as large as possible, given the market demand curve and the industry's cost structure.

There are three problems with the cartel solution to imperfect competition. First, cartel formations may be illegal. In the United States, for example, Section I of the Sherman Act of 1890 outlaws "conspiracies in restraint of trade," so would-be cartel members may expect a visit from the FBI. Similar laws exist in many other countries. A second problem with the cartel solution is that it requires that a considerable amount of information be available to the directors of the cartel—specifically, they must know the market demand function and each firm's marginal cost function. This information may be costly to obtain, and some cartel members may be reluctant to provide it. Finally, and most important, the cartel solution may be fundamentally unstable. Since each cartel member will produce an output level for which price exceeds marginal cost, each will have an incentive to expand output to increase its own profits. If the directors of the oligopoly are not able to police such "chiseling," the cartel solution may collapse. The difficulties of the OPEC cartel in dictating output levels to its members during the early 1980s attest to these problems. Ultimately, OPEC's production decisions were widely disobeyed (especially by non-Arab members of the cartel), and by 1984, prices had begun a precipitous decline.

Other Pricing Possibilities

The quasicompetitive and cartel models of pricing tend to determine the outer limits between which actual prices in an imperfectly competitive market will be set (for example, at point A in Figure 13.1). This band of outcomes may be very wide, so economists have tried to develop models to predict where market equilibrium will actually occur within these limits.[1] Developing these models is very difficult. For example, imagine developing a systematic description of how people play poker—complete with betting strategies, bluffing, and each player guessing what the other players are doing. No model can predict such behavior with complete accuracy. The outcomes depend on the skills of the players, the way the cards are running, and even on seemingly irrelevant factors like the time of night or the temperature of the room. Exactly the same types of problems arise in creating a model of pricing in markets with relatively few firms. In this case the outcome all depends on how the firms play the game.

The appendix to this chapter numerically illustrates some of the strategic issues involved in the pricing decisions in markets with two firms. It then proceeds from that example to discuss the theory of games and shows how that theory might be applied in economic situations. These discussions introduce the problems of modeling gamelike pricing decisions, and you should study them to understand what economists mean by strategic interactions among firms.

Kinked demand curve model
A model in which firms believe that price increases result in a very elastic demand, while price decreases result in an inelastic demand for their products.

Kinked Demand Curve Model

Two models of pricing in markets with few sellers have been widely discussed in economics. The **kinked demand curve model** was first developed by P. M.

---

[1]For example, if the elasticity of demand is -2, Equation 9.8 shows that $P = 2 \cdot MR$. Under a quasicompetitive solution $P = MC$; under the cartel solution, price is twice that level ($P = 2MC$). A model that can predict prices only within such a wide range is not very useful.

Figure 13.2
Kinked Demand Curve

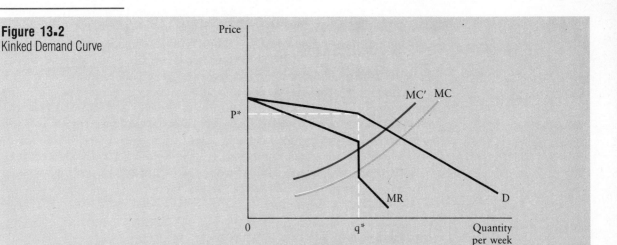

A firm in an oligopoly industry may believe it is faced by a demand curve (D) with a kink at the prevailing price (P*). If the firm considered raising its price, others would not follow: demand would appear to be very elastic since customers would shift to its competitors. Conversely, the firm may believe that if it lowered price, all its competitors would do the same. Demand would be relatively inelastic below P*. The kink at P* means that the MR curve will be discontinuous at this point. Therefore, firms may not respond to shifts in their marginal cost curves.

Sweezy in 1939 to explain why prices in markets with few firms tended to be inflexible.[2] It asserted that changes in costs were only rarely met by changes in market prices, and that when changes in market price did occur in oligopoly markets, they tended to be of rather large magnitudes. Although whether prices really do behave in this way is debatable, Sweezy tried to explain such price inflexibility by asking about the demand curve faced by a typical firm in an oligopoly market. He hypothesized that firms make their decisions in a cautious and pessimistic way. When contemplating lowering its price, a firm believes all its rivals will follow and, because it cannot gain a lot of extra sales by lowering price, demand is relatively inelastic for price decreases. If a firm were to raise its price alone, Sweezy assumes that the firm believes that others would not follow. For price increases, the firm will find demand very elastic, since its customers will switch to competitors' products whose prices have not been raised. This kinked demand curve possibility is labeled D in Figure 13.2. The prevailing market price is P*, and the firm sells quantity q*. Quantity sold would not increase greatly if the firm lowered its price (since rivals are

[2]P. M. Sweezy, "Demand under Conditions of Oligopoly," *Journal of Political Economy,* August 1939, pp. 568–573.

assumed to follow), but it would be decreased markedly if the firm raised its price.

If the firm believes that it is faced by a kinked demand curve, it may not react to small changes in costs. The marginal revenue curve associated with the kinked demand curve shows this reaction. The MR curve in Figure 13.2 is discontinuous at q*, reflecting the kinked nature of the assumed demand curve. Suppose that marginal cost were initially MC and that cost increases have shifted this curve to MC'. With this new marginal cost curve there will be no incentive for the firm to change either price or quantity, because marginal revenue is still equal to marginal costs and profits are being maximized. Prices will tend to remain fixed until some unifying event causes all firms to raise their prices at the same time.

Price Leadership Model

Price leadership model
Model in which one dominant firm takes reactions of all other firms into account in its output and pricing decisions.

A second model of pricing in markets with few sellers is called the **price leadership model.** It tends to accord with many real-world observations. In some markets one firm or group of firms is looked upon as the leader in pricing, and all firms adjust their prices to what this leader does. Two possible examples of price leadership are the computer industry (where IBM plays the role of a leader) and the commercial banking industry (where the prime rate tends to be determined by the major New York City banks).

Competitive fringe
Group of firms that act as price takers in a market dominated by a price leader.

A formal model of pricing in a market dominated by a leading firm is presented in Figure 13.3. The industry is assumed to be composed of a single price-setting leader and a **competitive fringe** of firms who take the leader's price as given in their decisions. The demand curve D represents the total demand curve for the industry's product, and the supply curve SC represents the supply decisions of all the firms in the competitive fringe. Using these two curves, the demand curve (D') facing the industry leader is derived as follows. For a price of P_1 or above the leader will sell nothing since the competitive fringe would be willing to supply all that is demanded. For prices below P_2 the leader has the market to itself since the fringe is not willing to supply anything. Between P_2 and P_1 the curve D' is constructed by subtracting what the fringe will supply from total market demand—that is, the leader gets that portion of demand not taken by the fringe firms.

Given the demand curve D', the leader can construct its marginal revenue curve (MR') and then refer to its own marginal cost curve (MC) to determine the profit-maximizing output level, Q_L. Market price will then be P_L. Given that price, the competitive fringe will produce Q_C and total industry output will be Q_T ($= Q_C + Q_L$).

This model does not answer such important questions as how the price leader in an industry is chosen, or what happens when a member of the fringe decides to challenge the leader for its position (and profits). The model does show how elements of both the perfectly competitive and the monopoly theories of price determination can be woven together to produce a model of

Figure 13.3
Formal Model of Price
Leadership Behavior

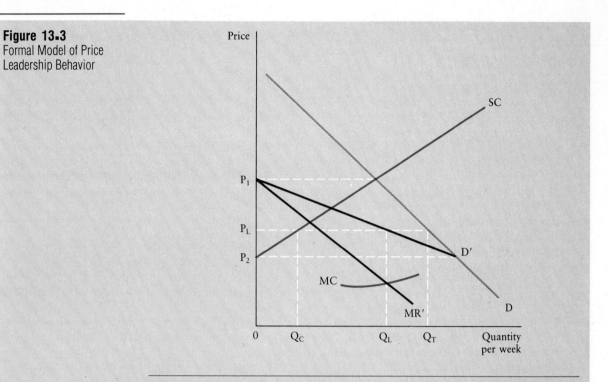

The curve D′ shows the demand curve facing the price leader—it is derived by subtracting what is produced by the competitive fringe of firms (SC) from market demand (D). Given D′, the firm's profit-maximizing output level is Q_L, and a price of P_L will prevail in the market.

oligopoly pricing. Such a model may explain industry behavior in some important situations, as "Applying Economics: OPEC Pricing Strategy" illustrates.

Product Differentiation

Up to this point we have assumed a homogeneous output. Demanders were assumed to be indifferent about which firm's output they bought, and the law of one price was assumed to hold in the market. These assumptions may not hold in many real-world markets. Firms often devote considerable resources to differentiate their products from their competitors' through such devices as quality and style variations, warranties and guarantees, special service features, and product advertising. These activities require firms to employ additional resources, and firms will choose to do so if profits are thereby increased. Product variation also results in a relaxation of the law of one price, since now the market will consist of goods that vary from firm to firm and consumers may have preferences about which supplier to patronize.

That possibility introduces a certain fuzziness into what we mean by the

OPEC Pricing Strategy

The Organization of Petroleum Exporting Countries (OPEC) was formed in the early 1960s. Altogether, OPEC members represented about half of total world oil production and perhaps 60 to 70 percent of total crude oil reserves. During its first 10 years, OPEC had relatively little influence on world oil prices. But during the 1973 Arab-Israeli war and its associated oil embargo, that situation changed dramatically. In slightly more than one year oil prices rose nearly fourfold—from about $2.50 to about $12 per barrel. After this initial price spurt, oil prices continued to rise (especially in reaction to supply disruptions, such as the Iranian revolution), although at a much slower rate. By 1982, crude oil sold for about $34 per barrel—a 14-fold increase over the span of a decade. This rising price of a basic energy commodity had major consequences for economies throughout the world, ranging from lowered thermostats and a marked shift toward smaller cars in the United States to major balance-of-payments problems for less developed countries. Since 1982 these problems have been alleviated by a sharp decline in oil prices. By early 1986 prices had fallen to about one-half of their 1982 levels.

Economists have developed two types of models to explain OPEC pricing. Both of these attempt to take account of the structure of OPEC membership, particularly the role played by Saudi Arabia and the nearby Persian Gulf states of Kuwait, Qatar, Bahrain, and the United Arab Emirates. These producers constitute more than one-third of total OPEC production and considerably more of its total crude oil reserves. The countries are relatively lightly populated compared to some other OPEC members, such as Indonesia, Nigeria, or Venezuela. They also seem to have substantial excess oil production capability. It is these features that make them crucial to the pricing story.

One approach to OPEC pricing treats the organization as a cartel. That is, the cartel coordinates the activities of its members so as to operate as a single-firm monopoly. Under this model, Saudi Arabia is able to hold the cartel together by restricting its own output by the amount necessary to achieve the profit-maximizing level. Saudi Arabia's unique geological position (it has more than 500 billion barrels of crude oil) and its small population make it possible for this cartel to persist much longer than has usually been the case for cartels, since there is no need to enforce major output restrictions on other producers. In exchange for Saudi coop-

---

Product group
Set of differentiated products that are highly substitutable for one another.

"market for a good," since now there are many closely related, but not identical, products. For example, if toothpaste brands vary somewhat from supplier to supplier, should we consider all these products to be in the same market or should we differentiate among fluoridated products, gels, striped toothpaste, smokers' toothpaste, and so forth? Although this question is of great practical importance in industry studies, we do not pursue it here. Instead, we will assume that the market is composed of a few firms, each producing a slightly different product, but that these products can usefully be considered a single **product group.** That is, each firm produces a product that is highly substitutable for its rivals. Although this definition has its own ambiguities (arguments about the definition of a product group often dominate antitrust law suits, for example), it should suffice for our purposes.

Firms' Choices

Let us assume that there are a few firms competing within a particular product group. Each firm can choose the amount to spend on differentiating its product

eration, other OPEC members must to some extent bend to that country's wishes. In particular, most observers agree that the Saudis exercise a moderating price influence within OPEC. Their large oil reserves make them more concerned than most other oil producers about possible long-run alternatives (such as nuclear or solar power) to oil-based energy being developed in response to oil's high price. They may seek price moderation to discourage these long-term alternatives.

Another view of the world oil market assumes a much greater degree of competitiveness than the cartel model. In this view, Saudi Arabia is treated as a price leader with other OPEC nations (and, indeed, all other oil producers) constituting a competitive fringe. Members of the competitive fringe, as shown in Figure 13.4, act as price takers. They produce where price is equal to marginal cost, and they do not engage in the type of output restrictions that cartel members would. If this model is correct, the elaborate, regular meetings of the OPEC oil ministers are simply a gaudy ritual with no particular significance for the actual pricing of oil. And Saudi Arabia's much-heralded position as a moderate in oil pricing simply derives from its position as a price leader with low marginal costs of production. Its behavior is consistent with the goal of long-run profit maximization, constrained by the competitive fringe.

On the whole, the evidence seems to be most consistent with the price leadership model of OPEC behavior. Even during the late 1970s prices seem to have been below those a cartelized monopoly would charge.[3] The sharp declines in 1984 and 1985 probably reflected a major shift in supply by the fringe producers as a result of significant oil discoveries, especially in non-OPEC countries.

To Think About

1. The sharp increase in oil prices between 1973 and 1982 is still a bit of a mystery to economists. Can such a large increase be fully explained with either the cartel or the price leadership model? In the absence of any very large increase in demand, wouldn't both these models predict rather modest price rises?

2. The history of most cartels has been one of failure to last for very long. Most seem to succumb to chiseling on price by their members. Is OPEC different? Does it provide a model for what producers of other raw materials (such as copper or tin) should do?

from those of its competitors. Again, the profit maximization model provides some insight about how firms will do this—they will incur additional costs associated with differentiation up to the point at which the additional revenue brought in by such activities equals each activity's marginal cost. With this view, producing differentiated products involves the same types of decisions that firms use in selecting any input.

Market Equilibrium

Although this description of firms' choices seems straightforward, the choices are actually quite complex. Since the demand curve facing any one firm de-

---

[3]By most estimates, the demand for oil is price inelastic at current price levels. Since an inelastic demand implies a negative marginal revenue, current prices are inconsistent with monopoly profit maximization.

Automobile Model Changes

One of the most important examples of product differentiation is the practice of annual model changes by U.S. (and, increasingly, most foreign) makers of automobiles. This strategy serves three basic functions for firms in the highly concentrated automobile industry. First, the annual model change differentiates this year's model from last year's and gives consumers a reason to switch from used cars to new ones. Second, the strategy provides each firm with the possibility of outguessing its rivals and garnering a larger share of the market. The importance of this motive is illustrated by the great secrecy surrounding the design of new models and the advertising blitz that accompanies their unveiling. Finally, some authors have argued that the annual model change provides an important barrier to entry in the automobile industry. Because of economies of scale associated with the model changeover, potential new firms are not able to compete successfully, and firms in the industry are able to earn profits above the competitive level.

Costs of annual automobile model changes are quite high. In a major study of automobile costs in the 1950s, Franklin M. Fisher, Zvi Griliches, and Carl Kaysen estimated that the total costs averaged $3 billion to $5 billion per year and amounted to nearly 25 percent of the total cost (including gasoline) of a car.[4] The author's principal findings are presented in Table 13.1 for the years 1950–1960. The Direct Costs column contains the amounts by which production costs exceeded those to produce a car with the same characteristics as a 1949 model. The data reflect the tendency throughout the 1950s of consumers to buy heavier cars with more horsepower and optional equipment (power steering and brakes, automatic transmissions, and so forth). Other components of the annual model change cost include retooling costs associated with making the required changes in capital equipment and costs of the extra gasoline required by the new models.

The dollar amounts in Table 13.1 are quite large: they exceed the total sales of many other industries during the period. The direct and retooling costs are presumably reflected in the prices of cars. Assessing the social desirability of these costs is difficult, however. On the one hand, it might be argued that the model change expenses were defensive and strategic in nature. Absence of such "wasteful" competition would release resources that could better be used elsewhere. On the other hand, consumers during the 1950s generally had the option of choosing automobiles with 1949 model characteristics, but they did not do so. It is therefore possible that resources invested in the model changeover provided more utility than they would have in an alternative use.

To Think About

1. Has the auto model changeover become less impor-

pends on the prices and product differentiation activities of its competitors, that demand curve may shift frequently and its position at any particular time may only be partly understood. The firm must make some assumptions in order to make decisions. And, whatever one firm decides to do may affect its competitors' actions.

Any model of "differentiated oligopoly" poses more complex strategic issues than the models for the homogeneous good case. Not surprisingly, there are few definite theoretical results about the nature of the market equilibrium that results from the differentiated oligopoly situation. Two very general conclusions might be mentioned, however. First, because of the differentiated

---

[4]Franklin M. Fisher, Zvi Gilriches, and Carl Kaysen, "The Cost of Automobile Model Changes since 1949," *Journal of Political Economy,* October 1962, pp. 433–451.

Table 13.1
Costs of Annual Automobile Model Changes, 1950–1960

Year	Direct Costs[a]	Retooling Cost[a]	Gasoline Costs[a]	Total Costs[a]	Total Passenger Car Production[b]	Total Costs per Car
1950	$ – 27	$ 20	$ 13	$ 6	6,659	$ 1
1951	267	45	36	348	5,331	65
1952	460	82	102	644	4,337	148
1953	436	246	161	844	6,135	138
1954	1,072	264	240	1,576	4,359	362
1955	2,425	469	372	3,266	6,201	527
1956	3,040	336	590	3,966	6,295	630
1957	4,048	772	806	5,626	6,218	905
1958	2,354	626	949	3,924	4,256	922
1959	3,675	532	1,147	5,354	5,568	962
1960	3,456	537	1,346	5,339	6,011	888

[a]Millions of dollars.
[b]Thousands of cars.
Source: Franklin M. Fisher, Zvi Griliches, and Carl Kaysen, "The Cost of Automobile Model Changes since 1949," *Journal of Political Economy,* October 1962, pp. 433–451.

tant in recent years? Don't automobile companies tend to stick with one basic model for several years? If so, why do you think they changed their product differentiation strategies?

2. The Fisher *et al.* study was conducted during a period when automobile imports were at low levels. What effects has the auto import boom of the 1970s and 1980s had on the market? Does the market now more closely resemble a competitive one? Which segments of the market have been most affected by imports?

nature of goods in the product group, price-taking behavior is unlikely. Each firm will believe that its activities have some effect on the price of its product. Price will exceed marginal revenue and marginal cost, and there may be some allocational inefficiency. Second, because of the uncertain demand facing each firm, information costs may be quite high. Firms may opt for strategies that economize on such costs. For example, they may adopt relatively simple "rules of thumb" in their decisions, such as adopting markup pricing (see Chapter 9) or aiming for a particular share of the market.

As a result of these types of behavior, market equilibria may be somewhat more stable over time than might at first be suggested by the complexities and uncertainties of the problem. Both prices and product types may converge around some median values, so that the homogeneous oligopoly models become appropriate. For example, product attributes may come to approximate those desired by the "typical" consumer, since any firm that departs very far from producing such a good may find itself outflanked by competitors. The tendency of television networks to produce the same types of shows and of political candidates to gravitate to the middle of the road in their positions are probably the most familiar instances of such behavior, but other occurrences come readily to mind. In "Applying Economics: Automobile Model Changes" we describe the costs associated with one product differentiation activity that has been closely studied.

Advertising and Resource Allocation

Because of its economic importance and controversial nature, advertising has been more intensively examined by economists than other aspects of behavior in differentiated oligopoly markets. Theoretical studies have covered advertising and resource allocation, empirical studies have been done on the effect of advertising on the demands for specific products, and legal investigations have been made into what should be done about false advertising claims.[5] Here we examine only the allocational issue. Specifically, we look first at two arguments that suggest that in an unregulated market, resources may be be overallocated to the provision of advertising messages. We conclude with some observations about the value of advertising information to consumers.

An analysis of advertising might start with the observation that the market for advertising messages is not separated from the market for the good being advertised. When someone purchases a box of laundry soap, he or she also pays for the advertising messages that the soap maker provides. In other words, a good and its associated advertising are **joint products**. This technical property of the way in which advertising messages are supplied may cause too many messages to be produced. As we have seen, firms will produce additional advertising messages up to the point at which the marginal revenue from the additional demand generated by a message is equal to the message's cost. This additional revenue reflects individuals' willingness to pay both for the goods and for the information provided by the advertising message. Looking at the advertising message alone, individuals value it at less than its production cost (since the good itself must have some value). If the information contained in the advertisement had been marketed separately, its market price would not exceed its production cost. Joint production therefore causes too many advertising messages to be produced.

The second argument that suggests that there may be too much advertising derives from a distinction (first made by Alfred Marshall) between constructive and combative advertising. Constructive advertising conveys useful information to increase the total demand for a product. Combative advertising, on the other hand, reflects the competition among different brands for a share of a fixed market. This kind of advertising is defensive in that any one firm is

Joint products
The inseparable combination of two goods in production, such as advertising, which is paid for by the consumer as part of the good being advertised.

---

[5]Some of these analyses (together with a wealth of empirical information) are reviewed in Richard Schmalensee, *The Economics of Advertising* (Amsterdam: North Holland Publishing, 1972), Chapter 1.

forced to do it because all the others do. An across-the-board reduction of advertising by all firms would not affect total demand at all, whereas a reduction by any one firm would be harmful to that firm. A reduction in combative advertising would free resources that could be productively employed elsewhere. In this sense, there may again be too much advertising.

Although these arguments are suggestive, a number of contrary points also have been raised. Advertising provides valuable information to consumers, usually without cost. Through advertising consumers can learn about products' prices, about quality differences among products, and about entirely new goods. Because each consumer can use this information without detracting from others' use of it, advertising has some attributes of a "public good" (see Chapter 19), and as we shall show, resources may actually be underallocated to such goods. Advertising also may have beneficial competitive effects on industry structure if the ability to promote a new firm's product reduces barriers to entry created by entrenched brands. For example, the highly successful Volkswagen advertising campaign of the early 1960s may have contributed significantly to opening the U.S. market to imports of small cars. To the extent there are economies of scale in producing advertising messages, however, these procompetitive effects may be mitigated by cost advantages that will be enjoyed by existing larger firms. There is no general answer to the questions of whether advertising helps or hinders competition and whether an appropriate level of resources will be devoted to producing advertising messages. A full evaluation will depend on the specific market circumstances. In "Applying Economics: Cigarette Advertising" we illustrate some of these complexities.

Entry by New Firms

The possibility of new firms entering an industry plays an important part in the development of the theory of perfectly competitive price determination. This possibility assures that any long-run profits will be eliminated by new entrants and that firms will produce at the low points of their long-run average cost curves. Under conditions of oligopoly, the first of these forces continues to operate. To the extent that entry is possible, long-run profits are constrained. If entry is completely costless, long-run economic profits will be zero (as in the competitive case).

Zero-Profit Equilibrium

Whether or not firms in an oligopolistic industry with free entry will be directed to the low point of their average cost curves depends on the nature of the demand curve facing them. If firms are price takers, the analysis given for the competitive case carries over directly. Since $P = MR = MC$ for profit maximization and since $P = AC$ if entry is to result in zero profits, production will take place where $MC = AC$ (that is, at minimum average cost).

If oligopolistic firms have some control over the price they receive (perhaps because each produces a slightly differentiated product), each firm will face a

APPLYING ECONOMICS

Cigarette Advertising

Prior to 1970, cigarettes were one of the most highly advertised products. Cigarette advertising constituted about 15 percent of all television advertising and a significantly higher fraction of advertising in magazines. Because of this dominance, expenditures on cigarette advertising have been extensively studied. The general conclusion of these studies is that advertising of cigarette brands closely approximates Marshall's notion of combative advertising—that is, it appears that advertising has a major impact on the choice of brand (a favorite example is the hugely successful "Marlboro Man" advertising campaigns of the 1960s), but that such advertising has relatively little effect on the overall level of smoking.[6]

In the late 1960s, cigarette advertising became an extremely controversial subject. As a result of the 1964 Surgeon General's Report linking smoking to lung cancer, Congress passed the Cigarette Labeling and Advertising Act. That Act required that all cigarette packs carry a warning label about the possible health hazard of smoking, and that the warning be prominently displayed in advertising. In response to requests from the American Cancer Society and others, the Federal Communications Commission also decided that the "fairness doctrine" required that free television air time be granted for antismoking commercials to combat advertising by cigarette companies. By 1970 antismoking commercials totaled about one-third of cigarette advertising time. In that year, however, Congress, impatient with the continued high level of cigarette sales despite their known health hazards, passed the Public Health Cigarette Smoking Act banning cigarette advertising from radio and television. Banning television advertising of cigarettes had the unintended side effect of sharply reducing antismoking commercials, since the fairness doctrine no longer applied.

In a 1972 paper, J. L. Hamilton tried to sort out the effects of these changes in the advertising environment on total cigarette sales.[7] He found that cigarette advertising increased average annual cigarette consumption by about 95 cigarettes per year (about 3 percent of average annual consumption). The health scare resulting from the Surgeon General's Report, on the other hand, was estimated to have reduced average sales by 253 cigarettes per year. Even more dramatic results were estimated by Hamilton for the antismoking commercials, which reduced average sales by an average of over 530 cigarettes per year. It appears that scenes of smoke-filled lungs and the appeal of actor Joseph Cotton who was dying of lung cancer left a more vivid impression on viewers than did the Marlboro Man.

To Think About

1. Did the advertising ban really hurt cigarette sales? Might it actually have helped such sales? Might the ban have helped cigarette companies? How hard do you think they fought the ban?

2. The cigarette example raises the question of how, if at all, the government should regulate advertising. Currently, various rules require that advertisements be "truthful" with respect to claims being made for a product or against a competitor's product. Do these rules seem necessary? Can't consumers decide for themselves whether advertising claims make sense?

Monopolistic competition
Market in which each firm faces a negatively sloped demand curve and there are no barriers to entry.

downward-sloping demand curve, and the competitive analysis may not hold. Entry still may reduce profits to zero, but now production at minimum average cost is not assured. This situation (which is sometimes termed **monopolistic competition** because it has features of both perfect competition and monopoly)

---

[6]For a summary of much of this literature, see Richard Schmalensee, *The Economics of Advertising* (Amsterdam: North Holland Publishing, 1972).

[7]J. L. Hamilton, "The Demand for Cigarettes: Advertising the Health Scare, and the Cigarette Advertising Ban," *Review of Economics and Statistics,* November 1972, pp. 401–411.

Figure 13.4
Entry Reduces Profitability
in Oligopoly

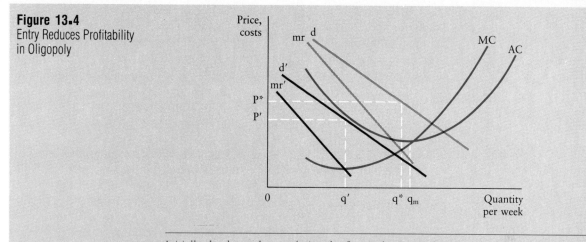

Initially the demand curve facing the firm is d. Marginal revenue is given by mr and
q^* is the profit-maximizing output level. If entry is costless, new firms attracted by the
possibility for profits may shift the firm's demand curve inward to d′, where profits are
zero. At output level q′ average costs are not a minimum, and the firm exhibits excess
capacity given by $q_m - q'$.

is illustrated in Figure 13.4. Initially, the demand curve facing the typical firm
is given by d and economic profits are being earned. New firms will be attracted by these profits, and their entry will shift d inward (because there are
now a larger number of firms to contend with a given market demand curve).
Indeed, entry can reduce profits to zero by shifting the demand curve to d′.
The level of output that maximizes profits with this demand curve, q′, is not,
however, the same as that level at which average costs are minimized, q_m.
Rather, the firm will produce less than that "efficient" output level and will
exhibit "excess capacity," given by $q_m - q'$. Some economists have hypothesized that this outcome characterizes industries such as service stations, convenience stores, and fast-food franchisers, where product differentiation is
prevalent but entry is relatively costless.[8]

Contestable Markets and Industry Structure

The conclusion that a zero-profit equilibrium with price above marginal cost
(such as that pictured in Figure 13.4) is sustainable in the long run has been

---

[8]This analysis was originally developed by E. H. Chamberlain, *The Theory of Monopolistic
Competition* (Cambridge, Mass.: Harvard University Press, 1950).

challenged recently by several economists.[9] They argue that the model neglects the effects of potential entry on market equilibrium by focusing only on the behavior of actual entrants. This argument introduces the distinction first made by Harold Demetz between competition *in* the market and competition *for* the market by showing that the latter concept provides a more appropriate perspective for analyzing the free entry assumption.[10] Within this broader perspective, the "invisible hand" of competition becomes even more constraining on firms' behavior, and perfect competition results are more likely to emerge.

Contestable market
Market in which entry and exit are costless.

The expanded examination of entry begins by defining a **contestable market** as one in which no potential competitor can enter by cutting price and still make profits (since if profit opportunities existed, potential entrants would take advantage of them). A perfectly contestable market drops the perfectly competitive assumption of price-taking behavior but expands a bit upon the concept of free entry by permitting potential entrants to operate in a hit-and-run manner, snatching up whatever profit opportunities are available. Such an assumption, as we will point out below, is not necessarily accurate in many market situations, but it does provide a different starting place for a simplified theory of pricing.

The equilibrium illustrated in Figure 13.4 is unsustainable in a contestable market, provided that there are two or more firms already in the market. In such a case a potential hit-and-run entrant could turn a quick profit by taking all the first firm's sales by selling q' at a price slightly below P' and making up for the loss this would entail by selling a further increment in output to another firm's customers at a price in excess of average cost. That is, because the equilibrium in Figure 13.4 has a market price that exceeds marginal costs, it permits a would-be entrant to take away one zero-profit firm's market and encroach a bit on other firms' markets where, at the margin, profits are attainable. The only type of market equilibrium that would be impervious to such hit-and-run tactics would be one in which firms earn zero profits and price at marginal costs. As we saw in Chapter 11, this requires that firms produce at the low points of their long-run average cost curves where P = MC = AC. Hence, even in the absence of price-taking behavior in markets with relatively few firms, contestability provides an "invisible hand" that guides market equilibrium to a perfectly competitive type of result.

This analysis can be taken one step further by showing how industry structure is determined. If, as in Chapter 11, we let q* represent that output level for which average costs are minimized and Q* represent the total market for

---

[9]See W. J. Baumol, "Contestable Markets: An Uprising in the Theory of Industry Structure," *American Economic Review*, March 1982, pp. 1–19, and W. J. Baumol, J. C. Panzar, and R. D. Willig, *Contestable Markets and the Theory of Industry Structure* (San Diego, Calif.: Harcourt Brace Jovanovich, 1982).

[10]Harold Demetz, "Why Regulate Utilities?" *Journal of Law and Economics*, April 1968, pp. 55–65.

Figure 13.5
Contestability and Industry Structure

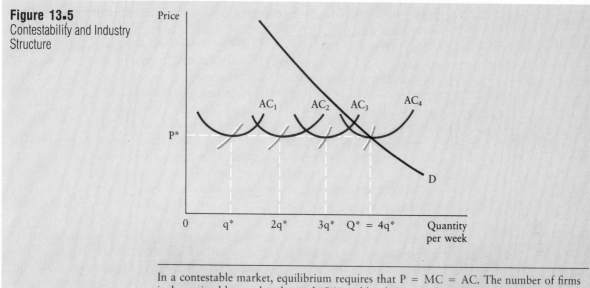

In a contestable market, equilibrium requires that P = MC = AC. The number of firms is determined by market demand (Q*) and by the output level that minimizes average cost (q*).

the commodity when price equals marginal (and average) cost, then the number of firms in the industry, n, is given by

$$n = \frac{Q^*}{q^*}.$$ [13.1]

Contrary to the perfectly competitive case, this number of firms may be relatively small. In Figure 13.5, for example, exactly four firms fulfill the market demand for Q*. The contestability assumption will insure competitive behavior, even though these firms may recognize strategic relationships among themselves. The ability of potential entrants to seize any possible opportunities for profit sharply constrains the types of behavior that are possible and thereby provides a well-defined equilibrium market structure.

Barriers to Entry

All of the analysis presented so far in this section has assumed free entry and exit. When various barriers prevent such flexibility, these results must be modified. Possible barriers to entry in the oligopoly case include many of those already discussed in connection with monopoly in Chapter 12. They also include those arising specifically out of some features of oligopolistic markets. Product differentiation, for example, may raise entry barriers by promoting strong brand loyalty. Or producers may so proliferate their brands that no room remains for would-be entrants to do anything different. As "Applying Economics: Entry Barriers in Breakfast Cereals" shows, this has been alleged to be true in the ready-to-eat breakfast cereal industry. The possibility of strategic pricing decisions may also deter entry if existing firms use them to convince firms wishing to enter that it would be unprofitable to do so. Firms may, for a time, adopt lower, entry-deterring prices in order to accomplish this goal, with the intent of raising prices once potential entrants disappear (assuming they do).

Finally, the completely flexible type of hit-and-run behavior assumed in the contestable markets theory may be subject to two other types of barriers in the real world. First, some types of capital investments made by firms may not be reversible. A firm cannot build an automobile assembly plant for a week's use and then dismantle it at no loss. In this case there are exit costs that will make recurrent raids on the industry unprofitable. Of course, in other cases, such as the trucking or airline industry, capital may be easily rented for short periods, and exit here poses few costs. So competitive-type results might occur in these industries. Second, the contestable market model requires that quantity demanded respond instantly to price differentials. If, instead, demanders switch slowly to a new product, potential entrants cannot attain market penetration quickly, and their ability to discipline firms in the market will be constrained.[11] The importance of all such restrictions for market behavior is ultimately an empirical question.

Industrial Organization Theory	So far in this chapter, we have been primarily concerned with a formal analysis of price determination in oligopolistic markets. Although this analysis offered a number of insights into the behavior of such markets, we also saw that it is very difficult to capture in a simple model all of the factors that may affect market outcomes. In recent years research in the field of industrial organization has expanded rapidly in an effort to provide details on those aspects of market behavior that are not easily captured by such models. This concluding section looks at some of this analysis. "Applying Economics: The IBM Case" illustrates how the tools of industrial organization are used in the field of antitrust.

It is customary to divide industrial organization into three topics: (1) market structure; (2) firm conduct; and (3) economic performance. *Market structure* is concerned with describing the industry. How many firms are there? What types of products are produced? Are there increasing returns to scale? Are there significant barriers to entry? Understanding such facts is necessary to analyzing *firm conduct*. Firm conduct concerns such matters as firms' output

---

[11]For some additional criticism of this type, see Michael Spence, "Contestable Markets and the Theory of Industrial Structure," *Journal of Economic Literature*, September 1983, pp. 981–990.

Entry Barriers in Breakfast Cereals

Production of ready-to-eat breakfast cereals in the United States is highly concentrated. The top four firms in the industry (Kellogg's, General Mills, General Foods, and Quaker) supply about 85 percent of total industry output. According to most estimates, the industry is highly profitable with significantly higher rates of return on firms' investments than the average manufacturing company enjoys. Despite these high profits, entry by new firms into the industry has been virtually nonexistent. Although many large food companies could conceivably enter the industry, they have chosen not to do so. Economies of scale in cereal production do not seem to explain this reluctance, since it appears that efficient size operations can be attained at a fairly small fraction of total industry output of about 2 to 3 percent. There must be some other explanation for the absence of entry.

In 1972 the U.S. Federal Trade Commission issued a complaint against the four largest cereal producers charging that through proliferating brands and intensive advertising the firms had erected substantial entry barriers, thereby insuring monopoly-type returns to themselves. The brand proliferation argument ran as follows: By creating a huge number of cereal brands (about 80 in 1972) the largest firms had substantially covered all the attributes (sweetness, crunchiness, grain composition, and so forth) that mattered to consumers. There was no room in the market for potential entrants who had no opportunity to differentiate their products successfully. Crucial to this argument were the related issues of intensive advertising and brand identification preventing potential entrants from duplicating the characteristics of an existing cereal at a lower price. That is, it was claimed that consumers would generally be unwilling to purchase a less expensive version of Cheerios, for example.[12]

Although this explanation of entry barriers is intriguing, it is not airtight. The notion that there is no room for new cereal brands implicitly assumes a limit to firms' ingenuity that may not, in fact, exist. For example, the introduction of natural cereals in the 1970s seems to have filled a market niche that had been overlooked by the major companies. Similarly, the belief that look-alike, cheap imitations of major brands will not sell seems to be contradicted by the growing number of house brand cereals offered by supermarkets in the 1980s. Finally, the FTC complaint alleged that the cereal companies acted in an implicit collusion to proliferate brands. The distinction between such collusion and simple head-to-head competition between major firms is difficult to make. To a large extent the case against the cereal makers remained unproven (indeed, it was dropped in early 1982) and the barriers to entry in the industry (if any) are still not completely explained.

To Think About

1. What advantages do large cereal producers have that permit them to develop new brands at relatively low cost? Why aren't such techniques available to other firms? Can you think of other products where "brand proliferation" is an important strategy for the firms involved (for example, how about cigarette firms)?

2. Brand proliferation is only one of many other possible strategies of creating entry barriers. Can you think of other ways that producers of differentiated products attempt to prevent the entry of rival producers? How would you explain their decisions to make such expenditures? What would determine their success?

---

[12]For a detailed development of this theory see Richard Schmalensee, "Entry Deterrence in the Ready-to-Eat Breakfast Cereal Industry," *The Bell Journal of Economics*, Autumn 1978, pp. 305–327.

The IBM Case

On the final day of the Johnson administration, an antitrust case was filed by the U.S. Justice Department against International Business Machines Corporation (IBM). During the ensuing 13 years, the case developed all the elements of a television soap opera. Successive Justice Department officials had considerable difficulty in designing a coherent case, legal careers were made and destroyed at the prestigious firm of Cravath, Swaine and Moore (IBM's attorneys), many economists made tidy consultants' fees on the case, and IBM even sought to have the judge in the case disqualified for being biased. In all, the case generated 66 million pages of documentation and probably cost taxpayers and IBM hundreds of millions of dollars. Despite these vast expenditures of physical and human resources, the IBM case was ultimately dropped by the Federal Government on January 8, 1982, on the argument it was "flimsy" and "without merit." This long-running and almost farcical saga illustrates several elements of industrial organization theory as it relates to modern antitrust litigation.

Consider first the question of what market IBM was alleged to have monopolized. In its original complaint, the Justice Department accused IBM of monopolizing the "general purpose computer" market in which, it was asserted, IBM had about a 70 percent share. In its defense, IBM continually sought to expand this market definition (to include all information-processing and retrieval systems, for example) and to show it was really a rather small fish in a big pond (which included, for example, American Telephone and Telegraph Company). At the time the case was dropped, the litigants had, after 13 years of debate, still not reached any agreement on the very basic question of what market IBM monopolized.

Similar ambiguities surrounded the legal arguments of whether IBM had "attempted to monopolize" the computer market. Three of the government's specific charges against IBM's conduct illustrate the dispute. First, the government alleged that IBM introduced "fighting machines" (particularly model 360-70) whose timing was targeted specifically to undermine competitors' efforts to develop new products. Second, it was argued that IBM's practice of selling its maintenance and programming services in a bundle with its machines made it difficult for competitors to gain a foothold in the market since they could not also offer such bundles. Finally, IBM's use of discounts for educational institutions was deemed anticompetitive because they resulted in a generation of students trained only on IBM equipment.

IBM, in its defense, attacked each of these conduct charges by asserting they simply reflected aggressive competition and good corporate citizenship. Introduction of new machines was, according to IBM, just normal business practice in the fast-moving computer industry. Similarly, IBM argued it bundled its services and equipment together simply to serve customers better. Other companies were, after all, free to adopt the same practice. Finally, educational discounts were, according to IBM, the natural response of a company seeking to promote general social well-being—to impugn their motives was unfairly cynical.

Most uninvolved observers of the IBM case saw some truths in both the government and IBM briefs. The decision to drop the case probably reflected the sensible judgment that the case had reached a stage where the costs of further litigation outweighed any potential gains from a government victory. In the 13 years since the case was filed, the computer industry had changed greatly, with hundreds of new firms being founded and IBM's share of the market falling rather sharply. It seems that, whatever had happened in the past, the computer industry is functioning rather well in the 1980s, and the social gains in tampering with its structure might be negligible.

To Think About

1. What market was it that IBM may have monopolized in the 1960s? If you were a government attorney, how would you define the relevant market? What if you were an attorney for IBM?

2. In the Alcoa case, Judge Learned Hand ruled that since Alcoa controlled nearly two-thirds of the primary aluminum production capacity in the United States, it was a monopoly. Was the two-thirds standard (which has been widely used since that time—for example, IBM's 70 percent share was deemed a "monopoly" based on this test) reasonable? Doesn't the strict definition of monopoly require 100 percent control of the market? Is there any reason to choose two-thirds? Why not one-half, three-fourths, or eleven-sixteenths?

Table 13.2
Representative Data on
U.S. Industrial Structure,
1977

Industry	Number of Firms	Total Output[a]	Total Value Added[a]	Percent Output Produced by			
				4 Largest	8 Largest	20 Largest	50 Largest
Motor vehicles	254	$76,518	$18,724	93%	99%	99+%	99+%
Steel mills	395	41,998	15,332	45	65	84	95
Pharmaceuticals	655	11,459	8,214	24	43	73	91
Aircraft	151	14,834	8,134	59	81	99	99+
Petroleum refining	192	91,689	14,424	30	53	81	94
Photographic equipment	702	9,945	6,732	72	86	90	94
Electronic computers	808	12,924	7,624	44	51	71	85
Commercial printing	10,964	9,360	5,338	6	10	17	26
Tires	121	8,971	4,347	70	88	97	99+
Sawmills	6,966	10,867	4,453	17	23	36	49
Toilet preparations	644	6,557	4,527	40	56	79	90
Cigarettes	8	6,377	3,803	90	100	100	100
Organic fibers	37	6,380	2,804	78	90	99	100
Bottled and canned soft drinks	1,758	10,007	4,085	15	22	36	50

[a]In millions.
Source: Statistical Abstract of the United States, 1981 (Washington, D.C.: U.S. Government Printing Office, 1981), table 1427.

and price decisions, product differentiation, advertising, investment decisions, research activities, and so forth—it investigates what firms do. Economic performance is concerned with appraising the desirability of particular markets. Criteria used in that appraisal include questions of economic efficiency, distributional equity, and the long-term growth of the industry.

Market Structure

Perhaps the most important types of information on market structure are those that concern the number, size, and general concentration of the firms in an industry. A representative selection of these data are illustrated in Table 13.2. Of particular interest to industrial organization economists are the concentration ratios—the percentages of total domestic shipments produced by the 4, 8, 20, and 50 largest firms. The figures indicate, for example, that production of motor vehicles, cigarettes, and organic fibers are all highly concentrated, with 4-firm concentration ratios of around 80 or higher. On the other hand, industries such as commercial printing, bottled soft drinks, and sawmills have a low concentration of production, with less than half of industry output being produced by the 50 largest firms. There appears to be a great variety among the structures of U.S. industries.

The types of data on industry concentration that are illustrated in Table 13.2 suffer from a number of shortcomings. Imports are not reflected in the data, and this may lead to a distorted picture of the degree of competition in industries (such as automobiles) where competition from foreign goods is strong. Similarly, the data presented are quite aggregated, and they may obscure concentration patterns in more narrowly defined markets. For example, the "toilet preparations" industry appears to be relatively unconcentrated on the basis of the data in the table, although some sectors of this market (such as toothpaste production) are very concentrated indeed. Many other problems of interpretation may arise in the data from the specific details of the industry in question. The low concentration in soft drinks, for example, becomes more problematic when it is recognized that many of the local bottlers represented in the data operate under exclusive areawide licenses from the Coca Cola or Pepsico companies. Despite all these difficulties, data such as those in Table 13.2 are about all the quantitative information that is available on real-world industrial structure, and such data are widely used.

Several other aspects of market structure have been systematically examined by industrial organization economists. Particular attention has been focused on barriers to entry because this concept plays a key role both in the model of perfectly competitive pricing in the long run and in the theory of contestable markets. Two types of entry barriers have been intensively studied: cost barriers derived from economies of scale and barriers created by firms' strategic decisions. Barriers of the latter type include those derived from firms' pricing decisions and from product differentiation. There is a vast amount of empirical information on all of these topics.[13]

A final structural concern has been the study of mergers. "Horizontal" mergers (that is, two firms producing the same types of goods) raise no particularly novel economic issues—they will clearly increase the concentration in an industry and therefore may create the kinds of allocational inefficiencies outlined previously in this chapter. More difficult to evaluate are "vertical" mergers, in which a given production process is integrated within one firm rather than relying on a network of sellers of intermediate products. For example, a merger of a computer chip maker and a computer assembler would represent such vertical integration. In this case the effects on the market price of the end product (computers) may be indeterminate. Vertical integration may produce cost efficiencies that tend to reduce prices, but it may also produce some degree of monopolistic control over prices of inputs. Hence, no clear conclusion is possible.

---

[13]The classic treatment of the entry issue is presented by J. S. Bain in *Barriers to New Competition* (Cambridge, Mass.: Harvard University Press, 1956). Bain estimates that a new product in a differentiated market may have to sell for 10 to 25 percent less than one already established in the market in order to win customer acceptance.

Finally, in recent years, "conglomerate" mergers have become common-place among firms in very different industries. Huge firms such as ITT or Textron operate in literally hundreds of markets, and this raises the question of whether those firms' subsidiaries behave in ways similar to independent firms in such markets. As with vertical mergers, a variety of analyses have been proposed, ranging from the notion that conglomerate firms provide "synergistic" cost savings and diversification for their subsidiaries to the hypothesis that conglomerates may aid in monopolization by engaging in cross-subsidization among subsidiaries.

Firm Conduct

The *firm conduct* aspect of industrial organization theory attempts to provide some real-world details that will supplement the various pricing models discussed earlier in this chapter. Because it has proved to be quite difficult to obtain detailed information about firms' strategic motives and assumptions (say, through interviews with managers), the focus of much firm conduct research has been on the narrower question of whether oligopolistic coordination in pricing decisions is possible or likely. Economists have examined the roles of explicit agreements, tacit understandings, price leadership, commonly used rules of thumb, and industrywide price lists as mechanisms for effecting such coordination. All of these at times have proved to be successful. But increasing legal scrutiny of such devices, combined with the instability in cartels created by incentives to chisel on price, have limited the possibility of success of these mechanisms.

Many other aspects of market organization tend to deter oligopolistic coordination. In particular, dynamic changes in either demand or cost conditions over time may make it very difficult for a would-be cartel to decide precisely how to maximize joint profits. The expected gains from such coordination may appear to be quite small. That judgment may be altered, however, if the cartel can devise some sort of coordinating device or if it can enlist government aid in the pursuit of its goals.

Industry Performance

The final aspect of industrial organization analysis concerns appraising *industry performance*. Traditionally, the primary focus here has been on examining the allocational efficiency of alternative industry structures. Two different types of criteria are employed. The first concerns the "static efficiency" of the industry, which is usually taken to mean how closely behavior in that industry approaches the perfectly competitive ideal. Industries with fairly large numbers of firms, low entry barriers, and prices close to marginal cost are regarded as "effectively" competitive. On the other hand, important departures from these ideals will reverse that assessment, and there may be static losses in social welfare as a result of such failures. A general conclusion of this type of research is that a large portion of the U.S. economy appears to be effectively competitive and that the degree of competition may have increased in recent years. For example, W. G. Shepherd finds that in 1980, 77 percent of U.S. national income was produced in industries that he classifies as effectively competitive, with 2 percent being produced under monopoly, 3 percent in industries with dominant firms, and 18 percent in "tight" oligopolies. He also reports that the share of oligopolies was roughly halved since the 1950s, resulting in a sharply rising incidence of competitive behavior. Shepherd attributes important roles to antitrust enforcement, increasing international trade, and government deregulation efforts in bringing about these results.[14]

A second set of allocational criteria concerns "dynamic" efficiency. These criteria focus on industry progress over time. In this case there is no well-defined ideal model to serve as a standard of judgment. Rather, the criteria involve a number of performance measures such as industry growth, productivity improvements, favorable relative price trends, and new product innovation. Much of this research stems from the initial work of Joseph Schumpeter (see Chapter 12) on the importance of entrepreneurial profit-seeking activity to the growth process. Developing and testing specific hypotheses about the effect of market structure on various performance measures have proved rather difficult, however.

In addition to allocational criteria, a number of noneconomic performance measures have also been examined by industrial organization theorists. Questions about the distribution of economic profits among industry participants or the impact of industry structure on relative wage rates have been examined to assess the possibility that departures from a competitive market may be desirable for equity reasons. Similarly, some authors have stressed the ability of various market organizations to generate employment for workers independent of whether such industries do so efficiently. Finally, the political influence of firms has been examined, with the goal of creating market structures (possibly competitive) that minimize that influence. As this partial list of additional criteria makes clear, the field of industrial organization may overlap with many other social science disciplines.

Summary

Many real-world markets resemble neither of the polar cases of perfect competition or monopoly. Rather, such markets are characterized by some degree of concentration and the individual firms have some effect on market price—they are not price takers—but no single firm exercises complete market control. In these circumstances there is no generally accepted model of market behavior. Aspects of both competitive and monopoly theory must be used

---

[14]W. G. Shepherd, "Causes of Increased Competition in the U.S. Economy," *Review of Economics and Statistics,* November 1982, pp. 613–626.

together with particular institutional details of the market in question in order to develop a realistic picture of behavior. Several specific issues that must be addressed in developing such a model are the following:

- The degree of market concentration and the importance of feedback effects in firms' decision-making processes.
- The importance of nonprice methods of competition, such as product differentiation and advertising.
- Entry conditions in the market and the constraints that potential entry places on attaining monopoly profits.
- The uncertainty faced by individual firms and the strategies they may adopt to cope with it.
- The potential benefits from monopolization of a market and the legal and resource costs associated with maintaining such a position.

Problems

13.1 Assume for simplicity that a monopolist has no costs of production and faces a demand curve given by

$$Q = 150 - P.$$

a. Calculate the profit-maximizing price-quantity combination for this monopolist. Also calculate the monopolist's profits.

b. Suppose a second firm enters the market. Let q_1 be the output of the first firm and q_2 the output of the second. Market demand is now given by:

$$q_1 + q_2 = 150 - P.$$

Assuming that this second firm also has no costs of production, use the Cournot model of duopoly (presented in the appendix) to determine the profit-maximizing level of production for each firm as well as the market price. Also calculate each firm's profits.

c. How do the results from parts a and b compare to what price and quantity would prevail in a perfectly competitive market? Graph the demand and marginal revenue curves and indicate the three different price-quantity combinations on the demand curve.

13.2 Use the analysis developed in this chapter and elsewhere in this part to explain the following price behavior:

a. Doctors charge poor patients less for identical services than they charge rich patients.

b. Banks announce a widely publicized prime rate and change it only occasionally.

c. Blacks pay more than whites for identical houses.

d. Insurance companies continue to solicit automobile insurance business in spite of their plea that "we lose money on every policy we write."

e. A certain brand of beer used to be sold in cans and returnable bottles (with a deposit required). It was less expensive to buy beer in bottles and throw them away than to buy beer in cans.

13.3 Some critics contend that U.S. automobile companies pursue a strategy of planned obsolescence: that is, they produce cars that are intended to become obsolete in a few years. Would that strategy make sense in a monopoly market? How might the production of obsolescence depend on the characteristics of market demand? How would oligopolistic competition affect the profitability of the strategy?

13.4 Suppose advertising expenditures are able to increase a firm's sales. How should a firm decide on the profit-maximizing level of advertising? What marginal rule should it use?

13.5 One of the major legal complaints against Standard Oil Company in the 1911 antitrust case concerned the practice of predatory pricing. That is, it was claimed that in some markets Standard Oil would price its product below average cost in an attempt to make competitors more willing to sell out their businesses. Would such a strategy be more effective than offering to buy out competitors directly? Develop a general theory of when predatory behavior might work (for a detailed analysis, see J. S. McGee, "Predatory Price Cutting: The Standard Oil (N.J.) Case," *Journal of Law and Economics*, October 1958, pp. 137–169).

13.6 In the Clorox case, Procter & Gamble was alleged to be a potential entrant into the liquid bleach market. Can you devise a way to use firms' cost curves and the demand curves facing the firms to differentiate among actual entrants? Potential entrants? Nonentrants? Use your analysis to suggest what the court should have looked for in this antitrust case.

*13.7 Suppose that the total market demand for crude oil is given by

$$Q_D = -2,000P + 70,000$$

where Q is the quantity of oil in thousands of barrels per year and P is the dollar price per barrel. Suppose also that there are 1,000 identical small producers of crude oil, each with marginal costs given by

$$MC = q + 5$$

where q is the output of the typical firm.

a. Assuming that each small oil producer acts as a price taker, calculate the typical firm's supply curve (q = ...), the market supply

---

*Denotes a rather difficult problem.

curve $(Q_S = \dots.)$, and the market equilibrium price and quantity (where $Q_D = Q_S$).

b. Suppose a practically infinite supply of crude oil is discovered in New Jersey by a would-be price leader and that this oil can be produced at a constant average and marginal cost of $AC = MC = \$15$ per barrel. Assume also that the supply behavior of the competitive fringe described in part a is not changed by this discovery. Calculate the demand curve facing the price leader.

c. Assuming that the price leader's marginal revenue curve is given by

$$MR = -Q/1,500 + 25,$$

how much should the price leader produce in order to maximize profits? What price and quantity will now prevail in the market?

d. Graph your result indicating the market demand curve, the supply curve for the competitive fringe, and the price leader's demand, MR, and MC curves.

e. Does consumer surplus increase as a result of the New Jersey oil discovery? How does consumer surplus after the discovery compare to what would exist if the New Jersey oil were supplied competitively?

APPENDIX TO CHAPTER 13

DUOPOLY MODELS AND GAME THEORY

Economists have developed several formal models that attempt to capture the interdependent nature of decisions in oligopoly markets. These models range from simple two-firm (*duopoly*) models through complex models that portray several different decisions being made by an arbitrary number of firms.[1] While none of the models has won the widespread acceptance that the monopoly and perfectly competitive models have, some of them are useful to demonstrate the nature of interdependence in a simple setting. In this appendix we develop a simple duopoly model that demonstrates market interdependence. A concluding section to the appendix examines the duopoly problem using game theory and offers an opportunity to survey that topic.

Basic Model: Monopoly Situation

Suppose the demand function for a good is given by

$$Q = 120 - P \qquad [13A.1]$$

where P is the market price of the good and Q is the quantity sold per week. This curve is shown in Figure 13A.1. Assume also that there are no costs of production.[2] Consequently, profit maximization requires that any firm produce that output level for which revenues are as large as possible. That is, output should be expanded to the point at which marginal revenue is zero (which then is equal to marginal cost). If there is only one firm facing the demand curve in Equation 13A.1, or if two firms decide to coordinate their decisions, this monopoly will choose to produce 60 units of output. At this output level P will be $60 and the monopoly's profits (and revenues) will be $3,600 (= $60 × 60). For the future development of a duopoly model, it is important to note how the profit-maximizing output level is chosen. In this case Q is chosen to be one-half of that quantity that would be demanded at a price of zero.[3] Our strategy now is to study possible demand curves that

---

[1]For survey of many of these models see K. J. Cohen and R. M. Cyert, *Theory of the Firm: Revenue Allocation in a Market Economy* (Englewood Cliffs, N.J.: Prentice-Hall, 1965), chapters 11 and 12.

[2]The assumption of zero costs is for convenience only. The models to be presented can be easily generalized to include any general cost function. To do so, however, would require the use of calculus.

[3]It is generally true for a *linear demand* curve that marginal revenue is equal to zero at $Q = 1/2Q_0$ (where Q_0 is the quantity demanded at a price of zero). Indeed, if marginal cost is any fixed number, marginal revenue equals marginal cost at $Q = 1/2Q_c$ (where Q_c is the quantity demanded when price equals marginal cost). Showing why these results hold is a simple application of our definition of marginal revenue—see Chapter 9.

Figure 13A.1
Monopolist's Output Choice

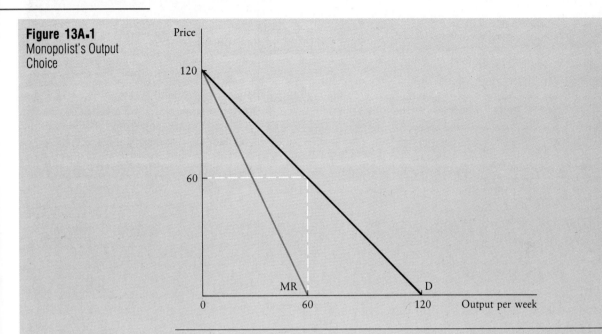

Given the market demand curve Q = 120 − P, a zero-cost monopolist would produce that output (60) for which marginal revenue is equal to 0. At this output, a price of $60 would prevail and profits would be $3,600. Notice that MR = 0 at an output level = 1/2Q₀ (where Q_0 is the quantity demanded at P = 0). This result holds for any linear demand curve.

might face the two firms in a duopoly and apply this basic result, which holds for any linear demand curve.

Cournot Model of Duopoly

Cournot model
A model of duopoly in which each firm assumes the other firm's output will not change if it changes its own output level.

A French economist, Augustin Cournot, presented the first formal model of duopoly in 1838.[4] In devising this **Cournot model,** the author assumed that each of the two firms in the market took the other firm's activities into account in only a very limited way. In particular, Cournot theorized that firm 1, say, chooses its output level (Q_1) on the assumption that the output of the firm 2 (Q_2) is fixed and will not be adjusted in response to firm 1's actions. Mathematically, total market output is given by

$$Q = Q_1 + Q_2 = 120 - P. \qquad [13A.2]$$

---

[4]Augustin Cournot, *Researches into the Mathematical Principles of the Theory of Wealth,* translated by N. T. Bacon (New York: Macmillan, 1897).

Assuming that Q_2 is fixed, the demand curve facing firm 1 is given by

$$Q_1 = (120 - Q_2) - P. \qquad [13A.3]$$

This simply says that some portion of market demand is assumed to be taken by firm 2, and firm 1 makes its choice from what is left. Using the rule discussed in the previous section, it is obvious that, facing a demand curve of the form in Equation 13A.3, firm 1's profit-maximizing output level would be given by

$$Q_1 = \frac{120 - Q_2}{2}. \qquad [13A.4]$$

Reaction function
In the Cournot model a function or graph that shows how much one firm will produce given what the other firm produces.

Consequently, the output level actually chosen by firm 1 will depend on the level of output that firm 2 is assumed to produce. For example, if firm 2 chooses to produce 60, firm 1 would choose 30 $[= (120 - 60)/2]$ and market price would be $30 $[= 120 - (Q_1 + Q_2) = 120 - 90]$. Equation 13A.4 is called the **reaction function** for firm 1 because it demonstrates how this firm reacts to firm 2's actions. This reaction function is shown graphically in Figure 13A.2.

Firm 2 might perform a similar analysis and arrive at a reaction function that expresses Q_2 as a function of Q_1 of the form

$$Q_2 = \frac{120 - Q_1}{2} \qquad [13A.5]$$

This reaction function is also shown in Figure 13A.2.

Market Equilibrium

Cournot equilibrium
A solution to the Cournot model in which each firm makes the correct assumption about what the other firm will produce.

So far we know how firm 1 reacts to firm 2's decisions and how firm 2 reacts to firm 1's decisions. These decisions are consistent with each other only at the point where the two lines intersect. At all other points the two firms' output choices are inconsistent because each firm expects the other to be producing at some output level other than that which it actually is. The point of intersection is the only **Cournot equilibrium** that can prevail in this two-firm market. It is easy to find this point of intersection by substituting Equation 13A.5 into Equation 13A.4 to get

$$Q_1 = \frac{120 - Q_2}{2} = \frac{120 - (120 - Q_1)/2}{2}$$

$$= \frac{120 - 60 + Q_1/2}{2} = 30 + \frac{Q_1}{4} \qquad [13A.6]$$

Figure 13A.2
Cournot Reaction
Functions in a Duopoly
Market

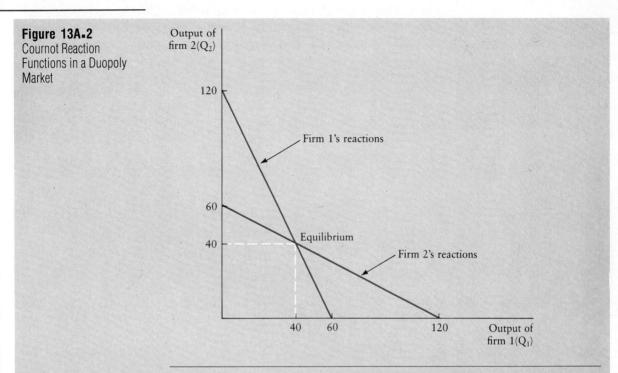

The reaction function for firm 1 shows how that firm will react on the assumption that firm 2's output choice is not affected by the level of Q_1 produced. The function for firm 2 shows a similar reaction for firm 2. Only at the point of intersection of the two curves ($Q_1 = 40$, $Q_2 = 40$) will both of the firms' assumptions be realized. This point of intersection is called the Cournot equilibrium point.

or

$$4Q_1 = 120 + Q_1 \qquad\qquad [13A.7]$$

or

$$Q_1 = 40. \qquad\qquad [13A.8]$$

Substituting this into Equation 13A.5 gives

$$Q_2 = \frac{120 - Q_1}{2} = 40. \qquad\qquad [13A.9]$$

In equilibrium both firms will produce 40, total output will be 80, and the market price will be $40 (= 120 − 80). Profits for each firm will therefore be $1,600 (= $40 × 40), and total industry profits will be $3,200.

The Cournot equilibrium solution is stable because each firm has adjusted its output to the output level being produced by the other firm. Total industry profits in the duopoly case ($3,200) are lower than under the monopoly case ($3,600). This is a result of the failure of the firms in the duopoly situation to coordinate their actions. Only if the firms collude will they be able to achieve the highest profits possible from the given demand curve. It is possible, however, that one of the duopoly firms can increase its profits by recognizing the way in which the other firm reacts to its output level.

Stackelberg Leadership Model

Suppose firm 1 recognizes that firm 2 reacts to its output as given by Equation 13A.5. If firm 2 faithfully follows such a response, firm 1 can increase its profits by making use of its knowledge of these reactions. Substituting Equation 13A.5 into the demand Equation 13A.3 gives

$$Q_1 = 120 - Q_2 - P = 120 - \frac{120 - Q_1}{2} - P$$

$$= 60 + \frac{Q_1}{2} - P \qquad [13A.10]$$

or

$$2Q_1 = 120 + Q_1 - 2P \qquad [13A.11]$$

and therefore

$$Q_1 = 120 - 2P. \qquad [13A.12]$$

By knowing firm 2's reaction, we have been able to derive the demand curve facing firm 1 as a function of its output only. Now, using the profit-maximizing rule, firm 1 should produce

$$Q_1 = 60 \qquad [13A.13]$$

since this is the output level at a price of 0 divided by 2 ($=120/2$). Now if firm 1 produces 60 and firm 2 is a faithful follower of its reaction function, it will produce

$$Q_2 = \frac{120 - 60}{2} = 30. \qquad [13A.14]$$

Consequently, industry output will be 90 and market price will be $30. The profits earned by firm 1 will be

Table 13A.1
Results of the Stackelberg Model (Profits for Each Firm under Various Strategies)

		Firm 2's Strategies	
		Leader	Follower
Firm 1's Strategies	Leader	1: $0 2: 0	1: $1,800 2: 900
	Follower	1: $ 900 2: 1,800	1: $1,600 2: 1,600

$$\pi_1 = \$30 \times 60 = \$1,800 \qquad [13A.15]$$

whereas the profits earned by firm 2 will be

$$\pi_2 = \$30 \times 30 = \$900. \qquad [13A.16]$$

By using its knowledge of firm 2's reaction function, firm 1 has been able to increase its profits. Of course, the profits of firm 2 have been seriously eroded in the process.

Price Leadership

Stackelberg model
A generalization of the Cournot model in which at least one firm knows the other's reaction function.

This model of a leader-follower relationship was first proposed by the German economist Heinrich von Stackelberg.[5] One ambiguous feature of the **Stackelberg model** is how to decide which firm will be the leader and which the follower. If each firm assumes the other is a follower, each will produce 60 and will be disappointed at the final outcome (with total output of 120, market price will, in the present example, fall to 0). On the other hand, if each acts as a follower, the situation will revert to the Cournot equilibrium discussed in the previous section. That equilibrium is, however, unstable: Each firm can perceive the benefits to being a leader and may try to choose its output accordingly. The various outcomes from stategic choices by each firm are shown in Table 13A.1. Because of the uncertainty and interdependence inherent in the model, each firm will try to be a leader, and this will have disastrous consequences for the profits of both. An ironclad agreement between the firms with each promising to adopt the follower strategy would lead to larger industry profits than those that are made when one or both of the firms try to adopt the leader strategy.[6]

---

[5]Heinrich von Stackelberg, *The Theory of the Market Economy*, translated by A. T. Peacock (New York: Oxford University Press, 1952), pp. 195–204).

[6]Of course, if we permit ironclad agreements, it is most profitable for the firms to coordinate their strategies and to act as a monopolist.

Figure 13A.3
Solutions to the Duopoly
Problem.

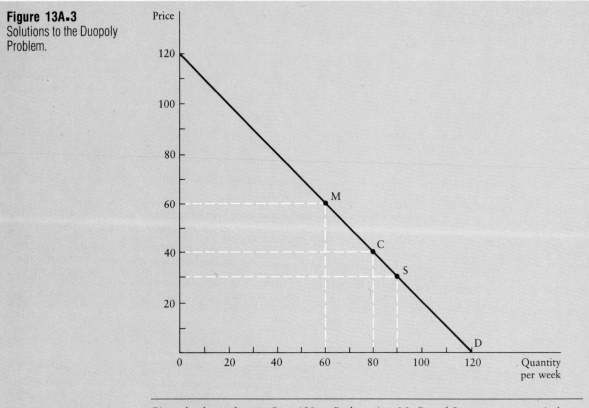

Given the demand curve $Q = 120 - P$, the points M, C, and S represent, respectively, the monopoly, Cournot, and Stackelberg solutions to the duopoly solution.

Comparison of the Models: Approaching the Competitive Solution

We have presented three solutions to the simple duopoly problem posed at the beginning of this appendix: (1) the monopoly solution; (2) the Cournot solution; and (3) the Stackelberg solution. These solutions are shown by the points M, C, and S respectively on the demand curve in Figure 13A.3. These points of market equilibrium approach the competitive solution (where $P = MC = 0$) as the more sophisticated models of duopoly behavior are examined. Indeed, as we showed in the previous section, if both firms attempt to take Stackelberg leadership roles, the competitive solution will be attained. In a sense, then, the uncertainty inherent in the duopoly model may provide a substitute for competition among many firms. There exists a number of more complex models of interdependent firm behavior for which that result also holds. Whether uncertainty in oligopolistic industries in the real world can provide an adequate substitute for competition, however, remains an open question. It all depends on how each firm views its relationship with other firms.

Strategy and the Theory of Games

Game theory
The study of the strategies used by the players in a game and the payoffs they receive.

Our discussion of duopoly shows that even in simple two-firm situations, strategy is important. This final section examines some of the ways in which economists have tried to capture the strategic relationship among firms in the formal study of **game theory.**

The basic structure of game theory consists of specifying the number of players in a game (or the number of firms in an industry), the strategies available to each player, and the outcomes that accrue to each player once a particular choice of strategies has been made. Obviously, a complete treatment of game theory is beyond the scope of this book.[7] However, since even an elementary discussion can provide many insights into real-world strategic choices, we will here briefly study the simplest type of games—two-person games.

Our discussion of two-person games involves two firms (now we call them A and B) that must choose how much to spend on advertising since this issue is often an important one in oligopoly markets. Suppose each firm has only two choices: a small advertising budget or a large one. We denote A's strategies by a_1 (a low advertising budget) and a_2 (a high budget). Similarly, B's strategies are denoted by b_1 (a low budget) and b_2 (a high budget). We now look at several different games in which these strategies might be used.

Zero-Sum Games

Zero-sum game
A game in which the amount which one player loses the other player wins.

In **zero-sum games** firms A and B are directly competitive. What A "wins," B "loses," and vice versa. This would be the case, for example, if total demand for the output of the two firms were absolutely fixed and consequently advertising would only affect the distribution of sales between the two firms. The *payoff matrix* for the first zero-sum game we consider here is shown in Table 13A.2. In this table A's strategies are shown vertically and B's strategies are recorded horizontally. The entries in the table record the outcomes (in terms of millions of dollars of profits) that accrue to A and B when the particular strategy choices are made. For example, the upper left corner of the matrix records the fact that when A "plays" a_1 and B "plays" b_1, A receives profits of $5 and B receives profits of $-\$5$. Similarly, when both firms have high advertising budgets, profits for each are zero. The other entries in the table should be interpreted in the same way. Total profits for the industry are always zero, indicating that the game is truly "zero-sum."

Assuming that both A and B fully understand the possible outcomes of the game, we can examine how they might decide on which strategy to pursue. For firm B, strategy b_2 dominates b_1: No matter what A does, B can do best by playing b_2. Against a_1, that strategy promises a gain of $5, and against a_2

[7]The central work in the field is John von Neumann and Oscar Morgenstern, *The Theory of Games and Economic Behavior* (Princeton, N.J.: Princeton University Press, 1949). A more intuitive coverage is provided in R. Duncan Luce and Howard Raiffa, *Games and Decisions* (New York: Wiley, 1957).

Table 13A.2
Payoff Matrix for
Equilibrium Zero-Sum
Game

		B's Strategies	
		b₁ (Low Budget)	b₂ (High Budget)
A's Strategies	a₁ (Low Budget)	A: + \$5 B: − 5	A: − \$5 B: + 5
	a₂ (High Budget)	A: \$0 B: 0	A: \$0 B: 0

it promises 0 profits. Firm A, on the other hand, has no dominant strategy: against b_1, strategy a_1 is preferred, but against b_2, strategy a_2 is preferred. There are numerous ways in which A might choose a strategy in this situation. One method would be for A to to adopt the pessimistic assumption that "no matter what I do, B will choose the strategy that harms me the most." Under this assumption, A should choose that strategy for which the worst possible outcome is as good as possible.[8] Here that choice would be a_2. By choosing a_2, A can assure itself zero profits no matter what B does. On the other hand, choosing a_1 runs some risk of getting a profit of − \$5. Consequently A chooses a_2, B chooses b_2, and both end up earning zero profits. The choice of a_2, b_2 is, in this situation, an *equilibrium* pair of strategies. If either A or B knew ahead of time what its competitor were going to do, it would not change its decision: Knowing B will choose b_2 does not alter A's determination to choose a_2, and vice versa.

Not all zero-sum games, have equilibrium strategies; there are *nonequilibrium* zero-sum games.[9] For example, consider the payoffs shown in Table 13A.3, which sum to 0. By following the pessimistic decision rule, A would choose strategy a_2 since under this choice it can at most suffer a profit loss of − \$5. If B is also pessimistic, it will choose b_1, which assures at least 0 profits. The choice a_2, b_1 is not, however, a stable equilibrium. For example, A might reason "I know B will choose b_1, so why should I suffer a loss of − \$5; instead, I'll choose a_1 and end up even." However, B can anticipate this trickery and opt for b_2 thus gaining profits of \$10 for itself and imposing a loss of \$10 on A. Of course, A will see this, and will choose a_2 to avoid the loss. The cycle can continue indefinitely since there is no equilibrium for the game. Each player will keep switching strategies in an effort to keep one step ahead of its competitor.

---

[8]This pessimistic way of choosing a strategy is called a "maximin" (or sometimes "minimax") decision rule.

[9]It can be shown, however, that most zero-sum games have equilibrium "mixed strategies" under which players use each of their strategies only a fraction of the time. See R. Duncan Luce and Howard Raiffa, *Games and Decisions* (New York, Wiley, 1957), Appendix 2.

Table 13A.3
Payoff Matrix for
Nonequilibrium
Zero-Sum Game

		B's Strategies	
		b_1 (Low Budget)	b_2 (High Budget)
A's Strategies	a_1 (Low Budget)	A: $0 B: 0	A: − $10 B: + 10
	a_2 (High Budget)	A: − $5 B: + 5	A: + $5 B: − 5

Nonzero-Sum Games

Most oligopoly situations are not zero-sum. It is not usually the case that what one firm gains the other loses but, rather, that a variety of outcomes is possible depending on the strategies that are chosen. A particularly fascinating non-zero-sum game is shown in Table 13A.4. This table is interpreted in exactly the same way as the previous two, except that the outcomes no longer sum to a constant value. In this game, strategy a_2 dominates a_1 for firm A: No matter what B does, A is better off with a_2. Similarly, b_2 dominates b_1 for firm B. Both firms will choose to have high advertising budgets and will each receive a profit of + $5. An ironclad agreement by both firms to pursue low advertising budgets, however, would result in a profit level of $7 for each. The difficulty with this twin low-budget strategy choice is that it is unstable. If A knows that B will choose b_1, it is to A's advantage to choose a_2 and increase its profits from + $7 to + $10. Similarly, if B knows A will choose a_1, B too has an incentive to cheat. Consequently, both firms, pursuing their own self-interest, will choose their second strategies even though rationality would suggest the twin low-budget strategy.

The Prisoner's Dilemma

Prisoner's dilemma
A game in which the players' most desirable outcome is unstable because each player has an incentive to cheat in the strategy actually chosen.

The game shown in Table 13A.4 is one example of what has come to be known as the **prisoner's dilemma.** The dilemma arises because the best choice of strategies is unstable and provides great incentives to cheat. Faced with the uncertainty inherent in the game, both players end up making a second-best choice. The term *prisoner's dilemma* to describe this situation comes from a game first discussed by A. W. Tucker in the 1940s, in which two people are arrested for a crime. The district attorney has little evidence in the case and is anxious to extract a confession. She separates the suspects and tells each, "If you confess and your companion doesn't, I can promise you a reduced six-month sentence, whereas your companion will, on the basis of your confession, get ten years. If you both confess you will each get a three-year sentence." Each suspect also knows that if neither one of them confesses the lack of

Table 13A.4
Nonzero-Sum Game

		B's Strategies	
		b_1 (Low Budget)	b_2 (High Budget)
A's Strategies	a_1 (Low Budget)	A: + $7 B: + 7	A: + $ 3 B: + 10
	a_2 (High Budget)	A: + $10 B: + 3	A: + $5 B: + 5

evidence will cause them to be tried for a lesser crime for which they would receive maximum two-year sentences if convicted.

The payoff matrix of this game is presented in Table 13A.5. This game closely resembles that shown in Table 13A.4, in that the "confess" strategy dominates for both A and B. However, an agreement between the two prisoners not to confess would reduce their terms from three to a maximum of two years (and possibly less). This "rational" solution is not stable, and there is an incentive for either prisoner to cheat on it.

A prisoner's dilemma type of game may occur in many real-world market situations. The example of advertising budgets may actually occur. Much advertising may be merely "defensive" in the sense that a mutual agreement to reduce advertising expenditures would be profitable to both parties. However, such an agreement would be unstable because one firm could increase its profits even further by cheating on the agreement. Similar situations arise in the tendency for airlines to show in-flight movies (there would be larger profits if all airlines stopped showing movies, but such a solution is unstable); in the instability of farmers' (and other cartel) agreements to restrict milk output since it is just too tempting for the individual farmer to try to sell more milk; or in the banking industry's move to "free" checking accounts (keeping service charges is more profitable, but this is unstable since one bank can greatly increase its deposits by offering free checks). As these examples show, the difficulty of enforcing agreements may be very detrimental to the profits of an industry. Again then, this is a situation where considerations of strategy may lead to competitive-type results.

The Duopoly Model as a Game

We can tie this discussion of game theory together with our prior examination of duopoly by noting the similarity between the outcomes of the Stackelberg model (in Table 13A.1) and the prisoner's dilemma. In both cases the players in the game have a preferred outcome; but that solution is fundamentally unstable because it provides incentives to cheat. As we showed in Chapter 13, this type of outcome is quite common in market situations (such as cartels)

Table 13A.5
The Prisoner's Dilemma

		Prisoner B	
		Confess	Not Confess
Prisoner A	Confess	A: 3 years B: 3 years	A: 6 months B: 10 years
	Not Confess	A: 10 years B: 6 months	A: 2 years B: 2 years

in which a gap between price and marginal cost provides participants with an incentive to chisel on price. As in the prisoner's dilemma, although such behavior is rational to each participant, it is collectively irrational to the cartel as a whole. Game theory, therefore, provides one more way of illustrating the ways in which competitive forces may come to dominate various types of markets.

Summary

This appendix is concerned with developing a few simple models that illustrate the strategic relationships among firms in oligopoly markets. Our principal observations about such models are:

- Solutions to a duopoly (two-firm) model depend importantly on how the firms treat each other's decisions. If the decisions are fully coordinated, monopoly results will occur.
- In the absence of perfect coordination, a variety of outcomes are possible. Some (such as the Stackelberg model of price leadership) may approach the competitive solution under which price is equal to marginal cost.
- Game theory provides a formal way of analyzing strategic choices made by various players. In zero-sum games (that is, those in which what one player wins the other loses) there will often exist equilibrium strategies that are stable in that no player has an incentive to change his or her choices once the other player's strategy is known.
- An important nonzero-sum is the prisoner's dilemma. In this game the solution involving each player's preferred strategy is unstable—there is an incentive for each player to cheat. The result of such cheating is to make both players worse off.
- Many of the features of game theory are reflected in oligopoly markets. For example, the incentive to chisel on price in a cartel is very similar to the prisoner's dilemma.

PRICING OF FACTORS OF PRODUCTION

Factors of production also have prices. Labor services are purchased for a wage rate per hour, machines have rental rates, and something must be paid for the use of land. In this part we investigate how those prices are determined. As a starting point it might be assumed that those prices (as is the case for the prices of goods) are established by the forces of supply and demand. People supply labor services, and these services are demanded by firms. Owners of capital and land are similarly willing to rent these resources to a firm for a price. In some way, then, prices are determined by the operation of the market.

Chapter 14 discusses the demand for factors of production. There are several ways in which the demand for inputs differs from the demand concepts we have been using so far. Most importantly, here firms are doing the hiring and their demand for any factor of production is a *derived demand*. It depends indirectly on the demand for the good that the firm produces. For example, the demand for the services of airline pilots depends on the demand for air travel. If the demand curve for air travel were to shift, the demand curve for pilots would also shift. A second important demand concept introduced in Chapter 14 is *economic rent*. Simply defined, any factor of production is said to earn rents when the factor is paid more than the amount necessary to keep the factor in its present employment. The most important example of such economic rent is the rent paid for the use of land. Since, to a first approximation, the supply of land is absolutely fixed, any payment to landowners is an economic rent in the sense that the payment does not induce additional supply—price is solely determined by demand.

Early economists (most notably David Ricardo) intensively studied the phenomenon of land rent, and in many respects their investigations provided a foundation for the marginal productivity theory of factor demand. This theory underlies most of the analysis of Chapter 14.

Much of the discussion in Chapter 14 assumes that firms hire inputs in perfectly competitive markets. That is, firms are assumed to be price takers in that their actions have no effect on the wage rate they must pay for labor or the rental rate they must pay for capital. In the final sections of Chapter 14, however, we explore the possibility that a firm may have some market power to affect factor prices. Specifically, we examine the situation of a monopsony (single buyer) and show how the market power possessed by the monopsony can lead to the same general kinds of distortions in the allocation of resources that we described in Chapter 12 for the case of monopoly.

The theory of demand in Chapter 14 is quite general— it applies to any factor of production. In Chapters 15 and 16 we take up several issues specifically related to pricing in the labor and capital markets. In Chapter 15 we discuss three particular aspects of the labor supply. First we analyze the simple labor supply decisions of one person and then construct a market supply of labor curve in much the same way we developed a market demand curve in Part 2. Next we briefly discuss occupational choice and the concept of compensating wage differentials. Finally, we take note of the fact that important portions of the labor market are characterized by the presence of unions, and we show how they can be incorporated into the general theory of how wages are determined.

In Chapter 16 we look at the market for capital. The central purpose of the chapter is to emphasize the connection between capital and the allocation of resources over time. Any economy's stock of capital equipment represents some output that was produced in the past to be used for production in the future. In Chapter 16 we analyze the choices people make in this process. We are especially interested in illustrating how the theory of capital and investment decisions can be incorporated into the models of firms' behavior from Part 3. The appendix to Chapter 16 presents some mathematical results about interest rates that are widely used in the study of capital and investment.

In *The Principles of Political Economy and Taxation*, David Ricardo wrote:

The produce of the earth . . . is divided among three classes of the community, namely, the proprietor of the land, the owner of the stock of capital necessary for its cultivation, and the laborers by whose industry it is cultivated. To determine the laws which regulate this distribution is the principal problem in Political Economy.[1]

The purpose of Part 5 is to take up Ricardo's "problem" and show how the prices of factors of production are determined. An understanding of this pricing mechanism not only provides insights into how the market works, but also helps us to understand how people get their incomes. The study of factor pricing completes our analysis of the circular flow of goods and payments for those goods throughout an economy. ▲

[1]David Ricardo, *The Principles of Political Economy and Taxation* (1817; reprinted, London: J. M. Dent and Son, 1965), p. 1.

CHAPTER 14

The Demand for Factors of Production

A simple way to start a discussion of pricing of factors is to assume that these prices are somehow established by supply and demand. Figure 14.1 depicts this concept. The factor supply curve (S) is drawn positively sloped on the assumption that higher factor rewards (which we will denote by v) will induce suppliers to offer more factor services (F) in the market place. Similarly the demand curve for the factor (D) is drawn with a negative slope on the assumption that demanders (principally firms) will hire a smaller quantity of the factor at higher levels of v. The price v* is therefore an equilibrium price at which the total quantity of factor services supplied is exactly equal to the quantity that is demanded. At a price above v* supply would exceed demand and there would be "unemployment" of this factor; for a price below v* there would be excess demand for the factor.

Assumptions about Supply

The curves in Figure 14.1 were drawn without very much careful thought. As in our examination of pricing in the goods market, the most interesting aspects of the analysis arise when we inquire into the more basic determinants of the shape of these curves. In this chapter we are primarily interested in studying the demand for a factor of production.

We assume here that there are a large number of suppliers of the factor in question. No single supplier can affect the price to be received; he or she will act as a price taker in making decisions. The market supply curve reflects the decisions of all suppliers as a group. This market supply curve can assume a wide variety of possible shapes. For example, the supply curve for land might be assumed to be very inelastic since the amount of land available is more or

Figure 14.1
Supply and Demand in
the Factor Market

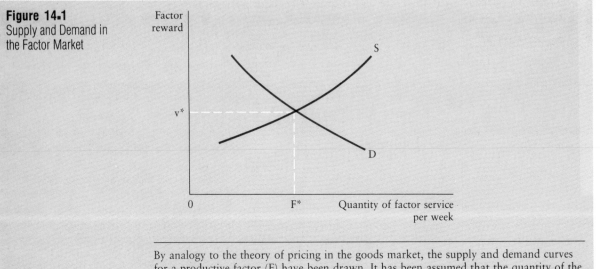

By analogy to the theory of pricing in the goods market, the supply and demand curves for a productive factor (F) have been drawn. It has been assumed that the quantity of the factor service supplied is an increasing function of the factor payment (v) and that the quantity demanded is a decreasing function of v. The factor reward v* is an equilibrium price, since at this price the quantity supplied is equal to the quantity demanded.

less fixed. The supply of other factors might be very elastic. For example, it is possible that relatively small increases in the wages of teachers might prompt a lot of people to consider the job. Whatever the shape of the supply curve, we usually assume that its position remains fixed throughout our analysis. In Chapters 15 and 16 we look at a few specific questions about the supply of labor and the supply of capital in detail.

Derived Demand

Derived demand
Demand for a factor of
production that is de-
termined by the demand
for the good it
produces.

The demand curve in Figure 14.1 is drawn downward sloping. A lower price for an input is assumed to cause firms to demand more of it. To understand why a firm would hire more of an input in response to a fall in its price, we must recognize that a firm's demand for any factor of production is a **derived demand**. Firms hire labor, capital, and land in order to produce output. The quantities they hire depend on how much output they are able to sell. General Motors' demand for production workers, for machinery, and for land and buildings depends on how many cars it can market. If the price of an input were to fall, the firm would increase its use of that input for two reasons. First, it would then be able to produce any output level more cheaply by using relatively more of this input. For example, a decline in wages might cause General Motors to use more workers and fewer machines on its assembly line. Second, if the firm, in response to the fall in the factor price, chose to produce

Figure 14.2
Economic Rent

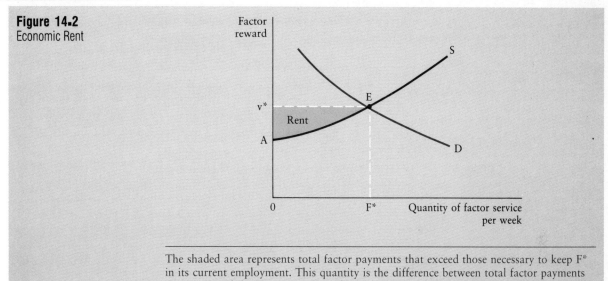

The shaded area represents total factor payments that exceed those necessary to keep F* in its current employment. This quantity is the difference between total factor payments (v*OF*E) and those payments a perfectly discriminating hirer might pay (AOF*E).

more output, it would demand even more inputs. For General Motors, for instance, costs of manufacturing cars would fall, and the firm might find it profitable to produce more of them and to hire more labor to do so.

Later in this chapter we analyze this sequence of events in more detail. For the moment, the discussion is sufficiently precise to indicate why a firm's demand curve for an input will be downward sloping. We now look a bit further at the supply-demand equilibrium pictured in Figure 14.1. In particular, we investigate the question of the "rent" earned by factors of production.

Economic Rent

Economic rent
The amount by which payments to a factor exceed the minimal amount required to retain it in its present use.

Rent plays an important role in the analysis of factor pricing. Because this term is used in a variety of contexts it is important to be precise about its economic meaning. We use the term **economic rent** to reflect the extent to which payments to a factor exceed the minimal amount required to retain it in its present use.

One example of economic rent that we have already examined is the long-run profits earned by a monopoly. Since those profits would not be earned if the monopoly's inputs were employed under perfect competition, they are a form of economic rent. Figure 14.2 illustrates a more general case. Since the supply curve records that amount of factor service that would be supplied at each price, the total dollar amount necessary to retain the level F* in this occupation is given by the area A0F*E. If firms could perfectly discriminate among factor suppliers by hiring one unit at a time at an amount necessary to draw *that unit* into employment, total factor payments would be A0F*E.[1] Competitive markets, however, do not work in this way. Rather, all units of an input are paid the same price, and this price (v*) is determined by what firms have to pay the last unit hired. Because all other units receive a return of v*, but might settle for somewhat less and still remain in their current employment, these "intramarginal" suppliers receive an economic rent. Total factor payments in the competitive case are given by v*0F*E, and total economic rents are given by the shaded area v*AE.

It is easy to see that the flatter (that is, the more elastic) the supply curve for a factor is, the smaller the area that represents economic rent is. If a supply curve were infinitely elastic (a horizontal line at the prevailing price), there would be no economic rent. At the other extreme, all of the return to a factor that is in fixed supply is in the nature of an economic rent.[2] The factor payments in such a situation are determined solely by demand, and there is no notion of lost opportunities on the part of the supplier of this fixed factor. It will always be supplied no matter what price is offered. Any return that is received is a result of the "accident" of where the demand curve happens to be.

Economic Rent and Opportunity Cost

It is important to recognize the relationship between the concepts of economic rent and opportunity cost. A factor of production that has many alternative uses will have a very elastic supply curve to any one employment. Since this factor can receive almost as high a price elsewhere, quantity supplied will be reduced sharply if an employer reduces its price offer even slightly. In such a case, economic rents would be small because the factor earns only slightly in excess of what it might earn elsewhere. For example, clerical workers have numerous employment opportunities, all of which offer approximately the same wage. The earnings of a clerical worker in, say, a life insurance firm represent virtually no economic rent, since the worker could earn almost exactly the same amount in employment by some other firm. On the other hand, there are factors of production that are uniquely suited to one employment and have a considerably lower value elsewhere. In that case, their supply curve to this employment is inelastic, reflecting the fact that a lower price would not cause a marked reduction in supply. Most of the earnings of such a factor would be called economic rent and would be measured by the difference between the factor's current earnings and earnings in its next best employment.

---

[1]This analysis is very similar to the analysis of consumer's surplus in Chapter 12.

[2]Some authors make a distinction between short-run and long-run rents. In the short run, when supply curves tend to be more inelastic, rent is referred to as quasirent to indicate that it may disappear when long-run supply response is permitted. The profits of perfectly competitive firms in the short run are one example of quasirent.

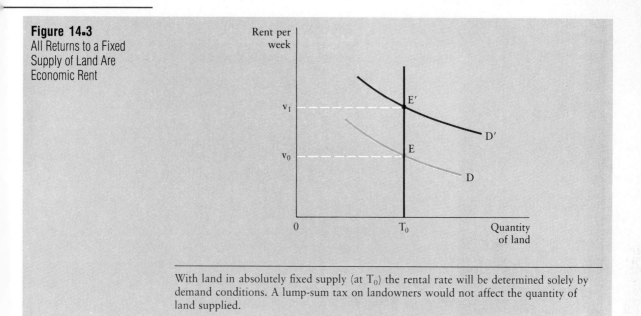

Figure 14.3
All Returns to a Fixed
Supply of Land Are
Economic Rent

With land in absolutely fixed supply (at T_0) the rental rate will be determined solely by demand conditions. A lump-sum tax on landowners would not affect the quantity of land supplied.

The high wages paid to players in professional baseball or basketball, for example, might be considered, in large part, as economic rent in the sense that the alternative earnings possibilities of these individuals (in occupations outside of their sport) may be relatively low.

Land Rent

The most common example of this analysis of economic rent is in the case of a fixed land supply. This situation is represented in Figure 14.3 by the vertical supply curve at the existing level of land (T_0). No matter what the level of demand is, this supply will be fixed. If demand were given by curve D, the rent on the land would be v_0, and the total return to the owner of the land is $v_0 0 T_0 E$. If, on the other hand, demand were given by the curve D′, the equilibrium rental rate would be v_1, and total rentals would be $v_1 0 T_0 E'$. The increase in price from v_0 to v_1, although it serves to ration the available land among demanders, has no effect on increasing supply. The nineteenth-century American economist Henry George[3] noted this fact and proposed that rents going to landowners be taxed at a very high level, since this taxation would

---

[3]Henry George, *Progress and Poverty: An Inquiry into the Cause of Industrial Depression and of Increase of Want with Increase of Wealth* (New York: Henry George, 1881).

have no effect on the quantity of land provided. While there are numerous complications in this proposal, George's idea of a single tax on land still has many adherents, particularly in the British Labour Party.

Although there are important historical reasons why the examination of economic rent centers on the returns to owners of land, we have seen that there is little economic reason for such a narrow view. Any factor of production for which alternative uses are slight will have a relatively inelastic supply to its most favorable employment. Most of the total return to this factor will represent economic rent, and this could be taxed away without creating a major reduction in supply. The price paid for rental of a favorably located parcel of land in Manhattan is largely economic rent in the same sense that the price Robert Redford receives for his acting is. In both cases, supply may be quite inelastic, and demand conditions will play the major role in determining price.

Ricardian Rent

In examining the rents earned on different parcels of land, one of the most important observations made by classical economists was that more fertile land tended to command a higher rent. David Ricardo, for example, carefully analyzed the way in which differential rents were related to land's fertility and to the demand for crops grown on the land.[4] Ricardo theorized that additional land of inferior quality would be cultivated up to the point at which the last acre planted earned exactly zero in economic rents. More fertile acres would earn positive rents, however, and these would represent a return based on the land's higher quality. Since the market price of any particular crop is determined by the costs of the marginal producer, and since rents are zero for this marginal producer, Ricardo concluded that economic rent should not be considered a cost element in determining the crop's price. Rather, rent is determined solely by the market demand for crops and by the availabilities of fertile land.

Graphic Presentation of Ricardo's Analysis

Ricardo's argument can easily be demonstrated graphically. Assume there are many parcels of land suitable for growing wheat. These parcels range from very fertile (low costs of production) to rather poor and rocky (high cost). The long-run supply curve for wheat can be constructed as follows. At low prices only the best land is used, as price rises, production continues on the fertile land, and additional crops are planted on land of poorer quality. At

---

[4]See Ricardo, *Political Economy and Taxation* (1817: Reprinted London: J. M. Dent and Son, 1965), Chapters 2 and 32.

Figure 14.4
Creation of Ricardian Rent
on Land of Differing
Fertility

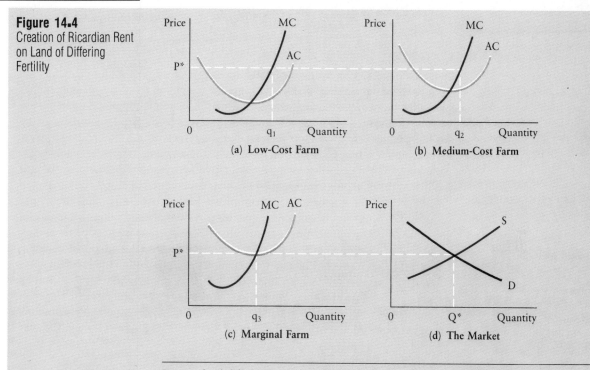

(a) **Low-Cost Farm**

(b) **Medium-Cost Farm**

(c) **Marginal Farm**

(d) **The Market**

Because land differs in quality, farms with the most fertile land will have lower costs. Since price will be determined by the costs of the marginal supplier, low-cost firms will earn pure economic profits. These profits might be called rent and will persist even in the long run since fertile land is in fixed supply.

still higher prices it will be profitable to utilize even lower quality land in production.

The market equilibrium is pictured in Figure 14.4. At the equilibrium price P*, owners of low-cost land parcels earn large economic profits (rent); those less favorably situated earn smaller rents; the marginal farm earns zero in rents. If it were possible to earn any rents on additional pieces of land, this land would be brought into cultivation. Those acres that are left unplanted must be of lower quality than those of the marginal farm. The equilibrium described in Figure 14.4 is stable in the long run. It is impossible for new entrants to earn a profit even though those farms already in the market, by virtue of controlling the best land, are able to do so.

Notice two things about this analysis. First, it shows how the demand for land is derived from the product market. The location of the market demand curve determines how much land will be cultivated and how much rent will be generated. Notice also that the existence of rent does not affect the price of wheat. Rather, wheat prices only reflect the higher production costs encountered on the "marginal" farm.

Generalizations of Ricardo's Analysis

Ricardo's analysis of rent can be generalized to any situation in which differing productivities of resources result in differing cost curves for the firms that own those resources. Other cases of land rents reflecting cost differences include high rental values of especially favorable locations for retail businesses; higher prices for homes located near transit lines; and the tendency of identical houses to sell for more when they are located in towns with good schools. For the case of natural resource deposits a similar analysis would hold. Those deposits from which resources can be obtained at low cost will command a rent relative to less accessible deposits. A major controversy over deregulation of natural gas prices in the United States, for example, concerned the distinction between "old" gas (that is, gas produced from older, lower cost wells) and "new" gas produced in more recent and costly locations. It was argued that old gas should continue to be produced under controlled prices so that owners of those low cost wells would not gain windfall profits (that is, rents) as a result of rising prices that only reflected production costs from new wells.

As you can see, Ricardo's analysis continues to provide insights into a number of important policy questions. "Applying Economics: Rent Capitalization of Commuting Costs in Washington, D.C." discusses the economic rents of housing located near the central city.

Marginal Productivity Theory of Factor Demand

Ricardian rent theory was an important predecessor of the development of marginalist economics. Ricardo's hypothesis that price is determined by the costs of the marginal producer in many ways represents the seed from which modern microeconomics grew. One major generalization of this hypothesis was the development of the marginal productivity theory of the demand for factors of production. This section investigates that theory in detail.

The basic concept of the marginal productivity theory of factor demand has already been stated in Chapter 9 when we discussed profit maximization. There we show that one implication of the profit maximization hypothesis is that the firm will make marginal input choices. More precisely, we showed that a profit-maximizing firm will hire additional units of any input up to the point at which the additional revenue from hiring one more unit is exactly equal to the cost of hiring that unit. If we use ME_K and ME_L to denote the marginal expense associated with hiring one more unit of capital and labor respectively, and let MR_K and MR_L be the extra revenue that hiring these units of capital and labor brings in, then profit maximization requires that

$$ME_K = MR_K;$$
$$ME_L = MR_L.$$

[14.1]

Our analysis in the remainder of this chapter applies this marginal concept in various situations.

Rent Capitalization of Commuting Costs in Washington, D.C.

One of the major ways suburban communities differ in their attractiveness to homebuyers is in their convenience to places of work. Among houses with otherwise similar characteristics (for example, square feet of living space, air conditioning, lot size, and so forth) it would be expected that those in easily accessible locations would command higher prices than those in locations requiring lengthy commuting. In other words, the low commuting costs involved in some locations would be expected to be "capitalized" into the market prices of houses, just as in Ricardo's analysis, land's superior fertility and ability to earn rent would be expected to be reflected in its market value.

The question of how commuting costs are reflected in property values has been examined in a number of studies. One of the most complete studies, by J. P. Nelson, focused on the Washington, D.C., metropolitan area for 1970.[5] By carefully controlling for the many other factors that influence the demand for housing, Nelson estimated that each minute of daily commuting time to major employment areas in Washington reduced house values by about $190. A home that sold for $50,000 in an area that involved commuting time of about half an hour would sell for about $44,300 if it were located in an area involving an hour commute. Housing prices in metropolitan areas throughout the United States suggest that this type of price decline with respect to commuting costs may be quite common. Not only do prices seem to reflect automobile commuting times, but houses located near major railroad lines (say in New York City suburbs in New Jersey or Connecticut) have higher prices than those located elsewhere.

One way Nelson was able to check his estimate of the extent to which commuting costs were capitalized in house values was to calculate the implicit value that people were placing on their own time by paying more for favorably located houses. By assuming a certain number of commuting trips per year he was able to calculate an implicit value of commuting time of around $1.85 per hour (or about one-third of workers' average aftertax wage rates in 1970). That figure was quite consistent with a variety of other studies showing how individuals make choices among ways of getting to work that show an implicit time value of between one third and one half the market wage.

To Think About

1. Can you think of factors in addition to commuting costs that might be reflected in housing costs? How might proximity to a park or to an environmental hazard affect prices? How might you use house values to estimate the social benefits or costs of these factors?

2. Some stores advertise that they have low prices because they don't have to pay "high downtown rents." Would Ricardo's analysis support this assessment?

Price-Taking Behavior

If, as we have been assuming, the firm is a price taker in the capital and labor market, it is easy to simplify the marginal expense idea. In this case, the firm can always hire an extra hour of capital input at the prevailing rental rate (v) and an extra hour of labor at the wage rate (w). Therefore, Equation 14.1

[5]J. P. Nelson, "Accessibility and the Value of Time in Commuting," *Southern Economic Journal,* January 1977, pp. 1321–1329.

reduces to

$$v = ME_K = MR_K;$$
$$w = ME_L = MR_L.$$

[14.2]

These equations simply say that a profit-maximizing firm that is a price taker for the inputs it buys should hire these inputs up to the point at which their unit cost is equal to the revenue they generate.

Marginal Revenue Product

To analyze the additional revenue yielded by hiring one more unit of an input is a two-step process. First we must ask how much output the additional input can produce. As we discussed in Chapter 8, this magnitude is given by the input's marginal physical productivity. For example, if a firm hires one more worker for an hour to make shoes, the worker's marginal physical productivity (MP_L) is simply the number of additional pairs of shoes per hour that worker can make.

Once the additional output has been produced, it must be sold. Assessing the value of that sale is the second step in analyzing the revenue yielded by hiring one more unit of an input. We have looked at this issue quite extensively in previous chapters—the extra revenue obtained from selling an additional unit of output is, by definition, marginal revenue (MR). So, if an extra worker can produce two pairs of shoes per hour and the firm can take in $4 per pair from selling these shoes, then hiring the worker for an hour has increased the firm's revenues by $8. It is this figure the firm will compare to the worker's hourly wage to decide whether he or she should be hired. So now our profit-maximizing rules become

$$v = ME_K = MR_K = MP_K \cdot MR;$$
$$w = ME_L = MR_L = MP_L \cdot MR.$$

[14.3]

Marginal revenue product
The extra revenue obtained from selling the output produced by hiring an extra worker or machine.

The terms on the right side of Equation 14.3 are called the **marginal revenue product** of capital and labor respectively since they show how much extra revenue is brought in by hiring one more unit. These are precisely what we need to study the demand for inputs and how the demand might change if wages or rental rates change.

A Special Case—Marginal Value Product

The profit-maximizing rules for input choices can be made even simpler if we assume that the firm we are examining sells its output in a competitive market. In that case, the firm will also be a price taker in the goods market, so the marginal revenues it takes in from selling one more unit of output is the market price (P). Using the result that MR = P, we now have

$$v = MP_K \cdot P; \qquad\qquad [14.4]$$
$$w = MP_L \cdot P$$

Marginal value product
A special case of marginal revenue product in which the firm is a price taker for its output.

as the conditions for a profit maximum.[6] We call the terms on the right hand side of Equation 14.4 the **marginal value product** (MVP) of capital and labor respectively, since they do indeed put a value on these inputs' marginal productivities. Our final condition for maximum profits in this simple situation is

$$v = MVP_K; \qquad\qquad [14.5]$$
$$w = MVP_L.$$

To see why these are required for profit maximization, consider again our shoe worker example. Suppose the worker can make two pairs of shoes per hour and that shoes sell for $4. The worker's marginal value product is $8 per hour. If the hourly wage is less than this (say $5 per hour), the firm can increase profits by $3 by employing the worker for one more hour; profits were not at a maximum. Similarly, if the wage is $10 per hour, profits would rise by $2 if one less hour of labor were used. Only if the wage and labor's marginal value product are equal will profits truly be as large as possible.

A Graphic Demonstration

Figure 14.5 shows this result graphically. The horizontal axis in the figure records the hours of labor hired, and the vertical axis shows the MVP for each of these levels.[7] We can construct an MVP curve for labor directly from the marginal physical product of labor curve (MP_L) introduced in Chapter 7 by multiplying MP_L by the market price of the firm's output. The resulting MVP_L is shown in Figure 14.5. The downward slope of that curve reflects the assumption of a diminishing marginal physical productivity: the more labor

---

[6]Equation 14.4 implies cost minimization. Dividing the two gives:

$$\frac{MP_L}{MP_K} = \frac{w}{v}$$

but in Chapter 7 we showed that RTS (of L for K) = MP_L/MP_K. A firm that pursues a marginal productivity approach to input demand will equate

$$RTS \text{ (of L for K)} = w/v$$

and this is what is required for cost minimization.

[7]Although here we analyze only the case of labor input, an analysis of the demand for capital input would proceed in exactly the same way. Throughout our discussion we assume the firm is a price taker in the output market so that the marginal value product is the correct demand concept.

Figure 14.5
Profit-Maximizing
Input Choice

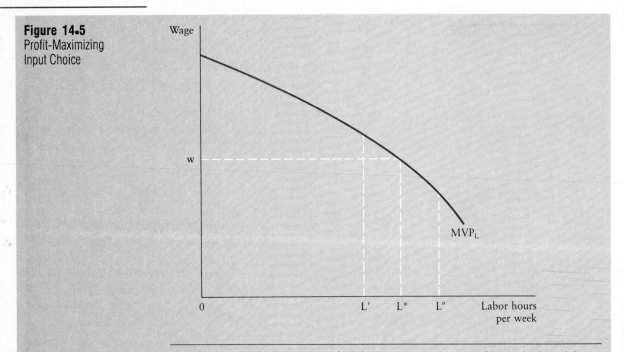

The marginal value product curve for labor (MVP_L) is constructed by multiplying labor's marginal physical productivity times the market price of the firm's output. The curve is downward sloping because of the assumption that labor exhibits a diminishing marginal physical productivity. At a wage of w, profit maximization requires that L^* units of labor input be hired.

hired, the lower will be labor's marginal physical productivity and the lower also will be its marginal value product.

The profit-maximizing amount of labor to hire can be found by recording labor's hourly wage rate (w) on the vertical axis. At that wage, profit maximization requires hiring L^* workers. Only for this level of labor input does $w = MVP_L$. For levels of labor input less than L^* (say L') labor's MVP will exceed the market wage and it would be profitable to hire more workers. Quantities of labor input greater than L^* (say L''), on the other hand, have an MVP that falls short of w, and profits would be increased by cutting back on employment. Only at L^* is the cost of hiring an extra worker exactly equal to the revenue that hiring the worker provides to the firm: only at L^* is the firm maximizing profits.

If w were to change we would expect the profit-maximizing quantity of labor input to change. We examine that possibility in the next section. In our investigation we continue to assume that the firm is a price taker for both the inputs it buys and the output it sells. The analysis would be only slightly changed if we studied a case of imperfect competition in the goods market. In this case marginal revenue (MR) would be less than market price (P) but

Figure 14.6
Change in Labor Input
When Wage Falls: Single-
Input Case

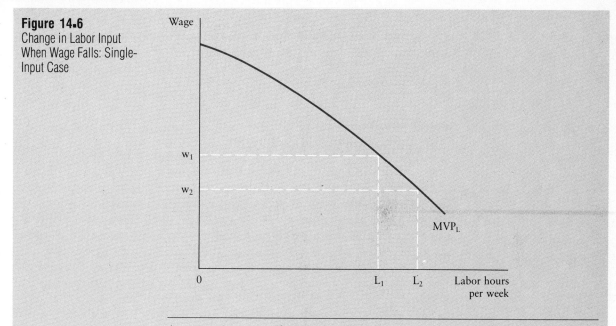

At a wage rate w_1, profit maximization requires that L_1 labor input be hired. If the wage rate falls to w_2, more labor (L_2) will be hired because of the assumed slope of the MVP_L curve.

it would be a simple matter to take that into account. However, the analysis is quite different if we drop the assumption that the firm is a price taker for the inputs it buys—a subject we study in detail later.

Responses to Changes in Input Prices

Suppose the price of labor (w) were to fall. We have showed why firms might demand more labor in response to such a change. In this section we provide a detailed analysis of why this is so.

Single-Input Case

As a simple first case, let us assume that a firm uses only labor to produce its output. The firm's marginal value productivity curve is shown in Figure 14.6. At a wage of w_1 the firm's profit-maximizing choice of labor input is given by L_1. The firm will persist in hiring L_1 units of labor so long as the conditions it faces do not change.

If the wage rate were to fall to w_2, more labor (L_2) would be demanded. At such a lower wage, more labor can be hired because the firm can "afford" to have a lower marginal physical productivity from the labor it employs. If it continued to hire only L_1 the firm would not be maximizing profits since, at the margin, labor would now be capable of producing more in additional revenue than hiring additional labor would cost. For the single input case, the assumption of a diminishing marginal productivity of labor insures that a fall in the price of labor will cause more labor to be hired.[8] The marginal value product curve shows this response.

A Numerical Example

As a numerical example of these input choices, let's look again at the hiring decision for Hamburger Heaven first discussed in the appendix to Chapter 8. Table 14.1 repeats the productivity information for the case in which Hamburger Heaven uses four grills (K = 4). As the table shows, the marginal productivity of labor declines as more workers are assigned to use grills each hour—the first worker hired turns out 20 (heavenly) hamburgers per hour, whereas the tenth hired produces only 3.2 hamburgers per hour. To calculate these workers' marginal value products we simply multiply these physical productivity figures by the price of hamburgers, $.20. These results appear in the final column of Table 14.1. With a market wage of $1 per hour, Hamburger Heaven should hire four workers. The marginal product value of each of these workers exceeds $1, so the firm earns some incremental profit on each of them. The fifth worker's MVP is only $.94, however, so it does not make sense to add that worker.

The number of workers hired is precisely the number required to minimize average cost with four grills in operation (see the appendix to Chapter 8). Profit maximization and cost minimization yield the same result. If the price of hamburgers had been higher than $.20, however, the MVP figures in the final column of Table 14.1 would have been higher, and the firm might have hired more workers (how many would be hired if hamburgers sold for $.25?). A rise in the price of hamburgers would provide an incentive for Hamburger Heaven to produce more burgers and, in the short run, to do so by adding more workers to use its fixed number of grills.

At a wage other than $1 per hour, Hamburger Heaven would hire a different number of workers. At $1.25 per hour, for example, only three workers would be hired. With wages of $.75 hour, on the other hand, seven workers would be employed. The MVP calculation provides complete information about Hamburger Heaven's short-run hiring decisions. Of course, a change in the wages of burger-flippers might also cause the firm to reconsider how many grills it uses—a subject that we now investigate.

---

[8]Since the marginal productivity of labor is positive, hiring more labor also implies that output will increase when w declines.

Table 14.1
Hamburger Heaven's
Profit-Maximizing Hiring
Decision

Labor Input per Hour	Hamburgers Produced per Hour	Marginal Product (Hamburger)	Marginal Value Product ($.20 per Hamburger)
1	20.0	20	$4.00
2	28.3	8.3	1.66
3	34.6	6.3	1.26
4	40.0	5.4	1.08
5	44.7	4.7	0.94
6	49.0	4.3	0.86
7	52.9	3.9	0.78
8	56.6	3.7	0.74
9	60.0	3.4	0.68
10	63.2	3.2	0.64

Two-Input Case

For the case where the firm can vary two (or more) inputs the story is considerably more complex. The assumption of a diminishing marginal physical product of labor can be misleading here. If w falls, there will be a change not only in labor input but also in capital input as a new cost-minimizing combination of inputs is chosen (see our analysis in Chapter 8). When capital input changes, the entire MP_L function shifts (labor now has a different amount of capital to work with) and our earlier argument cannot be made. The remainder of this section presents a series of arguments that establish that even in this case, a fall in w will lead to an increase in the quantity of labor employed.

Substitution Effect

In some ways analyzing the two-input case is similar to our analysis of the individual's response to a change in the price of a good in Chapter 4. When w falls we can decompose the total effect on the quantity of L hired into two components: a substitution effect and an output effect.

Substitution effect
In the theory of production, the substitution of one input for another while holding output constant in response to a change in the input's price.

In the **substitution effect,** if Q is held constant at Q_1, there will be a tendency to substitute labor for capital in the productive process. This effect is illustrated in Graph a in Figure 14.7. Since the condition for minimizing the cost of producing Q_1 requires that RTS = w/v, a fall in w will necessitate a movement from input combination A to combination B. Because the isoquants have been assumed to exhibit a diminishing RTS, it is clear from the diagram that this substitution effect must cause labor input to rise in response to the fall in w.

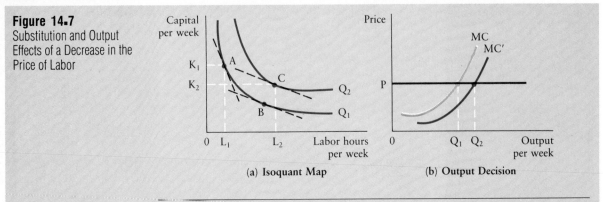

Figure 14.7
Substitution and Output
Effects of a Decrease in the
Price of Labor

(a) Isoquant Map   (b) Output Decision

When the price of labor falls, two analytically different effects come into play. One of
these, the substitution effect, would cause more labor to be purchased if output were held
constant. This is shown as a movement from point A to point B in Graph a. At point B
the cost-minimizing condition (RTS = w/v) is satisfied for the new, lower w.

The change in w/v will also shift the firm's expansion path and its marginal cost
curve. A normal situation might be for the MC curve to shift downward in response to a
decrease in w, as shown in Graph b. With this new curve (MC') a higher level of output
(Q_2) will be chosen. The hiring of labor will increase (to L_2) also from this output effect.

Output Effect

Output effect
The change in the
amount of an input that
the firm hires that re-
sults from a change in
output level. Output
changes because the
change in an input's
price affects the firm's
costs.

It is, however, not legitimate to hold Q constant. It is in considering a change
in Q—the **output effect**—that the analogy to a person's utility maximization
problem breaks down. The reason for this breakdown is that consumers have
budget constraints, whereas firms do not. Firms produce as much as the available demand allows, and their need for inputs is derived from these production
decisions. In order to investigate what happens to the quantity of output
produced, we must investigate the firm's profit-maximizing output decision.
A change in w, because it changes relative factor costs, will shift the firm's
expansion path. Consequently, all the firm's cost curves will be shifted, and
probably some output level other than Q_1 will be chosen.

Graph b in Figure 14.7 illustrates what might be considered the usual case.
It has been assumed that with this new expansion path the marginal cost curve
for the firm has shifted downward to MC' as a result of the fall in w. The
profit-maximizing level of output rises from Q_1 to Q_2.[9] The profit-maximizing
condition (P = MC) is now satisfied at a higher level of output. Returning to

[9]Price (P) has been assumed to be constant. If all firms in an industry were confronted with a
decline in w, all would change their output levels; the industry supply curve would shift, and
consequently P would change. So long as the market demand curve for the firm's output is
negatively sloped, however, the analysis in this chapter would not be seriously affected by this
observation.

Graph a, this increase in output will cause even more labor input to be demanded. The result of both the substitution and output effects will be to move the input choice to point C on the firm's isoquant for output level Q_2. Both effects work to increase L in response to a decrease in w.[10]

Summary of a Firm's Demand for Labor

We can summarize our findings about a firm's response to a fall in w by concluding a profit-maximizing firm will increase its hiring of labor for two reasons. First, the firm will substitute the now cheaper labor for other inputs that are now relatively more expensive. This is the substitution effect. Second, the wage decline will reduce the firm's marginal costs, thereby causing it to increase output and to increase the hiring of all inputs including labor. This is the output effect.

This conclusion holds for any input, and it can be reversed to show that an increase in the price of an input will cause the firm to hire less of that input. We have shown that the firm's demand curve for an input will be unambiguously downward sloping: the lower its rental price, the more of the input will be demanded.[11] The shape of the input demand curve with which we started our discussion (Figure 14.1) is therefore theoretically justified.

Responsiveness of Input Demand to Price Changes

Using the notions of substitution and output effects, we can show how responsive to price changes the demand for a factor might be. Suppose, for example, the wage rate rose. We already know that less labor will be demanded. Now we wish to investigate whether this decrease in quantity demanded will be large or small.

Ease of Substitution

First, consider the substitution effect. The decrease in the hiring of labor will depend on how easy it is for firms to substitute other factors of production

---

[10]No definite statement can be made about how the quantity of capital (or any other input) changes in response to a decline in w. The substitution and output effects work in opposite directions (as can be seen in Figure 14.7), and the precise outcome depends on the relative sizes of these effects.

[11]Actually, a proof of this assertion is not so simple as is implied here. The complicating factor arises when the input in question is "inferior," and it is no longer true that the marginal cost curve shifts downward when the price of such a factor declines. Nevertheless, it can be shown that, so long as the good that is being produced has a downward-sloping demand curve, the firm's demand for the factor will also be negatively sloped. For a mathematical proof, see E. C. Ferguson, *The Neoclassical Theory of Production and Distribution* (Cambridge: Cambridge University Press, 1969), pp. 136–153.

The Minimum Wage

The Fair Labor Standards Act of 1938 established a national minimum wage of $.25 per hour, with provisions for increasing this figure to $.40 per hour. Since that time, the minimum wage has been raised several times in response to general inflation and changing social values. The scope of minimum wage legislation has also been expanded over time, and most employees are now covered. Economists have been far from enthusiastic over this seemingly beneficial development in social legislation. They have argued that although minimum wages may benefit some workers, others suffer substantial unemployment.

A Graphic Analysis

Figure 14.8 illustrates the possible effects of a minimum wage. Graph a shows the supply and demand curves for labor. Given these curves, an equilibrium wage rate, w_1, is established in the market. At this wage, a typical firm hires l_1 and this choice of input is shown on the firm's isoquant map in Graph b. Suppose now that a minimum wage of ($w_2 > w_1$) is imposed by law. This new wage will cause the firm to reduce its demand for labor from l_1 to l_2. The reduction has two causes. First, the increase in the price of labor causes the firm to substitute capital for labor along the Q_1 isoquant. In addition to the substitution effect, there is a negative output to be reduced from Q_1 to Q_2. Consequently, the typical firm will reduce its demand for labor from l_1 to l_2. At the same time, more labor (L_3) will be supplied at w_2 than was

Figure 14.8

Effects of a Minimum Wage in a Perfectly Competitive Labor Market

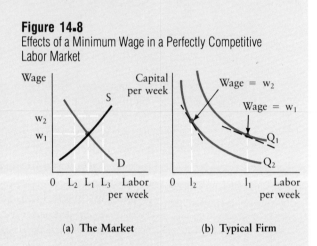

(a) **The Market**   (b) **Typical Firm**

Initially a wage rate of w_1 is set by the forces of supply and demand. At this wage rate a typical firm chooses to use l_1 units of labor. The imposition of a minimum wage (w_2) causes the firm to reduce labor usage to l_2 because it will both substitute capital (and other inputs) for labor and cut back output. All firms' demands will be reduced to L_2 at the new wage rate. Individuals wish to supply L_3, however, and there will be unemployment of $L_3 - L_2$.

supplied at the lower wage rate. The imposition of the minimum wage will result in an excess of the supply of labor over the demand for labor of $L_3 - L_2$. This excess

for labor. Some firms may find it relatively simple to substitute machines for workers, and for these firms the quantity of labor demanded will decrease substantially. Other firms may produce with a fixed proportions technology, and for them substitution will be impossible. In addition to the technical properties of the production function, the size of the substitution effect will depend on the length of time allowed for adjustment. In the short run, firms may have a stock of machinery that requires a relatively fixed complement of workers. Consequently, the short-run substitution possibilities are slight. Over the long run, however, the firm may be able to adapt its machinery to use less labor per machine; the possibilities of substitution may now be substantial. For example, a rise in the wages of coal miners will have little short-run substitution effect since existing coal-mining equipment requires a fixed complement of workers. In the long run, however, there is clear evidence that

supply is what we mean by "unemployment." At the new prevailing wage more individuals want to work than are able to find jobs. The extent of this unemployment will depend on the size of the substitution and output effects that come into play as firms are affected by the new wage.

Minimum Wages and Teenage Unemployment
There is some empirical evidence that changes in the minimum wage law have had serious effects in increasing teenage unemployment. Teenagers are the labor market participants most likely to be affected by minimum wage laws, since they usually represent the lower end of the spectrum of skills. An increase in minimum wages may cause employers to substitute capital and skilled labor for what has become more expensive, unskilled teenage labor. It may also cause large negative output effects, since the products produced by teenage employees (services, for example) usually have a fairly high price elasticity. In recent years, teenage unemployment has increased rapidly. Particularly hard hit have been teenage minority group members, for whom unemployment rates often exceed 30 percent. Although there are several factors that may account for such statistics (unstable employment opportunities, discrimination in employment, long periods of searching for jobs), many economists assign an important role to statutory changes in the minimum wage. For example, one study found that each 1 percent increase in the minimum wage

resulted in a reduction of 0.3 percent in teenagers' share of total employment.[12]

A particularly important example of this reduction is in the changing employment patterns of fast-food chains in response to rising minimum wages. These businesses are highly labor-intensive and sell a product (eating out) for which the demand is relatively price-responsive. The firms may find their sales falling off substantially in response to price rises stemming from minimum wage increases. In addition, the firms may attempt to substitute capital equipment (such as automatic hamburger turners) for teenage workers, thereby further reducing their demand for workers. In response to the 1977 minimum wage increase, for example, the McDonald's Corporation (reputedly the largest hirer of teenage workers in the United States) adopted a new program of research on labor-saving technology and made several changes in their teenage hiring practices. Since that time McDonald's has been in the forefront in supporting a proposal for a "subminimum" wage for teenagers.

To Think About
1. Does a minimum wage increase or decrease total wages received by workers affected by it? How does your answer depend on the elasticity of demand for labor?
2. How does a minimum wage affect the demand for workers who are paid wages above the minimum wage? Would these workers support legislation raising the minimum wage?

mining can be made more capital intensive by designing more complex machinery. In the long run, capital can be substituted for labor. "Applying Economics: The Minimum Wage" summarizes a particularly important example of this kind of effect.

Costs and the Output Effect

An increase in the wage rate will also raise firms' costs. In a competitive market this will cause the price of the good being produced to rise, and people will reduce their purchases of that good. This reduction in purchases is called the

[12]Finis Welch, "Minimum Wage Legislation in the United States," *Economic Inquiry,* September 1974, pp. 285–318.

output effect; because less output is being produced, less labor will be demanded. The output effect in this way reinforces the substitution effect. In order to investigate the likely size of the output effect, we must know (1) how large the increase in costs brought about by the wage rate increase is, and (2) how much quantity demanded will be reduced by a rising price. The size of the first of these components depends on how "important" labor is in total production costs, whereas the size of the second depends on how price-elastic the demand for the product is.

In industries for which labor costs are a major portion of total costs and for which demand is very elastic, output effects will be large. For example, an increase in wages for restaurant workers is likely to induce a large negative output effect in the demand for such workers, since labor costs are a significant portion of restaurant operating costs and the demand for meals eaten out is relatively price-elastic. An increase in wages will cause a big price rise, and this will cause people to reduce sharply the number of meals they eat out. On the other hand, output effects in the demand for pharmaceutical workers are probably small. Direct labor costs are a small fraction of drug production costs and the demand for drugs is price-inelastic. Wage increases will have only a small effect on costs, and any increases in price that do result will not cause demand for drugs to be reduced significantly.

This kind of *a priori* investigation of the sizes of substitution and output effects can take us only so far. In order to precisely estimate the effects of changes in factor prices on employment, real-world labor markets must be carefully examined using actual data.

Monopsony

Monopsony
A single hirer in a particular input market.

There are many situations in which the firm is not a price taker for the inputs it buys. It may frequently be necessary for the firm to offer a wage above that currently prevailing to attract more employees, or the firm may be able to get a better price on some equipment by restricting its purchases. In these situations it is most convenient to examine the polar case of **monopsony** (a single buyer) in a factor market. If there is only one buyer in this market, that firm faces the entire market supply curve. In order to increase its hiring of labor, say, by one or more units, the firm must move to a higher point on this supply curve. This will involve paying not only a higher wage to the last worker hired but also additional wages to those workers already employed. The marginal cost of the extra unit of labor therefore exceeds its wage rate, and some of the simplifications we made earlier no longer hold. Instead, for a monopsonist facing an upward-sloping supply curve for an input, the **marginal expense** will exceed the market price of the input. For labor input, for example, the marginal expense (ME_L) exceeds the market wage (w).

Marginal expense
The cost of hiring one more unit of an input. Will exceed the price of the input if the firm faces an upward-sloping supply curve for the input.

Notice the similarity between the concept of the marginal expense of an input and the marginal revenue for a monopolist. Both concepts are intended to be used when firms possess market power and their choices have an effect on prices. In such situations firms are no longer price takers. Instead, firms

Table 14.2
Labor Costs of Hiring
Bear Wardens in
Yellowstone Park

Hourly Wage	Workers Supplied per Hour	Total Labor Cost per Hour	Marginal Expense
$ 2	1	$ 2	$ 2
4	2	8	6
6	3	18	10
8	4	32	14
·10	5	50	18
12	6	72	22
14	7	98	26

will recognize that their actions affect prices and will use this information in making decisions.

A Numerical Illustration

This distinction is easiest to see with a numerical example. Suppose (as is probably the case) that the Yellowstone Park Company is the only hirer of bear wardens. Suppose also that the number of people willing to take this job (L) is a simple positive function of the hourly wage (w) given by

$$L = \tfrac{1}{2}w. \qquad [14.6]$$

This relationship between the wage and the number of people who offer their services as bear wardens is shown in the first two columns of Table 14.2. Total labor costs (w · L) are shown in the third column, and the marginal expense of hiring each warden is shown in the fourth column. The extra expense associated with adding another warden always exceeds the wage rate paid to that person. The reason is clear—not only does a newly hired warden receive the higher wage, but all previously hired wardens also get a higher wage. A monopsonist will take these extra expenses into account in its hiring decisions.

A graph can be used to help to clarify this relationship. Figure 14.9 shows the supply curve (S) for bear wardens. If, for example, Yellowstone wishes to hire three wardens, it must pay $6 per hour, and total outlays will be $18 per hour. This situation is reflected by point A on the supply curve. If the firm tries to hire a fourth warden, it must offer $8 per hour to everyone—it must move to point B on the supply curve. Total outlays are now $32 per hour, so the marginal expense of hiring the fourth worker is $14 per hour. By comparing the sizes of the total outlay rectangles, we can see why the marginal expense was higher than the wage paid to the fourth worker. That worker's hourly wage is shown by the gray rectangle—it is $8 per hour. The other three

Figure 14.9
Marginal Expense of Hiring
Bear Wardens

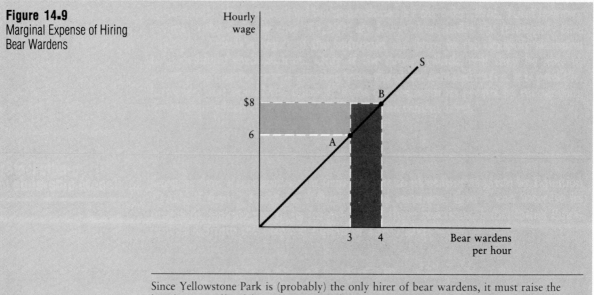

Since Yellowstone Park is (probably) the only hirer of bear wardens, it must raise the hourly wage offered from $6 to $8 if it wishes to hire a fourth warden. The marginal expense of hiring that warden is his or her wage ($8, shown in gray) plus the extra $2 per hour that must be paid to the other three wardens (shown in blue).

workers, who were previously earning $6 per hour, now earn $8. This extra outlay is shown in light blue. Total labor expenses for four wardens exceed those for three by the area of both the blue and gray rectangles. In this case, marginal expense exceeds the wage since the Yellowstone Company is the sole hirer of people in this unusual occupation.

Monopsonist's Input Choice

As for any profit-maximizing firm, a monopsonist will hire any input up to the point at which the additional revenue and additional cost of hiring one more unit are equal. For the case of labor this requires:

$$ME_L = MVP_L. \qquad [14.7]$$

In the special case of a price taker that faces an infinitely elastic labor supply ($ME_L = w$), Equations 14.5 and 14.7 are identical. However, if the firm faces a positively sloped labor supply curve, Equation 14.7 dictates a different level of input choice, as we now show.

Figure 14.10
Pricing in a Monopsonistic
Labor Market

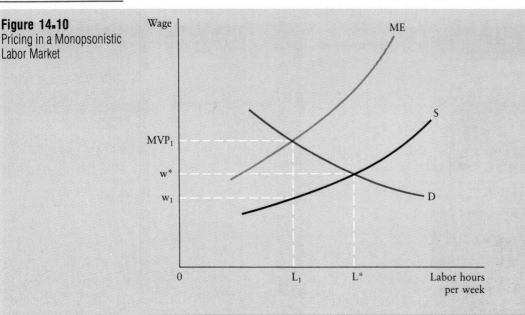

If a firm faces a positively sloped supply curve for labor (S), it will base its decisions on the marginal expense of labor curve (ME_L). Because S is positively sloped, ME_L lies above S. The curve S can be thought of as an average cost of labor curve, and the ME_L curve is marginal to S. At L_1 the equilibrium condition $ME_L = MVP_L$ holds, and this quantity will be hired at a market wage rate w_1.

A Graphic Demonstration

The monopsonist's choice of labor input is illustrated in Figure 14.10. The firm's demand curve for labor (D) is drawn negatively sloped, as we have shown it must be. The ME_L curve associated with the labor supply curve (S) is constructed in much the same way that the marginal revenue curve associated with a demand curve can be constructed. Because S is positively sloped, the ME_L curve lies everywhere above S. The profit-maximizing level of labor input for the monopsonist is given by L_1. At this level of input the condition of Equation 14.7 holds. At L_1 the wage rate in the market is given by w_1. The quantity of labor demanded falls short of that which would be hired in a perfectly competitive market (L^*). The firm has restricted input demand by virtue of its monopsonistic position in the market.

The formal similarities between this analysis and the monopoly analysis we presented in Chapter 12 should be clear. In particular, the "demand curve" for a monopsonist consists of a single point. In Figure 14.10 this point is given by L_1,w_1. The monopsonist has chosen this point as the most desirable of all those points on the supply curve S. A different point will not be chosen unless some external change (such as a shift in the demand for the firm's output or a change in technology) affects labor's marginal value product.

Monopsonistic Exploitation

In addition to restricting its input demand, the monopsonist pays an input less than its marginal value product. This result is also illustrated in Figure 14.10. At the monopsonist's preferred choice of labor input (L_1) a wage of w_1 prevails in the market. For this level of input demand, the firm is willing to pay an amount equal to MVP_1: this is the amount of extra revenue that hiring another worker would provide to the firm. At L_1 the monopsonist pays workers less than they are "worth" to the firm. In the absence of effective competition the monopsonist can persist in this behavior. Some authors refer to this gap between an input's MRP and its market price as (monopsonistic) *exploitation*. It should be clear from Figure 14.10 that the extent of this exploitation will be greater the more inelastic the supply of labor is to the monopsonist. The less responsive is labor supply to low wages, the more the monopsonist can take advantage of this situation.

Causes of Monopsony

To practice monopsonistic exploitation a firm must possess considerable power in the market for a particular input. If the market is reasonably competitive, monopsonistic exploitation cannot occur because other firms will recognize the profit potential reflected in the gap between MVPs and input costs. They will therefore bid for these inputs, driving their prices to equality with marginal value products. Under such conditions the supply of labor to any one firm will be nearly infinitely elastic (because of the alternative employment possibilities available) and the monopsonistic exploitation will be impossible. Our analysis suggests monopsonistic behavior will be observed in real-world situations in which, for some reason, effective competition for inputs is lacking. We now examine three causes of such an absence of competition: geography, specialized employment, and monopsonistic cartels.

Geography

Some firms may occupy a monopsonistic position by being the only source of employment in a small town. Because moving costs for workers are high, alternative employment opportunities for local workers are unattractive, and the firm may be able to exert a strong effect on wages paid. This possibility may, in part, explain the low wage rates that prevailed in the southern United States prior to World War II. Many small southern towns had isolated labor markets that were dominated by one or two firms. The term *company town* originated in this situation and carried a connotation of exploitation that may have been appropriate. A number of factors at work since World War II have tended to undermine these monopsonistic positions. The population has become more willing to relocate in response to wage rate differences. The entry of new firms into southern labor markets (together with improved methods of commuting to work) has further improved workers' alternative earnings possibilities. Finally, noncompetitive forces, such as increasing unionization and the expansion of the minimum wage law, have probably also had an effect on monopsonistic practices.

Specialized Employment

It may sometimes be the case that only one firm hires a particularly specialized type of input. If the alternative earnings prospects for that input are unattractive, its supply to the firm will be inelastic, presenting the firm with the opportunity for monopsonistic behavior. For example, marine engineers with many years of experience in designing nuclear submarines must work for the one or two companies that produce such vessels. Because other jobs would not make use of these workers' specialized training, alternative employment is not particularly attractive. Similarly, experienced telephone circuit designers may find they have to work for AT&T if they wish to capitalize on their skills. As a nonlabor example, the McDonald's Corporation for many years bought more than 50 percent of all frozen french fried potatoes produced in the United States; the corporation probably occupied a monopsonistic position in that market.

Monopsonistic Cartels

These examples suggest that monopsonistic hiring on specialized inputs is often associated with a monopoly position in the sale of an output (nuclear submarines, telephone service, or french fries). A particularly prevalent example of this relationship is in hiring by the federal government. Since the government occupies a monopoly position in the production of a number of goods requiring specialized inputs (space travel, armed forces, and national political offices, to name a few), it would be expected to be in a position to exercise monopsony power. In other cases a group of firms may combine to form a cartel in their hiring decisions (and, perhaps, in their output decisions too). "Applying Economics: Monopsony in the Market for Baseball Players" illustrates this relationship between a firm's monopoly position and monopsonistic hiring in a situation in which it is possible to obtain direct measures of workers' marginal value.

Discrimination in Hiring

If a monopsony can segregate the supply of a factor into two or more distinct markets, it may be able to increase profits. For example, a monopsony may be able to discriminate in hiring between men and women. Because the firm can readily identify which market a prospective employee belongs to, it will find it profitable to pay different wages in the two markets.

APPLYING ECONOMICS

Monopsony in the Market for Baseball Players

Our discussion of production cartels in Chapter 13 suggests that firms may be able to obtain monopoly profits by coordinating their output decisions. An identical argument can be made about firms' input decisions. If firms can coordinate their hiring, they can behave monopsonistically even though each firm individually has limited market powers. Usually this type of coordination is impossible because it is costly (or illegal) to enforce such agreements, and as in the monopoly case, there exist incentives to cheat (chiseling in this case involves raising wage offers). Occasionally, powerful cartels can achieve a successful monopsony. An important example is provided by major league baseball teams during the period in which the reserve clause was in effect. That clause combined with player drafts effectively bound each player to a single team and prevented interteam competition for salaries. Even though there were 18 major league clubs (or firms), their hiring was effectively cartelized—creating the potential for monopsonistic exploitation.

Numerical estimates of the degree of exploitation in major league baseball were constructed by G. W. Scully in a 1974 article.[13] Because baseball players' salaries are more or less a matter of public record, the principal problem Scully faced in measuring the effect of monopsony was to estimate the players' marginal value products. He adopted a two-step procedure. First, he examined the correlation between a team's winning percentage and its attendance figures. He concluded that winning did indeed produce additional revenues. Next he analyzed which aspects of individual player performance were most closely related to a team's overall performance. Two significant variables were identified: for hitters, the "slugging average" seemed most important, whereas for pitchers, the ratio of strikeouts to walks proved most relevant. Using statistics on these performance measures, Scully estimated marginal value products for players of differing abilities and compared these estimates to their salaries for the year 1969. A few of the estimates are presented in Table 14.3. These data show that most players' MVPs exceed their salaries by a substantial margin. Only for players with poor measures of performance do training and other costs result in low or even negative MVPs.

Table 14.3

Monopsonistic Exploitation in Major League Baseball, 1969

Hitters

Slugging Average	Hitters' Net MVP[a]	Estimated Salary
255	$ −39,100	$ 9,700
305	103,600	14,100
350	137,800	32,700
375	156,800	39,000
427	296,500	42,200
490	350,400	60,500
525	383,700	68,000

Pitchers

Ratio of Strikeouts to Walks	Pitchers' Net MVP[a]	Estimated Salary
1.50	$ −20,800	$ 9,000
2.00	132,000	16,500
2.30	169,200	36,900
2.79	349,600	47,200
3.09	405,300	66,800
3.54	479,700	86,300

[a]Estimated gross MVP less training and related costs. For poor players the net figure is negative.
Source: G. W. Scully, "Pay and Performance in Major League Baseball," *American Economic Review*, December 1974, p. 928.

---

[13]G. W. Scully, "Pay and Performance in Major League Baseball," *American Economic Review,* December 1974, pp. 915–930.

Scully concluded that in 1969 there was significant monopsonistic exploitation of better major league players. It was only a matter of time before players came to recognize the cartelizing effect of the reserve clause and took organized action against it. A players' strike in 1972 (coupled with legal action in a suit brought by St. Louis Cardinal outfielder Curt Flood) eventually led to the adoption of a free agent provision in players' contracts as a partial replacement of the reserve clause. Recent spectacular contract settlements for some star players are indicative of the bidding competition that has continued since the breakdown of the cartel.

To Think About
1. If players could be freely traded among teams, could monopolistic exploitation arise? Can you think of reasons other than wage restraint why organized baseball might resist such freedom of movement?
2. How might mergers between two rival leagues (for example, the American and National Football Leagues or the American and National Basketball Associations) affect players' salaries? Would players tend to favor or oppose such mergers? Do the mergers "substantially lessen" competition and thus constitute an antitrust violation?

Such a situation is shown in Figure 14.11. The figure assumes that men and women are equally productive and that the firm has a constant marginal value product of labor no matter how much labor is hired. This curve is shown by the horizontal MVP_L curve. The supply curves for men and women are shown in the figure as sharing the same vertical axis. Given these supply curves the firm will choose that quantity of labor in each market for which the marginal expense (ME) is equal to labor's marginal revenue product. Consequently, the firm will hire L_m from the men's market and L_w from the women's. The wage rate in the two markets will be w_m and w_w, respectively. The way we have drawn Figure 14.11, men's wages will exceed women's. This happens because women's labor supply is relatively inelastic.[14]

A similar analysis can be developed for any situation in which a monopsony can segregate the market for its inputs into two separate parts. In order to do so, it must be able to identify workers as belonging to particular markets so that its segmentation strategy will work. It must know how much of each kind of worker it is hiring. For this reason, wage discrimination among geographically distinct labor markets or among individuals with readily identifiable personal characteristics (sex, race, age) would be expected to be the types of discrimination most often encountered. "Applying Economics: Sex Discrimination" shows that some U.S. data are consistent with this model, but they raise more questions about discrimination than they answer.

---

[14]Women may, for example, have a more inelastic supply curve because they may have relatively few employment alternatives.

Figure 14.11
Discrimination in Hiring by
a Monopsonist

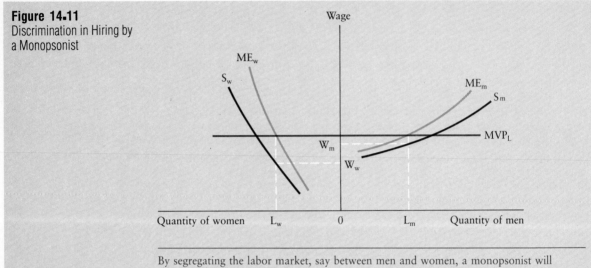

By segregating the labor market, say between men and women, a monopsonist will
minimize labor costs by choosing those quantities of labor such that the marginal revenue
product of labor is equal to the marginal expense in each market. In this diagram, the
wages of women (w_w) will be below the wages of men (w_m), even though the marginal
revenue product for both types of labor is identical.

Summary

In this chapter we examine firms' demands for the inputs they buy. The most
fundamental observation is that this demand is necessarily derived from the
demand for the output being produced. Firms don't hire workers just to have
them around. Rather, a firm's hiring decisions are one aspect of its desire to
maximize profits. In analyzing the demand for factors this connection between
factor and goods markets must be kept clearly in mind. Several specific conclusions emerge from our examination of this relationship:

- Factors of production may sometimes earn rents—payments in excess of
  their next best alternative employment—depending on the demand for
  their services.
- Firms will hire any input up to the point at which the marginal expense
  of hiring one more unit is equal to the marginal revenue yielded by selling what that input produces.
- If the firm is a price taker in both the market for its inputs and the
  market for its output, profit maximization requires that it employ that
  level of inputs for which the market price of the input (for example, the
  wage) is equal to the marginal value product of that input (for example,
  $P \cdot MP_L$).
- If the price of an input rises, the firm will hire less of it for two reasons.
  First, the higher price will cause the firm to substitute other inputs for

APPLYING ECONOMICS

Sex Discrimination

There is considerable evidence of wage discrimination along sexual lines in U.S. labor markets. For example, Table 14.4 shows median earnings in different occupations for men and women for the year 1983. Overall women's earnings averaged about 60 percent of those of men. Although some part of these male-female differences may be explained by objective characteristics (for example, age, educational differences, or the amount of job experience), a number of statistical studies have found that the gap in earnings continues to persist after controlling for these factors. Such findings are in general accord with the monopsony model of labor market discrimination. However, it is hard to believe that monopsony can be an important explanation for the wage differences that are observed. Very few (if any) firms in the United States are the only employer in the labor market from which they draw. If we are to apply the simple monopsony model, it must be assumed that all the firms in a particular labor market are able to collude perfectly in their discriminatory hiring decisions. Since economists generally believe that such collusion is very difficult to achieve (again there are incentives to cheat on any collusive agreement that is reached), they have instead turned their attention to examining how discrimination might arise in a competitive labor market. By understanding how discrimination arises in competitive markets, economists are in a position to suggest ways to combat it.

Wage Discrimination in Competitive Markets

An initial observation about discrimination in a competitive market is that it is costly to the discriminator. For example, a firm that decides not to hire female workers is raising its labor costs over what they would be if it hired workers solely on the basis of their skills. Similarly, a male worker who refuses to work with female workers is lowering the possible wage that might be received if he did not foreclose some of the employment options available. Finally, consumers who refuse to deal with female employees may be making their con-

Table 14.4
Median Earnings for Full Time, Year-Round Workers by Sex and Occupation, 1983

Occupation	Median Earnings for		Ratio Women ÷ Men
	Men	Women	
Manager and Professional	$30,086	$18,886	.63
Technical, Sales and Administration	22,497	13,522	.60
Service	14,688	9,228	.63
Precision Production	21,520	13,245	.62
Operators and Laborers	17,819	11,321	.64

Source: Statistical Abstract of the United States, 1986 (Washington, D.C.: U.S. Department of Commerce, 1986), Table 703.

sumption choices more costly. Discrimination persists, and this fact indicates that firms, workers, and consumers may be willing to pay these costs. For some reason individuals have a taste for discrimination and are willing to allocate resources to satisfy this taste. The importance of this observation is to demonstrate that discrimination is costly not only to those being discriminated against, but also to those doing the discriminating. Total income of both groups would be higher in the absence of discrimination.[15]

To Think About

1. What factors other than wage discrimination might explain the figures in Table 14.4? Should factors such as education, job skills, or work experience be controlled for in looking at male-female wage differences, or might these too reflect discrimination?
2. How would you explain the economic rationale for affirmative action programs that establish hiring guidelines for minorities and women? Under what conditions might such programs have an effect on the male-female wage differential?

---

[15]One of the first economists to study discrimination in detail was Gary S. Becker. In his book, *The Economics of Discrimination* (Chicago: University of Chicago Press, 1957), he develops a simple model that shows that discrimination harms both the majority and minority groups. This finding is in contrast to other views that discrimination in some way benefits the discriminator. Becker shows that discrimination in employment may indeed aid male (or in his case, white) workers, but it will hurt the owners of capital, and total income will decline.

the one whose price has risen. And, second, the higher price will raise the firm's costs and reduce the amount it is able to sell. This output effect also will cause fewer units of the input to be hired.

- If a firm is the sole hirer of an input (a monopsony), its hiring decisions will affect market wages. The marginal expense associated with hiring an additional unit of an input will exceed that input's price. Firms will take this into account in their hiring decisions—they will restrict hiring below what it would be under competitive conditions.
- If a firm has a monopsony in two markets, it may increase profits further by practicing input price discrimination among them.

Problems

14.1 Suppose the demand for labor is given by

$$L = -50w + 450$$

and the supply is given by

$$L = 100w$$

where L represents the number of people employed and w is the real wage rate per hour.

a. What will be the equilibrium levels for w and L in this market?
b. Suppose the government wishes to raise the equilibrium wage to $4 per hour by offering a subsidy to employers for each person hired. How much will this subsidy have to be? What will the new equilibrium level of employment be? How much total subsidy will be paid?
c. Suppose instead the government declared a minimum wage of $4 per hour. How much labor would be demanded at this price? How much unemployment would there be?
d. Graph your results.

14.2 Assume that the market for rental cars for business purposes is perfectly competitive with the demand for this capital input given by

$$K = 1,500 - 25v$$

and the supply given by

$$K = 75v - 500$$

where K represents the number of cars rented by firms and v is the rental rate per day.

a.   What will be the equilibrium levels for v and K in this market?
b.   Suppose that following an oil embargo gas prices rise dramatically so that now business firms must take account of gas prices in their car rental decisions. Their demand for rental cars is now given by

$$K = 1,700 - 25v - 300g$$

where g is the per gallon price of gasoline. What will be the equilibrium levels for v and K if g = $2? If g = $3?
c.   Graph your results.
d.   Since the oil embargo brought about decreased demand for rental cars, what might be the implication for other capital input markets as a result? For example, employees may still need transportation, so how might the demand for mass transit be affected? Since businesspeople also rent cars to attend meetings, what might happen in the market for telephone equipment as employees drive less and use the telephone more? Can you think of any other factor input markets that might be affected?

14.3   A landowner has three farms (A, B, and C) of differing fertility. The levels of output for the three farms with one, two, and three laborers employed are as given:

Number of Laborers	Level of Output		
	Farm A	Farm B	Farm C
1	10	8	5
2	17	11	7
3	21	13	8

For example, if one laborer were hired for each farm, the total output would be 10 + 8 + 5 = 23. This would represent a poor allocation of labor, since if the farm C laborer were assigned to farm A the total output would be 17 + 8 = 25.

a.   If market conditions caused the landowner to hire five laborers, what would be the most productive allocation of that labor? How much would be produced? What is the marginal product of the last worker?
b.   If we assume that farm output is sold in a perfectly competitive market with one unit of output priced at $1, and we assume that labor market equilibrium occurs when five workers are hired, what wage is paid? How much profit does the landowner receive?

14.4 Assume that the quantity of envelopes licked per hour by Sticky Gums, Inc. is $Q = 10,000\sqrt{L}$ where L is the number of laborers hired per hour by the firm. Assume further that the envelope-licking business is perfectly competitive with a market price of $.01 per envelope. The marginal product of a worker is given by

$$MP_L = 5,000/\sqrt{L}.$$

a. How much labor would be hired at a competitive wage of $10? $5? $2? Use your results to sketch a demand curve for labor.
b. Assume that Sticky Gums hires its labor at an hourly wage of $10. What quantity of envelopes will be licked when the price of a licked envelope is $.10? $.05? $.02? Use your results to sketch a supply curve for licked envelopes.

*14.5 Suppose there are a fixed number of 1,000 identical firms in the perfectly competitive concrete pipe industry. Each firm produces the same fraction of total market output and each firm's production function for pipe is given by

$$q = \sqrt{KL}$$

and for this production function

$$RTS \text{ (L for K)} = K/L.$$

Suppose also that the market demand for concrete pipe is given by

$$Q = 400,000 - 100,000P$$

where Q is total concrete pipe.

a. If $w = v = \$1$, in what ratio will the typical firm use K and L? What will be the long-run average and marginal cost of pipe?
b. In the long-run equilibrium what will be the market equilibrium price and quantity for concrete pipe? How much will each firm produce? How much labor will be hired by each firm and in the market as a whole?
c. Suppose the market wage, w, rose to $2 while v remained constant at $1. How will this change the capital-labor ratio for the typical firm, and how will it affect its marginal costs?

---

*Denotes a problem that is rather difficult.

    d.   Under the conditions of part c, what will the long-run market equilibrium be? How much labor will now be hired by the concrete pipe industry?

    e.   How much of the change in total labor demand from part b to part d represents the substitution effect resulting from the change in wage and how much represents the output effect?

14.6 Suppose that the supply curve for labor to a firm is given by

$$L = 100w$$

and the marginal expense of labor curve is given by

$$ME_L = L/50$$

where w is the market wage. Suppose also that the firm's demand for labor (marginal revenue product) curve is given by

$$L = 1,000 - 100MRP_L.$$

    a.   If the firm acts as a monopsonist, how many workers will it hire in order to maximize profits? What wage will it pay? How will this wage compare to the MRP_L at this employment level?

    b.   Assume now that the firm must hire its workers in a perfectly competitive labor market, but it still acts as a monopoly when selling its output. How many workers will the firm hire now? What wage will it pay?

    c.   Graph your results.

14.7 Carl the clothier owns a large garment factory on an isolated island. Carl's factory is the only source of employment for most of the islanders and thus Carl acts as a monopsonist. The supply curve for garment workers is given by

$$L = 80w$$

and the marginal expense of labor curve is given by

$$ME_L = L/40$$

where L is the number of workers hired and w is their hourly wage. Assume also that Carl's labor demand (marginal value product) curve is given by

$$L = 400 - 40MVP_L.$$

a. How many workers will Carl hire in order to maximize his profits and what wage will he pay?

b. Assume now that the government implements a minimum wage law covering all garment workers. How many workers will Carl now hire and how much unemployment will there be if the minimum wage is set at $3 per hour? $3.33 per hour? $4.00 per hour?

c. Graph your results.

d. How does the imposition of a minimum wage under monopsony differ in results as compared with a minimum wage imposed under perfect competition (assuming the minimum wage is above the market determined wage)?

14.8 Under what conditions would you expect the imposition of a minimum wage to:

a. Have no effect on wages or on the number of workers employed?

b. Increase wages and leave the number of workers unaffected?

c. Increase wages and decrease the number of workers?

d. Increase both wages and the number of workers?

*14.9 The Ajax Coal Company is the only employer in its area. It can hire any number of female workers or male workers it wishes. The supply curve for women is given by

$$L_f = 100w_f$$

$$ME_f = L_f/50$$

and for men by

$$L_m = 9W_m^2$$

$$ME_m = \tfrac{1}{2}\sqrt{L_m}$$

where w_f and w_m are, respectively, the hourly wage rate paid to female and male workers. Assume that Ajax sells its coal in a perfectly competitive market at $5 per ton and that each worker hired (both men and women) can mine two tons per hour. If the firm wishes to maximize profits, how many female and male workers should be hired and what will the wage rates for these two groups be? How much will Ajax earn in profits per hour on its mining machinery? How will that result compare to one in which Ajax was constrained (say by market forces) to pay all workers the same wage based on the value of their marginal products?

14.10 Assume employers have no "taste for discrimination" against blacks but that the white employees do. A white employee considers the "psychic wage" to be a combination of the money wage and the percentage of blacks in the firm. That is, a white worker demands higher wages in order to work with blacks. Both blacks and whites offer their services in a perfectly competitive market and are equally productive. The wages for whites and blacks are given by

$$v = \text{MVP}(1 + \text{percent of blacks in firm})$$

and

$$w = \text{MVP}$$

respectively. How might you expect a cost-minimizing firm to adjust the racial mix of its employees?

CHAPTER 15

Pricing of Labor

In this chapter we examine some aspects of factor pricing that are particularly related to the labor market. Because we have discussed the demand for labor (or any other factor of production) in some detail, in this chapter we are concerned primarily with the supply of labor. The theory of labor supply provides another useful application of the model of individual choice developed in Part 2. With this model it is possible to explain many of the important trends in the United States labor market. These trends include the decline in the average workweek since the 1890s and the marked recent increases of married women in the labor force. A second reason for examining the economics of labor supply is to provide some insight into the job choices people make. The concept of compensating wage differentials we develop for this purpose also has uses that extend far beyond traditional questions of occupational choice. This chapter also examines labor unions. Because unions are important, powerful participants in the labor markets of most western countries, any treatment of labor supply would be incomplete without such an examination. In addition, the tools used to study union behavior and bargaining can be applied to other situations in which both buyers and sellers exercise some market power. Chapter 15 not only applies some of the tools developed previously to new issues, but also presents additional concepts that play an important role in economists' descriptions of the market mechanism.

Allocation of Time

Part 2 analyzes how an individual will choose to allocate a fixed amount of income among a variety of available goods. People must make similar choices in deciding how they will spend their time. The number of hours in a day (or in a year) is absolutely fixed, and time must be used as it passes by. It is not possible, in a literal sense, to "save" some time today so that it can be used tomorrow. Given this fixed amount of time, any person must decide how many hours to work; how many hours to spend consuming a wide variety of goods, ranging from cars and television sets to operas; how many hours to devote to self-maintenance; and how many hours to sleep. By studying the division of time people choose to make among these activities, economists are able to understand the decision to work. By viewing work as only one of a number of choices open to people in the way they spend their time, it is possible to understand why work decisions may be adjusted in response to changing opportunities.

A Simple Model of Time Use

We first assume that there are only two uses to which any person may devote his or her time, either engaging in market work at a wage rate of w per hour or not working. We refer to nonwork time as **leisure,** but this word does not mean idleness in our use of it. Time that is not spent in market work can be used to work in the home, for self-improvement, or for consumption (it takes time to use a television set or a bowling ball).[1] All of these activities contribute to a person's well-being, and time will be allocated to them in what might be assumed to be a utility-maximizing way.

Leisure
Time spent in any activity other than market work.

More specifically, we assume that utility depends on consumption of market goods (C) and on the amount of leisure time (H) available. Figure 15.1 presents an indifference curve map for this utility function. The diagram has the familiar shape introduced in Chapter 3, and it shows those combinations of C and H that yield an individual various levels of utility.

To discuss utility maximization we must first analyze the budget constraint that faces this person. If the period we are studying is one day, the individual will work $24 - H$ hours. That is, he or she will work all of the hours not devoted to leisure. For this work she or he will earn w per hour and will use this to buy consumption goods.

The Opportunity Cost of Leisure

Each extra hour of leisure this person takes reduces his or her income (and consumption) by w dollars. The hourly wage therefore reflects the opportunity cost of leisure. In a very real sense, people have to pay this cost for each hour

w = opportunity cost of leisure

---

[1]For a more theoretical treatment of the allocation of time, see G. S. Becker, "A Theory of the Allocation of Time," *The Economic Journal*, September 1965, pp. 493–517. The author treats the household as both a provider of labor services and a producer of utility, which is made by combining time with goods. The household is seen to be bound by a time constraint and must allocate available time among a number of activities. The implications drawn by Becker are far-reaching and affect most of the traditional theory of individual behavior.

Figure 15.1
Utility-Maximizing Choice
of Hours of Leisure and
Work

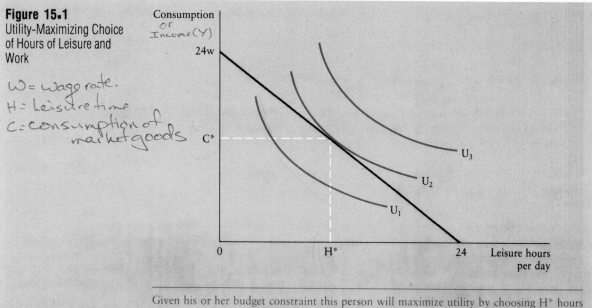

W = wage rate.
H = Leisure time
C = consumption of
       market goods

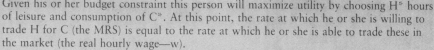

Given his or her budget constraint this person will maximize utility by choosing H* hours
of leisure and consumption of C*. At this point, the rate at which he or she is willing to
trade H for C (the MRS) is equal to the rate at which he or she is able to trade these in
the market (the real hourly wage—w).

they do not work. The wage rate used to make these calculations should be
a real wage in that it should reflect the prevailing price level for consumer
goods. A nominal wage of $1 per hour provides the same purchasing power
when the typical item costs $.25 as does a wage of $100 per hour when that
item sells for $25. In either case, the person must work 15 minutes to buy the
item. Alternately, in both cases, the opportunity cost of taking one more hour
of leisure is to do without four consumption items. "Applying Economics:
The Opportunity Cost of Time" looks at these cases of competing uses of time
and illustrates how these ideas can explain the choices people make.

Utility Maximization

To show the individual's utility-maximizing choices of consumption and leisure, we must first graph the relevant budget constraint. This is done in Figure
15.1. If this person doesn't work at all, he or she can enjoy 24 hours of leisure.
This is shown as the horizontal intercept of the budget constraint. If, on the
other hand, this person works 24 hours per day, he or she will be able to buy
24 · w in consumption goods. This establishes the vertical intercept in the
figure. The slope of the budget constraint is −w. This reflects our prior discussion of opportunity costs—each added hour of leisure must be "purchased"
by doing without w worth of consumption items.

APPLYING ECONOMICS

The Opportunity Cost of Time

Although the discussion in Chapter 15 refers only to choices between labor and leisure time, the concepts are quite general. Choices that people must make among competing uses of time can usually be analyzed within a utility-maximizing framework, and it is often possible to gain considerable insights by recognizing the opportunity costs involved. In this example we discuss three such applications: transportation choices, the economics of child bearing, and job search activities.[2] Each of these applications builds directly on the observation that the opportunity cost of time spent not working is given by the market wage rate.

Transportation Choices

In choosing among alternative ways of getting to work, people will take both time and dollar costs into account. Transportation planners are particularly interested in how people respond to differences in such costs so they can predict the effect on demand of improvements in highways or in public transit systems. Most studies have found that commuters are quite sensitive to time costs, especially those associated with walking to a bus or train station or with waiting for the bus or train to come.[3] By examining people's willingness to pay to avoid

such waits, these studies generally conclude that people value travel time at about one-half of their market wage. For example, studies conducted in connection with the Bay Area Rapid Transit System (BART) in San Francisco concluded that fares involved in using the system were less than one-fourth of the total costs people faced. Far more important were the time costs involved in getting to suburban BART stations, waiting for trains, and walking from the downtown BART stations to the final destination. Given the size of these costs it is not surprising that most commuters in the Bay Area continue to use private cars for their trips despite the availability of one of the most modern transit systems in the world.

The Economics of Childbearing

People's decisions to have children are affected by a number of social, religious, and economic factors. Economists have tended to focus primarily on the costs associated with having children and how those costs vary among individuals. One of the most important costs is the forgone wages of parents who choose to care for their children rather than to pursue market employment. Indeed, by some estimates, this cost is far in excess of all other costs of childbearing combined. That type

Given this budget constraint, this person will maximize utility by choosing to take H* hours of leisure and to work the remaining time. With the income earned from this work, he or she will be able to buy C* units of consumption goods. At the utility-maximizing point, the slope of the budget ($-w$) is equal to the slope of indifference curve U_2. In other words, the marginal rate of substitution of leisure hours for consumption will be equal to the real wage rate he or she can earn. That is, this person will choose a bundle of leisure and consumption such that the rate at which he or she is willing to trade H for C is equal to the rate at which he or she is able to trade them in the market by working.

If this were not true, utility would not be as large as possible. For example,

---

[2] An additional important application of the time allocation model to examining individuals' investments in human capital is discussed in the next chapter.

[3] See, for example, T. A. Domencich and Daniel McFadden, *Urban Travel Demand* (Amsterdam: North Holland Press, 1975).

of calculation has led some authors to speculate that increasing real wages for women in the United States since World War II are the principal reason for the decline in the birth rate during that period. Since raising children has become relatively more expensive, people have chosen to "consume" fewer of them. Similarly, the lower birth rates in North America and Western Europe as compared to the less developed world might be attributed to wage rate differences (and hence cost of children differences) between these regions.[4]

Job Search Theory

In seeking new jobs, people are often faced with considerable uncertainty about available openings. Consequently, they must invest some time (and possibly other resources, such as telephone calls or advertising) in finding a suitable job match. To the extent that people must reduce work time to accommodate their job search plans, the hourly cost of search can be approximated by the market wage. The higher an individual's market wage, the more likely he or she would be to adopt search techniques that economize on time (such as using an employment agency). If, on the other hand, search time

is subsidized (say, by unemployment insurance benefits), search time may be prolonged in the hope of finding a better job. For this reason, some economists believe that unemployment insurance benefits may contribute to unemployment itself. By one estimate, a 10 percent increase in weekly unemployment benefits is associated with about one-half week of additional unemployment.[5]

To Think About

1. Why do empirical studies of commuting patterns find that people value their time at about one-half the market wage? Doesn't our theory suggest that the value should be the full wage rate? Can you think of reasons why the MRS of commuting time for work time might differ from the MRS of leisure for work time?

2. The evidence about people's job search activities is that receipt of unemployment insurance benefits causes them to be more choosy about the jobs they take. Isn't that a good thing? Isn't it important that people find the best job for which they are qualified rather than being forced to take the first opportunity because of economic necessity? Is there an "optimal" degree of selectivity?

suppose a person's MRS were equal to 2, indicating a willingness to give up two units of consumption to get an additional hour of leisure. Suppose also that the real wage is $4. By working one more hour he or she is able to earn enough to buy four units (that is, $4 worth) of consumption. This is clearly an inefficient situation. By working one hour more, this person can buy four extra units of consumption. But he or she required only two units of consumption to be as well off as before. By working the extra hour, this person earns two ($= 4 - 2$) units of consumption more than required. Consequently he or she could not have been maximizing utility in the first place. A similar proof can be constructed for any case in which the MRS differs from the

[4]For a seminal contribution to the economics of fertility, see G. S. Becker, "An Economic Analysis of Fertility," in *Demographic and Economic Change in Developed Countries* (Princeton, N.J.: Princeton University Press, 1960).

[5]For a summary of some studies of this effect see Daniel Hamermesch, *Jobless Pay and the Economy* (Baltimore: Johns Hopkins University Press, 1976).

market wage. That proves that the two trade-off rates must be equal for a true utility maximum.

Flexibility of Work

Before we examine how these choices might be affected by a change in the real wage rate, it is important to ask whether the theory developed here has any relevance to the real-world decisions people must make. While we all are relatively free to determine what we will do in our spare time, it might be argued that we do not have the freedom of choice in selecting our own hours of work, which is implied by the time allocation model. Most jobs require that you work about 40 hours a week, and this figure is not very flexible in response to people's preferences. Nevertheless, the freedom of choice in hours of work that we have been assuming may be justified in several ways. First, the model might apply to a very long period, perhaps a lifetime. Over such a period you have considerable flexibility in the number of hours to be worked since you may choose to work 40 hours during some weeks (or years) and zero hours during others. By moving in and out of the labor market at different stages in their lifetimes, people can adjust hours of work rather precisely.

A second and similar justification for our model is to regard it as applying to the average person. At any one point of time, some individuals will work 40 hours and others will not work. Consequently, average hours of work will depend on how many people fall into each category. If nearly everyone works, the average person will work about 40 hours, whereas if 50 percent of all people work 40 hours and 50 percent do not work, the average person will be working 20 hours. A final way to justify the assumption of time flexibility is to note that people do have considerable freedom in choosing the jobs they will take. By choosing among the comforts and discomforts of particular jobs people can be thought of as making a marginal choice, even though actual hours of work are fixed by the employer. For example, someone taking a low-paying job as a surfing instructor can be regarded as choosing an occupation with a significant leisure component, and he or she is thereby adjusting the hours of actual work. We examine some additional questions about occupational choice in the section of this chapter on compensating wage differentials.

Income and Substitution Effects of a Change in the Real Wage Rate

A change in the real wage rate can be analyzed the same way we studied a price change in Chapter 4. When w rises, the price of leisure becomes higher—people must give up more in lost wages for each hour of leisure consumed. The **substitution effect** of an increase in w on the hours of leisure will therefore be to reduce them. As leisure becomes more expensive there is reason to consume less of it. However, the **income effect** of a rise in the wage will increase leisure. Since leisure is a normal good, the higher income resulting from a higher w will increase the demand for it. Hence income and substitution effects work in the opposite direction. It is impossible to predict whether an

Substitution effect of a change in w
Movement along an indifference curve in response to a change in the real wage. A rise in w causes an individual to work more.

Income effect of a change in w
Movement to a higher indifference curve in response to a rise in the real wage rate. If leisure is a normal good, a rise in w causes an individual to work less.

increase in w will increase or decrease the demand for leisure time. Since leisure and work are mutually exclusive ways to use time, it is also true that it is impossible to predict what will happen to the number of hours worked. When the wage rises, the substitution effect tends to increase hours worked. The income effect, because it increases the demand for leisure time, tends to decrease the number of hours worked. Which of these two effects is the stronger is an important empirical question whose answer depends on people's preferences for consumption and leisure.

A Graphic Analysis

Figure 15.2 illustrates two possible reactions to an increase in w. In both graphs the initial wage rate is w_0 and the optimal choices of consumption and leisure are given by C_0 and H_0. When the wage rate increases to w_1 the utility-maximizing combination moves to C_1, H_1. This movement can be divided into two effects. The substitution effect is represented by the movement along the indifference curve U_0 from C_0, H_0 to S. This effect works to reduce the number of hours of leisure in both parts of Figure 15.2. People substitute consumption for leisure since the relative price of leisure has increased.

The movement from S to C_1, H_1 represents the income effect of a higher real wage. Since it is assumed that leisure time is a normal good, increases in income will cause more leisure to be demanded. Consequently, the income and substitution effects induced by the increase in w work in opposite directions. In Graph a in Figure 15.2 the demand for leisure is reduced by the rise in w; that is, the substitution effect outweighs the income effect. On the other hand, in Graph b the income effect is stronger, and the demand for leisure increases in response to an increase in w. This person actually chooses to work fewer hours when w increases. In our analysis of demand we would have considered this result unusual—when the price of leisure rises this person demands more of it. For the case of consumption goods, income and substitution effects usually work in the same direction and both cause quantity to decline when price increases. In the case of leisure, however, income and substitution effects work in opposite directions. An increase in w makes a person better off because he or she is a *supplier* of labor. In the case of a consumption good, an individual is made worse off by a rise in price because he or she is a *consumer* of that good. Consequently, it is not possible to predict how a person will respond to a wage increase—he or she may work greater or fewer hours depending on his or her preferences.

Individual Supply Curve for Labor

Using this model of time use, we can now discuss labor supply in detail. In Figure 15.3 we have drawn an individual's supply of labor curve by calculating the number of hours he or she is willing to work at every possible real wage

Figure 15.2
Income and Substitution
Effects of a Change in the
Real Wage Rate

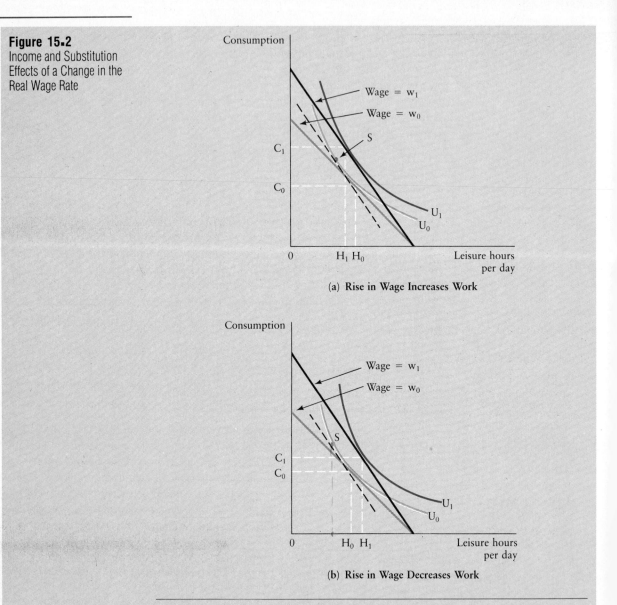

(a) **Rise in Wage Increases Work**

(b) **Rise in Wage Decreases Work**

Since the individual is a supplier of labor, the income and substitution effects of an
increase in the real wage rate work in opposite directions in their effect on the hours of
leisure demanded (or on hours of work). In Graph a the substitution effect (movement to
point S) outweighs the income effect, and a higher wage causes hours of leisure to decline
to H_1. Hours of work, therefore, increase. In Graph b the income effect is stronger than
the substitution effect, and H increases to H_1. Hours of work in this case fall.

Figure 15.3
Two Shapes for an Individual's Supply Curve for Labor

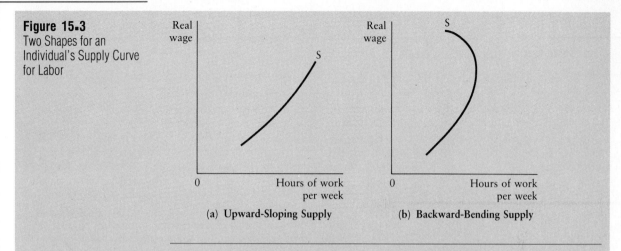

(a) **Upward-Sloping Supply**   (b) **Backward-Bending Supply**

In Graph a a higher real wage induces the individual to supply more labor. The substitution effect of the higher wage outweighs the income effect. In Graph b, on the other hand, the supply curve for labor is backward bending. For relatively high wage rates, the income effect of a higher wage outweighs the substitution effect and causes the individual to demand more leisure.

Backward bending labor supply curve
Labor supply curve in which higher real wages cause less labor to be supplied because the income effect outweighs the substitution effect.

rate. In Graph a the individual's supply curve is drawn with an upward slope: at higher real wage rates this person chooses to work longer hours. The substitution effect of a higher wage outweighs its income effect. This need not always be the case, however, as Graph b shows. There the supply curve is **backward bending**—once real wages exceed a certain level, even higher wage rates induce this person to work fewer hours. Such a curve is entirely consistent with the theory of labor supply we have developed. At relatively high wage rates, an increase in the wage may cause people to choose to work fewer hours, since the income effect may be stronger than the substitution effect. In this situation a person uses his or her higher real wage rate to "buy" more leisure. High-priced lawyers taking Wednesday afternoons off to play golf is a rational response to their situations—though it does result in the loss of some legal fees.

Do people's labor supply curves more nearly resemble that shown in Graph a or Graph b in Figure 15.3? Although there is substantial evidence that short-run labor supply curves have a positive slope (consider, for example, the positive effect on hours of work that offering higher overtime wages has), it appears that over the long run labor supply curves at times may have been backward bending. In 1890 the average workweek in the United States in the manufacturing industry was about 60 hours. Real wages in 1890 were about $2.80 per hour (in terms of 1985 prices). By 1929 the workweek in manufacturing had dropped to 40 hours, in spite of the fact that real wages had risen to about $4.90 per hour. American workers chose to take a large part of their increasing incomes in the form of leisure, and this is consistent with the notion of a backward-bending supply curve. Since 1929, real wages in

APPLYING ECONOMICS

The Volunteer Army and the Draft

The question of the elasticity of the supply of labor played an important role in the mid-1960s debate over the costs of establishing an all-volunteer army in the United States. If the supply of labor to the military were elastic, volunteers could be attracted with relatively small increases in existing pay schedules. An inelastic supply, on the other hand, would require sharp increases in defense costs as a result of the elimination of military conscription.

To study this issue, W. Y. Oi in 1967 calculated a supply curve for military personnel.[6] His basic results are presented in Table 15.1. There is clear evidence that increases in military pay encouraged enlistments. For example, Oi showed that an increase in the first-term pay of enlistees from the then-present level of $2,500 to a level more nearly approximating civilian wages (about $3,600 for unskilled 18-year-olds in 1965) would have increased enlistments by 40 percent. Notice, however, that the supply curve tended to become more inelastic as potential wages were raised still further. Raising wages from $4,700 to $5,900 would attract only 13 percent more enlistments. This may indicate that people's willingness to enlist voluntarily in the military varies widely across the population and those with preferences against serving can be attracted only at very high wages.

Following cessation of hostilities in Viet Nam in the early 1970s, the U.S. military moved rapidly toward the establishment of an all-volunteer force. Experiences since

Table 15.1
Supply Curve of Voluntary Enlistments in the Armed Forces in 1965

Annual First-Term Pay	Enlistments
$2,500	260,000
3,600	365,000
4,700	415,000
5,900	470,000

Source: W. Y. Oi, "The Economic Cost of the Draft," American Economic Review, May 1967, pp. 39–62.

manufacturing have continued to rise (to about $9 per hour in 1985), but the workweek has not fallen much below 40 hours per week. It appears that in recent years the substitution effect of higher wages has almost exactly balanced the income effect—at least for manufacturing workers. Of course, these numbers only represent average wages. Across occupations and industries relative wages changed over time and this had the effect of causing people to change the kinds of jobs they took. As "Applying Economics: The Volunteer Army and the Draft" shows, the supply curve of labor to any one occupation is undoubtedly upward-sloping and possibly quite elastic.

---

[6]W. Y. Oi, "The Economic Cost of the Draft," American Economic Review, May 1967, pp. 39–62. Oi's calculations have been simplified in this example, and they do not correspond exactly to those in the original article. The cost figures do not include forgone rents that would be earned by "true" volunteers in moving to a volunteer army (because they would be paid more under the new pay scales than was necessary to attract them into the army).

that time have been quite consistent with what had been predicted by Oi and others; that is, enlistments proved to be rather responsive to military pay. One recent study of the years 1967 to 1979, for example, found that the supply elasticities for enlistments in the army and navy exceed one and are especially high for later years in which the threat of a draft had largely disappeared.[7] Interestingly, these authors also found that supply elasticities to the marines and air force were much lower than for the other armed services. For the case of the marine corps, they attributed this finding to the special nature of that branch of the armed forces: it appears that a segment of the population wants to join almost regardless of wages. The air force is also a special case because of the specialized training it provides. The allure of high-wage civilian jobs following service in the air force appears to outweigh the effects of current wages on enlistments.

Of course, military planners also have been forced to recognize that the supply elasticity of enlistments is a two-way street. If military wages lag behind compa-rable civilian wages, enlistments (especially in the army and navy) may fall precipitously. Because military pay costs have already come to represent almost 24 percent of the total U.S. defense budget, there is considerable resistance to raising wages faster. But, the alternative of returning to a draft, especially in peacetime, seems even less palatable.

To Think About

1. The "costs" of hiring soldiers are usually taken to be only the wages they are paid. With a military draft, is that a correct way to account costs? How would you measure the costs of military service to a draftee? Should these be added to the actual costs the military incurs?

2. Some people say that a draft is the only fair·way to raise an army since only with a draft would the burden of military service be "equally shared." Do you agree? Ideally, how would the costs of military service be shared under a draft relative to the costs under a volunteer force? How did the draft of the 1960s actually work in practice?

Market Supply Curve for Labor

We can construct a market supply of labor curve from individual supply curves by "adding" them up. At each possible wage rate, we add together the quantity of labor offered by each person in order to arrive at a market total. One particularly interesting aspect of this procedure is that as the wage rate rises, more people may be induced to enter the labor force. That is, rising wages may induce some people who were not previously employed to take jobs. Figure 15.4 illustrates this possibility for a simple case of two individuals. For a real wage below w_1, neither person chooses to work. Consequently, the market supply curve of labor (Graph c) shows that no labor is supplied at real wages below w_1. A wage in excess of w_1 causes person 1 to enter the labor

---

[7]See Colin Ash, Bernard Udis, and R. F. McNowan, "Enlistments in the All-Volunteer Force: A Military Personnel Supply Model and Its Forecasts," *American Economic Review*, March 1983, pp. 145–155.

Figure 15.4
Construction of the Market
Supply Curve for Labor

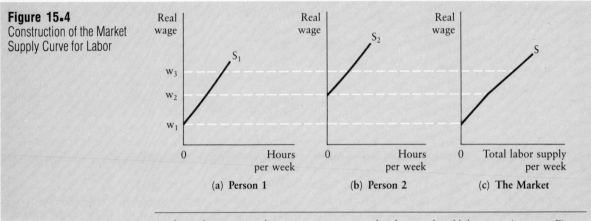

(a) Person 1 (b) Person 2 (c) The Market

As the real wage rises there are two reasons why the supply of labor may increase. First, higher real wages may cause each person to work more hours. Second, higher wages may induce more people (for example, person 2) to enter the labor market.

market. However, so long as wages fall short of w_2, person 2 will not work. Only at a wage rate above w_2 will both people choose to take a job. As Graph c in Figure 15.4 shows, the possibility of the entry of these new workers makes the market supply of labor somewhat more responsive to wage rate increases than would be the case if we assumed that the number of workers were fixed. Changing wage rates may not only induce current workers to alter their hours of work, but perhaps more importantly, they may change the composition of the work force. As "Applying Economics: Changing Labor Force Participation for Married Women and Older Males" shows, such effects have been especially pronounced for older men and married women in the United States over the past 25 years.

Occupational Choice and Compensating Wage Differentials

So far this chapter has primarily treated the labor market as a single market. All labor was assumed to be of the same quality and all jobs were assumed to be equally attractive so we could speak of *the wage* as being set by supply and demand in one market. In reality, of course, wages differ greatly among individuals and among jobs.

There are three reasons for these differentials. First, workers have different levels of skills. These differences in skills may cause some workers to be more productive than others; in a competitive market for labor, those with greater skills will earn higher wages. Second, some workers may receive wages that are essentially monopoly rents. If workers can successfully limit access to certain jobs they may succeed in improving their own wages. Finally, wage rates may differ among jobs because some jobs are more pleasant than others. More enjoyable jobs will attract a large supply of applicants, and this may cause the wage rates to be lower than in less desirable ones.

Changing Labor Force Participation for Married Women and Older Males

Probably the two most significant trends in labor market behavior in the United States during the past three decades has been (1) the increasing tendency for married women to hold paying jobs; and (2) the decline in work by older men. Both of these trends are illustrated in Table 15.2. For women in the prime age category 25–34, the increase in labor force participation has been spectacular. The fraction of married women aged 25–34 who are in the work force more than doubled between 1960 and 1984. Many reasons have been proposed to explain this major social phenomenon.

Economists have tended to focus on expanding job opportunities and real wages for women as a principal explanation. Because married women have good alternative uses for their time (work in the home rather than work in the market) substitution effects from higher real wages would be expected to be large, so labor supply will increase in response to higher wages. Sociologists, on the other hand, tend to attribute the increasing work by married women to political and cultural factors. That is, they attribute the change to a shift in the supply curve rather than a move along it in response to higher wages. In this view, the fact that it has become "more acceptable" for married women to work outside of the home coupled with both a diminished desire to have children and an increasing enforcement of antidiscrimination laws is primarily responsible for the trend. Whatever the cause,

these labor force statistics show greater responsiveness in labor supply behavior of a large segment of the population than was believed likely in earlier times.

Interestingly, the labor force trend for older married men has been precisely opposite to that for younger married women. As Table 15.2 shows, between 1960 and 1984 the labor force participation rate for married men over 65 fell to less than half its initial level. The pattern is all the more puzzling given the improvement in the health of older men that had occurred over this period. Such improvements should have resulted in more rather than less work activity by this group. Similarly, anti–age-discrimination legislation should also have resulted in a trend opposite to that observed.

Although it is possible that the figures simply reflect a backward bending supply of labor in response to higher wages, most economists have instead focused on issues of retirement as being the primary cause. Most importantly, the rapid growth in Social Security coverage of the elderly coupled with rising real benefit amounts may have encouraged increasingly large numbers of workers to retire in recent years. Other provisions of the program (such as reduction in benefits that results when the elderly do take jobs) have had a similar effect of discouraging work. Policymakers have been especially concerned about these trends (most importantly because they threaten the financial integrity of Social Security) and have taken some steps to try to reverse them.[8]

Table 15.2
Labor Force Participation Rates, 1960–1984

Year	Married Females Age 25–34	Married Males Age 65 and Over
1960	27.7%	37.1%
1965	32.1	31.1
1970	39.3	30.2
1975	48.3	23.7
1980	59.3	20.4
1984	64.0	17.3

Source: Statistical Abstract of the United States, 1985, Table 669.

To Think About
1. How does income taxation affect the labor supply decisions of married women? Can you predict the effect of taxes on their wages? How about the effect of taxes on the wages of their husbands? Would special tax treatment of the earnings of married couples increase or decrease labor supply by married women?
2. Would the availability of Social Security benefits at retirement cause people to work more or less during their prime working years? Might your answer depend on whether Social Security encourages people to retire earlier than they would in the absence of the program?

---

[8]For a more complete discussion of these issues in the theory of labor supply see R. G. Ehrenberg and R. G. Smith, *Modern Labor Economics*, 2d ed. (Glenview, Ill: Scott, Foresman, 1985), Chapters 6 and 7.

In this section we restrict our attention to this third reason for wage differentials. Even though we implicitly assume that all workers are equally skilled and that there are no monopoly elements in the wage-setting process, wage differentials can (and do) arise. (In the next chapter we briefly discuss differential skill levels in the context of "human capital" theory. We discuss the concept of monopoly rent in Chapter 14, and we return to this subject when we study unions later in this chapter.)

The notion that differing characteristics of jobs may lead to differential wages has long been noted by economists. In *The Wealth of Nations,* for example, Adam Smith observed that

> . . .the whole of the advantages and disadvantages of the different employments of labour . . . must, in the same neighbourhood, be either equal or continually tending to equality. If in the same neighbourhood there is any employment either more or less advantageous than the rest, so many people would crowd into it in the one case, and so many would desert it in the other, that its advantages would soon return to the level of other employments. . . .
>
> [But] pecuniary wages . . . are everywhere in Europe extremely different according to the different employments of labour . . . this difference arises partly from certain circumstances in the employments themselves, which, either really, or at least in the imaginations of men, make up for a small pecuniary gain in some and counter-balance a great one in others. . . .[9]

Smith then stresses the difference between the "whole advantages and disadvantages" of a particular job and the wages paid for the job. Even with perfect freedom of access to jobs and no skill differentials, wage rate differences can persist because of differences in the attractiveness of certain jobs. The market operates to equate the total attractiveness of jobs, not just the pecuniary rewards of these jobs. To capture such effects economists define **compensating wage differentials** as differences in wages that arise because of differing characteristics of jobs. The wage rate differences "compensate" for the differing job characteristics.

Compensating wage differentials
Differences in wages caused by differing job characteristics.

A Graphic Demonstration

Figure 15.5 illustrates a simple example of the way in which compensating differentials might arise. It assumes that there are two jobs: one "pleasant," the other "unpleasant." The demand curves of firms for workers to fill those jobs are assumed to be the same for both jobs. There are no differences in the skills of workers that might lead to differing marginal value products. The demand curve for both jobs is represented by the curve D.

Because the jobs differ in their attractiveness, the supply of labor to them

---

[9]Adam Smith, *The Wealth of Nations,* Cannan ed. (New York: Modern Library, 1937), Chapter 10, p. 1.

Figure 15.5
Compensating Wage
Differentials

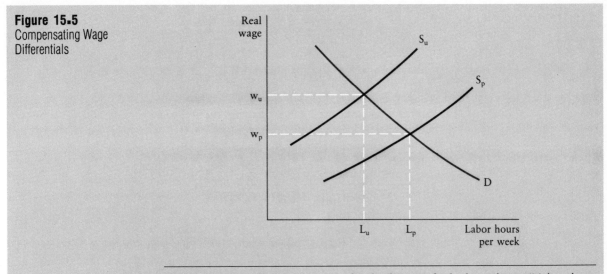

The demand curve for labor is assumed to be the same for both a "pleasant" job and an "unpleasant" one. However, the supply curves (S_p and S_u, respectively) differ for the two types of jobs. This causes wages to differ between the jobs. The higher wage rate for the unpleasant job (w_u) is said to "compensate" for the nature of the job.

will differ, however. The curve S_u represents the supply curve to the unpleasant job, and the equilibrium wage is given by w_u. At this wage firms in the unpleasant industry will demand L_u hours of labor input, and this is what individuals are willing to supply. Similarly, the curve S_p represents the supply curve of workers to the pleasant job. This curve lies to the right of the S_u curve because of the differences in the jobs. At any given wage individuals are willing to supply more labor to the pleasant job. Through the interaction of supply and demand, an equilibrium wage rate of w_p will be established for the pleasant job. This wage will be below w_u and the difference between w_u and w_p is the wage differential that compensates for the unpleasantness of the first job.

The equilibrium shown in Figure 15.5 is stable: there is no incentive for a worker to transfer from one job to the other. As Smith predicted, the "net advantages" of the two jobs have been equalized. Measuring these differentials is not only interesting in itself, but the information may be useful for a variety of other purposes, as "Applying Economics: Compensating Wage Differentials" shows.

Labor Unions

Workers may at times find it useful to join a labor union in order to pursue goals that can more effectively be achieved through group action. Sometimes joining a union is completely voluntary. In many cases, however, compulsory

APPLYING ECONOMICS

Compensating Wage Differentials

Obtaining numerical estimates of the size of compensating wage differentials is a difficult and controversial problem. Accurate measurement requires that other influences on wage rates (skills, monopoly or monopsony power, and so forth) be controlled for, so that observed wage differences can be correctly attributable to individuals' supply reactions to the characteristics of jobs.

Tables 15.3 and 15.4 provide some very tentative estimates that are intended to capture such effects. The first of these reports the results of a study by Richard Thaler and Sherwin Rosen of the way in which differences in the risk of loss of life on a job affect wages.[10] Table 15.3 shows that jobs that have high mortality rates also have higher annual wages (other things being the same). Thaler and Rosen point out that in 1967 individuals chose among jobs as if they were putting an implicit value of about $176,000 on their own lives. In other words, employees seem willing to accept an increase in the annual probability of dying on a job of one-tenth of 1 percent in exchange for $176 extra in annual salary. While that conclusion is controversial and may, for a variety of reasons, be too low (for instance, it disregards the costs that a person's death may impose on his or her family), there are many situations in which assigning some estimated value for a life is essential. Workplace health and safety legislation, for example,

must reach some compromise between the benefits of safer methods of production and the costs of such safety. It is perhaps possible to design a 100 percent safe coal mine, but the costs of doing so might be prohibitive.

Table 15.3
Compensating Wage Differentials for Differential Death Rates, by Occupations, 1967

Occupation	Additional Annual Deaths per 100,000	Estimated Increment to Annual Salary
Bartenders	179	$315
Boilermakers	230	405
Fire fighters	44	77
Lumberjacks	256	451
Mine operatives	176	310
Police and detectives	78	137
Taxicab drivers	182	320
Teamsters	114	201

Source: R. Thaler and S. Rosen, "The Value of Saving a Life: Evidence from the Labor Market" in N. E. Terleckyj, ed., *Household Production and Consumption* (New York: National Bureau of Economic Research, 1975), pp. 265–298. Data computed from Tables 1 and 3.

membership (the closed shop) is required in order to maintain the viability of the union organization. If all workers were left on their own to decide on membership, their rational decision might be not to join the union (to avoid dues and other restrictions). They would still benefit from the higher wages and better working conditions that may have been won by the union. What appears to be rational from each individual worker's point of view may prove to be irrational from a group point of view, since the union is undermined by these "free riders." Compulsory membership is therefore a common means of maintaining an effective union and preventing other workers from getting a free ride. This section examines the goals that an effective union might pursue, and how this pursuit will affect the price of labor.

---

[10]Richard Thaler and Sherwin Rosen, "The Value of Saving a Life: Evidence from the Labor Market" in N. E. Terleckyj, ed., *Household Production and Consumption* (New York: National Bureau of Economic Research, 1975), pp. 265–298.

Values for lives must, at least implicitly, be used in making decisions about how much safety to build in, and Thaler and Rosen's study provides a basis for devising a way to assign such values.

Because it is very difficult to define "working conditions" of jobs in objective and quantifiable ways, measuring compensating differentials for "unpleasant" jobs is even more difficult than measuring differentials associated with risks of loss of life. The results of R. E.

Table 15.4
Compensating Wage Differentials for Unpleasant Working Conditions in 1967

	Addition to Wage Provided by Job Attribute			
	White Males	Black Males	White Females	Black Females
Repetitive jobs	10.3%	7.7%	22.3%	25.6%
Jobs in a poor work environment	6.8	−7.7	3.3	19.5

Source: R. E. B. Lucas, "Hedonic Wage Equations and Psychic Wages in the Returns to Schooling," *American Economic Review*, September 1977, Table 1, p. 554.

B. Lucas's attempt at measurement are reported in Table 15.4.[11] These results show that, on the whole, people do seem to receive somewhat higher wages for jobs that are repetitive in nature or that require working in an unpleasant environment (that is, one characterized by heat, cold, noise, or some other unpleasant feature). As with the numbers for the death risk of jobs, however, these results should be regarded only as broadly indicative of underlying economic forces. The measurement methods used were probably too crude to place much faith in the precise values obtained.

To Think About

1. Isn't it rather crass to use people's employment choices to put a value on their lives? Isn't there some better way that is more humane and less hard-hearted? Indeed why bother to put a value on life at all? Isn't all life essentially beyond valuation?
2. How can the idea of compensating wage differentials be reconciled with the everyday observation that some very unpleasant jobs (such as those of trash collectors or day laborers) are not paid very well whereas executives in fancy, comfortable offices may be paid a great deal? Isn't a theory that suggests that unpleasant jobs are paid more highly just completely contrary to your experiences?

Unions' Goals

As in our discussion of the theory of the firm, we start our analysis of union behavior by describing the goals a union might seek. A first assumption we might make is that the goals of a union represent what its members want. This assumption avoids the problem of union leadership and disregards the personal aspirations of those leaders, which may be in conflict with rank-and-file goals. Union leaders are therefore assumed to be conduits for expressing the desires of the membership. In the United States union goals have tended to be oriented toward bread-and-butter issues. The programs of major unions

[11]R. E. B. Lucas, "Hedonic Wage Equations and Psychic Wages in the Returns to Schooling," *American Economic Review*, September 1977, Table 1, p. 554.

have not emphasized the promotion of radical social change except briefly in the early 1900s. Rather, unions have attempted to exert an effect solely in the labor market to which they are suppliers, and in this they have had some success.

Strong unions can be treated in the same way as monopoly firms. The union faces a demand curve for labor; because it is the sole source of supply, it can choose the point on this curve at which it will operate. The point that is actually chosen by the union will obviously depend on what particular goals it has decided to pursue. Three possible choices are illustrated in Figure 15.6. The union may, for example, choose to offer that quantity of labor that maximizes the total wage bill ($w \cdot L$). If this is the case, it will offer that quantity for which the marginal revenue from labor demand is equal to zero. This quantity is given by L_1 in Figure 15.6, and the wage rate associated with this quantity is w_1. The point E_1 is therefore the preferred wage-quantity combination. Notice that at wage rate w_1 there may be an excess supply of labor, and the union must somehow allocate those jobs that are available among the workers who want them. It may, for example, adopt a seniority or apprenticeship scheme that preserves high-wage jobs for its most senior workers.

Another possible goal that the union may pursue would be to choose to supply the quantity of labor that maximizes the total economic rent obtained by its members. In this way the union would be acting in a way similar to a monopoly firm by maximizing the "profits" (that is, wages in excess of opportunity costs) of its members. To do so would require the union to choose that quantity of labor for which the additional total wages obtained by having one more employed union member (the marginal revenue) is equal to the extra cost of luring that member into the market. The union should therefore choose that quantity, L_2, at which the marginal revenue curve crosses the supply curve. The wage rate associated with this quantity is w_2, and the desired wage-quantity combination is labeled E_2 in the diagram. Again, this combination requires that some workers who desire to work at the prevailing wage are left unemployed. Perhaps the union may "tax" (by charging dues) the large economic rent earned by those who do work in order to transfer income in the form of layoff benefits to those who don't.

A third possibility would be for the union to aim for maximum employment of its members. This would involve choosing the point w_3, L_3, which is precisely the point that would result if the market were organized in a perfectly competitive way. No employment greater than L_3 could be achieved, since the quantity of labor that union members supply would be reduced for wages less than w_3.

Other Union Goals: Job Security and Fringe Benefits

Although the union goals illustrated in Figure 15.6 are those that are easiest to diagram, the list is by no means exhaustive. Two other important goals that unions may seek, for example, are job security and a variety of nonwage

Figure 15.6
Three Possible Points on
the Labor Demand Curve
That a Monopoly Union
Might Choose

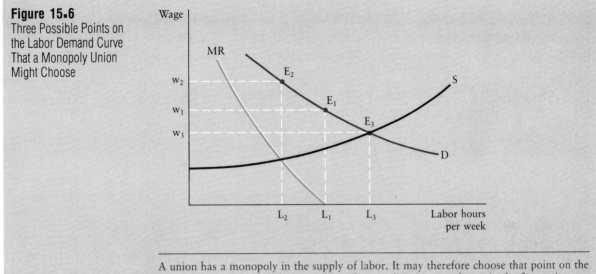

A union has a monopoly in the supply of labor. It may therefore choose that point on the demand curve for labor that it prefers. Three such points are shown in the figure. At point E_1 total labor payments $(w \cdot L)$ are maximized; at E_2 the economic rent that workers receive is maximized; and at E_3 the total amount of labor hired is maximized.

fringe benefits. Job security is particularly important in industries such as durable goods manufacturing or construction in which there are major cyclical influences on product demand and on the demand for labor. Unions may seek to reduce the risks of such fluctuations for their members by establishing contractual rights to jobs. In that way the variability in workers' wage incomes will be reduced, and (as we show in Chapter 6) this reduction raises workers' utility.

Fringe benefits such as pensions, vacations, insurance coverage, and generally better working conditions are also of considerable value to workers. Because such benefits are frequently of low public visibility in negotiating sessions and are often nontaxable to workers, they have come to constitute an increasingly important part of firms' total labor costs.

There are two ways in which recognition of such alternative union (or for that matter, any worker's) goals should be used to modify the analysis presented previously in this chapter. First, the price of labor should be generalized to include indirect forms of compensation in addition to the usual hourly wage rate. Obviously, firms and workers bargain over the total package of compensation, not just one part of it. Related to this is a second observation: Unions may be willing to forgo wage rate increases to obtain other types of benefits. They may, as "Applying Economics: Unionization of Fire Fighters" shows, opt for more leisure time instead of higher wages. Although diagramming such other goals may be difficult, these goals do play a major role in many labor negotiations.

Unionization of Fire Fighters

Our analysis so far has suggested that unions may, in the absence of effective competition, be able to exert some influence on the terms of labor contracts. Here we examine the unionization of fire fighters by the International Association of Fire Fighters (IAFF). The market for fire fighters is one in which union influences could be particularly pronounced. Because there is no effective private competition for the services provided by municipal fire departments, once the IAFF gains recognition as the bargaining agent with a city, it does not have to be concerned about the erosion of that position through competition. Similarly, a city's demand for fire fighters is likely to be inelastic with respect to wage changes since demand for fire prevention services is itself inelastic and there are few possibilities for substituting capital for labor.

A 1971 study by Orley Ashenfelter tended to support the presumption that unionization of fire fighters can have significant labor market effects.[12] Table 15.5 summarizes Ashenfelter's findings for 1966 for small (population 25,000 to 50,000) and moderate-size (population 50,000 to 100,000) cities. Three bargaining goals of the

IAFF were examined: hourly wage rates, annual salaries, and weekly hours of work. The hours-of-work goal was included because firefighters typically work long hours on duty waiting for calls (the typical workweek is about 56 hours) and there is some public sympathy for reductions in those hours. Of course, a reduction in hours not accompanied by a proportionate reduction in annual salary implies an increase in the hourly wage. Bargaining over hours is one way in which the IAFF may have been able to achieve higher wages.

Table 15.5 shows that fire fighters represented by the IAFF tended to work 6 to 8 percent fewer hours than did nonunionized fire fighters. Those reductions in hours were not matched by reductions in annual salaries in unionized cities—indeed, annual salaries tended to be slightly higher in such cities. Consequently, hourly wages paid to fire fighters represented by the IAFF were 9 to 16 percent higher than those paid to nonunion workers. The unique nature of fire fighting may result in these data overstating the economic impact of unions in the economy as a whole. But, most studies of other industries have also concluded that the effects of unions on relative wage rates are in the 10 to 20 percent range.[13] It appears that unions do have a substantial influence on wage determination.

Table 15.5
Effects of Unionization of Fire Fighters, All U.S. Cities, 1966 (Percent Difference between Union and Nonunion Cities)

	Small Cities	Moderate-Size Cities
Percent difference in weekly hours	−5.8%	−8.5%
Percent difference in annual salary	+10.1	+1.0
Percent difference in hourly wage	+16.0	+9.4

Source: O. Ashenfelter, "The Effect of Unionization on Public Sector Wages: The Case of Fire Fighters," *Industrial and Labor Relations Review*, January 1971, pp. 191–202. Abstracted from Tables 2 and 3.

To Think About
1. Fire fighters are not usually hired by private firms. Rather, they work for municipal governments. How would you develop a theory of these governments' demands for workers? Would their demand curves be negatively sloped? How, for example, might a town respond to an increase in the wages of fire fighters?
2. Might fire fighters' unions have a positive effect on productivity that largely offsets the higher wages they obtain? Or might the union, through various restrictive work rules, actually reduce productivity? Can you think of any evidence that might support either of these possibilities?

---

[12]O. Ashenfelter, "The Effect of Unionization on Public Sector Wages: The Case of Fire Fighters," *Industrial and Labor Relations Review*, January 1971, pp. 191–202.

[13]Some authors have suggested that the effects of unions on costs of production may not be this great since unionized workers may also be more productive than nonunionized workers. For a discussion of the issues, see R. B. Freeman and J. L. Medoff, *What Do Unions Do?* (New York: Basic Books, 1984).

Summary

In this chapter we have examined several questions about the supply of labor and how supply decisions may affect wage rates. Our primary conclusions are:

- The market wage rate represents the opportunity cost of leisure for individuals. It shows how nonwork time can be traded for income (and consumption) in the marketplace.
- A utility-maximizing individual will choose to work that number of hours for which the MRS of leisure for consumption is equal to the market wage. That is, he or she will equate the rate at which they are willing to trade leisure for consumption to the market opportunity cost of that leisure.
- A change in the wage has both substitution and income effects on people's choices. The effects work in opposite directions. A higher real wage, for example, will have a substitution effect that encourages people to work more, but an income effect that encourages them to work less.
- If jobs differ in their attractiveness, this will show up in the supply of labor for those jobs. Differentials in wage rates will arise that compensate people for differing job characteristics.
- If workers join together to form a union, they may exert some monopoly power in the labor market. The supply decisions made by the monopoly union will depend on what goals it chooses to pursue. It is likely that unions can raise market wages for those who get jobs.

Problems

15.1 Suppose there are 8,000 hours in a year (actually there are 8,760) and that an individual has a potential market wage of $5 per hour.

   a. What is the individual's full potential income if he or she could work 8,000 hours? If he or she chooses to devote 75 percent of this income to leisure, how many hours will be worked?
   b. Suppose a rich uncle dies and leaves the individual an annual income of $4,000 per year. If he or she continues to devote 75 percent of full income to leisure, how many hours will be worked?
   c. How would your answer to part b change if the market wage were $10 per hour instead of $5 per hour?
   d. Graph the individual's supply of labor curve implied by parts b and c.

15.2 Mrs. Smith has a guaranteed income of $10 per day from an inheritance. Her preferences require her always to spend half her potential income on leisure (H) and consumption (C).

   a. What is Mrs. Smith's budget constraint in this situation?
   b. How many hours will Mrs. Smith devote to work and to leisure in order to maximize her utility given that her market wage is $1.25? $2.50? $5.00? $10.00?

c. Graph the four different budget constraints and sketch in Mrs. Smith's utility-maximizing choices. (Hint: when graphing budget constraints, remember that when H = 24, C = 10, not 0.)

d. Graph Mrs. Smith's supply of labor curve.

*15.3 Suppose the supply curve for labor to a firm has the form

$$L = 100w$$

where w is the market wage. Suppose that the marginal expense of hiring workers is:

$$ME_L = L/50.$$

Suppose also that the firm's demand (marginal revenue product) curve has the form

$$L = -50MVP_L + 450.$$

a. If the firm is a monopsonist, how many workers will it hire in order to maximize profits? What wage will it pay?

b. If the supply of labor is monopolized, how many workers should be provided to the firm in order to maximize the total wage bill (wL)? What will the wage rate be?

c. If the market has both a monopsony on the demand side and a monopoly on the supply side what can you say about the "equilibrium" outcome? How will this compare to the competitive solution?

15.4 Suppose a union has a fixed supply of labor to sell. If the union desires to maximize the total wage bill, what wage rate will it demand? How would your answer change if unemployed workers were paid unemployment insurance at the rate u per worker and the union now desired to maximize the sum of the wage bill and the total amount of unemployment compensation?

15.5 Use the time allocation model in Chapter 15 to discuss the effects on an individual's hours of work of

a. The receipt of a substantial amount of outside income.

b. The imposition of a tax on wages.

c. An increase in the general price level with no concomitant increase in wages.

d. National legislation of a maximum workweek of 35 hours.

15.6 Mr. Peabody has a utility function of $U = \sqrt{C \cdot H}$ and is maximizing his utility at U = 20 when he works 14 hours a day. Would he be will-

---

*Denotes a problem that is rather difficult.

ing to give up an hour of his leisure to drive Mrs. Atterboy to the wrestling match if she offered him $5?

15.7 Use the concept of the opportunity cost of time to discuss:

    a. Who you might expect to pay the higher fares to fly the faster Concorde to Europe.

    b. Who you would expect to be more likely to stand in long lines and even camp out overnight to purchase tickets to a sporting event.

    c. For whom greens fees are a larger fraction of the total cost of a golf game—a prospering physician or a peanut vendor.

    d. How the degree of traffic congestion affects who drives to work and who takes mass transit.

*15.8 A welfare program for low income people offers a family a basic grant of $6,000 per year. This grant is reduced by $.75 for each $1 of other income the family has.

    a. How much in welfare benefits does the family receive if it has no other income? If the head of the family earns $2,000 per year? How about $4,000 per year?

    b. At what level of earnings does the welfare grant become zero?

    c. Assume that the head of this family can earn $4 per hour and that the family has no other income. What is the annual budget constraint for this family if it does not participate in the welfare program? That is, how are consumption (C) and hours of leisure (H) related?

    d. What is the budget constraint if the family opts to participate in the welfare program? (Remember, the welfare grant can only be positive.)

    e. Graph your results from parts c and d.

    f. Suppose the government changes the rules of the welfare program to permit families to keep 50 percent of what they earn. How would this change your answer to parts d and e above?

    g. Using your results from part f, can you predict whether the head of this family will work more or less under the new rules described in part f?

CHAPTER 16

Pricing of Capital

The study of capital as a factor of production is extremely important in economics. For example, economics has traditionally assigned an important role to capital accumulation as a source of economic growth. One of the major reasons for increasing income over time is the increasing amount of productive equipment workers have at their disposal. To understand where this equipment comes from and the incentives that lead to its accumulation requires that we study capital. Similarly, Keynesian economic theory assigns an important role to investment as one component of aggregate demand. Since net investment comes about because firms want to change the amount of capital they have available, it is again important to understand the factors that go into the firms' decisions. For this reason, capital theory is central to modern macroeconomics. The purpose of Chapter 16 is to provide a simple analysis of capital pricing that is relevant to all of these issues.

Definition of Capital

Capital stock
The total amount of machines, buildings, and all other manmade, nonlabor resources in an economy.

When we speak of the **capital stock** of an economy we mean the total amount of machines, buildings, and other manmade, nonlabor resources that are in existence at some point in time. These assets represent some portion of an economy's past output that was not consumed then. This output was instead set aside to be used for production in the future. All societies, from the most primitive to the most complex, engage in capital accumulation. A bushman's taking time off from hunting to make arrows, people in a modern society using part of their incomes to buy houses, or governments taxing citizens in order to purchase dams and post office buildings are all engaging in essentially the same sort of activity—some portion of the economy's current output is being set aside for use in producing additional goods in future periods. Present

Figure 16.1
Two Views of Capital
Accumulation

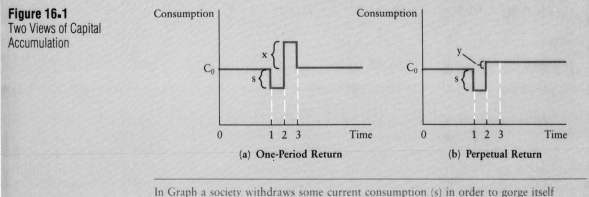

In Graph a society withdraws some current consumption (s) in order to gorge itself (with x extra consumption) in the next period. The one-period rate of return would be measured by x/s − 1. The society in Graph b takes a more long-term view and uses s to increase its consumption perpetually by y. The perpetual rate of return would be given by y/s.

sacrifice for future gain is the essential aspect of capital accumulation. The next section introduces the concept of a rate of return in order to show why people engage in such an activity.

Rate of Return

Rate of return
The increase in future output made possible by investing one unit of current output in capital accumulation.

The process of capital accumulation is pictured schematically in Figure 16.1. In both panels of the figure, society is initially consuming level C_0 and has been doing so for some time. At time 1 a decision is made to withhold some output (amount s) from current consumption for one period of time. Starting in time 2 this withheld consumption is in some way put to use producing future consumption. An important concept connected with this process is the **rate of return** earned on the consumption that is put aside. In Graph a, all of the withheld consumption is used to produce additional output only in time 2. Consumption is increased by amount x in time 2 and then returns to its prior level, C_0. Society has saved for one period in order to have an orgy in the next one. A measure of the one-period rate of return from this activity would be

$$r_1 = \frac{x}{s} - 1. \qquad [16.1]$$

If x > s (if more consumption comes out of this process than went into it) we would say that the one-period rate of return to capital accumulation is positive. For example, if withholding 100 units from current consumption permitted society to consume an extra 110 units next year, the rate of return would be .10 (= 110/100 − 1) or 10 percent.

In Graph b of Figure 16.1 society is assumed to take a more long-term view in its consumption activities. Again, an amount s is set aside at time 1. Now, however, this set-aside consumption is used to raise the consumption level for all periods in the future. If the permanent level of consumption is raised to $C_0 + y$, we define the perpetual rate of return to be

$$r_\infty = \frac{y}{s}.$$ [16.2]

If capital accumulation succeeds in raising C_0 permanently, r_∞ will be positive. For example, suppose society set aside 100 units of output in time 1 to be devoted to capital accumulation. If this capital would permit output to be raised by 10 units for every period in the future (starting at time 2) the perpetual rate of return would be 10 percent.

When economists speak of the rate of return to capital accumulation, they have in mind something between these two extremes. Somewhat loosely they define the rate of return in an economy to be the terms at which presently produced goods that are not currently consumed can be turned into goods that can be consumed at some future date. The next section makes this definition more precise.

Determination of the Rate of Return

The act of capital accumulation essentially consists of withholding some output from current consumption, investing this output in some sort of equipment, and using the equipment to produce output in the future. The rate of return measures the terms on which this process can be accomplished. In a market economy the actual rate of return will depend on the technical possibilities for turning present goods into future goods, and on the preferences of people for present versus future goods. An equilibrium rate of return will reflect both the return to capital accumulation that is technically feasible and the return that individuals are willing to accept.

A Supply-Demand Analysis

Future goods
Goods that are purchased today by setting aside some present output as capital whose output is then consumed in the future.

Determination of this equilibrium rate of return can be illustrated by considering the supply and demand for what we might call **future goods.** Such goods are purchased today by setting aside some capital investment, and when the output from that capital is consumed this is a future good. Simple examples of future goods include wine or trees for lumber. Once produced (or, in the case of trees, planted) these goods increase in value over time—they offer a rate of return. Although purchasing machinery in the U.S. economy is much more complicated than planting trees, the activities are similar in that they represent trading present goods for future ones. It is that process we wish to study.

Figure 16.2
The Market for Future
Goods

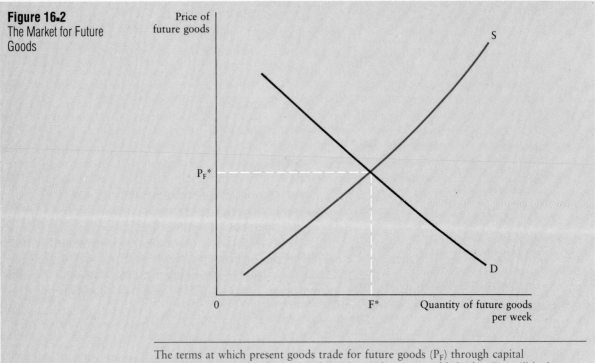

The terms at which present goods trade for future goods (P_F) through capital accumulation is set by demand and supply conditions. It is likely that P_F^* will be less than one. We define the rate of return (r) by the formula $1/1 + r = P_F^*$. Since $P_F^* < 1$, r will be positive.

The market for future goods is pictured in Figure 16.2. The horizontal axis shows the quantity of future goods traded (F). On the vertical axis we have recorded the price of future goods (P_F). This price records the number of current goods (for example, pounds of seedlings) sacrificed to get one future good (for example, one pound of lumber). The demand curve for future goods is drawn sloping downward on the assumption that the lower their price, the greater the quantity people will demand. In other words, the smaller the required sacrifice of present goods, the greater will be people's demands for goods in the future. The supply curve for future goods slopes upward because of the assumption that the process of setting aside capital for the production of future goods may run into diminishing returns. As the amount of future goods produced increases, the marginal cost (in terms of the present investment required) of producing them rises. Expanding the production from a wood lot requires progressively more in the way of initial investment of workers' time, soil improvements, and care in spacing seedlings.

Equilibrium Price of Future Goods

Equilibrium in the market shown in Figure 16.2 is at P_F^*, F^*. At that point the supply and demand for future goods are in balance, and the required amount of current goods will be put into capital accumulation in order to produce F^* in the future.[1]

There are a number of reasons to expect that P_F^* will be less than one: that is, it will cost less than the sacrifice of one current good to "buy" one good in the future. On the demand side it might be argued that people require some reward for waiting. Everyday slogans ("a bird in the hand is worth two in the bush," "live for today") and more substantial realities such as the uncertainty of the future and the finiteness of life suggest that people are generally impatient in their consumptive decisions. Capital accumulation such as that shown in Figure 16.1 will take place only if the current sacrifice is in some way worthwhile.

There are also supply reasons for believing P_F^* will be less than one. All of these involve the idea that capital accumulation is "productive": sacrificing one good currently will yield more than one good in the future. Tree farmers, vineyard operators, and cheesemakers "abstain" from selling their wares currently in the belief that time will make them more valuable in the future.[2] Similarly, building steel mills or power stations may ultimately yield more in the future value of output than was used to produce these capital goods. "Applying Economics: The Rate of Return to Storing Wine" illustrates a particularly rewarding example of this productivity of time.

The Equilibrium Rate of Return

We can now show the relationship of the rate of return (r) to what we have called the price of future goods by the formula

$$P_F^* = \frac{1}{1 + r}. \tag{16.3}$$

Since we believe that P_F^* will be less than one, r will be positive. For example, if $P_F^* = .9$, r will equal approximately .1, and we would say that the rate of return to capital accumulation is 10 percent.[3] By withholding one good from

---

[1]This is a much simplified form of an analysis originally presented by Irving Fisher in *The Rate of Interest* (New York: Macmillan, 1907).

[2]For a discussion of these examples in the context of "Austrian" capital theory, see Marc Blaug, *Economic Theory in Retrospect* (Homewood, Ill.: Irwin, 1962), Chapter 12.

[3]More precisely, if $P_F^* = .9$, r will be .11111... since $.9 = \dfrac{1}{1 + .1111...}$.

The Rate of Return to Storing Wine

Laying down rare wine to age is a particularly simple yet rewarding example of capital accumulation—present consumption of wine is forgone in the hope of obtaining more enjoyable consumption in the future. Although there are no objective standards to measure how much a wine's taste improves each year, prices for bottles of wine of various ages provide a good estimate of the returns obtained by oenophiles. In a 1981 study, Elizabeth Jaeger examined results for the Hueblein Wine Auction for red bordeaux and California cabernet sauvignon over the period 1969–1977.[5] Overall, she calculated that wines being auctioned yielded average annual rates of return of over 20 percent, a figure well in excess of returns available on financial investments (such as Treasury bills) during the period. At least for these particular years, it appears that aging of wine offered a substantial incentive to delay consumption.

One question immediately suggested by these results is why returns to storing wine are so high. Jaeger suggests the principal explanation is that storing wine is a risky enterprise. Besides the problem of protecting wine against breakage and temperature changes, there is major uncertainty as to whether a particular vintage will age properly. The chemistry involved in the changing properties of wine over time is very delicate. Undetectable differences in rare wines when they are first bottled may lead to major discrepancies in their quality as they age. Discovering that a particular red vintage is aging poorly can lead to sharp price drops, reflecting the wine's lowered quality. Jaeger finds some evidence to support this explanation for wine's high rates of return by comparing older and younger vintages. She calculates a much higher rate of return on the younger vintages since these are subject to great risks and potential disappointments. Older vintages, on the other hand, have shown that they age well, and purchasing them involves a lesser risk. For these older vintages, rates of return were not significantly higher than those obtainable on relatively safe financial investments.

To Think About

1. When is the right time to sell wine that is rising in value? Should a winery hold onto its product until it has ceased to appreciate further? Or should the product be sold while it is still rising in value? What is the opportunity cost of keeping wine in the barrel?
2. How does the rate of return on other investments affect the behavior of winery owners with respect to aging their product? Would an increase in alternative returns result in fine wines being aged for longer or shorter periods? Do you think wine fanciers really make such calculations?

current consumption, the consumption of future goods can be increased by 1.1. The rate of return and P_F are equivalent ways of measuring the terms on which present goods can be turned into future goods.[4] In the remainder of this chapter we assume that the equilibrium rate of return r has been estab-

---

[4]It is important to make a distinction between the rate of return (r) and interest rates (R) actually observed in real-world markets (say, on savings accounts or on bonds). Since we live in a world of inflation, market interest rates will reflect both the rate of return on capital accumulation and the expected change in prices (since lenders will want to be compensated for the fact that they will be repaid in devalued dollars). If the proportional change in the price level is given by P_e, R and r are related by:

$$R = r + P_e.$$

For example, if r = .05 (5 percent) and P_e = .04 (4 percent) the market interest rate will be R = .09 (9 percent).

[5]Elizabeth Jaeger, "To Save or Savor: The Rate of Return to Storing Wine," *Journal of Political Economy,* June 1981, pp. 584–592.

lished by the process shown in Figure 16.2. That rate provides a measure of the benefits of capital accumulation to all people who are considering it. We show how they take account of r in all of the decisions they make that concern the allocation of resources over time.

Rental Rate on Machines and the Theory of Investment

So far in this chapter we have not talked about the firm's demand for capital. We can now do so using the concepts we have developed. Presumably a firm will rent machines in accordance with the same principles of profit maximization derived in Chapter 14. Specifically, a profit-maximizing firm will hire that number of machines for which the marginal value product (MVP) from hiring one more is equal to the machine's market rental rate (v).

This section first investigates the determinants of machines' market rental rates and assumes that firms rent all the equipment they use. Later, the section examines the particular problems raised because most firms buy machines rather than rent them and own them until they are no longer useful.

Determinants of Market Rental Rates

Consider a firm in the business of renting machines to other firms. Hertz and Avis rent automobiles, banks lease computers and aircraft to other operators, and Taylor Rental rents everything from punch bowls to chain saws. Here we assume that all capital equipment is handled in this way. Suppose that the rental firm owns a machine that has a current market value of P. If it sold the machine outright, it could get P for it. How much will the firm charge its clients for the use of the machine? The owner of the machine faces two kinds of costs: depreciation on the machine and the opportunity cost of having its funds tied up in a machine rather than in an investment earning interest. If it is assumed that depreciation costs per period (say each year) are a constant percent (d) of the machine's market price and that the market rate of return on other investments is given by r, then the total costs to the machine owner for one year are given by

$$dP + rP = P(r + d). \qquad [16.4]$$

If we assume that the machine rental market is perfectly competitive, no pure profits can be earned by renting machines. The workings of the market will insure that the rental rate per year for the machine (v) is exactly equal to the long-run costs of the machine owner. Hence we have the basic result that

$$v = P(r + d). \qquad [16.5]$$

The annual rental rate is the sum of interest and depreciation costs that the rental company incurs. For example, suppose that the rate of return on alternative investments is 5 percent per year (that is, .05) and that the physical depreciation rate is 4 percent per year (.04). Suppose also that the current market price of a particular machine is $100. In this simple example, the machine would have a rental rate of $9 [$100 × (.05 + .04)] per year. The opportunity cost of the funds invested in the machine is $5, and the remaining $4 reflects the physical costs of deterioration.

A Nondepreciating Machine

In the case of a machine that does not depreciate (d = 0), Equation 16.5 can be written in a simpler way:

$$\frac{v}{P} = r. \tag{16.6}$$

This simply says that in equilibrium an infinitely long-lived (nondepreciating) machine is equivalent to a perpetual bond and must yield the market rate of return. The rental rate as a percent of the machine's price must be equal to r. If v/P exceeds r everyone would rush out to buy machines, since they yield more than the prevailing interest rate. For example, if v = $10 per year and machines sell for $100, a firm in the machine rental business will earn 10 percent on the funds it invests in machines. If alternative investments yield only 5 percent, the rental business is a very profitable one and new firms would enter it. Alternatively, if v/P is below r no one would be in the business of renting out machines, since more could be made on alternative investments. Hertz would do better putting its funds in a bank rather than investing in cars.

Ownership of Equipment

To this point our analysis has assumed that firms rent all of the machines they use. Although such rental does take place in the real world, it is more common that firms own the machines they use. A firm will buy a machine and use its services in combination with the labor the firm hires to produce output. Ownership of machines makes the analysis of the demand for capital slightly more complicated than of the demand for labor. By recognizing the important distinction between a stock and a flow, we can show that these two demands are quite similar.

A firm uses capital services to produce output. These services are a flow magnitude. It is the number of machine hours that is relevant to the productive process (just as it is labor hours), not the number of machines per se. Frequently, the assumption is made that the flow of capital services is proportional to the stock of machines (100 machines can, if fully employed for one hour, deliver 100 machine hours of service). These two different concepts are often used synonymously. If during a period a firm desires a certain number of machine hours, this is usually taken to mean that the firm needs a certain number of machines to provide them. The firm's demand for capital services is also a demand for capital.

A profit-maximizing firm in perfect competition will choose its level of inputs so that the marginal value product from an extra unit of any input is equal to its cost. This result holds also for the demand for machine hours. The cost of capital services is given by the rental rate (v) in Equation 16.5. This cost is borne by the firm whether it rents the machine in the open market or owns the machine itself. In the former case, machine rental is an explicit cost; in the latter case, it is an implicit cost since the firm could rent out its equipment to another user if it chose to do so. In either case the opportunity cost of machine use is given by the market rental rate v. The fact of ownership is, to a first approximation, irrelevant to the determination of cost, and we can treat all firms as if they rent capital equipment. Firms that own machines can be viewed as renting those machines from themselves.

Theory of Investment

Investment
The purchase of new capital.

If a firm finds that it desires more capital services than can be provided by its currently existing stock of machinery, it has two choices. First, it may hire the additional machines that are needed in the rental market. This would be formally identical to its decision to hire additional labor. Second, the firm can buy new machinery to meet its needs. This second alternative is the one most often chosen; we call the purchase of new equipment by the firm **investment**.

Investment demand is an important component of aggregate demand in macroeconomic theory. Frequently it is assumed that this demand for plant and equipment (that is, machines) is inversely related to the rate of return on alternative investments. Using the analysis we developed in this part of the text, we can demonstrate the links in this argument. A fall in r will, *ceteris paribus*, decrease the rental rate on capital (Equation 16.5). Because forgone investment returns represent an implicit cost for the owner of a machine, a fall in r in effect reduces the cost of capital inputs. This fall in v implies that capital has become a relatively less expensive input and, as we showed in Chapter 14, this will prompt firms to increase their capital use. Firms may then either rent additional machines from others or buy new equipment for their own use.

It is this latter effect (the buying of new equipment) that is termed investment. The relationship between changes in r and investment is just one aspect of the theory of firms' demand for factors of production. Because the rate of return is an important determinant of the rental rate on capital, a fall in r has an effect on investment by causing firms' demands for capital services to increase. If the firm's current stock of machinery cannot deliver the desired number of machine hours, investment in new machinery will take place.

Tax Policy and Investment

Until now we have assumed that the costs that face a potential user of capital are of only two types: (1) implicit costs arising from forgone interest on the funds invested in a machine, and (2) explicit costs of the machine's physical deterioration. Taxes represent a third type of cost that can also influence decisions on capital use. In the United States and many other countries the corporate profits tax is not only an important source of government revenue, it also is a major policy tool that influences the level of investment decisions.[6] This section uses the model we have developed to explain how the profits tax affects investment and to provide some evidence on the effects of various elements of the tax code.

A Graphic Demonstration

When taxes are imposed on the net output of capital equipment, Equation 16.5 must be modified to take them into account. Now there are three costs that a machine owner must pay: interest, physical depreciation, and taxes. Consequently, the rental rate on a machine will now be

$$v = P(r + d) + T \qquad [16.7]$$

where T represents the taxes on a machine that must be paid by the owner. A higher T implies a higher rental cost, and a lower T implies a lower cost. Figure 16.3 shows the effect that a reduction in T (and v) and will have on the firm's desired level of capital inputs. Initially, the rental rate on capital is given by v_1; the firm produces Q_1 by using K_1 units of capital input per period.

Now suppose T declines. Using Equation 16.7, this will cause a machine's rental rate to fall to v_2. As was the case for labor, this fall in the rental rate will create both substitution and output effects, which cause more capital to be hired. In Graph a in Figure 16.3 the substitution effect causes the optimal input combination to move to point B on the Q_1 isoquant. The fall in v also causes the firm's marginal cost curve to shift downward to MC′. Output is increased to Q_2; at this output level, the firm now wishes to hire K_2 units of capital input. Since the firm may not have a sufficient stock of capital equipment on hand to provide this level of services, it may have to buy additional equipment. In other words, it may engage in investment. This is the sequence of events by which changes in governmental tax policy are related to the generation of investment incentives. In "Applying Economics: Effects of Tax

---

[6]Although this tax is termed a profits tax, as we showed in Chapter 9 it is not a tax on economic profits, but rather on both economic profits and on the net output (marginal value product) of machines. It is this taxation of machines' net incomes that affects investment decisions. A tax only on economic profits would have no such effect since it would not affect profit-maximizing or cost-minimizing decisions.

Figure 16.3
Effects of a Reduction in
Taxes on the Demand for
Capital Services

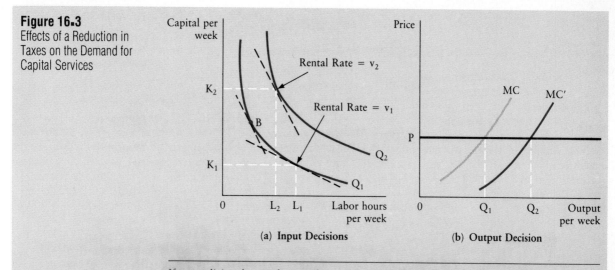

(a) Input Decisions

(b) Output Decision

If tax policies change the rental rate on capital, this will change the demand for capital services. For example, a reduction in taxes will cause the rental rate to fall from v_1 to v_2. This will create both substitution (from K_1, L_1 to B) and output (from B to K_2, L_2) effects, which cause the quantity of capital services demanded to increase (from K_1 to K_2). This increased demand for services may prompt firms to buy new machines.

Policies on Investment" we examine the success of some specific tax measures that were intended to spur investment in this way.

Present Discounted Value and Investment

Present discounted value
The present value of funds payable in the future after taking account of the opportunity cost of interest forgone.

The theory of firms' demand for capital is usually presented in a form rather different from that we have developed. This alternative form is termed the **present discounted value** theory of investment demand. Rather than treating the renting of machines similarly to the hiring of labor and centering attention on the rental rate (as we have done), this approach analyzes the specific decision to purchase a machine. The theory concerns the demand for machines rather than the demand for the services of machines. The distinction between the two approaches is, however, not very important. Besides discussing the notion of present discounted value, this section also shows that this approach results in the same behavior as does the rental rate approach we have been using.

Present Discounted Value

In order to describe the present discounted value criterion for investment, we must first discuss the procedure that should be used to add up sums of money that are to be received in different time periods, since the purchaser of a

Effects of Tax Policies on Investment

Federal tax policies have been widely used to influence the overall level of investment over the past 25 years. While the general thrust of these policies has been to increase investment by lowering taxes, changes in the general tax rate have not been the primary way this has been accomplished. Rather, complex changes have been made in accounting procedures, and special credits have been allowed for investment. Although it would be inappropriate to describe these changes in detail, a brief sketch of the three most important policies will indicate how investment incentives have been provided.

Table 16.1
Change in Gross Investment in Equipment as a Result of Federal Tax Policy, 1963 (Billions of 1954 Dollars)

	Manufacturing Equipment	Non-manufacturing Equipment
Total gross investment	$8.461	$17.982
Change due to:		
Accelerated depreciation	0.549	1.141
Useful lifetime guidelines	0.315	0.656
Investment tax credit	0.867	1.808
Total effect of federal tax policy	1.731	3.605
Tax effect as a percent of total gross investment	20.5%	20.0%

Source: R. E. Hall and D. W. Jorgenson, "Tax Policy and Investment Behavior," *American Economic Review,* June 1967, pp. 391–414, Tables 3, 4, and 5.

Accelerated Depreciation
In 1954, federal tax policy was changed to allow firms to write off the costs of their investments in plant and equipment more rapidly than previously. That policy allowed firms to postpone the taxes owed on the income generated by newly purchased machinery. In essence, firms received an interest-free loan of their tax liability from the government. By one estimate this relatively subtle change in accounting principles reduced the rental rate on capital by as much as 20 percent.[7]

Useful Lifetime Guidelines
Another provision for accelerated depreciation was instituted in 1962. Under this provision the useful lifetimes of various types of equipment for tax purposes were shortened. For example, the minimum useful life of a car was reduced from four to three years. This made it possible for firms to gain further benefits from accelerated depreciation, and effective rental rates on capital were reduced another 2 or 3 percent.

Investment Tax Credit
An additional tax change in 1962 was the institution of an investment tax credit for machinery and equipment purchases. Under that policy, 7 percent of the amount firms invested could be taken as a credit against taxes due. That policy reduced effective rental rates by 7 percent—essentially the federal Treasury paid 7 percent of all machinery and equipment purchases.

Effects of the Tax Policies in the Early 1960s
Table 16.1 shows the estimated effect of each of these tax policies on firms' total gross investment in equipment in 1963. As our theoretical discussion suggested, the reduction in rental rates had a substantial effect on the demand for capital equipment, increasing total pur-

---

[7]R. E. Hall and D. W. Jorgenson, "Tax Policy and Investment Behavior," *American Economic Review,* Vol. LVII, No. 3 (June 1967), pp. 391–414. All of the other numbers for the 1960s in this example are also taken from this source.

chases by about 20 percent over what they would have been under older, less generous tax laws. Clearly, tax policy provides a powerful lever with which the federal government can affect investment, and through investment, the overall pace of economic activity. The relatively high levels of employment experienced during the mid-1960s in the United States may have been in part the result of such policies.

Tax Policies of the Reagan Administration

In the first year of the Reagan administration, a similar set of investment-oriented tax policies was enacted as part of the Economic Recovery Tax Act of 1981. Changes introduced under this Act included a new form of accelerated depreciation (Accelerated Cost Recovery System—ACRS) and an increased investment tax credit. Adoption of the ACRS was a particularly important innovation. It eliminated the prior concept of "useful lifetime guidelines" for determining depreciation allowances and substituted a simplified scheme in which any asset fell into one of four classes with tax lives of 3, 5, 10, or 15 years. For most capital assets these lives were considerably shorter than had been the case previously. Most notably, the depreciation period for all equipment used to conduct research and development activities was reduced to a short three years when the previous guidelines had required much longer periods. Adoption of the ACRS also brought much greater uniformity into the tax treatment of various industries' investments. For example, under prior laws, depreciation periods for producers' equipment ranged from over 14 years for ships and boats to over 12 years for turbines to 5 years for trucks and tractors. Similarly, depreciation periods for buildings ranged from 17 to more than 40 years. Under the ACRS, depreciation periods were set at a uniform 5

years for most equipment and 10 or 15 years for buildings. It was hoped that such changes would result in a more uniform tax treatment of investment decisions across industries, thereby mitigating some of the anomalies that had developed under the prior system.

The overall effect of the ERTA changes was to reduce taxes substantially (reducing effective rental rates) on firms' capital investments. Indeed, some analysts even suggested that the tax rates under ERTA on many types of equipment were negative; that is, the government was effectively subsidizing this type of investment.[8] Possibilities for this subsidy having a major effect on firms' investment behavior were rather limited, however. The tax law was again changed in 1982 (under the pompously titled Tax Equity and Fiscal Responsibility Act), and the prior subsidy was largely eliminated. Indeed, this latter law raised the tax rates on some types of investment to above their pre-1981 levels. The likely overall effect of the Reagan changes on actual investment incentives was therefore unclear.

To Think About

1. Why does the government adopt policies to encourage investment? Won't private markets do enough investment without government subsidies? What goals is the government trying to achieve with such tax policies? Are there better ways to do so?

2. Depreciation policies are usually based on the actual purchase price of a machine. Is this definition of depreciation consistent with economists' notions of production costs? What are the actual costs involved in using a machine? Are these necessarily related to the machine's price perhaps many years ago? How does the failure to use accurate cost measures for firms' depreciation affect their investment decisions?

---

[8]See Donald Fullerton and Y. K. Henderson, "Long Run Effects of the Accelerated Recovery System," *National Bureau of Economic Research Working Paper* No. 828 (revised, February, 1983).

machine will collect net income (or, more properly, the marginal value product) from the machine over several periods into the future. Although some formal aspects of this subject are presented in the appendix to this chapter, it is possible here to provide an intuitive explanation of the logic that economists employ.

The most basic observation is that one dollar today is worth more than a dollar that is not to be received until a later date. If a dollar is available today it can be invested and earn interest at the prevailing rate, r. Conversely, if a dollar is not received until next year, some interest must be forgone. The current dollar is more valuable. Specifically, a dollar today will grow to $1 + r$ dollars next year. We might define the present value of $1 to be paid next year as $1/(1 + r)$. This is the amount that, if invested today at an annual interest rate r, will yield $1 in one year. If you invest $.95 today at 5 percent, you will have $1 next year. The present value of $1 to be received one year from now is $.95.

It is easy to generalize the idea of present value to any number of periods. If $1 is invested for two years, for example, it will grow to $1 \cdot (1 + r) \cdot (1 + r) = \$1 \cdot (1 + r)^2$. The present value of $1 payable in two years would be $1/(1 + r)^2$. This is the amount that would have to be invested today in order to obtain $1 in two years. These results can be summarized by

$$\text{Present value of \$1 payable in one year} = \frac{\$1}{(1 + r)}.$$

$$\text{Present value of \$1 payable in two years} = \frac{\$1}{(1 + r)^2}.$$

$$\text{Present value of \$1 payable in three years} = \frac{\$1}{(1 + r)^3}.$$

$$\text{Present value of \$1 payable in n years} = \frac{\$1}{(1 + r)^n}. \qquad [16.8]$$

In order to illustrate the implications of the present value concept, Table 16.2 shows the present value of $1 payable in one, two, three, ten, and twenty years in the future for five possible interest rates. For example, if r is 4 percent, the present value of $1 payable in one year is $.962. If about $.96 is invested today at 4 percent, it will grow to $1 by the end of one year. If the interest rate is 7 percent, an investment of only $.26 will grow to $1 in 20 years. In general, the present value of a dollar to be paid at some date in the future declines as the interest rate increases. The higher r is, the more heavily future payments are discounted since the opportunity costs of lost interest are greater. Similarly, for a fixed interest rate, dollars payable in the distant future are worth less than those payable in the near term. Again, such distant payments are discounted more heavily because of the greater opportunity costs involved. Published tables and calculators are available for calculating present values and these can be most helpful for economic analyses that involve sums of money payable over time.

Table 16-2
Present Value of $1
Payable at Various Dates

Interest Rate (r)	1 Year	2 Years	3 Years	10 Years	20 Years
3%	$.970	$.943	$.915	$.744	$.554
4	.962	.925	.889	.676	.456
5	.952	.907	.864	.614	.377
6	.943	.890	.840	.558	.312
7	.935	.873	.816	.508	.258

Present Discounted Value Approach to Investment Decisions

When a firm buys a machine, it is in effect buying a stream of net revenues in future periods. In order to decide whether or not to purchase the machine, the firm must assign some value to this stream. Since the revenues will accrue to the firm in many future periods, the logic of the preceding argument suggests that the firm should compute the present discounted value of this stream. Only by doing so will the firm have taken adequate account of the effects of interest payments. This is the alternative approach often used to explain the investment decision.

Consider a firm in the process of deciding whether to buy a particular machine. The machine is expected to last n years and will give its owner a stream of monetary returns (that is, marginal value products) in each of the n years. Let the return in year i be represented by R_i. If r is the present interest rate, and if this rate is expected to prevail for the next n years, the present discounted value (PDV) of the machine to its owner is given by:

$$PDV = \frac{R_1}{1 + r} + \frac{R_2}{(1 + r)^2} + \ldots + \frac{R_n}{(1 + r)^n}. \qquad [16.9]$$

This represents the total value of the stream of payments that is provided by the machine, once adequate account is taken of the fact that these payments occur in different years. If the PDV of this stream of payments exceeds the price (P) of the machine, the firm should make the purchase. Even when the opportunity costs of the interest payments that the firm could have earned on its funds had it not purchased the machine are taken into account, the machine promises to return more than it will cost to buy, and firms would rush out to buy machines. On the other hand, if P exceeds the machine's PDV, the firm would be better off to invest its funds in some alternative that promises a rate of return of r. When account is taken of forgone interest, the machine does not pay for itself. No profit-maximizing firm would buy such a machine.

In a competitive market the only equilibrium that can prevail is if the price of a machine is equal to the present discounted value of the net revenues from the machine. Only in this situation will there be neither an excess demand for machines nor an excess supply of machines. Market equilibrium requires that:

$$P = PDV = \frac{R_1}{1 + r} + \frac{R_2}{(1 + r)^2} + \ldots + \frac{R_n}{(1 + r)^n}. \qquad [16.10]$$

We now use this condition to show a simple situation in which the present value approach to making investment decisions yields the same results as the rental rate approach.

Present Discounted Value and the Rental Rate

For simplicity, assume that machines do not depreciate and that the marginal value product is the same in every year. This uniform return will then also equal the rental rate for machines (v), since that is what another firm would be willing to pay for the machine's use during the period. With these simplifying assumptions we may write the present discounted value from machine ownership as:

$$PDV = \frac{v}{(1 + r)} + \frac{v}{(1 + r)^2} + \ldots + \frac{v}{(1 + r)^n} + \ldots \qquad [16.11]$$

where the dots (. . .) indicate that payments go on forever. But since in equilibrium P = PDV, the appendix to this chapter shows how we can solve Equation 16.11 as

$$P = \frac{v}{r} \qquad [16.12]$$

or

$$r = \frac{v}{P} \qquad [16.13]$$

which is the same as Equation 16.6 (v/P = r). For this case the present discounted value criterion gives results identical to those outlined earlier using the rental rate approach

We have again demonstrated the algebraic relationship between a machine's current price, the rental rate on the machine, and the market rate of interest. In particular, an increase in r will decrease the machine's PDV, and firms will be less willing to buy machines for the same reasons as we discussed before—opportunity costs are too high. This result is quite general. The present discounted value approach to investment and the rental rate approach are alternative ways of phrasing the same idea. However, as "Applying Economics: The Economist and the Car Dealer" shows, PDV calculations can be useful

APPLYING ECONOMICS

The Economist and the Car Dealer

In 1985 an economist well known to this author ventured into an automobile showroom to buy a new car. He quickly settled on a no-frills family car with a final price tag of $10,000 (in round numbers). Before reaching final agreement with the salesman, the nervous economist was introduced to the manager of the firm who was supposed to close the deal.

The manager's pitch was a smooth one. "You look like a sensible and frugal buyer," he said. "Do I have a deal for you! We have just signed a great financing package with a local bank to make car loans. I can let you have this car now and all you have to do is pay back $3,100 per year for the next four years. You will pay back $12,400—$10,000 for the car and $2,400 in finance charges. If you instead pay for the car with $10,000 in cash you'll lose, say, 7 percent each year by taking your money out of the bank. This amounts to $2,800 over four years. By financing with us you save $400."

This final appeal to opportunity cost sounded good to the economist, but he smelled a rat. How could the car dealer (or dealer's bank) offer more favorable financing than the economist made on his account at that same bank? Something was wrong. As the startled car dealer looked on, the economist pulled out his calculator to evaluate the present value of the repayment scheme being proposed. He used 7 percent as his opportunity cost:

$$\text{PDV of auto loan} = \frac{\$3{,}100}{(1.07)} + \frac{\$3{,}100}{(1.07)^2} + \frac{\$3{,}100}{(1.07)^3}$$
$$+ \frac{\$3{,}100}{(1.07)^4} = \$10{,}500.$$

So this loan was actually more costly than paying for

the car with cash even after accounting for opportunity costs. To cinch the analysis the economist pressed the dealer to reveal the true interest rate in his offer (which by law he was required to do). After some complaints about how such figures "distort the real picture," he announced the true cost as 9.2 percent—considerably more than the economist made in his paltry savings account. The "deal" being offered was no deal at all. After a bit more verbal sparring, the economist was handed back to the salesman (who seemed embarrassed by the whole episode) and proceeded to buy the car with cash. He has not taken the car back to this dealer for service since then, however.

The trick in the car dealer's offer is obvious. He was not offering to lend the purchase price of the car for four years. Instead, the scheme he proposed (similar to all consumer credit purchase schemes) required repayment of some of the loan's principal each year. Effectively, the economist would have been borrowing much less than $10,000 for the entire period. The car dealer's opportunity cost calculations were misleading, and the economist was (at least on this occasion) saved from a costly mistake by a simple application of the present value concept.

To Think About
1. Suppose the car dealer had allowed his entire $12,400 charge to be paid at the end of four years. Then, would his argument be correct? How much would the economist save by taking such a deal?
2. How would you compute the "true" interest charge on the car dealer's offer? Does this figure actually "distort the true picture"? In general, do laws requiring disclosure of true interest charges seem desirable?

in a wide variety of other contexts. The next two sections use the present value concept to study two additional applications of capital theory: human capital and the pricing of resources that are in fixed supply.

Human Capital

One important application of the theory of capital concerns a very different kind of investment from what we have been discussing so far—the investment that a person can make in himself or herself. People can invest in themselves in a variety of ways. They can acquire a formal education, they may accept apprenticeships and learn skills on the job, they can spend considerable efforts in looking for better jobs, or they can purchase various kinds of medical services that maintain them in good health. All of those activities can be looked upon as "investments" since both time and money are sacrificed currently in the hope that this will somehow pay off in the future.

Human capital
Capital in the form of learned abilities acquired through training, education, or experience.

By acquiring skills or buying good health, people are adding to their stock of **human capital** in much the same way that the purchase of machines by firms adds to the firms' stock of physical capital. There is substantial evidence that most additions to human capital are quite productive—they help people to increase their earnings in future years. In fact, it has been found that there are many investments that individuals make in themselves that yield returns substantially in excess of the prevailing rate of return on other investments.[9] In this section we discuss how such calculations are made with specific evidence in the next "Applying Economics" example. Finally, we describe some of the ways in which human capital differs from physical capital.

Calculating the Yield on an Investment

Conceptually, it is an easy matter to compute the rate of return (or yield) that an individual receives from an investment in human capital (or on any other kind of capital investment, for that matter). Suppose that the cost of an investment that someone is intending to make is given by C. Suppose also that the investment is expected to raise this person's earnings in each year in the future and that these additions to earnings are given by $I_1, I_2, \ldots, I_n$. What we wish to know is what interest rate i will discount these earnings increments to make them exactly equal to C. Mathematically, we know C and I, and we wish to find that value of i that solves the equation:

$$C = \frac{I_1}{(1 + i)} + \frac{I_2}{(1 + i)^2} + \ldots + \frac{I_n}{(1 + i)^n} + \ldots . \qquad [16.14]$$

The value of i that solves Equation 16.14 would be called the rate of return on this particular investment (see the appendix to this chapter for a discussion of this calculation). "Applying Economics: Yields on Investments in Schooling and On-the-Job Training" illustrates some results that are typically obtained from this kind of calculation.

---

[9]For a thorough analysis of the educational aspects of human capital formation, see G. S. Becker, *Human Capital,* National Bureau of Economic Research (New York: Columbia University Press, 1964). For a treatment of the human capital approach to the study of medical expenditures, see Michael Grossman, *The Demand for Health,* National Bureau of Economic Research Occasional Paper 119 (New York: Columbia University Press, 1972).

Limitations of the Human Capital Approach

Although this analogy between human and physical capital provides many insights into the nature of people's decisions about gaining skills and education, it should not be pushed too far. Human capital has a number of special properties that make it unique among the assets an individual can buy. Contrary to other assets, human capital cannot (in the absence of slavery) be sold. The owner of human capital is inextricably tied to his or her investment. Although a person may "rent" out this investment to employers for a wage, he or she may not sell it in the way a firm might sell a machine it no longer needed. Human capital also depreciates in a rather unusual way. It is totally lost upon the death of its owner. This makes the investment rather risky. Finally, the acquisition of human capital may take substantial time. Whereas a firm seeking to buy a drill press may only have to spend five minutes to make a phone call, people who wish to improve their skills must usually invest considerable time, perhaps years, in doing so. The irreversibility of time makes this process of human capital investment all the more risky.

Pricing of Finite Natural Resources

As a final application of the results of basic capital theory we consider how markets will price finite natural resources over time. At times, much concern has been expressed about the possible exhaustion of some finite resources. In the mid 1970s, for example, considerable attention was focused on the adequacy of known petroleum reserves. On other occasions concern has also been expressed about the supply of a wide variety of finite resources ranging from diamonds to fresh water. Our principal concern here is the implications of the fact that these resources are in finite supply for their pricing.

Scarcity Costs

Scarcity costs
The opportunity costs of forgone future production that cannot be made because of current production that uses finite resources.

What makes the production of exhaustible resources different from the production of any other economic good is that current production from a finite resource stock reduces the amount of the resource available for the future. This might be contrasted to the usual case of production in which firms' activities during one year have no effect on their production activities the next year. Producers of an exhaustible resource must take an additional cost into account in their current production decisions: the opportunity cost of forgone sales in the future. To study that cost formally, economists define the **scarcity costs** associated with current production of an exhaustible resource as the opportunity costs of forgone future sales that cannot be made because of that current production. Recognition of such costs does not imply that firms will produce no output, constantly hoarding their resources for some future time. But they will be careful to incorporate the full opportunity costs of current sales in their decisions.

APPLYING ECONOMICS

Yields on Investments in Schooling and On-the-Job Training

The two most important human capital investments people make are in formal schooling and in on-the-job training. Costs of investment in schooling are of two types. First are explicit costs such as tuitions and fees, transportation costs, and other incidental expenses. A second, and probably larger, component of schooling costs is the implicit opportunity costs of forgone earnings while in school. Because people could hold jobs instead of attending school, potential earnings on those jobs must be considered a cost of formal education. A similar opportunity cost argument suggests that if people forsake some earnings in order to learn skills that will be useful to them in the future, these forgone earnings are a cost of accumulating job skills. Since most skills that are specific to a particular occupation are probably learned on the job, wages will be lower during this learning period. The costs of on-the-job training are composed primarily of these temporarily forgone wages.

A 1970 study by Thomas Johnson attempted to estimate the dollar costs of these two types of human capital investments.[10] A few of the author's results for males in 1959 are presented in Table 16.3. The table shows that on-the-job training costs are about the same for individuals of differing educational levels. Most workers require about the same degree of initial preparation when starting out on a job. As would be expected, the costs of formal schooling rise rapidly for individuals with higher educational levels. Workers with less than a high school education have invested relatively little in formal schooling (less than $4,000—composed primarily of forgone earnings). More than three-quarters of such workers' total human capital investments are in on-the-job training. For more highly educated people, formal schooling costs may be quite high. Those with education beyond the college level have a total investment that may average over $40,000 (in 1959 dollars). Again, the principal component of this cost is the earnings college graduates forgo when they attend graduate school.

The investments in human capital shown in Table 16.3 seem to pay off in increasing total lifetime incomes. For example, on average, individuals with a college education earned nearly $100,000 more over their lifetimes than did those with only a high school education. The final column of Table 16.3 presents the percentage yields on total human capital investments. These yields were calculated using a formula similar to Equation 16.14. All of the yields are positive, indicating that formal schooling and on-the-job training do indeed pay off in increased earnings. The yields diminish for higher levels of formal education, however, and this suggests some kind of diminishing return to human capital investments may exist. As for any other economic activity, it appears to be possible to push investments in human capital too far. Indeed, more recent data tend to indicate that the returns to college education have fallen below

The implications of scarcity costs for pricing are illustrated in Figure 16.4. In the absence of those costs, the industry supply curve for the resource would be given by S and that curve would, as usual, reflect the marginal costs of actually producing (that is, drilling, mining, or refining) the resource. Scarcity costs (related to the finiteness of the ultimately available resource supply) shift firms' marginal cost curves upward. The new market supply curve is S'. The gap between S' and S reflects the opportunity costs associated with forgone future sales. Current output is reduced (from Q^* to Q') when firms recognize

---

[10]Thomas Johnson, "Returns from Investment in Human Capital," *American Economic Review*, September 1970, pp. 546–560.

Table 16.3
Investments in Human Capital and the Yield of Those Investments for White Males in the Northern United States, 1959

Years of Education Completed	Investment in Schooling	Investment in On-the-Job Training	Total Investment in Human Capital	Total Lifetime Income	Yield on Investment in Human Capital
9–11	$ 3,760	$15,316	$19,076	$220,025	24.6%
12	9,408	14,704	24,112	245,433	21.5
13–15	11,293	17,170	28,463	278,323	17.5
16	27,800	18,216	46,016	341,856	15.5
17+	40,738	23,033	63,771	380,626	13.5

Source: Thomas Johnson, "Returns from Investment in Human Capital," *American Economic Review*, September 1970, pp. 546–560, Table 3.

those in Table 16.3, primarily because of the rapid increase in the number of college graduates over the past 20 years. All of the yields in Table 16.3 are, however, well above yields on alternative investments that people might make (savings accounts, bonds, and so forth) and this may reflect the unique nature of human capital investments.

To Think About

1. If education offers such a high return, why should it be subsidized by the government? Doesn't the high return give people an adequate incentive to purchase their own education? Can you think of reasons why one might want to subsidize, say, elementary and secondary education? Do these reasons also apply to professional training such as medical or law school?

2. If workers obtain higher wages as a result of on-the-job training, who pays for that training? Do firms have an incentive to provide the training or do workers in effect pay for it by accepting low wages when they are new on the job?

the finiteness of the resource supply. This reduction reflects firms' preference for withholding some of the resource from current supply in order to be able to sell it in the future.

Scarcity Costs and Resource Prices

The actual value of scarcity costs depends on firms' perceptions about what resource prices will be in the future. Knowledge of those prices is required if owners are to be able to calculate correctly the opportunity costs associated with current sales out of their resource stocks. As a simple example, suppose a firm that owns a silver mine knows that silver will sell for $1 per ounce in 20 years. Since the amount of silver in the mine is fixed, selling an ounce today

Figure 16.4
Scarcity Costs Associated
with Exhaustible Resources

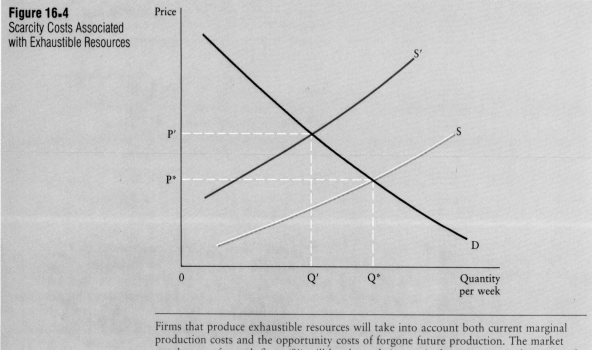

Firms that produce exhaustible resources will take into account both current marginal
production costs and the opportunity costs of forgone future production. The market
supply curve for such firms (S′) will be above their marginal cost curves to the extent of
those scarcity costs.

will mean forgoing this $1 sale in 20 years. If we assume that the real interest
rate is 5 percent, Table 16.2 shows that the present value of this opportunity
cost is $.38. Assuming the mine owner is indifferent between selling the silver
in 20 years or today, the current market price should also be $.38 per ounce.
That is the only price that reflects an equilibrium between present and future
sales. Any lower current price would encourage the mine owner to leave the
silver in the ground since it will be worth more later even taking account of
forgone interest in the meantime. A current price above $.38 would, on the
other hand, cause the owner to sell as much silver as possible today and not
wait for 20 years.

   Our calculation of scarcity costs proceeds by comparing the price of silver
to its actual production costs. If the marginal cost of producing an ounce of
silver is $.20 an ounce, then scarcity costs would be $.18 per ounce since that
is the amount by which the current equilibrium price exceeds marginal production cost. In this case, the fact that price exceeds marginal cost is not a
sign of inefficiency. Instead, it shows that all costs are fully reflected in the
price.

   An important implication of this discussion is that in the absence of any
changes in production costs or in expectations about future prices, the market
price of silver would be expected to increase over time at the rate of return

What Should the Price of Oil Be?

Did the 1982 market price of crude oil (about $34 per barrel) reflect scarcity costs arising from the finite nature of oil reserves, or did it more properly reflect (perhaps temporary) monopoly rents? The possibility that the price represented actual marginal costs of production can be readily dismissed since there was general agreement that the marginal costs of the lowest cost producer (Saudi Arabia) were around $2 to $3 per barrel.

In order to assess scarcity costs in 1982, we have to assume something about the future price of oil. Although there is considerable disagreement on that subject, there is some consensus that by the year 2020 (38 years from 1982) energy will be generally available from new technologies (solar, fusion, tidal, geothermal, and so forth) at the equivalent of $50 to $70 per barrel of oil (in 1982 prices).[11] Taking the upper range of these numbers and assuming that r is 4 percent gives

$$\text{PDV of a barrel of oil} = \frac{\$70}{(1.04)^{38}} = \$15.77 \quad [16.15]$$

as the equilibrium present value. The 1982 market price was more than twice what appeared to be dictated by the scarcity value of oil.

The Organization of Petroleum Exporting Countries cartel may have exercised quite a bit of monopoly influence in setting the market price. Experiences since 1982 are consistent with this interpretation. The worldwide recession of 1982–1983 put severe pressure on the OPEC pricing structure. By 1985 there was serious bickering within the cartel over how to allocate production among its members, and this resulted in further price weakness. By early 1986 the market price for oil had fallen into the $14 to $15 range, suggesting that most of OPEC's power to determine prices had been eroded and that the price of oil now closely reflected both production and scarcity costs.

To Think About
1. The notion that OPEC acted as a monopoly cartel and raised the price of crude oil is based on a simple, single-period model of monopoly behavior. How does the recognition that oil is a finite resource affect that model? If OPEC sharply raises oil prices currently, won't it find that it has too much oil left to sell at some date in the future? What restraints on current behavior of the cartel are provided by the need to sell oil profitably in the future?
2. The model of finite resource pricing that we present assumes the amount of resources is known. How would the analysis change if the quantities of resource reserves were not known accurately and could only be discovered through exploration? How would unexpected new finds affect resource prices?

on alternative investments. If r is 5 percent, for example, real silver prices would be expected to rise at 5 percent a year.[12] Only by following that path would prices always equal the present value of $1 in 20 years.

This result can be shown intuitively from another perspective. Any firm will evaluate its resource holdings in the same way as any other investment. Investments in resources should yield the same return r as those alternatives.

---

[11]See, for example, W. D. Nordhaus, "The Allocation of Energy Resources," *Brookings Papers on Economic Activity*, 1973, No. 3, pp. 529–570.

[12]Since r is a "real" rate of return (that is, corrected for inflation), the prediction here is that the price of the resource relative to the price of all other goods should rise at the rate r. This result was first rigorously shown by Harold Hotelling in "The Economics of Exhaustible Resources," *Journal of Political Economy*, April 1931, pp. 137–175.

Only if the real prices of finite resources increase at the rate r will they provide such a return to their owners. If prices were rising slower than r, natural resources would be an inferior investment and owners should put their funds elsewhere. A rate of price rise above r per year is also unsustainable in the long run because investors would bid up the current price of resources to reflect their investment desirability. This bidding up of prices would continue until the possibility for further increases in excess of r was eliminated. This principle of the pricing of scarce finite resources can be used to study a variety of economic issues, as "Applying Economics: What Should the Price of Oil Be?" illustrates.

Summary

The fundamental concept introduced in this chapter is the rate of return (or real interest rate), which shows the terms at which present goods can be exchanged for future goods. It is this "price" that ties together economic decisions made in different time periods. The rate of return is a primary influence on the allocation of resources over time. We show these effects in several contexts:

- The rate of return, because it represents an important opportunity cost incurred by firms that own machines, directly affects firms' input choices. A higher rate of return raises the rental costs of capital and thereby discourages investment.
- The real interest rate is also important for calculating the present value of payments to be made in different time periods. Such payments can only be compared once the opportunity costs of interest forgone are taken into account.
- Human capital represents a particular type of investment that people may make in themselves. Rates of return on such investments may be rather high, possibly because of the risky features of such investments.
- Finite resources pose important allocational problems because using some quantity of them in one year precludes use of those resources in later years. The logic of interest rate computations suggests that the relative price of finite resources should increase over time at a rate equal to the real rate of interest.

Problems

16.1 Mr. Moneybags is thinking of buying a bond issued by the ABC Corporation. Mr. Moneybags' economist friend tells him that a fair price for the bond is the bond's present discounted value. The face value of the bond is $10,000, which will be given to Mr. Moneybags at the end of five years. In addition, the bond promises to pay five "coupons" of $1,000 at the end of each year. Assuming the market interest rate (i) is 12 percent annually, what is a fair price for the bond? What if i = 8 percent instead? What is the relationship between bond prices and interest rates?

16.2 The president of the Acme Landfill Company has estimated that the purchase of 10 more deluxe dump trucks can bring in added revenues of $100,000 a year for the life of the trucks. The trucks have a life span of seven years and cost $50,000 each. If the company can earn a 10 percent rate of return on investments in alternative ventures, should it go ahead and purchase the trucks? What if the company found that it could only earn a 9 percent return on its alternative investments? Should it go ahead with the purchase?

16.3 A high pressure life insurance salesman was heard to make the following argument: "At your age a $100,000 whole life policy is a much better buy than a similar term policy. Under a whole life policy you'll have to pay $2,000 per year for the first four years, but nothing more for the rest of your life. A term policy will cost you $400 per year, essentially forever. If you live 35 years, you'll pay only $8,000 for the whole life policy, but $14,000 for the term policy. Surely the whole life is a better deal."

Assuming the salesman's life expectancy assumption is correct, how would you evaluate this argument? Specifically, calculate the present discounted value of the premium costs of the two policies assuming that the interest rate is 10 percent.

16.4 Suppose J. P. Miser obtains utility from present and future consumption (C_1 and C_2) and that she has a certain amount of dollars (Y) to allocate between these goods.

   a. If the interest rate is r, what will the budget constraint in this problem be?
   b. Using the budget constraint from part a, show graphically how Y will be allocated between C_1 and C_2 to maximize utility. What will the tangency condition for a utility maximum be in this situation?
   c. Suppose r were to increase. What will happen to the utility-maximizing choices for C_1 and C_2?

*16.5 Assume that an individual expects to work for 40 years, then retire with a life expectancy of an additional 20 years. Suppose also that the individual's earnings rise at a rate of 3 percent per year and that the interest rate is also 3 percent (the overall price level is constant in this problem). What (constant) fraction of income must the individual save in each working year to be able to finance a level of retirement income equal to 60 percent of earnings in the year just prior to retirement?

16.6 The No-Flite Golfball Company manufactures cut-proof golfballs and is thinking of investing in a new name. Its media personnel have come up with two suggestions: "Astro-Flite" and "Jack Nickless." It is cheaper to switch to Astro-Flite since the second name will involve legal fees for dealing with a well-known golfer who is likely to get upset by the

---

*Denotes a problem that is rather difficult.

whole thing. The second name, however, is expected to bring in more business than the first. If the costs and payoffs are as given below, and the firm expects to go out of business in five years, is it worth it to make a name switch, and if so, to which name?

	Cost	Yearly Return	Interest Rate
Astro-Flite	$3,800	$1,000	10%
Jack Nickless	5,000	1,400	10

Would your answer change if the interest rate were 15 percent?

16.7 Some foresters suggest that timber plots be managed so as to achieve "maximum sustainable yield." Would an economist agree that a single tree should be grown to maturity before it is cut down and sold as lumber (since trees begin to grow more slowly as they get older)? How would an economist manage a whole forest of trees? How might the problem be complicated by a forest of trees of widely different ages (and growth rates)?

*16.8 Suppose scotch increases in value as it ages. In particular, the value of scotch at any time t is given by $V = 100t - 6t^2$ and the proportional growth rate in that value is $100 - 12t/V$. Graph this scotch function. At what value of t is V as large as possible? Is that when the scotch should be bottled? If the interest rate is 5 percent, when should the scotch be bottled?

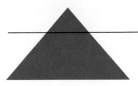

COMPOUND INTEREST

People encounter compound interest concepts almost every day. Calculating returns on bank accounts, deciding on the true cost of an automobile loan, or buying a home with a mortgage all involve the use of interest rate computations. This appendix shows how some of those computations are made. The methods introduced are useful not only in economics classes, but in many personal economic decisions too.

Interest

Interest
Payment for the current use of funds.

Interest is payment for the time value of money. A borrower gets to use funds for his or her own purposes for a time and in return pays the lender some compensation. Interest rates are usually stated as some percentage of the amount borrowed (the principal). For example, an annual interest rate of 5 percent would require that someone who borrowed $100 would pay $5 per year in interest.

Throughout this appendix we assume that the market has established an annual interest rate, i, and that this interest rate will persist from one year to the next. It is a relatively simple matter to deal with interest rates that change from one period to another, but we do not consider them here. We are also not particularly interested in whether i is a "nominal" interest rate (such as a rate quoted by a bank) or a "real" interest rate that has been adjusted for any inflation that may occur over time.[1] The mathematics of compound interest is the same for both nominal and real interest rates.

Compound Interest

Compound interest
Interest paid on prior interest earned.

If you hold funds in a bank for more than one period, you will receive **compound interest**—that is, you will receive interest not only on your original principal but also on the interest that you earned in prior periods and left in the bank. Compounding is relatively complicated and results in rather dramatic growth over long periods.

If you invest $1 at the interest rate of i, at the end of one year you will have

$$\$1 + \$1 \cdot i = \$1 \cdot (1 + i). \qquad [16A.1]$$

---

[1]Nominal and real interest rates can be related by the formula $i = r + \bar{p}$ where i is the nominal interest rate per year, r is the real interest rate, and $\bar{p}$ is the expected annual rate of inflation.

For example, if i is 5 percent at the end of one year, you will have

$$\$1 + \$1 \cdot (.05) = \$1 \cdot (1.05) = \$1.05. \qquad [16A.2]$$

If at the end of the first year you leave your money in the bank, you will now earn interest on both the original \$1 and on your first year's interest. At the end of two years you will therefore have

$$\$1(1 + i) + \$1 \cdot (1 + i) \cdot i$$
$$= \$1 \cdot (1 + i)(1 + i)$$
$$= \$1 \cdot (1 + i)^2 \qquad [16A.3]$$

To understand Equation 16A.3 it is helpful to expand the term $(1 + i)^2$. Remember from high school algebra that

$$(1 + i)^2 = 1 + 2i + i^2. \qquad [16A.4]$$

At the end of two years, \$1 will grow to

$$\$1 \cdot (1 + i)^2 = \$1 \cdot (1 + 2i + i^2)$$
$$= \$1 + \$1 \cdot (2i) + \$1 \cdot i^2. \qquad [16A.5]$$

At the end of two years you will have the sum of three amounts:

1. Your original \$1.
2. Two years' interest on your original \$1—\$1 $\cdot$ 2i.
3. Interest on your first year's interest—$[(\$1 \cdot i) \cdot i] = \$1 \cdot i^2$.

If, again, the interest rate is 5 percent, at the end of two years you will have

$$\$1 \cdot (1.05)^2 = \$1 \cdot (1.1025) = \$1.1025. \qquad [16A.6]$$

This represents the sum of your original \$1, two years' interest on the \$1 (that is, \$.10), and interest on the first year's interest (5 percent of \$.05, which is \$.0025). The fact that you will have more than \$1.10 is a reflection of compounding. As we look at longer and longer periods of time, the effects of this compounding become much more pronounced.

If you now leave these funds, which after two years amount to $\$1 \cdot (1 + i)^2$, in the bank for another year, at the end of this third year you will have

$$\$1 \cdot (1 + i)^2 + \$1 \cdot (1 + i)^2 \cdot i$$
$$= \$1 \cdot (1 + i)^2(1 + i)$$
$$= \$1 \cdot (1 + i)^3. \qquad [16A.7]$$

Table 16A.1

Effects of Compound Interest for Various Interest Rates and Time Periods with an Initial Investment of $1

Years	Interest Rate			
	1 Percent	**3 Percent**	**5 Percent**	**10 Percent**
1	$1.01	$ 1.03	$ 1.05	$ 1.10
2	1.0201	1.0609	1.1025	1.2100
3	1.0303	1.0927	1.1576	1.3310
5	1.051	1.159	1.2763	1.6105
10	1.1046	1.344	1.6289	2.5937
25	1.282	2.094	3.3863	10.8347
50	1.645	4.384	11.4674	117.3909
100	2.705	19.219	131.5013	13,780.6123

For an interest rate of 5 percent, this amounts to

$$\$1 \cdot (1 + .05)^3 = \$1 \cdot (1.157625) = \$1.157625. \qquad [16A.8]$$

The fact that you get more than simply your original $1 and three years' simple interest ($.15) again reflects the effects of compounding.[2]

By now the pattern should be clear. If you leave your $1 in the bank for any number of years, n, you will have, at the end of that period,

$$\text{Value of \$1 compounded for n years} = \$1 \cdot (1 + i)^n. \qquad [16A.9]$$

With a 5 percent interest rate and a period of 10 years, you would have

$$\$1 \cdot (1.05)^{10} = \$1 \cdot (1.62889\ldots) = \$1.62889. \qquad [16A.10]$$

Without compounding you would have had $1.50—your original $1 plus 10 years' interest at $.05 per year. The extra $.12889 comes about through compounding.

To illustrate the effects of compounding further, Table 16A.1 shows the value of $1 compounded for various time periods and interest rates.[3] Notice how compounding becomes very important for long periods. For instance, Table 16A.1 shows that, at a 5 percent interest rate, $1 grows to be $131.50 over 100 years. This represents the original $1, simple interest of $5 ($.05 per year for 100 years), and a massive $125.50 in interest earned on prior interest. At higher interest rates the effect of compounding is even more pronounced

---

[2]As an exercise, you may wish to expand $(1 + i)^3$ and see whether you can explain the meaning of each of the four terms in the expression.

[3]Because these computations are burdensome, they are often made using either a calculator or interest rate tables. Calculators capable of doing fairly sophisticated interest calculations can be purchased for about $20 in 1987.

since there is even more prior interest on which to earn interest. At a 1 percent interest rate, only about 26 percent of the funds accumulated over 100 years represent the effects of compounding. At a 10 percent interest rate more that 99.9 percent of the huge amount accumulated represents the effects of compounding.

The use of one dollar in all of the computations we have made so far was for convenience only. Any other amount of money grows in exactly the same way. Investing $1,000 is just the same as investing a thousand one-dollar bills—at an interest rate of 5 percent this amount would grow to $1,050 at the end of one year [$1,000 · (1.05)]; it would grow to $1,629 at the end of ten years [$1,000 · (1.629)]; and to $131,501 at the end of one hundred years [$1,000 · (131.501)].

Algebraically, D dollars invested for n years at an interest rate of i will grow to

$$\text{Value of \$D invested for n years} = \$D \cdot (1 + i)^n. \quad [16A.11]$$

"Applying Economics: Compound Interest Gone Berserk" illustrates some particularly extreme examples of using this formula.

Present Discounted Value

Because interest is paid on invested dollars, a dollar you get today is more valuable than one you won't receive until next year. You could put a dollar you receive today in a bank and have more than a dollar in one year. If you wait a year for the dollar you will do without this interest that you could have earned.

Economists use the concept of **present discounted value** (sometimes termed *present value*) to reflect this opportunity cost notion. The present discounted value of the dollar you will not get for one year is simply the amount you would have to put in a bank now to have $1 at the end of one year. If the interest rate is 5 percent, for example, the present value of $1 to be obtained in one year is about $.95—if you invest $.95 today you will have $1 in one year, so $.95 accurately reflects the present value of $1 in one year.

More formally, if the interest rate is i, the present discounted value of $1 in one year is $1/(1 + i)$ since

Present discounted value
The current value of funds payable in the future. After taking account of the opportunity cost of interest forgone.

$$\$1/(1 + i) \cdot (1 + i) = \$1. \quad [16A.12]$$

If i = 5 percent, the present discounted value (PDV) of $1 in one year is

$$\text{PDV} = \$1/(1.05) = \$.9524 \quad [16A.13]$$

and

$$\$.9524 \cdot (1.05) = \$1. \quad [16A.14]$$

APPLYING ECONOMICS

Compound Interest Gone Berserk

The effects of compounding can be gigantic if a sufficiently long period is used. Consider the author's two favorite examples:

Manhattan Island
Legend has it that in 1623 Dutch settlers purchased Manhattan Island from the native Americans living there for trinkets worth about $24. Suppose these native Americans had invested this $24 at 5 percent interest for the 364 years between 1623 and 1987. Using Equation 16A.11, in 1987 they would have

$$\$24 \cdot (1.05)^{364} = \$24 \cdot (51,630,325)$$
$$= \$1,239,127,807.$$

Over 364 years, their $24 would have grown to more than $1 billion. With a higher interest rate (say 10 percent) the figure would be much larger—exceeding by far the entire value of Manhattan Island in 1987.

Horse Manure
In the 1840s the horse population of Philadelphia was growing at nearly 10 percent per year. Projecting this growth into the future, the city fathers began to worry about excessive crowding and potential pollution of the streets from manure. So they passed restrictions on the number of horses allowed in the city. It's a good thing! If the 1840 horse population of 50,000 had continued to grow at 10 percent per year into the 1980s there would have been quite a few:

$$\text{Number of horses} = 50,000 \cdot (1 + i)^{140}$$
$$= 50,000 \cdot (1.10)^{140}$$
$$= 50,000 \cdot (623,700)$$
$$= 31,185,000,000.$$

With these 31 billion horses the manure problem would have been severe—amounting to perhaps 200 feet per year over the entire city. The City of Brotherly Love (the author's hometown) was spared this fate through timely governmental action.

To Think About
1. The tongue-in-cheek nature of these examples suggests there is probably something wrong with such simplistic applications of compound interest. For each of the examples explain carefully why the calculations are pure nonsense.
2. At high interest rates, compounding can produce spectacular results even for relatively short time periods. In the late 1970s for example, it was possible to invest in bonds that yielded 15 percent per year. How much would you have to invest now at 15 percent to have $1 million in, say, 45 years when you retire? Do you think this calculation is "reasonable"? What does it overlook?

A similar computation would result for any other interest rate. For example the PDV of $1 payable in one year is $.971 if the interest rate is 3 percent, but $.909 when the interest rate is 10 percent. With a higher interest rate, the PDV is lower because the opportunity costs involved in waiting to get $1 are greater.

Waiting two years to get paid involves even greater opportunity costs than waiting one year since now you forgo two years' interest. At an interest rate of 5 percent, $.907 will grow to be $1 in two years—that is, $1 = $.907 · $(1.05)^2$. Consequently, the present value of $1 payable in two years is only $.907. More generally, for any interest rate, i, the present value of $1 payable in two years is

$$\text{PDV of \$1 payable in two years} = \$1/(1 + i)^2 \qquad [16A.15]$$

Table 16A.2

Present Discounted Value
of One Dollar for Various
Time Periods and Interest
Rates

Year until Payment Is Received	Interest Rate			
	1 Percent	3 Percent	5 Percent	10 Percent
1	$.99010	$.97087	$.95238	$.90909
2	.98030	.94260	.90703	.82645
3	.97059	.91516	.86386	.75131
5	.95147	.86281	.78351	.62093
10	.90531	.74405	.61391	.38555
25	.78003	.47755	.29531	.09230
50	.60790	.22810	.08720	.00852
100	.36969	.05203	.00760	.00007

Note: These amounts are the reciprocals of those in Table 16A.1

and for the case of a 5 percent interest rate

$$\text{PDV of \$1 payable in two years} = \$1/(1.05)^2$$

$$= \$1/1.1025$$

$$= \$.907. \qquad\qquad [16A.16]$$

The pattern should now be obvious. With an interest rate of i the present value of $1 payable after any number of years, n, is simply

$$\text{PDV of \$1 payable in n years} = \$1/(1 + i)^n. \qquad [16A.17]$$

Calculating present values is the reverse of computing compound interest. In the compound interest case (Equation 16A.9) the calculation requires multiplying by the interest factor $(1 + i)^n$ whereas in the present discounted value case (Equation 16A.17) the calculation proceeds by dividing by that factor. Similarly, the present value of any number of dollars ($D) payable in n years is given by:

$$\text{PDV of \$D payable in n years} = \$D/(1 + i)^n. \qquad [16A.18]$$

Again, by comparing Equations 16A.11 and 16A.18 you can see the different ways that the interest factor $(1 + i)^n$ enters into the calculations.

In Table 16A.2 the author has again put his calculator to work to compute the present discounted value of $1 payable at various times and for various interest rates. The entries in this table are the reciprocals of the entries in Table 16A.1 since compounding and taking present values are different ways of looking at the same process. In Table 16A.2 the PDV of $1 payable in some particular year is smaller, the higher is the interest rate. Similarly, for a given interest rate, the PDV of $1 is smaller the longer it is until the $1 will be paid.

APPLYING ECONOMICS

Zero Coupon Bonds

Federal Treasury bonds sometimes include coupons that promise the owner of the bond a certain semiannual interest payment. For example, a thirty-year $1 million bond issued in 1987 with a 10 percent interest rate would include 60 semiannual coupons that represent the government's promise to pay $50,000 (that is, half of 10 percent of $1 million) on January 1 and July 1 of each year. The image of a Scrooge-like "coupon clipper" collecting regular interest payments in this way is a popular figure for financial cartoonists.

Unfortunately, this form of bond is not particularly convenient for investors. Bonds (and their attached coupons) may be lost, cashing the coupon necessitates a trip to the bank, and there is no easy way to reinvest interest payments to obtain the benefits of compounding. As a remedy for some of these problems in the late 1970s some financial firms began to introduce *zero coupon* bonds based on the Treasury obligations. These worked as follows: A brokerage firm would buy a bond (say the $1 million bond described above). Then it would "strip" the coupons from the bond and sell these as separate investments. For example, it would sell a coupon representing a $50,000 interest payment on January 1, 2010 to an investor who wished to invest his or her funds until then.

How much would such a stripped coupon be worth? The present discounted value formula gives the answer.

If the interest rate is 10 percent, the present value of $50,000 payable in 2010 (23 years from January 1, 1987) is

$$\frac{\$50,000}{(1 + i)^{23}} = \frac{\$50,000}{(1.10)^{23}} = \frac{\$50,000}{8.954} = \$5,583.$$

So the coupon would sell for $5,583 and would grow to nearly nine times this amount by 2010 when it was redeemed. Such a financial investment offers considerable advantages to an investor who does not want to be bothered with semiannual coupons, and zero-coupon bonds have proven to be quite popular.

To Think About
1. Does an investor who buys a zero-coupon bond have to leave his or her funds in that investment until the payment is due? Would someone who sells before this due date lose all interest earned? Are zero-coupon investments more risky than ordinary bonds?
2. Do the financial institutions offering zero-coupon bonds have to use Treasury coupons for their promises of future payments? Couldn't they just make the promises themselves and sell them in the market? What advantages are offered by using Treasury bond coupons as the basis for zero-coupon investments?

With a 10 percent interest rate, for example, a dollar that will not be paid for 50 years is worth less than one cent ($.00852) today. "Applying Economics: Zero Coupon Bonds" shows how such PDV calculations apply to a rapidly growing type of financial asset.

Discounting Payment Streams

Dollars payable at different points of time have different present values. One must be careful in calculating the true worth of streams of payments that occur at various times into the future—simply adding them up is not appropriate. Consider a situation which has irritated the author for some time. Many state lotteries promise grand prizes of $1 million that they pay to the winners over 25 years. But $40,000 per year for 25 years is not "worth" $1 million. Indeed, at a 10 percent interest rate the present value of such a stream is only $363,000—much less than half the amount falsely advertised by the state. This section describes how such a calculation can be made. There is really nothing new to learn about discounting streams of payments—performing the calculations always involves making careful use of the general discounting formula in Equation 16A.18. However, repeated use of that formula may be very time consuming (if a stream of income is paid, say, at one hundred different times in the future), and our main purpose here is to present a few shortcuts.

Consider a stream of payments that promises one dollar per year starting next year and continuing for three years. By applying Equation 16A.18 it is easy to see that the present value of this stream is

$$PDV = \frac{\$1}{(1 + i)} + \frac{\$1}{(1 + i)^2} + \frac{\$1}{(1 + i)^3}. \qquad [16A.19]$$

If the interest rate is 5 percent, this value would be:

$$\frac{\$1}{1.05} + \frac{\$1}{(1.05)^2} + \frac{\$1}{(1.05)^3}$$

$$= \$.9523 + \$.9070 + \$.8639$$

$$= \$2.7232. \qquad [16A.20]$$

Consequently, just as for the lottery, one dollar a year for three years is not worth three dollars, but quite a bit less because of the need to take forgone interest into account in making present value calculations.

If the promised stream of payments extends for longer than three years, additional terms should be added to Equation 16A.19. The present value of $1 per year for 5 years is

$$PDV = \frac{\$1}{(1 + i)} + \frac{\$1}{(1 + i)^2} + \frac{\$1}{(1 + i)^3} + \frac{\$1}{(1 + i)^4} + \frac{\$1}{(1 + i)^5} \quad [16A.21]$$

which amounts to about $4.33 at a 5 percent interest rate. Again, one dollar per year for five years is not worth five dollars.

Equation 16A.21 can be generalized to any number of years (n) by just adding the correct number of terms:

$$PDV = \frac{\$1}{(1 + i)} + \frac{\$1}{(1 + i)^2} + \cdots + \frac{\$1}{(1 + i)^n}. \qquad [16A.22]$$

Table 16A.3 uses this formula to compute the value of one dollar per year for various numbers of years and interest rates. Several features of the numbers in this table are important to keep in mind when discussing present values.

Table 16A.3
Present Value of $1 per Year for Various Time Periods and Interest Rates

Years of Payment	Interest Rate			
	1 Percent	3 Percent	5 Percent	10 Percent
1	$ .99	$ .97	$ .95	$ .91
2	1.97	1.91	1.86	1.74
3	2.94	2.83	2.72	2.49
5	4.85	4.58	4.33	3.79
10	9.47	8.53	7.72	6.14
25	22.02	17.41	14.09	9.08
50	39.20	25.73	18.26	9.91
100	63.02	31.60	19.85	9.99
Forever	100.00	33.33	20.00	10.00

As noted previously, none of the streams is worth in present value terms the actual number of dollars paid. The figures are always less than the number of years for which one dollar will be paid. Even for low interest rates the difference is substantial. With a 3 percent interest rate, one dollar per year for 100 years is worth only $31 in present value. At higher interest rates, the effect of discounting is even more pronounced. A dollar each year for 100 years is worth less than one-tenth of the total amount received in present value terms with an interest rate of 10 percent.

Perpetual Payments

The value of a stream of payments that goes on "forever" at one dollar per year is reported as the final entry in each column of Table 16A.3. To understand how this is calculated we pose the question in a slightly different way. How much ($X) would you have to invest at an interest rate of i to yield one dollar a year forever? That is, we wish to find $X that satisfies the equation

$$\$1 = i \cdot \$X. \qquad [16A.23]$$

But this just means that

$$\$X = \$1/i \qquad [16A.24]$$

Perpetuity
A promise of a certain number of dollars each year, forever.

which is the way the entries in the table were computed. For example, the present value of $1 per year forever with an interest rate of 5 percent is $20 (= $1/.05). With an interest rate of 10 percent the figure would be $10 (= $1/.10). Such a permanent payment stream is called a **perpetuity**. Although these are technically illegal in the United States (although many people set up "permanent" endowments for cemetery plots, scholarships and prize funds) other countries do permit such limitless contracts to be written. In the United Kingdom, for example, perpetuities originally written in the 1600s are still bought and sold. Equation 16A.24 shows that even though such perpetuities in principle promise an infinite number of dollars (since the payments never cease), in present value terms they have quite modest values. Indeed, for relatively high interest rates, there isn't much difference between getting one dollar a year for 25 or 50 years and getting it forever. At an interest rate of 10 percent, for example, the present value of a perpetuity (which promises an infinite number of dollars) is only $.92 greater than a promise of a dollar a year for only 25 years. The infinite number of dollars to be received after year 25 are only worth 92 cents![4]

Varying Payment Streams

The present value of a payment stream that consists of any given number of dollars per year can be calculated by multiplying the value of one dollar per year by that amount. In the lottery illustration with which we began this section, for example, we calculated the present value of $40,000 per year for 25 years. This is 40,000 times the entry for one dollar per year for 25 years at 10 percent from Table 16A.3—40,000 · $9.08 = $363,200. The present value of any other constant stream of dollar payments can be calculated in a similar fashion.

When payments vary from year to year, the computation can become more cumbersome. Each payment must be discounted separately using the formula given in Equation 16A.18. We can show this computation in its most general form by letting D_i represent the amount to be paid in any year i. Then the present value of this stream would be

---

[4]Using the formula for perpetuities provides a simple way of computing streams that run for only a certain number of years. Suppose we wished to evaluate a stream of $1 per year for 25 years at a 10 percent interest rate. If we used Equation 16A.22 we would need to evaluate 25 terms. Instead, we could note that a 25-year stream is an infinite stream less all payments for year 26 and beyond. The present value of a perpetual stream is

$$\frac{\$1}{i} = \frac{\$1}{.10} = \$10$$

whereas the present value of a perpetual stream that starts in year 25 is

$$\frac{\$10}{(1 + i)^{25}} = \frac{\$10}{(1 + .10)^{25}} = \frac{\$10}{(10.83)} = \$.92.$$

The value of a 25-year stream is

$$\$10 - \$.92 = \$9.08$$

which is the figure given in Table 16A.3.

More generally, a stream of $1 per year for n years at the interest rate i has a present value of

$$PDV = \frac{\$1}{i} - \frac{\$1/i}{(1 + i)^n}.$$

Mortgage Market Innovations

High interest rates in the late 1970s and early 1980s made it very difficult for young people to afford to buy a house using an ordinary mortgage. With such a mortgage, the borrower agrees to pay a fixed amount each month for the duration of the mortgage (usually 30 years). For example, with an interest rate of 10 percent a would-be buyer of a $100,000 home would have to pay $10,600 in annual mortgage payments ($883 per month) because the present value of $10,600 per year for 30 years is precisely the $100,000 needed to buy the house. Since such high mortgage payments were not affordable by many young people—especially in the early years of trying to establish a family when their incomes were fairly low—they sought alternative payment schedules that more closely met their economic circumstances.

It is important to understand the nature of the problem people faced. They were not "too poor" to afford a $100,000 house in any absolute sense. But, they were at an early stage in their careers when their earnings were low and were expected to grow. They also could reasonably expect the values of their homes to increase, if only they could get into the market in the first place.

In response to these needs, banks devised mortgages with payment streams that more closely met people's life patterns. There are, of course, an infinite number of possible payment streams that have a present value of $100,000 so there was plenty of room for innovations. Here we illustrate two of them.

Balloon Payments

With a balloon payment mortgage, some interest charges are pushed to the end of the mortgage in order to reduce monthly costs early in the mortgage. For example, a borrower could reduce his or her annual payments to about $8,800 ($733 per month) by agreeing to make a single balloon payment of $300,000 at the end of 30 years (presumably when the house would have appreciated substantially).

Graduated Payments

With this scheme, mortgage payments would increase over time to reflect the borrower's increased earnings. For example, the borrower could agree to pay $7,000 per year for the first ten years, $15,000 for the next ten years, and $23,000 for the final ten years and still get $100,000 currently to buy the house.

Numerous other schemes were devised during the early 1980s to further cushion the initial shock of mortgage payments. As interest rates fell in the middle of the decade, the attractiveness of these innovations declined as people seemed to prefer a fixed payment scheme.

To Think About

1. Doesn't paying $300,000 at the end of 30 years seem like a huge amount to save only $2,000 per year in mortgage payments? Explain why the balloon payment has to be so large to obtain a sizable reduction in payments.

2. Why don't people always opt for graduated payment schemes (assuming their incomes will grow)? Why might people want to spend a higher fraction of their income on housing when they are young than when they are old? Does the desire for fixed payments come more from lenders than borrowers?

$$PDV = \frac{D_1}{1 + i} + \frac{D_2}{(1 + i)^2} + \frac{D_3}{(1 + i)^3} + \cdots + \frac{D_n}{(1 + i)^n}. \quad [16A.25]$$

Here each D could be either positive or negative depending on whether funds are to be received or paid out. In some cases the computations may be rather complicated (as "Applying Economics: Mortgage Innovations" illustrates) so it may be a good idea to get a calculator that does the drudgery for you.

Frequency of Compounding

So far we have talked only about interest payments that are compounded once a year. That is, interest is paid at the end of each year and does not itself start to earn interest until the next year starts. In the past that was how banks worked. Every January 1 depositors were expected to bring in their bank books so that the past year's interest could be added to them. People who withdrew money from the bank prior to January 1 often lost all the interest they had earned so far in the year.

Recently, however, banks and all other financial institutions have started to use more frequent, usually daily, compounding. This has provided some extra interest to investors, because more frequent compounding means that prior interest earned will begin itself to earn interest more quickly. In this section we use the tools we have developed so far to explore this issue.

As before, assume the annual interest rate is given by i (or in some of our examples 5 percent). But now suppose the bank agrees to credit interest two times a year—on January 1 and on July 1. If you deposit $1 on January 1, by July 1 it will have grown to be $1 $(1 + i/2)$ since you will have earned half a year's interest. With an interest rate of 5 percent, you will have $1.025 on July 1. For the second half of the year you will earn interest on $1.025, not only on $1. At the end of the year you will have $1.025 $\cdot$ (1.025) = $1.05063, which is slightly larger than the $1.05 you would have with annual compounding. More generally, with an interest rate of i, semiannual compounding would yield

$$\$1(i + 1/2)(1 + i/2) = \$1(1 + i/2)^2 \qquad [16A.28]$$

at the end of one year. That this is superior to annual compounding can be shown with simple algebra:

$$\$1 \cdot (1 + i/2)^2 = \$1(1 + i + i^2/4)$$
$$= \$1 \cdot (1 + i) + \$1 \cdot i^2/4 \qquad [16A.29]$$

which is clearly greater than $1 $\cdot$ (1 + i). The final term in Equation 16A.29 simply reflects the interest earned in the first half of the year (i/2) times the interest rate in the second half of the year (i/2). This is the bonus earned by semiannual compounding.

We could extend this algebraic discussion to more frequent compounding—quarterly, monthly, or daily—but little new information would be added. More frequent compounding would continue to increase the effective yield that the 5 percent annual interest rate actually provides. Table 16A.4 shows how the frequency of compounding has this effect over time periods of various durations. The gains of using monthly rather than annual compounding are fairly large, especially over long periods of time when small differences in effective yields can make a big difference. Gains in going from monthly to daily compounding are fairly small, however. The extra yield from compound-

Table 16A.4
Value of $1 at a 5 Percent Annual Interest Rate Compounded with Different Frequencies and Terms

Years on Deposit	Frequency			
	Annual	**Semiannual**	**Monthly**	**Daily**
1	$ 1.0500	$ 1.0506	$ 1.0512	$ 1.0513
2	1.1025	1.1038	1.1049	1.1052
3	1.1576	1.1596	1.1615	1.1618
5	1.2763	1.2801	1.2834	1.2840
10	1.6289	1.6386	1.6471	1.6487
25	3.3863	3.4371	3.4816	3.4900
50	11.4674	11.8137	12.1218	12.1803
100	131.5013	139.5639	146.9380	148.3607

ing even more frequently (every second?) are even smaller.[5] Most banks currently utilize daily compounding both because they have been forced to do so by competitive pressures and because they find it fairly easy to adopt computer programs to make such payments.

Calculating Yields

Yield
The interest rate at which the present discounted value of the returns from an investment are exactly equal to the investments' current cost.

The compound interest formulas we have introduced so far can be easily reversed to solve for the interest return promised on an investment if the payments and the investment's present value are known. As a very simple example, suppose someone promises to give you $105 in one year if you give them $100 today. Obviously the interest rate promised here (what is more formally called the **yield**) is 5 percent. By comparing this yield to the yield on other investment options available, you can decide whether to give your $100 to this person.

In general, if an investment promises to pay D dollars n years from now and will charge you P dollars for this promise, we can use Equation 16A.18 to write

$$P = D/(1 + i)^n \qquad [16A.30]$$

but now we wish to solve this equation for the yield, i. To find the yield on a promise of, say, $1,000 in 10 years that costs $400 today, we would write

$$\$400 = \$1,000/(1 + i)^{10} \qquad [16A.31]$$

---

[5]An approximation to daily compounding is provided by the instantaneous compounding formula
$$\text{Value of } \$1 \text{ in year } n = e^{in}$$
where i is the annual interest rate and e is the base of natural logarithms (= 2.71828. . . .). For an explanation see Walter Nicholson, *Microeconomic Theory: Basic Principles and Extensions,* 3 ed. (Hinsdale, Ill.: Dryden, 1985), pp. 591–594.

and manipulate this expression to solve for i:

$$(1 + i)^{10} = \$1,000/\$400 = 2.5$$

or

$$(1 + i) = (2.5)^{1/10}. \qquad [16A.32]$$

At this stage you will need either a calculator or a set of yield tables since raising numbers to strange exponential powers is not easy to do by hand. Performing such a calculation gives

$$(1 + i) = (2.5)^{1/10} = 1.096 \qquad [16A.33]$$

or

$$i = .096. \qquad [16A.34]$$

So this investment has a yield of 9.6 percent.

In more complex cases investments will often promise different payments in various future periods and the rights to these payments can be purchased for some present cost. For example, when a firm buys a machine it is really purchasing the right to the stream of future profits that the machine generates. Calculating the yield (or what is sometimes called the *internal rate of return*) on such an investment again requires use of the present value formulas introduced earlier. Suppose that an automobile repair shop is thinking of buying an electronic engine tester that costs $10,000. The shop will earn $2,000 each year on this tester and will be able to sell it for $5,000 in five years when a new model becomes available. What is the yield in buying the tester? Using the present value formula in Equation 16A.25 gives

$$\$10,000 = \frac{\$2,000}{(1 + i)} + \frac{\$2,000}{(1 + i)^2} + \frac{\$2,000}{(1 + i)^3} + \frac{\$2,000}{(1 + i)^4}$$

$$+ \frac{\$2,000}{(1 + i)^5} + \frac{\$5,000}{(1 + i)^5} \qquad [16A.35]$$

—that is, the present cost of the tester ($10,000) should be equated to the present value of $2,000 per year for five years plus the present value of the price the machine will bring when it is sold.

Solving Equation 16A.35 by hand for the yield, i, is no simple task, but it can be easily done by modern calculators. The author's calculator provides a solution of i = 12.15 percent as the yield on this testing machine. The repair shop can compare this yield to that available on other equipment it might buy or to the return banks are offering to decide whether to purchase the tester.

Making such yield calculations therefore offers a convenient way of comparing the returns available from alternative investments that may provide very different payment streams. Our example in Chapter 16, "Applying Economics: The Economist and the Car Dealer" shows how these kinds of calculations can provide valuable information to would-be users of credit.

Summary

This appendix surveys the mathematical calculations that surround compound interest concepts. Dollars payable at different points of time are not identical (since those payable in the distant future require the sacrifice of some potential interest) and it is important to be careful in making comparisons among alternative payment schedules. In discussing this issue we show that

- In making compound interest calculations, it is necessary to take account of interest that is paid on prior interest earned. The interest factor $(1 + i)^n$—where n is the number of years over which interest is compounded—reflects this compounding.
- Dollars payable in the future are worth less than dollars payable currently. To compare dollars that are payable at different dates requires using present discounted value computations to allow for the opportunity costs associated with forgone interest.
- Evaluating payment streams requires that each individual payment be discounted by the appropriate interest factor. It is incorrect simply to add together dollars payable at different times.
- More frequent compounding leads to higher effective returns since prior interest paid begins to earn interest more quickly. There is an upper limit to the increased yield provided, however.
- The present discounted value formula can also be used to calculate yields on investments. The availability of such yields provides a convenient way to compare alternative investments in which the actual payment streams may be quite different.

GENERAL EQUILIBRIUM AND WELFARE

So far in this book we have taken a "positive" approach toward economic analysis. That is, we have developed in detail many models of the forces of supply and demand that seek to explain how markets actually operate. As we explain in Chapter 1, this approach closely parallels what physical scientists do—they develop models to explain and predict events that happen in the real world. In this final part of the book, we will move away from positive analysis a bit and adopt a slightly more normative approach. Our primary concern here is to explain how well private markets succeed in allocating scarce resources.

In *The Wealth of Nations* Adam Smith theorized that market forces operate like an "invisible hand" in guiding available resources into their best use.[1] Here we explore the extent to which Smith was right. We show that, as was usually the case, Smith's insights were remarkably astute—there is a clear connection between smoothly functioning markets and the efficient allocation of resources. But, there are also some important limitations of markets' liability to achieve desirable results in certain situations, and we examine these also.

Chapter 17 focuses on Smith's invisible hand hypothesis. It starts by describing how a smoothly operating market system might work. This discussion stresses the interconnections between different markets and describes in rather broad terms what a general equilibrium (many market) model of perfectly competitive markets might look like. The chapter then takes up the problem of defining what it means for an economy to allocate its resources "efficiently." The chapter shows that reliance on competitive markets will succeed in allocating resources efficiently. That is, we show that Adam Smith's hypothesis about the power of the invisible hand is essentially correct. This result, showing the connection between competitive markets and economic efficiency, is the most important conclusion of modern welfare economics.

There are economic forces that interfere with the ability of a competitive market to allocate resources effciently. We have already described one of these forces, monopoly, in Chapter 12. Two other problems are briefly mentioned in Chapter 17—difficulties posed by third-party effects (such as industrial pollution) that are not reflected in market prices; and difficulties posed by "public goods" that may have to be produced by the government and funded through compulsory taxation. These topics are taken up in detail in Chapters 18 and 19, respectively.

Chapter 17 concludes with a discussion of the issues of fairness or equity in the allocation of resources and shows some difficulties in defining and achieving that fairness.

The relationship between competitive pricing and efficiency is examined in a slightly different way in the

---

[1] Adam Smith, *The Wealth of Nations* (1776; New York: Modern Library, 1965), p. 423.

Appendix to Chapter 17. There we introduce a widely used mathematical tool, linear programming, and show how it can be employed to solve problems in allocating resources. Particular attention is devoted to the duality between the solutions to allocational problems and the prices that might bring the solutions about.

Chapter 18 examines the allocational problems caused by externalities—problems caused by effects of one person's actions on someone else (for example, harming people's health through pollution) that are not reflected in market transactions. The chapter first defines the notion of externalities precisely and illustrates the problems they cause. The chapter then focuses on possible solutions to the externality problem. Particular attention is devoted to the role that the legal definition of private property rights might have in this process. Chapter 18 concludes with some illustrations of how a full specification of such rights may significantly reduce problems associated with externalities. Chapter 18 offers a number of insights into the nature and economic function of private property.

One particular type of externality occurs in connection with what economists call public goods. Once these goods are produced, everyone benefits from them, whether or not they pay anything for these benefits. National defense is the traditional example—once an army is established, it protects everyone regardless of how much they pay for it with their taxes. Because of this feature of public goods, they are usually produced by governments and paid for through compulsory taxation. In Chapter 19 we study this process. Not only do we examine the problems that public goods pose for a market economy, we also investigate why the provision of public goods by the government may pose problems as well. This final chapter of the book considers some of the public choices that are made in allocating scarce resources. ▲

General Equilibrium and Economic Efficiency

Parts 4 and 5 of this book develop a variety of models to explain how markets work. For the most part, we have looked at the market for some specific commodity or factor of production and tried to explain how the forces of demand and supply operated to determine its price. In this chapter (and indeed in this final part of the book) we are interested in the question of how well markets function. Specifically, we develop a definition of what it means to allocate resources efficiently, and we then examine whether markets can achieve this goal.

We are examining a question first posed in the eighteenth century by Adam Smith, who saw in market forces an "invisible hand" that guides resources to their best use. Although the vast number of transactions that take place in an economy may seem like utter chaos, Smith viewed them as in fact being quite orderly in moving resources from where they are least valued to where they are most valued. A primary purpose of Chapter 17 is to investigate Smith's ideas rigorously and to show that, with some important limitations, his insights were essentially correct.

Perfectly Competitive Price System

Before starting our examination of Smith's invisible hand notion, we must describe the particular model of the economy we will be using. This model is a generalization of the supply-demand model of perfectly competitive price determination introduced in Chapter 11. Here we assume that all markets are of this type, and refer to this set of markets as a **perfectly competitive price system**. The assumption is that there are in this simple economy some large number of homogeneous goods. Included in this list of goods are not only consumption items but also factors of production (whose pricing is described

Perfectly competitive price system
An economic model in which individuals maximize utility, firms maximize profits, there is perfect information about prices, and every economic actor is a price taker.

① individuals maximize utility
② firms maximize profits
③ perfect information
④ everyone is a price taker.

in Part 5). Each of these goods has an equilibrium price, established by the action of supply and demand.[1] At this set of prices, every market is cleared in the sense that suppliers are willing to supply that quantity that is demanded and consumers will demand that quantity that is supplied. We also assume that there are no transaction or transportation charges and that both individuals and firms have perfect knowledge of these prices.

As in Part 4, each good obeys the law of one price: a good trades at the same price no matter who buys it or which firm sells it. If one good were traded at two different prices, people would rush to buy the good where it was cheaper and firms would try to sell all their output where the good was more expensive. These actions in themselves would tend to equalize the price of the good. In the perfectly competitive market, then, each good must have only one price. This is why we may speak unambiguously of *the* price of a good.

The perfectly competitive model assumes that people and firms react to prices in specific ways:

1. There are assumed to be a large number of people buying any one good. Each person takes all prices as given. Each adjusts behavior to maximize utility, given the prices and his or her budget constraint. People may also be suppliers of productive services (for example, labor), and in such decisions they also regard prices as given.[2]
2. There are assumed to be a large number of firms producing each good, and each firm produces only a small share of the output of any one good. In making input and output choices, firms are assumed to operate to maximize profits. The firm treats all prices as given when making these profit-maximizing decisions. The firm's activities, either as a supplier of goods or as a demander of factor inputs, have no effect on market prices.

These assumptions should be familiar to you since we have been making them throughout this book. Our purpose here is to show how an entire economic system operates when all markets work in this way.

An Illustration of General Equilibrium

A major distinction between this model and the perfectly competitive models we have used previously is that now we are interested in studying an entire system of many interconnected markets, not just a single market in isolation.

[1]One aspect of this market interaction should be made clear from the outset. The perfectly competitive market only determines relative (not absolute) prices. In this chapter, we speak of relative prices. It makes no difference whether the prices of apples and oranges are \$.10 and \$.20, respectively, or \$10 and \$20. The important point in either case is that two apples can be exchanged for one orange in the market.

[2]Since one price represents the wage rate, the relevant budget constraint is in reality a time constraint. This is the way we treat individuals' labor-leisure choices in Chapter 15.

Figure 17.1
The Market for Tomatoes and Several Related Markets

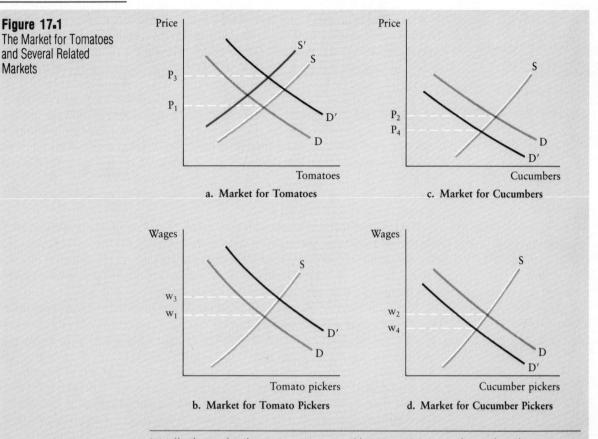

a. Market for Tomatoes

c. Market for Cucumbers

b. Market for Tomato Pickers

d. Market for Cucumber Pickers

Initially the market for tomatoes is in equilibrium (at P_1) as are the markets for tomato pickers, cucumbers, and cucumber pickers. An increase in demand for tomatoes will disturb these equilibria. Virtually all of the supply and demand curves will shift in the process of establishing a new, general equilibrium.

That is, we wish now to take a "general equilibrium" view of the economy rather than the partial equilibrium approach used in Parts 4 and 5. To illustrate this approach, Figure 17.1 shows the market for one good, say tomatoes, and three other markets related to it: (1) the market for tomato pickers; (2) the market for a related product—cucumbers; and (3) the market for cucumber pickers. Suppose that initially all of these markets are in equilibrium as shown by the sets of shaded supply and demand curves in the four panels of Figure 17.1. That is, the equilibrium price of tomatoes is given by P_1, wages of tomato pickers by w_1, the price of cucumbers by P_2, and the wages of cucumber pickers by w_2. Since these prices act to equate the amount supplied and demanded in each of these markets, the general equilibrium shown in Figure 17.1 will persist from week to week until something happens to change it.

Assume now that such a change does occur. Imagine a situation where the government announces that tomatoes have been found to cure the common cold, so everyone decides to eat more of them. An initial consequence of this discovery is that the demand for tomatoes will shift outward to D'. In our previous analysis this shift would cause the price of tomatoes to rise and that would be, more or less, the end of the story. Now, however, we wish to follow the repercussions of what has happened in the tomato market into the other markets shown in Figure 17.1. A first possible reaction would be in the market for tomato pickers. Since tomato prices have risen, the marginal value product of labor used to harvest tomatoes will rise, so the demand curve for labor in Graph b in Figure 17.1 will shift to D'. This will tend to raise wages of tomato pickers, which will, in turn, raise the costs of tomato growers. The supply curve for tomatoes (which, under perfect competition, just reflects growers' marginal costs) will shift to S'.

What happens to the market for cucumbers? Since people have an increased desire for tomatoes, they may reduce their demands for cucumbers because these vegetables don't cure colds. The demand for cucumbers will shift inward to D', and cucumber prices will fall. That will reduce the demand for cucumber workers, and the wage associated with that occupation will fall.

We could continue this story indefinitely. We could ask how the lower price of cucumbers affects the tomato market. Or we could ask whether cucumber pickers, discouraged by their falling wages, might consider picking tomatoes, shifting the supply of labor curve in Graph b in Figure 17.1 outward. To follow this chain of events further would add little to our story. Eventually we would expect all four markets in Figure 17.1 to reach a new equilibrium, such as that illustrated by the solid supply and demand curves in the figure. Once all the repercussions have been worked out, the final result would be a rise in tomato prices (to P_3), a rise in the wages of tomato pickers (to w_3), a fall in cucumber prices (to P_4), and a fall in the wages of cucumber pickers (to w_4). This is what we mean then by a smoothly working system of perfectly competitive markets. Following any disturbance, all of the markets can eventually reestablish a new set of equilibrium prices at which quantity demanded is equal to quantity supplied in each market.[3] It is this model—or, as in "Applying Economics: Modeling the Impact of Taxes with a Computer," a more complex form of this model involving hundreds, perhaps even millions of interconnected markets—that we will use to investigate the question of economic efficiency.

---

[3]Actually, the question of whether many markets can establish a set of prices that brings equilibrium to each of them is a major and difficult theoretical question. For a simple discussion and some references see Walter Nicholson, *Microeconomic Theory: Basic Principles and Extensions,* 3d ed. (Hinsdale, Ill.: Dryden Press, 1985), pp. 684–694.

APPLYING ECONOMICS

Modeling the Impact of Taxes with a Computer

Chapter 11 illustrates how the competitive model might be used to analyze the impact of taxes on a single market. A primary shortcoming of that approach is that it does not allow a very complete description of the various effects a tax may have. For example, we show that an excise tax on a good is partly paid by consumers and partly paid by firms, with the respective shares being determined by elasticities of demand and supply. This conclusion tells us very little about who really bears the burden of the tax. We have no idea how that burden is shared among different consumers of the good, nor do we know who finally pays the firms' share (it could be owners of the firms, workers in the firms, or some combination of the two). Simple models of supply and demand are just not rich enough in detail to answer such questions.

The development of large scale computers and sophisticated programs for modeling the economy has changed this situation dramatically. Now it is possible to use general equilibrium models of the economy to obtain very detailed appraisals of the impact of taxes. Some of these models divide the economy into as many as 50 or more industries and equally many different types of consumers. A graphic representation of such models might look like Figure 17.1 but with more than 100 different markets represented. Coping with the information necessary to compute equilibrium prices in all of these markets without a computer would be impossible. Using the speed and capacity of modern computers makes it a fairly simple process.

These large general equilibrium models of the economy have yielded major and sometimes surprising conclusions about the effects of taxes on an economy. Generally, these effects are bigger than have been usually discovered using partial equilibrium methods.[4] One study of the entire tax system of the United Kingdom,

for example, concluded that distortions introduced by that system resulted in a deadweight loss (similar to the loss from monopoly described in Chapter 12) of 6 to 9 percent of total gross national product. The taxes also caused a transfer of nearly one-quarter of all income from high-income to low-income households. The study found that the British tax system imposed particularly heavy costs on its manufacturing industries—perhaps providing an explanation for recent poor industrial performance in that country. Studies of the U.S. tax system tend to reach similar, though perhaps not so dramatic, conclusions. For example, some authors have reported that, at the margin, the U.S. tax system involves large deadweight losses. Collecting one dollar in extra taxes imposes very large costs (perhaps as much as two dollars) on people who pay them. These studies suggest that moving to simpler tax schemes, such as a flat rate consumption tax, would reduce these losses substantially.

To Think About

1. Suppose the government were to institute a tax on each gallon of gasoline sold. How would you analyze the economic effects of this tax with a partial equilibrium model? What further repercussions of the tax would this simple model miss? How many markets do you think you should study to gain a fairly complete picture of the impact of the tax?

2. In most general equilibrium models of taxation the final results of who pays taxes are reported as how aftertax incomes of various groups of people are affected. There is no notion that firms pay any taxes at all. What do you make of this? How do you reconcile the commonsense (and politically popular) idea that firms do indeed pay taxes with the general equilibrium notion that ultimately only people pay taxes?

---

[4]For a summary of many of these models, see John B. Shoven and John Walley, "Applied General Equilibrium Models of Taxation and International Trade," *Journal of Economic Literature*, September 1984, pp. 1007–1051.

Efficiency in Production

We start our analysis of economic efficiency by describing what it means to say that an economy with fixed amounts of resources has used these resources "efficiently." To do this, we use the production possibility frontier concept first introduced in Chapter 1. We show here that an economy that is on its production possibility curve is allocating its resources efficiently. On the other hand, if production takes place inside the frontier, resources are being poorly allocated and moving them around would improve matters. Before we can show all of this, we first define production efficiency.

Definition of Efficiency

A major problem with defining efficient production is that any economy produces many different goods. For this reason it is impossible to talk about producing as much total output as possible. There is simply no way to add together apples, oranges, automobiles, and aircraft carriers into something called output.[5] Instead, we adopt what may seem a relatively complicated definition. Under this definition an allocation of resources is said to be **technically efficient** if it is impossible to increase the output of one good without cutting back on the production of something else. Alternatively, resources are said to be allocated inefficiently if it is indeed possible, by moving resources around, to increase output of one good without sacrificing anything.

For example, suppose an economy produces only two products, wine and cloth. An allocation of resources under which more wine could be produced without having to reduce cloth output would be inefficient—there is no reason why the resources should not be shuffled around to yield more wine output. On the other hand, if increasing wine output meant cutting back on cloth output, the initial allocation would be efficient since output cannot be unambiguously increased. By using this definition of efficiency, it is never necessary to compare wine and cloth directly to decide whether or not resources are allocated efficiently. Rather, wine is compared only to wine (to see whether output of it has increased), and cloth is compared only to cloth.

> **Technically efficient allocation of resources** An allocation of the available resources such that producing more of one good requires producing less of some other good.

RTS between inputs is the same.

Efficient Input Use

As a starting point in our discussion of efficiency in production, we can treat the entire economy as a single firm that uses fixed amounts of two inputs, capital (K) and labor (L), to produce two different goods (called X and Y). The firm must decide only how to allocate the two inputs between producing

---

[5] Since we do not wish to introduce prices into our discussion of efficiency, it is not possible to add up different goods by valuing them at their market prices. The price system might be used to achieve economic efficiency, but prices cannot be used to define the concept itself.

[Handwritten margin notes: RTS — rate at which one input can be substituted for another while holding production constant. Efficient allocation: ① resources are fully employed ② RTS between inputs is the same.]

X and Y. The firm will be operating efficiently if it is not possible for it to reallocate its inputs in such a way that output of X can be increased without necessarily cutting back on Y. The condition that will bring about such an efficient allocation involves the firm's rate of technical substitution (RTS) first mentioned in Chapter 8. There we define the RTS as the rate at which a firm can substitute one input (say, labor) for another (say, capital) while holding the output of a particular good constant. The RTS is the (negative of) the slope of a production isoquant. Using this concept, it is easy to show that the firm has allocated its resources efficiently if it has them fully employed and if the RTS between the inputs is the same for both goods the firm produces.

An Intuitive Proof

We can present an intuitive proof of this assertion. The first part of the rule is obvious: if a firm leaves any portion of its available inputs unemployed, it is not operating efficiently. By putting the unemployed factors to work, the firm could increase its output of one good without having to cut back elsewhere. Being fully employed is not, however, sufficient to insure efficiency. The firm must also allocate its resources so that the technical rate of trade-off between inputs (the RTS) is the same in each output the firm produces.

To see this, let's suppose that a firm has 100 hours of labor and 100 machine hours to devote to the production of cars and trucks. Suppose that the firm (rather arbitrarily) decides to allocate half of each of the inputs to the production of cars and the other half to the production of trucks. With 50K and 50L producing cars, the RTS might be 2. The same number of cars could be produced with 48K and 51L. Assume, alternatively, that the RTS in truck production is 1. The same truck output could be produced with 51K and 49L. This alternative allocation of the available inputs is superior to the initial equal allocation. The 100 labor hours are still being used (51 in car production, 49 in truck production). However, even though outputs of both cars and trucks are the same under the revised allocation as under the equal allocation, there is now one machine hour left over. This extra machine hour can be used in either car or truck production to increase output over what it initially was. The initial allocation (with unequal RTS) was therefore inefficient.

Edgeworth box diagram A graphic device for illustrating all of the possible allocations of two goods (or two inputs) which are in fixed supply.

Edgeworth Box Diagram

A particularly useful device for studying the allocation of fixed amounts of resources to alternative uses is the **Edgeworth box diagram.**[6] The basics for

[6] Named for F. Y. Edgeworth (1854–1926), who in 1881 derived the concept of a contract curve in his *Mathematical Physics: An Essay on the Application of Mathematics to the Moral Sciences* (New York: August M. Kelley, 1953).

Figure 17.2
Construction of Edgeworth
Box Diagram for
Production

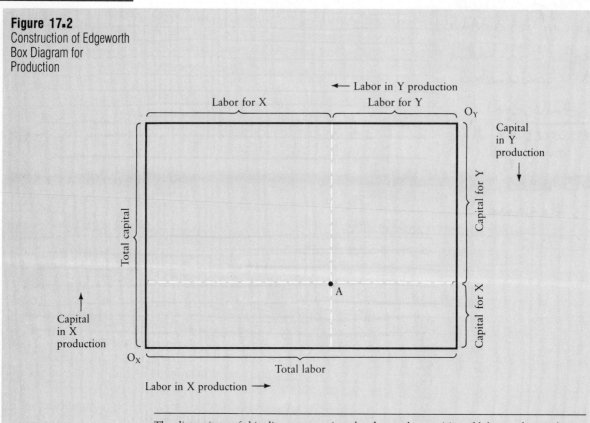

The dimensions of this diagram are given by the total quantities of labor and capital
available. Quantities of these resources devoted to X production are measured from
origin O_X; quantities devoted to Y are measured from O_Y. Any point in the box
represents a fully employed allocation of the available resources to the two goods.

constructing this diagram are illustrated in Figure 17.2. As its name implies,
the diagram is a rectangular box with dimensions given by the amounts of
capital and labor available. In Figure 17.2 the length of the box represents
total labor hours and the height of the box represents total capital hours. Now
we let the lower left corner of the box represent the "origin" for measuring
capital and labor devoted to production of good X. The upper right corner
of the box represents the origin for resources devoted to Y. Using these conventions, any point in the box can be regarded as a fully employed allocation
of the available resources between goods X and Y. Point A, for example,
represents an allocation in which the indicated number of labor hours are
devoted to X production together with a specified number of hours of capital.
Production of good Y uses whatever labor and capital is left over. At point
A, for example, Figure 17.2 shows the exact amount of labor and capital used
in the production of good Y. Any point in the box has a similar interpretation.

Figure 17.3
Box Diagram of Efficiency
in Production

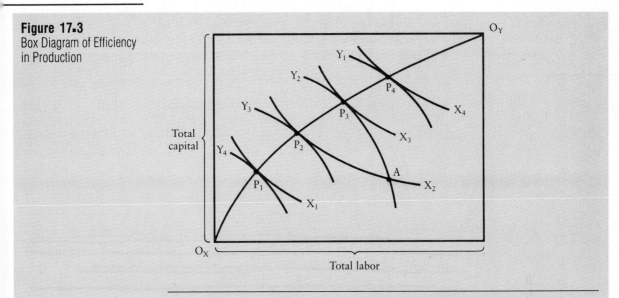

This diagram adds production isoquants for X and Y to Figure 17.2. It then shows technically efficient ways to allocate the fixed amounts of K and L between the production of the two outputs. The line joining O_X and O_Y is the locus of these efficient points. Along this line the RTS (of L for K) in the production of good X is equal to the RTS in the production of Y.

The Edgeworth box shows every possible way the existing capital and labor might be used. Now we wish to discover which of these allocations are efficient.

Efficient Allocations

To discover these efficient allocations we must introduce the isoquant maps (see Chapter 7) for the two goods X and Y, since these show how much can be produced with various levels of capital and labor input. Figure 17.3 contains the isoquant map for good X using O_X as an origin. This isoquant map looks exactly like the ones we used before. For good Y, however, the trick of the Edgeworth box diagram is to use O_Y as an origin and rotate the usual diagram 180°. If you turn your book upside down, you will see that the isoquant map for good Y has the usual shape when viewed from that angle. We have been able to put both the isoquant maps on the same diagram and these will help us to identify the efficient allocations.

Our arbitrarily chosen point A is clearly not efficient. With capital and labor allocated in this way, Y_2 is produced together with X_2. By moving along the Y_2 isoquant to P_3 we can hold Y output constant and increase X output to X_3. Point A was not an efficient allocation since we were able to increase output of one good (X) without decreasing output of the other good (Y). Point A is inefficient because production of goods X and Y uses the available resources in the wrong combination, not because some of these resources were not used at all. Both point A and point P_3 represent fully employed allocations of the available resources. But, the allocation at point P_3 results in good X using more capital and less labor while Y uses more labor and less capital than at point A (check this for yourself!). This new allocation is a better way to use the available resources.

Which points in Figure 17.3 are the efficient ones? A bit of intuition should suggest to you that only points such as P_1, P_2, P_3, and P_4 are. These represent allocations where the isoquants are tangent to each other. At any other point in the box diagram, the two goods' isoquants will intersect, and we can show inefficiency as we did for point A. At the points of tangency, however, this kind of unambiguous improvement cannot be made. In going from P_2 to P_3, for example, more X is being produced, but at the cost of less Y being produced, so P_3 is not more efficient than P_2—both of the points are efficient. Tangency of the isoquants for good X and good Y implies that their slopes are equal. That is, the RTS of capital for labor is equal in X and Y production just as our intuitive example suggests must be the case for efficiency.

The curve joining O_X and O_Y that includes all of these points of tangency shows all of the efficient allocations of capital and labor. Points off this curve are inefficient in that unambiguous increases in output can be obtained by reshuffling inputs among the two goods. Points on O_X, O_Y are all efficient allocations, however. More X can be produced only by cutting back on Y production.

Production Possibility Frontier

Production possibility frontier
A figure illustrating the technically efficient output possibilities for an economy with fixed amounts of inputs.

We can use the information from Figure 17.3 to construct a **production possibility frontier,** which shows those alternative outputs of X and Y that can be produced with the fixed amounts of capital and labor. In Figure 17.4 the various efficient points from Figure 17.3 have been transferred onto a graph with X and Y outputs on the axes. At O_X, for example, no resources are devoted to X production; consequently Y output is as large as possible with the existing resources. Similarly, at O_Y, the output of X is as large as possible. The other points on the production possibility frontier (say P_1, P_2, P_3, and P_4) are derived in an identical way from Figure 17.3.

The production possibility curve clearly exhibits the notion of efficiency we have been using. Any point inside the frontier is inefficient because output can be unambiguously increased. The allocation of K and L represented by point A, for example, is inefficient because output levels in the shaded area are both attainable, and preferable, to A. If you look again at Figure 17.3, you can see how the available resources might be reallocated to obtain those more efficient points.

Rate of Product Transformation

The slope of the production possibility frontier shows how X output can be substituted for Y output when total resources are held constant. For example,

Figure 17.4
Production Possibility
Frontier Derived from
Figure 17.3

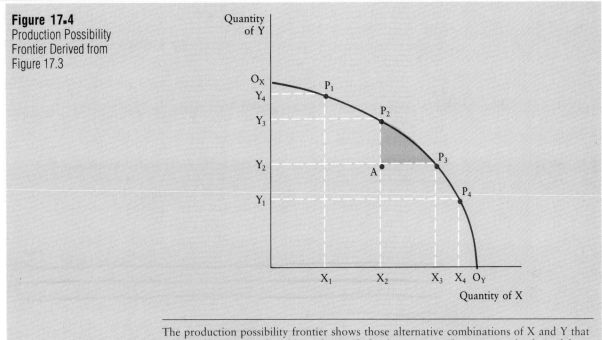

The production possibility frontier shows those alternative combinations of X and Y that can be efficiently produced by a firm with fixed resources. The curve can be derived from Figure 17.3 by varying inputs between the production of X and Y while maintaining the conditions for efficiency. The slope of the production possibility curve is called the rate of product transformation (RPT).

for points near O_X on the production possibility frontier, the slope is a small negative number, say $-\frac{1}{2}$, implying that by reducing Y output by one unit, X output could be increased by two. Near O_Y, on the other hand, the slope is a large negative number, say -5, implying that Y output must be reduced by five units to permit the production of one more X. The slope of the production possibility frontier shows the possibilities that exist for trading Y and X in production. We call this slope the **rate of product transformation (RPT)** of good X for good Y. This concept indicates the number of units by which Y output must be reduced in order to increase X output by one unit.

Rate of product transformation
The slope of the production possibility frontier which shows the opportunity costs involved in producing more of one good and less of some other good.

Increasing RPT and the Shape of the Production Possibility Frontier

In Figure 17.4 we have drawn the production possibility frontier so that the RPT increases as X output increases. In moving clockwise along the frontier, progressively greater and greater amounts of Y must be given up in order to increase X output by one unit. Such a shape can be justified intuitively by arguing that increases in X (or Y) output eventually run into diminishing returns. For output combinations near O_X, most resources are devoted to Y production. Some of these resources may be more suited to X production than they are to Y production. When X output is increased slightly, it is only reasonable to assume that these particular resources will be shifted into X output first. Such a shift will not reduce Y output very much, but it will increase X significantly. Near O_X, therefore, the RPT will be small. On the other hand, near O_Y, X output has been expanded greatly. To increase X further requires that resources be drawn out of Y production that are very good at producing Y but not good at producing X. Consequently, Y will have to be cut back significantly to get only one more unit of X. Near O_Y, the RPT will be high. An increasing RPT accords well with an intuitive idea that it is possible to push output of X too far.

Rate of Product Transformation Is the Ratio of Marginal Costs

Much of the above argument is rather imprecise. Terms such as *too far* and *good at producing* X are too vague to be relied on for careful analysis. To show that the shape of the production possibility frontier in Figure 17.4 is rigorously justified, we must make use of the following result: the RPT (of X for Y) is equal to the ratio of the marginal cost of X (MC_X) to the marginal cost of Y (MC_Y). That is,

$$\text{RPT (of X for Y)} = \frac{MC_X}{MC_Y}. \qquad [17.1]$$

Although we will not prove this result mathematically here, we do provide an intuitive proof. Suppose only labor is used in the production of X and Y. Assume that, at some point on the production possibility frontier, the marginal cost of producing more X is 4 (that is, assume that it takes four units of labor input to produce an additional unit of X output). Suppose also that the marginal cost of Y (in terms of the additional labor required to produce one more unit) is 2. In this situation it is clear that, since the total supply of labor is fixed, two units of Y must be given up in order to free enough labor to produce one more unit of X. We would therefore say that the RPT (of X for Y) is 2. But this is simply the ratio of the marginal cost of X to the marginal cost of Y (that is, 4/2); at least for this simple case, Equation 17.1 holds. A more complete analysis would indicate that the equation holds even when there are many inputs being used to produce X and Y.

We are now in a position to show why the production possibility frontier has a concave shape. Such a shape is based on the presumption that the production of both X and Y exhibits increasing marginal costs. As production of either of these outputs is expanded, marginal costs are assumed to rise. Consider moving along the frontier in a clockwise direction. In so doing the production of X is being increased, whereas that of Y is being decreased. By the assumption of increasing marginal costs, then, MC_X is rising while MC_Y falls. But, by Equation 17.1, this means that the RPT is rising as X is substituted for Y in production. The concave shape of the production possibility frontier is then justified by the assumption of increasing marginal costs.

Production Possibility Frontier and Opportunity Cost

The reason we have spent so much space in developing the concept of the production possibility frontier is that it is probably the single most important tool for studying technical efficiency in production. The curve clearly demonstrates that there are many combinations of goods that are technically efficient. The curve also shows that producing more of one good necessitates cutting back on the production of some other good. As we described in Chapter 1, this is precisely what economists mean by the term *opportunity cost*. The cost of producing more X can be most readily measured by the reduction in Y output that this entails. The cost of one more unit of X is therefore best measured as the RPT (of X for Y) at the prevailing point on the production possibility frontier. The curve clearly shows the supply opportunities that are available in an economy. As "Applying Economics: Production Possibilities for 'Guns and Butter'" shows, knowing something about such possibilities can be very important for public decision making.

An Efficient Mix of Outputs

The goal of an economic system is to satisfy human wants. Being technically efficient in production (that is, being on the production possibility frontier) may not be at all desirable if the "wrong" combination of goods is being produced. It does little good for an economy to be an efficient producer of yo-yos and xylophones if no one wants these goods. Similarly, an economy in which large amounts of resources are devoted to frivolous purposes by the government (say, building statues to the ruling leadership) may not be truly efficient even though production of statues itself is on the production possibility frontier. In order to assure overall **economic efficiency** in the allocation of resources, we need some way to tie people's preferences to the economy's productive abilities. The condition necessary to insure that the right goods are produced is that people's marginal rates of substitution (MRS—defined in Chapter 3 as the amount of one good a person is willing to give up to get some of another good) must equal the economy's rate of product transformation (RPT). That is, the rate at which people are willing to trade one good for another must equal the rate at which the goods can be traded for each other in production.

Economically efficient allocation of resources A technically efficient allocation of resources in which the output combination also reflects people's preferences.

An Intuitive Proof

As an example, suppose people were willing to trade three apples for one orange, but resources were allocated so that one apple could be traded for one orange in production. In this situation, resources would not be efficiently allocated between the two goods. Too few oranges are being produced since people place a relatively higher evaluation on oranges than is their opportunity cost in production. To grow one additional orange, it would be necessary to cut back the apple harvest by one. But, people would willingly sacrifice three

Production Possibilities for "Guns and Butter"

Traditionally when economics textbooks introduce the production possibility frontier, they label the axes "guns" and "butter" to record the notion that an economy can produce various combinations of defense ("guns") and nondefense ("butter") items. During wartime the economy reallocates resources toward guns, whereas in more peaceful periods a relatively larger share of resources is devoted to butter. Use of the production possibility frontier concept can be helpful in understanding the kinds of opportunity costs that might be included in such moves.

In the early 1960s there was considerable interest in what the economic dislocations of disarmament might be. At that time, defense spending amounted to about 10 percent of gross national product, and a number of studies attempted to estimate what the effects of a fairly sharp reduction (say, cutting in half) might be. In many respects the issue was one of deciding how specialized the inputs devoted to defense were. If such inputs had uses that were highly specific to defense, the adjustment costs might be large since these inputs could not be easily employed elsewhere. If, on the other hand, inputs were easily transferable between sectors, opportunity costs of adjustment might be low.

The studies of this issue that were conducted in the early 1960s tended to conclude that for modest reductions in defense spending, these adjustment costs would be relatively small.[7] Many products that are bought by the military can be readily sold to civilians (for example, food), and even for some goods that have solely defense uses (such as military aircraft), problems involved in converting to civilian production may have been rather minor. Only for highly specialized industries such as

ordinance or defense-related research and development did these authors see substantial dislocations.

By 1985 the share of GNP devoted to national defense had fallen to about 7 percent. Because the decline from 10 to 7 percent took place over a relatively long period and because it took place within a growing economy, there were few special costs associated with this decline. However, some people believe that in the late 1980s it would be more difficult in economic terms to convert from defense-related production to civilian production than was the case in the 1960s. An increasing array of military goods (for example, nuclear submarines or antimissile defense systems) have no obvious civilian counterpart, and it is generally believed that practically all defense goods have become much more technically sophisticated and specialized in recent years. Although there may be good reasons to adopt policies aimed toward disarmament, the opportunity costs of converting resources to civilian use could be high.

To Think About

1. If defense expenditures were reduced, what industries would be affected? Can you answer that question simply by asking what things would the Defense Department no longer buy? Or should you look further back in the chain of supply?
2. Currently, nearly half of all research and development expenditures in the United States are financed by the Defense Department. How might that affect the long-term growth of the economy? Do research and development in defense result only in improved weapons or do they spill over into civilian sectors of the economy?

apples for another orange. Consequently, they are better off to the extent of two apples—they only had to give up one apple, not three, to get the orange. As with the other examples of comparing trade-off rates in this book, any

---

[7]For a summary, see Roger E. Bolton, ed., *Defense and Disarmament: The Economics of Transition* (Englewood Cliffs, N.J.: Prentice-Hall, 1966).

Figure 17.5
Efficiency of Output Mix

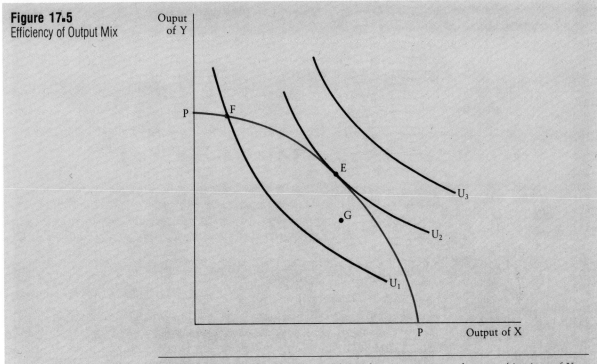

In this economy, the production possibility frontier represents those combinations of X and Y that can be produced. Every point on it is efficient in a technical sense. However, only the output combination at point E is a true utility maximum for the typical person. Only this point represents an economically efficient allocation of resources. At E that person's MRS is equal to the rate at which X can be traded for Y in production (the RPT).

time the rate at which people are willing to trade two goods differs from the rate at which the goods can be technically traded, a beneficial reallocation can be made.

A Graphic Demonstration

Figure 17.5 illustrates this requirement for economic efficiency in the mix of outputs. It assumes that there are only two goods (X and Y) being produced and that there is just one typical person in society. Those combinations of X and Y that can be produced are given by the production possibility frontier. Any point on the frontier represents a point of technically efficient production. By superimposing this typical person's indifference curve map on Figure 17.5, we see that only one point on the frontier provides maximum utility. This point of maximum utility is at E, where the frontier is tangent to the typical person's highest indifference curve, U_2. At this point of tangency the person's MRS (of X for Y) is equal to the technical RPT (of X for Y), which is the required condition for economic efficiency in the mix of outputs being produced. Point E is preferred to every other point on the production possibility frontier. In fact, for any other point, such as F, on the frontier, there exist points that are inefficient but that are preferred to F. In Figure 17.5 the technically inefficient point G is preferred to the technically efficient point F. It would be preferable from the typical person's point of view to produce inefficiently rather than to consume the "wrong" combination of goods even though these are produced in an efficient way. Point E (which *is* an economically efficient point) is superior to any such second best solutions.

Figure 17.5 shows, at least for a simple case, how resources might be allocated efficiently in an economy. The requirement that inputs be used efficiently in the production of two goods yields the production possibility curve as an illustration of these technically efficient allocations. To choose among these technically efficient allocations, however, requires that we introduce people's preferences. These demand influences then determine which of the potential output combinations that might be supplied is economically efficient. With this model of an efficient allocation of resources, we are now ready to examine how it might be brought about through the operations of perfectly competitive markets.

Efficiency of Perfect Competition

We illustrate the economic efficiency of perfect competition in two steps. First, we provide a very brief proof of why firms' desires to minimize costs will result in their using an efficient mix of inputs—that is, we show that firms will be on the production possibility frontier. Then, we present a more detailed proof of why competitive markets will result in the "right" final combination of goods being produced.

Efficiency in Input Use

If all inputs are traded in perfectly competitive markets, every firm will act as a price taker in making its decisions about which inputs to use. In this case, as we show in Chapter 8, a firm will choose an input combination for which the rate of technical substitution (RTS) is equal to the ratio of the inputs' prices (w/v). But, since every producer of each good faces the same input prices, w and v, they will all be equating their RTS to the same w/v. The desire to minimize costs will lead them to choose the same RTS, as is required for efficiency. Since w and v are equilibrium prices of labor and capital respectively, we also know that both inputs will be fully employed. If, in total, firms wished to have fewer workers than were available, the wage would fall to restore equilibrium between the quantity demanded and quantity supplied. Consequently, the workings of competitive markets for inputs insures that both inputs are fully employed, and firms' desire to minimize costs insures that they are efficiently employed among various uses. Smith's invisible hand (that is, the market) leads firms to one of the technically efficient allocations illustrated in Figure 17.4.

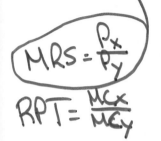

utility
maximization

$MRS = \dfrac{P_X}{P_Y}$

$RPT = \dfrac{MC_X}{MC_Y}$

Since MRS = RPT

∴ $RPT = \dfrac{P_X}{P_Y}$

economically
efficient allocation
of resources (p. 511)

Efficiency in Output Mix

A proof that the operations of competitive markets will also lead to an efficient choice of outputs is equally straightforward. Such markets will determine the equilibrium prices for goods X and Y—we can call these equilibrium prices P_X^* and P_Y^*. These prices are taken as given by both demanders and suppliers. For demanders, utility maximization (as we show in Chapter 3) will lead each person to equate his or her marginal rate of substitution (MRS) to the ratio of these prices (P_X^*/P_Y^*). In maximizing profits, each competitive firm will produce where price equals marginal cost—that is, $P_X^* = MC_X$ and $P_Y^* = MC_Y$. But earlier in this chapter, we showed that the rate of product transformation between two goods (RPT) is given by the ratio of the good's marginal costs:

$$RPT = MC_X/MC_Y. \qquad [17.2]$$

Therefore, profit maximization will result in

$$RPT = MC_X/MC_Y = P_X^*/P_Y^*. \qquad [17.3]$$

Consequently, profit-maximizing firms equate the rate at which they can trade X for Y in production to P_X^*/P_Y^* just as people do in maximizing utility. The RPT of X for Y will equal the MRS and that, combined with the notion that demand must equal supply for each good, meets the requirements for economic efficiency described in Figure 17.5.

A Graphic Demonstration

Figure 17.6 illustrates this result. The figure shows the production possibility frontier for a two-good economy, and the set of indifference curves represents people's preferences for these goods. First, consider any initial price ratio P_X/P_Y. At this price ratio, firms will choose to produce the output combination X_1, Y_1. Only at this point on the production frontier will the ratio of the goods be equal to the ratio of their marginal costs (and equal to the RPT). On the other hand, given this budget constraint (line C), individuals collectively will demand X_1', Y_1'.[8] Consequently, there is an excess demand for good X (people want to buy more than is being produced), whereas there is an excess supply of good Y. The workings of the marketplace will cause P_X to rise and P_Y to fall. The price ratio P_X/P_Y will rise; the price line will move clockwise along the production possibility frontier. That is, firms will increase

---

[8]It is important to recognize why the budget constraint has this location. Since P_X and P_Y are given, the value of total production is $P_X \cdot X_1 + P_Y \cdot Y_1$. This is the value of GNP in the simple economy pictured in Figure 17.6. It is also the total income accruing to people in society. Society's budget constraint passes through X_1, Y_1 and has a slope of $-P_X/P_Y$. This is precisely the line labeled C in the figure.

Figure 17.6
How Perfectly Competitive
Prices Bring about
Efficiency

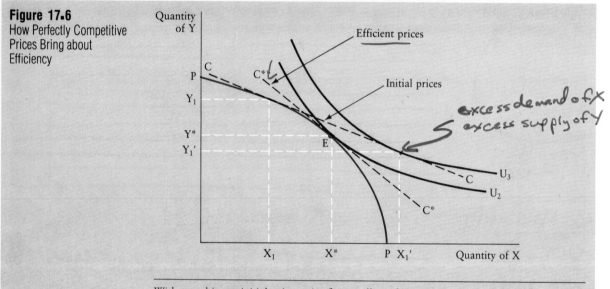

With an arbitrary initial price ratio, firms will produce X_1, Y_1; society's budget constraint will be given by line C. With this budget constraint, individuals demand X_1', Y_1'; that is, there is an excess demand for good X_1 ($X_1' - X_1$) and an excess supply of good Y_1 ($Y_1 - Y_1'$). The workings of the market will move these prices toward their equilibrium levels P_X^*, P_Y^*. At those prices, society's budget constraint will be given by the line C^* and supply and demand will be in equilibrium. The combination X^*, Y^* of goods will be chosen, and this allocation is efficient.

their production of good X and decrease their production of good Y. Similarly, people will respond to the changing prices by substituting Y for X in their consumption choices. The actions of both firms and individuals eliminate the excess demand for X and the excess supply of Y as market prices change.

Equilibrium is reached at X^*, Y^* with an equilibrium price ratio of P_X^*/P_Y^*. With this price ratio, supply and demand are equilibrated for both good X and good Y. Firms, in maximizing their profits, given P_X^* and P_Y^*, will produce X^* and Y^*. Given the income that this production represents for people, they will use that income to purchase precisely X^* and Y^*. Not only have markets been equilibrated by the operation of the price system, but the resulting equilibrium is also economically efficient. As we showed previously, the point X^*, Y^* provides the highest level of utility that can be obtained given the existing production possibility frontier. Figure 17.6 provides a simple general equilibrium proof that the results of supply and demand interacting in competitive markets can produce an efficient allocation of resources.

Prices, Efficiency, and Laissez-Faire Policies

We have shown that a perfectly competitive price system, by relying on the self-interest of people and of firms, and by utilizing the information carried by prices, can produce an economically efficient allocation of resources. In a sense, this finding provides "scientific" support for the *laissez-faire* position taken by many economists. For example, Adam Smith's assertion that:

> The natural effort of every individual to better his own condition, when suffered to exert itself with freedom and security, is so powerful a principle that it is alone, and without any assistance, not only capable of carrying on the society to wealth and prosperity, but of surmounting a hundred impertinent obstructions with which the folly of human laws too often encumbers its operations. . . .[9]

has been shown to have considerable validity. As Smith noted, it is not the public spirit of the baker that provides bread for people to eat. Rather, bakers (and other producers) operate in their own self-interest in responding to market signals (Smith's invisible hand). In so doing, their actions may be coordinated by the market into an efficient, overall pattern. Rather than being chaotic, the market system, at least in this simple model, imposes a very strict logic on how resources are used.

That efficiency theorem raises many important questions about the ability of markets to arrive at these perfectly competitive prices and about whether the theorem should act as a guide for government policy (for example, should governments avoid interfering in markets as suggested by "Applying Economics: Gains from Free Trade and Political Obstacles to Achieving Them"?). The rest of this chapter makes a start toward answering this question. Examining the efficiency of the price system and possible roles for government intervention generally occupy us for the remainder of this book.

Why Markets Fail to Achieve Economic Efficiency

Showing that perfect competition is economically efficient depends crucially on the assumptions that underlie the competitive model. In this section we examine some of the real-world problems that may prevent markets from generating such an efficient allocation. We see that many of these are quite likely to occur (although we generally delay our discussion on what to do about them until later chapters).

The factors that might interfere with perfect competition can be classed into three general groupings that include most of the cases occurring in the real world: *imperfect competition, externalities,* and *public goods.* We discuss each separately below.

Imperfect Competition

Imperfect competition
A market situation in which buyers or sellers have some influence on the prices of goods or services.

Imperfect competition in a broad sense includes all those situations in which economic actors (that is, buyers or sellers) exert some market power in deter-

---

[9]Adam Smith, *The Wealth of Nations* (1776; New York: Random House, Modern Library ed., 1937), p. 508.

Gains from Free Trade and Political Obstacles to Achieving Them

High tariffs on grain imports were imposed by the British government following the Napoleonic Wars. Debate over the effects of these "Corn Laws" dominated the politics of Great Britain during the period 1820–1845. A principal focus of the debate concerned the effect that elimination of tariffs would have on the welfare of British consumers and on the incomes of various groups in society. Here we examine the free trade question in both its historical and more recent forms.

The production possibility frontier in Figure 17.7 shows those combinations of grain (X) and manufactured goods (Y) that could be produced by English factors of production. Assuming (somewhat contrary to fact) that the Corn Laws completely prevented trade, market equilibrium would be at E with the domestic, pre-trade price ratio shown in the figure. Removal of the tariffs would reduce this price ratio to the price ratio that prevailed in the rest of the world. Given that new ratio, England would produce combination A and consume combination B. Grain imports would amount to $X_B - X_A$ and these would be financed by export of manufactured goods equal to $Y_A - Y_B$. Overall utility would be increased by the opening of trade. Figure 17.7 illustrates that there may be substantial gains from trade. (For some estimates of the dollar values of such gains, see Table 6.3 on page 136).

By referring to the Edgeworth production box diagram that lies behind the production possibility frontier (Figure 17.3), it is also possible to analyze the effect of tariff reductions on factor prices. The movement from point E to point A in Figure 17.7 is similar to a movement from P_3 to P_1 in Figure 17.3. Production of X is decreased and production of Y is increased by such a move, and Figure 17.3 shows the reallocation of capital and labor made necessary by such a move. If we assume that grain production is relatively capital intensive (that

is, it uses a lot of land), the movement from P_3 to P_1 causes the ratio of land to labor to rise in both industries. This will, in turn, cause the relative price of capital to fall (since effectively, each acre of land now has fewer workers on it). Figure 17.3 suggests that repeal of the Corn Laws would be harmful to capital owners (that is, landlords) and helpful to laborers. It is not surprising that landed interests fought repeal of these laws.

Modern Resistance to Trade

That trade policies may affect the relative incomes of various factors of production continues to exert a major influence on political debates about such policies. In the United States, for example, exports tend to be intensive in their use of skilled labor, whereas imports tend to be intensive in unskilled labor input. By analogy to our discussion of the Corn Laws, it might be expected that further movements toward free trade policies would result in rising relative wages for skilled workers and in falling relative wages for unskilled workers. It is not surprising that unions representing skilled workers (the Machinists, certain segments of the United Auto Workers, and the Petroleum and Atomic Workers) tend to favor free trade, whereas unions of unskilled workers (those in textiles, shoes, and related businesses) tend to oppose it.

Adjustment Costs

A careful study of Figure 17.7 indicates another reason why workers in firms that produce imported goods may be opposed to moves toward more open world trade. The reallocation of production from point E to point A in Figure 17.7 requires that factors of production be transferred out of X (import) production into Y (export) production. Making such a reallocation may impose costs on workers. They may have to move to

Figure 17.7

Analysis of the Corn Laws Debate

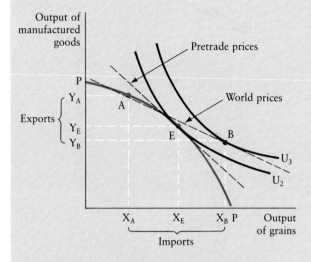

Reduction of tariff barriers on grain would cause production to be reallocated from point E to point A. Consumption would be reallocated from E to B. If grain production were relatively capital intensive, the relative price of capital would fall as a result of these reallocations.

new communities, search for new jobs, or learn new skills. All of these activities are costly to the individuals involved. Even though society as a whole benefits from trade expansion (overall utility increases from U_2 to U_3), individual workers may not be so lucky.

Trade Adjustment Policy

In order to share the costs of adjusting to trade policies, most countries offer some sort of governmental assistance to trade-affected workers. As part of the Trade Expansion Act of 1962, for example, the United States enacted a program of Trade Adjustment Assistance to provide jobless benefits and other services to workers in industries affected by trade expansion. In 1974 all of these benefits were substantially liberalized, primarily by making it easier for workers to establish that they had been harmed by imports. In many respects the adjustment assistance provisions of the 1962 and 1974 trade acts represented "bribes" to entice those workers who would be hurt by increasing imports to refrain from actively opposing such policies. Unfortunately, what in principle seemed a reasonable policy in practice proved quite difficult to administer. In particular, determination of which workers were actually injured by trade became largely a political question, and substantial amounts of adjustment assistance went to workers who suffered relatively small import-related costs. In 1981 the program was significantly scaled back and refocused more explicitly on workers suffering major losses from expanded trade.[10]

To Think About

1. This example shows that the typical consumer gains from the opening of trade. Use Figure 17.7 to discuss under what circumstances these gains would be relatively large. When might they be small or nonexistent? Is it possible that the opening of trade might actually make the typical consumer worse off?
2. Figure 17.7 shows that a nation will tend to export goods that have a lower relative price domestically than they do in the international market (in this case, good Y). What factors will determine such differences in relative prices—that is, what factors determine a country's "comparative advantage" in international trade?

[10]For a discussion, see Walter Corson and Walter Nicholson, "Trade Adjustment Assistance under the Trade Act of 1974," in R. G. Ehrenberg, ed., *Research in Labor Finance*, Vol. 4 (Greenwich, Conn.: JAI Press, 1982).

Figure 17.8
The Production of Good X under Monopoly Conditions Prevents Economic Efficiency

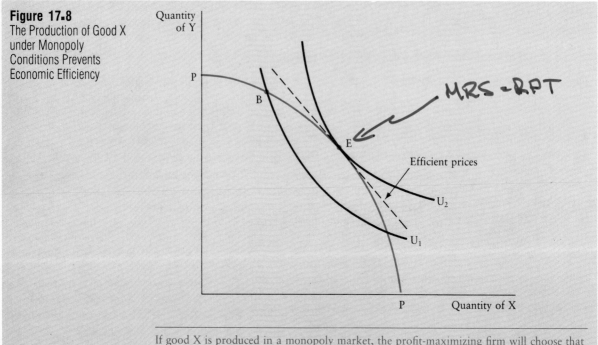

If good X is produced in a monopoly market, the profit-maximizing firm will choose that output combination for which the marginal revenue from selling X is equal to marginal cost. Production will take place at a point such as B. Too little X will be produced as a result of the monopolization of its market.

[handwritten margin notes:]
MRS=RPT=
$\frac{MC_x}{MC_y} = \frac{P_x}{P_y}$

MC < P

MC = MR
profit maximization

mining price. Markets that are organized as oligopolies or in which there is a monopsony on the demand side are considered in this category in addition to the usual case of monopoly. The essential aspect of all such markets is that marginal revenue (or marginal expense in the case of a monopsony) is different from market price since the firm is no longer a price taker. As we show in Chapter 12, a profit-maximizing monopoly, by equating marginal revenue with marginal cost, will not produce where price is equal to marginal cost. Because of this behavior, relative prices will no longer accurately reflect relative marginal costs, and the price system no longer carries the information necessary to insure efficiency.

As an example, consider the efficiency conditions for the economy diagrammed in Figure 17.8. Point E represents an economically efficient allocation: at that point the MRS (of X for Y) is equal to the RPT (of X for Y). A perfectly competitive price system could generate this allocation. Suppose instead that one of the goods, X, is produced under monopoly conditions, whereas Y is produced under conditions of perfect competition. The profit-maximizing output choice now is that combination of X and Y for which marginal revenue is equal to marginal cost in each market. For good X this will create a gap between the price paid by consumers and the good's marginal cost. That is, for good X

$$MC_X = MR_X < P_X \qquad [17.4]$$

even though for good Y

$$MC_Y = MR_Y = P_Y. \qquad [17.5]$$

This will result in a choice of outputs such as that represented by point B, with less X and more Y being produced than is optimal, given the existing preferences and technology.[11] The existence of a monopoly, by creating a gap between price and marginal cost, has caused the economic efficiency of the price system to fail. No longer do people and firms use the same concept (price) in making their decisions. Instead, it is marginal revenue that is relevant to firms' decisions and price that is relevant to individuals' decisions. Under conditions of imperfect competition, these two will differ and an inefficient mix of outputs will be chosen.

Externalities

A price system can also fail to allocate resources efficiently when there are relationships among firms or between firms and people that are not adequately represented by market prices. Examples of such occurrences are numerous. Perhaps the most common one is the case of a firm that pollutes the air with industrial smoke and other debris. This is called an **externality**. It is an effect of the firm's activities on people's well-being that is not taken into account through the normal operation of the price system. While a more complete discussion of the nature of externalities is presented in the next chapter, here we can describe why the presence of such nonmarket effects interferes with the ability of the price system to allocate resources efficiently.

The basic problem with externalities is that firms' private costs no longer correctly reflect the social costs of production. In the absence of externalities, the costs a firm incurs accurately measure social costs. The prices of the resources the firm uses represent all the opportunity costs involved in production. When a firm creates externalities, however, there are additional costs—those that arise from the external damage. The fact that pollution from burning coal to produce steel causes diseases and general dirt and grime is as much a cost of production as are the wages paid to the firm's workers. Both types

Externality
The effect of one party's economic activities on another party's well-being that is not taken into account by the price system.

---

[11]This is a "general equilibrium" proof of the result first illustrated in Figure 12.4 where the differential effects of monopoly and perfect competition are demonstrated in a partial equilibrium framework. Figure 17.7 clearly shows that the presence of a monopoly in good X will cause resources to be directed into the production of other goods.

Figure 17.9
Externalities May Cause an
Inefficient Allocation of
Resources

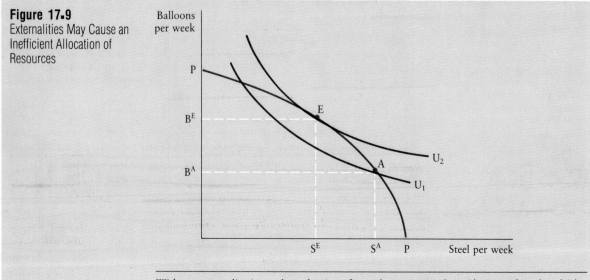

With an externality in steel production, firms choose to produce S^A units of steel and B^A units of balloons. Because of externalities involved in steel production, the market prices at A do not reflect individuals' true marginal rates of substitution. The allocation A is therefore inefficient and results in a lower utility level than does the efficient allocation E.

of costs should be considered in a full assessment of the social costs of steel production. However, the firm only responds to the private costs of steel production in deciding how much steel to produce. It disregards the social costs of its pollution. This again results in a gap between market price and (social) marginal cost and therefore leads to a misallocation of resources.

This result is illustrated in Figure 17.9. Again, in this figure, point E records an efficient allocation of resources at which the RPT is equal to the social MRS. Suppose now there is an externality in the production of good X, say steel, but none in good Y, say balloons. In this case, market prices do not lead economic agents to the efficient point E. Rather, firms choose to produce at point A where the RPT is equal to the ratio of equilibrium market prices. Although supply and demand are in equilibrium at these prices, such private decisions consider only the direct consumption values of steel and balloons: the steel-produced pollution is not taken into account. At point A the true marginal rate of substitution is less than the slope of the production possibility frontier, indicating that people are less willing to give up balloons to get more steel than is indicated by the market prices of those goods. The externality causes steel to be overproduced relative to the efficient allocation. Overall utility is reduced from U_2 to U_1 by this misallocation. In Chapter 18 we investigate a number of additional types of externalities, and we examine several ways in which the allocational problems they cause might be corrected.

③ Public Goods

A third possible failure of the price system to yield an efficient allocation of resources stems from the existence of goods that can be provided to new users at zero marginal cost and must be provided on a nonexclusive basis to everyone. Such goods include national defense, inoculations against infectious diseases, criminal justice, and pest control. The distinguishing features of these goods are that providing benefits to one more person costs nothing and that they provide benefits to everyone. Once the goods are produced, it is impossible (or at least very costly) to exclude anyone from benefiting from them. In such a case price cannot equal marginal cost (which is zero). There is also an incentive for each person to refuse to pay for the good in the hope that others will purchase it and thereby provide benefits to all. The pervasive nature of this incentive will ensure that not enough resources are allocated to such goods. To avoid this underallocation, communities (or nations) may decide to have the government produce these goods and finance this production through compulsory taxation. For that reason, such goods are frequently termed **public goods.** In Chapter 19 we treat the problems raised by public goods in detail.

Public goods
Goods that provide nonexclusive benefits to everyone in a group and which can be provided to one more user at zero marginal cost.

What to Do about These Problems

Any economic system will undoubtedly have all of these kinds of problems. Can solutions be found that still permit the market system to do its job efficiently? Some solutions do seem possible. In Chapter 12, for example, we discuss several possible solutions to the allocational inefficiencies posed by monopolies. In Chapter 18 we discuss several solutions to the externality problem. In other cases, however, correcting problems with the competitive price system may be much more difficult. In Chapter 19, for example, we show how devising solutions to the public goods problem is particularly vexing. There seems to be no guarantee that if we leave the production of public goods to the political process (say, voting in a democracy) this will result in the correct amount of public goods being produced. In many other cases the route to achieving an efficient allocation of resources also may not be clear. Each problem requires a careful examination to see whether it is possible to move toward economic efficiency.

Efficiency and Equity

So far in this chapter we have discussed the concept of economic efficiency and whether an efficient allocation of resources can be achieved through reliance on market forces. We have not mentioned questions of *equity* or fairness in the way goods are distributed among people. In the concluding section of this chapter we take up these questions. We show not only that it is very difficult to define what an equitable distribution of resources is, but also that there is no reason to expect that allocations that result from a competitive price system (or from any other method of allocating resources, for that matter) will be equitable.

An Exchange Economy

Exchange efficiency
An allocation of the available goods such that no one person can be made better off without necessarily making someone else worse off.

MRS between goods is the same.

To study the equity issue, we can explore the particularly simple case of allocating a fixed amount of two goods between two people. In Chapter 6 we briefly discuss this situation and show that it may often be possible for both people in such a situation to be made better off through trading. Following our discussion earlier in this chapter, we call an allocation in which such an unambiguous improvement can be made "inefficient." An *efficient allocation* of goods among the people in our **exchange economy,** on the other hand, is one in which any one of the people can be made better off (through obtaining a different set of goods) only by making someone else worse off. Before we investigate the equity question, it will be helpful if we examine efficiency in this situation in more detail.

Conditions for Efficient Exchange: An Intuitive Proof

If an allocation of goods in this exchange situation is to be efficient, the goods should be distributed among people so that the marginal rate of substitution (MRS) between any two goods is the same for everyone.[12] To show this result, let us suppose there are only two goods (say, apples and oranges) and two people (Smith and Jones) in society. We will also assume that there are 50 apples and 100 oranges to be divided among Smith and Jones. Would an equal allocation of these commodities to each person be efficient?

The answer to this question depends on the people's preferences. Suppose that the MRS for Smith is 2/1 when he gets 25 apples and 50 oranges. Smith is willing to give up two oranges to get one more apple under the proposed equal allocation. On the other hand, suppose that Jones' MRS is 1/1. Under the equal allocation scheme (with 25 apples and 50 oranges) she would be willing to trade one orange for one apple. Under these assumptions, it is easy to see that the proposed equal allocation is not efficient. Take two oranges from Smith; trade one of these to Jones for one apple (notice that Jones is willing to make this trade). Now give this apple to Smith so that he will be as well off as before the two oranges were taken. We have now found a new allocation in which Smith (with 26 apples and 48 oranges) and Jones (with 24 apples and 51 oranges) are each as well off as they were under the original equal allocation. With this new allocation, however, there is one orange left over. It may be given to either Smith or Jones, making the recipient better off

---

[12]We have already shown this result in Chapter 6. You may wish to review the simple example presented there.

Figure 17.10
Edgeworth Box Diagram of
Efficiency in Exchange

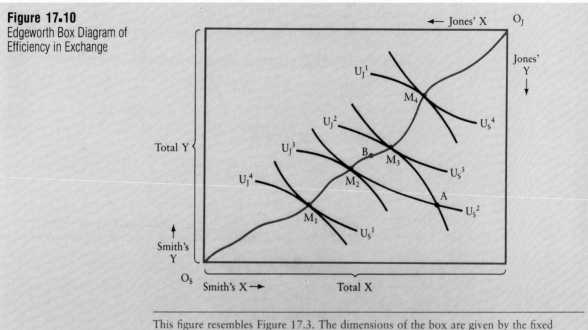

This figure resembles Figure 17.3. The dimensions of the box are given by the fixed amounts of X and Y that are available in this economy. Indifference curves for two people (Smith and Jones) are also shown in the box. The points on the curve O_S, O_J are efficient in the sense that at these allocations Smith cannot be made better off without making Jones worse off, and vice versa. An allocation such as A, on the other hand, is inefficient since both Smith and Jones can be made better off (by choosing B, for example). Along O_S, O_J the MRS for Smith is equal to that for Jones. The line O_S, O_J is called the contract curve.

than he or she was before. What we have shown is that the initial (equal) allocation was not efficient. There exists some alternative allocation in which Smith could be made better off without making Jones any worse off.

Edgeworth Box Diagram

The numbers in this example were purely arbitrary. Any allocation in which the MRSs of two people differ can be shown to be inefficient. Whenever the goods are allocated so that the rates at which individuals are willing to trade one good for another differ, these goods can be reallocated in an unambiguously better way; that is, a more efficient allocation can be found.

There may be many different allocations that are efficient, and we can most easily demonstrate these by using the Edgeworth box diagram introduced in Figure 17.2. The Edgeworth box in Figure 17.10 has dimensions given by the total (fixed) quantities of the two goods (call these goods simply X and Y). The horizontal dimension of the box represents the total quantity of X available, whereas the height of the box is the total quantity of Y. The point O_S is considered to be the origin for Smith. Quantities of X for Smith are measured along the horizontal axis rightward from O_S; quantities of Y, along the vertical axis upward from O_S. Any point in the box can be regarded as some allocation of X and Y to Smith. For example, at point A, Smith gets the amounts shown in the figure. The useful property of the Edgeworth box is that the quantities received by Jones are also recorded by point A. Jones gets that part of the total quantity that is left over. That is, Jones' quantities are measured from O_J. The quantities assigned to Smith and Jones in this manner exactly exhaust the total quantities of X and Y available.

Finding an Efficient Point

Any point in the Edgeworth box represents an allocation of the available goods between Smith and Jones, and all possible allocations are contained within the box. The reader may wish to choose any point in the box and demonstrate that this point represents a unique division of goods X and Y to Smith and Jones. To discover which of the points are efficient, we must introduce preferences. In Figure 17.10 Smith's indifference curve map is drawn with origin O_S. Movements in a northeasterly direction represent higher levels of utility to Smith. In the same figure, Jones' indifference curve map is drawn with the corner O_J as an origin. As we did for the isoquant map in Figure 17.3, we have taken Jones' indifference curve map, rotated it 180°, and fitted it into the northeast corner of the Edgeworth box. Movements in a southwesterly direction represent increases in Jones' utility level.

Using these superimposed indifference curve maps, it is possible to find the efficient points in the diagram. Consider any fixed utility level for Jones, say U_J^2. The definition of efficiency requires that Smith's utility level be maximized for this given level of Jones' utility; not to do so would be inefficient. The point of maximum utility for Smith in this case is point M_3, where Smith's indifference curve (U_S^3) is just tangent to the curve U_J^2. At this point of tangency, the MRS (of X for Y) for Smith is equal to that for Jones; the efficient conditions we discussed earlier hold.

Contract curve
A graphic representation of all the efficient allocations of goods in an Edgeworth box diagram of exchange.

Pareto optimal allocation of resources
Allocations in which no one person can be made better off without necessarily making someone else worse off (see also exchange efficiency).

Contract Curve

Within the Edgeworth box there are a number of tangencies such as M_3. A few of these (M_1, M_2, and M_4) are labeled in Figure 17.10. Each of these points is efficient since Smith's utility is as large as possible given some preassigned level for Jones' utility. Similarly, for any specific level of Smith's utility, Jones' utility is as large as possible at these points. The locus of all these efficient points is called the **contract curve**. It shows those efficient allocations that people might make through free bargaining among themselves. Points on the contract curve are sometimes called *Pareto optimal* allocations after the Italian economist Vilfredo Pareto, who first discovered this concept of exchange efficiency. In Figure 17.10 this contract curve is given by the line running from O_S to O_J. For every allocation on the contract curve Smith cannot be made better off without making Jones worse off. The utilities of Smith and Jones are directly in conflict as is required by the definition of efficiency. This is not true for points off the contract curve. For example, an allocation such as point A, which is off the contract curve, is inefficient in that both people can be made better off by moving to a point on the contract curve. This would be true, for instance, if the allocation B (or any point between M_2 and M_3) were chosen rather than point A. At B both Smith and Jones are better off than they were at A. Point A represents an inefficient way of allocating X and Y. Both Smith and Jones can strike bargains that are superior to point A. "Applying Economics: Exchange in a POW Camp" shows that such bargains might be struck even under the most trying of circumstances.

Utility Possibilities and the Equity Problem

Allocations along the contract curve show the possible levels of utilities that Smith and Jones might obtain by making efficient bargains with each other. If we are willing to assume for the moment that utility is measurable, we can show these possibilities in much the same way we did for production possibilities earlier in this chapter. This **utility possibility frontier** is shown in Figure 17.11. Information to construct this curve is taken directly from Figure 17.10. All the efficient allocations shown in Figure 17.10 (such as M_1, M_2, M_3, and M_4) appear on the frontier in Figure 17.11. Inefficient allocations (such as point A) appear inside the frontier, clearly showing that both people can be made better off than they are at such an interior point.

> **Utility possibility frontier**
> A diagram illustrating all the Pareto optimal allocations of utility among the individuals in an economy.

Although all of the allocations along the utility possibility frontier in Figure 17.11 are *Pareto optimal*, some people might consider some of these allocations "fairer" than others. With allocations near O_S, for example, Jones gets most of the goods available whereas Smith gets very few. That situation is reversed near O_J where Smith is in a far more favorable position. The **equity** problem for any economic system is to devise rules or procedures for deciding which allocations are indeed unfair and what, if anything, should be done about them. Here we examine two aspects of this question: (1) problems in defining and achieving equity and (2) the connections among equity, efficiency, and perfect competition.

> **Equity**
> The fairness of the distribution of goods or utility.

Defining and Achieving Equity

A primary problem with developing an accepted definition of "fair" or "unfair" allocations of resources is that not everyone agrees with what the concept means. For some people, practically any allocation might be called "fair" providing no one breaks any laws in arriving at it—for these people, only acquisition of goods by theft would be called "unfair." Others may base their notions of fairness on a dislike for inequality. Only allocations in which people

APPLYING ECONOMICS

Exchange in a POW Camp

Prisoner of war (POW) camps provide an illustration of ways in which voluntary exchange arrangements may arise even in the most trying of circumstances. The basic goods available to the prisoners in such situations are usually determined by what they are given by their captors and by what goods come through other sources (for example, the Red Cross). Very little actual production takes place. Still, as R. A. Radford shows in a famous article detailing his experiences as a POW during World War II, elaborate arrangements may develop for reallocating the available goods in more efficient ways.[13] Radford shows, for example, that most prisoners were given essentially the same set of basic necessities, but customary rates of exchange among these commodities rapidly developed to reflect the prisoners' preferences. Tins of jam typically traded for one-half pound of margarine, whereas tins of diced carrots were worth practically nothing in exchange.

Bartering one good for another involves a potential inefficiency. A person who wants to trade jam for margarine has to find someone willing to make the trade. It is this problem that leads all modern societies to adopt money as a way of facilitating exchange. With a monetary system, one need not find someone willing to trade margarine for jam but can instead trade the jam for money and then use the money to buy margarine. In the POW camps there was no money in the usual sense, but as Radford shows, cigarettes came to play this role. Every commodity had a customary price in terms of cigarettes, and relative cigarette prices reflected relative rates of exchange between commodities. During periods when many Red Cross packages were received, cigarette sup-

plies rose and there was a general inflation of goods' prices in terms of cigarettes. This reflects the monetarist notion that general inflation represents "too much money chasing too few goods." Similarly, Gresham's law (that bad money drives out good) was reflected by the fact that only relatively poor quality cigarettes were used for making transactions—the better ones were smoked instead.

Radford also observed a form of international trade in the POW camps. Since French and British troops were imprisoned in separate areas, different prices developed for goods in these communities. Coffee, for example, was more highly valued in terms of cigarettes among French prisoners than among British prisoners. Risk-taking entrepreneurs who were willing to move between the camps (usually by bribing guards) could get "rich" by buying coffee from the British and selling it to the French.

To Think About

1. Suppose a POW camp's only source of jam was from monthly Red Cross packages. Would you expect sharp declines in jam prices just after the packages arrive? If you, as a prisoner, observed such a regular pattern, what would you do?
2. Some medical officers at the POW camps argued that use of cigarettes as money was unfair to smokers, since they might harm their health by selling their food rations for more cigarettes. The medical officers favored "price controls" on some food items. How would you evaluate this argument for price controls? How effective do you think such controls would be?

receive about the same levels of utility (assuming these levels could be measured and compared) would be regarded as fair. For the first type of people, practically any allocation on the utility possibility frontier would be fair providing it did not involve force or theft. For people of the second type, only allocations near the 45° line (where the utilities of Smith and Jones are equal) would be fair. Welfare economists have devised a number of other specific notions of

[13]R. A. Radford, "The Economic Organization of a POW Camp," *Economics*, November 1945, pp. 189–201.

Figure 17.11
Utility Possibility Frontier

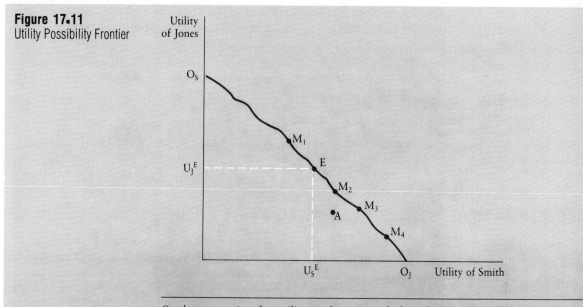

On the assumption that utility can be measured, the utility possibility frontier can be derived from the Edgeworth exchange box (Figure 17.10). The curve O_S, O_J shows those combinations of utility that are achievable. One possible criterion for choosing among these points would be to require equality of utilities. This would dictate choice of point E.

fairness but many of these tend to give conflicting conclusions about which allocations are or are not equitable.[14] There is simply no agreement on the issues.

Even if everyone agreed on what a fair allocation of resources (and utility) is, there would still be the question of how such a situation should be achieved. Can we rely on free exchange among people to achieve fairness, or will something more be required? Figure 17.11 shows why voluntary solutions may not always succeed. Suppose, for example, that everyone agrees that the only fair allocation is one of equal utilities. Perhaps everyone remembers his or her childhood experiences in dividing up a cake or candy where equal shares seemed to be the only reasonable solution. The desired allocation would be point E in Figure 17.11. On the other hand, suppose Smith and Jones start out at point A—in which Smith is in a fairly favorable situation. As we described previously, any allocation between M_2 and M_3 is preferable to point A because both people would be better off by making such a move. In this case, however, the point of equal utility (E) does not fall in this range. Smith

---

[14]For a survey of these equity concepts, see Amartya Sen, "Social Choice Theory," in K. J. Arrow and M. D. Intriligator, *Handbook of Mathematical Economics,* Vol. III (New York: North Holland, 1986), pp. 1106–1127.

Initial endowments
The initial holdings of goods from which trading occurs in exchange.

would not voluntarily agree to a move to point E since that would make him worse off than at point A. He would prefer to refrain from any trading rather than accept the "fair" allocation E. In the language of welfare economics, the **initial endowments** (that is, the starting place for trading) of Smith and Jones are so unbalanced that voluntary agreements will not result in an equal allocation of utilities. If point E is to be achieved, some coercion must be used to get Smith to accept it.

Equity, Efficiency, and Perfect Competition

The previous section shows that there is no particular reason to expect that a voluntary system of bargaining among people (such as occurs under perfect competition) will necessarily result in an equitable allocation of the available resources. Initial endowments may be too skewed or the concept of equity may itself be too vague to permit such a result. There is no "invisible hand" guiding a competitive system toward equitable solutions. It we insist on equity, it may be necessary to opt for some governmental coercion (such as taxes to transfer income among people) to get people to agree to allocations they would not voluntarily accept.

Adopting coercive methods to achieve equity may involve problems too. For example, in several places in this book we have shown how taxes may affect people's behavior and result in deadweight losses that arise from this distortion. Using government's power to transfer income (that is, utility) may therefore be a costly activity—achieving equity may involve some losses of efficiency. In our simple analysis of exchange, taxing Smith to provide goods for Jones may cause him to use some of his initial endowment to avoid such taxes by bribing the tax collectors. More generally, taxation may affect people's willingness to work and to produce goods, thereby affecting the amounts of goods available as reflected by the size of the Edgeworth box diagram with which we started our analysis. There may consequently be some trade-off between achieving equitable allocations of resources and achieving efficient allocations. "Applying Economics: Modeling the Impact of Taxes with a Computer" earlier in this chapter suggests that such efficiency costs may be quite high, but the issue is a very broad one that has not been resolved by economists.

Summary

We begin this chapter with a description of a general equilibrium model of a perfectly competitive price system. In that model, prices of every good are determined by the forces of supply and demand, and everyone takes prices as given in their economic decisions. We then arrive at the following conclusions about such a method for allocating resources:

- Profit-maximizing firms will use resources in a technically efficient way to produce goods because each firm will choose a combination of inputs for which the RTS is equal to the ratio of the inputs' prices. Firms will therefore operate on the production possibility frontier.

- Profit-maximizing firms will also produce an economically efficient mix of outputs. The workings of supply and demand will insure that the technical rate at which one good can be transformed into another in production (the rate of product transformation—RPT) is equal to the rate at which people are willing to trade one good for another (the MRS). Adam Smith's invisible hand brings considerable coordination into seemingly chaotic market transactions.

- Factors that interfere with the ability of prices to reflect marginal costs under perfect competition will prevent an economically efficient allocation of resources. Such factors include imperfect competition, externalities, and public goods. The latter two factors are discussed in detail in the next chapters.

- Even in a very simple exchange situation, there are no forces to insure that voluntary transactions will result in equitable final allocations. Achieving equity (if that term can be adequately defined at all) may require some coercion to transfer income. Such interventions may involve substantial costs in terms of economic efficiency.

Problems

17.1 Suppose the production possibility frontier for cheeseburgers (C) and milkshakes (M) is given by

$$C + 2M = 600.$$

a. Graph this function.
b. Assuming that people prefer to eat two cheeseburgers with every milkshake, how much of each product will be produced? Indicate this point on your graph.
c. Given that this fast food economy is operating efficiently, what price ratio (P_C/P_M) must prevail?

17.2 Consider an economy with just one technique available for the production of each good, food and cloth:

Good	Food	Cloth
Labor per unit output	1	1
Land per unit output	2	1

a. Supposing land is unlimited but labor equals 100, write and sketch the production possibilities frontier.
b. Supposing labor is unlimited but land equals 150, write and sketch the production possibilities frontier.

   c. Supposing labor equals 100 and land equals 150, write and sketch the production possibilities frontier. (Hint: What are the intercepts of the production possibilities frontier? When is land fully employed? Labor? Both?)

   d. Explain why the production possibility frontier of part c is concave.

   e. Sketch the relative price of food as a function of its output in part c.

   f. If consumers insist on trading four units of food for five units of cloth, what is the relative price of food? Why?

   g. Explain why production is exactly the same at a price ratio of $P_F/P_C = 1.1$ as at $P_F/P_C = 1.9$.

   h. Suppose that capital is also required for producing food and cloth and that capital requirements per unit of food are 0.8 and per unit of cloth 0.9. There are 100 units of capital available. What is the production possibilities curve in this case? Answer part e for this case.

*17.3 Suppose the production possibility frontier for guns (X) and butter (Y) is given by

$$X^2 + 2Y^2 = 900.$$

   a. Graph this frontier.

   b. If individuals always prefer consumption bundles in which $Y = 2X$, how much X and Y will be produced?

   c. At the point described in part a, what will be the RPT and what price ratio will cause production to take place at that point? This slope should be approximated by considering small changes in X and Y around the optimal point.

   d. Show your solution on the figure from part a.

17.4 "Jack Sprat can eat no fat, his wife can eat no lean." Construct an Edgeworth box diagram for this pair (assuming fixed quantities of fat and lean) and indicate the contract curve.

17.5 Smith and Jones are stranded on a desert island. Each has in his possession some slices of ham (H) and cheese (C). Smith is a very choosy eater and will eat ham and cheese only in the fixed proportions of two slices of cheese to one slice of ham.

    Jones is more flexible in his dietary tastes and has a utility function given by $U_J = 4H + 3C$. Total endowments are 100 slices of ham and 200 slices of cheese.

   a. Draw the Edgeworth box diagram that represents the possibilities for exchange in this situation. What is the only price ratio that can prevail in any equilibrium?

   b. Suppose that Smith initially had 40H and 80C. What would the equilibrium position be?

---

*Denotes a problem that is rather difficult.

c. Suppose that Smith initially had 60H and 80C. What would the equilibrium position be?

d. Suppose that Smith (much the stronger of the two) decides not to play by the rules of the game. Then what could the final equilibrium position be?

17.6 The country of Extrenum produces only skis (S) and waterskis (W), using capital (K) and labor (L) as inputs. The production functions for both S and W are fixed proportions. It takes two units of labor and one unit of capital to produce a pair of skis. Waterskis, on the other hand, require one unit of labor and one unit of capital. If the total supply of capital is 100 units, construct the production possibility curve for this economy. Are all inputs fully employed at every point on the production possibility curve? How do you explain any unemployment that might exist?

*17.7 Robinson Crusoe obtains utility from the quantity of fish he consumes in one day (F), the quantity of coconuts he consumes that day (C), and the hours of leisure time he has during the day (H) according to the utility function:

$$\text{Utility} = F^{1/4} \, C^{1/4} \, H^{1/2}.$$

Robinson's production of fish is given by

$$F = \sqrt{L_F}$$

(where L_F is the hours he spends fishing), and his production of coconuts is determined by

$$C = \sqrt{L_C}$$

(where L_C is the time he spends picking coconuts). Assuming that Robinson decides to work an eight-hour day (that is, H = 16), graph his production possibility curve for fish and coconuts. Show his optimal choices of those goods.

17.8 There are 200 pounds of food on an island that must be allocated between two marooned sailors. The utility function of the first sailor is given by:

$$\text{Utility} = \sqrt{F_1}$$

where F_1 is the quantity of food consumed by the first sailor. For the second sailor, utility (as a function of food consumption) is given by:

$$\text{Utility} = \frac{1}{2}\sqrt{F_2}$$

a. If the food is allocated equally between the sailors, how much utility will each receive?
b. How should food be allocated between the sailors to assure equality of utility?
c. Suppose that the second sailor requires a utility level of at least 5 to remain alive. How should food be allocated so as to maximize the sum of utilities subject to the restraint that the second sailor receive that minimum level of utility?
d. What other criteria might you use to allocate the available food between the sailors?

*17.9 Suppose that there are two individuals in an economy. Utilities of those individuals under five possible social states are shown in the following table.

The individuals do not know which number (1 or 2) they will be assigned when the economy begins operating. They are uncertain about the actual utility they will receive under the alternative social states. Which social state will be preferred if an individual adopts the following strategies in his or her voting behavior to deal with this uncertainty?

State	Utility 1	Utility 2
A	50	50
B	70	40
C	45	54
D	53	50.5
E	30	84

a. Choose that state that assures the highest utility to the least well-off person.
b. Assume that there is a 50–50 chance of being either individual and choose that state with the highest expected utility.
c. Assume that, no matter what, the odds are always unfavorable in that there is a 60 percent chance of having the lower utility and a 40 percent chance of higher utility in any social state. Choose the state with the highest expected utility given these probabilities.
d. Assume that there is a 50–50 chance of being assigned either number, and that each individual dislikes inequality. Each will choose that state for which:

$$\text{Expected utility} - |U_1 - U_2|$$

is as large as possible (where the $|...|$ notation denotes absolute value).
e. What do you conclude from this problem about the social choices under a veil of ignorance as to an individual's specific identity in society?

17.10 In an economy with two individuals (A and B), discuss the results of exchange in the following situations:

 a. Perfect competition in which A and B accept prices as given by the market.
 b. A is a monopolist and can set any price it chooses.
 c. A is a perfect price discriminator and can charge a different price for each unit traded.

 Does each of these lead to a Pareto efficient solution? It would be useful to work with an Edgeworth box diagram to present your solution.

17.11 The country of Podunk produces only wheat and cloth, using as inputs land and labor. Both are produced by constant returns to scale production functions. Wheat is the relatively land-intensive commodity.

 a. Explain in words or with diagrams how the price of wheat relative to cloth (p) determines the land-labor ratio in each of the two industries.
 b. Suppose that p is given by external forces (this would be the case if Podunk were a small country trading freely with a large world). Show, using the Edgeworth box, that if the supply of labor increases in Podunk, the output of cloth will rise and the output of wheat will fall.

LINEAR PROGRAMMING, PRICING OF INPUTS, AND DUALITY

This appendix introduces the mathematical tool of linear programming and uses this tool to demonstrate some additional relationships between the efficient use of resources and the pricing of those resources. Since a detailed treatment of linear programming is beyond the scope of this book, our analysis here is brief.[1]

The Problem

We examine here only one specific example of linear programming techniques. In this example, an economy is assumed to have fixed amounts of various productive inputs, and a central planner must choose how to allocate these inputs to the production of two goods, cars and trucks. In order to avoid introducing demand we assume that prices of the two goods are determined outside of our model and do not change. We assume that the price of each truck (P_T) is $4,000 and that the price of each car (P_C) is $5,000. The sole goal of the central planner in our simple economy is to allocate the available resources to car and truck production so that the total value of output is as large as possible. That is, the goal is to choose car output (C) and truck output (T) so that

$$\text{Total value} = TV = P_T \cdot T + P_C \cdot C$$

$$= 4000 \cdot T + 5000 \cdot C \qquad [17A.1]$$

is as large as possible given available resources.

A Graphic Demonstration

Before we approach the solution to this problem using linear programming, the general kind of solution we might derive can be demonstrated by applying the tools presented earlier. The most direct way to proceed is by using a graphic analysis. In Figure 17A.1 the production possibility frontier is drawn for the economy. The curve PP represents those combinations of cars and

---

[1]For an interesting though fairly difficult survey of linear programming techniques, see Robert Dorfman, P. A. Samuelson, and R. M. Solow, *Linear Programming and Economic Analysis* (New York: McGraw-Hill, 1958).

Figure 17A.1
Value Maximization in a
Hypothetical Economy

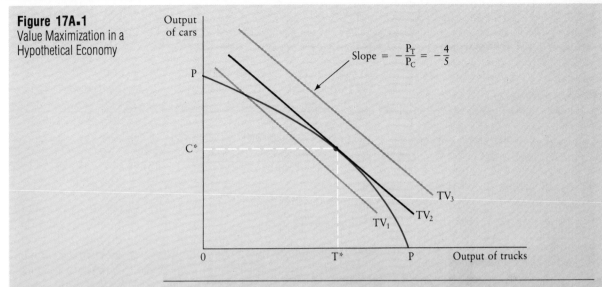

PP represents the feasible combinations of cars and trucks that can be produced with available resources. If a central planner wishes to maximize the total value of production (TV), the combination C*, T* should be produced. At this output combination, the RPT (of trucks for cars) is equal to the ratio of these goods' prices (P_T/P_C).

trucks that can be produced given the inputs available. Our goal is to choose that point on the PP frontier that provides maximum revenues. This maximization process is shown in the figure. The several parallel straight lines (labeled TV_1, TV_2, TV_3) record those combinations of cars and trucks that provide equal value. The combinations lying along TV_3 provide more in total value than do those on TV_2, which in turn provide more value than do those on TV_1. The slope of these lines is given by

$$-P_T/P_C \, (= \, -\$4{,}000/\$5{,}000 \, = \, -4/5)$$

since this ratio of prices tells how cars can be traded for trucks in the market while keeping the total value for output constant.

The total value of cars and trucks produced is as large as possible when output combination C*, T* is chosen. This combination produces total revenues of TV_2, and it is the only combination that is capable of providing this amount. All other feasible output combinations on PP provide less total value than does this optimal choice. At C*, T* the production possibility frontier is exactly tangent to the total value line TV_2. This type of result should by now be familiar to you. At the optimal point, the rate at which cars can technically be traded for trucks is equal to the rate at which these two goods can be traded in the market. In other words, the rate of product transformation (of trucks for cars) is equal to the price ratio P_T/P_C.

Table 17A.1
Resources and Technology in a Hypothetical Economy

Resource	Total Available	Required to Produce 1 Truck	Required to Produce 1 Car
Labor	720 labor-hours	1 labor-hour	2 labor-hours
Machines	900 machine-hours	3 machine-hours	1 machine-hour
Steel	1800 tons	5 tons	4 tons

A Linear Programming Statement of the Problem

Linear programming
A mathematical technique for finding the maximum (or minimum) value for a linear function whose variables are subject to linear constraints.

Linear programming is a mathematical technique that is particularly suited to solving our problem. The technique was developed as a systematic way to find the maximum values of linear functions (such as Equation 17A.1) when the variables in these functions—C and T—are constrained in the values they can take on. In order to show how this technique works, we must first examine the factors in the economy that constrain the output choices that are feasible.

There are two types of constraints on the amount that can be produced by an economy: total quantities of various inputs are fixed, and certain technical rules (that is, production functions) must be followed in turning these inputs into outputs. For the purposes of our car-truck example, we assume that there are only three inputs: labor, machines, and steel. The quantities of these inputs that are assumed to be available are shown in the second column of Table 17A.1. No production plan can be implemented that uses more than 720 labor-hours, 900 machine hours, or 1800 tons of steel.

Production Functions for Cars and Trucks

Table 17A.1 also indicates the amount of each input required to produce one car or one truck. It takes one labor-hour, three machine-hours, and five tons of steel to build a truck; it takes two labor-hours, one machine-hour, and four tons of steel to build a car. The production techniques shown in Table 17A.1 are fixed proportions: no substitution between inputs is possible. This kind of linear technology is one characteristic of most linear programming problems.

Resource Constraints

We can now examine the constraints that these amounts of inputs place on the combinations of cars and trucks that can be produced. With C representing the number of cars to be produced and T the number of trucks, the first line of Table 17A.1 shows that all possible choices of T and C must obey the inequality

$$1 \cdot T + 2 \cdot C \le 720.$$

[17A.2]

That is, the quantity of labor employed in truck production (one labor-hour to build one truck) plus the quantity employed in car production (two labor-hours per car) cannot exceed the 720 labor-hours available. Equation 17A.2 might be called the "labor-hours" constraint in production.

Similar constraints exist for machines and for steel. Again, these can be taken directly from Table 17A.1. The machine-hour constraint is

$$3 \cdot T + 1 \cdot C \le 900 \qquad \text{[17A.3]}$$

and the steel constraint is

$$5 \cdot T + 4 \cdot C \le 1800. \qquad \text{[17A.4]}$$

These constraints record that no more machines or steel may be used in production than are available.

Given these three resource constraints, our problem is to find values of T and C that satisfy all constraints and to make the total value of output, shown in Equation 17A.1:

$$TV = 4000 \cdot T + 5000 \cdot C$$

as large as possible. That, then, is our linear programming problem.

Construction of the Production Possibility Frontier

One very time-consuming solution to the problem would be to list all the combinations of C and T that satisfy the three constraints, calculate the total value obtained from each combination, and choose that one with the largest value. A far more efficient procedure makes use of graphic techniques. Figure 17A.2 graphs the three resource constraints. Since any feasible combination of C and T must satisfy *all* three constraints, we are interested only in those points in the diagram that fall on or below all three lines. The heavy line in Figure 17A.2 indicates the outer perimeter of such feasible choices. Combinations of cars and trucks on or inside this curve can be produced. Those outside the perimeter cannot be produced because there are not enough resources to do so.

For example, should the central planner in the economy decide to produce only cars, the heavy line indicates that 360 could be produced. In producing only cars, the economy "runs out" of labor-hours first (there is enough steel to produce 450 cars and enough machine-hours to produce 900 cars). For trucks, on the other hand, the binding constraint is machine availability. There are only enough machine-hours to build 300 trucks. Other combinations of cars and trucks on or inside the heavy line in Figure 17A.2 similarly satisfy all the constraints. The curve is just the production possibility frontier for the simple economy we have described.

Figure 17A.2
Construction of the Production Possibility Frontier for the Linear Programming Problem

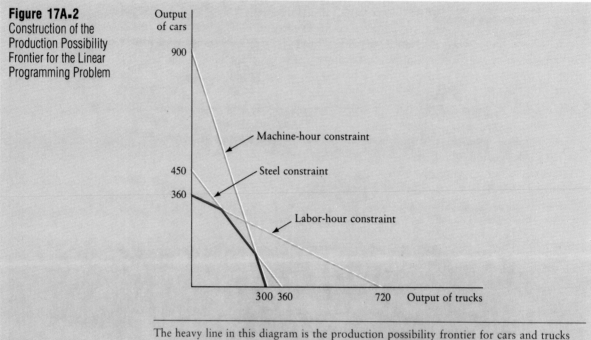

The heavy line in this diagram is the production possibility frontier for cars and trucks applied by the input constraints. It is the perimeter of the set of output combinations that satisfies all the constraints.

Linear Programming Solution of the Problem

We can use the production possibility frontier derived in Figure 17A.1 to solve our maximum value problem in much the same way that the problem was solved in Figure 17A.1. Figure 17A.3 again shows the production possibility frontier together with several lines of equal revenue. From the figure, we can see that the value-maximizing point is output combination C^*, T^*, where the labor-hour constraint and the steel constraint intersect.[2] (Refer back to Figure 17A.2 to check that these are indeed the constraints that intersect at C^*, T^*.) Solving the two constraints for C^* and T^* gives:

$$1T + 2C = 720 \text{ (labor-hour constraint)}$$

$$5T + 4C = 1800 \text{ (steel constraint)} \qquad [17A.5]$$

---

[2]This point, in a sense, satisfies the rule that the RPT should equal the ratio P_T/P_C. The RPT along the labor-hour constraint is $-1/2$; along the steel constraint the RPT is $-5/4$. The vertex at C^*, T^* includes all slopes between $-1/2$ and $-5/4$. But the ratio $-P_T/P_C$ is given by $-4/5$, which lies between these two values. Hence, C^*, P^* is the revenue-maximizing point. In linear programming problems, the optimal solution will usually occur at corners, such as the one illustrated.

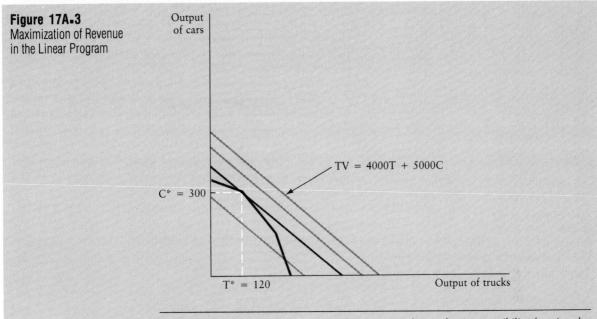

Figure 17A-3
Maximization of Revenue
in the Linear Program

By superimposing several lines of equal revenue on the production possibility frontier, the point of maximum revenue can be found. This point occurs where the labor-hour and steel constraints intersect.

or, from the labor-hour constraint,

$$T = 720 - 2C. \qquad \text{[17A.6]}$$

Therefore, by substitution into the steel constraint,

$$5(720) - 10C + 4C = 1800$$
$$-6C = -1800. \qquad \text{[17A.7]}$$

Hence, our optimal solution is

$$C^* = 300$$
$$T^* = 120. \qquad \text{[17A.8]}$$

That means that 120 trucks should be produced along with 300 cars. The revenue provided by these outputs is $1,980,000; this is the maximum value possible given the resource constraints. At this production level not all the available machine-hours are being used. Production of 300 cars and 120 trucks requires only 660 machine hours, whereas 900 are available. The observation that at the value-maximizing output level there are unused machines has important implications for the pricing of machines, as we will now demonstrate.

Duality and the Pricing of Inputs

Dual linear programming problem
A minimization problem related to a primal linear programming maximization problem; often involves computation of appropriate resource prices.

So far we have said nothing about the price of inputs in this linear programming problem. The economy had the inputs on hand, and the central planner set about the task of maximizing the value of the economy's output. A linear programming problem related to this *primal* maximization problem is the *dual* **linear programming problem** of finding the proper input prices associated with the optimal choice of C and T. Formally, these dual input prices solve the following linear programming problem:

Minimize

$$M = 720P_L + 900P_K + 1800P_S \qquad [17A.9]$$

subject to

$$P + 3P_K + 5P_S \geq 4000$$

$$2P_L + P_K + 4P_S \geq 5000 \qquad [17A.10]$$

where P_L, P_K, and P_S are the per unit prices of labor, capital, and steel.

This dual problem can be given an economic interpretation. We are asked to find prices for the inputs that minimize the total value of all inputs available (that is, minimize total cost). These prices must not be too low (they can't all be zero). The two inequalities in Equation 17A.10 require that neither the production of cars nor trucks earns a pure economic profit. For example, the first inequality says that the costs of producing one truck (that is, the cost of one labor-hour, three machine-hours, and five tons of steel) should not be less than the price of a truck ($4,000). Similarly, the input costs must be sufficiently high that their cost is not less than the price of a car ($5,000).

Without going into formal detail, it should be clear that the dual problem is related in some way to the original problem. All the constants that appeared in the primal problem also appear in the dual problem, but in different places. In particular, quantities of inputs that appeared in the original constraints now appear as coefficients in the dual objective function (Equation 17A.9) and vice versa. Also the constraints of the primal problem seem to have been "turned on their side" in the dual problem.

Solution to the Dual Problem

A graphic solution to the dual linear programming problem is not presented here because it would require a three-dimensional graph to show all three input prices. It must be taken on faith that the solution to the dual program turns out to be

$$P_L = \$1,500$$

$$P_K = \$0$$

$$P_S = \$500. \qquad\qquad [17A.11]$$

These are the prices of labor, machines, and steel that minimize Equation 17A.9 and obey the two constraints given by Equation 17A.10. You may wish to check if this is indeed true.

There are several important features about this solution:

- With these input prices, the inequalities in Equation 17A.10 are exactly satisfied. Neither good is produced at a loss. Hence, both goods can be produced in the economy without needing a subsidy.
- The value of M with these input prices is $1,980,000. It is no coincidence that this is identical to the maximum value for the total value of output that we found in the primal problem. Such a relationship holds between the primal and the dual solutions of all linear programs. Here this equality resembles the income-output identity in the *National Income and Product Accounts*. The total value of output is equal to the total value of inputs.
- The input that had some extra amount left over in the primal problem (machine-hours) is given a price of $0 in the dual problem. This result tells economists that adding machines in this economy would have no effect on the value of output. Since labor and steel are the inputs that prevent output being increased, on the other hand, these inputs are given positive prices. The values given in Equation 17A.11 for P_L and P_S indicate how much extra value would be provided by one more unit of these inputs. You may wish to show, for example, that an increase in labor-hours by one unit will cause the total of output to increase by $1,500 if we allow the economy to produce fractional parts of cars and trucks.[3]

Further Observations on Duality

These linear programming problems demonstrate the relationship between the optimal choice of outputs and the correct choice of input prices. The optimal allocation of a fixed amount of inputs to the production of a variety of possible

---

[3]The firm will produce five-sixths of an additional car in this situation but will cut truck production by two-thirds of a truck. Consequently, total revenue is changed by $5/6 \cdot \$5,000 - 2/3 \cdot \$4,000$, which is about $1,500.

outputs always has associated with it a dual problem that involves the optimal pricing of those inputs available. The solution of one problem is equivalent to the solving of the other.[4] This relationship has been widely used.

The computation of input prices from a linear programming model can be very useful for economic planning in less developed economies. Such "shadow prices" can provide information about how important certain inputs are, and occasionally such computed prices may differ greatly from the actual prices of the inputs. For example, there are institutional reasons (labor unions, minimum wages, and so forth) why some groups of workers may have high wages even though labor is an overabundant resource in the particular country. On the other hand, linear programming models may suggest that the "real" value of labor is rather low, and planners should adopt production techniques that utilize labor to a greater extent than would seem economically warranted by looking only at market wage rates.

In a similar way linear programming has been used by corporations in order to make more efficient management decisions. One such use arises when a firm wishes to decentralize its decision making. To do so, the firm often divides its operations among several profit centers, which are responsible for all production decisions within a specific area. One problem with which the management of such decentralized firms must contend is how to charge each profit center for the general company inputs (plant and equipment, administrative staff, advertising staff) it uses. Only by correctly choosing the bookkeeping prices of these inputs can the firm's management be sure that the decisions of the manager of each profit center will produce desirable overall results. Linear programming has been used extensively for calculating the prices of such intracompany resources.

These two examples merely hint at the huge number of applications that linear programming has had. Others include such widely different uses as the planning of natural gas pipelines and railway yards, investigating the optimal portfolio of stocks for a mutual fund to own, and studying the movement of seasonal labor forces in Africa. In many of these applications, a linear program's duality features are utilized.

Summary

This appendix describes the use of the mathematical tool of linear programming as a way to solve economic problems. In addition to illustrating the technique with a simple example, it also discusses the importance of the dual

---

[4]Linear programming problems may not always have solutions. If a linear programming problem and its associated dual have "feasible" solutions (solutions that satisfy the constraints of the problems) then they each have optimal solutions that have the properties listed above. For an elegant and concise discussion of the relationship between primal and dual linear programming problems with applications to a variety of allocational problems, see David Gale, *The Theory of Linear Economic Models* (New York: McGraw-Hill, 1960).

relationship between allocating resources efficiently and the correct pricing of these resources. The specific findings in the appendix are:

- Linear programming can sometimes be used to find the maximum (or minimum) value for a linear function when the values of some of the variables in the function are subject to linear constraints.
- The optimal solution found by linear programming will have many of the characteristics of efficiency illustrated in Chapter 17. Specifically, the marginal rate of product transformation will be approximately equal to the relative prices of goods being produced.
- Solving the dual to a linear programming problem can provide optimal prices for scarce resources. Resources that are not scarce will be assigned a price of zero in such solutions.

CHAPTER 18

Externalities and Property Rights

Externalities are interactions among economic actors that are not adequately reflected in the market. Our goal in this chapter is to analyze why markets fail to allocate resources effciently in this situation. We also show various ways in which the problems posed by externalities can be controlled. More generally, our study of externalities provides insights into the nature and problems of private property; the issue of property rights is an underlying theme of this chapter.

Before launching into a detailed analysis, we should be precise in defining exactly what an externality is, since there has been substantial confusion over this point in economics. An **externality** is an effect of one economic actor's activities on another actor's well-being that is not taken into account by the normal operations of the price system. This definition stresses the direct, nonmarket effect of one actor on another. The definition does not include effects that take place through the market. If I buy an item that is on sale before you do, I may keep you from getting it and thereby affect your well-being. That is not an externality since the effect took place in a market setting and does not affect the ability of markets to allocate resources efficiently. Before examining why nonmarket effects may distort the allocation of resources, our definition may be made more concrete by giving a few examples.

Externality
The effect of one party's economic activities on another party that is not taken into account by the price system.

Examples of Externalities

Externalities can occur between any two economic actors. Here we illustrate both negative (harmful) and positive (beneficial) externalities between firms. We then examine externalities between people and firms, and conclude by considering a few externalities between people.

Externalities between Firms

Consider two firms—one producing eyeglasses, another producing charcoal (this is an actual example from 19th century English law). The production of charcoal is said to have an external effect on the production of eyeglasses if the output of eyeglasses depends not only on the amount of inputs chosen by the eyeglass firm but also on the level at which the production of charcoal is carried on. Suppose these two firms are located near each other, and the eyeglass firm is downwind from the charcoal firm. In this case, the output of eyeglasses may depend not only on the level of inputs the eyeglass firm uses itself but also on the amount of air pollution that may affect its precision grinding wheels. The level of pollutants, in turn, is determined by the output of charcoal. Increases in charcoal output would cause fewer high quality eyeglasses to be produced even though the eyeglass firm has no control over this negative effect.[1]

The relationship between two firms may also be beneficial. Most examples of such positive externalities are rather bucolic in nature. Perhaps the most famous, proposed by James Meade, involves two firms, one producing honey by raising bees and the other producing apples.[2] Because the bees feed on apple blossoms, an increase in apple production will improve productivity in the honey industry. The beneficial effects of having well-fed bees is a positive externality to the beekeeper. Similarly, bees pollinate apple crops and the beekeeper provides an external benefit to the orchard owner. Later in this chapter we examine this situation in greater detail since, surprisingly enough, the beekeeper–apple grower relationship has played an important role in economic research on the significance of externalities.

Externalities between Firms and People

Firms' productive activities may impact directly on individuals' well-being. As we show in Chapter 17, for example, a firm that produces air pollution imposes costs on people living near the firm in the form of ill health and increased dust and grime. Similar effects arise from firms' pollution of water (for example, mining firms that dump their waste into Lake Superior, reducing the lake's recreational value to people who wish to fish there), misuse of land (strip mining that is an eyesore and may interfere with water supplies), and production of noise (airports that are located near major cities). In all of these cases, at least on first inspection, it seems that firms will not take these external costs into consideration when making decisions on how much to produce.

---

[1]We will find it necessary to redefine the assumption of "no control" considerably as the analysis of this chapter proceeds.

[2]James Meade, "External Economies and Diseconomies in a Competitive Situation," *Economic Journal*, March 1952, pp. 54–67.

Of course, people may also have external effects on firms. Drivers' auto pollution harms the productivity of citrus growers, cleaning up litter and graffiti is a major expense for shopping centers, and the noise of Saturday night rock concerts on college campuses probably affects motel rentals. In each of these cases there may be no simple way for the affected parties to force the producers of the externalities to take the costs of their actions into account.

Externalities between People

Finally, the activity of one person may affect the well-being of someone else. Playing a radio too loud, smoking cigars, or driving during peak hours are all consumption activities that may negatively affect the utility of others. Planting an attractive garden or shoveling the snow off one's sidewalk may, on the other hand, provide beneficial externalities. These activities will not be reflected in market transactions among the people involved. We will now examine the implications of this failure to account for externalities in the allocation of resources.

Externalities, Markets, and Allocational Efficiency

It has traditionally been argued that the presence of externalities such as those we have just described can cause a market to operate inefficiently. We discuss the reasons for this briefly in Chapter 17, and repeat these reasons here using the example of eyeglass and charcoal producers. Production of eyeglasses is assumed to produce no externalities, but is assumed to be negatively affected by the level of charcoal output. We now show that resources will be allocated inefficiently in this situation. For an efficient allocation of resources it is required that price be equal to social marginal cost in each market (see Chapter 17 for a discussion of this point).[3] If the market for eyeglasses is perfectly competitive (as we assume both markets to be), their price will indeed be equal to this good's private marginal cost. Indeed, since there are no externalities in eyeglass production, there is no distinction between private and social marginal cost in this case.

For charcoal production, the story is more complex. The producer of charcoal will still produce that output for which price is equal to private marginal cost. This is a direct result of the profit-maximization assumption. However, because of the negative effect that production of charcoal has on eyeglass production, it will not be true that private and social marginal costs of charcoal production are equal. Rather, the true **social cost** of charcoal production is equal to the private cost *plus* the cost that its production imposes on eyeglass firms in terms of reduced or inferior output. The charcoal producer firm does

Social costs
Costs of production that include both input costs and costs of the externalities that production may cause.

---

[3]The proof presented in Chapter 17 is both more elegant and formally more correct than the one presented here because it develops the analysis in terms of relative rather than absolute marginal costs.

Figure 18.1
An Externality in Charcoal
Production Causes an
Inefficient Allocation of
Resources

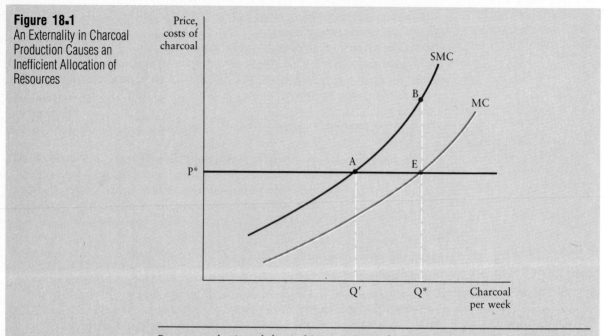

Because production of charcoal imposes external costs on eyeglass makers, social
marginal costs (SMC) exceed private marginal costs (MC). In a competitive market the
firm would produce Q* at a price of P*. At Q*, however, SMC > P* and resource
allocation could be improved by reducing output to Q'.

not recognize this effect and produces where price is equal to private marginal
cost (which is lower than social marginal cost). The social marginal cost of
charcoal production exceeds the good's price: this is a clear sign that too much
charcoal is being produced. Society would be made better off by reallocating
resources away from charcoal production and toward the production of other
goods (including eyeglasses). In this case, relying on the free operation of the
market (and the self-interest of the charcoal firm) has not produced an efficient
allocation of resources. Because of the externality in charcoal production, the
price system no longer carries the correct information about costs that is
necessary to achieve efficiency.

A Graphic Demonstration

Figure 18.1 illustrates the misallocation of resources that results from the
externality in charcoal production. Assuming that the charcoal producer is a
price taker, the demand curve for its product is simply a horizontal line at the
prevailing market price (say P*). Profits are maximized at Q* where price is
equal to the private marginal cost of producing charcoal (MC). Because of the
externality that charcoal production imposes on eyeglass makers, however,

the social marginal cost of this production (SMC) exceeds MC as shown in Figure 18.1. At Q*, the social marginal cost of producing charcoal exceeds the price people are willing to pay for this output (P*). Resources are misallocated, and production should be reduced to Q′ where the social marginal cost and price are equal. In making this reduction, total social costs (area Q′Q*BA) are reduced to a greater extent than are expenditures on charcoal (given by area Q′Q*EA). This comparison shows how the allocation of resources is improved by a reduction in charcoal output since costs are reduced to a greater extent than are consumers' expenditures on charcoal. Consumers can presumably spend this money on something else that involves lower social costs than charcoal. Now we examine various ways in which this desirable reduction in charcoal output might be brought about.

Traditional Ways of Coping with Externalities

To study possible solutions to the problems that externalities pose for the allocation of resources, we assume that production techniques are fixed and that the externality is a necessary fact of life.[4] Under this assumption, prescriptions such as "ban charcoal pollution" or "force charcoal producers to use alternative production techniques that yield less soot" are outside the frame of analysis. Introducing other ways of coping with externalities would considerably complicate our analysis without adding to an understanding of the issue. Even in our restricted case, there are still two approaches that may bring about improved efficiency—taxation and merger.

Taxation

The government could impose a suitable excise tax on the firm generating the externality. Presumably this tax would cause the output of charcoal to be cut back and would cause resources to be shifted into other uses. This classic remedy to the externality problem was first lucidly put forward in the 1920s by A. C. Pigou.[5] Although it has been somewhat modified, it remains the "standard" answer given by economists. The central problem for regulators becomes one of obtaining sufficient empirical information so that the correct tax structure can be enacted.

---

[4]It is also assumed that the detrimental effects of the production of charcoal do not affect anyone else in the economy other than eyeglass producers. Similarly, the discussion of externalities usually takes place within a partial equilibrium framework in which the rest of the economy is assumed to be perfectly competitive.

[5]A. C. Pigou, *The Economics of Welfare*, 4th ed. (London: Macmillan, 1946). Pigou also stresses the desirability of providing subsidies to firms that produce beneficial externalities. More recent literature has stressed that such taxes and subsidies must be based directly on the costs (or benefits) of the externalities (rather than on the total costs of the goods themselves) if efficiency is to be achieved.

Figure 18.2
Taxation Solution to the
Externality Problem

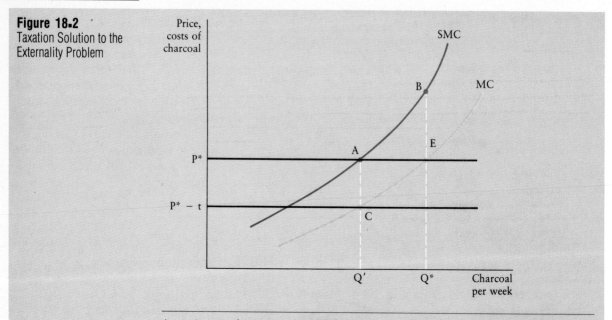

An excise tax of amount t would reduce the net price of charcoal to P* − t. At that price
the firm would choose to produce the socially optimal level of charcoal output (Q').

The taxation solution is illustrated in Figure 18.2. Again MC and SMC
represent the private and social marginal costs of charcoal production, and
the market price of charcoal is given by P*. An excise tax of amount t (see
Chapter 10) would reduce the net price received by the firm to P* − t, and
at that price the firm would choose to produce Q'. The tax causes the firm to
reduce its output to the socially optimal amount. At Q' the firm incurs private
marginal costs of P* − t and imposes external costs on eyeglass makers of t
per unit. The per-unit tax paid by consumers of charcoal is therefore exactly
equal to the extra costs that charcoal producers impose on eyeglass producers.[6]
"Applying Economics: Effects of a Tax on Power Plant Emissions" shows
how such a **Pigovian tax** might work in practice.

Pigovian tax
A tax or subsidy on an
externality that brings
about an equality of
private and social
marginal costs.

Merger and Internalization

A second traditional cure for the allocational problems caused by externalities
between two firms would be for these firms to merge. If there were a single

---

[6]If the charcoal firm here represents an entire industry, then the tax would, as in Chapter 10,
raise the market price of charcoal. If the industry exhibited constant costs, in the long run price
would rise by the exact amount of the tax and demand would be reduced to the socially optimal
level by that price rise.

APPLYING ECONOMICS

Effects of a Tax on Power Plant Emissions

Electric power plants that burn coal emit a variety of unhealthy byproducts, most importantly sulfur (which is believed to cause, among other things, "acid" rain). Existing environmental regulations require such power plants to achieve certain emission standards, mainly by "scrubbing" the coal fumes in their exhaust stacks. Since that process is very costly, a number of economists and other observers have suggested that taxing sulfur emissions might obtain the same results at much lower resource costs. Specifically, a 1973 proposal by Wisconsin Senator William Proxmire would have taxed sulfur emissions at an initial rate of 5 cents per pound, with the rate rising to 20 cents over a period of years. By providing utilities with an incentive to shift to lower

Table 18.1
Estimated Effects of a Tax on Sulfur Emissions and Coal Production

	Tax per Pound				
	0¢	5¢	10¢	15¢	20¢
Emissions (millions of tons)	11.4	10.0	8.5	7.5	6.7
Coal production (millions of tons)					
Appalachia	308	301	292	277	259
Midwest	150	135	93	89	78
West	49	56	74	84	90
U.S. total	507	492	459	450	427

Source: A. Schlottmann and L. Abrams, "Sulfur Emissions Taxes and Coal Resources," *Review of Economics and Statistics*, February 1977, pp. 50–55; Tables 2 and 3.

sulfur coal, this plan would have substantially mitigated the need for scrubbing.

A. Schlottman and L. Abrams attempted to estimate the effects of the tax proposed by Proxmire on both coal production and sulfur emissions in the United States.[7] A summary of their results is presented in Table 18.1. Overall, the authors estimated that a 5 cent per pound tax would reduce annual sulfur emissions by about 1 million tons (a 12 percent reduction), with the 20 cent tax leading to nearly a 5 million ton reduction (a greater than 40 percent reduction). These reductions came partly from a reduced level of coal use and partly from a shift in coal supplies from regions with high sulfur content coal (parts of Appalachia and the Midwest) to regions with low sulfur content coal (the West). These changes would have imposed additional costs on utilities both because of the need to switch to imported oil as a fuel and because of the increased costs involved in transporting coal. Such costs may be rather small compared to alternative ways of dealing with sulfur, or to the health hazards involved in continuing high levels of sulfur emissions.

To Think About
1. Would an excise tax on coal have the same effect as Proxmire's proposed tax on sulfur emissions? How would such a tax affect utilities' choices of inputs? Relative to the emissions tax, how would the excise tax affect utility firms' willingness to invest in anti-pollution equipment?
2. Some authors have suggested that the government should create licenses that permit firms to dump a certain amount of pollutants into the environment. These licenses would then be sold to the highest bidder. Would the economic results of such a licensing arrangement resemble those of an emissions tax? Does the idea of creating licenses to engage in pollution seem like a good one?

---

[7]A. Schlottman and L. Abrams, "Sulfur Emission Taxes and Coal Resources," *Review of Economics and Statistics*, February 1977, pp. 50–55.

Internalization of an externality
Incorporation of the social marginal costs of an externality into an economic actor's decisions (as through taxation or merger).

firm producing both charcoal and eyeglasses, this firm would recognize the detrimental effect that charcoal production has on its glass-grinding equipment. In effect, the combined firm would now pay the full social marginal costs of charcoal production because it now incurs these costs directly. In other words, the firm's manager would now take the marginal cost curve for charcoal production to be SMC and would produce Q', where price equals this marginal cost. This is exactly what is required for efficiency. Economists would say that the externality in production has been **internalized** as a result of the merger.

Examples of Internalization

Attempts to internalize externalities in production are not uncommon. It is often the case that a firm will expand in size with the purpose of encompassing all the spillover effects of its activities. Firms may, for example, merge in an attempt to capture external benefits. Recreational site developers (such as ski slopes, golf courses, or resort hotels) often operate the service industries (such as motels, gas stations, and shops) near their projects. In this way they are able to internalize any effects that the appearance of such service firms may have on customers and plan an attractive overall environment.

Another important example of attempting to internalize external effects is the recent move toward the creation of regional metropolitan governments. It has been argued that geographically limited city governments cannot handle many current urban problems because these problems spill over into neighboring communities. New York's air pollution problems, for example, are not confined to the city itself but affect communities in New Jersey and Connecticut as well. New York City also provides benefits to neighboring communities by acting as a commercial and cultural center. Since many of the people who benefit from having such activities available do not live or work in New York City, there is no feasible way to get them to support the central city through taxes. By adopting a regional government, all such spillover effects would be internalized and policies that were optimal from a regional point of view could be pursued.

Property Rights, Allocation, and Equity

One important question we might still ask about this analysis is if the charcoal producer's actions impose a cost on the eyeglass maker, why doesn't the eyeglass maker "bribe" the charcoal firm to cut back on its output? Presumably the gain of a cutback to the eyeglass firm (the reduction in external costs is given by area ACEB in Figure 18.2) would exceed the loss of profits to charcoal makers (area ACE in the figure), and some bargaining arrangement might be worked out that would monetarily benefit both parties. Both firms would be irrational not to recognize such a possibility, and it would seem that the benefits of internalization could be obtained without actually going through a merger.

Property rights
The legal specification of who owns a good and the trades the owner is allowed to make with it.

Common property
Property that may be used by anyone without cost.

Private property
Property that is owned by specific people who may prevent others from using it.

We can make this observation somewhat clearer by introducing the concept of property rights to show how these rights might be traded between the two firms. Simply put, **property rights** are the legal specification of who owns a good and of the types of trades that the owner is allowed to make with others. Some goods may be defined as **common property** that is owned by society at large and may be used by anyone; others may be defined as **private property** that is owned by specific people.

Private property may either be *exchangeable* or *nonexchangeable*, depending on whether the good in question may or may not be traded. In this book we have been primarily concerned with exchangeable private property, and these are the type of property rights we will consider here.[8]

Costless Bargaining and the Free Market

For the purposes of the two-firm externality example, it is interesting to consider the nature of the property right that might be attached to the air shared by the charcoal and eyeglass firms. Suppose property rights were defined so as to give sole rights to use of the air to one of the firms, but that the firms were free to bargain over exactly how the air might be used. It might be thought that if rights to the air were given to the charcoal producer, pollution would result; whereas, if rights were given to the eyeglass firm, the air would remain pure and grinding machines would work properly. This might not be the case, because this conclusion disregards the bargains that might be reached by the two parties. Indeed, several authors have argued that if *bargaining is costless*, the two parties left on their own will arrive at the efficient output (Q'), and this result will be true regardless of who "owns" the rights to use the air.

Ownership by the Polluting Firm

Suppose the charcoal firm has the right to use the air as it wishes. It must then impute the costs (if any) related to this ownership into its cost function. What are the costs associated with air ownership? Again the opportunity cost notion provides the answer. For the charcoal firm, its costs of using the air for its exhaust are what someone else is willing to pay for this resource in its next best alternative use. In our example, only the eyeglass maker has some alternative uses for the air (to keep it clean). But the amount that this firm would be willing to pay for clean air is precisely equal to the external damage done

---

[8]Two important examples of privately owned goods that are not exchangeable are a person's human capital (this could be sold only in a society that permitted slavery) and a person's vote (a private good that is provided by the state).

by the pollution. If the charcoal firm calculates its costs correctly, its marginal cost curve (including the implicit cost of air use rights) becomes SMC in Figure 18.2. The firm will therefore produce Q′ and sell the remaining air use rights to the eyeglass maker for a fee of some amount between ACE (the lost profits from producing Q′ rather than Q* tons of charcoal) and ACEB (the maximum amount the eyeglass maker would pay to avoid having charcoal output increased from Q′ to Q*).

Ownership by the Injured Firm

A similar allocational result would occur if eyeglass makers owned the rights to use the air as they pleased. In this case the charcoal producer would be willing to pay any amount up to the total profits it earns for the right to pollute the air (assuming there is no less damaging way to make charcoal). The eyeglass maker will accept these payments so long as they exceed the costs imposed on it by the charcoal firm's pollution. The ultimate result of bargaining will be for the charcoal firm to offer a payment for the right to "use" the air to dispose of the amount of soot and ash associated with output level Q′. The eyeglass maker will not sell the rights for any further pollution into the air because what the charcoal firm would be willing to pay falls short of the cost of this additional pollution. Again, as when the charcoal firm had the air use rights, an efficient allocation can be reached by relying on voluntary bargaining between the two firms. In both situations some production of charcoal takes place, and there will be some air pollution. Having no charcoal output (and no pollution) would be inefficient in the same sense that producing Q* is—scarce resources would not be efficiently allocated. In this case there is some "optimal level" of air pollution that may be achieved through bargains between the firms involved.

The Coase Theorem

We have shown that the two firms left on their own can arrive at the efficient output level (Q′). Assuming that bargaining costs are zero, both parties will recognize the advantages of striking a deal. Each will be led by the "invisible hand" to the same output level that would be achieved through an ideal merger. Interestingly, that solution will be reached no matter how air use rights are assigned. The pollution-producing firm has exactly the same incentives to choose an efficient output level as does the injured firm. The ability of the two firms to bargain freely causes the true social costs of air pollution to be recognized by each in their decisions. This result is sometimes referred to as the **Coase theorem** after the economist Ronald Coase, who first proposed it in this form.[9]

Coase theorem
If bargaining is costless, the social cost of an externality will be taken into account by the parties and the allocation of resources will be the same no matter how property rights are assigned.

---

[9]See Ronald Coase, "The Problem of Social Cost," *Journal of Law and Economics*, October 1960, pp. 1–44.

Distributional Effects

There are distributional effects that do depend on who is assigned air use rights. If both firms appear in court demanding rights to use the air as they wish, the court's decision on how these rights should be assigned will have important distributional effects. If the charcoal firm is given the air rights, it will get the fee paid by the eyeglass maker, which will make the charcoal producer at least as well off as it was producing Q^*. If the eyeglass firm gets the rights, it will receive a fee for air use that at least covers the damage the air pollution does. Because in our example allocation will be unaffected by the way in which property rights are assigned, any assessment of the desirability of certain assignments must be made on equity grounds.[10] For example, if the owners of the charcoal firm were very wealthy and those who make eyeglasses were poor, we might argue that ownership of the air use rights should be given to eyeglass makers on the basis of distributional equity. If the situation were reversed, courts might give the charcoal firm the rights. The price system may in principle be capable of solving problems in the allocation of resources caused by externalities but, as always, the price system will not necessarily achieve equitable solutions.[11]

The issue of equity in the assignment of property rights arises in every allocational decision, not only in the study of externalities. The issue of which firm should be assigned the air rights is not essentially different from the question of which person has the right of ownership to a particular house. In either case a government could decide that the prevailing system of property rights is undesirable, and it might redefine those rights. The issue of income distribution is no more intertwined with the problem of externalities than it is with any other allocational question.

The Role of Bargaining Costs

The analysis of this section depends crucially on the assumption of zero bargaining costs. If the costs (real or psychological) of striking bargains were high, the workings of this voluntary exchange system might not be capable of achieving an efficient result. The allocation of resources would also probably not be independent of the way in which property rights are assigned. In the

---

[10]This conclusion requires that the changing distribution of wealth implied by different assignments of property rights has no effect on the allocation of goods. Loosely speaking, it is assumed that the demand and cost curves of Figure 18.2 will not shift in response to the changing distribution of wealth. It is assumed that "income effects" are unimportant.

[11]Matters of equity cannot be established here on *a priori* grounds but require a detailed examination of the welfare level of each agent. It would be inappropriate to argue that the charcoal firm has an inalienable right to the use of the air, or that eyeglass makers have a basic right to clean air. The desires of the two firms are strictly competitive and any arguments about the intrinsic rights of one party can symmetrically be applied to the other. For some fascinating examples of this symmetry in legal cases see Ronald Coase, "The Problem of Social Cost," *Journal of Law and Economics*, October 1960, pp. 1–44.

APPLYING ECONOMICS

Bargains in the Orchard—Bees and Apples

Earlier in this chapter we mentioned Meade's example of the beneficial externalities between beekeepers and apple growers—bees pollinate apples, and apples provide nectar for honey. Since the costs of bargaining between these two producers are probably low, our analysis suggests that there may be incentives to internalize these externalities through private contracts.

Cheung's investigation of beekeeping in Washington state shows that such contracts are very well developed.[12] Terms of contracts between beekeepers and farmers typically take into account both the benefits that various crops provide to beekeepers (in the form of honey) and the benefits that farmers get from having bees pollinate their crops. For crops such as clover and alfalfa, which have high honey yields, beekeepers usually pay rent to farmers for the right to have their bees use the farmers' land. On the other hand, apple and cherry growers must "rent" bees to provide pollination because the honey yield from those crops is low. Although Meade's externality example has a certain bucolic ap-

peal, to economists actual economic incentives seem to have limited its relevance in the real world. A quick look in the Yellow Pages in any farm area would show that trading in the services of bees is a viable business. As the Coase theorem would predict, voluntary arrangements seem to have eliminated the distorting effects of the externality.

To Think About

1. Not every beekeeper enters into contracts with growers for nectar. Instead, many allow their bees to forage (and pollinate) anywhere the bees choose to go. What sort of factors would determine whether there were formal contracts between beekeepers and growers?

2. Can you think of other examples of beneficial externalities in which some kind of payment is made by the beneficiary? For example, how do apartment and condominium complexes pay for landscaping services? Or, how do mall owners pay for indoor plants, fountains, and parking lot maintenance?

next section we examine an important type of externality for which bargaining costs are indeed quite high—environmental externalities. We show that for such externalities it is unlikely that the competitive market will attain an efficient outcome. Still, as "Applying Economics: Bargains in the Orchard—Bees and Apples" shows, the price system has a much greater power to handle externalities than might be presumed.

Bargaining Costs and Environmental Externalities

It is a commonplace observation that markets seem to have failed to cope with externalities related to the environment. Firms and individuals routinely pollute the air and water through their disposal activities; noise levels in urban areas are often so high as to be harmful to residents' health; and the array of signs and posters along most major highways creates what some people regard as "visual pollution." In view of the analysis of the previous section, a natural first question to ask about these externalities is why they have not been in-

[12]S. N. S. Cheung, "The Fable of the Bees: An Economic Investigation," *Journal of Law and Economics*, April 1973, pp. 11–33.

ternalized through bargaining. It would seem that those who are harmed by the externalities could bargain with those who create them and thereby improve the allocation of resources. A principal reason this does not happen is the *high bargaining costs* that are associated with most environmental externalities. It is frequently difficult to organize people harmed by these externalities into an effective bargaining unit and to calculate the monetary value of the losses suffered.[13] Similarly, most legal systems have been set up primarily to adjudicate disputes between two specific plaintiffs rather than to represent the rights of large, diffuse groups. Each of these factors makes bargaining costs extremely high in most cases of environmental spillovers. The lack of effective bargaining over these in the real world would seem to imply that the transaction costs involved may exceed by a substantial amount the possible efficiency gains that can be obtained by successful bargaining.

Bargaining Costs and Allocation

In cases characterized by high transactions or bargaining costs, the assignment of ownership rights can have significant allocational effects. If, as is normally the case, disposal of refuse into air and water is treated as use of common property, this in effect assigns use rights to each firm. The firm may use the air and water around it in any way it chooses, and high bargaining costs will prevent it from internalizing any external costs into their decisions. For this reason, pollution-producing activities may be operated at a higher level than would be optimal unless specific types of regulations (such as Pigou-type taxes) are employed.

Specification of ownership rights may also be an important determinant of the methods of production that are adopted. Because cost curves will be affected by the way in which these rights are distributed when bargaining costs are high, incentives for adopting different techniques of production can be generated. If the full social cost of pollution-producing techniques is imposed on polluters, for example, these techniques will appear less profitable than they otherwise would. When a dynamic view is taken of the economic process, the assignment of property rights may have significant effects on the evolution of technology. For example, it was not until strong anti–air-pollution laws were imposed on electric utility generation that low-sulfur fuels came into general use. Similarly, development of geothermal and solar electricity generation may proceed more rapidly than would have been the case had the external costs of more traditional methods of electricity generation not been imposed on producers through government regulations that require installa-

---

[13]Many of the problems that arise in the provision of public goods are important impediments to group antipollution action. Once pollution is abated, it is abated for everyone. The benefits are nonexclusive. Consequently, it may be to the advantage of each person to adopt the position of a free rider. See Chapter 19 for a further discussion of this free rider issue.

The Phosphate Ban and Clean Clothes

Most modern laundry detergents contain phosphates. These are added to provide greater cleaning power and to impart a longer useful life to fabrics. Phosphates also encourage the growth of algae and other water-based plants (phosphates are a major ingredient in fertilizer), which may be potentially harmful to the environment. Increased organic matter in lakes and streams leads to a reduced oxygen content of the water, and this may kill fish.

Legislators and regulators have been quite concerned about phosphates from detergents making their way into streams and rivers. In the late 1970s several localities banned the sale of laundry detergents containing phosphates, and some states have followed suit. Because these bans are easy to impose and seem to represent only trivial inconvenience for consumers (there are other types of detergents available), they have not involved the extensive debate that many other environmental regulations have.

Although phosphate bans may be politically expedient, our analysis in this chapter suggests that such dramatic measures seldom produce efficient results. Alternative, more carefully targeted actions may result in resources being used more wisely. For example, a 1984 study of phosphate bans in Wisconsin and North Carolina estimates that these imposed costs of about $50 to $70 per household per year in the form of extra laundry additives needed, increased fabric wear, and decreased wash quality.[14] Gains in terms of improved water quality were generally not detectable. Even if there were gains for water quality, the author shows that these could be obtained more cheaply (for about one-fourth to one-third the cost) by adoption of waste water treatment methods than by banning phosphate detergents. In this case, the politics of the regulatory process seems to have resulted in at least as much inefficiency in the allocation of resources as did the initial externality it was intended to cure.

To Think About

1. What other regulatory strategies (instead of an outright ban) might be used to address the phosphate problem? How would a Pigovian tax operate in this case? Would it be preferable to a ban? Why didn't government officials follow such an approach?

2. Some people argue that economists' proposals of pollution taxes (or similar licensing arrangements) are wrong since they "let people with the money simply pay for doing wrong." Do you agree? Aren't strict regulatory controls (or, better yet, outright bans on pollution) a better approach to preserving the environment?

---

tion of air cleaning equipment. Of course, as "Applying Economics: The Phosphate Ban and Clean Clothes" shows, such regulations may not always necessarily be efficient either.

The Evolution of Property Rights

Legal assignments of property rights change over time. Some goods that were at one time commonly owned (most land, for example) have in more recent times become primarily private property. Similarly, some goods that were at one time private (such as roads, bridges, lighthouses, and fire companies) have increasingly become publicly owned. Traditionally, such changes have been

---

[14]The report is summarized in W. Kip Viscusi, "Phosphates and the Environmental Free Lunch," *Regulation*, September/December 1984, pp. 53–55.

regarded as primarily legal or political in origin. Although economic analysis could illustrate the implications of various property rights assignments, it was believed to have little to say about how assignments were in fact made.

More recently, several economists have argued that the way societies choose to define property rights are strongly motivated by economic considerations. In particular, it has been suggested that private property rights come into existence when it becomes economical for those affected by externalities to internalize them through transactions in private property; that is, when the benefits of coping with the externalities exceed the costs of enforcing private property rights.[15] In broad terms, the hypothesis is that legal institutions (notably the way in which property rights are defined) evolve over time toward economically efficient outcomes. Although it would be inappropriate here to investigate the wide variety of implications for the analysis of law that stems from this hypothesis, "Applying Economics: Land Contracts in the California Gold Rush" shows how one type of land contract changed very rapidly in response to market pressures.

Common Property

Resources are termed *common property* if they can be used by anyone without a direct charge. As our discussion of air and water pollution showed, this is frequently the case for the natural environment—enforcement of private property rights is simply too costly. Other examples of common property include the radio and television spectrum (although rights to particular wavelengths have been created by the government), fishing and mining in the oceans or Antarctica, and the use of outer space. In this section we examine some of the problems that arise in the use of common property. As a specific example we examine the case of ocean fishing, but similar issues arise in all cases of common ownership.

Ocean fisheries are, in most cases, common property.[16] Anyone wishing to catch fish need only rent or buy a boat and proceed to a desirable location. Because most fishing grounds are treated as common property, there may be a tendency for the areas to be overfished from a long-run viewpoint. Each fisherman will adopt a policy of increasing his or her catch up to the point at which the marginal cost of catching additional fish is equal to the price of fish. Although such a policy may lead to short-run profit maximization, it also runs the risk of so depleting the stock of fish that the future catch may be endangered. Because the fisheries are "owned" in common, individual fishermen will not take these additional costs of resource depletion into account.

---

[15]See Harold Demsetz, "Toward a Theory of Property Rights," *American Economic Review, Papers and Proceedings*, May 1967, pp. 347–359.

[16]This section is based on H. S. Gordon, "The Economic Theory of a Common-Property Resource: The Fishery," *Journal of Political Economy*, April 1954, pp. 124–142; and on Anthony Scott, "The Fishery: The Objectives of Sole Ownership," *Journal of Political Economy*, April 1955, pp. 116–124.

Land Contracts in the California Gold Rush

The degree to which externalities affect the allocation of resources can have an impact on how property rights are defined in legal contracts. Since legal agreements among people can take a wide variety of forms, it is likely that contractual provisions will be chosen that prove mutually beneficial. Changes in the general economic environment would be likely to change the provisions that are regarded as optimal. An interesting example is provided by land contracts in California gold fields during the period 1848–1860.[17] Because California had only recently become independent from Mexico when gold was discovered in 1848, there were few explicit statutes enforced on miners claiming land. Rather, a group of miners would stake out a claim and rely primarily on their own devices to prevent "claim-jumping." Usually a group of 6–10 miners would band together to enforce and protect their claim to an area. Among the miners on a given claim, sharing contracts initially predominated. That is, the miners would work together in panning for gold and would share equally the output that resulted from the process. This type of contract offered two advantages over a more individualistic approach to mining. First, risk was reduced since every miner would obtain the same share of output rather than facing the probability of choosing the wrong mining location. Second, miners could achieve some economies of scale in building the equipment necessary for efficiency searching stream banks and beds and in policing their claims against others.

By late 1849, population in the California gold fields had expanded rapidly, producing pressures to change the form of mining contracts. Greater population necessitated larger numbers of miners on each claim (mainly in order to protect the claim). That resulted in greater problems of shirking the work by some miners involved in sharing contracts. Also the risk reduction benefits of sharing contracts declined as claim characteristics became better understood and secondary markets in mine property developed. Hence, the form of mining contracts began to change toward a simple land contract. Under that contract, each miner on a claim was given property rights to a specific land parcel. By mid-1850 the land contract became instituted into the U.S. mining laws. Sharing contracts in California proved to be a short-lived contractual response to the special conditions of 1848.

To Think About

1. Why were sharing contracts more efficient for small-mining claims than for large ones? More generally, are output-sharing arrangements more difficult to develop in large organizations than small ones? How might your observations apply to communal farms or similar types of arrangements?

2. Suppose an investor provided the funding to find and develop a gold mine. What kind of contract would you expect to be developed between this owner and the miners? How might the miners be paid—with a direct salary, with a share of the gold, or with a share of the mine's profits?

It would not be in any one fisherman's interest to cut back on output this year in order to aid in "conservation," since others will not do so. If the fishery were owned by a single person or firm, a different logic might prevail. In that situation, the owner would recognize the effect that policies adopted today will have on next year's catch and would adjust current output decisions accordingly.

---

[17]This example is based on J. Umbeck, "A Theory of Contract Choice and the California Gold Rush," *Journal of Law and Economics*, October 1977, pp. 421–437.

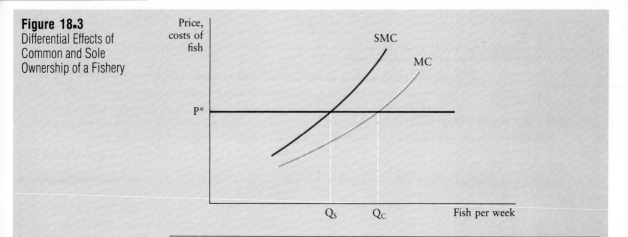

Figure 18.3
Differential Effects of Common and Sole Ownership of a Fishery

Under common ownership, fishermen will recognize only current operating costs as reflected by MC. They will, therefore, produce output level Q_C. If the fishery is owned by a single firm, the depleting effects of current operations will be taken into account. This firm would produce at a point (Q_S) where price is equal to a comprehensive measure of marginal costs (SMC).

A Graphic Demonstration

This argument is illustrated in Figure 18.3. Suppose that the price of fish is given by P* and the marginal cost curve for the current year's output is given by MC. Under common ownership, each fishing firm will produce output level Q_C since this output level maximizes current profits. If the fishery were solely owned by one firm, that firm would consider both the present and future operating costs of its actions. Since increasing the current year's catch tends to reduce the catch (and the profits) in future years, the firm will regard its marginal cost curve as being SMC. This curve reflects both current operating costs and the future costs of reduced harvests. The sole owner would choose to produce output level Q_S since this provides maximum profits when full costs are taken into account.

This analysis shows that when resources are commonly owned they may be overused. Under common ownership, each fishing firm imposes an external cost on others by not recognizing the effect its fishing has on future harvests. A firm given sole ownership of the fishery would internalize this externality and would operate the fishery on a sustained yield basis. Moves in recent years by several countries such as the United States, Canada and Chile to define 200-mile "economic zones" beyond the traditional 12-mile territorial limit can be viewed as an application of this principle. By expanding their limits, these countries are attempting to create a property right to surrounding fish-

Oysters and Lobsters

Because shellfish are found along the continental shelf in relatively isolated beds, enforcement of property rights in such resources is less costly than for ocean fisheries. These property rights may be enforced by the state as for any other legal right, or they may be enforced informally by custom, heredity, and a shotgun. Whatever the source of the property rights, our analysis suggests that shellfish producers who operate under a system of private property will recognize the divergence between private and social marginal costs and will, in the long run, be more productive than those who fish on common property.

Some direct evidence on this possibility was provided in a 1975 study of oyster production by R. J. Agnello and L. P. Donnelley.[18] The authors noted that states differ widely in the proportion of privately owned oyster grounds. In Virginia, for example, about 74 percent of oysters produced are from privately owned grounds, whereas in neighboring Maryland the figure is less than 17 percent. The authors found there was clear evidence that oyster producers were more productive in states with a high level of private property. In Virginia, for example, the average physical productivity of oyster fishermen was nearly 60 percent higher than in Maryland. More generally, the authors found that a 10 percent increase in the proportion of oyster grounds that were privately owned led to an increase of 338 pounds in the annual oyster catch of each producer. They attribute this result to the greater efficiency with which private oyster beds can be managed.

A similar result was obtained by F. W. Bell in a study of lobstering.[19] In this case, however, the author found that property rights were only weakly enforced (by custom rather than by law) and that the common property nature of most production decisions led to overproducing. In 1966, the author calculated there may have been twice as many lobster traps in use as would be dictated by efficiency considerations. A reduction in the number of traps to the optimal level would have increased the catch by nearly 10 pounds per trap. The author suggested that such a reduction might be brought about through state regulation, but our analysis indicates that it might better be achieved through a more complete definition of property rights in the industry.

To Think About

1. Many New England towns used to have "commons." This was land owned by the town that anyone could use—primarily as a place for livestock to graze. What would you expect might happen to such common land? Do New England towns still have commons? How do they regulate the use of this land?

2. How does the common property problem arise in the case of hunting? Can you think of any animals that were severely threatened by this problem? How do you explain cases where over-hunting does not seem to be a serious problem?

eries and thereby to internalize the negative externalities of overfishing. "Applying Economics: Oysters and Lobsters" shows how this process can be carried even further in coastal areas where enforcement of property rights is easier than it is in the deep oceans.

---

[18]R. J. Agnello and L. P. Donnelley, "Property Rights and Efficiency in the Oyster Industry," *Journal of Law and Economics*, October 1975, pp. 521–533.

[19]F. W. Bell, "Technological Externalities and Common Property Resources: An Empirical Study of the U.S. Northern Lobster Industry," *Journal of Political Economy*, January/February 1972, pp. 148–158.

Summary

We begin this chapter with a demonstration of the misallocation of resources that is created by an externality. That misallocation occurs because of a divergence between private and social marginal costs that leads economic actors, acting in their own self-interest, to make choices that are not efficient. Using this concept we show:

- The traditional method for correcting the allocational bias of an externality, first proposed by A. C. Pigou, is to impose an optimal tax on the firm creating the externality.
- When bargaining costs are low and property rights are fully specified, no governmental intervention may be required to cope with an externality. Private negotiations between the parties may result in an efficient allocation regardless of how the property rights are actually assigned (the Coase theorem).
- Some externalities, such as those associated with environmental pollution, involve high bargaining costs. In this case, taxation or regulation may be required to achieve an efficient allocation (although regulation does not guarantee such a result).
- Common property poses the problem of overuse because individual decision makers take no account of the costs involved in using the property. In some cases, private property–types of arrangements will arise as a way of solving these problems.

Problems

18.1 A firm in a perfectly competitive industry has patented a new process for making widgets. The new process lowers the firm's average cost curve, meaning this firm alone (although still a price taker) can earn real economic profits in the long run.

a. If the market price is $20 per widget and the firm's marginal cost curve is given by MC = .4q where q is the daily widget production for the firm, how many widgets will the firm produce?

b. Suppose a government study has found that the firm's new process is polluting the air and estimates the social marginal cost of widget production by this firm to be SMC = .5q. If the market price is still $20, what is the socially optimal level of production for the firm? What should the amount of a government-imposed excise tax be in order to bring about this optimal level of production?

c. Graph your results.

18.2 On the island of Pago-Pago there are two lakes and 20 fishermen. Each fisherman gets to fish on either lake and gets to keep the average catch on that lake. On Lake X the total number of fish caught is given by:

$$F^X = 10L_X - \tfrac{1}{2}L_X{}^2,$$

where L_X is the number of fishermen on the lake. The amount an additional fisherman will catch is $MP_X = 10 - L_X$.

For Lake Y the relationship is

$$F^Y = 5L_Y$$

and

$$MP_Y = 5.$$

a. Under this organization of society, what will the total number of fish caught be?

b. The chief of Pago-Pago, having once read an economics book, believes that she can raise the total number of fish caught by restricting the number of fishermen allowed on Lake X. What is the correct number of fishermen on Lake X to allow in order to maximize the total catch of fish? What is the number of fish caught in this situation?

c. Being basically opposed to coercion, the chief decides to require a fishing license for Lake X. If the licensing procedure is to bring about the optimal allocation of labor, what should the cost of a license be (in terms of fish)?

d. Does this problem prove that a "competitive" allocation of resources may not be optimal?

*18.3 Suppose that the oil industry in Utopia is perfectly competitive and that all firms draw oil from a single (and practically inexhaustible) pool. Each competitor believes that he or she can sell all the oil he or she can produce at a stable world price of $10 per barrel, and that the cost of operating a well for one year is $1,000.

Total output per year (Q) of the oil field is a function of the number of wells (N) operating in the field. In particular,

$$Q = 500N - N^2,$$

and the amount of oil produced by each well (q) is given by:

$$q = \frac{Q}{N} = 500 - N.$$

The output from the Nth well is given by:

$$MP_N = 500 - 2N.$$

---

*Denotes a problem that is rather difficult.

a. Describe the equilibrium output and the equilibrium number of wells in this perfectly competitive case. Is there a divergence between private and social marginal cost in the industry?

b. Suppose that the government nationalizes the oil field. How many oil wells should it operate? What will total output be? What will the output per well be?

c. As an alternative to nationalization, the Utopian government is considering an annual license fee per well to discourage overdrilling. How large should this license fee be to prompt the industry to drill the optimal number of wells?

*18.4 Three types of contracts are used to specify how tenants of a plot of agricultural land may pay rent to the landlord. Rent may be paid (1) in money (or a fixed amount of agricultural produce); (2) as a fixed proportionate share of the crop; or (3) in "labor dues," by working on other plots owned by the landlord. How might these alternative contract specifications affect tenants' production decisions? What sorts of transaction costs might occur in the enforcement of each type of contract? What economic factors might affect the type of contract specified in different places or during various historical periods?

18.5 There is currently considerable controversy concerning product safety. Two extreme positions might be termed *caveat emptor* (let the buyer beware) and *caveat vendor* (let the seller beware). Under the former scheme, producers would have no responsibility for the safety of their products: buyers would absorb all losses. Under the latter scheme this liability assignment would be reversed; firms would be completely responsible under law for losses incurred from unsafe products. Using simple supply and demand analysis, discuss how the assignment of such liability might affect the allocation of resources. Would safer products be produced if firms were strictly liable under law?

18.6 Inventors are not usually able to capture all the profits arising from their inventions. Inventions tend to become public property that can be freely used without paying royalties to the inventor. Develop a supply-demand diagram that demonstrates how this externality may cause too few inventions to be produced. How might the adoption of patent laws mitigate this problem by granting property rights to inventions? What inefficiencies might be created by patents?

18.7 Develop an example of interpersonal externalities similar to the one that illustrates interfirm externalities in Chapter 18. Show how the assumption of zero bargaining costs permits exchanges among the two persons to bring about an optimal allocation of resources even in the presence of this type of externality.

18.8 Suppose a monopoly produces a harmful externality. Use the concept of consumer surplus to analyze whether an optimal tax on the polluter would necessarily be a welfare improvement.

CHAPTER 19

Public Goods and Public Choice

Chapter 17 shows that some goods are not necessarily suited to production through private markets since they have zero marginal costs of serving another person and benefit everyone. These goods tend to be produced by the government and are paid for through compulsory taxation. Our goal in Chapter 19 is to study some of the issues that arise in this process. We begin by defining public goods and examining the problems that such goods pose for the allocation of resources under a competitive market system. We then show why these goods will often be produced by governments and show that it is at least possible that such actions could result in an efficient allocation of resources. In the final sections of the chapter, we examine the ways governments actually work and raise some doubts about whether they will ultimately choose such efficient solutions. Our general purpose in this final chapter is to investigate the behavior of the government as an important economic actor.

Public Goods

What does a government do? Economists might define governmental activities with one general statement: A government produces public goods. The general term *public goods* in this definition could refer to all those effects a government has on the members of society. These effects include all the tangible goods and services provided by the government (for example, national defense, postal services, education, and so forth) and are also intended to include the various intangible benefits (or costs) of citizenship, such as provision of justice or building national character. In a sense, governments are not very different from other organizations (such as labor unions, professional associations, fraternities and sororities, or the American Legion) that provide benefits to, and impose obligations on, their members. The distinguishing characteristic of government is its ability to produce public goods on a very large scale and to finance these goods with compulsory taxes.

Attributes of Public Goods — ① nonexclusive — ② nonrival

The above discussion of public goods is circular—governments are defined as producers of public goods, and public goods are defined to be the stuff that government produces. Many economists (most notably, Paul Samuelson) have tried to attach a more specific, technical definition to the term *public good*.[1] The purpose of such a definition is to differentiate those goods that are public by nature from those that are suitable for private markets.[2] The most common definitions of public goods stress two attributes that seem to characterize many of the goods governments produce: nonexclusivity and nonrivalry.

Nonexclusivity

One property that distinguishes public goods is whether people may be excluded from the benefits the goods provide. For most private goods, such exclusion is indeed possible. I can easily be excluded from consuming a hamburger if I don't pay for it. In some cases, exclusion is either very costly or impossible. National defense is the standard example. Once an army or navy is set up, everyone in a country benefits from its protection whether or not they pay for it. Similar comments apply on a local level to such goods as mosquito control or inoculation programs against disease. In these cases, once the programs are implemented, all of the residents of a community benefit from them and no one can be excluded from those benefits, regardless of whether he or she pays for them. These **nonexclusive goods** can be contrasted to exclusive private consumption goods (such as automobiles or motion pictures) for which exclusion is a simple matter. Those who do not pay for such private goods do not receive the services these goods promise.

Nonexclusive goods Goods that provide benefits to everyone. No one can be excluded from such benefits.

Nonrivalry

A second property that characterizes many public goods is nonrivalry. A **nonrival good** is one for which benefits can be provided to additional users at a zero marginal social cost. For most goods, consumption of additional amounts

Nonrival goods Goods for which additional consumers may use them at zero marginal costs.

---

[1] See Paul A. Samuelson, "The Pure Theory of Public Expenditure," *Review of Economics and Statistics*, November 1954, pp. 387–389.

[2] Usually the implication is that governments should not produce private goods since the competitive market will do a better job of this.

involves some marginal costs of production. Consumption of one more hot dog, for example, requires that various resources be devoted to its production. For some goods, however, this is not the case. Consider one more automobile crossing a highway bridge during an off-peak period. Since the bridge is already there anyway, one more vehicle crossing it requires no additional resources and does not reduce consumption of anything else. One more viewer tuning into a television channel involves no additional cost even though this action would result in additional consumption taking place. Consumption by additional users of such a good is nonrival in that this additional consumption involves zero marginal social costs of production; such consumption does not reduce other people's ability to consume.

Categories of Public Goods

The concepts of nonexclusivity and nonrivalry are in some ways related. Many goods that are nonexclusive are also nonrival. National defense and mosquito control are two examples of goods for which exclusion is not possible and for which additional consumption takes place at zero marginal cost. Many other instances might be suggested.

These concepts are not identical. Some goods may possess one property, but not the other. It is, as shown in Chapter 18, impossible (or at least very costly) to exclude some fishing boats from ocean fisheries, yet one more boat imposes social costs in the form of a reduced catch for all concerned. Similarly, use of a bridge during off-peak hours may be nonrival, but it is possible to exclude potential users by erecting toll booths. Table 19.1 presents a cross-classification of goods by their possibilities for exclusion and their rivalry. Several examples of goods that fit into each of the categories are provided. Many of the examples (in boxes other than the upper left corner in the table—exclusive, rival private goods) are often produced by the government. Nonrival goods are sometimes privately produced—there are private bridges, swimming pools, and highways that consumers must pay to use even though this use involves zero marginal cost. For these goods, nonpayers can be excluded from consuming them, so a private firm may be able to cover its costs. Still, even in this case the resulting allocation of resources will be inefficient because price will exceed marginal cost.[3]

Public goods

Goods that provide non-exclusive benefits to everyone in a group and which can be provided to one more user at zero marginal cost. Goods which are both nonexclusive and nonrival.

We will define **public goods** as having both of the properties listed in Table 19.1. That is, such goods provide nonexclusive benefits and can be provided to one more user at zero marginal cost. Public goods are both nonexclusive and nonrival.

---

[3]This would not be the case if the good were provided free and financed by tax revenues or other types of contributions.

Table 19.1
Types of Public and
Private Goods

		Exclusive	
		Yes	No
Rival	Yes	Hot dogs, automobiles, houses	Fishing grounds, public grazing land, clean air
	No	Bridges, swimming pools, highways (at off-peak hours)	National defense, mosquito control, justice

Public Goods and Market Failure

Our definition of public goods illustrates why private markets may not produce them in adequate amounts. For exclusive private goods, the purchaser of that good can entirely appropriate the benefits of the good. If Smith eats a pork chop, for example, that means the chop yields no benefits to Jones. The resources used to produce the pork chop can be seen as contributing only to Smith's welfare, and he or she is willing to pay whatever this is worth. The resource cost of a private good can be "attributed" to a single person.

For a public good, this will not be the case. In buying a public good, any one person would not be able to appropriate all the benefits the good offers. Since others cannot be excluded from benefiting from the good and since others can use the good at no cost, society's potential benefits from the public good will exceed the benefits that accrue to any single buyer. The resource cost should not be attributed solely to one purchaser. However, the potential purchaser will not take the potential benefits of this purchase to others into account in his or her expenditure decisions. Consequently, private markets will tend to underallocate resources to public goods.

As an example of the allocational problems raised by the nature of public goods, suppose a consumer is deciding to purchase either an automobile or an elaborate mosquito sprayer. The automobile and the mosquito sprayer have the same price, but the automobile yields more direct utility to the consumer. The automobile will be bought since that is the utility-maximizing decision for this person to make. From a social point of view, that may not be the best allocation of resources. The automobile increases social welfare only to the extent that this one person derives benefits from its use. Mosquito control can provide benefits to many people in addition to its benefits to the purchaser. The purchaser will not take those extra benefits into account in his or her decision (even though they can be provided to others at zero cost). From a social point of view, resources may be underallocated to mosquito control (and to public goods in general).

A Graphic Demonstration

Problems raised by the nature of public goods can be demonstrated with partial equilibrium analysis by examining the demand curve associated with

Figure 19.1
Derivation of the Demand
for a Public Good

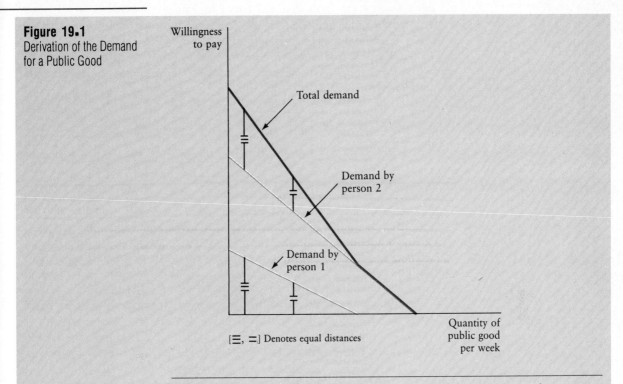

Since a public good is nonexclusive, the price that people are willing to pay for one more
unit (their marginal valuations) is equal to the sum of what each individual would pay.
Here person 1's willingness to pay is added vertically to person 2's to get the total
demand for the public good.

such goods. In the case of a private good, we found the market demand curve
(see Chapter 5) by summing people's demands horizontally. At any price, the
quantities demanded by each person are summed up to calculate the total
quantity demanded in the market. The market demand curve shows the marginal evaluation that people place on an additional unit of output. For a public
good (which is provided in about the same quantity to everyone) we must add
individual demand curves vertically. To find out how society values some level
of public good provision, we must ask how each person values this level of
output and then add up these valuations.

This idea is represented in Figure 19.1 for a situation with two people. The
total demand curve for the public good is the vertical sum of each person's
demand curve. Each point on the curve represents what person 1 and person
2 together are willing to pay for the particular level of public goods production. Producing one more unit of the public good would benefit both people;
so, to evaluate this benefit, we must sum each person's evaluation of the good.
This is shown in Figure 19.1 by adding what person 1 is willing to pay to
what person 2 is willing to pay. In private markets, on the other hand, the
production of one more unit benefits only the person who ultimately consumes

it.[4] Because each person's demand curve in Figure 19.1 is below the total demand for the public good, no buyer is willing to pay what the good is worth to society as a whole. Therefore, although "Applying Economics: Are Lighthouses Public Goods?" offers a warning about jumping to conclusions, in many cases private markets seem to undervalue the benefits of public goods and underallocate resources to them.

Voluntary Solutions to the Problem

Since public goods cannot be traded efficiently in competitive markets, a number of economists have examined how such goods might be provided by the government and financed through taxation. One approach investigates whether an efficient allocation of resources to public goods might come about voluntarily; that is, people would agree to be taxed in exchange for the benefits that the public good provides. Perhaps the earliest statement of how such an equilibrium might arise was provided by the German economist Erik Lindahl in 1919.[5] Lindahl's argument can be illustrated graphically for a society with only two individuals (again the ever-popular Smith and Jones). In Figure 19.2 the curve labeled SS shows Smith's demand for a particular public good. Rather than using the price of the public good on the vertical axis, we instead assume that the share of the public good's cost that Smith must pay varies from 0 percent to 100 percent. The negative slope of SS indicates that at a higher tax "price" for the public good, Smith will demand a smaller quantity of it.

Jones' demand for the public good is derived in much the same way. Now, however, we record the proportion paid by Jones on the right-hand vertical axis of Figure 19.2 and reverse the scale so that moving up the axis results in a lower tax price paid. Given this convention, Jones' demand for the public good (JJ) has a positive slope.

The two demand curves in Figure 19.2 intersect at C, with an output level of OE for the public good. At this output level Smith is willing to pay, say,

---

[4]If MC_P and MC_G represent the marginal costs of a public and a private good, respectively, then (somewhat loosely) the conditions for optimality in the production of a private good are given by

$$MC_G = MV_G^1 = MV_G^2 = \ldots = MV_G^n$$

and for the public good by

$$MC_P = MV_P^1 + MV_P^2 + \ldots + MV_P^n$$

where MV_G^i and MV_P^i are the marginal valuations (that is, the amount an individual is willing to pay for one more unit) of the two goods. For a more extensive discussion, see Paul A. Samuelson, "The Pure Theory of Public Expenditure," *Review of Economics and Statistics*, November 1954, pp. 387–389.

[5]Most of Lindahl's writings are in German. Excerpts from them are reprinted in translation in R. A. Musgrave and A. T. Peacock, eds., *Classics in the Theory of Public Finance* (London: Macmillan, 1958).

Are Lighthouses Public Goods?

Lighthouses have played an important role in the development of the theory of public goods. Our categories in Table 19.1 suggest that lighthouses have both properties that tend to be associated with public goods: (1) the light provided is a nonexclusive good, offering guidance to everyone who sees it; and (2) the light is nonrival since an additional ship can make use of it at zero marginal cost. It is not surprising that lighthouses are often used as textbook examples of public goods.

Just because lighthouses have the characteristics of public goods does not mean that they must be owned and operated by the government. Private ownership is still possible, provided the owners have some way to collect from those who use the lighthouse. In a fascinating history of lighthouses in England, Ronald Coase shows that during the seventeenth and eighteenth centuries most were indeed privately owned.[6] Owners were then provided with the legal right to collect "light dues" from shipowners who visited British ports. Apparently, the business of operating lighthouses was a thriving one during this period, and many enterprising entrepreneurs entered the market in response to profit opportunities.

In 1836 the British Parliament granted an exclusive franchise to operate all lighthouses to Trinity House, a quasigovernmental body. The era of private ownership came to an end. Reasons for Parliament's decision are somewhat unclear. Some members argued that monopoly provision of lighthouse services through the government would be more efficient (though, as for many cases of multiplant monopolies, the source of such efficiencies is not obvious). Others adopted a more political stance, arguing that lighthouses simply should be government-owned as a source of national pride (or, indeed, of political patronage). Regardless of which of these arguments was finally persuasive, the debate showed that in some cases whether the government decides to produce a particular good may be less a matter of the good's technical properties than of prevailing political institutions and attitudes.

To Think About

1. Lighthouses may not provide nonexclusive benefits—conceivably a lighthouse keeper could turn off the light for ships that haven't paid their dues. With modern communications equipment, especially radar for ship sightings, this is even more feasible today than in eighteenth-century England. Would adoption of a system of communications that resulted in lighthouses' output becoming an exclusive good improve the efficiency of resource allocation?

2. In the case of lighthouses and other public goods that might be "privatized" (for example, elementary education through a system of government-financed vouchers), is it necessary for the government to set prices for these goods? How would light dues be determined if they were not set by the government?

60 percent of the good's cost whereas Jones pays 40 percent. That point C is an equilibrium is suggested by the following argument. For output levels less than OE, the two people combined are willing to pay more than 100 percent of the public good's cost. They will vote to increase its level of production (but see the warnings about this statement in the next section). For output levels greater than OE, the people are not willing to pay the total cost of public goods being produced and may vote for reductions in the amounts being provided. Only for output level OE is there a **Lindahl equilibrium** where

Lindahl equilibrium Balance between people's demand for public goods and the tax shares they must pay for them.

[6]Ronald Coase, "The Lighthouse in Economics," *Journal of Law and Economics*, October 1974, pp. 357–376.

Figure 19.2
Lindahl Equilibrium in the
Demand for Public Goods

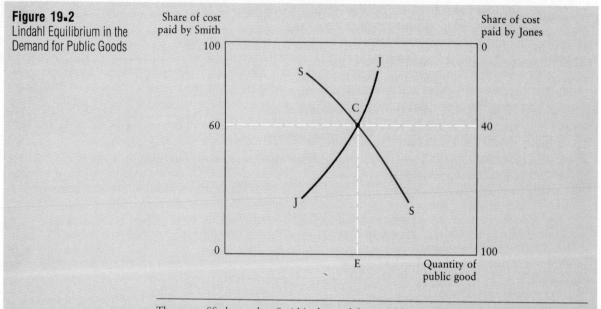

The curve SS shows that Smith's demand for a public good increases as the tax share that Smith must pay falls. Jones' demand curve for the public good (JJ) is constructed in a similar way. The point C represents a Lindahl equilibrium at which OE of the public good is supplied with Smith paying 60 percent of the cost. Any other quantity of the public good is not an equilibrium since either too much or too little funds would be available.

the tax shares precisely pay for the level of public goods' production under-taken by the government.

Not only does this allocation of tax responsibilities result in an equilibrium in people's demands for public goods, but it is also possible to show that this equilibrium is efficient.[7] The tax rate shares introduced in Lindahl's solution to the public goods problem play the role of "pseudo" prices that mimic the functioning of a competitive price system in achieving efficiency. Unfortunately, for reasons we now examine, this solution is at best only a conceptual one.

Discovering the Demand for Public Goods: The Free Rider Problem

Deriving the Lindahl solution requires knowledge of the optimal tax share for each person. A major problem arises in how such data might be collected. Although, through their voting patterns, people may provide some information about their preferences for public goods (a topic we take up later in this

---

[7] For a derivation, see Walter Nicholson, *Microeconomic Theory: Basic Principles and Extensions*, 3d ed. (Hinsdale, Ill.: The Dryden Press, 1985), pp. 714–715.

chapter), that information is usually too sketchy to permit tax shares to be computed. Most voting methods do not record the intensity of people's desires for various public goods. As an alternative, a government might ask people how much they are willing to pay for particular packages of public goods, but the results of this poll might be extremely inaccurate. In answering the question, people may feel that they should understate their true preferences for fear they will ultimately have to pay what the good is worth to them in the form of taxes. From each person's point of view, the proper strategy is to understate true preferences in the hope that others will bear the burden of paying taxes. Since, for a traditional public good, no one can be excluded from enjoying its benefits, the best position to occupy is that of a **free rider**. Each person, by acting in his or her own self-interest, may ensure that society underestimates the demand for public goods and underallocates resources to their production.

Free rider
A consumer of a nonexclusive good who does not pay for the good in the hope that other consumers will.

The free rider problem arises in all organizations that provide collective goods to their members. For example, labor unions generally are able to obtain better wages and working conditions in unionized plants. Workers in such plants have an incentive to enjoy the benefits of unionization while at the same time refusing to join the union. They thereby avoid the payment of dues. In order to combat such free rider problems, unions quite often insist on a "closed," or "union," shop. Similar problems arise in collecting blood on a voluntary basis. Since people know that they will get all the blood they need if they have to be hospitalized, the tendency is to be a free rider and refrain from donating.

As these examples illustrate, the free rider problem can be solved only by some sort of compulsion. This compulsion may arise out of a sense of group solidarity or civic pride (people do give blood in America, and far more do in England), or it may require legal or quasilegal force (as in the union case). For governments the necessity to tax people to force them to pay for public services is inescapable, and some voting schemes have been proposed that gather the sort of information required for a Lindahl equilibrium. None of these offers a particularly effective solution to the free rider problem, however. As "Applying Economics: Searching for Free Riders" illustrates, this type of behavior seems relatively common and a variety of social mechanisms are used to control it.

Local Public Goods

Some economists have suggested that the public goods problem may be more tractable on a local than on a national level.[8] Because individuals are relatively free to move from one locality to another, they may indicate their preferences for local public goods by choosing to live in communities that offer them

---

[8]See C. M. Tiebout, "A Pure Theory of Local Expenditures," *Journal of Political Economy*, October 1956, pp. 416–424.

APPLYING ECONOMICS ── ▲

Searching for Free Riders

The notion that people will behave as free riders when making decisions about public goods seems intuitively reasonable. It draws directly on the model of rational decision making that we develop in Part 2. Finding actual examples of free rider behavior in the real world is difficult, however. Of course, everyone has experiences of people shirking group responsibilities (the author's children tend to disappear when it's time to do yardwork). A major problem arises in deciding whether this represents free riding or simply indicates that the good being provided is of little value to a person (perhaps the children don't care what the yard looks like). Since preferences are difficult if not impossible to measure, the search for free riders has turned in other directions.

Some researchers have tried to demonstrate free rider behavior in experiments. The subjects (usually college students) are given some money that they may either keep or contribute to some public good (often a pot of money) that they will share equally. For example, five students might each be given $10 and told that they can keep the $10 or put some of it into a common fund that will be doubled and split evenly. If every student contributes $10, each will receive $20 in return. Each person has an incentive to cheat on this deal. If one student doesn't contribute and the four others do, the one who doesn't contribute will get to keep the original $10 and will receive $16 more ($40 contributed and then dou-

bled, then split five ways) for a total of $26. Each person has an incentive to be a free rider. What is individually rational is collectively irrational if everyone is a free rider, since everyone then ends up with only $10.

Results of such simple experiments do indicate that free ridership exists and may become more significant as an experiment is repeated.[9] Sometimes as many as half or more of the students involved take the free rider position. In many cases, cooperative behavior tends also to appear. Especially if the students can talk together, they may choose cooperative solutions that outwit the game and the professor who is conducting it. There will, however, usually continue to be some students who will cheat on such cooperative strategies to their own advantage.

To Think About

1. How do you solve the free rider problems that arise in your own living arrangements? Who (if anyone) cleans the room, buys essential provisions, or plans the parties? By what methods do you control free riding?

2. Charities also face a free rider problem in getting people to contribute. What are some of the methods used by charities such as United Way, the Red Cross, or the local public television station to coerce would-be free riders into contributing?

utility-maximizing public goods taxation packages. "Voting with one's feet" provides a mechanism for revealing public goods demand in much the same way that "dollar voting" reveals private goods demand. People who wish high quality schools or a high level of police protection can "pay" for them by choosing to live in highly taxed communities. Those who prefer not to receive such benefits can choose to live elsewhere. Similar arguments apply to other types of organizations that offer packages of public goods for their members— people can choose which package of goods they prefer by choosing which clubs to join. Whether such actions can completely reveal the demand for

─────────────

[9]For a summary of some of these experiments, see T. S. McCaleb and R. E. Wagner, "The Experimental Search for Free Riders," *Public Choice*, September 1985, pp. 479–490.

public goods (even on a local level) remains an unsettled question, however. We now examine more common ways in which people express their demands for public goods—through the political process.

Direct Voting and Resource Allocation

Voting is used to decide on allocational questions in many institutions. In some instances, people vote directly on policy questions. That is the case in New England town meetings and many statewide referenda (such as that discussed later in "Applying Economics: The Tax Revolt and Proposition 13"), and for many of the public policies adopted in Switzerland. Direct voting also characterizes the social decision procedure used for many smaller groups and clubs such as farmers' cooperatives, university faculties, or the local Rotary Club. In other cases, societies have found it more convenient to utilize a representative form of government in which people directly vote only for political representatives, who are then charged with making decisions on policy questions.

To study how public choices are made, we begin with an analysis of direct voting. Direct voting is important not only because such a procedure may apply to some cases but also because elected representatives often engage in direct voting (such as in the U.S. Congress), and the theory we illustrate applies to those instances also. Later in the chapter we take up special problems of representative government.

Majority Rule

Because so many elections are conducted on a majority rule basis, we often tend to regard that procedure as a natural and, perhaps, optimal one for making social choices. But a quick examination suggests that there is nothing particularly sacred about a rule requiring that a policy obtain 50 percent of the vote to be adopted. In the U.S. Constitution, for example, two-thirds of the states must adopt an amendment before it becomes law. And 60 percent of the U.S. Congress must vote to limit debate on controversial issues. Indeed, in some institutions (Quaker meetings, for example), unanimity may be required for social decisions. Our discussion of the Lindahl equilibrium concept suggests that there indeed does exist a distribution of tax shares that would obtain unanimous support in voting for public goods. But arriving at such unanimous agreements may be very time-consuming and may be subject to strategic ploys and free rider behavior by the voters involved. To examine in detail the forces that lead societies to move away from unanimity and to choose some other determining fraction would take us too far afield here. We instead assume throughout our discussion of voting that decisions are made by majority rule. You may be able to think of some situations that might call for a decisive proportion of other than 50 percent.

Table 19.2
Preferences That Produce
the Paradox of Voting

Voter	Order of Preferences		
Smith	A	B	C
Jones	B	C	A
Fudd	C	A	B

A = Low-spending policy.
B = Medium-spending policy.
C = High-spending policy.

The Paradox of Voting

In the 1780s the French social theorist M. de Condorcet observed an important peculiarity of majority rule voting systems—they may not arrive at an equilibrium but instead may cycle among alternative options. Condorcet's paradox is illustrated for a simple case in Table 19.2. Suppose there are three voters (Smith, Jones, and Fudd) choosing among three policy options. These policy options represent three levels of spending on a particular public good (A = low, B = medium, and C = high), but Condorcet's paradox would arise even if the options being considered do not have this type of ordering associated with them. Preferences of Smith, Jones, and Fudd among the three policy options are indicated by the order listed in the table. For example, Smith prefers option A to option B and option B to option C, but Jones prefers option B to option C, and option C to option A. The preferences described in Table 19.2 give rise to Condorcet's paradox.

Consider a vote between options A and B. Option A would win, since it is favored by Smith and Fudd and opposed only by Jones. In a vote between options B and C, option B would win, again by two votes to one. But in a vote of option C versus option A, option C would win, and consequently social choices would cycle. In subsequent elections, any choice that was initially decided upon could be later defeated by an alternative, and no equilibrium would ever be reached. In this situation, the option finally chosen will depend on such seemingly unrelated issues as when the balloting stops or how items are ordered on an agenda rather than being derived in some rational way from the preferences of voters.

Single-Peaked Preferences and the Median Voter Theorem

Condorcet's voting paradox arises because of the degree of irreconcilability in the preferences of voters. We might ask whether restrictions on the types of preferences allowed might yield situations where equilibrium voting outcomes are more likely. A fundamental result about this probability was dis-

Figure 19.3
Single and Peaked
Preferences and the
Median Voter Theorem

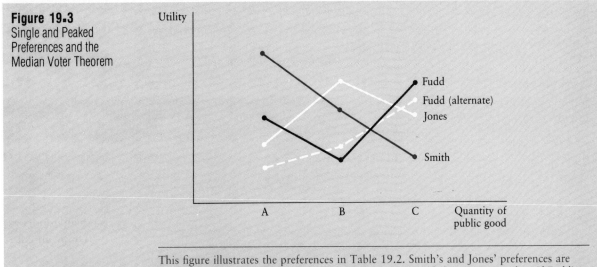

This figure illustrates the preferences in Table 19.2. Smith's and Jones' preferences are single-peaked, but Fudd's have two peaks, and these yield the voting paradox. If Fudd's instead had been single-peaked (the dashed lines), option B would be chosen as the preferred choice of the median voter (Jones).

covered by Duncan Black in 1948.[10] Black showed that equilibrium voting outcomes always can occur in cases where the issue being voted upon is one-dimensional (such as how much to spend on public goods) and where voters' preferences are "single-peaked."

To understand what *single-peaked* means, consider again Condorcet's paradox. In Figure 19.3 we illustrate the preferences that gave rise to the paradox by assigning hypothetical utility levels to options A, B, and C that are consistent with the preferences recorded in Table 19.2. For Smith and Jones, preferences are single-peaked—as levels of public goods' expenditures rise, there is only one local utility-maximizing choice (A for Smith, B for Jones). Fudd's preferences, on the other hand, have two local peaks (A and C). It is these preferences that produced the cyclical voting pattern. If, instead, Fudd had preferences represented by the dashed line in Figure 19.3 (where now C is the only local peak), there would be no paradox. In that case, option B would be chosen since that option would defeat both A and C by votes of two to one. Here B is the preferred choice of the *median voter* (Jones) whose preferences are "between" the skewed preferences of Smith and the revised preferences of Fudd.

---

[10]Duncan Black, "On the Rationale of Group Decision Making," *Journal of Political Economy*, February 1948, pp. 23–24.

Voting for School Budgets on Long Island

Decisions about spending for public schools provide examples of public choice theory in which the median voter theorem may be applicable. Voters have rather definite preferences about the proper level for such spending and, on the whole, those preferences are probably single-peaked. For this reason, voting patterns in elections related to school financing questions have been more intensively studied by economists than any other public issue.

For example, Robert Inman examined voting patterns in 58 Long Island (New York) school districts that determine their annual funding for schools through a budget referendum.[11] He found that levels of per-pupil spending in these towns were heavily influenced by the income of the median voter and by the share of taxes this voter would be expected to bear. Although higher income voters can expect to pay higher taxes (principally because they own more expensive houses upon which school property taxes are levied), the author still found that high median income districts will choose to spend more on education than low income districts—that is, a high income elasticity of demand for education tends to dominate voters' decisions.

Although Inman's results suggested that the median voters (in his case, moderate income, middle-aged

homeowners with children) tend to dominate the voting patterns, he also found that some smaller segments of the population may affect the voting results. Most important of these groups are older voters whose children have already passed through the public schools. These voters tend to reduce desired public school spending somewhat. Other groups, such as renters and Catholic parents (who may not send their children to public schools) also tend to have some influence in his results. In most cases, however, preferences of the median voter prove to be decisive in setting school budgets.

To Think About
1. In many localities, school budgets are determined by elected school boards, not by direct referenda. How do you think such indirect budget-setting procedures would affect the results of the median voter theorem? What pressures might bring about systematic departures of actual spending from what might be chosen by the median voter?
2. Are there ways in which median voter groups could encourage other groups to vote with them on school budget issues? How, for example, might median voters blunt the low spending preferences of older voters, renters, or people who send their children to private schools?

Median voter
A voter whose preferences for a public good represent the middle point of all voters' preferences for the good.

Black's result is quite general and applies to any number of voters. If choices are one-dimensional and preferences are single-peaked, majority rule will result in selection of that project which is most favored by the **median voter**. Therefore, that voter's preference will determine what social choices are made. "Applying Economics: Voting for School Budgets on Long Island" shows that in some cases this theory can explain observed decisions on public spending fairly well.

Unfortunately, the median voter theorem may be of only limited general importance, since many issues of public choice, unlike voting for school budgets, are not one-dimensional. Consider, for example, choosing among alternative environmental policies. These may involve varying levels of spending, choices of locations for polluting firms, and types of pollution permitted. In such a

---

[11]Robert Inman, "Testing Political Economy's 'As If' Proposition: Is the Median Income Voter Really Decisive?" *Public Choice*, 1978, pp. 45–65.

Table 19.3
Intensity of Preferences
and Logrolling

Voter	Utility Gain or Loss		
	Project A	Project B	Project C
1	−5	2	2
2	−5	6	6
3	3	2	10
4	3	−5	−5
5	3	−7	−7

case, people's preferences are likely to be both varied and quite complex. In describing how people vote on these issues, the single-peaked notion loses much of its intuitive appeal and there are no simple median voter theorems.

Intensity of Preferences and Logrolling

So far, we have discussed voting schemes in which voters can choose which of two options they prefer but have no opportunity to express the intensity of their feelings. In these situations majority rule can result in adoption of policies that are only mildly favored by the majority but are despised by a minority. To prevent that, minority voters may adopt logrolling (or vote-trading) techniques.

Table 19.3 provides an example of logrolling. In it the preferences about three projects (in terms of utility gains or losses) for five voters are recorded. If all the projects are voted on individually, all will pass—always by a vote of three to two. That these outcomes may not be desirable can be seen by summing the utility levels (assuming that can be done) for each project; by this criterion, only project C is "worthwhile." Both A and B yield a net negative utility level to society as a whole. These projects might be blocked through logrolling. Suppose voters 1 and 5 agree to "trade" votes; that is, voter 1 agrees to oppose project B, providing voter 5 will oppose project A. Such a trade makes both people better off than they would be should both projects be adopted. With the trading of votes, both projects fail by three to two votes.[12]

Simple vote trading does not guarantee that all projects that are, on the average, beneficial will be accepted and those that are harmful will be turned down. Consider a two-way choice between projects A and C. In that case, voters 1 and 5 can still profitably trade votes, insuring that both project A (undesirable) and project C (desirable) are defeated. As this example suggests,

---

[12]This trade imposes a negative externality on voters 2 and 3 (who are worse off without both projects than with both) and a positive externality on voter 4.

there is no very close connection between the concept of free trading in votes and choosing efficient resource allocations. No general efficiency theorems are possible. Nevertheless, the prevalence of "back-scratching" and "pork barrel" politics in legislative bodies is a prevalent and fascinating phenomenon that deserves considerably greater study.

Analysis of Representative Government

In a representative government, voters vote for candidates, not policies. Successful candidates represent their constituencies in making policy choices. Here we examine a few of the issues that have been raised about this kind of indirect representation of individual preferences.

As in the theory of the firm, we start our analysis by examining the motives of government leaders. It might, for instance, be proposed that government leaders act for the "social good." At least two realities argue against assuming such benevolent motivations. First, the notion of "social good" is extremely ill-defined. It is just not true that everyone in society has the same view of the way things should be. Second, the assumption of such benevolent political leadership is in marked contrast to the self-interest assumption that underlies both the theory of the individual and the theory of the firm developed earlier. There seems no very persuasive reason why people should change their basic motivations upon elevation to political office.

Majority Principle and Pluralism

One interesting theory of leadership motivation has been put forward by Anthony Downs. In *An Economic Theory of Democracy*, he hypothesizes that

> parties in democratic politics are analogous to entrepreneurs in a profit-seeking economy. So as to attain their private ends, they formulate whatever policies they believe will gain the most votes, just as entrepreneurs produce whatever products will gain the most profits. . . .[13]

In other words, parties act to *maximize political support*. In order to pursue this goal, parties must contend with uncertainty in many respects. A party is uncertain how any particular policy choice will affect political support. This is true not only because it may be hard to find out who benefits from government action, but also because policies must be adopted before the policies of the party (or parties) out of power are known. This strategic advantage of those out of power is significantly modified, however, by the control that the party in power has over the public's access to information.

---

[13]Anthony Downs, *An Economic Theory of Democracy* (New York: Harper & Row, 1957), p. 295.

It would be impossible to summarize the numerous insights and testable hypotheses that follow from Downs' basic assumption. Perhaps the most interesting general conclusion the author draws is that the party in power will generally adopt a *majority principle* in its policy decisions. It will pursue only those policies for which more votes are gained than are lost, and it will pursue such policies up to the point at which the marginal gain in votes from those benefiting from the policy equals the marginal loss in votes from those being hurt by the policy. The analogy between party motivation and profit maximization is quite close.

Downs' view of the nature of the political process can be contrasted with another, more commonly held view. This alternative conception examines the *pluralistic* nature of democratic government. Social decisions are assumed to be made by the interaction of many powerful special interest groups. Presumably these groups wield some influence over political leaders by virtue of campaign contributions, friendship, superior knowledge of special issues, or perhaps by direct measures of corruption. Whatever the avenues of control, it is assumed that pressure groups are the primary molders of the legal system.

Two assessments of pluralism have been put forward. The first optimistically predicts that the interaction of numerous pressure groups will, in some sense, produce a socially desirable outcome. Laws that are ultimately passed represent an equilibrium among numerous groups. Because no one group has significant power (at least not on all issues), the resulting equilibrium will generally be representative of the society as a whole.

Special-Interest Groups and Rent-Seeking Behavior

This beneficial assessment of pluralism has been questioned by many authors. One of the most interesting objections was put forward by Mansur Olson.[14] He pointed out that there is a systematic bias in a pluralistic society that causes only certain kinds of pressure groups to exercise political power. In particular, Olson argues that only pressure groups that represent narrow special interests will arise; pressure groups representing the broad public interest will be weak or nonexistent. The reason for this tendency, Olson explains, lies in the nature of the public good provided by a special interest group to its members. For a close-knit group, each member can recognize the benefits of group action, and there may be strong sanctions against being a free rider. Groups such as the National Rifle Association or the United Automobile Workers may be quite effective in pursuing their goals through government action. In some cases the gains will be largely psychological—for example, members of the Sierra Club like knowing that national parks will be protected and enlarged. In other cases the gains will be monetary. In the early 1980s, for example, some U.S. auto-

---

[14]See Mansur Olson, *Logic and Collective Action* (Cambridge, Mass.: Harvard University Press, 1965), especially Chapters 5 and 6.

Rent Seeking through Agricultural Marketing Orders

The agricultural marketing order program operated by the U.S. Department of Agriculture provides a good example of how the rent-seeking activities of narrow special interest groups can affect legislation. Under the program, the government imposes supply restrictions on 47 relatively minor agricultural commodities, including almonds, cranberries, navel oranges, lemons, spearmint oil, raisins, and, most recently, kiwi fruit. These supply restrictions take a variety of forms including limiting what planters may grow, prorationing orders on how much may be sold during any given week, and restricting the kinds of technology that can be used for production in the industry. The reasons given for such constraints on supply vary. Most often, these are claimed to be needed in order to "assure stable prices" or to "guarantee" that the produce supplied is of sufficient quality.

Most economists who have examined the programs carefully, however, conclude that their primary result is to increase both overall costs to consumers and growers' profits. Even seemingly minor restrictions can be quite effective in this regard. For example, it is estimated that restrictions on the number of lemons that may be harvested cost consumers about $45 million per year and that the overall impact of the program for lemons is probably much higher because of the limits placed on new production techniques such as "shrink-wrap" packaging. For navel oranges, costs as high as $72 mil-

lion per year arise from the use of quality grading systems that restrict the supply of fresh oranges sold and require that many navel oranges be crushed for concentrate—a use for which they are ill-suited.[15]

Of course, none of these costs contributes a very large part of the typical person's spending for food. Overall, it is doubtful that the programs add a few tenths of 1 percent to such costs. Kiwi fruits and cranberries are simply not important enough in people's budgets for them to get very excited about the restrictions. For the growers involved, however, the supply restrictions may be extremely important. It is not surprising, therefore, that grower organizations tend to dominate congressional lobbying about the market order program.

To Think About

1. A purported benefit of the market order program is to stabilize prices for the goods involved. How might the program have this effect? Would a stabilized, high price be preferable to fluctuating prices for consumers?

2. Why are market order programs accepted by Congress? After all, cranberries or almonds are only grown in a few congressional districts. Why don't the vast majority of members (who have no growers in their districts) vote to stop the programs since at least some of their constituents would be made better off by such a move?

---

mobile companies pressed for "voluntary" export restraints with the Japanese, presumably with the goal of increasing their profits. Similarly, specialized groups of agricultural producers may find it in their economic interest to enlist the government's help in restricting supply, as shown in "Applying Economics: Rent Seeking through Agricultural Marketing Orders." Economists call these activities examples of **rent-seeking behavior.** Special interest groups who feel they may have success in obtaining profits by seeking government favors will probably do so. Such behavior is simply another application of the profit maximization hypothesis.

Rent-seeking behavior
Firms or individuals influencing government policy to increase their own profits.

---

[15]See, for example, T. M. Lenard and M. P. Mazur, "Harvest of Waste: The Marketing Order Program," *Regulation*, May/June, 1985, pp. 19–26.

For representing broad questions of public interest, Olson sees a problem. In such cases the direct gains to the people who participate in the political process may be small even though social gains from the policies they advocate may be large. People will have a tendency to refrain from such political activities—they will be susceptible to the free rider problem. Consider, for example, the benefits of free trade. Economists have expounded on these benefits for years, but any single person would probably gain little direct benefit from petitioning the government for free trade. Although the total social benefits of a free trade policy may be quite large, the gains are spread so broadly over the population that no one person (unless he or she happens to be a Toyota dealer) would be interested in spending the time and effort necessary for a successful lobbying effort. According to Olson, broad issues of public interest will be underrepresented and special interests will be overrepresented in the political process.

Reelection Constraint

By combining Downs' and Olson's theories of government action, we can construct a realistic third alternative. It is undoubtedly true that pressure groups exercise considerable influence over legislation, and Olson is probably right when he theorizes that the public interest will be underrepresented. However, Olson's model does not take sufficient account of the motives of political leaders. Lobby groups probably do give utility (and money!) to political leaders, and these leaders may follow the dictates of the lobbyists. But a legislator does not have an unconstrained utility-maximization problem. Rather, he or she must operate subject to the *constraint of reelection*. The legislator must pay some attention to what Downs calls the majority principle, although this attention will by no means be absolute. Public-interest lobby groups can be seen as attempting to make individual voters aware of the benefits and costs of certain government actions. Such voter awareness may make a legislator's reelection constraint more binding and may mitigate the void of power on public issues noted by Olson.

Bureaucracies

Although governmental policies in a representative democracy are enacted by elected officials, they are usually implemented by and operated through bureaucratic agencies. Because those agencies typically possess monopoly power in the production of the services with which they are charged, it is possible that they exercise an independent influence on the direction of policy. For example, Niskanen hypothesizes that government agencies seek to maximize their budgets (perhaps because high budgets yield utility to bureaucrats).[16] A

---

[16]W. A. Niskanen, *Bureaucracy and Representative Government* (Chicago: Aldine, 1971).

The Tax Revolt and Proposition 13

In recent years a number of states have passed tax limitation statutes, and a constitutional amendment has been proposed to serve the same purpose at the federal level. This tax revolt had its origin in California with the passage of Proposition 13 in 1977. That ballot initiative required that property in California be taxed at a maximum rate of 1 percent of the 1975 fair market value and imposed sharp limits on tax increases in future years. It resulted in a decline in local property tax revenues of nearly 60 percent between fiscal 1978 and fiscal 1979.

There are two hypotheses about why voters demanded such a drastic change in policy. The first views Proposition 13 as a demand for changing the sources of local tax revenues without reducing local expenditures significantly. In this view, citizens were largely content with the existing levels of local services, but wanted state tax sources (primarily income and sales taxes) to take over a larger share of the burden. A second hypothesis views Proposition 13 as a statement by voters that local government had grown too large and that voters wished to see a cutback in both taxes and expenditures.

In a 1979 paper, Attiyeh and Engle examined voting patterns on Proposition 13 in an attempt to differentiate between these hypotheses.[17] They found such patterns tended to contradict the notion that voters simply wished to change the sources of local government financing. For example, communities in which property tax levies had been rising most dramatically did not appear to disproportionately favor Proposition 13. On the other hand, the authors found clear evidence that voters wished a reduction in both tax rates and expenditures, although their results suggested that a somewhat less dramatic reduction might have received even more voter support. In all, Attiyeh and Engle's results imply that local government in California had expanded beyond the bounds a majority of voters believed to be optimal. The success of Proposition 13 clearly showed, however, that there were limits to that expansion.

To Think About
1. Since World War II the fraction of GNP devoted to government has risen in virtually every Western country. How do you explain this rise? Would a law that limited government spending to a set fraction of GNP be a good idea?
2. Many American politicians favor a balanced-budget amendment to the U.S. Constitution. Does the analysis of this chapter provide any reasons for thinking this amendment is a good idea? What kinds of economic arguments might you use to support the amendment? What arguments might be used to oppose it?

major implication of that hypothesis is that in the bargaining between elected officials and bureaucracies, decisions will be reached that tend to overallocate resources to the public sector (relative to what would be preferred by the median voter).

Several authors have attempted to estimate such allocational effects empirically.[18] They generally conclude that the data are consistent with the budget-maximization hypothesis. However, this empirical work is, of necessity, quite preliminary. More sophisticated modeling awaits the development of better data sources and more precise analytic models. "Applying Economics: The

---

[17]Richard Attiyeh and Robert F. Engle, "Testing Some Propositions about Proposition 13," *National Tax Journal*, June 1979, pp. 131–146.

[18]See, for example, T. E. Borcherding, *Budgets and Bureaucrats: The Sources of Government Growth* (Durham, N.C.: Duke University Press, 1975).

Tax Revolt and Proposition 13" illustrates some of the problems in analyzing how voters feel about whether actual levels of resources allocated to the government are too high.

Summary

In this chapter we examine the economic theory of public goods and of the public choices that lead to the government providing such goods. Studying such subjects is a fairly recent activity for economists, and the theory described here is far from complete. We simply do not understand how resources are allocated through political "markets" as well as we understand how they are allocated in private markets. Still, applying economic logic to what are basically political issues leads to a number of important conclusions:

- Pure public goods have the property of nonexclusivity and nonrivalry—once the good is produced, no one can be excluded from receiving the benefits it provides, but additional people may benefit from the good at zero cost.
- These properties pose a problem for private markets since people will not choose to purchase an efficient amount of such goods. For this reason, resources may be underallocated to public goods.
- In theory, compulsory taxation can be used to provide public goods in efficient quantities by charging taxpayers what the goods are worth to them. However, measuring this demand may be impossible because each person has an incentive to act as a free rider in stating his or her preferences.
- Direct voting may produce paradoxical results. However, in some cases, majority rule will result in the adoption of those policies favored by the median voter.
- Analysis of representative government is made complicated by the need to consider the actual motives of elected political leaders. In some cases, such leaders will make choices in ways that maximize political appeal (that is, maximize votes). Narrow special interests and bureaucracies may often result in other choices being made, however.

Problems

19.1 Suppose there are only two people in society. The demand curve for person A for mosquito control is given by

$$q_a = 100 - P.$$

For person B the demand curve for mosquito control is given by

$$q_b = 200 - P.$$

a. Suppose mosquito control is a pure public good—that is, once it is produced everyone benefits from it. What would be the optimal level of this activity if it could be produced at a constant marginal cost of $50 per unit?

b. If mosquito control were left to the private market, how much might be produced? Does your answer depend on what each person assumes the other will do?

c. If the government were to produce the optimal amount of mosquito control, how much will this cost? How should the tax bill for this amount be allocated between the individuals if they are to share it in proportion to benefits received from mosquito control?

19.2 Suppose there are three people in society who vote on whether the government should undertake specific projects. Let the net benefits of a particular project be $150, $140, and $50 for persons A, B, and C respectively.

a. If the project costs $300 and these costs are to be shared equally, would a majority vote to undertake the project? What would be the net benefits to each person under such a scheme? Would total net benefits be positive?

b. Suppose the project cost $375 and again that costs were to be shared equally. Now would a majority vote for the project and total net benefits be positive?

c. Suppose (presumably contrary to fact) votes can be bought and sold in a free market. Describe what kinds of results you might expect in parts a and b.

19.3 Suppose that education provides both private benefits and nonexclusive public benefits to individuals. Any particular level of educational output provides equal amounts of these types of benefits. How should resources be allocated in order to attain efficient production of this semipublic good? How might production of the good be financed?

*19.4 Suppose that there are N individuals in an economy with three goods. Two of the goods are pure nonexclusive public goods, whereas the third is an ordinary private good.

a. What conditions must hold for resources to be allocated efficiently between either of the public goods and the private good?

b. What conditions must hold for resources to be allocated efficiently between the two public goods?

19.5 In an economy characterized by a hierarchy of government units (for example, federal, state, and local governments), what criteria might be used to determine which public goods are produced by which level of government? How would economies of scale in production affect your answer?

---

*Denotes a problem that is rather difficult.

SOLUTIONS TO ODD-NUMBERED PROBLEMS

This section contains brief solutions to all of the odd-numbered problems in this book. These solutions should be helpful both for students trying to solve the specific problems and as a general review for many of the concepts presented.

Chapter 2

2.1

a.   If $x = 0$, then $y = 15$.

b. $y = 0$, $0 = 15 + 3x$
$$-3x = 15$$
$$x = -5.$$

c. $x = 3$, $y = 15 + 3(3) = 15 + 9 = 24$.
$x = 4$, $y = 15 + 3(4) = 15 + 12 = 27$.
If x increases by 1, y increases by 3.

d.   (graph)

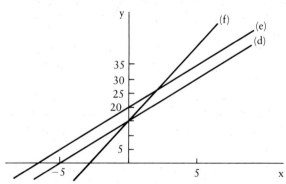

e.   (graph)
i.   If $x = 0$, then $y = 20$.
ii. $y = 0$, $0 = 20 + 3x$
$$-3x = 20$$
$$x = -20/3 = -6\ 2/3.$$
iii. $x = 3$, $y = 20 + 3(3) = 20 + 9 = 29$.
$x = 4$, $y = 30 + 3(4) = 20 + 12 = 32$.
If x increases by 1, y increases by 3.

f.   (graph)
i.   If $x = 0$, $y = 15$.

ii. $y = 0$, $0 = 15 + 5x$
$$-5x = 15$$
$$x = -3.$$
iii. $x = 3$, $y = 15 + 5(3) = 15 + 15 = 30$.
$x = 4$, $y = 15 + 5(4) = 15 + 20 = 35$.
If x increases by 1, y increases by 5.

2.3

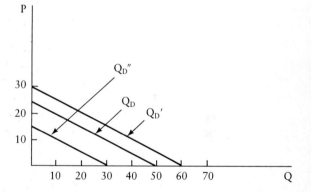

The algebraic solution proceeds as follows.

a. $Q_D = 40 - 2P + .001\ I$, $I = 10,000$,
so $Q_D = 50 - 2P$.
If $P = 0$, then $Q_D = 50$.
If $P = 10$, then $Q_D = 50 - 2(10) = 30$.
If Q_D equals 0, then $0 = 50 - 2P$
$$2P = 50$$
$$P = 25.$$

b. $I = 20,000$ changes Q_D to $Q_{D'} = 60 - 2P$.
If $P = 0$, then $Q_D = 60$.
If $P = 10$, then $Q_D = 40$.

If Q_D equals 0, then $0 = 60 - 2P$

$$2P = 60$$
$$P = 30.$$

c. $Q_D = 40 - 2P + .001\ I,\ P = P_P + 10$
Substituting:
$$Q_{D''} = 40 - 2(P_P + 10) + .001\ I$$
$$= 40 - 2P_P - 20 + .001\ I$$
$$= 20 - 2P_P + .001\ I.$$
If $I = 10{,}000$, then $Q_{D''} = 30 - 2P_P$.
If $P_P = 10$, then $Q_D = 10$.
If $P_P = 0$, then $Q_D = 30$.
If Q_D equals 0, then $0 = 30 - 2P_P$
$$2P_P = 30$$
$$P_P = 15.$$

2.5

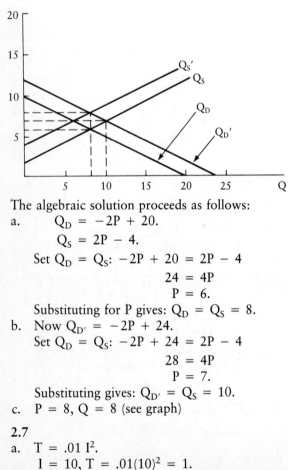

The algebraic solution proceeds as follows:
a. $Q_D = -2P + 20.$
$$Q_S = 2P - 4.$$
Set $Q_D = Q_S$: $-2P + 20 = 2P - 4$
$$24 = 4P$$
$$P = 6.$$
Substituting for P gives: $Q_D = Q_S = 8$.
b.   Now $Q_{D'} = -2P + 24.$
Set $Q_D = Q_S$: $-2P + 24 = 2P - 4$
$$28 = 4P$$
$$P = 7.$$
Substituting gives: $Q_{D'} = Q_S = 10$.
c. $P = 8, Q = 8$ (see graph)

2.7
a. $T = .01\ I^2.$
$I = 10, T = .01(10)^2 = 1.$
Taxes $= \$1{,}000.$

$I = 30, T = .01(30)^2 = 9.$
Taxes $= \$9{,}000.$
$I = 50, T = .01(50)^2 = 25.$
Taxes $= \$25{,}000.$

b.
	Average Rate	Marginal Rate
$I = 10{,}000$	10%	20%
$I = 30{,}000$	30	60
$I = 50{,}000$	50	100

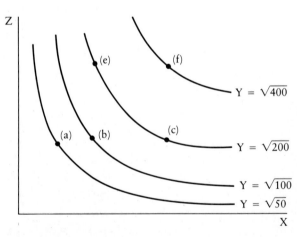

2.9

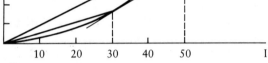

a. $2X + Z = 20, Z = -2X + 20, -Z/X =$
$-2, Z = 2X, X = 5, Z = 10.$
b. $X + Z = 20, Z = -X + 20, -Z/X =$
$-1, Z = X = 10.$
c. $X + 2Z = 40, Z = -1/2X + 20, -Z/X =$
$-1/2, X = 20, Z = 10.$
d. $X + 5Z = 100, Z = -1/5X + 20,$
$-Z/X = -1/5, X = 50, Z = 10.$
e. $2X + Z = 40, Z = -2X + 40, -Z/X =$
$-2, X = 10, Z = 20.$
f. $X + Z = 40, Z = -X + 40, -Z/X =$
$-1, Z = 20 = X.$

Chapter 3

3.1

a. $\dfrac{\$8.00}{\$.40/\text{apple}} = 20$ apples can be bought.

b. $\dfrac{\$8.00}{\$.10/\text{orange}} = 80$ oranges can be bought.

c. 10 apples cost:
10 apples × $.40/apple = $4.00, so there is $8.00 − $4.00 = $4.00 left to spend on oranges, which means $\dfrac{\$4.00}{\$.10/\text{an orange}} = 40$ oranges can be bought.

d. One less apple frees $.40 to be spent on oranges, so $\dfrac{\$.40}{\$.10/\text{orange}} = 4$ more oranges can be bought.

e. $8.00 = $.40 × number of apples + $.10 × number of oranges = .40A + .10 · O

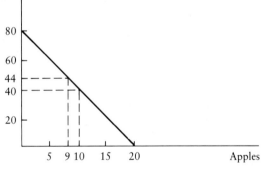

3.3

The figure below shows two intersecting indifference curves. By the definition of indifference curves, combination A must be indifferent to B and B must be indifferent to C. But, by the assumption that more is preferred to less, combination C must be preferred to A. Consequently, the curves in the figure exhibit intransitivity.

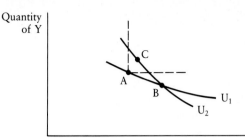

3.5

To graph the indifference curves, use U^2 instead of U. U = 10 means $U^2 = 100 = D \cdot C$. Hence, indifference curves are rectangular hyperbolas.

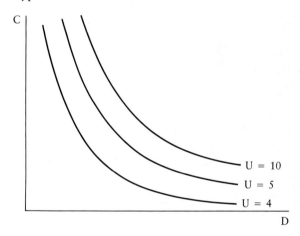

2D + 4C = 64.
D = 32 − 2C.
$U = \sqrt{D \cdot C} = \sqrt{(32 - 2C)(C)} = \sqrt{128}$.
$2C^2 - 32C + 128 = 0$.
(C − 8) (2C − 16) = 0 or C = 8.
Therefore D = 16.

3.7

U(M) = U(G, V) Preferences require that G = 2V. Extra G or V provides no extra utility if the other ingredient isn't available also. Indifference curves are L-shaped.

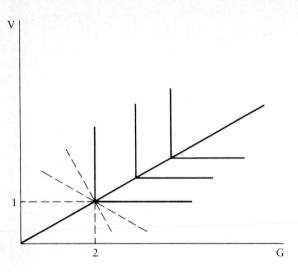

No matter what the relative prices are (the slope of the budget constraint) the maximum utility tangency will always be at the vertex of an indifference curve where G = 2V.

3.9

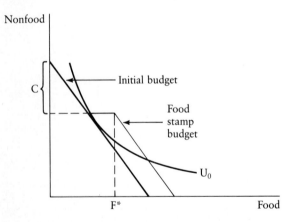

This person will participate in the Food Stamp program if (as in graph) can reach a utility level higher than U_0 by doing so. With cash, post-transfer constraint would extend the line to the nonfood axis making it desirable for all to participate.

Chapter 4

4.1

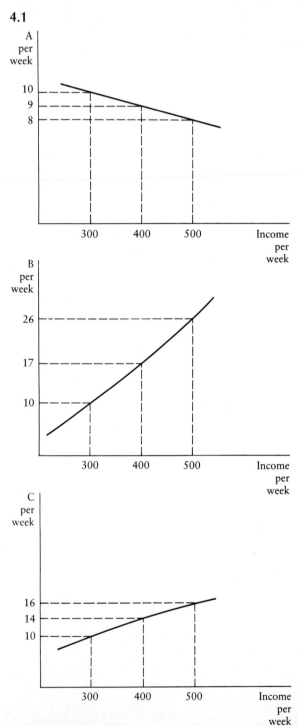

Note: A is inferior, B is a luxury, C is a necessity.

4.3

In the figure, Mr. Wright is required to buy X_0 of clothing. Given this constraint, he can only attain utility level U_0. With an unconstrained choice U_1 can be attained.

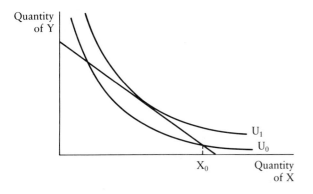

4.5

If both were inferior goods, then an increase in income would result in choosing less of each good. Since there are only two goods available, this will result in some income not being spent.

4.7

If the price of X rises, the quantity purchased will also rise. Hence the amount available to spend on Y falls, so since the price of Y is unchanged, the quantity of Y bought must fall.

4.9

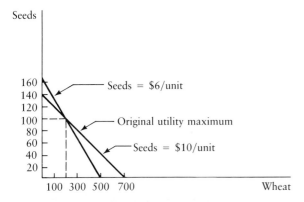

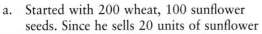

a. Started with 200 wheat, 100 sunflower seeds. Since he sells 20 units of sunflower

seeds, he can buy 100 more units of wheat (will consume 300 in all).

b. If he continues to sell 20 units of sunflower seeds, he will only be able to get an additional $120/$2 = 60 units of wheat, so he'd be worse off. It is clear from the graph that the new constraint is northeast (Sam can be better off) of the old one only where Sam consumes more sunflower seeds than he produces, so he must sell wheat and buy sunflower seeds with the new prices.

c. In this case, the income effect is not the usual one since the lower sunflower seed price does not imply a higher real income, as in the usual case, since Sam's income is a function of the price of sunflower seeds. (Graphically, the lower price causes a rotation around the point 200 wheat, 100 sunflower seeds rather than around the wheat intercept.)

Chapter 5

5.1

$Q = 500 - 50P$.

a. If P = 2, Q = 400.
   If P = 3, Q = 350.
   If P = 4, Q = 300.
   If P = 0, Q = 500.

b.

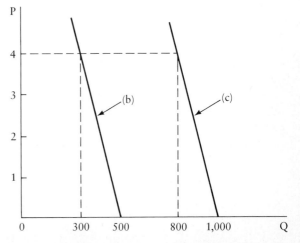

c.   Q = 1000 − 50P.
     If P = 2, Q = 900.
     If P = 3, Q = 850.
     If P = 4, Q = 800.
     If P = 0, Q = 1000.
     (See previous graph.)

5.3
a.
	Tom	Dick	Harry	Total
P = 50	0	0	0	0
P = 35	30	20	0	50
P = 25	50	60	25	135
P = 10	80	120	100	300
P = 0	100	160	150	410

b.   "Total" column in part a.

c.

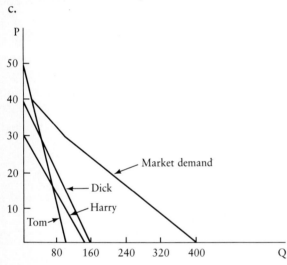

d.   Above graph.

5.5
a.   If price of X rises by 1 percent, quantity will
     fall by 2 percent since e_{x,p_x} = −2. Therefore
     X will be 980.
b.   If the price of Y rises by 1 percent, quantity
     of X will rise by 0.5 percent since e_{x,p_y} =
     0.5. Therefore, X will be 1005.
c.   If income rises by 1 percent, quantity of X
     demanded will increase by 0.8 percent since
     $e_{x,I}$ = 0.8. Therefore, quantity of X de-
     manded will increase to 1008.

5.7
A numerical example will be sufficient here.
Since ham and cheese are used in a fixed relationship, there is really only one good—ham and
cheese sandwiches. Since this is the only good,
the price elasticity of demand for it must be
−1—that is, P · Q is constant.
a.   If P_H = P_C then ham constitutes one-half
     the price of a sandwich. If P_H rises by, say,
     10 percent, cost of a sandwich rises by 5
     percent so quantity purchased falls by 5 per-
     cent. Elasticity is, therefore, 5%/10% =
     −1/2.
b.   For similar reasons, using the same numeri-
     cal example, cross price elasticity is −1/2.
c.   If P_H = $2P_C$, ham now constitutes two-
     thirds the cost of a sandwich. If P_H rises by
     10 percent, the cost of a sandwich rises by
     6.6 percent and quantity must fall by 6.6
     percent. Elasticity is 6.6%/10% = −2/3.
     Similar logic shows that cross price elasticity
     is −1/3.

5.9
e_{x,p_x} = −.6, e_{x,p_y} = −.8, $e_{x,I}$ = ?. A 1 percent
rise in income is the same as a 1 percent drop in
P_X, P_Y. With such a drop, X would increase by
0.6 + 0.8 = 1.4%. Hence, $e_{X,I}$ = 1.4.

Chapter 6

6.1
If Jack gives up three cords of firewood in return
for two bushels of corn, both men are better off.
Jack is willing to give up three cords for one
bushel so he receives an "extra" bushel and is
better off. Steve is willing to give up two bushels
for one cord but actually receives two "extra"
cords and is much better off. (This is one of
many possible solutions.)

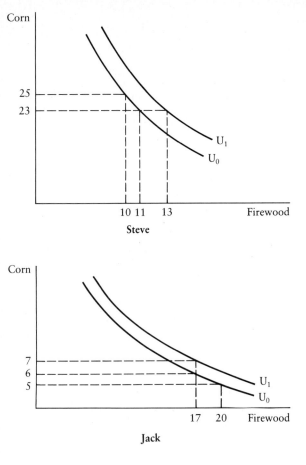

Steve

Jack

6.3

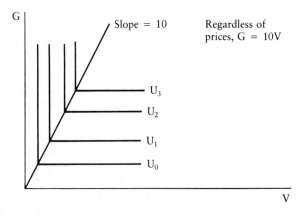

G

Slope = 10

Regardless of prices, G = 10V

U_3

U_2

U_1

U_0

V

Base year index:

$$\frac{I_2}{I_1} = \frac{P_{G1}\,G_2 + P_{V1}\,V_2}{P_{G1}\,G_1 + P_{V1}\,V_1}$$

$$= \frac{P_{G1}\,G_2 + P_{V1}\,(10G_2)}{P_{G1}\,G_1 + P_{V1}\,(10G_1)}$$

$$= \frac{G_2(P_{G1} + 10P_{V1})}{G_1(P_{G1} + 10P_{V1})}$$

$$= \frac{G_2}{G_1}.$$

Current year index:

$$\frac{I_2}{I_1} = \frac{P_{G2}G_2 + P_{V2}V_2}{P_{G2}G_1 + P_{V2}V_1}$$

$$= \frac{P_{G2}G_2 + P_{V2}\,(10G_2)}{P_{G2}G_1 + P_{V2}\,(10G_1)}$$

$$= \frac{G_2(P_{G2} + 10P_{V2})}{G_1(P_{G2} + 10P_{V2})}$$

$$= \frac{G_2}{G_1}.$$

6.5

a. $U_{1986} = \sqrt{40 \cdot 40} = 40.$
    $U_{1987} = \sqrt{20 \cdot 80} = 40.$

b. $I^{86} = P_X{}^{86}\,X^{86} + P_Y{}^{86}Y^{86} = \$1 \cdot 40 +$
    $\$1 \cdot 40 = \$80.$
    $I^{87} = P_X{}^{86}\,X^{87} + P_Y{}^{86}Y^{87} = \$1 \cdot 20 +$
    $\$1 \cdot 80 = \$100.$
    $\dfrac{I^{87}}{I^{86}} = \dfrac{5}{4} > 1$, so real income in 86 prices is
    higher in 1987.

c. $I^{86} = P_X{}^{87}X^{86} + P_Y{}^{87}Y^{86} = \$4 \cdot 40 +$
    $\$1 \cdot 40 = \$200.$
    $I^{87} = P_X{}^{87}X^{87} + P_Y{}^{87}Y^{87} = \$4 \cdot 20 +$
    $\$1 \cdot 80 = \$160.$
    $\dfrac{I^{87}}{I^{86}} = \dfrac{4}{5} < 1$, so real income in 87 prices is
    lower in 1987.

d. Results of calculations depend on which prices are used. It may be necessary to use some combination of the two indices to get a true picture.

6.7

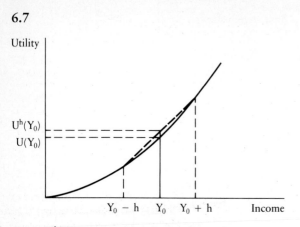

Since $U^h > U$, the individual will gamble, even on unfair bets. This would be limited by the individual's resources; he or she could eventually run out of money by taking unfair bets.

6.9

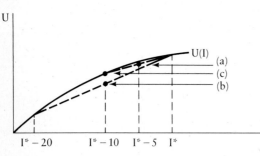

Note $U_c > U_b$, hence increasing fine is more effective. Chief is wrong.

Chapter 7

7.1

a. $K = 6. \; Q = 6K + 4L = 6(6) + 4L = 36 + 4L.$
     If $Q = 60, 4L = 60 - 36 = 24, L = 6.$
     If $Q = 100, 4L = 100 - 36 = 64, L = 16.$

b. $K = 8. \; Q = 6K + 4L = 6(8) + 4L = 48 + 4L.$
     If $Q = 60, 4L = 60 - 48 = 12, L = 3.$
     If $Q = 100, 4L = 100 - 48 = 52, L = 13.$

c. $RTS = \dfrac{2}{3}$: If L increases by one unit, can

keep Q constant by decreasing K by two-thirds units.

7.3

a.

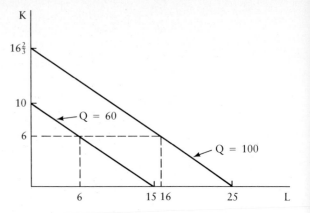

b. $AP_L = \dfrac{Q}{L} = \dfrac{100}{\sqrt{L}}$

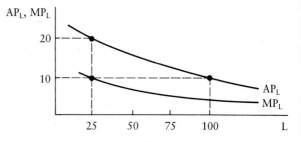

c.   Graph above. Since the AP_L is everywhere decreasing, then each additional worker must be contributing less than the average of the existing workers, bringing the average down. Therefore, the marginal productivity must be lower than the average.

7.5

$Q = KL - .8K^2 - .2L^2$. Average Productivity

$\frac{Q}{L} = K - .8\frac{K^2}{L} - .2L = 10 - \frac{80}{L} - .2L.$

a. Average productivity reaches maximum at
L = 20, Q = 40. MP_L = 0 at L = 25.

b.

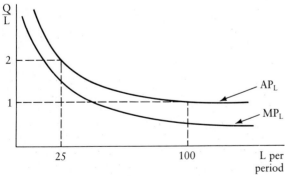

c. K = 20. $Q = 20L - 320 - .2L^2$. Q/L =

$20 - \frac{320}{L} - .2L.$

Average productivity reaches maximum at
L = 40, Q = 472. MP_L = 0 at L = 50.

7.7

$Q = K^{1/2}L^{1/2}$

a. $AP_L = \frac{Q}{L} = \left(\frac{K}{L}\right)^{1/2}.$ $AP_K = \left(\frac{L}{K}\right)^{1/2}.$

b. K = 100. $AP_L = \frac{10}{\sqrt{L}}.$

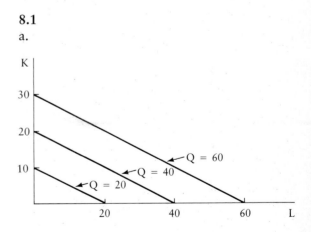

c. It is unusual that MP_L never actually reaches
zero.

d.

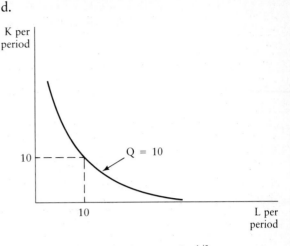

e. $RTS = \frac{MP_L}{MP_K} = \frac{AP_L}{AP_K} = \frac{(K/L)^{1/2}}{(L/K)^{1/2}} = \frac{K}{L}.$

K = 10, L = 10. RTS = 1.
K = 25, L = 4. RTS = 6.25.
K = 4, L = 25. RTS = .16.
Yes, it does exhibit diminishing RTS.

Chapter 8

8.1

a.

K

30

20

10

Q = 60
Q = 40
Q = 20

20   40   60   L

RTS = 1/2 since if L is increased by one, K
can be reduced by one-half while holding Q
constant.

b. Since RTS = $\frac{1}{2} < \frac{w}{v} = 1$, the manufacturer will use only K. For Q = 20, K = 10;

$Q = 40; K = 20; Q = 60, K = 30.$ The manufacturer's expansion path is simply the K axis. Note that if $v = \$3$, say, RTS $= \frac{1}{2} > \frac{w}{v} = \frac{1}{3}$, the manufacturer will use only L. For $Q = 20, L = 20; Q = 40, L = 40; Q = 60, L = 60.$ In this case the manufacturer's expansion path is the L axis.

8.3
Isoquants can have positive slopes, providing one input has a negative marginal product. For that reason, such regions of isoquant maps will not observed.

8.5

a. $Q = 2\sqrt{K \cdot L}.\ K = 100,\ Q = 2\sqrt{100 \cdot L}.$

$Q = 20\sqrt{L}.\ \sqrt{L} = \frac{Q}{20}.\ L = \frac{Q^2}{400}.$

$STC = vK + wL = 1(100) + 4\frac{(Q^2)}{400} = 100 + .01Q^2.$

$SAC = \frac{STC}{Q} = \frac{100}{Q} + \frac{Q}{100}.$

b. $SMC = \frac{Q}{50}.$ If $Q = 25,\ STC = 100 + \frac{(25)^2}{100} = 106.25.$

$SAC = \frac{100}{25} + \frac{25}{100} = 4.25.$

$SMC = \frac{25}{50} = .50.$

If $Q = 50,\ STC = 100 + \frac{(50^2)}{100} = 125.$

$SAC = \frac{100}{50} + \frac{50}{100} = 2.50.$

$SMC = \frac{50}{50} = 1.$

If $Q = 100,\ STC = 100 + \frac{(100)^2}{100} = 200.$

$SAC = \frac{100}{100} + \frac{100}{100} = 2.\ SMC = \frac{100}{50} = 2.$

If $Q = 200,\ STC = 100 + \frac{(200^2)}{100} = 500.$

$SAC = \frac{100}{200} + \frac{200}{100} = 2.50.$

$SMC = \frac{200}{50} = 4.$

c.

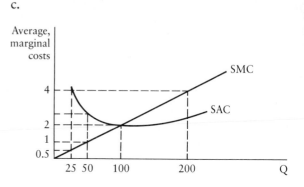

d. As long as the marginal cost of producing one more unit is below the average cost curve, average costs will be falling. Similarly, if the marginal cost of producing one more unit is higher than the average cost, then average costs will be rising. Therefore, the SMC curve must intersect the SAC curve at its lowest point.

8.7
To minimize, costs should equate the marginal productivities of labor in each plant. If labor were more productive in one plant than another, costs could be lowered by moving workers.

a. $MP_{L1} = MP_{L2}.\ 5/2\sqrt{L_1} = 5/\sqrt{L_2}.$
$2\sqrt{L_1} = \sqrt{L_2}.\ L_2 = 4L_1.\ Q_1 = 5\sqrt{L_1};\ Q_2 = 10\sqrt{L_2} = 10\sqrt{4L_1} = 20\sqrt{L_1}$
Hence $Q_2 = 4Q_1.$

b. $4Q_1 = Q_2,$ so $Q_1 = 1/5\ Q.\ Q_2 = 4/5\ Q$ where Q is total output.

$STC\ (\text{Plant 1}) = 25 + wL_1 = 25 + \frac{Q_1^2}{25}.$

$STC\ (\text{Plant 2}) = 100 + wL_2 = 100 + \frac{Q_2^2}{100}.$

$STC = STC\ (\text{Plant 1}) + STC\ (\text{Plant 2})$

$= 25 + \frac{Q_1^2}{25} + 100 + \frac{Q_2^2}{100}$

$= 125 + \frac{(1/5\ Q)^2}{25} + \frac{(4/5\ Q)^2}{100}$

$$= 125 + \frac{1/25 \ Q^2}{25} + \frac{16/25 \ Q^2}{100}$$

$$= 125 + \frac{20/25 \ Q^2}{100}$$

$$= 125 + \frac{Q^2}{125}.$$

$$MC = \frac{2Q}{125}. \quad AC = \frac{125}{Q} + \frac{Q}{125}.$$

$$MC(100) = \frac{200}{125} = \$1.60. \ MC \ (125) =$$

$2.00.

MC (200) = $3.20.

c.   In the long run, because of constant returns to scale, can change K so doesn't really matter where production occurs. Could split evenly or produce all output in one plant. TC = K + L = 2Q. AC = 2 = MC.

d.   If there were decreasing returns to scale, then should let each firm have equal share of production. AC and MC, not constant any more, they are increasing functions of Q, so do not want either plant to be too large.

8.9

Each average cost curve reaches a minimum when its slope is 0. This occurs at only one point on the AC curve. Consequently, other tangencies cannot also be minima. The draftsman was correct.

Chapter 9

9.1

a.   Set P = MC. 20 = .2q + 10. 10 = .2q. q = 50.

b.   Maximum profits = TR-TC = (50·20) $-[.1(50)^2 + 10(50) + 50] = 1000$ $- 800 = 200.$

9.3

If P is constant, the TR = P·q is simply a straight line through the origin. Profits will be maximized where the slope of the TR curve (which is the price) is equal to the slope of the TC curve (that is to marginal cost).

9.5

Here the demand curve has a constant elasticity of -2. Hence, $MR = P(1 + \frac{1}{e}) = \frac{1P}{2}$, but $P^2 = \frac{256}{Q}$, so $P = \frac{16}{\sqrt{Q}}$ so $MR = \frac{8}{\sqrt{Q}}$.

For profit maximization, $MR = MC$, $\frac{8}{\sqrt{Q}} = .001Q$, $8000 = Q^{3/2}$.

Hence, $Q = 400$. $P = \frac{16}{20} = .80$.

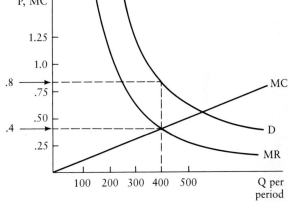

9.7

a. $TR = P \cdot Q = \frac{(100 - Q) \cdot Q}{2} =$

$$50Q - \frac{1}{2} Q^2.$$

MR = 50 − Q.
Noncalculus proofs can be done graphically or with a table.

b.   Max. π: MR = MC.
MR = 50 − Q. MR = MC: 50 − Q = 10.
Q = 40, P = 30, π = P·Q − 10Q = 1200 − 400 = 800

c.   Max. revenue: MR = 0. 50 − Q = 0.
Q = 50, P = 25, π = P·Q − 10Q = 1250 − 500 = 750.

d.   Constraint π = 768. 50Q − Q²/2 − 10Q = 768.
Use quadratic formula or factor:

$Q = (32, 48)$, but trying to maximize revenue so will choose $Q = 48$, $P = 26$.

e.

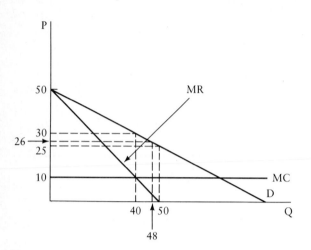

Chapter 10

10.1

For temporary price changes, hiring and severance costs might be regarded as marginal costs since they arise in connection with short-term changes in input use. For permanent price changes, however, these are more like fixed costs since they do not affect hourly wage rates.

10.3

a. $STC = vK + wL$
    $= 10 \cdot 100 + wL$
    $= 1,000 + 5L.$

    but $q = 10\sqrt{L}$, so $L = \dfrac{q^2}{100}$.

    Hence, $STC = 1,000 + q^2/20$.

b. Use $P = MC$.
    $20 = .1q$, so $q = 200$.
    $L = q^2/100$, so $L = 400$.

c. If $P = 15$, $P = MC$ implies $15 = .1q$, or $q = 150$, $L = 225$.

d. Cost will be 175 to reduce L from 400 to 225. With $q = 150$, profits = TR − TC = $15(150) - (1,000 + .05q^2) = 2,250 - (1,000 + 1,125) = 125$.

After paying severance cost of 175 the firm will incur a loss of 50.

e. If the firm continues to hire 400 workers it will have no severance costs and profits of TR − TC = $15(200) - (1,000 + .5(200^2)) = 3,000 - (1,000 + 2,000) = 0$, which is better than in part d. An output level of 180 ($L = 324$) would yield an overall profit for the firm.

10.5

If manager owned none of the firm would choose benefits up to point where MRS = 0. This seems unreasonable since owners would certainly place constraints on such behavior.

10.7

a. Again we use $P = MC$.
    $30 = .02q$, so $q = 1,500$.
    Profits = TR − TC = $30(1500)$
    $- (.01q^2 + 10,000)$
    $= 45,000 - (22,500 + 10,000)$
    $= 12,500.$

b. Now costs = $.75 \cdot STC$
    $= .0075q^2 + 7,500.$
    $SMC = .75 (.02q) = .015q.$
    $P = MC$ implies $30 = .015q$ or $q = 2,000$.
    In this case
    Profits = TR − TC = $30(2,000)$
    $- (.0075q^2 + 7,500)$
    $= 60,000 - (30,000 + 7,500)$
    $= 22,500.$

c. Ted would pay up to $22,500 - 12,500 = 10,000$ per week for the company.

Chapter 11

11.1

a. Set supply equal to demand to find equilibrium price:
    $Q_S = 1000 = Q_D = 1600 - 600P.$
    $1000 = 1600 - 600P$
    $600 = 600P$
    $p = 1/lb.$

b. $Q_S = 400 = 1600 - 600P.$
    $600P = 1200.$
    $P = 2/lb.$

c. $Q_S = 1000 = 2200 - 600P.$
$1200 = 600P.$
$P = 2/lb.$
$Q_S = 400 = 2200 - 600P.$
$600P = 1800.$
$P = 3/lb.$

d.

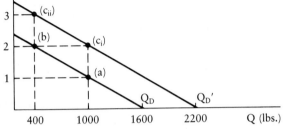

11.3

a. Supply $= 100,000$. In equilibrium, $100,000 = Q_S = Q_D = 160,000 - 10,000P$ or $P = 6$.

b. For any one firm, quantity supplied by other firms is fixed at 99,900. Demand curve is $Q_{D'} = 160,000 - 10,000P - 99,900 = 60,100 - 10,000P$.
If quantity supplied is 0, $Q_{S'} = 0 = Q_{D'} = 60,100 - 10,000P$. $P = 6.01$.
If quantity supplied is 200, $Q_{S'} = 200 = Q_{D'} = 60,100 - 10,000P$, or $P = 5.99$.
Elasticity $-$ Slope of demand $\times$ P/Q for market.

$$e_{Q,P} = -10,000 \cdot \frac{6}{100,000} = -.6.$$

For a single firm, demand is much more elastic: $e_{Q,P} = -10,000 \cdot \frac{6}{100} = -600.$

A change in quantity supplied does not affect price very much.

11.5

a. Short run: MR $= P$ so $P = MC$.
$P = q^2 + 20q + 100.$
$P = (q + 10)^2.$
$\sqrt{P} = q + 10.$
$q = \sqrt{P} - 10.$

b. $P = 121$. $q = \sqrt{121} - 10 = 1.$
$P = 169$. $q = \sqrt{169} - 10 = 3.$
$P = 256$. $q = \sqrt{256} - 10 = 6.$

c. $\pi = $ TR $-$ TC. $P = 121$.
$\pi = 1 \cdot (121) - [.33(1)^3 + 10(1)^2 + 100(1) + 48].$
$= 121 - 158.33 = -37.33.$
$P = 169.$
$\pi = 3(169) - [.33(3)^3 + 10(3)^2 + 100(3) + 48].$
$= 507 - 446.91 = 60.09.$
$P = 256.$
$\pi = 6(256) - [.33(6)^3 + 10(6)^2 + 100(6) + 48].$
$= 1536 - 1079.28 = 456.72.$

11.7

$C = q^2 + wq = q^2 + .002Qq.$

a. If $w = 10$, $C = q^2 + 10q$. MC $= 2q + 10 = P$. Hence $q = P/2 - 5$.
Industry Supply: $Q = \sum_{1}^{1000} q = 500P - 5000.$
at $P = 20$, $Q = 5000$; at $P = 21$, $Q = 5500$.

b. Here MC $= 2q + .002Q$. Set $= P$.
$q = P/2 - .001Q.$
Total $Q = \sum_{1}^{1000} q = 500P - Q$. Therefore,
$Q = 250P.$
$P = 20$, $Q = 5000.$
$P = 21$, $Q = 5250.$
Supply is more steeply sloped in this case of interactions—increasing production bids up the wages of diamond cutters.

11.9

a. In long-run equilibrium, AC $= P$ and MC $= P$, so AC $= MC$.
$$.01q - 1 + \frac{100}{q} = .02q - 1.$$
$$\frac{100}{q} = .01q.$$
$$\frac{10,000}{q} = q. \quad q^2 = 10,000. \quad q = 100$$
gallons.

$$AC = .01(100) - 1 + \frac{100}{100} = 1 - 1 + 1$$

$= 1.$

$MC = .02(100) - 1 = 2 - 1 = 1.$

b. In the long run, $P = MC$, $P = \$1$.
$Q_D = 2,500,000 - 500,000(1) =$
2,000,000 gallons. The market supplies
2,000,000 gallons, so $\dfrac{2,000,000 \text{ gallons}}{100 \text{ gallons/station}} =$
20,000 gas stations.

c. In the long run, $P = \$1$ still since the AC
curve has not changed.
$Q_D = 2,000,000 - 1,000,000(1) =$
1,000,000 gallons.
$\dfrac{1,000,000 \text{ gallons}}{100 \text{ gallons/stations}} = 10,000$ gas stations.
Shift in demand results in cutting the num-
ber of gas stations in half.

11.11

a. LR supply is horizontal at $P = MC = AC$
$= 10$.

b. $Q = 1500 - 50P^* = 1000$. Each firm produces $q = 20$, $\pi = 0$. There are 50 firms.

c. $MC = q - 10$, $AC = .5q - 10 + 200/q$.
$AC = $ min when $AC = MC$.
$.5q = 200/q$, $q = 20$.

d. $P = MC = q - 10$. $q = P + 10$ for
industry.
$$Q = \sum_{1}^{50} q = 50P + 500.$$

e. $Q = 2000 - 50P$. if $Q = 1000$, $P = 20$.
Each firm produces $q = 20$, $\pi = 20(20 - 10) = 200$.

f. $50P + 500 = 2000 - 50P$. $P = 15$, $Q = 1250$. Each firm produces $q = 25$, $\pi = 25(15 - AC) = 25(15 - 10.5) = 112.5$.

g. $P = 10$ again, $Q = 1500$, 75 firms produce
20 each. $\pi = 0$.

Chapter 12

12.1

a. $P = 53 - Q$.

For maximum profits, set $MR = MC$:
$MR = 53 - 2Q = MC = 5$.
$Q = 24$, $P = 29$.
$\pi = TR - TC = 24 \cdot 29 - 24 \cdot 5 = 696 - 120 = 576$. Consumer surplus $=$
$\dfrac{1}{2}(53 - 29) \cdot 24 = 288$.

b. $MC = P = 5$. $P = 5$, $Q = 48$.

c. Consumer's surplus $= \dfrac{1}{2}(48)^2 = 1152$.

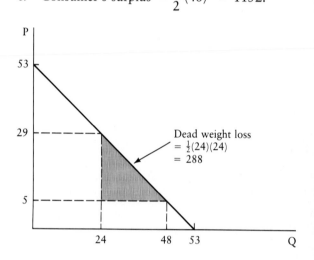

12.3

a. $AC = MC = 10$, $Q = 60 - P$, $MR = 60 - 2Q$.
For profit max., $MC = MR$. $10 = 60 - 2Q$, $2Q = 50$, $Q = 25$, $P = 35$.
$\pi = TR - TC = (25)(35) - (25)(10) = 625$.

b. $AC = MC = 10$, $Q = 45 - .5P$. $MR = 90 - 4Q$.
For profit max., $MC = MR$, $10 = 90 - 4Q$, $80 = 4Q$, $Q = 20$, $P = 50$.
$\pi = (20(50) - (20)(10) = 800$.

c. $AC = MC = 10$, $Q = 100 - 2P$, $MR = 50 - Q$.
For profit max., $MC = MR$, $10 = 50 - Q$, $Q = 40$, $P = 30$.
$\pi = (40)(30) - (40)(10) = 800$.

d.

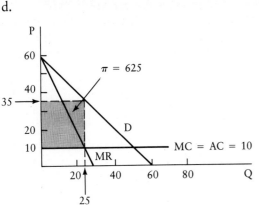

Part a

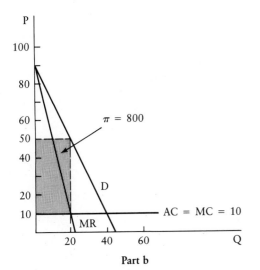

Part b

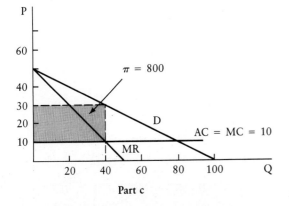

Part c

The supply curve for a monopoly is a single point, namely, that quantity for which MC = MR. Any attempt to connect equilibrium points (price-quantity points) on the market demand curves has little meaning and brings about a strange shape. One reason for this is that as the demand curve shifts, its elasticity (and its MR curve) often changes, bringing about varying patterns of price and quantity changes.

12.5
A multiplant monopolist will still produce where MR = MC and will equalize MC among factories.
$MR = 100 - 2(q_1 + q_2)$ and $MC_1 = MC_2$.
$q_1 - 5 = .5q_2 - 5$. $q_1 = .5q_2$.
$MR = 100 - 2(.5q_2 + q_2)$.
$MR = MC_2$. $100 - 2(1.5q_2) = .5q_2 - 5$.
$3.5q_2 = 105$.
$q_2 = 30$ and $q_1 = 15$, so $Q_T = 45$.
In this case, $P = 55$ and MC is 10 in each plant.

12.7
D' is the aftertax demand curve.

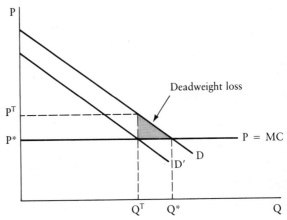

Chapter 13

13.1
$Q = 150 - P$. $MC = 0$.
a. A zero cost monopolist would produce that output for which MR is equal to 0 (MR =

MC = 0). MR = 0 at one-half of the demand curve's horizontal intercept ($1/2 \cdot 150$ = 75). Q = 75. P = 75.
$\pi = (75)(75) = \$5625$.

b. $q_1 + q_2 = 150 - P$.
Demand curve for firm 1: $q_1 = (150 - q_2) - P$.
Profit-maximizing output level: $q_1 = \dfrac{150 - q_2}{2}$.

Demand curve for firm 2: $q_2 = (150 - q_1) - P$.
Profit-maximizing output level: $q_2 = \dfrac{150 - q_1}{2}$.

Market equilibrium:
$$q_1 = \frac{150 - (150 - q_1)/2}{2}.$$

$$q_1 = \frac{150 - 75 + q_1/2}{2} = 37.5 + \frac{q_1}{4}.$$

$4q_1 = 150 + q_1$.
$3q_1 = 150$.
$q_1 = 50$, $q_2 = 50$, $P = 50$.
$\pi 1 = \pi 2 = \$2,500$. π total = 5,000.

c. Under perfect competition P = MC = 0.
Q = 150, P = 0, π = 0.

P

150
140

120

100

80 ——————————•Q = 75 P = 75

60
50 ——————————•Q = 100 P = 50
40

20   D

                            •Q = 150 P = 0

      20 40 60 80 100 120 140 150   Q

              MR

13.3

Most literature suggests that "planned obsolescence" is a profitable strategy for a monopoly, but not so under perfect competition since en-

trants would produce more durable commodities. The difficult part of the theory of durability is how to treat the market for used goods and the degree of substitutability between new and used goods.

13.5

McGee's conclusion is that predatory pricing would not be profit-maximizing because of the losses suffered on the potential monopolist's own output.

13.7

$Q_D = -2,000P + 70,000$.

a. 1000 firms. MC = q + 5.
Price taker: set MC = P. q + 5 = P.
q = P − 5.
$$Q_S = \sum_{1}^{1000} q = 1,000P - 5,000.$$
To find equilibrium, set $Q_D = Q_S$.
$-2,000P + 70,000 = 1,000P - 5,000$.
$3,000P = 75,000$. P = 25, Q = 20,000.

b. Demand for leader = Market demand − Quantity supplied by fringe.
$Q_{DL} = (-2,000P + 70,000) - (1,000P - 5,000)$.
$Q_{DL} = -3,000P + 75,000$.

c. $MR_L = \dfrac{-Q_1}{1,500} + 25$. $MC_L = 15$.
For profit max., set $MR_L = MC_L$.
$$\frac{-Q_L}{1,500} + 25 = 15.$$

$$10 = \frac{Q_L}{1,500}. \quad Q_L = 15,000, P = 20.$$
Total $Q_D = 30,000$.

d.

P

35

25

20 ——————————

15

5

      15,000   30,000   60,000 70,000   Q

Market demand

$Q_{S fringe}$

Demand for price leader

$AC_L = MC_L = 15$

MR_L

e. Yes, consumer surplus does increase:
For P = 25, Consumer surplus = 100,000.
For P = 20, Consumer surplus = 225,000.
For P = 15, Consumer surplus = 400,000

Chapter 14

14.1

Demand L = −50w + 450. Supply: L = 100w.

a. S = D. 100w = −50w + 450. w = 3, L = 300.

b. D: L = −50(w − s) + 450.
s = subsidy.
w = $4. L_s = 400 = −50(4 − s) + 450.
s = 3.
Total subsidy is 400 × 3 = $1200.

c. w = $4. D = 250. S = 400. U = 150.

d.

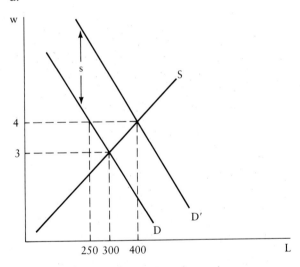

14.3

a. Five laborers: put them where MP_L is greatest.
First laborer goes to A, second goes to B, third goes to A, fourth goes to C, fifth goes to A.
Output = 21 + 8 + 5 = 34.
MP of last worker is 4.

b. P · MP_L = $1 × 4 = $4 = w.

Five laborers, wL = $20
π = TR − TC = PQ − wL = $34 − $20 = $14.

14.5

a. w = v = $1, so K and L will be used in a one-to-one ratio.
TC = w · L + v · K = L + K = 2L, so
$$AC = \frac{2L}{q} = \frac{2L}{\sqrt{KL}} = \frac{2L}{\sqrt{LL}} = 2 \text{ and MC} = 2.$$

b. P = 2, so Q = 400,000 − 100,000(2) = 200,000 pipe.
$$q = \frac{200,000 \text{ pipe}}{1,000 \text{ firms}} = 200 \text{ pipe/firm.}$$
q = 200 = $\sqrt{L \cdot K}$ = L, so 200 workers are hired per firm, 200,000 by the industry.

c. w = $2, v = $1, so K/L = 2
TC = wL + vK
   = 2L + K = 4L = $2\sqrt{2}q$.
so AC = MC = $2\sqrt{2}$.

d. P = $2\sqrt{2}$. Q = 400,000 − 100,000($2\sqrt{2}$) = 117,157.
$$L = \frac{117,157}{\sqrt{2}} = 83,000 \text{ workers hired by}$$
the industry.

e. If Q = 200,000 at the new wage,
$$L = \frac{200,000}{\sqrt{2}} = 141,000 \text{ workers would}$$
have been hired by the industry.
So if Q were unchanged, 59,000 fewer workers would have been hired. This reduction is the substitution effect.
The remaining 58,000 fewer workers are the result of the lower output. This is the output effect.

14.7

Supply: L = 80w. $ME_L = \frac{L}{40}$. Demand: L = 400 − $40MVP_L$.

a. For monopsonist, $ME_L = MVP_L$. L = 400 − $40MVP_L$. 40 MVP_L = 400 − L.
$$MVP_L = 10 - \frac{L}{40}.$$
$$\frac{L}{40} = 10 - \frac{L}{40}. \quad \frac{2L}{40} = 10. \quad L = 200.$$

Get w from supply curve:

$$w = \frac{L}{80} = \frac{200}{80} = \$2.50.$$

b. For Carl, the marginal expense of labor now equals the minimum wage, and in equilibrium the marginal expense of labor will equal the marginal revenue product of labor.

$$w_m = ME_L = MVP_L$$
$$w_m = \$3.00.$$

Carl's Demand	Supply
$L = 400 - 40MVP_L$	$L = 80w$
$= 400 - 40(3)$	$= 80(3)$
$= 280.$	$= 240.$

Demand > supply. Carl will hire 240 workers, with no unemployment.

To study effects of minimum, try \$3.33 and \$4.00

$$w_m = \$3.33.$$

$L = 400 - 40(3.33)$	$L = 80(3.33)$
$= 267.$	$= 267.$

Demand = supply, Carl will hire 267 workers, with no unemployment.

$$w_m = \$4.00$$

$L = 400 - 40(4.00)$	$L = 80(4.00)$
$L = 240$	$L = 320$

Supply > demand, Carl will hire 240 workers, unemployment = 80.

c.

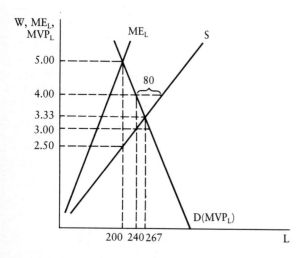

d. Under perfect competition, a minimum wage means higher wages but fewer workers employed. Under monopsony, a minimum wage may result in higher wages and more workers employed as shown by cases studied in part b.

14.9

Here marginal value product is \$10 per hour:

$$ME_m = \frac{\sqrt{L_m}}{2} = 10, \text{ so } L_m = 400, \text{ } w_m = \frac{20}{3} = 6.67.$$

$$ME_f = \frac{L_f}{50} = 10, \text{ so } L_f = 500, \text{ } w_f = 5. \text{ } L_T = 900 \text{ per hour.}$$

Profits on machinery = $9000 - 5(500) - 6.66(400) = 3833.$

If same wage $w = MVP_L = 10$, $L = 1000 + 900 = 1900.$

Profits = $19,000 - 1900 \cdot w = 19,000 - 19,000 = 0.$

Chapter 15

15.1

a. 8000 hrs/year × \$5/hr = \$40,000/yr.
    ¾ × 40,000/yr = \$30,000/yr at leisure.
    $$\frac{\$30,000}{5} = 6,000 \text{ hours of leisure. Work} = 2,000 \text{ hours.}$$

b. ¾ × \$44,000/yr = \$33,000/yr at leisure.
    $$\frac{\$33,000}{5} = 6,600 \text{ hours of leisure. Work} = 1,400 \text{ hours.}$$

c. Now full income = \$84,000.
    ¾ × \$84,000 = \$63,000.
    Leisure = 6,300 hours. Work = 1,700 hours. Hence, higher wage leads to more labor supply. Note that in part a, labor supply is perfectly inelastic at 2,000 hours.

d.

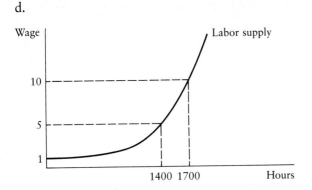

15.3

a. $ME_L = L/50$
    Demand: $L = -50MVP_L + 450.$
$$MVP_L = -L/50 + 9 = ME_L$$
$$= L/50.$$
$$L = 225.$$
Get w from Supply: $225 = 100w.$ w = $2.25.

b. $w = -L/50 + 9.$ MR $= -L/25 + 9.$ Set equal to zero to maximize wage bill: $L = 225.$ Here $w = -L/50 + 0 = \$4.50.$

c. Somewhere "between" a. and b. bargaining will determine the final outcome. Under competition, S = D: w = 3, L = 300. Bilateral monopoly outcome will have $L < 300.$

15.5

a. This will result in a simple income effect on the demand for leisure.

b. A tax on wages will cause both income and substitution effects on labor supply. It is equivalent to a change in the real wage.

c. This will result in a fall in the real wage and a concomitant reduction in supply (if the supply curve is positively sloped).

d. Will have no effect on those who choose to work less than 35 hours. Will reduce utility and money income for those who would choose to work more than 35 hours.
    Note: none of these outcomes takes into ac-count possible reactions in the demand for labor to the proposed situations.

15.7

a. Executives who value their time greatly.

b. Someone with a great desire to see the event and who did not value time greatly.

c. Total cost of golf game includes opportunity cost. Therefore, total cost for physicians is much greater. Green fees are greater function of total cost for vendor.

d. As traffic congestion gets worse, time costs .of commuting by car will rise. This may have the greatest effect on relative commuting costs for high wage commuters. They may be the first to switch.

Chapter 16

16.1

If i = 12%, Price = PDV $= \dfrac{1,000}{(1 + .12)}$
$$+ \frac{1,000}{(1 + .12)^2} + \frac{1,000}{(1 + .12)^3} + \frac{1,000}{(1 + .12)^4}$$
$$+ \frac{1,000}{(1 + .12)^5} + \frac{10,000}{(1 + .12)^5}. \text{ PDV} = \$9,279.$$

If i = 8%, Price = PDV $= \dfrac{1,000}{(1 + .08)}$
$$+ \frac{1,000}{(1 + .08)^2} + \frac{1,000}{(1 + .08)^3} + \frac{1,000}{(1 + .08)^4}$$
$$+ \frac{1,000}{(1 + .08)^5} + \frac{10,000}{(1 + .08)^5}. \text{ PDV} = \$10,799.$$

When interest rates go down, bond prices go up. It is an inverse relationship.

16.3

Assuming premiums paid at end of year, $PDV_{\text{whole life}} = \$6,340.$ $PDV_{\text{term}} = \$3,858.$ The salesman is wrong. The term policy represents a better value to this consumer.

16.5

Let Y_t = Income in year t = $Y_0(1.03)^t$
S_t = Savings in year t = $sY_t = sY_0(1.03)^t$

Accumulated savings $= \sum_{t=0}^{40} s_t(1.03)^{40-t}$

$$= \sum_{t=0}^{40} sY_0(1.03)^t(1.03)^{40-t}$$

$$= 40sY_0(1.03)^{40}.$$

PDV of dissavings:

$$PDV = \sum_{t=0}^{20} .6Y_0(1.03)^{40} \cdot (1.03)^{-t}.$$

Equate the two streams to solve for s:

$$s = \frac{PDV}{40\ Y_0(1.03)^{40}}$$

$$= \frac{.6\ Y_0(1.03)^{40} \sum_0^{20} (1.03)^{-t}}{40\ Y_0(1.03)^{40}}$$

$$= \frac{.6(15.9)}{40} = .24$$

which is much higher than the average savings rate in the United States (about 5 percent).

16.7

Each tree should be cut down when the rate of interest (opportunity cost) is equal to the tree's rate of growth. Maximum sustainable yield proceeds to the point where growth becomes zero. It neglects the opportunity cost of interest.

Chapter 17

17.1

Production possibility frontier

a.

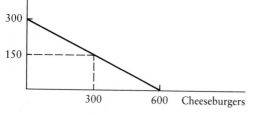

b. $M = 1/2C.\ C + 2M = 600.$
$C + 2(1/2C) = 600.$
$2C = 600.\ C = 300.\ M = 150.$

c. $-$slope $= RPT = \frac{1}{2}.$ Under efficient econ-

omy, $RPT = MRS = \frac{P_c}{P_m}$ so $\frac{P_c}{P_m} = \frac{1}{2}.$

17.3

a. Production possibility frontier:

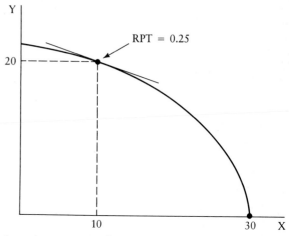

b. If $Y = 2X$, $X^2 + 2(2X)^2 = 900$.
$9X^2 = 900$; $X = 10$, $Y = 20$.

c. If $X = 9$ on the production possibility

frontier, $Y = \sqrt{\dfrac{819}{2}} = 20.24.$

If $X = 11$ on the frontier, $Y = \sqrt{\dfrac{779}{2}} =$

19.74.

Hence, RPT is about 0.25.

17.5

Smith's indifference curves are L-shaped with the vertex at a ratio of 1 H to 2 C.
Jones' indifference curves are straight lines with a slope of $-\frac{3}{4}$.

a.

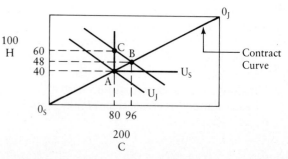

b. 40 H, 80 C (Point A) is the contract curve.

c. 60 H, 80 C is not on contract curve. Could move to point A, point B, or anywhere in between.

d. Smith might grab all 100 H, 200 C for herself.

17.7

$H = 16$, $L_F + L_C = 8$. $F^2 + C^2 = 8$.

$U = 4F^{1/4}C^{1/4}$.

$C = F$ since the goods enter utility symmetrically.

$C = F = 2$, $H = 16$, $U = 4\sqrt{2} = 5.66$.

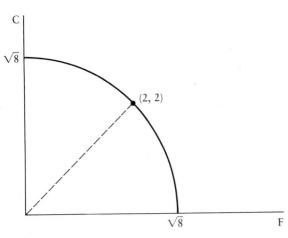

17.9

a. D

b. E

c. $E(U) = .6(L) + .4(H)$.

$EU_A = 50$, $EU_B = 52$, $EU_C = 48.6$, $EU_D = 51.5$, $EU_E = 50$. .... Choose B.

d. Max $E(U) - |U_1 - U_2|$.

Values: A: $50 - 0 = 50$.

B: $55 - 30 = 25$.

C: $49.5 - 9 = 40.5$.

D: $51.75 - 2.5 = 49.25$.

E: $57 - 54 = 3$.

Choose A.

e. It shows that a variety of different social choices might be made depending on the criteria being used.

Chapter 18

18.1

a. $MC = .4q$. $P = \$20$. Set $P = MC$.

$20 = .4q$. $q = 50$.

b. $SMC = .5q$.

Set $P = SMC$. $20 = .5q$. $q = 40$.

At optimal production level of $q = 40$, the marginal cost of production is $MC = .4q = .4(40) = 16$, so the excise tax $t = 20 - 16 = \$4$.

c.

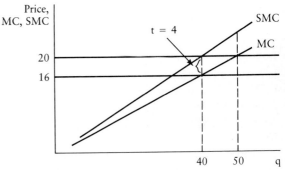

18.3

$AC = MC = 1000/\text{well}$

a. Produce where revenue/well $= 1000 = 10q = 5000 - 10N$. $N = 400$. There is an externality here because drilling another well reduces output in *all* wells.

b. Produce where $MVP = MC$ of well.

Total value $= 5000 N - 10N^2$. $MVP = 5000 - 20N = 1000$. $N = 200$.

Let Tax $= X$. Want revenue/well $- X = 1000$ when $N = 200$. At $N = 200$, average revenue/well $= 3000$. Charge $X = 2000$.

18.5

Under *caveat emptor*, buyers would assume all losses. The demand curve under such a situation might be given by D. Firms (which assume no liability) might have a horizontal long-run supply curve of S. A change in liability assignment would shift both supply and demand curves. Under *caveat vendor*, losses (of amount L) would now be incurred by firms, thereby shifting the long-run supply curve to S′.

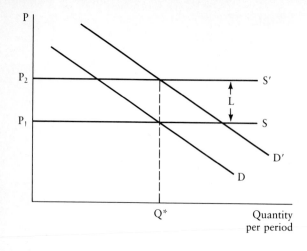

Individuals now no longer have to pay these losses and their demand curve will shift upward by L to D'. In this example then, market price rises from P_1 to P_2 (although the real cost of owning the good has not changed) and the level of production stays constant at Q^*. Only if there were major information costs associated with either the *caveat emptor* or *caveat vendor* positions might the two give different allocations. It is possible also that L may be a function of liability assignment (the moral hazard problem) and this would also cause the equilibria to differ.

18.7

One example of this type of externality would be an individual who refused to trim a hedge that bordered a neighbor's property. The neighbor might, if he or she valued a trimmed hedge, offer to trim it (at least one side of it) thereby internalizing the externality. In general, one might expect that such agreements are common since bargaining costs are low when only two individuals are involved.

Chapter 19

19.1

a. Marginal valuation for a = $P = 100 - q_a$; for b, Marginal valuation = $P = 200 - q_b$. Because of the public good nature of mosquito control there should be added "vertically." Marginal value = $300 - 2q$ (since $q_a = q_b$). Set this = 50, gives q = 125.

b. Free rider problem could result in having no production.

c. Total cost = $50 \times 125 = \$6,250$. Area under demand curve for a = \$4,688; for b = \$17,188. May want to share costs in proportion to these values.

19.3

Resources should be allocated so that the sum of people's marginal valuations of education's public benefits plus the private benefit for the marginal buyer equals the marginal cost of producing one more unit. It might be financed through a combination of compulsory taxes and user fees. For example, elementary and secondary education might be publicly financed (if it provided all public goods) whereas university education might be funded privately if its benefits were private.

19.5

If different localities have different tastes for a certain public good, then it should be produced by local governments. But if the good can be supplied uniformly over the whole state (example, state police), then it should be produced by the state. Diseconomies of scale may make it more efficient to produce countrywide or statewide services on a statewide or local basis.

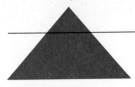

GLOSSARY

Accounting cost The concept that goods or services cost what was paid for them. (p 182)

Agent The role of making economic decisions for another party, such as the manager of a firm being hired to act for the owner. (p 257)

Asymmetric information A situation in which buyers and sellers have different amounts of information about a market transaction. (p 317)

Average cost Total costs divided by output—A common measure of cost per unit. (p 190)

Average productivity The ratio of total output produced to the quantity of a particular input employed. (p 162)

Backward bending labor supply curve Labor supply curve in which higher real wages cause less labor to be supplied because the income effect outweighs the substitution effect. (p 439)

Barriers to entry Factors that prevent new firms from entering a market or industry. (p 323)

Budget constraint The limit that income places on the combinations of goods and services that an individual can afford. (p 64)

Capital stock The total amount of machines, buildings, and all other manmade, nonlabor resources in an economy. (p 455)

Cartel model A model of oligopoly pricing in which firms coordinate their decisions to act as a multiplant monopoly. (p 355)

Ceteris paribus assumption In economic analysis, holding all other factors constant so that only the factor being studied is allowed to change. (p 50)

Coase theorem If bargaining is costless, the social cost of an externality will be taken into account by the parties and the allocation of resources will be the same no matter how property rights are assigned. (p 556)

Cobweb model A model of price adjustment in which some trading takes place at non-equilibrium prices. (p 318)

Common property Property that may be used by anyone without cost. (p 555)

Comparative statics The investigation of new choices people make when conditions change, as compared to the choices they made under the former conditions. (p 79)

Compensating wage differentials Differences in wages caused by differing job characteristics. (p 444)

Competitive fringe Group of firms that act as price takers in a market dominated by a price leader. (p 358)

Complements Two goods such that when the price of one increases, the quantity demanded of the other falls. (p 98)

Compound interest Interest paid on prior interest earned. (p 481)

Constant cost industry An industry in which the entry or exit of firms has no effect on the cost curves of the firms in the industry. (p 292)

Consumer Price Index (CPI) The current value of the market basket of goods and services purchased by a typical household compared to a base year value of the same market basket. (p 135)

Consumer surplus The difference between the total revenue that would be collected under perfect price discrimination and the amount actually paid by consumers. (p 334)

Consumption bundles The combinations of goods or services that an individual chooses. (p 52)

Contestable market Market in which entry and exit are costless. (p 368)

Contour lines Lines in two dimensions that show the sets of values of the independent variables that yield the same value for the dependent variable. (p 36)

Contract curve A graphic representation of all the efficient allocations of goods in an Edgeworth box diagram of exchange. (p 526)

Cournot equilibrium A solution to the Cournot model in which each firm makes the correct assumption about what the other firm will produce. (p 382)

Cournot model A model of duopoly in which each firm assumes the other firm's output will not change if it changes its own output level. (p 381)

Cross-price elasticity of demand The percentage change in the quantity demanded of a good in response to a 1 percent change in the price of another good. (p 120)

Deadweight loss A loss of consumer surplus that is not transferred to another economic actor. (p 335)

Decreasing cost industry An industry in which the entry of firms decreases the costs of the firms in the industry. (p 302)

Dependent variable In algebra, a variable whose value is determined by another variable. (p 24)

Derived demand Demand for a factor of production that is determined by the demand for the good it produces. (p 396)

Differentiated good A good that differs from producer to producer. (p 275)

Differentiated oligopoly A market in which relatively few firms produce a differentiated good. (p 275)

Direct approach To verify economic models, the direct approach examines the validity of the assumptions on which the model is based. (p 15)

Dual linear programming problem A minimization problem related to a primal linear programming maximization problem; often involves computation of appropriate resource prices. (p 542)

Economic cost The cost concept that goods or services cost the amount required to keep them in their present use: the amount that they would be worth in their next best alternative use. (p 182)

Economic profits The difference between total revenue and total economic costs. (p 183)

Economic rent The amount by which payments to a factor exceed the minimal amount required to retain it in its present use. (p 397)

Economically efficient allocation of resources A technically efficient allocation of resources in which the output combination also reflects people's preferences. (p 511)

Edgeworth box diagram A graphic device for illustrating all of the possible allocations of two goods (or two inputs) which are in fixed supply. (p 505)

Efficient wage A wage above the market wage paid to encourage a worker to remain with a firm. (p 257)

Elasticity The measure of the percentage change in one variable brought about by a 1 percent change in some other variable. (p 113)

Engel curves Curves that record the relationship between the quantity demanded of a good and total income. (p 82)

Equilibrium price The price at which the quantity demanded by buyers of a good is equal to the quantity supplied of the good by sellers. (p 278)

Equity The fairness of the distribution of goods or utility. (p 527)

Excess demand The extent to which quantity demanded exceeds quantity supplied at a particular price. (p 311)

Exchange efficiency An allocation of the available goods such that no one person can be made better off without necessarily making someone else worse off. (p 524)

Expansion path The locus of cost-minimizing input combinations a firm will choose to produce various levels of output (when the prices of inputs are held constant). (p 188)

Expected value For a gamble with a number of uncertain outcomes, the outcome that will occur on average. (p 142)

Externality The effect of one party's economic activities on another party's well-being that is not taken into account by the price system. (p 521, p 547)

Fair games Games with an expected value of zero. (p 144)

Firm Any organization that turns inputs into outputs. (p 157)

Fixed costs Costs associated with inputs that are fixed in the short run. (p 198)

Fixed-proportions production function A production function in which the inputs must be used in a fixed ratio to one another. (p 170)

Free rider A consumer of a nonexclusive good who does not pay for the good in the hope that other consumers will. (p 577)

Future goods Goods that are purchased today by setting aside some present output as capital whose output is then consumed in the future. (p 457)

Game theory The study of the strategies used by the players in a game and the payoffs they receive. (p 387)

General equilibrium model An economic model of several related markets. (p 14)

Giffen's Paradox A situation in which the increase in a good's price leads people to consume more of the good. (p 95)

Homogeneous demand Demand does not change when prices and income increase in the same proportion. (p 81)

Homogeneous good A good that is identical from producer to producer. (p 275)

Homogeneous oligopoly A market in which relatively few firms produce a homogeneous good. (p 275)

Human capital Capital in the form of learned abilities acquired through training, education, or experience. (p 472)

Imperfect competition A market situation in which buyers or sellers have some influence on the prices of goods or services. (p 517)

Income effect The part of the change in quantity demanded of a good whose price has changed that is caused by the change in real income that results from the price change. (p 85)

Income effect of a change in w Movement to a higher indifference curve in response to a rise in the real wage rate. If leisure is a normal good, a rise in w causes an individual to work less. (p 437)

Income elasticity of demand The percentage change in the quantity demanded of a good in response to a 1 percent change in income. (p 120)

Increase or decrease in demand The change in demand for a good caused by changes in the price of another good, income, or preferences. Graphically represented by a shift of the entire demand curve. (p 104)

Increase or decrease in quantity demanded The increase or decrease in quantity demanded caused by a change in the good's price. Graphically represented by the movement along a demand curve. (p 104)

Increasing cost industry An industry in which the entry of firms increases the costs of the firms in the industry. (p 296)

Independent variable In an algebraic equation, a variable that is unaffected by the action of another variable and may be assigned any value. (p 24)

Index number An average of many different trends into one number. (p 135)

Indifference curve All the combinations of goods or services that provide the same level of utility. (p 56)

Indirect approach To verify economic models, the indirect approach asks if the model can accurately predict real-world events. (p 16)

Individual demand curve A graphic representation of the relationship between the price of a good and the quantity of it demanded by a person. (p 99)

Inferior good A good that is bought in smaller quantities as income increases. (p 83)

Initial endowments The initial holdings of goods from which trading occurs in exchanges. (p 530)

Intercept The value of Y when X equals zero. (p 26)

Interest Payment for the current use of funds. (p 481)

Internalization of an externality Incorporation of the social marginal costs of an externality into an economic actor's decisions (as through taxation or merger). (p 554)

Investment The purchase of new capital. (p 463)

Isoquant A curve that shows the various combinations of inputs that will produce the same amount of output. (p 163)

Isoquant map A contour map of a firm's production function. (p 163)

Job-specific skills Skills learned on a job about how to do that specific job better. (p 252)

Joint products The inseparable combination of two goods in production, such as advertising, which is paid for by the consumer as part of the good being advertised. (p 364)

Kinked demand curve model A model in which firms believe that price increases result in a very elastic demand, while price decreases result in an inelastic demand for their products. (p 356)

Labor theory of value Relative prices of goods are determined only by the relative amounts of labor used to make them. (p 9)

Law of one price All trades between sellers and buyers for the same good are conducted at one price. (p 275)

Leisure Time spent in any activity other than market work. (p 432)

Lindahl equilibrium Balance between people's demand for public goods and the tax shares they must pay for them. (p 575)

Linear function An equation that is represented by a straight line graph. (p 25)

Linear programming A mathematical technique for finding the maximum (or minimum) value for a linear function whose variables are subject to linear constraints. (p 538)

Long run The period of time in which a firm may consider all of its inputs to be variable in making its decisions. (p 196)

Long-run elasticity of supply The percent change in quantity supplied in the long run in response to a 1 percent change in price. (p 300)

Marginal cost The cost of producing one more unit of output. (p 191)

Marginal expense The cost of hiring one more unit of an input. Will exceed the price of the input if the firm faces an upward-sloping supply curve for the input. (p 414)

Marginal physical productivity The additional output that can be produced by one more unit of a particular input while holding all other inputs constant. (p 159)

Marginal rate of substitution (MRS) The rate at which

an individual is willing to trade one good for another while remaining equally well off. (p 54)

Marginal rate of technical substitution   The negative of the slope of an isoquant. This shows the amount by which capital input can be reduced while holding the output constant when one more unit of labor input is added. (p 165)

Marginal revenue   The extra revenue a firm receives when it sells one more unit of output. (p 229)

Marginal revenue product   The extra revenue obtained from selling the output produced by hiring an extra worker or machine. (p 404)

Marginal value product   A special case of marginal revenue product in which the firm is a price taker for its output. (p 405)

Market   A hypothetical "place" where buyers and sellers determine the price of a good. (p 275)

Market demand   The total quantity of a good or service demanded by all potential buyers. (p 109)

Market demand curve   The relationship between the total quantity demanded of a good or service and its price holding all other factors constant. (p 110)

Market period   A short period of time during which quantity supplied is fixed. (p 278)

Markup pricing   Determining the selling price of a good by adding a percentage to the cost of producing it. (p 240)

Median voter   A voter whose preferences for a public good represent the middle point of all voters' preferences for the good. (p 582)

Microeconomics   The study of the economic choices individuals and firms make. (p 6)

Models   In economics, theories that capture the essentials of how the economy works. (p 7)

Monopolistic competition   Market in which each firm faces a negatively sloped demand curve and there are no barriers to entry. (p 366)

Monopoly   A market in which there is only one seller of a good. (p 275)

Monopoly rents   The profits that a monopoly earns in the long run. (p 329)

Monopsony   A single hirer in a particular input market. (p 414)

Natural monopoly   A firm that exhibits diminishing average cost over a broad range of output levels. (p 341)

Nonexclusive goods   Goods that provide benefits to everyone. No one can be excluded from such benefits. (p 570)

Nonrival goods   Goods for which additional consumers may use them at zero marginal costs. (p 570)

Normal good   A good that is bought in greater quantities as income increases. (p 83)

Normative analysis   Theories that make judgments about how the economy's resources should be used. (p 17)

Opportunity cost   The cost of a good or service as measured by the alternative uses that are forgone by producing the good or service. (p 181)

Output effect   The change in the amount of an input that the firm hires that results from a change in output level. Output changes because the change in an input's price affects the firm's costs. (p 410)

***Pareto optimal* allocation of resources**   Allocations in which no one person can be made better off without necessarily making someone else worse off (see also exchange efficiency). (p 526)

Partial equilibrium model   An economic model of a single market. (p 12)

Perfect competition   A market in which there are assumed to be a large number of buyers and sellers for a good who do not individually affect the good's price. Entry into the market is assumed to be costless. (p 275)

Perfect price discrimination   Selling a good one unit at a time for the maximum amount demanders will pay. (p 333)

Perfectly competitive price system   An economic model in which individuals maximize utility, firms maximize profits, there is perfect information about prices, and every economic actor is a price taker. (p 500)

Perpetuity   A promise of a certain number of dollars each year, forever. (p 489)

Pigovian tax   A tax or subsidy on an externality that brings about an equality of private and social marginal costs. (p 552)

Positive economic analysis   Theories that explain how resources actually are used in an economy. (p 17)

Present discounted value   The present value of funds payable in the future after taking account of the opportunity cost of interest forgone. (p 465, p 484)

Price discrimination   The practice of charging different prices for a good in different markets. (p 339)

Price elasticity of demand   The percentage change in the quantity demanded of a good in response to a 1 percent change in its price. (p 113)

Price leadership model   Model in which one dominant firm takes reactions of all other firms into account in its output and pricing decisions. (p 358)

Price taker   A firm or individual whose decisions regarding buying or selling have no effect on the prevailing market price of a good or service. (p 231)

Prisoner's dilemma   A game in which the players' most desirable outcome is unstable because each player has an incentive to cheat in the strategy actually chosen. (p 389)

Private property   Property that is owned by specific people who may prevent others from using it. (p 555)

Probability   The relative frequency with which an event will occur. (p 142)

Product group   Set of differentiated products that are highly substitutable for one another. (p 360)

Production function   The mathematical relationship between inputs and outputs. (p 157)

Production possibility frontier   A figure illustrating the technically efficient output possibilities for an economy with fixed amounts of inputs. (p 508)

Property rights   The legal specification of who owns a good and the trades the owner is allowed to make with it. (p 555)

Public goods   Goods that provide nonexclusive benefits to everyone in a group and which can be provided to one more user at zero marginal cost. Goods which are both nonexclusive and nonrival. (p 523, p 571)

Quadratic function   An equation that includes terms in X^2. (p 31)

Quasicompetitive model   A model of oligopoly pricing in which each firm acts as a price taker. (p 354)

Rate of product transformation   The slope of the production possibility frontier which shows the opportunity costs involved in producing more of one good and less of some other good. (p 509)

Rate of return   The increase in future output made possible by investing one unit of current output in capital accumulation. (p 456)

Reaction function   In the Cournot model a function or graph that shows how much one firm will produce given what the other firm produces. (p 382)

Rent-seeking behavior   Firms or individuals influencing government policy to increase their own profits. (p 586)

Rental rate (v)   The cost of hiring one machine for one hour. (p 182)

Returns to scale   The rate at which output increases in response to proportional increases in all inputs. (p 167)

Revenue maximization   A goal for firms in which they work to maximize their total revenue rather than profits. (p 239)

Risk aversion   The tendency of people to refuse to accept fair games. (p 144)

Scarcity costs   The opportunity costs of forgone future

production that cannot be made because of current production that uses finite resources. (p 473)

Short run   The period of time in which a firm must consider some inputs absolutely fixed in making its decisions. (p 196)

Short-run average variable cost   Total variable costs divided by quantity produced. These costs are avoidable if the firm produces no output. (p 204)

Short-run elasticity of supply   The percent change in quantity supplied in the short run in response to a 1 percent change in price. (p 285)

Short-run supply curve   The relationship between market price and quantity supplied of a good in the short run. (p 281)

Shutdown price   The price below which the firm will choose to produce no output in the short run. Equal to minimum average variable cost. (p 245)

Simultaneous equations   A set of equations with more than one variable that must be solved together for a particular solution. (p 38)

Slope   The direction of a line on a graph. Shows the change in Y that results from a change in X. (p 26)

Social costs   Costs of production that include both input costs and costs of the externalities that production may cause. (p 549)

Stable equilibrium   A situation in which market forces cause price to move to its equilibrium level. (p 320)

Stackelberg model   A generalization of the Cournot model in which at least one of the firms knows the other's reaction function. (p 385)

Subscripts   The use of small numbers at the bottom of variables to identify them as separate variables. (p 40)

Substitutes   Two goods such that if the price of one increases, the quantity demanded of the other rises. (p 98)

Substitution effect   In the theory of production, the substitution of one input for another while holding output constant in response to a change in the input's price. (p 409)

Substitution effect   The part of the change in quantity demanded of a good whose price has changed that is caused by substitution of the good that is now relatively cheaper for the other that is now relatively more costly. A movement along an indifference curve. (p 84)

Substitution effect of a change in w   Movement along an indifference curve in response to a change in the real wage. A rise in w causes an individual to work more. (p 437)

Supply response   The change in quantity of output in response to a change in demand conditions. (p 277)

Survivorship principle   The idea that in competitive markets, only profit-maximizing firms are likely to survive. (p 238)

Tax incidence theory   The study of the final burden of a tax after considering all market reactions to it. (p 295)

Technically efficient allocation of resources   An allocation of the available resources such that producing more of one good requires producing less of some other good. (p 504)

Theory of choice   The interaction of preferences and income that causes people to make the choices they do. (p 50)

Theory of value   Study of the factors that determine relative prices. (p 8)

Transactions costs   Costs involved in making market transactions and in gathering information with which to make those transactions. (p 315)

Transitive   The property that if A is preferred to B, and B is preferred to C, then A must be preferred to C. (p 52)

Unstable equilibrium   A situation in which market forces cause price to move away from its equilibrium level. (p 320)

Utility   The pleasure, satisfaction, or need fulfillment that people get from their economic activity. (p 50)

Utility possibility frontier   A diagram illustrating all the Pareto optimal allocations of utility among the individuals in an economy. (p 527)

Variable costs   Costs associated with inputs that can be varied in the short run. (p 198)

Variables   The basic elements of algebra, usually called X, Y, and so on, that may be given any numerical value in an equation. (p 24)

Wage rate (w)   The cost of hiring one worker for one hour. (p 182)

Water-diamond paradox   If water is so much more important to life than diamonds, how can diamonds be more expensive than water? (p 9)

Yield   The interest rate at which the present discounted value of the return from an investment is exactly equal to the investment's current cost. (p 493)

Zero-sum game   A game in which the amount which one player loses the other player wins. (p 387)

AUTHOR INDEX

SUBJECT INDEX

Page numbers of running glossary entries appear in boldface type.